CW00796199

Electrostatics:

Principles, Problems and Applications

Electrostatics:

Principles, Problems and Applications

Jean Cross

CSIRO Division of Textile Physics, Ryde, Australia

Adam Hilger, Bristol

© IOP Publishing Limited 1987

All rights reserved. No part of this publication may be reproduced, stored in a retrieval system or transmitted in any form or by any means, electronic, mechanical, photocopying, recording or otherwise, without the prior permission of the publisher.

British Library Cataloguing in Publication Data

Cross, J.A. (Jean A.)
  Electrostatics: principles, problems
  and applications.
  1. Electrostatics
  I. Title
  537′.2   QC571

  ISBN 0-85274-589-3

Consultant Editor: **A E De Barr**

Published under the Adam Hilger imprint by IOP Publishing Limited
Techno House, Redcliffe Way, Bristol, BS1 6NX, England

Typeset by Datapage International Limited, Dublin, Ireland
Printed in Great Britain by J W Arrowsmith Ltd, Bristol

Contents

Preface   ix

Notation   xi

1   Historical Background and Elementary Theory   1
    1.1   Historical background   1
    1.2   Fundamental definitions   5
    1.3   Orders of magnitude   12
    1.4   Summary of electrostatic equations in uniform fields   13
    1.5   Gauss's law—the electric field due to an assembly of
          charges   16

2   Electrification of Solids and Liquids   17
    2.1   Contact and frictional charging   17
    2.2   Corona charging   46
    2.3   Charging by the capture of small particles   60
    2.4   Induction charging   61
    2.5   Double-layer charging   64
          References   85

3   Measurements and Instrumentation   91
    3.1   Introduction   91
    3.2   Potential dividers and resistance probes   92
    3.3   Electrometers and electrostatic voltmeters   92
    3.4   Field meters and non-contacting voltmeters   96
    3.5   Charge measurement—the Faraday cup   108
    3.6   Measurement of the charge and mobility of individual
          particles   110
    3.7   Field and potential probes   115
    3.8   The use of the Kerr and Pockels effect for measurement
          of electric fields   124

3.9	Capacitance meters	128
3.10	Measurement of resistance and resistivity	129
3.11	Energy of electrostatic sparks	136
	References	140
4	**Electrostatics in Gas Filtration**	**144**
4.1	Introduction	144
4.2	Electrostatic precipitation	146
4.3	Electron beam desulphurisation and denitrisation	163
4.4	Electrostatically enhanced cyclone separators	164
4.5	Electrostatic scrubbers and granular bed filters	166
4.6	Electrostatically enhanced fabric filters	183
	Appendix	189
	References	192
5	**Miscellaneous Applications**	**198**
5.1	Electrostatic atomisation	198
5.2	Electrostatic spray coating	209
5.3	Electrostatic separation	237
5.4	Electrokinetic phenomena in liquids	248
5.5	Dielectrophoresis	269
5.6	Applications of the corona discharge	276
5.7	Electrodynamic containment and control of particles	285
5.8	Applications of electromechanical forces	294
5.9	Electrostatic copying	299
5.10	Electrostatics in the textile industry	302
5.11	Electrostatic crystals	306
5.12	Electrostatic generators	308
	References	312
6	**Hazards and Problems**	**326**
6.1	Fire and explosion hazards	326
6.2	Electrostatic sparks	342
6.3	Non-electrostatic sparks	366
6.4	Electrostatic eliminators	369
6.5	Antistatic agents	376
6.6	Electrostatic problems in the electronics industry	383
6.7	Adhesion	386
	Appendix	410
	References	415
7	**Theory**	**425**
7.1	Fundamental laws of electrostatics	425
7.2	Capacitance and capacitors	434

7.3	Polarisation	437
7.4	Identification of field lines and equipotentials	442
7.5	Electric field and potential by solution of Laplace's equation	460
7.6	Earnshaw's theorem	477
7.7	Corona discharge theory	477
	Appendix	487
	References	489
Index		**492**

Preface

Electrostatics is the term given to the study of the interactions between electrically charged bodies. Strictly speaking this includes the study of the forces which hold individual electrons and ions together to form atoms, the chemical forces which bind the atoms together and much of the science of plasma physics and electrochemistry. For the purposes of this book, however, electrostatics will be defined simply as the study of the cause and effects of charge accumulation in solids and liquids.

Electrostatic effects were first reported more than 2500 years ago, when Thales found that a piece of amber that had been rubbed with silk would pick up small particles. In spite of this early detection of electrostatic attraction, it was not until the early twentieth century that the electron as an elementary particle of matter was separately identified, or that the reason for charge separation could reasonably be described. Even today it is not possible to predict with certainty whether a particular material will charge positive or negative, or to make more than a very rough estimate of the magnitude of the charge that will be produced. These uncertainties have led to electrostatics being often discounted as a serious science and its many applications have been underrated. In recent years, however, there has been a reawakening of interest, led by the need to understand the electrostatic causes of explosions and the rapid development of industrial applications such as electrostatic powder coating and electrostatic photocopying. The apparent inconsistencies of electrostatic effects are becoming better understood, so they can be controlled and used in a wide range of industrial processes.

The applications of electrostatics and the problems which may be caused by unwanted static are of interest to a wide range of different industries including, for example, metal finishing, mining, the food industry and the chemical industry. A basic understanding of the subject is needed by managers, safety officers and plant engineers, as well as the people who design and study electrostatic equipment. The objective of this book is to provide a reference text which gives an introduction to the fundamental principles of electrostatics, and describes the uses to which electrostatic forces can be put and the problems created by unwanted static charge in industry. In many cases the subjects covered reflect the requests for information that I have received both as an industrial consultant at Southampton University in England and as a scientist at CSIRO in Australia. The book should fill the gap I have found in the literature on many of these questions.

The book is written at a level which will be comprehensible to professional and technician engineers, or scientists of any discipline who may have no formal electrical training. The use of calculus has been avoided where possible and in all cases the introductory section on each topic is descriptive rather than mathematical. Where this approach leads to a loss of generality, or an oversimplification, a more precise mathematical treatment is also given. However these sections may be passed over without losing the sense of the text as a whole. Comprehensive references are provided to enable the interested reader to follow up each topic in greater detail.

Sufficient basic theory to understand the chapters concerning the applications and problems of electrostatics is presented in the first chapter. More advanced theory, including the derivation of some of the formulae stated in the rest of the book is given in Chapter 7. The book updates and complements the excellent text on the applications of electrostatics edited by A D Moore ('Electrostatics and its Applications' Wiley 1973). Electrostatic generators have received little attention over the last fifteen years and are omitted from this text but some topics, for example electrostatic forces in gas cleaning, have been treated in more detail.

The potential hazards of charge accumulation in a flammable environment are well known. The circumstances under which hazardous electrostatic sparks can occur are reviewed, and the means by which a potential hazard can be evaluated and eliminated are discussed. Although sparks due to friction and impact and RF sparks are not electrostatic in nature, they are often confused with electrostatic sparks and a section on these two phenomena is therefore included.

Electrostatic forces can be a nuisance when they cause unwanted adhesion. The relevance of electrostatic forces to powder collection on surfaces and powder flow and agglomeration is discussed.

Although the importance of electrostatics in industry has increased greatly over the last twenty or thirty years, modern electrostatics is still rarely included in undergraduate or technical studies. This book should provide a text which can be used for teaching purposes as well as a reference book for workers in industry.

Notation

Except where otherwise specified the following symbols are used throughout this book.

a	particle radius
b	mobility
c	velocity of light
d	distance
e	the charge on an electron ($= 1.602 \times 10^{-19}$ C)
g	acceleration due to gravity
h	heat transfer coefficient
i	$(-1)^{1/2}$
k	Boltzmann's constant ($= 1.380 \times 10^{-23}$)
l	length
m	mass
p	moment of a dipole (or const $= 3\varepsilon_r/(\varepsilon_r + 2)$)
q	charge
r	radial coordinate
s	distance
t	time
u	velocity
v	volume
w	migration velocity
A	area
C	capacitance, Cunningham correction factor
D	density
D	electric displacement, diffusion constant
E	electric field
E_b	breakdown field
F	force

I	current
J	current density
K	arbitrary constant
L	length
N	number density
P	polarisation, P-Legendre polynomial
Q	charge density, Q-Legendre polynomial
Q_s	surface charge density
Q_v	volume charge density
R	resistance
$\mathscr{R}$	Reynolds' number
T	temperature
U	energy
V	voltage
W	energy
Y	Young's modulus

α	polarisability or specific collecting area of a precipitator
γ	surface tension–surface free energy
δ	Debye length
ε_0	permittivity of free space ($= 8.854 \times 10^{-12}$ F m^{-1})
ε_r	relative permittivity (relative dieletric constant)
ε	permittivity (dielectric constant) $= \varepsilon_0\varepsilon_r$
ζ	zeta potential
η	viscosity
θ	angle in polar or cylindrical coordinates
λ	wavelength
v	Poisson's ratio
ξ	efficiency
ρ	resistivity
σ	conductivity
τ	time constant
φ	work function (polar angle)
χ	susceptibility
Ψ	Euler's constant ($= 0.577$)

Chapter 1   Historical Background and Elementary Theory

1.1 HISTORICAL BACKGROUND

The attraction of small particles of straw to an amber rod which had been rubbed with silk was recorded around 600BC but there was little recorded advance in the study of the phenomenon until the sixteenth century, when William Gilbert (1540–1603) found that materials other than amber had similar properties. He coined the term 'electrical' to describe the effect, taking the word from $\varepsilon\lambda\varepsilon\kappa\tau\rho\sigma\nu$, the Greek word for amber. He built the first electroscope to detect electric charge, (simply a pivoted needle that was attracted to a charged body) and called materials which could be made to charge by friction 'electrics' and metals which did not charge 'non-electrics'. Electrical repulsion was discovered not long after by Otto von Guericke who showed that if a charged rod was brought near iron filings they would be first attracted then repelled. He built the first electrostatic generator from a rotating sulphur sphere which rubbed against a cloth to build up a charge. He discovered that it was not necessary to touch the sphere physically to transfer charge, mere proximity being sufficient. He also discovered that electricity would pass down a linen thread.

In 1733 Du Fay suggested that attraction and repulsion between charged bodies resulted from two different types of electricity. The first, which was characteristic of amber, thread and paper he called 'resinous' and the second, which was characteristic of glass, rock crystal and precious stones he called 'vitreous'. Bodies charged with the same type of electricity were found to repel each other while those charged oppositely were attracted. Du Fay proposed that the two types of electricity were weightless fluids (imponderable fluids) and experiments were carried out to try to collect it in various receptacles. A suitable vessel in which charge could be stored was eventually designed independently by Von Kleist and Musschenbroek. This is now known as a Leyden jar, after the town in which Musschenbroek worked. Metal foil conductors were placed on the inner and outer walls of a dry glass container. The inner conductor was electrified by connecting it to an electrical machine and the outer was earthed, either directly, or through the experimenters hand. If the inner and outer conductors were then connected together a spark occurred and if the experimenter touched the inner and outer can simultaneously he received an electric shock.

Electrostatic demonstrations became the rage. It was found that sparks could ignite gunpowder and alcohol, and demonstrations were carried out suspending people from insulating ropes and drawing sparks from them.

At this stage there were two theories proposed; Du Fay's two-fluid theory and a single-fluid theory put forward by Benjamin Franklin. Franklin suggested that electricity was a fluid existing in all bodies. If the bodies contained an equilibrium quantity of electricity they were neutral. Vitreous electricity was considered to be an excess of the fluid (i.e. a positive quantity of fluid) and resinous electricity was attributed to a lack of fluid (i.e. a negative quantity of fluid). Franklin explained the operation of the Leyden jar by assuming that when a quantity of electricity was poured into the inner conductor the same quantity was obliged to leave the outer by repulsion. When the two conductors were connected together equilibrium was re-established by means of a spark. Although we now know that there are two types of electric charge, the words positive and negative have been retained rather than the terms vitreous and resinous originally used in the two-fluid theory.

Franklin is best known for recognising the connection between electricity and lightning. (Prior to Franklin's work, thunderstorms were believed to be caused by the explosion of sulphurous gases.) In 1752 he reported the results of his experiments as follows.

> Make a kite with silk handkerchiefs and a cross of cedar. To the top of the cross fix a sharp pointed wire a foot or so above the wood. Tie a silk ribbon to the end of the line and a key at the join between the silk and the line. Raise the kite in a thunder storm and stand under cover so the silk remains dry and the twine does not touch the door. Loose filaments of the twine stand out in all directions and a plentiful supply of electricity streams out from the key. Thereby is the sameness of electrical matter with that of lightning completely demonstrated.

The study of electricity was completely qualitative up until 1753 when the pith ball electroscope was invented and the deflection of two similarly charged lightweight balls, suspended on a fine thread, was used as a measure of the amount of charge on the balls. Thirty years later Coulomb invented a simple torsion balance which allowed him to measure the force exerted by charged bodies. He found that electrical forces, like magnetic forces, obeyed an inverse square law, i.e. the force, F, between two equally charged bodies can be described by the equation

$$F = \frac{Cq^2}{d^2}$$

where q is the charge on each body, d is the spacing and C is a constant.

At this time there was no definition of the unit of charge. The constant C was therefore chosen to be one and the unit of charge was defined so that the force between two bodies of unit charge was one dyne. This is the basis of the esu (electrostatic units) system which is found in many of the older textbooks.

By the end of the eighteenth century the two-fluid theory was gaining popularity over the single-fluid theory, mainly because of the difficulty of visualising how the lack of an electrical fluid in two bodies could produce repulsion. However, several scientists were beginning to be uneasy about the growth in the number of imponderable fluids which had to be assumed to exist to account for heat, light, sound, magnetism and the two types of electricity.

By this time it was possible to generate electricity by friction, by heating certain crystals, by experimenting with electric fishes and by drawing electricity from the atmosphere. During the next hundred years the connections between electrical and magnetic energy and the more conventional chemical, mechanical and heat energy were made. A major breakthrough in this area came in 1795 when Volta made the first battery by placing two pieces of metal in a damp cloth and showing that an electric current flowed between them. Five years later Carlisle and Nicholson found that this current would decompose water. This demonstrated for the first time that there was a connection between ponderable and imponderable matter, but the nature of the connection was not discovered until the twentieth century.

With the invention of the battery and the ability to produce continuous currents came the discovery that a current flowing in a wire would influence a magnet, and the link between electricity and magnetism was made. During the nineteenth century the nature of this relationship was studied in detail and the mathematical rules describing the behaviour of electricity and magnetism were developed.

A major problem which taxed scientists of the eighteenth and nineteenth centuries was how to account for the way electrical forces can act at a distance. It was at first postulated that some substance emerged from the charged bodies to exert the mysterious force, but experiments repeatedly showed that an electrical force could be transmitted through insulators, although they did not allow the electric fluid to flow. Two methods of considering the phenomenon developed independently. The mathematicians developed a self-consistent theory, based on centres of force which were able to act at a distance. They attempted no physical explanation of how this might occur. Action at a distance was simply defined as due to a 'field' in the intervening space. Faraday, proposed that there were lines of force with experimentally derived properties travelling through all of space. Faraday's concept of field lines is frequently the simplest way to visualise and predict electrostatic phenomena. It is therefore worth considering his ideas in detail.

The concept of field lines was first introduced to describe the action between two magnets. The magnetic line of force or field line was defined as a line whose direction at any point coincides with the direction of the magnetic force. This direction could be demonstrated by iron filings or small magnets which aligned themselves along the direction of the magnetic field. The similarity between electrical and magnetic effects had been demonstrated in several experiments, for example, Coulomb showed that the forces both obey an inverse square law. Faraday carried out experiments which showed that the amount of charge which could be stored in a Leyden jar, or between two flat plates, depended on the nature of the insulating material between the two surfaces. He recognised the similarity between this and the change in magnetic force when an iron core was placed in an electromagnet and suggested that the electric force could be visualised by field lines in the same way as the magnetic force. An electric field line was therefore defined as 'the path followed by a small positive charge in the vicinity of an electrically charged body'. An electric line of force, or field line, may be assumed to start on unit positive charge and end on unit negative charge and the strength of the force exerted on a charged body depends on the density of field lines in space.

Electric field lines can be displayed in two dimensions by applying a high voltage between foil electrodes on a glass plate. Freshly powdered gypsum crystals (hydrated calcium sulphate), scattered on the plate and gently tapped will arrange themselves along electric field lines in the same way as iron filings show the direction of a magnetic field.

In 1873 Maxwell published a treatise in which he translated the ideas of Faraday into a more conventional mathematical formulation and showed that the two ways of considering electric fields were equivalent. He pointed out that the experimental laws of electricity and magnetism were completely consistent with the hypothesis that there is a physical medium between the two bodies, which is in a state of stress, such that there is a tension along the lines of force and an equal pressure in all directions perpendicular to them. Although the lines are simply a technique to allow us to visualise something which is not visible, the analogy allows us to solve many electrical and magnetic problems.

A second major contribution of Faraday to the understanding of electrostatics was his introduction of the concept of induced electric charge. He envisaged an insulating material as a collection of a large number of isolated small conductors, each containing equal quantities of positive and negative electricity and therefore uncharged. He proposed that charge was able to move within the conductors but not between them. Application of an electric field separated the positive and negative charge to opposite ends of the conductor which became 'polarised' (This idea is now known to be substantially true with materials made up from neutral atoms containing positive ions and electrons.) The hypothesis explains why a capacitor with a dielectric material between the plates will store more charge than the two plates in a vacuum. When a voltage is applied to the plates the charges move within the small conductors in the dielectric so that positive charge moves slightly towards the negative plate and vice versa. This partially neutralises the charge applied to the plates hence more charge is able to be stored for the same build-up of potential across the capacitor.

The mathematical formulation of electrical and magnetic theory developed in the nineteenth century remains largely unchanged although the mechanisms were greatly clarified with the discovery in the early twentieth century that matter was made up of elementary charged particles. When Maxwell and the other mathematicians developed their theories electricity was still considered to be a fluid, but in the absence of the knowledge of the electron and the proton this was as close to the truth as could be reached. In 1892 Maxwell wrote

> In most expositions of this theory (the two fluids theory) the two electricities are called 'fluids' because they are capable of being transferred from one body to another and are, within conducting bodies, extremely mobile. The other properties of fluids, such as their inertia, weight and elasticity are not attributed to them by those who have used the theory for mathematical purposes; but the use of the word 'fluid' has been apt to mislead the vulgar, including many men of science who are not natural philosophers, and who have seized upon the word fluid as the only term in the statement of the theory which seemed intelligible to them. The mathematical treatment of the subject has been greatly developed by writers who express themselves in terms of the two fluids theory. Their results however have been deduced entirely from data which can be proved by experiment, and which must therefore be true whether we adopt the two fluids theory or not.

Much of the general theory developed in the following pages and in Chapter 7 may be found in 'A Treatise on Electricity and Magnetism' by James Clerk Maxwell, first published in 1873 and reprinted in its third edition in 1955.

1.2 FUNDAMENTAL DEFINITIONS

1.2.1 Charge

The original definition of unit electric charge was derived from the experiments of Coulomb to be 'that quantity of electricity which when placed at unit distance from an equal quantity of charge repels it with unit force'. The distance (d) was measured in centimetres, the force (F) in dynes and the units of electric charge (q) were called electrostatic units (esu). Thus like charges repel and unlike attract with a force F given by the Coulomb law:

$$F = \frac{Cqq'}{d^2}. \tag{1.1}$$

The constant C is set to one to define the electrostatic unit of charge. The theories of electrostatics and electrodynamics grew up independently and the esu system of units is not directly compatible with the conventional unit of electric current, the ampere. If the charge is to be defined in coulombs ($1\ \mathrm{C\,s}^{-1} = 1\ \mathrm{A}$) and the force and distance are to be expressed in the conventional SI units of newtons and metres then the constant, C, in the Coulomb equation is no longer one but becomes

$$C = 1/4\pi\varepsilon_0$$

ε_0 is a constant called the permittivity of free space. In order to make the units of coulombs and newtons compatible ε_0 has the units of farads per metre where the farad is the SI unit of capacitance. One coulomb is equivalent to 2.998×10^9 esu (SI units will be used throughout this text). When a current flows in a metal, the charge carriers all have the same elementary unit charge. This is usually designated by e, the charge on a single electron. This charge is equivalent to 1.602×10^{-19} C.

1.2.2 Electric field

The force on a charge q due to the presence of a second charge q' a distance d away is said to be due to the electric field, E, produced by the charge q':

$$F = qE. \tag{1.2}$$

From the Coulomb law the force on q is equal to

$$F = \frac{q'}{4\pi\varepsilon_0 d^2}. \tag{1.3}$$

Therefore the electric field due to the charge q' is given by

$$E = \frac{q'}{4\pi\varepsilon_0 d^2}. \tag{1.4}$$

1.2.3 Potential, voltage or electromotive force

Electric potential is defined as the work done in moving unit charge unit distance against unit electric field, i.e. if the unit charge is moved a distance s against a uniform electric field E then the potential difference between the two positions of the unit charge is

$$V = Es \qquad (1.5)$$

i.e.

$$E = V/s. \qquad (1.6)$$

The electric field is thus the rate of change of potential with distance. (At this stage the polarity of E and V have not been considered.) A potential may be assigned to a point in space or to a surface. The potential at a point is the work done in moving unit charge to that position from a position of zero potential.

The unit of electric potential (the volt) is the same as work/unit charge or energy/unit charge. It is not a force although the historical term 'electromotive force' or EMF is still sometimes used instead of the terms 'voltage' or 'potential'.

1.2.4 Field lines and equipotentials

The electric field and potential are not easy concepts to visualise and various mechanical analogies are often made. For example, the electric potential can be related to the work done in moving a ball of unit weight to the top of a hill. Lines of equal potential may be drawn, which are the contour lines of the hill. If the ball is released it will roll down the hill, following a path which is perpendicular to the contour lines. These are equivalent to electric field lines, which are the paths followed by a unit positive charge.

Using this analogy, it can be seen that, if the potential increases from left to right, the movement of a positive charge will be from right to left. The field and the voltage therefore have opposite signs and $E = -V/s$.

In more general mathematical terms, applicable where the electric field is not uniform, the relationship between electric field and potential may be written

$$V = - \int E \, ds \qquad (1.7)$$

$$E = -dV/ds. \qquad (1.8)$$

In three dimensions this is written

$$E = -\operatorname{grad} V = -\nabla V. \qquad (1.9)$$

The use of field lines to visualise the physical effect of an electric field can be illustrated by considering a conducting cylinder in a uniform electric field set up between two parallel electrodes (figure 1.1). There can be no potential difference along a conducting surface. Therefore the equipotentials close to any conductor must be parallel to it. No point in space can simultaneously be at two potentials therefore the equipotential lines cannot cross. If these

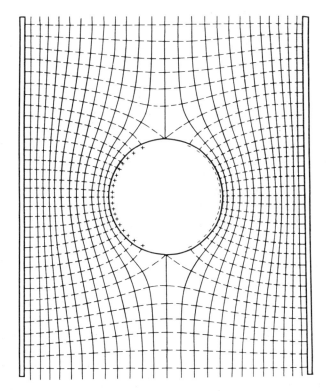

Figure 1.1 Field lines and equipotentials for a cylinder in a uniform field. Full curves are equipotentials and broken curves are field lines.

two criteria are considered, the equipotential lines must take the general form shown by the full curves in figure 1.1. Field lines are perpendicular to equipotentials, and are shown by the broken curves in figure 1.1. It can be seen that if charged particles of a single polarity are introduced they will follow the field lines and move towards the isolated conductor, which will become charged. Charge will flow to the conductor until the repulsion is sufficient to counteract the distortion in the electric field, caused by the presence of the conductor. This quantity of charge depends on the size of the conductor and the electric field, but not on how much free charge is present. The full calculation for a spherical conductor is given in §2.2.4.

Electric field lines can be considered to begin and end on a charge, therefore a high density of field lines implies a high charge density and a high electric field.

1.2.5 Capacitance

The capacitance of an article is a measure of its ability to store charge. When an isolated conductor is given a charge q, it attracts or repels other charges, and may be said to have a potential V. The ratio of the charge on the conductor and the potential to which it rises is called its capacitance, C

$$C = q/V. \qquad (1.10)$$

The value of the capacitance depends on the size and geometry of the conductor and its position with respect to earth. Calculations of capacitance for various geometries are given in Chapter 7 and the results for a few simple systems are presented in §1.4.3. The SI unit of capacitance is the farad.

In conventional electrical calculations voltages are fixed by a battery or power supply and the current flow varies according to the load or resistance of the circuit. In electrostatics the charge is static and cannot flow freely. If the capacitance of the object on which the fixed charge is stored, changes, for example because an isolated charged object is moved, then the potential of the object must change. This means that the measurement of an electrostatic voltage does not indicate the amount of static charge present, unless the capacitance can be estimated. There is no fundamental difficulty with a voltage varying as an article is moved and it is only our familiarity with electrodynamics which makes this appear unusual.

1.2.6 Dielectric constant or permittivity

Charge can be stored on a capacitor made up from two conductors such as two parallel plates or concentric cylinders. In this case the capacitance depends on both the geometry and the nature of the material between the two conductors. The ratio of the capacitance of two conductors with an insulating material between them, and the same conductors in vacuum, is called the dielectric constant or permittivity of the insulating material. It is normally expressed as a multiple of the permittivity of free space ε_0 (defined by the Coulomb law). Thus the permittivity of a material is $\varepsilon_r \varepsilon_0$ where ε_r is the relative dielectric constant or relative permittivity of the material.

For a vacuum ε_r is one and for air it is very close to one. The dielectric constant of a material is loosely related to its conductivity. A perfect conductor has a dielectric constant of infinity. For most solid insulators the relative dielectric constant is between one and ten but for polar liquids, and some crystalline materials, it may be significantly higher. When a potential is applied across a slab of insulator between two metal plates, charge is displaced in the insulator and appears at the plates. The amount of this charge, and hence the capacitance of this arrangement, depends on the polarisability of the insulator. The relative dielectric constant of a material is therefore a measure of the extent to which its atoms and molecules polarise. If an oscillating voltage is applied to the plates of a capacitor the relative dielectric constant, and hence the capacitance, will be a function of the frequency of the oscillating voltage.

The force between two charged particles is modified by the permittivity of the medium in which they are situated and the Coulomb law in a medium of relative permittivity ε_r is

$$F = \frac{qq'}{4\pi\varepsilon_0\varepsilon_r d^2}.\qquad(1.11)$$

1.2.7 Resistivity

When a potential is applied across the ends of a conductor charge flows, thus creating an electric current. The ratio between the voltage and the current is called the resistance. Obviously current can flow more easily through a sample of larger cross sectional area and more voltage is required to push the charge through a longer sample. Therefore resistance depends on the size of the sample. However, the resistance of a sample of unit length with unit cross sectional area is a property of the material and is called the resistivity. Resistivity, ρ, is related to resistance, R, by the equation

$$\rho = RA/d\qquad(1.12)$$

where A is the area and d the length of the sample. Resistivity is a bulk property of the material and is measured in ohm metres (Ω m). The

Table 1.1 Conductivities of common materials ($S\,m^{-1}$).

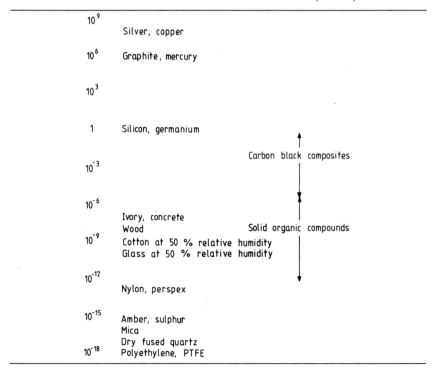

reciprocal of resistivity is the conductivity, σ, which is measured in siemens. (This is the same unit as Ω^{-1} which used to be called the mho.)

It is important to distinguish between bulk resistivity and surface resistivity. The surface resistivity of a material is the resistance measured between two electrodes which have the same length as spacing. The resistance measured in this way will be the same, whatever the dimensions of the electrodes, provided this square geometry is retained. Surface resistivity is measured in ohms, the same unit as a linear resistance, but it is sometimes written as ohms per square to indicate that the standard geometry was used.

Resistivities of materials cover an extremely wide range. From table 1.1 it can be seen that the difference in resistivity between copper at $10^{-8}\,\Omega\,m$ and polyethylene at $10^{18}\,\Omega\,m$ is 26 orders of magnitude. Within the range of materials generally considered to be insulators one may find resistivities ranging over nine orders of magnitude from $10^9\,\Omega\,m$ for soda glass to $10^{18}\,\Omega\,m$ for polyethylene or PTFE. For low-voltage work one tends to assume that insulators are materials that conduct no charge at all and conductors are materials that conduct almost perfectly. In electrostatic problems one is interested in the movement of very small amounts of charge by relatively large voltages and the ability of insulating materials to conduct slightly becomes important.

1.2.8 Time constant for charge decay

It is often important in considering electrostatic problems to estimate the time that charge will take to decay away. This will depend on the size of the capacitance on which the charge is stored and the resistance through which it can flow to earth. The rate at which charge flows through the resistance is proportional to the voltage on the capacitor. This is proportional to the remaining charge. Therefore the charge decays fast at first, when the charge and voltage are high, and more slowly when the charge and voltage are reduced. The linear relationship between the rate of charge flow and the capacitance and voltage leads to an exponential decay of charge which has the form shown in figure 1.2. Mathematically, this is written as

$$q = q_0 \exp(-t/\tau) \qquad (1.13)$$

or

$$q = q_0\, e^{-t/\tau}$$

where q is the charge at time t, q_0 is the charge before the decay begins, τ is the time constant which is equal to RC and e is a mathematical constant which has the approximate value 2.718. The time constant is the time taken for the charge to reach approximately 37 % of its initial value. Equation

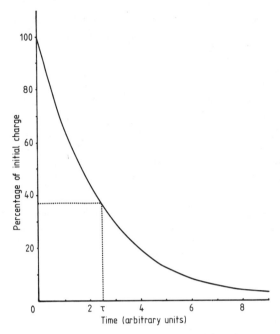

Figure 1.2 The exponential decay of charge with a time constant τ.

(1.13) may also be written as

$$\ln q = \ln q_0 - t/\tau$$

or

$$2.30 \log q = 2.30 \log q_0 - t/\tau.$$

Therefore, if q is plotted on log/linear graph paper with the time t on the linear scale, exponential decay will produce a straight line whose slope is $-(1/2.3)\tau$. This enables the time constant to be found simply from experimental measurements of the decrease in charge with time.

The time constant may be written in terms of the dielectric constant of the material and its resistivity

$$\tau = \varepsilon_r \varepsilon_0 \rho. \tag{1.14}$$

1.3 ORDERS OF MAGNITUDE

The electrostatic force is the force which binds atoms and molecules together, yet in the macroscopic world it is so small that only very lightweight particles can be picked up by an electrostatically charged rod. One reason for this apparent paradox is the low charge levels achieved in practice. For example, the charge flowing in a wire carrying 1 A is $1\,\mathrm{C\,s^{-1}}$. Thus, on the basis of current flow, the Coulomb is a realistic unit. However, when the Coulomb law is used to calculate the force between two charges of 1 C, one metre apart,

$$F = qq'/4\pi\varepsilon_0 d^2$$
$$= 1/(4\pi \times 8.8 \times 10^{-12})$$
$$= 9.04 \times 10^9 \text{ N}. \tag{1.15}$$

This is equivalent to the gravitational force on the object weighing 10^9 kg which is obviously totally unrealistic. The amount of charge which can be built up in practice must be much less than 1 C.

In practice it is just possible to lift a 5 mm diameter polystyrene sphere weighing approximately 100 mg using a field of 500 kV m^{-1}. Equating the electrical force lifting the particle to the force due to gravity:

$$qE = mg \tag{1.16}$$

and the charge is found to be 2×10^{-9} C. The charge density on the surface of the sphere is therefore 2.5×10^{-5} C m^{-2}.

One electron has a charge of 1.6×10^{-19} C. Therefore, this charge density is equivalent to approximately 1.6×10^{14} extra electrons per square metre on a negatively charged surface. The atomic density on a solid surface is of the order of 2×10^{19} atoms m^{-2}. Therefore, if charge resides on the surface monolayer of atoms only about eight atoms per million are charged.

The maximum charge which can be built up on a surface is limited by the breakdown strength of the air. When the electric field in air reaches a value of approximately 3×10^6 V m^{-1} the air ionises and the surface charge is dissipated. It will be shown in §1.5 that the surface charge needed to create this field is 2.64×10^{-5} C m^{-2}.

The low percentage of charged atoms needed to give the surface its limiting charge explains why electrostatic phenomena are so notoriously unpredictable. If only one surface atom in 125 000 is charged, then it follows that surface impurity levels of a few parts per million can significantly alter the charge on a surface. It can also be seen that if there were not some mechanism preventing every atom on a surface from becoming charged, then electrostatic forces in the real world would be extremely large.

1.4 SUMMARY OF ELECTROSTATIC EQUATIONS IN UNIFORM FIELDS

A general theory of electrostatics which can be used to solve problems where charge densities and electric fields are not uniform involves differential calculus and will be discussed in Chapter 7. However, many electrostatic problems can be solved approximately, assuming that electric fields and charge densities are uniform. The equations of electrostatics then become very simple and are summarised below.

1.4.1 The Coulomb law

The force between two charges q and q' a distance d apart in a medium of relative dielectric constant ε_r is

$$F = qq'/4\pi\varepsilon_0\varepsilon_r d^2. \tag{1.17}$$

This law was originally found experimentally. A justification that it is precisely true is given in Chapter 7.

1.4.2 Electric field

The electric field, E, is defined by the equation

$$F = qE. \tag{1.18}$$

Therefore, the electric field due to a charge q' is

$$E = q'/4\pi\varepsilon_0\varepsilon_r d^2. \tag{1.19}$$

The electric field may also be expressed in terms of the rate of change of potential with distance. The electric field between parallel planes with a potential difference V between them is

$$E = -V/d. \tag{1.20}$$

1.4.3 Capacitance

By definition

$$C = q/V. \tag{1.21}$$

The energy stored in a capacitance is

$$U = \tfrac{1}{2}CV^2 = \tfrac{1}{2}qV = \tfrac{1}{2}q^2/C. \tag{1.22}$$

The capacitance between two parallel plates of area A, separated by a slab of a dielectric medium of thickness, d, and relative dielectric constant, ε_r, is given by

$$C = \varepsilon_0\varepsilon_r A/d. \tag{1.23}$$

The capacitance of an isolated conducting sphere of radius r in a medium of dielectric constant ε_r is

$$C = 4\pi\varepsilon_0\varepsilon_r. \tag{1.24}$$

(a)

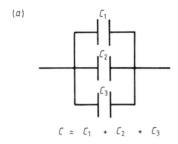

$$C = C_1 + C_2 + C_3.$$

(b)

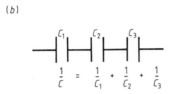

$$\frac{1}{C} = \frac{1}{C_1} + \frac{1}{C_2} + \frac{1}{C_3}$$

Figure 1.3 Capacitances in (a) parallel and (b) series.

The combined effect of a number of capacitors in series (figure 1.3(b)) is

$$1/C = 1/C_1 + 1/C_2 + 1/C_3 \ldots \qquad (1.25)$$

The combined effect of a number of capacitors in parallel (figure 1.3(a)) is

$$C = C_1 + C_2 + C_3 \ldots \qquad (1.26)$$

1.4.4 Resistance

Resistance is defined as the ratio of voltage to current

$$R = V/I. \qquad (1.27)$$

For conductors R is a constant but for insulators the resistance may change with the applied voltage.

The resistance of a piece of material depends on its dimensions. The resistance of a sample with unit area and unit length is called the resistivity and is a property of the material

$$\rho = Rd/A. \qquad (1.28)$$

Electrical conductivity is the reciprocal of resistivity

$$\sigma = 1/\rho. \qquad (1.29)$$

The combined effect of a number of resistances in series is given by

$$R = R_1 + R_2 + R_3 \ldots \qquad (1.30)$$

The combined effect of resistances in parallel is given by

$$1/R = 1/R_1 + 1/R_2 + 1/R_3. \qquad (1.31)$$

1.4.5 Time constant for charge decay

The time constant of an exponential decay, τ, is the time taken for the quantity concerned to reach $1/e$ (approximately 37 %) of its initial value. For decay of charge from a capacitor C through a resistance R

$$\tau = RC. \tag{1.32}$$

For the decay of charge from a material of dielectric constant ε_r and resistivity, ρ

$$\tau = \varepsilon_0 \varepsilon_r \rho. \tag{1.33}$$

1.5 GAUSS'S LAW—THE ELECTRIC FIELD DUE TO AN ASSEMBLY OF CHARGES

Gauss's law states that if an imaginary surface, of area S, is drawn round a uniform density of charge, then the component of the electric field at the surface, which is perpendicular to the surface, is proportional to the total charge enclosed, i.e.

$$E = \sum q / S\varepsilon_0 \varepsilon_r \tag{1.34}$$

where $\sum q$ is the sum of the charges enclosed by the surface. The Gauss law may be used to calculate the maximum density of charge which can be sustained before the air ionises (at an electric field of 3×10^6 V m^{-1}). For example, consider a sphere with a surface charge density of Q_s (C m^{-2}). If we take as the imaginary Gaussian surface another sphere which is only just outside the charged sphere, it may be considered to have the same surface area S as the sphere itself. The total charge enclosed is the surface density of charge multiplied by the surface area, i.e. $\sum q = Q_s \times S$. From the Gauss law

$$E = (Q_s \times S)/(S \times \varepsilon_0) = Q_s/\varepsilon_0. \tag{1.35}$$

The maximum electric field is 3×10^6 V m^{-1}, therefore the maximum charge density is

$$Q_{max} = 3 \times 10^6 \times 8.8 \times 10^{12}$$

$$= 2.64 \times 10^{-5} \, \text{C m}^{-2}.$$

This is the maximum charge density which can be sustained on any surface in air. As discussed earlier, a charge density of 2.64×10^{-5} C m^{-2} is equivalent to only a few surface atoms out of every million being charged.

In most practical situations the charge on a surface, or the mean charge density on a collection of particles, is limited, not by the ability of the surfaces to acquire a charge, but by the ionisation of the air. The Gauss law is therefore used frequently to obtain an estimate of the charge which will exist in a given industrial situation.

Chapter 2 Electrification of Solids and Liquids

2.1 CONTACT AND FRICTIONAL CHARGING

When two insulating materials are rubbed together, the surfaces acquire a net electric charge, with one becoming negative and the other positive. For many materials, it is only necessary to touch the surfaces together, then separate them to transfer a measurable charge. Most frictionally charged surfaces have both positively and negatively charged areas, but one polarity predominates, determining the net charge of the surface. The distribution of charge on a surface can be displayed by dusting the surface with positive and negatively charged pigments of different colours. For example, a mixture of one part carmine, five parts flowers of sulphur and three parts lycopodium, will charge so that the carmine is attracted to positive areas of surface and the lycopodium to negative areas. (The lycopodium can be rendered more visible by dyeing it blue by dispersing 70 g in 100 ml of methyl violet (Hull 1949).)

Materials may be arranged in a table according to the amount of positive charge which is transferred (i.e. every material charges positive against materials below it in the table). This is known as the triboelectric series and is analogous to the electrochemical series of metals. In practice, the order of materials in the triboelectric series is not unambiguous and a number of different series have been published by different authors.

At first sight it is surprising that frictional charging has been recognised for nearly three thousand years, yet we still do not really understand its causes. However, charge transfer is a surface phenomenon which, as discussed in §1.3, involves at most only eight out of every million surface atoms. Surface changes of a few parts per million can therefore have a substantial influence on the amount of charge exchanged.

During contact between two materials, charge moves from one to the other. Therefore, in order to understand the phenomenon, it is necessary to consider the energy of the electrons and ions at the surfaces of the two materials and the way in which they move both within and between materials.

2.1.1 Electron energies in materials

Electrons in a single isolated atom move in orbits around the nucleus. Each electron has a particular energy depending on the distance of the orbit from the nucleus. An electron is not able to change energy continuously, but must jump between the defined orbits, gaining or losing a discrete amount of energy (a quantum of energy). The defined orbits round the nucleus are considered to be energy levels which are either occupied or unoccupied by an electron. When atoms are brought together to form a solid, they influence each other, with the result that the orbits become less precisely defined and the electrons can have a range of energies around the original discrete level. The outer electrons of the atoms have a greater influence on each other than the inner ones and therefore the energy levels representing the outer orbits of the atoms cover a wider range of energy than the inner orbits. Electrons may still only have an energy within a fixed range and are said to be in energy bands instead of energy levels. The inner electrons of the atom affect each other only slightly and are in narrow bands called core bands. The outer, or valence electrons are smeared into a wider band known as the valence band. Energy levels which correspond to excited states of the outer electrons form a conduction band. According to quantum mechanical laws, each band can only contain a fixed number of electrons and when this number is reached the band is full. Between the allowed ranges of energy are forbidden energy bands. The spread in the energies of electrons as atoms are brought together to form a solid is illustrated in figure 2.1.

This simple band model can explain the difference in electrical conductivity between metals, insulators and semiconductors. A material is only able to conduct if outer electrons lie in an energy band which is partially empty. If the band is full, there are two electrons for every possible energy which can exist in the band, the maximum which is allowed by quantum mechanical rules. This means no electron in the band can increase its energy and electrons cannot be accelerated by an electric field. The material is therefore an insulator (figure 2.2(b)).

At any temperature above absolute zero there is a chance that a few electrons will have sufficient energy to cross the forbidden gap to the empty conduction band. These electrons are then free to accelerate. They also leave empty energy levels, or 'holes', within the valence band which allow a few valence electrons to change energy. The number of mobile electrons and holes within an insulator is very low and electronic conduction in insulators

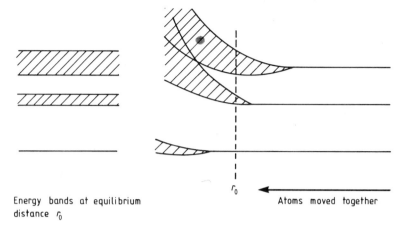

Energy bands at equilibrium
distance r_0

Atoms moved together

Figure 2.1 The formation of energy bands. The sharp energy levels of individual atoms widen as the atoms are brought together because of interactions between the electrons of different atoms.

is also very low. Some insulators (for example, glasses and some polymers) have ions which are relatively loosely bound to the main structure and can move in an electric field. In these materials ionic conductivity exceeds electronic conductivity.

In a metal the outer electrons are either in a partially empty valence band, or the equilibrium spacing is such that a full valence band overlaps the empty conduction band, as shown in figure 2.2(a). In either case the electron is able to increase its energy within the band, and the material is a conductor. The highest filled energy level at absolute zero temperature is known as the Fermi energy.

The above theory, which considers the changes in the electron energies as atoms are brought together, is known as the tight-binding approximation since atoms are considered to remain tightly bound entities which have a

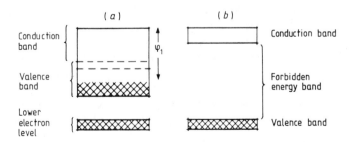

Figure 2.2 The band structure of (a) a metal and (b) an insulator. The cross hatching indicates the filled energy levels and φ_1 is the metal work function.

relatively small effect on each other. It is able to explain differences between metals and insulators and is a reasonable approximation for many insulators, however, it is unable to explain a number of experimentally observed properties of materials. For example, measurements of the conductivity of metals show that the distance travelled by electrons between collisions with the lattice is many times the spacing between the atoms. According to the tight-binding approximation, one would expect an electron to be scattered at every atomic site. This anomaly is explained by taking into account the wave-like nature of electrons, i.e. the probability of finding an electron at any position can be described by a wave which satisfies an equation first derived by Schrödinger (see, for example, Eisberg 1961). The outer electrons of an atom can be considered to be waves which propagate freely through the lattice of the crystal. These waves are only scattered by breaks in the periodicity of the lattice, caused by thermal oscillations or by imperfections in the crystal. Just as an oscillating string can only vibrate with certain frequencies, depending on its length, so the electron wave can only have certain frequencies and energies depending on the periodicity of the crystal. The wave model therefore also predicts a band structure with allowed and forbidden ranges of electron energy.

An important feature of the model is that waves propagate throughout the crystal, and electrons do not belong to any atom in particular, i.e. they are 'delocalised'. This treatment of electrons in a material is known as the 'nearly-free-electron model', because the ions of the crystal lattice are considered to have only a small effect on the outer electrons. The electrons are always both waves and particles and are delocalised in both metals and insulators, provided the atoms are sufficiently close together and are arranged in a regular array.

2.1.2 Electron energies in a metal

The nearly-free-electron model is a good description of the energy of electrons in a metal and many of the properties of metals can be explained by assuming that the outer electrons form a sea of electrons, free to move throughout the crystal lattice. The density of electron energy states, per unit energy range, for these free electrons, is shown by the broken curve in figure 2.3. At a temperature of absolute zero the electrons will take up the lowest allowed energy in the band and the highest occupied energy level is called the Fermi energy. At non-zero temperature electrons will have thermal energy, therefore some will have energies slightly above the Fermi energy, leaving some empty energy levels just below the Fermi energy, as illustrated in figure 2.3. The energy required to move an electron from the top of the energy distribution, out of the metal to infinity, is called the work function. For the majority of metals this is around four electron volts (eV) and depends on surface impurity atoms such as adsorbed gases. The zero of energy is usually

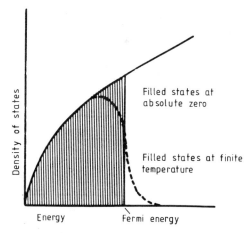

Figure 2.3 Density of energy states as a function of energy.

defined as the vacuum level (i.e. the energy of an electron as it leaves the material with zero velocity). The electrons at the Fermi level in the metal therefore have an energy of the order of -4 eV (where 1 eV is the energy required to move an electron through a potential of 1 V).

2.1.3 Electron energies in crystalline insulators and semiconductors

At a temperature of absolute zero both crystalline insulators and semiconductors have a full valence band and an empty conduction band. The main distinction between the two types of material is the size of the energy band gap. A semiconductor has a band gap of the order of 1 eV and at a finite temperature some electrons in the valence band are likely to have sufficient thermal energy to cross the gap and reach the conduction band. A crystalline insulator has a forbidden energy gap of up to 12 eV and a much higher temperature is required to excite electrons to the conduction band. In most insulators the electrons lie in a full energy band which is well below the Fermi energy of a metal while the empty conduction band of the insulator is at the vacuum level and is well above the Fermi energy.

If an insulator or semiconductor contains impurity atoms the electrons associated with that atom are in a slightly different environment to the other electrons in the crystal. An impurity atom may therefore give rise to an additional energy level which is outside the normally allowed range. This additional energy level may be occupied by an electron, but the situation can also be envisaged where the impurity atom has a different number of electrons than the atoms of the parent lattice. An extra electron will give rise to a filled energy level close to the conduction band, whereas the lack of an electron will give an unoccupied energy level close to the valence band. Both situations allow the possibility of a small number of charge carriers moving and hence some conduction.

The simple band theory breaks down for both molecular crystals and ionic crystals. In molecular crystals there is a relatively large distance between molecules. As the distance between individual atoms increases, the interaction between their electron orbits is less, and the bands become very narrow. Eventually it is no longer possible to consider the electrons to be delocalised. They still have an energy which lies within narrow bands, but the energy for each electron is separate, both in energy and space. In ionic crystals, the interaction between the electrons and the lattice is not negligible. As an electron moves through a lattice its electric field affects the ions of the crystal lattice and the lattice distorts and becomes polarised. The combination of the electron and its associated lattice distortion can be treated as if it were a different type of charged particle called a polaron. Ionic crystals are seldom of practical interest in electrostatics, therefore the properties of the polaron are not considered further here. Reviews of polaron theory are given by Austin and Mott (1969) and O'Dwyer (1973).

2.1.4 Electron energies in amorphous insulators and localised states

In the nearly-free-electron model, the delocalised nature of the electron and the band structure of electron energies are a consequence of the periodicity of the crystal. Many insulators of interest in electrostatics are either totally amorphous, or partly so. Anderson (1958) showed that for a sufficiently random lattice of one dimension, all states of an electron are localised. This means that if one tries to find a wave motion for electrons that is compatible with the Schrödinger wave equation and a disordered lattice, one finds that all solutions have a maximum value at one particular position and decay exponentially to zero as they move away from that position.

Frisch and Lloyd (1960) calculated the number of electron states of each energy for a disordered system of ions. They considered both the case of electrons influenced by a low density of strong scatterers (equivalent to a tight-binding approximation) and the case of a high density of weak scatterers (equivalent to the nearly-free-electron model). They found that for a low density of strong scatterers there was a pronounced minimum in the density of electron states as a function of energy, however, for a completely random distribution of ions the minimum did not reach zero and there was no completely forbidden gap.

In a real three-dimensional structure, Mott (1968) predicted that there would be both localised and non-localised states, with localised states within the range of energies where the density of states is low, i.e. in the pseudo-band gap of the material. Thus, in real amorphous materials there is still effectively a forbidden energy gap but there will be some electrons with energies within that gap localised at one position in the material.

The energies of electrons in an amorphous insulator are shown schematically in figure 2.4.

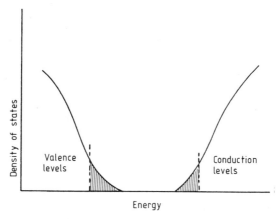

Figure 2.4 Density of states for an insulator with a disordered structure (after Mott 1968). Shaded portions represent localised states.

2.1.5 Other localised electron energy states

We have seen so far that there are localised energy levels within the band gap due to amorphous structures and due to impurity atoms. There will also be energy levels within the band gap, localised at the surface of the material. These will be associated with the impurities which tend to congregate at the surface and with the break in the normal structure of the material at the surface.

In covalently bonded solids most of the additional available energy levels (or electron traps) are due to impurity atoms. In molecular solids, electron traps may be associated with the ends of molecular chains or with cross linking but they may also be due to polarisation fluctuations in side groups of long molecular chains (Duke and Fabish 1976).

Duke and Fabish suggest that side groups can form intrinsic charge-carrying ion sites in a polymer, which are somewhat analogous to ions in a liquid. These molecular ion sites may be electron donors or acceptors. Some side group molecules exist in a free state as a gas for which the electron energy levels are known. Duke and Fabish calculate that when the inter-molecular and intramolecular interactions are taken into account the energy levels for the charged molecules bound in the solid, will be similar to the Fermi energy of a metal. The energies are predicted to fluctuate by about 0.5 eV from site to site, because of thermal fluctuations and differences in the local environment at each molecule. They therefore envisage a double Gaussian distribution of localised states, representing donor and acceptor molecules, lying within the insulator band gap and centred at about -4 eV as shown in figure 2.5 (Fabish *et al* 1976, Duke *et al* 1978, Fabish and Duke 1977).

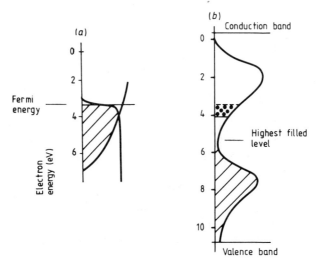

Figure 2.5 Schematic diagram of energetics for (*a*) metal and (*b*) insulator contact for carrier injection into insulator acceptor states (Duke and Fabish model) (after Fabish and Duke 1978). Shaded areas represent filled energy states.

2.1.6 Ions in materials

Ionic conduction is observed in some crystalline insulators, in electrolytes (solutions or melts of compounds which readily dissociate into positive and negative ions), in many amorphous materials (such as glasses and some polymers) and in electrolytic layers on surfaces with adsorbed water. For these materials ionic transfer may play a part in charge transfer between materials and the theory of ionic motion within and between materials will be relevant.

2.1.7 Electrolytic conduction

An electrolyte may be defined as an assemblage of atoms or molecules of which at least some are mobile ions. Electrolytes may be either solids or liquids but liquid electrolytes have received the most study. Ions in a liquid may arise from dissociation of the host medium or from impurities. When a voltage is applied, positive ions (cations) migrate towards the cathode and negative ions (anions) towards the anode. At the electrodes the ionic charge carriers in the liquid must be converted to electron charge carriers in the metal by means of chemical reactions. A number of competing processes may occur. For example, an electron from the cathode may neutralise the mobile ion or it may neutralise the positive part of another ionic compound, leaving the negative part to either react with the mobile ion, or migrate to the anode. In liquids the electrode reactions are normally complicated, with a number of different processes occurring together and reaching a chemical equilibrium.

Since ions are transferred through the material, electrolysis results in the liberation of material at the electrodes. The ion transport obeys Faraday's laws:

(i) The mass of a given substance liberated at one electrode is proportional to the current which has passed.

(ii) The mass of a given material liberated at an electrode is proportional to its electrochemical equivalent. (The electrochemical equivalent is the atomic weight divided by the valency where the valency is the number of charges carried by the ion.)

The flow of current in an electrolyte obeys a modified version of the Ohm law. No current flows until the voltage exceeds a critical value, known as the decomposition potential, V_c, but at higher voltages the current flow obeys the relation

$$V - V_c = IR$$

where R is the resistance of the liquid.

In a liquid with a low concentration of ions the conductivity is proportional to the concentration of ions. For higher concentrations, the conductivity increases less rapidly with concentration, because each ion attracts to itself an atmosphere of oppositely charged ions which retard its progress.

Solid electrolytes behave in a very similar way to liquid electrolytes. Faraday's laws are still obeyed, but in a solid there may be a substantial component of electronic conductivity, which leads to an apparent deviation from the expected behaviour. In a solid the energies and mobilities of the ions are usually such that only one species of ion contributes to the conductivity and the multiple electrode reactions which are a feature of electrolysis in a liquid do not occur.

2.1.8 Ionic conduction in dielectric liquids

In dielectric (relatively insulating) liquids ions may be produced as a result of dissociation or they may be injected at one or both electrodes.

The current flow in a dielectric liquid is not proportional to the applied voltage. The current–voltage curve tends to be irreproducible and to depend on the nature of the electrodes and the number of previous tests. It is also very sensitive to the growth rate of the voltage.

The current–voltage curve generally has three distinct parts:

(i) At low fields there is a quasi-ohmic behaviour (corresponding to electrolytic conduction).

(ii) At intermediate fields the current increases more slowly than predicted by the Ohm law and the current tends to saturate. This is associated with the formation of regions of space charge in the liquid.

(iii) At high fields the conductivity increases rapidly as extra charge is injected from the electrodes.

2.1.9 Ionic conduction in dielectric solids

Typically a polymer has an electrical conductivity between 10^{-12} and 10^{-18} and glass around 10^{-10} S m^{-1}. The conductivity is related to the number of charge carriers by the equation

$$\sigma = neb \tag{2.1}$$

where n is the density of charge carriers, e is the charge on an ion and b is the ion mobility. If the mobility is of the order of 10^{-11} m^2 V^{-1} s^{-1}, and e is equal to one electron charge $(1.6 \times 10^{-19}$ C), a conductivity of 10^{-10} S m^{-1}, implies a carrier concentration of 10^{18} m^{-3}. Comparing this with typical atomic density of around 10^{28} m^{-3}, it can be seen that only an extremely low density of charge carriers (i.e. one atom in 10^{10}) is necessary for significant conduction.

In a crystalline insulator, relatively free ions are formed as a result of crystal defects. In a glass, ions, such as the alkalis which are introduced to give the glass specific properties, or hydrogen from water, take up interstitial positions in the silica network to which they are only loosely bound. In a polymer, relatively free ions are derived from residual polymerisation catalyst, from plasticisers and other additives, from dissociation products of the polymer itself and from adsorbed water. In all cases the ion will move by a thermally activated process, i.e. at a temperature, T, the ion will have a probability, P, of having enough energy to hop to an adjacent stable position which is given by

$$P = A \exp(U/kT) \tag{2.2}$$

where U is the energy of the barrier which must be overcome, T is absolute temperature (K) and k is the Boltzmann constant. It can be shown that the current density of ions flowing in an applied field E will be given by

$$j = \sinh(eaE/2kT) \tag{2.3}$$

where a is the distance between neighbouring stable positions and e is the charge on an ion (Mott and Gurney 1948).

2.1.10 Ions on surfaces

If electronic surface states are occupied there may be a charged layer at the surface of an insulator. This will result in the accumulation of a layer of counter charges, extending deeper into the material, forming a surface double layer. Figure 2.6(*a*) shows a schematic representation of the energy states at a polymer surface (Lewis 1978).

When a gas is absorbed onto a surface, it is usually assumed that charge transfer occurs. This will result in an ionic surface double layer and a potential barrier which inhibits the movement of electrons from the material as shown schematically in figure 2.6(*b*).

Most surfaces in air will be covered by a layer of water ranging in thickness between a monolayer to a macroscopic thin film. Where a continuous film is formed the water provides a medium for dissociation of ions. Ions of one polarity will be preferentially attracted to the surface and again a charged double layer is formed. The properties of charged double layers at a solid–liquid interface are discussed in more detail in §2.5.

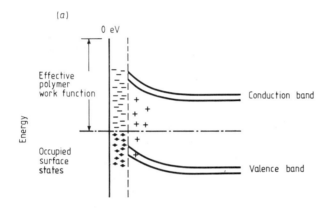

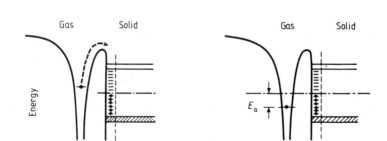

Figure 2.6 (*a*) Double layer at a polymer surface with negative charge in the surface states and counter positive charge in the bulk polymer. (*b*) Ionic transfer to surface leaving a neutral gas molecule. In the right-hand figure an activation energy E_a is required. The gas provides a potential barrier to the movement of charge from the insulator.

The influence of water on hydrophobic surfaces is less well understood. With a monolayer or less of water, the absorbed molecules cannot be considered to have the properties or structure of the liquid. Awakuni and Calderwood (1972) could detect no surface conduction on polyethylene or PTFE even in a saturated-water atmosphere, however significant water adsorption and conductivity were observed if the surfaces were oxidised. It was found that with a quartz surface, conductivity was only significant after a full monolayer had been adsorbed, whereas with an oxidised PTFE surface, water adsorption of less than a monolayer would increase conductivity, implying that individual water molecules formed mobile ions on the surface of this material.

There is a vast literature on the study of atomically clean surfaces and much still to be understood in this area. Real surfaces, particularly the surfaces of polymers and highly insulating materials, in the presence of adsorbed gases and water vapour, are even less well understood. Here only a brief indication has been given of some of the factors which complicate an understanding of surface phenomena such as contact charging.

2.1.11 Experiments on charge transfer between a metal and an insulator

A number of experiments were carried out in the 1960s which showed that the amount of charge transferred to an insulator, in a simple (non-sliding) contact, by each of a series of metals, was proportional to the metal work function. For example, Davies (1967a,b, 1969) mounted dielectric specimens on an earthed drum which was rotated against a wheel made from five different metals. The charge density on the dielectric specimens and the work functions of the metal segments were monitored continuously as the drum and the wheel were rotated in opposite directions. The metal work function was found by measuring the contact potential difference against an oscillating gold reference electrode. The apparatus was evacuated to prevent breakdown of the air as the surfaces separated. For each polymer, the charge density was approximately proportional to the metal work function. This allowed an effective work function to be assigned to the polymers as shown in table 2.1.

Arridge (1967) contacted nylon against a wide range of metals and obtained the linear relationship shown in figure 2.7. Strella found the effective work functions of nineteen materials, four of which were the same as those tested by Davies (Strella 1970, unpublished results cited in Seanor 1972). Strella obtained higher effective work functions than Davies, and the materials appeared in a different order (table 2.1). In general, both estimates of polymer work functions, and the order of materials in the triboelectric series, differ between different workers. Table 2.2 presents the results of a number of different triboelectric series published since 1924 (Bauser 1974). The order of materials in a triboelectric series is not always unique, even in one series of tests, and there is a lack of reproducibility between tests which reflects the inhomogeneities of polymer surfaces.

Table 2.1 Polymer work functions.

Material	Work function (eV)	
	Davies (1969)	Strella (1970)
− PVC	4.85 ± 0.20	5.13
Polyimide	4.36 ± 0.06	
Polycarbonate	4.26 ± 0.13	4.80
PTFE	4.26 ± 0.05	5.75
PET	4.25 ± 0.10	
Polystyrene	4.22 ± 0.07	
+ Nylon 66	4.08 ± 0.06	4.30–4.54
− Teflon (PTFE)		5.75
Polychlorotrifluoethylene		5.30
Polychlorinated propylene		5.14
PVC		5.13
Polychlorinated ether		5.11
Poly-4-chlorostyrene		5.11
Poly-4-chloro-4-methoxy-styrene		5.02
Polysulphone		4.95
Polyepichlorohydrin		4.95
Polystyrene		4.90
Polyethylene		4.90
Polycarbonate		4.80
Polyethylene-vinyl acetate		4.79
Polymethylmethacrylate		4.68
Polyvinylacetate		4.38
Polyvinylbutyral		4.30
Poly-2-vinylpyridine-styrene		4.27
Nylon 66		4.30–4.54
+ Polyethylene oxide		3.95–4.50

It is common to assign a value of work function to an insulator, but it can be seen from the earlier discussion that the most energetic electrons in an insulator do not have a single value of energy throughout the material as they do in a metal. Electron energies in an insulator are a function of position, surface impurities and the local atomic structure as well as the chemical nature of the material and the work function of an insulator is therefore an experimental quantity, defined in terms of electron flow from a particular sample to a contacting metal. It has no fundamental standard value from sample to sample.

Table 2.2 The triboelectric series.

(a) Montgomery (1959)

Material	Polymer type
+ Wool	
Nylon	
Viscose	Cellulose
Cotton	
Silk	
Acetate rayon	Cellulose acetate
Lucite or Perspex	PMMA
Polyvinyl alcohol	
Dacron	Copolyester of ethylene glycol and terephthalic acid
Orlon	Polyacrylonitrile
PVC	
Dynel	Copolymer acrylonitrile/vinyl chloride
Velon	Copolymer vinylidene chloride/vinyl chloride
Polyethylene	
− Teflon	PTFE

(b) Webers (1963)

Material	Polymer	Source
+ Polyox	Polyethylene oxide	Union Carbide
Polyethylene amine		Chemirad
Gelatin		
Vinac	Polyninyl acetate	Colton chemical
Lucite 44	Polybutyl methacrylate	Du Pont
Lucite 42	Polymethyl methacrylate	Du Pont
Acryloid A101	Polymethyl methacrylate	Rohm and Haas
Zelec DX	Polycation	Du Pont
Polyacrylamide		Cyanamid
Cellulose acetate/butyrate		Eastman
Acysol	Polyacrylic acid	Rohm and Haas
Carbopol	Polyacid	BF Goodrich
Polyethylene terephthalate		
Polyvinyl butyral		Du Pont
− Polyethylene		

(c) Williams (1976)

Material	Polymer	Source
+ Lucite 2041	Methyl methacrylate	Du Pont
Dapon	Diallyl phthalate	
Lexan 105	Poly-bisphenol-A-carbonate	GE
Formvar	Polyvinylformal	Monsanto
Estane	Polyurethane	Goodrich
Du Pont 49000	Polyester	Du Pont
Durez	Phenol formaldehyde	Durez
Ethocel 10	Ethyl cellulose	Hercules
Polystyrene 8X	Polystyrene	Kopper
Epolene C	Polyethylene	Eastman
Polysulphone P-3500	A diphenyl sulphone	Union Carbide
Hypalon 30	Chlorosulphonated PE	Du Pont
Cyclolac H-1000	Acrylonitrile-butadiene-styrene terpolymer	Borg Warner

Table 2.2 (*continued*)

(c) Williams (1976)

Material	Polymer	Source
Uncoated iron		
Cellulose acetate butyrate		
Epon 828/V125	Epoxy amine curing agent	Shell/General Mills
Polysulphone P-1700		Union Carbide
Cellulose nitrate		
− Kynar	Polyvinyldene fluoride	Penwalt

(d) Bauser (1974). All references in footnote are given in Bauser (1974).

	Friction							Contact		
Reference	a	b	c	d	e	f	g	h	i	j
RH (%)	52–69	33	15			18			30	$(10^{-5}\,\tau)$

+ Mica
Wool
PVA

PMMA
PA 66
Wool (knitted)
Silk
Viscose
Cotton
Silk

PVAc
PMMA
PVA
Silk (woven)
PVC
PVA
Ebonite

Cellulose acetyl/butyrate
Cotton
PVC
Ebonite
PS
PET
PS

Polyvinylbutyrate

Polyacrylonitrile
Sulphur

PVC,h
PE
PTFE
Polyimide
− PVC

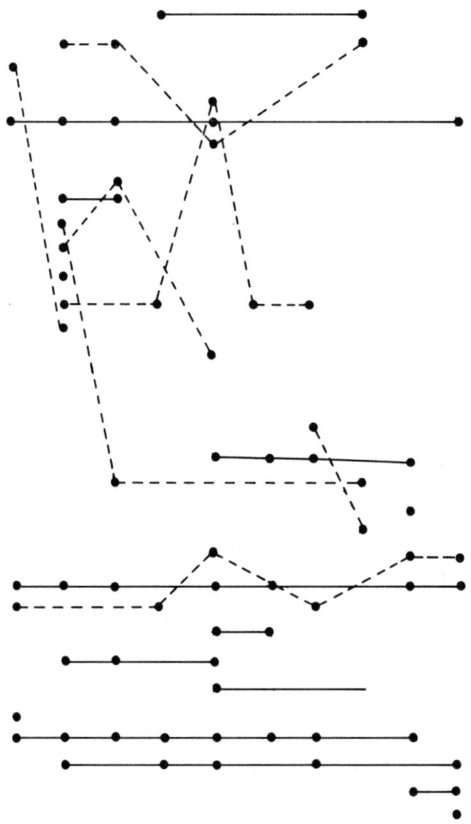

a, Sasaki (1969); b, Hersh and Montgomery (1956); c, Ballou (1954); d, Fukuda and Fowler (1958); e, Henniker (1962); f, Webers (1963); g, Rose and Ward (1957); h, Silsbee (1924); i, Coste (1970); j, Davies (1969).

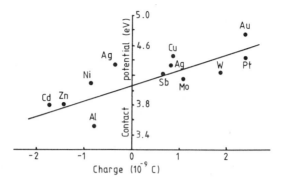

Figure 2.7 Variation of charge on nylon 6.6 with contact potential of different metals (after Arridge 1967). Undrawn, TiO_2 filled nylon, tested under nitrogen.

Recent and detailed experimental work has found that the simple linear relationship between the charge transferred and the metal work function is not universal. Cunningham and Hood (1970a,b) found a linear relationship after a single contact, but the slope of successive lines decreased as more and more contacts were made at the same position. They suggested that the real area of contact decreased with time, and did not attempt to assign values of work function to the polymers. Lowell (1976) went to considerable trouble in his experiments to ensure that the charge was produced by a single, non-sliding, contact and found that the quantity of charge transferred to polyethylene, PTFE and PET was independent of the metal work function. However, after multiple contacts, or sliding, the linear dependence observed by other experimenters was found. The quantity of charge transferred increased roughly as the logarithm of the number of contacts (figure 2.8). For PTFE and polyethylene, the increase in charge with the number of contacts continued to well beyond a thousand contacts, but with PET the charge saturated. The duration of the contact and the time between contacts had no effect and if the surface was discharged and the experiment repeated the same results were obtained. This proved that the increase in the charge transferred could not be due to an increased contact area due to permanent deformation of the surface.

The quantity of charge transferred to diamond also increases with the number of contacts although this material is too hard to deform during contact. It was found that the rise in charge with number of contacts was influenced by the conductivity of the diamond, which was varied by illuminating it with light of different intensities. When the sample was in the dark, and the resistivity consequently high, there was no increase in charge for up to a hundred contacts (Homewood *et al* 1983). The way in which the charge increased with the number of contacts was different for diamond and for polymers, and experiments showed that conduction was almost certainly not the mechanism responsible for the increase in charge in polymeric materials.

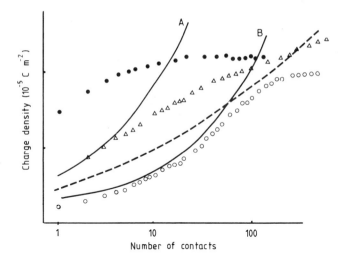

Figure 2.8 Charge density of polymers as a function of the number of contacts (from Lowell 1976). $\bigcirc$, PET/Al; $\bullet$, PET/Hg (arbitrary units); $\triangle$, PTFE/Pt ($\times 20$). Broken curve, theory based on the hypothesis that the charge increase is due to a variation in the position of the contact. Full curves, theory based on the hypothesis that the charge is transferred to the bulk material by mechanical deformation: A, $t/r = 0.02, f = 0.25$; B, $t/r = 0.01, f = 0.1$. Here, t is tunnelling depth, r is redistribution depth and f is the fraction of traps which move into polymer.

Lowell (1976), working with polyethylene, PET and PTFE, found no dependence of charge transfer with the duration of the contact, but a time dependence has been observed for polystyrene (Furhmann and Kurschner 1981). This was attributed to the presence of a low-energy barrier between the Fermi level of the metal and the acceptor states in the polymer. Furhmann and co-workers proposed a simple analogue computer model of electrification by intermittent contact (Henneke *et al* 1979). A time dependence of charging was also observed by Davies (1967a,b). He found that in single-contact charging between aluminium and polyethylene the charge transferred increased with time for up to ten minutes. He proposed that the effect could be accounted for either by electrical relaxation effects as charge spread away from the contact point or by an increase in the true contact area with time.

In the most recent work of Lowell and his co-workers, the effect of the metal work function on the quantity of charge transferred has been investigated with greatly improved statistics. The apparatus has been automated, and each result for the charge transferred between a metal and a polymer is built up from measurements of between 60 and 120 individual contacts at different positions on the sample. The distribution of the amount of charge transferred was not Gaussian for either PTFE or nylon, with both materials producing results with a tail of large charges. The mean charge transferred to PTFE was independent of metal work function but the charge transferred to nylon increased as the work function of the metal increased as shown in figure 2.9. It can be seen that there was a general trend towards a linear relationship, but the charge transferred from a number of metals was significantly removed from the general trend, and several others differed by more than would be expected from the standard error (Akande and Lowell 1985).

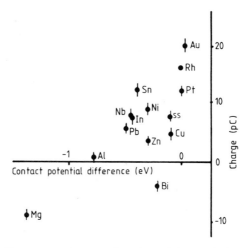

Figure 2.9 Charge transfer as a function of the work function of the contacting metal for nylon 66 (from Akande and Lowell 1985).

Non-linear relationships between charge transfer and metal work function have also been reported (Bauser *et al* 1970, Bauser 1974). For example, Kittaka and Murata (1971) (cited in Bauser 1974) found that the charge transferred to polyacrylester increased sharply as the work function of the metal exceeded 4.5 eV and Zimmer (1970) observed a curved relationship with polyvinyl carbazole.

In summary there is a general trend for the amount of charge transferred in the contact between a polymer and a series of metals to increase approximately linearly with the metal work function. There is considerable scatter in the results and some individual metals and polymers cannot be fitted to the general results.

2.1.12 Theoretical models of electron transfer

The observation of a linear relationship between the charge transferred and metal work function (which is the energy required to leave the metal) implies that electrons are the major species transferred during contact. A number of models have been put forward, most are based on the model of an insulator as a wide band gap semiconductor.

Let us first consider the energies of electrons in the partially full bands during a simple contact (no rubbing or sliding) between two different metals (figure 2.10). The work functions of the two materials are, in general, not equal, and an electron is able to lower its energy by flowing from one metal to the other. This results in a charge imbalance which eventually prevents further charge flow. The charge which has been transferred creates a potential difference between the two metals, known as the contact potential difference. When the metals are separated again the capacitance between the surfaces decreases. Therefore, for constant charge, the potential between the surfaces rises and charge is driven back across the interface, so that after separation the surfaces are essentially neutral. When an insulator is placed in contact with a metal, the full valence band of the insulator lies between -7 and -12 eV, the empty conduction band is near the vacuum level (0 eV) and the metal Fermi level is somewhere between -3 and -6 eV. Electrons in the metal cannot gain energy to reach the empty insulator conduction band, nor can they move to the insulator valence band which is full. Electron flow between a metal and an insulator therefore relies on the presence of energy states within the insulator band gap.

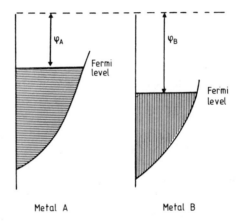

Figure 2.10 Energy distribution of electron states in two metals at absolute zero before contact. When metals are placed in contact electrons in A can lower their energy by flowing to B. φ_A and φ_B are the work functions of the metals.

From the discussion in §§2.1.1–2.1.5, we know that the simple band model is likely to be a poor representation of the electron energy levels in polymers, which are the materials most often involved in contact charging. However, for these materials there are likely to be localised levels throughout the entire energy range. Some of these will be localised at the surface and some within the bulk material. There is very little independent evidence concerning the distribution of these energy levels, in space or in energy, and the various theories of charge transfer use different models to explain the linear relationship between the charge transferred and the metal work function. The review presented here is not exhaustive but gives a general idea of the thinking involved.

Davies (1970) assumed that electrons were injected with a uniform volume density into the bulk states of the material to a depth λ. He calculated the value of the volume charge density, Q, by integrating Laplace's equation (see Chapter 7) and assuming the surface charge density σ was λQ. With these assumptions the surface charge density is proportional to the difference in work functions of the metal and the polymer. Chowdry and Westgate (1974a,b) disputed the requirement that the electron injection depth would be independent of the work function, as assumed by Davies, but showed that a linear relationship would also be obtained if the states were assumed to be uniformly distributed in energy.

Bauser (1970) and Krupp (1971) preferred a model which involved only surface states and obtained a linear dependence of charge on metal work function by assuming that these states were uniformly distributed in both space and energy.

Duke and Fabish and their co-workers at the Xerox corporation (Duke and Fabish 1976, Duke *et al* 1978, Fabish and Duke 1977) rejected the hypothesis that localised bulk states are due to impurities or morphological effects, citing evidence that the states were invariant with different methods of polymer preparation and varied systematically with the molecular structure of the monomeric units of the polymer. They proposed that charge transfer could only occur to a narrow window of bulk and surface energy states in the insulator, which had an energy which was close to the metal Fermi energy. They proposed that these states were due to molecular ion levels of side group molecules as discussed in §2.1.5. Evidence for the energy selectivity of the charge exchange process was provided by the observation that contacting with different metals showed an additive effect.

Lowell (1976) felt it was unlikely that electrons could move from the surface sufficiently quickly to fill bulk states in highly insulating polymer materials, and disputed that the localised energy levels would be uniformly distributed in energy (as must be the case in many of the earlier models). His experimental results on polyethylene, PTFE and PET showed that a number of contacts were required before a linear relationship between charge transfer and work function was obtained. He proposed that during contact the electrons entered only those states which were within 5 nm of the surface, and therefore were close enough to the interface for electrons to tunnel into them. Bulk states were filled in multiple contacts by a process in which charge was redistributed during, or after, each contact. He found pronounced differences when mercury, rather than a hard solid, was the contacting metal and postulated that the redistribution was produced mechanically. He suggested that successive contacts disturbed the microstructure of the polymer near the surface so that some of the filled traps were moved away into the bulk, and that empty states were brought closer to the surface.

Further changes would occur as the polymer recovered when the contact was removed. According to this model, charging ceased when the charge on the polymer surface was large enough to prevent further tunnelling from the metal to the polymer traps. The limiting charge therefore depended on the energy difference between the electrons at the Fermi energy of the metal and the level of the traps, but the amount of charge transferred in a single contact did not depend on the metal work function, provided the energy of the surface traps was lower than the Fermi energy of the metal.

The linear relationship can also be explained without having to assume that there is a uniform energy distribution of states if the density of states is high enough (Hays 1974) or if back tunnelling occurs on separation of the metal and the insulator (Lowell 1979).

The experimental results that show a non-linear relationship between charge transfer and the metal work function, can also be explained on the basis of electron transfer by choosing a suitable energy distribution of electron states in the insulator. Non-linearity could also be due to differences in the area of intimate contact between the polymer and the metal, particularly where little pressure is applied to the contact. Coste and Pechery (1981) have investigated this using an optical technique to measure the true contact between a film and a roller. They found that more charge was transferred when the surface roughness was low and the percentage of true contact high. The relationship between contact area and charge density was not linear (figure 2.11). This may be because the measurement of contact area is unable to take account of the true contact on the scale of a fraction of a nanometer, which may be significant in charge exchange. Alternatively, there may be redistribution of charge after transfer as proposed by Lowell.

The distribution of electrons between bulk and surface states has been investigated experimentally by Fabish *et al* (1976). They studied the spatial distribution of charge in polymers by measuring the surface potential using the Kelvin–Zisman reciprocating capacitor technique (Zisman 1932). The surface potential is the integral of the local electric field over the thickness of the film. If the charge lies totally on the surface of the polymer the film potential, ΔV, is related to the surface charge density, σ_s, and the film thickness, d, by

$$\Delta V = (\sigma_s/\varepsilon_0\varepsilon_r)d. \qquad (2.4)$$

If the states are uniformly distributed through the bulk of the film with density ρ then

$$\Delta V = (\rho/2\varepsilon_0\varepsilon_r)d^2. \qquad (2.5)$$

The form of the dependence of the surface potential on film thickness therefore gives information on whether surface or bulk states are involved. It was found that low work function metals interacted mainly with bulk states whereas high work function metals filled mainly surface states. Bulk states were filled to a depth of 4 μm below the surface. It was also found that a

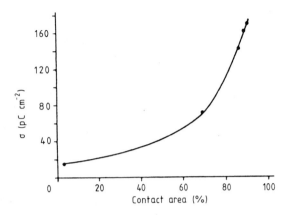

Figure 2.11 Relationship between charge density and contact area (at a pressure of 10 kg cm^{-2}) (from Coste and Pechery 1981).

metallic substrate on which a polymer film was supported could exert an influence for films up to a thickness of 15 μm. Lowell calculated that electrons will be transferred from surface to bulk states by tunnelling only to a depth of about 2 nm (Lowell 1976), and the high penetration depth for charge measured in the Fabish experiments may be due to mechanical redistribution of states or to injection under the influence of the electric field between the surface and the substrate metal. Controlled surface enrichment of a polyblend by the addition of increasing quantities of a fluoropolymer has shown that charging in contact with other polymers is related to composition to a depth of about 1.5 nm (Williams 1976).

The transfer of charge from surface to bulk states has also been observed by Barnes *et al* (1981). The surface potential was measured as a function of position and time after contact with a metal electrode using an induction probe with a resolution of 80 μm. The charge transferred on a single contact could easily be monitored and, for insulating polymers, was typically 10^{-6} C m^{-2}. The charge remained localised for relatively long periods, but the surface potential gradually decayed with time. Toomer and Lewis (1980) suggested a number of reasons for this decay including transfer from surface to bulk states.

All the theories of electronic transfer must assume a particular distribution of electron energy levels. For specific materials there is some independent evidence of the positions of some states (Wintle 1974, Duke *et al* 1978) but in most cases the charge transfer experiments are unsupported by independent measurements and the proposed energy levels can only be considered to be plausible models.

Most theories assume that the amount of back tunnelling when the materials are separated is negligible and that the final charge, after separation in a vacuum, is the same as the charge that was present when the surfaces were in contact. When the surfaces are separated, the electric field between them rises as discussed above. This effectively increases the energy of the trapped electron. If the electron is trapped in an energy level well below the metal Fermi energy, the probability of it gaining sufficient energy from the field to leave the insulator is low. In fact, if a uniform distribution of states with energy is assumed, it can be calculated that the trapping density of charge is insufficient to give significant back tunnelling (Lowell 1976). However, if the electron traps are all approximately at the same energy as the Fermi energy in the metal, as proposed by Duke, Fabish and colleagues, then the possibility of significant back flow cannot be excluded.

Fabish *et al* (1976) have investigated back tunnelling by observing the charge transferred to a polymer film on a metal backing as a function of the film thickness. The field in the region between the contacting surfaces as they separate is a function of the relative size of the capacitance between the surfaces and the capacitance between the film surface and the substrate. They explain their results assuming that all surface states are emptied by back flow of charge and that the residual charge is due to charges trapped in bulk states. Krupp (1971), Wagner (1956) and Peterson (1954a,b) also believed back currents to be significant.

2.1.13 Charging of solids by ion transfer

Most of the literature in the English speaking journals over the last twenty years has concentrated on the electronic theory of charge transfer. However, Russian workers suggest that charging is due to a combination of electron transfer from the metal to the insulator and positive- or negative-ion transfer from the insulator to the metal (Postnikov 1978). The supporters of the ionic theories point out that real surfaces of metals or insulators are covered by adsorbed layers, which are frequently ionic in nature, or contain a charged double layer. The presence of these contamination layers provides an additional potential barrier through which electrons must pass in order to move between materials. Ion charge transfer theories can account for some observations which are difficult to explain on the basis of an electronic model. For example, glass may be made to charge positively or negatively depending on whether it was previously in contact with an acid or an alkali (Shaw and Jex 1928). Ruckdeschal (1973) carried out experiments with organic glasses and identified the proton as the most likely charge carrier. Ionic theories are not incompatible with the observed dependence of charge transfer on metal work function because most semiempirical equations for the surface free energy of a metal (which governs ion adsorption) include the metal work function.

A number of different theories have been published, most of which discuss ion transfer only in qualitative terms. For example, Harper (1967) suggested that the mobile ions formed by electrolytic dissociation in moisture films are transferred. (In his experiments hydrophobic materials such as polyethylene produced much less charge than did hydrophilic materials such as glass.) Kornfeld (1969) suggested that solid insulating materials have a characteristic electric charge due to the accumulation of vacancies of a single polarity at sites on the surface of the material. Normally this charge is compensated by selective adsorption of oppositely charged ions and the surface is neutral. On contact or friction the compensating layers on the two materials are mixed and the compensation is destroyed leaving a residual charge on each surface.

The most recent ionic theory is due to Shinbrot (1985). He takes Harper's value of 0.26 eV for the potential barrier due to an adsorbed water layer 10 nm thick and calculates the electron transmission probability to be 10^{-7}. He then considers two surfaces each with a surface double layer as shown in figure 2.12 and calculates the probability that individual dipole elements (for example, the dipole in the position ringed in the figure) will flip over to give a polarity reversal. The result is combined with a calculation of the probability that oppositely charged ions will link across the interface to give an estimate of the probability of ionic charge transfer. Shinbrot concludes that charging will be exclusively ionic unless fields exceeding 10^6 V m^{-1} are present at the interface.

Figure 2.12 Dipole layers at contacting rough surfaces (after Shinbrot 1985).

It is observed that when materials are rubbed together, fragments of one material become attached to the other, i.e. the break point on separation is a few molecules below the surface. Mass transfer in both directions has been detected between all combinations of polytetrafluoroethylene, polyethyleneterephthalate and polycarbonate and between all of these polymers and gold, silver and platinum. The amount of material transferred exceeded by several orders of magnitude the amount necessary to give rise to a typical measured charge transfer on the basis of one electronic charge transferred per atom.

The theory of charge transfer is still in its infancy and evaluation of the various models requires a much better understanding of the nature of the surfaces of polymers and other insulators, including the electron energy levels and the nature of the impurity layers.

2.1.14 Frictional charging

Most of the experiments cited so far make some attempt to ensure that electrification is due to a single contact and is carried out in vacuum, to avoid charge loss by air breakdown as the surfaces are separated. In practice, charging is produced by rubbing surfaces together in air.

It is found that when two like materials are rubbed together the quantity of charge transferred is as great as in the friction between unlike materials. The polarity of the charge taken by each surface depends on whether the contact is a point or a line (i.e. which sample is rubbed and which is doing the rubbing). The most likely explanation of this phenomenon is that the temperature of the contact point affects the charge transfer. It is often found that the amount of charge transferred during rubbing is affected more by the energy of rubbing than by the nature of the materials. It is therefore important to separate true contact charging from frictional charging and failure to do this has resulted in some confusing results in the published literature.

Haenen (1979) showed that, when a series of metals and polymers were rubbed together at least fifty times, the charge transferred, q, could be related to the force of the contact, F, by the equation

$$q \propto F^{\alpha} \tag{2.6}$$

α lay between 0.3 and 1 and was a function mainly of the metal but, to a lesser degree, the polymer.

Generally, there is an increase in charge with rubbing velocity (e.g. Montgomery 1959). However, peaks have also been found as shown in figure 2.13. Zimmer (1970) studied the charging of plastics when they were rubbed against a metal brush as a function of the rubbing velocity. He found that in some cases (for example, polyethyleneterephthalate) the polarity of the charge transferred to the polymer changed from negative to positive as the speed of rubbing increased (figure 2.14). He found that for polymers which showed this effect it was also possible to change the polarity of the charge transferred by a simple contact by increasing the temperature. Temperatures of between 90 and 180 °C were required. His results are shown in table 2.3.

In practice charging occurs in air rather than in a vacuum. The high field between the surfaces as they separate will cause the air to ionise. The ions neutralise the surface charge but tend to overcompensate so the portion of the surface where the discharge occurs has the opposite polarity to the initial frictional charge. The surface may thus have areas of different charge

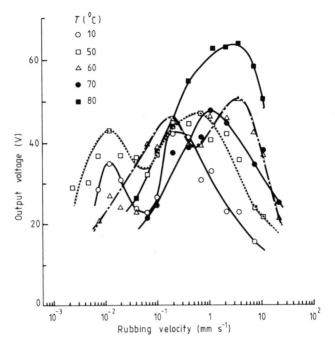

Figure 2.13 Variation of electrification with rubbing velocity at different temperatures, 30 % relative humidity, 61 mN normal load (after Ohara 1979).

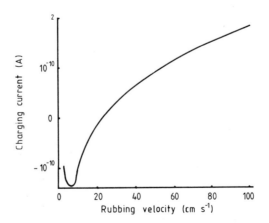

Figure 2.14 Charging current plotted against rubbing velocity (after Zimmer 1970). Polyethylene terephthalate disc rubbed against a metal brush.

Table 2.3 Change in polarity of contact charging with temperature.

Polymer	Charge density (at room temp.) ($\times 10^{-5}\,C\,m^{-2}$)	Transition temperature (°C)	Charge density (at transition temp.) ($\times 10^{-5}\,C\,m^{-2}$)
ABS (Novodur W)	− 4.7	160	+5.6
ABS (Novadur PM)	−16.5	130	+7.05
PMMA (Plexiglass)	−70.5	90	+3.76
Polyester	−70.5	180	+9.4
Polyphenylenoxide	−70.5	150	+4.7
ABS (Novadur PK)	−185	—	—
Polyvinylchloride	−235	—	—

(Hull 1949). Areas of differing polarity can also be produced by non-uniformities which lead to surface states of different energy at different positions.

The charge which remains on the surface after the contact is broken depends not only on discharge through the air but also on the rate at which the charge spreads through the material. This varies with the nature of the material and with the polarity of the charge. Table 2.4 lists the half-lives of positive and negative charges for a number of polymers. The charge leakage rate is dependent on factors other than the resistivity of the materials and it is not always clear why the decay of the two polarities should differ. For example, it is not surprising that positive charge should have a tendency to cling to the ionised carboxyl groups in polyacrylic acid, but in other cases the reasons are less obvious.

Table 2.4 The half-lives of positive and negative charges.

Polymer	Half-lives	
	Positive	Negative
Poly-n-vinylimidazole	0.18	0.24
Cellophane	0.30	0.30
Poly-N-N-dimethylacrylamide	0.66	0.48
Polyacrylic acid	1.50	0.96
Wool	2.50	1.55
Cotton	3.60	4.80
Polyvinylfluoride	8.00	8.70
Poly-n-vinylpyrrolidone	41.00	15.80
Polyacrylonitrile	667	687
Nylon 66	936	720
Polyvinylalcohol	8470	3770

Cooke (1954), Jewell-Thomas (1957) and Donald (1958) found that the charge on particles sliding down a metal chute followed the equation

$$q \propto q_0[1 - \exp(-t/\tau)] \tag{2.7}$$

where t is the contact time and τ is a time constant characteristic of the material.

Cunningham (1970) found that the same rule was obeyed when polymer films were passed over a grounded metal rollar and that τ was linearly related to the surface resistivity of the film. However this was not confirmed by Williams (1964), who measured the charge acquired by glass beads as they rolled down a metal chute with a polymer film. The coating was a di-methylaminoethyl methacrylate/methacrylic acid copolymer, which allowed quarternary ammonium carboxylate groups to be introduced into the polymer in a controlled way. These groups acted as an antistatic additive by increasing the polymer moisture content. Williams was therefore able to measure the charge transferred as a function of resistivity. He confirmed that equation (2.7) was valid but found that τ was proportional to the logarithm of the surface resistivity rather than to the resistivity itself.

Coste and Pechery (1977) found that the moisture content of the polymer was an important factor. They passed polymer films over metal rollers, one of which could be run at a speed which differed from that of the film, to provide a source of friction. Three distinct types of behaviour, illustrated in figure 2.15, were found:

(i) The charge density grew to a constant value. This type of curve was obtained when the roller travelled at the same speed as the film (i.e. there was little friction) (see figure 2.15(a)).

(ii) The charge density passed through a maximum then decreased and changed polarity to reach a new equilibrium state (see figure 2.15(b)).

(iii) The charge density reached a maximum then decreased to a new steady state without changing polarity (see figure 2.15(c)).

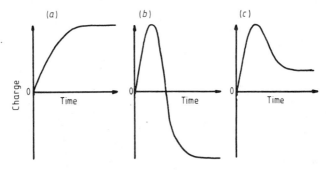

Figure 2.15 Types of behaviour observed for the build-up of charge density with time (after Coste and Pechery 1977).

For some polymers type-(ii) behaviour was observed whenever there was relative motion between the belt and the roller. For others the polarity reversed only over certain ranges of relative belt velocity, belt load and relative humidity. Outside these ranges type-(iii) behaviour was observed.

These results were interpreted in terms of both a change in temperature of the surface and its tendency to adsorb water.

The frictional charging process is so complicated it is seldom possible to predict from a knowledge of the materials how much charge will be transferred in a particular circumstance. In practice, since the charge depends on the force and velocity of the contact, the charge acquired by a particular material depends as much on the energy of rubbing as on the materials involved.

2.1.15 Limiting charge applied by friction

When surfaces are charged by friction in air, the surface charge density is frequently able to reach the Gaussian limit where the electric field above the surface reaches the level where the air ionises. The nature of the surfaces producing the charge is then not important. It is shown in §1.5 (and more generally in §7.1.5) that Gauss's law limits the charge density on an isolated surface to $2.64 \times 10^{-5}\,\mathrm{C\,m^{-2}}$.

The charge on the surface of dispersed particles will be even lower than this value if the electric field due to the total volume of charge reaches the breakdown limit of air. For example, when the particles are flowing through a pipe, the field at the pipe walls must be less than the breakdown limit of the air.

Let us assume that there are n kg of powder per cubic metre of air in a pipe of radius R. The volume charge density, Q_v, is given by

$$Q_v = nq/m \;\mathrm{C\,m^{-3}}$$

where q/m is the charge-to-mass ratio of the particles. Since the field at the pipe walls is uniform Gauss's law may be written

$$ES = Q_v V/\varepsilon_0 = nqV/m\varepsilon_0$$

where S is the surface area and V the volume of length L of the pipe. The maximum charge-to-mass ratio of the powder in the pipe is found by setting E to the breakdown field, E_b. The pipe surface area is $2\pi RL$ and its volume is πR^2. This gives a maximum charge-to-mass ratio of

$$(q/m)_{max} = \frac{2\varepsilon_0 E_b}{nR}. \tag{2.8}$$

A high charge limit therefore requires a small pipe radius R and a low density of particles in the pipe.

If the particle mass is written as $4\pi r^3 D$ (where D is the density of the particle)

$$q_{max} = \frac{8E_b\pi\varepsilon_0 r^3 D}{3nR}.$$ (2.9)

The maximum charge on a single particle, q_{max}, can be calculated using equation (1.34)

$$E = \sum q/S\varepsilon_0\varepsilon_r$$

i.e.

$$\sum q'_{max} = E_b \times 4\pi r^2 \varepsilon_0.$$ (2.10)

It can be seen that the pipe limit is below the single-particle limit while $2rD/3nR < 1$. In practice this means that frictional charging is only efficient when the density of dust is low and the dust is conveyed in a small pipe.

When particles are charged by friction, the magnitude of the charge transferred is higher, the greater the energy put into the friction. Devices which are designed to charge powder by friction therefore usually involve either forcing a small quantity of powder at high speed through a narrow tube or spinning particles in a small electric fan. It also follows that the charge acquired during industrial processing of powdered materials is more a function of the process than the materials. Higher charges are built up the higher the amount of energy put into the process and the lower the amount of powder involved. This is discussed further in Chapter 6 and in §2.5.

In vacuum, ionisation and breakdown are inhibited and the electric field above a surface can rise until field emission occurs, i.e. until negative surfaces spontaneously emit electrons and positive surfaces emit ions. Negative field emission normally requires surface fields exceeding 1×10^9 V m^{-1}, while for positive field emission the field must be an order of magnitude higher. The surface charge density needed to create these fields can be calculated from Gauss's law using the field emission limit instead of E_b.

2.2 CORONA CHARGING

Charging by friction is not very predictable or easily controlled so that when a surface must be charged in a defined way a corona discharge is commonly used. This provides ions of a single polarity which charge the surface to a limit which can be controlled.

2.2.1 Introduction to the corona discharge

A corona discharge is produced when a high voltage is applied between two electrodes, one of which has a small radius of curvature. The non-uniform electric field causes an electrical discharge in a limited region near the sharp electrode, at voltages below the spark breakdown voltage of the gap. Typical corona geometries are a cylinder with a wire at its axis or a point and a plane as illustrated in figure 2.16. In the region close to the sharp electrode the electric field is very high and exceeds the breakdown field of the gas. Any electron entering this region will be accelerated, so that by the time it collides with an atom it has sufficient energy to detach an electron, leaving a positive ion and an additional electron. This electron is also accelerated producing its own electron/ion pair and the result is an avalanche of electrons formed close to the point. Light is emitted during the ionisation process and, in air, a bluish glow can be seen round the sharp electrode which gives the discharge the name 'corona'.

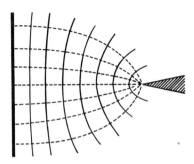

Figure 2.16 Point to plane before corona onset: broken curves, field lines; full curves, equipotentials.

Since positive ions and electrons are very different from each other, the behaviour of the discharge depends on the polarity of the sharp electrode. When a negative high voltage is applied to a pointed electrode in air naturally occurring negative ions, which enter the high-field region, split to form an electron and a neutral atom. The electron accelerates away from the negative point, driven by the high electric field, and gains sufficient energy to ionise any atom with which it collides. The electron multiplication process continues until new electrons are formed far enough away from the point that they are unable to gain sufficient energy from the electric field between collisions to ionise an atom. Meanwhile, the positive ions are attracted to the negative point electrode. They too gain energy from the high electric field and, on collision with the electrode, release secondary electrons which add to the discharge. Photoionisation also takes place.

In air (or any gas which contains electronegative atoms such as oxygen or fluorine) electrons which have insufficient energy to form an electron/positive ion pair attach to a neutral atom to form a negative ion. These ions (or the electrons in a non-attaching gas) form the only significant current outside the ionisation region.

When the sharp electrode is positive, electrons created by ionisation in the high-field region are attracted to the point and positive ions drift towards the plane. The positive ions undergo many collisions with neutral molecules and lose energy to them but do not cause ionisation. They reach the cathode with a rather low energy and do not create significant secondary electrons. The electrons created in the ionisation region travel towards the positive point, forming avalanches of electron/ion pairs in the gas. With a positive corona discharge, secondary emission from the sharp electrode is of less importance than in a negative corona, but photons from the corona glow may produce ionisation in the gas, or cause photoemission from the electrodes. Again, most of the current in the space outside the ionisation region is carried by ions of the polarity of the point.

With a positive voltage applied to a wire the corona has the appearance of a bluish sheath over the entire surface. With a negative voltage the corona is concentrated into tufts at points along the wire. On a smooth conductor the points are evenly spaced and their number increases with current. The diameter of the corona glow increases with applied voltage.

For both positive and negative discharges the majority of the interelectrode space contains slow-moving ions of a single polarity (that of the sharp electrode). These make frequent collisions with neutral molecules, which are similar in size to the ions. This results in a transfer of momentum from the ions to the molecules and there is a bulk movement of the gas in the direction of the electric field, which is known as the ion wind. This is generated by the ions and powered by the energy these gain from the electric field, but the wind is a bulk movement of the gas and not of the ions alone. Typically the ion wind has a speed of the order of 1 m s^{-1}.

The ions created in the corona discharge modify the electric field between the two electrodes. They have the effect of decreasing the field near the sharp electrode and increasing it near the passive electrode. The result is that although the field in the absence of ions is not uniform, the field across the drift region of the corona discharge when ions are present, can be assumed to be constant. As a rough approximation it may be taken to lie between V/X and $V/2X$ where X is the electrode spacing and V the applied voltage.

A corona discharge is frequently described in terms of its current–voltage characteristic. This is only slightly different for the two polarities and in practice the most important difference is that positive points tend to arc at a lower voltage than negative points. Where possible a negative corona is therefore usually chosen for corona charging applications.

The voltage at which the corona discharge starts (the corona inception voltage) is fairly sharply defined with the current jumping suddenly from a negligible level to about $1 \ \mu A$. The current then rises with increasing voltage following an equation of the form

$$I = KV(V - V_0) \qquad (2.11)$$

where V_0 is the corona inception voltage and K is a constant depending on geometry. This equation applies reasonably well to both point/plane and cylindrical geometries. The current–voltage characteristic is discussed in more detail in Chapter 7.

In summary the corona discharge can be assumed to consist of a high field ionisation region close to the point in which there are both positive and negative ions, and a uniform field region where the field lies between V/X and $V/2X$ and in which there is only one polarity of charge (the same polarity as the point). This picture is oversimplified, however the approximations made are generally satisfactory for calculations of corona charging.

2.2.2 Calculation of the limiting charge on a plane

Ions from a corona discharge may be used to charge a plane surface. For an isolated, insulating sheet, the charge density is limited by the ionisation of the air, which occurs when the field above the surface reaches approximately $3 \times 10^6 \, \mathrm{V \, m^{-1}}$. This breakdown field may be designated E_b. The electric field, E, above a surface is related to the charge density by the Gauss law as discussed earlier.

The surface charge density corresponding to the breakdown field is therefore

$$Q_s = \varepsilon_0 E_b$$
$$= 2.64 \times 10^{-5} \, \mathrm{C \, m^{-2}}.$$

The field of a corona discharge at the plane electrode is normally of the order of $3 \times 10^5 \, \mathrm{V \, m^{-1}}$, i.e. a surface charge density of only $2.6 \times 10^{-6} \, \mathrm{C \, m^{-2}}$ is sufficient to repel further ions.

The maximum surface charge density can be increased by placing an earthed sheet behind the insulating plane. An image charge is then set up in the metal sheet which reduces the field above the surface. For a thin insulator, totally isolated except for the metal plate, all charges are paired and the field above the surface is zero. The surface charge and its image can be considered to form a capacitor for which all the electric field lies between the plates. In any real situation pairing is not complete so that the capacitance between the insulating surface and other objects will be significant and there will be a low electric field above the surface.

When the field above the surface is low the charge may be limited by leakage rather than air breakdown. An approximate estimate of the limiting surface potential V_p can be made if the current–voltage characteristic of the corona discharge in the absence of the insulating material on the plate is known. It may be assumed that the leakage current is given by

$$I_1 = V_p/R \tag{2.12}$$

where R is the resistance between the surface and earth. (For insulating materials Ohm's law is usually not obeyed and R depends on V_p.)

As charge from the corona builds up on the surface, V_p rises and the leakage current, I_1 also rises. However, as the surface voltage increases, the potential difference between the corona point and the surface decreases. The charging current, I_c, therefore decreases. The limiting charge on the surface is reached when the charging current equals the leakage current.

The corona current is related to the potential difference between the corona point and the plane $V - V_p$ by equation (2.11), therefore

$$I_c = K(V - V_p)(V - V_p - V_0).$$

The constant K can be determined from the current–voltage characteristic of the corona when a metal plate replaces the insulating surface. Equating I_1 to I_c gives an equation in V_p, where the corona starting voltage V_0, the corona constant K and the resistance R can all be measured.

If it is required to apply a controlled uniform charge to a flat insulating surface a grid may be placed above it. The potential on this grid controls the corona current and the penetration of charge to the substrate and so can be used to vary the surface voltage.

2.2.3 Corona charging of particles

When a particle is placed in a uniform electric field it will polarise and therefore attract ions of different polarities over different halves of its surface. Thus a neutral particle charged by exposing it to a single polarity of ion or a charged particle can be discharged in a bi-ionised field.

The quantity of charge arriving at a particle depends on the electric field at the surface of the particle. The arguments by which the maximum particle charge is calculated can be followed qualitatively by considering a conducting sphere in a uniform electric field. The field is distorted as a consequence of the difference between the relative dielectric constant of the conducting sphere ($\varepsilon_r = \infty$) and the air ($\varepsilon_r = 1$). It can easily be seen that this distortion must occur because the conducting surface of the sphere and the plane electrodes which provide the uniform field must all be equipotentials. The field lines must therefore be distorted in order to remain perpendicular to the equipotentials. (This is illustrated for a cylinder in figure 1.1 and the field distortion due to a dielectric or a conducting sphere is discussed in detail in Chapter 7.)

A conducting sphere in a uniform field is illustrated in figure 2.17. Positive ions in the field will travel along the field lines in the direction of the arrows and negative ions will move in the reverse direction. Therefore, when a

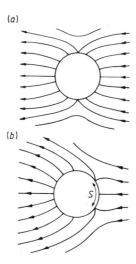

Figure 2.17 Field at a conducting sphere in a uniform field: (*a*), uncharged; (*b*), with a positive charge.

particle is placed in the mono-ionised uniform field of a corona discharge, the ions follow the field lines and the particle charges. As charge is gained the potential of the particle changes and the field distortion is modified so that the particle collects ions over a smaller area of surface. Figure 2.17(*a*) illustrates the field lines round an uncharged particle showing that positive and negative ions would collect over equal areas of the surface. Figure 2.17(*b*) shows a particle which has acquired a positive charge. Positive ions are now collected over the reduced area *S*. It can also be seen that, if this particle is in a field in which both polarities of ion are present (for example, from an AC corona discharge) it collects negative ions over a larger portion of its surface and will be neutralised, restoring the electric field to the form shown in 2.17(*a*). If the ions of the two polarities do not have the same mobility, the particle will collect the ions over equal areas, but will collect the polarity with the higher mobility faster, therefore it will not reach zero charge.

In a mono-ionised field, due to a DC corona discharge, a saturation charge is reached when the attractive field due to the field distortion equals the repulsive field due to the charge on the particle, and charging ceases. The maximum charge which can be acquired by a particle in a uniform electric field, in which there is only one polarity of ions, can be calculated by equating the force due to the distorted field (which is calculated by solving Laplace's equation) to the force of repulsion from the charged particle. This calculation was first reported by Pauthenier and Moreau-Hanot (1932). The saturation charge is therefore often known as the Pauthenier limit and this mechanism of charging is known as field charging or Pauthenier charging.

It will be shown in the next section that (q_{max}), for the general case of conducting or insulating particles is given by

$$q_{max} = 4\pi\varepsilon_0 a^2 pE \tag{2.13}$$

where

$$p = 3\varepsilon_r/(\varepsilon_r + 2)$$

p varies between three for a conducting particle (relative dielectric constant ∞) and one for an insulating particle of relative dielectric constant one.

It can be seen from this equation that the maximum charge is proportional to the electric field and the square of the particle radius, and it depends weakly on the relative dielectric constant of the particle but it does not depend on the density of charging ions. This affects only the time it takes for the particle to reach the saturation charge.

The charge on a particle at any time t is given by

$$q = q_{max}[1/(1 + \tau/t)] \tag{2.14}$$

where τ, the time taken for the particle to reach half the saturation charge, is given by

$$\tau = 4\varepsilon_0/N_0 eb \tag{2.15}$$

where N_0 is the density of ions (number m^{-3}) and b is the ion mobility. b is defined by the equation

$$b = u/E$$

where u is the ion velocity in a field E.

Equation (2.15) can be written in terms of the current density, J, and the electric field, E, using the relationships

$$J = N_0 eu$$

and

$$u = Eb$$
$$\tau = 4\varepsilon_0 E/J. \tag{2.16}$$

For a typical corona discharge $J = 10^{-4}$ A m^{-2} and $E = 3 \times 10^5$ V m^{-1}, therefore

$$\tau \simeq 0.1 \text{ s}$$

i.e. a particle will have reached 50 % of its charge in 0.1 s and 90 % of its charge in 1 s. The particle charging time is a function of the mobility of the charge carriers so that particles will charge much more quickly when electrons rather than positive ions are the charge carriers.

2.2.4 Calculation of the maximum charge of a sphere in a corona discharge

The net force on an ion approaching the surface of a charged particle is the sum of the force of attraction to the sphere (caused by the distortion of the electric field due to the presence of the particle) and the force of repulsion from the charge already on the particle. The field E at the surface of an uncharged conducting sphere in a uniform applied electric field. E_0 is derived in Chapter 7 and is given by

$$E = 3E_0 \cos \theta \qquad (2.17)$$

where $\theta = 0$ is the direction of the applied field. This is an attractive field and therefore has a positive sign. The repulsive field at the sphere surface due to a charge, q, on the sphere is given by $- q/4\pi\varepsilon_0 a^2$ where a is the radius of the sphere.

The saturation charge occurs when these two terms are equal and $3E_0 \cos \theta$ is a maximum, i.e. $\cos \theta = 1$. Therefore q_{max} is given by

$$3E_0 = q_{max}/4\pi\varepsilon_0 a^2$$
$$q_{max} = 12\pi\varepsilon_0 E_0 a^2. \qquad (2.18)$$

It is shown in Chapter 7 that if the particle is a dielectric of relative permittivity ε_r, the modified field at its surface is $Ep \cos \theta$, where $p = 3\varepsilon_r/(\varepsilon_r + 2)$. Therefore, for a dielectric sphere the maximum charge achieved before the repulsive electric field due to the charge on the particles repels all further charge is

$$q_{max} = 4\pi\varepsilon_0 E_0 pa^2. \qquad (2.19)$$

The relative dielectric constants of nearly all insulating materials lie between one and ten so that p will be between 1 and 2.5. For a conducting particle ε_r is infinite so $p = 3$ and equation (2.19) reduces to the equation for a conducting sphere derived above.

The electric field in the uniform field region of the corona discharge is usually an order of magnitude below the breakdown limit. That is, E_0 in equation (2.18) is normally up to a factor of ten less than E_b in equation (2.10) and the charge acquired by friction under good conditions can exceed the charge applied by a corona discharge.

2.2.5 Calculation of the rate of charging of spheres in a corona discharge

The rate at which the sphere charges is equal to the number of charges arriving at its surface per second, integrated over the surface of the sphere, i.e.

$$\frac{dq}{dt} = \int N_0 eu \, dA$$

where N_0 is the number of ions per unit volume, e is the charge per ion and u the velocity of the ion.

For an ion of mobility b

$$u = Eb$$

therefore

$$\frac{dq}{dt} = \int N_0 ebE \, dA. \tag{2.20}$$

The field, E, at the surface of the particle at any time is the resultant of the original electric field E_0, distorted by the presence of the sphere ($E_0 p \cos \theta$) and the field due to the charge q which has already reached the sphere ($q/4\pi\varepsilon_0 r^2$).

Therefore, substituting for E in equation (2.20)

$$\frac{dq}{dt} = N_0 eb \int (3E_0 p \cos \theta - q/4\pi\varepsilon_0 r^2) 2\pi r^2 \sin \theta \, d\theta$$

$$= 2\pi r^2 N_0 eb \int (3E_0 p \cos \theta - qE_0 p/q_{max}) \sin \theta \, d\theta$$

where $q_{max} = 4\pi\varepsilon_0 r^2 pE_0$ (equation (2.19)). When this is integrated

$$\frac{dq}{dt} = \pi a^2 E_0 N_0 peb(1 - q/q_{max})^2 \tag{2.21}$$

when this too is integrated it is found that

$$q = q_{max}[1/(1 + \tau/t)].$$

$\tau = 4\varepsilon_0/N_0 eb$ is the time taken for the particle to reach half its final charge; this depends on the mobility of the charge carriers and their number density.

2.2.6 Neutralisation of a particle in a bi-ionised field

If a particle is in an electric field E_0 with a current density J_+ in one direction and a current density J_- in the other then the final particle charge is given by

$$q_{max} = 4\pi\varepsilon_0 pr^2 E_0[(1 - \xi)/(1 + \xi)] \tag{2.22}$$

where

$$\xi = (J_-/J_+)^{1/2} \qquad 0 \leqslant \xi \leqslant 1.$$

(The proof is given in §7.5.)

The time dependence of the charge on the particle is given by Moore (1973)

$$q = \frac{q_{max}(1 - e^{-\alpha t})}{1 - [(1 - \xi)/(1 + \xi)] e^{-\alpha t}} \tag{2.23}$$

where

$$\alpha = (J_+ J_-)^{1/2}/\varepsilon_0.$$

2.2.7 Diffusion charging

Diffusion charging arises from collisions between ions and particles because of the random thermal motion of the ions in the gas.

The field charging, or Pauthenier charging, mechanism described above gives a charge which is proportional to the square of the particle radius. The charge acquired by small particles is therefore low, and when the particle radius is less than about 1.5 μm diffusion charging can become important.

A simple calculation of the charge acquired by a particle from the diffusion mechanism can be made using the standard kinetic theory of gases, (see, for example, Jeans 1962). According to this theory, the probability that an ion will have an energy which is greater than the repulsive potential W, due to the charge already collected by the particle, is given by the equation

$$N = N_0 \exp(W/kT) \tag{2.24}$$

where N is the number of ions of energy greater than W, N_0 is the number of ions per unit volume, k is Boltzmann's constant ($= 1.38 \times 10^{-3}$ J K^{-1}) and T is the absolute temperature. The repulsive energy, W, between an ion with a charge, e, and a particle of radius, a, and charge, q, is

$$W = qe/4\pi\varepsilon_0 a.$$

The number of times per second that an ion collides with a stationary particle gives the rate of change of charge, dq/dt. It depends on:

(i) the number density of ions which have sufficient energy to reach the particle,
(ii) their velocity, u_i, and
(iii) the cross sectional area of the particle, πa^2, i.e.

$$dq/dt = \pi a^2 N u_i = \pi a^2 e u_i N_0 \exp(qe/4\pi\varepsilon_0 akT). \tag{2.25}$$

The charge q at a time, t, is found by integrating this expression

$$q = \frac{(4\pi\varepsilon_0 akT)}{e} \ln\left(\frac{aN_0 q^2 u_i t}{4\varepsilon_0 kT} + 1\right). \tag{2.26}$$

There is no theoretical maximum charge that may be gained by a particle by the diffusion charging mechanism because, for any charge, there is a small, but finite, probability that eventually there will be an ion with sufficient energy to overcome the potential due to the charge on the particle. The maximum charge is therefore limited by discharge, when the field round the particle reaches about 3×10^6 V m^{-1}, not by the mechanism itself.

The relative importance of Pauthenier charging and diffusion charging according to the simple kinetic theory is illustrated in figure 2.18. For particle diameters between 0.04 and 1.5 μm both mechanisms may play a part.

Several theories have been published which attempt to describe particle charging for the conditions where both processes are applicable. For example, Murphy *et al* (1959) and Smith and McDonald (1976) based theories on the assumption that the charging mechanism was mainly due to the thermal motion of the ions and that the electric field acted as a perturbation on this process. The field was assumed to assist charging in two ways: (i) the ions were able to gain kinetic energy from the field to help them overcome the repulsive force of the charged particle and (ii) the ion distribution near the particle was allowed to alter. Liu and Yeh (1969) and Smith and McDonald (1976), used different techniques to solve the diffusion equation for the ion density near a charged particle and obtained results in reasonable agreement with experimental results. Recently there has been increased interest in the charging of small aerosol particles (<50 nm in diameter) and several theories have been published which take into account the image charge forces. Four of the most widely used theories are surveyed by Davison and Gentry (1983) and the same authors have also considered

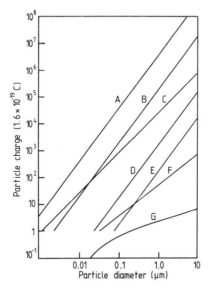

Figure 2.18 Particle charge limits (after Davies 1966). The curves are: A, the ion limit, $E_s = 2 \times 10^{10}$ V m^{-1}; B, the electron limit, $E_s = 10^9$ V m^{-1}; C, the Rayleigh limit, $\tau = 2.1 \times 10^{-6}$; D, the frictional charge limit and field charging, $E = 3 \times 10^6$ V m^{-1}; E, field charging, $E = 3 \times 10^5$ V m^{-1}; F, diffusion charging; G, bipolar equilibrium.

the effect of the dielectric constant of the aerosol particle (Davison and Gentry 1985).

In practice the electric field and the charge carrier mobility and density are seldom accurately known and an adequate estimate of the charge on particles between 50 nm and 1 μm is obtained by summing the charges calculated from the classical Pauthenier and kinetic theory equations (Hewitt 1957). However, if the ion current density is less than two orders of magnitude greater than the particle density, a more sophisticated theory may be required.

2.2.8 Results of experiments on charging in a corona discharge

The charge acquired by particles of approximately 1 μm diameter in a corona discharge has been measured by Edmonson (1961), Hewitt (1957), Pauthenier and Moreau-Hanot (1932), Penney and Lynch (1957) and White (1963). The Pauthenier and Moreau-Hanot results also covered the size range up to 100 μm. All experiments show reasonable agreement with the Pauthenier/Moreau-Hanot theory for field charging. In most of these experiments the particles were smooth spheres but Hignett (1967) measured the charge on fly ash particles in the range 2.5–100 μm, for which only the smallest were smooth spheres. The charging rate of these particles was considerably lower than predicted by theory. For example, 1 s was required to produce 80 % of the charge on a 13.5 μm particle instead of 0.1 s as would be predicted for a spherical particle. However, particles larger than 50 μm in diameter reached a maximum charge which was above the predicted limit—possibly because of the high surface area of the irregular particles compared with smooth spheres.

At the smaller end of the size range, Hewitt (1957) measured the relationship between particle charge and the particle size, the ion current density and the external field, using dioctyl-phthalate spheres with diameters in the range 0.1 to 1.3 μm. The following results were obtained:

(i) The electric mobility of the particle (which depends on the particle charge and mass and is a measure of its ability to move in an electric field) was a minimum for particles between 0.02 and 0.4 μm in diameter.

(ii) The external field affected the charging rate for particles as small as 0.14 μm in diameter.

(iii) When there was no electric field the classical diffusion charging theory applied.

(iv) When the electric field was high and the particles greater than 1 μm in diameter the Pauthenier charging equation applied.

(v) The sum of the charges, calculated using the classical diffusion and field charging equations, adequately described the experimental results over a wide range of conditions.

2.2.9 Chemical dependence of field charging

Charging theories all assume that once an ion reaches a particle it will stick to it. There is some evidence that this is not always the case and that the probability of an ion remaining on the particle depends on the surface chemistry (Sampuran-Singh 1981). Problems have occasionally been experienced in achieving the maximum charge on some polymer powders and there seems to be a relationship between poor charging and the lack of polar groups on the surface. Two explanations have been proposed. The first suggestion is that particles without polar groups tend to have a more highly resistive surface, preventing the spread of charge round the particle surface. The side of the particle receiving the ions then becomes highly charged and repels further ions before the other side of the particle has reached saturation. (This implies that the particles were not spinning in the air stream which is a matter of debate.) The second explanation proposes that a binding mechanism is necessary to hold the ions to the collector particle. This would be provided by a polar molecule which would attract the opposite polarity of charge to the surface. This view is supported by the observation that nylon powder (which has negative OH polar molecules on its surface) will charge more efficiently when the corona discharge is positive and it is difficult to apply a high negative charge to nylon by means of a corona discharge. This has been attributed to the need to overcome the high positive frictional charge acquired by this material, but a low negative charge is measured even with very long corona charging times and its seems more likely that there is a chemical dependence of ionic charging.

2.2.10 Moving particles

When the particles are moving with respect to the electric field one might expect that an allowance would have to be made for aerodynamic forces. However, Whipple and Chalmers (1944) studying the collection of ions by a spherical charged collector when an electric field was applied parallel to the direction of air flow found that, in most cases, the air velocity had no effect. (This work was carried out to investigate the way that rain droplets charge as they fall to earth.)

Figure 2.19 shows the paths of negative ions towards a neutral particle with zero air flow and with an air flow of velocity $v = 2bE$ in the same direction as the ion movement (b is the ion mobility and E is the field, therefore this air flow is twice the ion velocity far from the particle). If y is the distance from the axis of the limiting ion path for intersection, Whipple and Chalmers show that y^2 is given by

$$y^2 = \frac{b(3Ea^2 + q/4\pi\varepsilon_0)^2}{3Ea^2(v + bE)}. \tag{2.27}$$

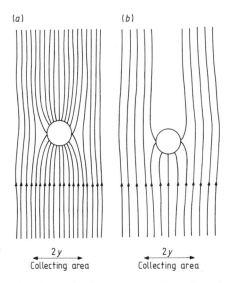

Figure 2.19 Paths of negative ions to an uncharged conducting particle: (a), stationary; (b), moving with velocity 2bE (after Whipple and Chalmers 1944).

When there is zero charge on the particle and the air velocity v is also zero this reduces to $3a^2$, i.e. an uncharged conducting sphere captures ions from a cylinder with an area of cross section three times the cross section of the sphere.

The rate of capture of ions is given by

$$G = \frac{\pi n b (3Ea^2 + q/4\pi\varepsilon_0)^2}{3Ea^2} \tag{2.28}$$

where q is the particle charge. This is independent of the air velocity and applies to a charge q which lies between $\pm 12\pi\varepsilon_0 a^2$. (In practice the particle charge is seldom outside this range.)

When there is relative motion of the sphere and the air, the sphere captures ions from a smaller cross sectional area but more ions cross any cross section per unit time. The two effects just balance and the saturation charge is independent of the relative velocity of the sphere and the air. (The above equations assume a negative charge but apply to a positive charge travelling in the same electric field if the polarity of q is changed.)

If the ions are travelling in the field in the same direction as the particle is moving the particle velocity can affect the charge. For example, the particles may travel so fast that the ions are unable to catch up with them and charging is reduced. In this case y^2 becomes

$$y^2 = \frac{-4bq}{4\pi\varepsilon_0(v - bE)}. \tag{2.29}$$

If q is positive then the air velocity must be less than bE if y^2 is to be positive and y have a real value.

2.3 CHARGING BY THE CAPTURE OF SMALL PARTICLES

A particle may also become charged by the capture of smaller charged particles rather than ions. In this case the effect of the polarisation of both particles in the electric field must be considered, and both particles have inertia so they will not necessarily follow the field and aerodynamic flow lines. Kraemer and Johnstone (1959) and Nielson and Hill (1976a,b) have looked at this problem which has also been reviewed by Clift (1984).

The first approach taken was to consider the forces between a very small inertialess particle and a larger spherical collector particle and to equate the electrostatic forces between the particles to the forces due to the fluid resistance. The electrostatic forces considered were:

(i) The Coulomb force between a charged particle and the charged collector.

(ii) The electrical image force between the charged particle and a neutral collector.

(iii) The force on a charged particle towards a collector in an electric field (this is the Pauthenier problem discussed above).

(iv) The attraction between a charged particle and the dipole induced by it in the collector.

(v) The attraction between the charged collector and the dipole induced by it in the particle.

(vi) The attraction between the charged particle and the dipole induced in the collector by the other charged particles.

The complete problem is not soluble analytically and the processes were treated separately. Usually, under particular circumstances, several of the mechanisms can be shown to be negligible. For example, mechanism (v) can be shown to be proportional to d^2/D^5, where d is the diameter of the particle and D the diameter of the collector. If the collector is much larger than the particle this force is weak. If there is no externally applied field mechanism (iii) is absent.

Kraemer and Johnstone (1955) identified dimensionless groups which characterise each of the forces and calculated the collection efficiencies of charged particles by a spherical collector in Stokes's flow, using a computer model. Nielson and Hill (1976a,b) extended the work to particles with inertia and different forms of flow. Both present their results as graphs of collection efficiency as a function of the dimensionless parameter relevant to that type of collection process.

2.4 INDUCTION CHARGING

Induction charging is applicable only to materials which are electrically conducting. It can best be described by considering a particle on a plane electrode in an electric field as shown in figure 2.20. The rod-shaped particle becomes polarised in the field due to the sphere. Charge can flow freely between the conducting particle and the plane electrode so that the particle is left with a net charge opposite in polarity to the upper electrode. This produces a force of attraction to the upper electrode which will lift a lightweight particle with its net charge. On reaching the upper electrode the particle loses its charge. It remains polarised and this time the negative charge flows to earth and the positive charge is left on the particle. Particles placed between two plane electrodes oscillate between them changing polarity on contact with each electrode in turn. Particles charged to a single polarity may be extracted from the system by means of a hole in one of the planes.

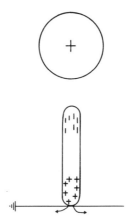

Figure 2.20 Induction charging of rod in the electric field between sphere and plane.

An important feature of induction charging is that it is possible for a conductor to become charged by contacting an earth *providing an electric field is present*. For example figure 2.21 shows a man, wearing boots with non-conducting soles, standing beneath a positively charged plastic belt. He will become polarised, with positive charges repelled towards his feet, but the charge is unable to flow to earth because of his insulating footwear. If the man reaches up and touches an earthed roller on the conveyor he will lose the negative charge at the top part of his body by conduction to the earth. The positive charge is still repelled to his feet by the electric field due to the charge on the belt. When the man walks out from under the belt he will still

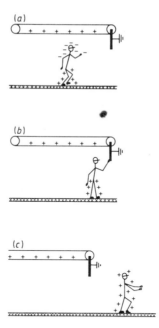

Figure 2.21 Induction charging of personnel: (*a*), charge separates in field due to charged belt; (*b*), charge is lost from top of body; (*c*), person is left with net charge.

have this positive charge, although he has only touched an earthed conductor. If the man had been wearing conductive footwear, he could still have gained a charge while he was under the belt, but the charge would flow from him to earth as soon as he was removed from the influence of the electric field.

Liquids may also be charged by induction. A charge is induced on the liquid surface and, under suitable conditions, the electrostatic pressure on the charged surface is sufficient to force it up into a cone from which surplus charge is ejected in the form of charged droplets. If an electric field is applied to liquid issuing from a capillary the jet will be broken up into droplets which will again be charged by induction. The induction charging of liquids is closely tied up with the disruption of liquid surfaces and the process of atomisation and double-layer charging. This is discussed further in §§2.5.8 and 5.1.

2.4.1 Calculation of the charge and force on a particle

The magnitude of the charge and the force F acting on conducting particles resting on an earthed plane in a uniform electric field has been calculated by Felici (1966). When the particle is a hemisphere of radius a the solution is straightforward because the hemisphere and its image in the plate become a sphere in a uniform field. This is the same problem that must be solved to calculate the maximum charge applied in a corona discharge (§2.2.4).

The field at the surface of a conducting sphere in a uniform field is shown in §7.5 to be

$$E = 3E_0 \cos \theta$$

and the charge per unit area induced by the field is

$$Q_s = 3\varepsilon_0 E_0 \cos \theta.$$

The total charge, q, is found by integrating this over the hemisphere:

$$q = 3\varepsilon_0 E_0 \pi a^2. \tag{2.30}$$

While the particle is on the plane it experiences a force of repulsion due to the uniform applied electric field

$$F_d = qE_0$$

and a force of attraction F_i due to the image force tending to hold the particle on the plane

$$F_i = q^2/4\pi\varepsilon_0 4a^2$$
$$= qE_s/4. \tag{2.31}$$

$E_s = q/4\pi\varepsilon_0 a^2$ is the field created by the charged sphere itself. The particle is detached if $E_0 > E_s/4$.

Once the particle has been detached, the image force decreases rapidly and only the force due to E_0 is significant. The net force acting on the particle tending to remove it from the plane is thus significantly less than the force on the same particle once it has been detached. The particle therefore accelerates as it leaves the plane.

The calculations of Felici for the charge and force on particles of other geometries are given in table 2.5.

Table 2.5 Induction charging of particles.

Particle shape	Force on particle while on substrate	Charge on particle
Hemisphere radius, a	$\frac{9}{4}\pi\varepsilon_0 E_0^2 a^2$	$3\pi\varepsilon_0 E_0 a^2$
Semi-ellipse major axis $a \geqslant$ minor axis, b	$\pi\varepsilon_0 E_0^2 a^2 \dfrac{\ln(a/b) - \frac{1}{2}}{\ln(2a/b) - 1}$	$\dfrac{\pi\varepsilon_0 E_0 a^2}{\ln(2a/b) - 1}$
Sphere radius, a	$4\pi\varepsilon_0(1.37E_0^2 a^2)$	$4\pi\varepsilon_0(1.64E_0 a^2)$

The force acting on a conducting sphere in the field of a parallel-plate capacitor has also been calculated by Lebedev and Skal'skaya (1962) who also found the charge on the sphere to be $1.64E_0a^2$ and the electrostatic force acting to lift it from the plate to be $1.37E_0^2$.

Induction charging relies on the conduction of charge from the particle to the electrode. The time constant for charge movement is given by $\tau = \varepsilon_r\varepsilon_0\rho$, where $\varepsilon_0 = 8.8 \times 10^{-12}$, $\varepsilon_r \geqslant 1$ is the relative dielectric constant of the material and ρ is its resistivity. It can be seen that relatively resistive materials such as glasses (whose resistivity is of the order of 10^{10}–$10^{12}\ \Omega$ m) may charge slowly by this mechanism. For these materials the effectiveness of induction charging is often a function of the relative humidity and moisture adsorbed at the particle contacts.

2.4.2 Electrostatic dispersion

Since individual particles are charged and lifted from a horizontal electrode, induction charging may be used to disperse a bed of powder in either a dielectric liquid or a gas. It has been found that for dense dispersions and reasonably high fields the particles do not all travel all the way between the electrodes but, as the field is increased, an increasing number collide with other particles and reverse direction. Szirmai has observed that the particles do not simply rebound but are accelerated away after contact as predicted by Felici. In the densest regions of a dispersion there are tight clusters of powder particles which rapidly oscillate amongst themselves making little headway in the direction of either of the electrodes (Szirmai 1980, 1981). Szirmai also observed that charge exchange could occur between particles which passed close to each other without contact. He carried out extensive studies of the minimum dispersing field and the current–voltage characteristic of the system and the particle velocities, measuring the properties of the charged particles by observing the height to which they rose above the upper electrode after passage through a hole.

2.5 DOUBLE-LAYER CHARGING

2.5.1 General principles

When an ionic material is dissolved in a liquid of high dielectric constant the ions are dissociated and will move in opposite directions in an electric field. For example, common salt is a positively charged sodium ion bound to a negatively charged chlorine ion and the force of attraction between the two is given by the Coulomb law:

$$F = \frac{qq'}{4\pi\varepsilon_r\varepsilon_0 r^2}.$$

When the dielectric constant of the medium (ε_r) increases, the force decreases and the compound dissociates. Water has a particularly high dielectric constant and there is usually considerable dissociation of ionic compounds. Aqueous solutions are therefore electrically conducting. It is extremely difficult to obtain a perfectly pure liquid and in real terms any liquid which has not been extensively purified will contain some free ions. These are normally paired so that the liquid is, on average, electrically neutral, but under some circumstances the ions can be separated and the liquid acquires a net charge. Charge separation occurs on a microscopic scale in a liquid at any interface (solid–liquid, gas–liquid or liquid–liquid). One polarity of charge will be held, relatively tightly bound at the interface, with ions of the other polarity attracted to the bound charge, but held much more weakly, to form a diffuse layer. The diffuse layer cannot approach the interface more closely than a few molecular diameters and it extends into the liquid a distance which depends on the liquid conductivity. For water-based liquids, where the conductivity is greater than $10^{-6}\,\text{S m}^{-1}$ the diffuse layer is only a few molecules thick. For liquids where the conductivity is of the order of $10^{-11}\,\text{S m}^{-1}$ or lower, the outer charged layer extends a macroscopic distance from the interface. If the conductivity is low enough the diffuse layer may extend the whole way across a tube resulting in a uniform density of charge. Polar molecules in the liquid will be attracted to the free charge and also aligned in the electric field. Figure 2.22 shows a schematic diagram of the double layer in a liquid where there are also polar molecules (Moore 1973).

Charging of liquids, or of solid particles in liquids, normally takes place because the moving liquid carries with it the outer loosely bound layer of

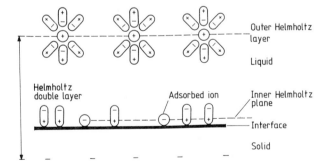

Figure 2.22. Schematic diagram of a solid–liquid interface (from Moore 1973). © John Wiley 1973. Reprinted by permission of John Wiley and Sons, Inc.

charge, leaving the inner layer attached to the solid surface. The potential in the fluid at the plane of slip is called the zeta potential.

As liquid flows, for example through a pipe, it carries with it charge from the diffuse layer. If the charging process is to continue, this charge must be replenished by charge moving through the walls of the pipe. Currents measured between tube walls and the ground are of the order of 10^{-9}–10^{-14} A. These low levels of current are able to flow through insulating pipes and liquid charging is not limited to contact with conductors.

The amount of charge built up by liquid flowing in a pipe is limited by three factors:

(i) The rate at which ions can diffuse to the pipe walls to be discharged.

(ii) The build-up of charge downstream. (In long pipes this amounts to a complete rebuilding of the double layer.)

(iii) The conductivity of the liquid. (The nature of the ions which causes that conductivity affects the polarity but not the magnitude of the charge.)

The rate at which charge flows to earth depends on the time constant τ equal to $\varepsilon_r \varepsilon_0 \rho$ (where ε_r is the relative dielectric constant of the liquid and ρ is its resistivity). Therefore, a highly conducting liquid cannot store charge. A perfectly pure insulating liquid will also not charge because it has insufficient dissociated ions. The charge generation rate therefore builds up as the conductivity increases, reaches a maximum when the liquid conductivity is of the order of 10^{-10} S m^{-1}, then decreases and ionic aqueous solutions are again uncharged. The range of conductivity over which charging is observed is 10^{-13}–10^{-7} S m^{-1} and charge densities in liquids range between 10^{-2} and 10^{-6} C m^{-3}. It has been found that metal tubes give the highest charging rate (with very little difference between different metals) but charging still occurs in glass, rubber and plastic pipes. Turbulent flow produces more charge than laminar flow and rough pipes produce more charge than smooth. (Even when the roughness is too small scale to affect the state of turbulence.)

Liquids are charged whenever an interface is disrupted, therefore charge is also generated during atomisation of a liquid, when it splashes against a surface or when a dispersion of solid particles or an emulsion is stirred.

2.5.2 The electrostatic double layer at a liquid–solid interface

Ions become attached to the interface between a metal and a liquid in three ways.

(i) By image forces between ions in the liquid and the metal (one polarity being more strongly held because it is smaller).

(ii) By specific chemical adsorption of an ionic species from the liquid.

(iii) By injection from the metal as a result of electrolytic effects. (In most of the early analyses electrolysis was not included, but Felici (1984) has recently shown that it can be extremely important.)

At an interface between a liquid and an insulating solid it is also possible for chemical groups on the insulator surface to dissociate, or for the charge balance of a surface to be changed when a constituent of the insulator is replaced by one of lower valency (Ottewill 1975). As a consequence of these processes any interface is charged and ions of opposite polarity to the interfacial charge (counter ions) are attracted to it while ions of the same polarity are repelled.

The distribution of charge in the double layer is extremely important because it determines the way the potential varies with distance from the solid surface, which controls physical parameters such as the stability of colloids, their movement in an electric field and the separation of electrostatic charge by liquid motion. An early theory due to Helmholtz (1879) assumed that the counter ions were parallel to the charged surface at a distance of about one molecular diameter. The potential then falls to zero very rapidly, as shown in figure 2.23(*a*), and the double layer can be treated as a parallel-plate capacitor. This can only be a first approximation, because thermal agitation must tend to diffuse the ions held in the liquid. The Helmholtz model was superseded by the Gouy–Chapman model (Gouy 1910, Chapman 1913). In this model the counter ions were assumed to form a diffuse layer, with the concentration and the potential falling off rapidly with distance at first, and then more gradually as shown in figure 2.23(*b*). This model was useful for plane surfaces with a low charge density and for distances not too close to the surface, but was inadequate for small distances and high charges because it neglected the diameters of the ions which were treated as point charges. This theory was therefore modified by Stern (1924) who assumed the liquid side of the double layer could be divided into two parts, a single layer of strongly held counter ions held close to the bound surface charge and a more diffuse layer of the same polarity. According to Stern, the potential falls off rapidly and linearly at first and then more gradually as shown in figure 2.23(*c*). The bound counter ions in the Stern layer can even change the sign of the potential as shown in figure 2.23(*d*). Double-layer theories are reviewed by Haydon (1974) and Dukhin (1974).

The distribution of ions in the diffuse part of the layer is controlled by thermal diffusion and is therefore governed by the Boltzmann equation (Adamson 1976), i.e. for ions the same polarity as the interface

$$n_+ = n_0 \exp\left(\frac{\lambda e \Psi_x}{kT}\right). \tag{2.32}$$

Here n_+ is the concentration of ions, λ is the ion valency, Ψ_x is the potential at distance x from the surface, k is Boltzmann's constant, T is the absolute temperature and e is the elementary electron charge.

The distribution of counter ions is given by

$$n_- = n_0 \exp\left(\frac{\lambda' e \Psi_x}{kT}\right). \tag{2.33}$$

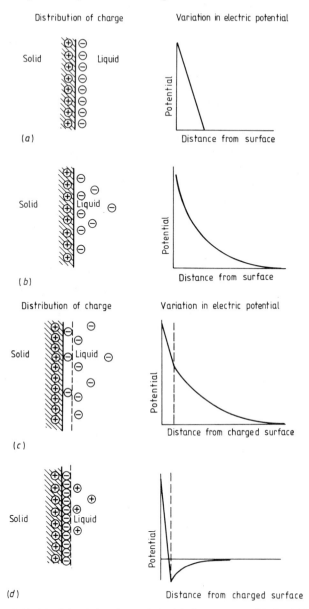

Figure 2.23 Models of the charged double layer at a solid–liquid interface; (*a*), Helmholtz model; (*b*), Gouy–Chapman model; (*c*), Stern model; (*d*), Stern model showing reversal of sign of charged surface.

This leads to a potential which decreases exponentially from the surface (Ottewill 1975):

$$\Psi_x = \Psi_0 \exp(-\kappa x). \tag{2.34}$$

The extent of the layer is inversely proportional to κ, which is given by

$$\kappa^2 = \frac{2e^2 n_0}{\varepsilon_r \varepsilon_0 k T} = \frac{1}{\delta_0^2} \qquad (2.35)$$

$1/\kappa = \delta_0$ is the Debye length of the double layer, i.e. a measure of the diffuse layer thickness.

The properties of the double layer can be explored by means of impedance measurements. Figure 2.24 shows a schematic diagram of a simple metal–electrolyte interface as presented by Parsons (1971).

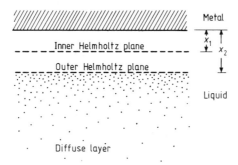

Figure 2.24 The Helmholtz double layer.

At low frequencies the impedance of the interface can be considered to be two capacitances in series, the first depends on the properties of the region between the metal interface and the inner Helmholtz plane and the other on the properties of the diffuse layer. The inner capacitance can be approximated to two planes of charge with a spacing x_i, equal to the distance between the surface and the inner Helmholtz plane; C_1 (the capacitance per unit area) is then given by $\varepsilon_r \varepsilon_0 / x_1$. With a relative permittivity ε_r between two and six (typical of most non-polar liquids, and x_1 of the order of molecular dimensions, C_1 is between 0.12 and 1 F m^{-2}.

The capacitance of the diffuse layer is more difficult to calculate, but Parsons estimates that it may be given by

$$C_2 = (\varepsilon_r \varepsilon_0 / \delta_0)\, \cosh(\varphi e / 2kT) \qquad (2.36)$$

where the Debye length, δ_0, is given by equation (2.35) and φ is the potential difference between the outer Helmholtz plane and the bulk of the liquid (Parsons 1971).

Relatively insulating liquids have a low density of charge carriers therefore δ is high, C_2 is small and the impedance of the interface is dominated by the diffuse layer.

2.5.3 The zeta potential

Problems involving liquid–solid interfaces are often discussed in terms of the zeta potential. This is defined as the potential at the plane of slip between the surface and the liquid as they move with respect to each other. The zeta potential for colloid particles may be measured by observing the motion of a particle in an electric field (Adamson 1976). It is given by

$$\zeta = \eta\mu/\varepsilon_0\varepsilon_r \qquad (2.37)$$

where η is the fluid viscosity, μ is the electrophoretic mobility ($= u/E$) and u is the particle velocity in a field E.

The zeta potential is a conveniently measurable quantity which defines the motion of particles in liquids in an applied electric field, but it cannot be identified with any known feature of the double-layer charge distribution and is essentially an experimental quantity.

2.5.4 Electrode reactions

As liquid moves through a pipe it carries with it charge from the diffuse layer. If the charging process is to continue this charge must be replenished by a charge moving through the walls of the pipe. The nature of the charge carriers in the pipe and liquid differ, therefore there must be an electrode reaction at the pipe wall. Two types of reaction may be distinguished; reactions where electrons are exchanged with species in the solution (redox reactions), and reactions where a chemical species is transferred between the electrode and the liquid (deposition reactions). The rate at which charge is replenished depends on the rate at which these chemical reactions can occur, which itself depends on the rate at which reactants are transported by diffusion to and from the interface. The chemistry of possible charge exchange reactions between hydrocarbons and a metal pipe are complicated, and although it is possible to speculate on the reactions which may lead to a particular measured charge density in the liquid, it is not possible to predict charge levels (Parsons 1971). Analysis of the problem from an electrochemical point of view is complicated by the fact that in insulating liquids, for which electrostatic charging is important, the diffuse charge layer is large and may exceed the diffusion layer thickness.

2.5.5 The theory of charge generation in liquids flowing through pipes

The calculation of the charge separated when a liquid flows through a metal pipe requires the combination of parameters that determine the distribution of charge in the liquid (e.g. the dimensions of the double layer, the electrical resistivity of the liquid, the ionic mobility and the material of the pipe) with those that determine the flow pattern of the liquid (flow velocity, liquid viscosity and the diameter, length and roughness of the pipe). Most of the calculations which attempt to relate the charge acquired to these parameters ignore the electrochemistry of the system and consider it entirely from an electrostatic point of view.

A simple model due to Klinkenberg and van der Minne assumed that the velocity of the liquid near the pipe walls was constant, or varied linearly with distance from the wall, and proved that the streaming current was then proportional to the zeta potential (Klinkenberg and van der Minne 1958, Klinkenberg 1964). This theory gave a qualitative explanation of current generation, but could not explain the complex dependence of charge on liquid and flow properties, which is observed in practice. Later models attempted to deal with more complicated velocity profiles and to derive the zeta potential from fundamental liquid properties. However, since the electrochemistry of the boundary between a hydrocarbon liquid and a metal is not well understood, all relied on adjustable parameters to obtain a fit to experimental data.

It is generally agreed, from both experimental and theoretical evidence, that insulating liquids in turbulent flow in a long pipe obey an equation of the form:

$$I_\infty = A u^m d^n \tag{2.38}$$

where I_∞ is the streaming current for infinite pipe length, A is a constant which depends on the liquid, u is the velocity, d the pipe diameter and m and n are exponents. Detailed theories have been proposed by Koszman and Gavis (1962a,b), Gibbings and Hignett (1966), Touchard (1978), Touchard and Dumarque (1978), Abedian and Sonin (1982), Walmsley and Woodford (1981a) and Walmsley (1982, 1983a,b). Walmsley (1983a,b) and Walmsley and Woodford (1981a,b) also review the earlier theories.

It is usually assumed that liquid flowing in a pipe has a core with uniform charge density maintained by turbulent mixing and a laminar layer near the pipe wall where the influence of turbulence is negligible. The theories then choose different velocity distributions across the pipe, different boundary conditions to represent charge transfer at the pipe wall and different models for regeneration of charge in the liquid. For example, Gavis and Koszman (1961) supposed that one polarity of ion diffused to the pipe wall where it was discharged, the other polarity being unreactive. They also assumed that the conductivity of the liquid remained constant, i.e. that the number density of free ions was constant and charge was regenerated by dissociation in the liquid. They then set up equations representing the transport of ionic charge in the liquid by conduction, diffusion and convection. The influence of the electric field was incorporated using Poisson's equation and the effect of turbulence, by introducing an eddy diffusivity term. They showed that for liquids of all resistivities in turbulent flow in electrically conducting pipes the current for a long pipe obeyed the general equation:

$$I_\infty = A_1 u^{1.88} d^{0.88} F(G) \tag{2.39}$$

where F is a function of G

$$G = (d^2/R_e^{1.75}\tau v) \tag{2.40}$$

and

$$A_1 = \frac{\pm 0.35RT\,\varepsilon_r\varepsilon_0(v/D)^{0.25}(1 - C_s/C_0)}{nFv^{-0.88}}. \tag{2.41}$$

For high-resistivity liquids and turbulent flow

$$i_\infty = A_1 u^{1.88} d^{0.88}. \tag{2.42}$$

In these equations

$\quad u$ = the flow velocity,
$\quad R_e$ = the Reynolds number (du/v),
$\quad d$ = the pipe diameter,
$\quad v$ = the kinematic viscosity,
$\quad \tau$ = the charge relaxation time constant = $\varepsilon_r\varepsilon_0\rho$,
$\quad \rho$ = the resistivity of the liquid,
$\quad C_0$ = the concentration of discharging ions in the bulk of the fluid,
$\quad C_s$ = the concentration of discharging ions at the tube wall,
$\quad R$ = the gas constant,
$\quad F$ = the Faraday number,
$\quad D$ = the molecular diffusivity of charge.

If $I_\infty/(u^{1.88}d^{0.88})$ is put equal to Y, and experimental results are displayed by plotting log Y against log G, equation (2.39) predicts that a continuous curve will be obtained. For high-resistivity liquids in turbulent flow (the conditions normally of relevance to electrostatic charging) for which equation (2.42) applies, log Y plotted against log G gives a straight line at log $Y = $ log A_1. The validity of these equations has been confirmed for small-diameter metal pipes by Koszman and Gavis (1962a,b) and Gibson and Lloyd (1970). Log Y is constant providing log G is less than approximately -5 but for higher values of log G the value of log Y falls as predicted.

Walmsley and Woodford (1981a,b) looked in more detail at the effect of different flow regimes. They related the current I to the volume flow rate Q by the equation

$$I = 4Qe \int z(1 - z^2)(N_+(z) - N_-(z))\,\mathrm{d}z \tag{2.43}$$

where z is the radial position as a fraction of the pipe radius and $N_+(z)$ and $N_-(z)$ were the concentration of positive and negative ions at position z.

The concentrations of ions was found by choosing a model for ion production, ion loss and ion transport within the liquid. The assumptions made by Walmsley and Woodford were:

(i) Ion production proceeds at a constant rate by dissociation.

(ii) Ion losses occur by recombination and by adsorption at the pipe wall.

(iii) In the steady state the rate of ion production and loss are equal.

(iv) The recombination rate is diffusion limited and ion mobilities are related to diffusivities by the Einstein equation.

(v) The electric field is related to the density of charge by Poisson's equation.

To complete the model, boundary conditions were specified to define the rate at which ions were adsorbed at the pipe wall.

In their papers dealing with laminar flow Walmsley and Woodford (1981a,b) assumed that the rate of adsorption of an ion was proportional to the concentration of that species close to the wall. With this assumption, the current was found to depend on the ratio of the adsorption rates of positive and negative ions, the ratio of the diffusivities of positive and negative ions, the electrical conductivity and the average adsorption rate of positive and negative ions.

If either the ionic adsorption rates or the ionic diffusivities of the two species of ion differed, then positive and negative ions were lost to the walls at different rates and the liquid became charged. These two parameters were therefore the source of the streaming current. Their magnitude and polarity were affected by the liquid conductivity and it was found that differences in adsorption dominated at high conductivities and differences in diffusivity at low conductivities. If the two processes lead to charge of the opposite polarity being lost to the walls, it is possible that the streaming current polarity will change when an additive is used to increase the electrical conductivity. In laminar flow the radial distributions of charge and velocity are not affected by the liquid motion so the current is proportional to the flow velocity.

In later papers the model was extended to turbulent flow by changing the velocity profile used in the model and by adding a radially varying eddy diffusivity term (the same for both polarities of ion). The possibility of charge being injected, as well as adsorbed at the pipe walls, was also included.

Four ranges of electrical conductivity were distinguished, the limits of the ranges depending on the pipe radius, r, the mean diffusivity, D, and the thickness of the laminar sublayer near the pipe wall, δ, (which in turn depends on the degree of turbulence):

(i) At very low conductivities ($\sigma \ll D\varepsilon_r\varepsilon_0/r^2$) the diffuse charged layer is spread uniformly across the tube. Changing from laminar to turbulent flow therefore had no effect on the charge generation.

(ii) At slightly higher conductivities ($D\varepsilon_r\varepsilon_0/r^2 < \sigma < D\varepsilon_r\varepsilon_0/r\delta$) the charge resides close to the wall in laminar flow but is spread through the tube by turbulent flow.

(iii) At intermediate conductivities ($D\varepsilon_r\varepsilon_0/r\delta \ll \sigma \ll D\varepsilon\varepsilon_0/\delta^2$) the charge layer is close to the top of the wall in laminar flow and is spread across the pipe by turbulence, but there is also a significant region of non-uniform charge in the laminar sublayer. The thickness (δ) of this layer decreases as the turbulence increases, with $\delta \propto R_e^{-0.875}$. This results in a mean charge density that increases as δ^{-1} or $R_e^{0.875}$ as predicted by Koszman and Gavis (1962a).

(iv) At high conductivities ($\sigma > D\varepsilon_r\varepsilon_0/\delta^2$) the charge layer is so thin that it lies within the laminar sublayer even during turbulent flow. The transition to turbulent flow therefore produces very little effect.

None of the theories take into account the pipe roughness which is experimentally observed to increase charge generation. Koszman and Gavis suggest that calculations of charging for safety purposes should allow a factor of ten for the possible effect of pipe roughness. It has been suggested that the reason for the increase in charge with pipe roughness is that the velocity gradient of the liquid in the pipe is in fact as important as the mean velocity which appears in the charging theories.

2.5.6 Experimental results of charge generation during liquid flow in conducting pipes

It is generally agreed that the current flowing in turbulent flow in a long pipe obeys an equation of the form

$$I_\infty = Au^m d^n \tag{2.44}$$

where d is the pipe diameter, u is the liquid velocity, and m and n are exponents. Experimental results have verified this equation but differ in the values assigned to the exponents. Koszman and Gavis (1962a,b) found theoretically that the values of m and n were 1.88 and 0.88 respectively and confirmed these figures in experimental work using heptane flowing in pipes of various materials between 0.2 and 2.3 mm diameter (Koszman and Gavis 1962a,b).

For larger diameter pipes (25–200 mm), carrying motor spirit, with resistivity 10^{11}–10^{14} Ω m, a significantly higher dependence on pipe diameter was measured by Schon (1965) who proposed an equation:

$$I_\infty = A(ud)^\alpha \tag{2.45}$$

where α had the value 1.8–2.0.

Gibson and Lloyd (1970) carried out a series of experiments using 29 m lengths of stainless-steel pipe with diameters ranging between 0.016 and 0.109 m and liquid flow velocities between 1 and 10 m s^{-1}, representing conditions likely to be directly relevant to the transport of liquids in industry. Uncontaminated toluene, with a resistivity of the order of 3×10^{10} Ω m, and samples of toluene with different quantities of an antistatic additive, reducing the resistivity to 5×10^9 and 5×10^8 Ω m, were tested. Data followed the general form of the theory proposed by Koszman and Gavis (1962a) but differed in detail. Equation (2.44) was obeyed with $m = 2.4$ and $n = 1.6$. When data were taken over a narrow velocity range at high velocities, the best-fit value of m was 1.91, which was much closer to the Koszman and Gavis figure of 1.88, which had been verified for small pipes. However, the diameter dependence of current was not similar for the large and small pipes over any velocity range. With the most conducting sample, m had a strong dependence on pipe diameter, and an equation of the form of equation (2.44) was not valid.

(a) *Effect of pipe length*

The charge on liquid emerging from a pipe is nearly proportional to pipe length for short pipes, but the dependence on pipe length decreases as the pipe length increases. The dependence of charge on pipe length is usually assumed to be exponential. Thus Klinkenberg and van der Minne (1958) give an equation for the ratio of the charge density from a finite pipe length L to the charge Q_∞ from an infinite pipe

$$Q/Q_\infty = 1 - \exp(-LR_\mathrm{e}) \qquad (2.46)$$

and Koszman and Gavis (1962a,b) suggest that

$$I/I_\infty = 1 - \exp(-L/u\tau) \qquad (2.47)$$

where u is the average turbulent flow velocity and τ is the charge relaxation time. However, Walmsley (1983a,b) showed that the exponential law will only apply if the adsorption rates at the surface are high, and that the length scale required for saturation is R_e/T rather than R_e, as proposed by the Klinkenberg model (T is the transference number of the more rapidly adsorbing charge carriers).

For pipes of finite length the streaming current can tend to saturate as the velocity is increased (i.e. there is a fall in the mean charge density leaving the pipe as the velocity is increased). This may be due to a finite ion adsorption rate at the pipe wall, which defines the maximum current which can be supplied by a fixed area of pipe wall.

(b) *Effect of liquid resistivity*

Equations (2.39)–(2.41) indicate that the charging current depends on the liquid viscosity, dielectric constant and electrical resistivity. Minor changes in contamination can affect the resistivity significantly while making only small changes to the liquid viscosity and dielectric constant, therefore it is the liquid resistivity which dominates its charging properties. Numerous experiments have been carried out demonstrating that there is a maximum in the charging current as a function of resistivity. The position of the maximum lies within the range 10 to 1000 pS m^{-1} and is a function of the nature of the ions and the velocity of flow. Figure 2.25 shows an example of the effect of the flow velocity on the charge of heptane flowing in a 250 mm long platinum pipe (Koszman and Gavis 1962a,b) and figure 2.26 shows the effect of changing the resistivity of aircraft fuel. The current flow in an infinitely

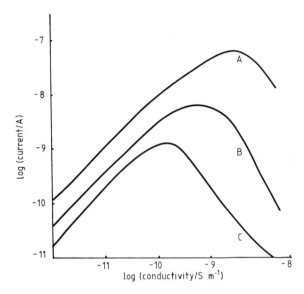

Figure 2.25 Charging current as function of conductivity: A, flow of 10.9 m s^{-1}; B, flow of 3.36 m s^{-1}; C, flow of 1.5 m s^{-1} (from Koszman and Gavis 1962a,b).

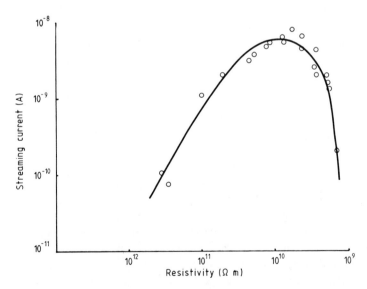

Figure 2.26 The effect of resistivity on the charging of JP-4 aircraft fuel (from Leonard and Carhart 1969).

long pipe can be calculated from the current to a pipe of length L by equation (2.47).

For high electrical resistivities, for which equation (2.42) applies, the streaming current in an infinite pipe should be independent of liquid conductivity. Koszman and Gavis confirm this for heptane in small-diameter pipes. Their results are reproduced in figure 2.27.

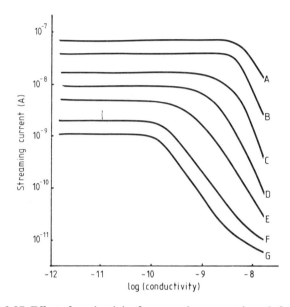

Figure 2.27 Effect of conductivity for streaming current in an infinite pipe (from Koszman and Gavis 1962a,b): A, 10.9 m s^{-1}; B, 7.7 m s^{-1}; C, 4.8 m s^{-1}; D, 3.36 m s^{-1}; E, 2.38 m s^{-1}; F, 1.5 m s^{-1}; G, 1.05 m s^{-1}.

2.5.7 Charge generation in insulating pipes

Experimental studies of liquid charging have mostly concentrated on aqueous solutions in glass or metal tubes, with some work on hydrocarbons in metal tubes. There is less information on charging of hydrocarbons in glass tubes or charging of any liquid in highly insulating tubes.

Koszman and Gavis included glass in their study of heptane charging, and found very little difference in the size of the streaming current from that obtained with a stainless-steel tube.

Cross *et al* (1977) investigated the charging of xylene in a Pyrex glass system and found a significant dependence of charging on the properties of the pipe wall. For example, changes of polarity could be induced by baking the glass pipe to 400 °C or by treating the surface with hydrophobic silane. Xylene was pumped round a circulatory system which included a reservoir several times the volume of the rest of the system. The current flowing to metal flanges, or to metal bands placed round the outside of the glass pipe, varied in both magnitude and polarity with position round the system. The positions of zero charge between polarity reversals in the system were normally in the straight sections of pipe. In this system bends or constrictions could produce charge levels in the liquid which are above the equilibrium value for the straight sections. Thus excess charge generated in one part of the system could relax in a subsequent section. There was evidence that the liquid conductivity increased with the charge density while the liquid was circulated.

The currents flowing in the system increased linearly with the square of velocity for velocities up to 1.2 to 1.5 m s^{-1}, but then tended to level off, however, the current flowing into the reservoir increased faster with velocity at high velocities as shown in figure 2.28. In this system which was built to represent an industrial installation, the state of the surface of the pipe wall was difficult to control and the liquid had a different equilibrium charging rate at different parts of the system, a quantitative analysis was therefore not possible, however the experiments illustrated the complications of predicting charge generation in a real system.

The charging of liquids flowing in plastic pipes has been studied by Gibson (1971). Liquids with conductivities between 10^{-10} and 10^{-12} S m^{-1} were found to give an initially high current, which decreased over the first few minutes of flow (figure 2.29). More conducting liquids (10^{-8} S m^{-1}) behaved more like liquids of all resistivities in conducting pipes, giving a more or

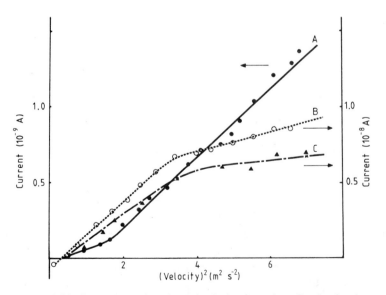

Figure 2.28 Current as a function of velocity for xylene flowing in glass pipes (from Cross *et al* 1977): A, current to reservoir; B, current to glass; C, current to flange.

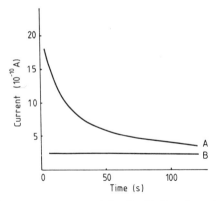

Figure 2.29 The current generated by liquid flow in polyethylene: A, liquid resistivity $10^{10}\,\Omega$ m; B, liquid resistivity $10^8\,\Omega$ m (from Gibson 1971).

less constant current. The final current was generally slightly lower than that produced by a liquid of similar resistivity and velocity in a conducting pipe.

2.5.8 Charge generation during stirring

Stirring produces the same order of magnitude of charging as pipe flow. As before, a maximum is found in the quantity of charge produced as a function of conductivity. The nature of the additive used to change the conductivity affects the position of the peak charge density (figure 2.30).

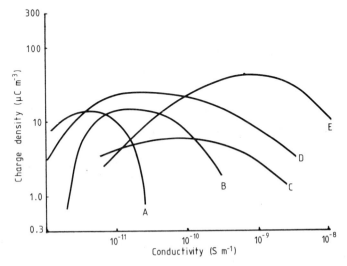

Figure 2.30 Charging of xylene with various additives as a function of conductivity: A, sodium dioctylsulphosuccinate; B, Shell ASA 3; C, Petrosul 742; D, 1-decene polysulphone (from Krämer 1981).

2.5.9 Charging of suspensions

When a suspension of a solid in a liquid is stirred, charge may be transferred to the liquid as a result of the movement of the double layer at the liquid–solid interface. It has been demonstrated experimentally that a suspension of solid particles in a liquid may achieve much higher charge levels than the pure liquid. Vos and co-workers at Shell Research Laboratories (Vos 1971) found that xylene (with a conductivity of about 50 pS m^{-1}) gave increased charge levels when stirred with suspensions of small particles. When the conductivity of the liquid was increased to 2000 pS m^{-1}, by means of an antistatic additive, the charge density decreased to the same value produced in the absence of suspended particles. The charge density of agitated suspensions increased with stirrer speed and depended more strongly on the particle size than on the chemical composition of the suspended particles. It was found, for example, that a suspension of epoxy resin produced the highest charge when the particle diameter was between 0.3 and 4 mm. Both particles smaller than 0.3 mm and those larger than 4 mm produced less charge (figure 2.31). For silica particles (also suspended in xylene) Krämer found that the optimum size was 0.1 to 0.2 mm (Krämer 1981).

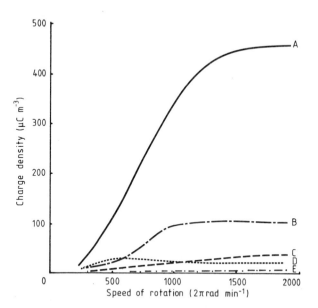

Figure 2.31 The charge density of xylene and various suspensions as a function of the speed of rotation (solids 40 kg m^{-3}): A, epoxy resin 0.3–4.0 mm; B, glass beads 0.1 mm; C, silocel 0.5 mm; D, epoxy resin 4.0 and 0.3 mm; E, xylene (conductivity 1–2 pS m^{-1}) (from Vos *et al* 1974).

One might expect that emulsions would produce similar charge levels to suspensions. Experimental work is limited and it has been found that emulsifiers, included to produce a stable emulsion for laboratory tests, tend to increase the electrical conductivity of the liquid, therefore there are insufficient data to predict the charging behaviour of emulsions in insulating liquids. However, it has been observed that small amounts of immiscible water in a hydrocarbon liquid significantly increase charge generation in many industrial processes.

2.5.10 Electrostatic disruption of liquid surfaces

When a liquid is broken up into droplets, the droplets are frequently charged. This effect was noted by Lenard in 1892 who observed that there was a negative space charge in the fine mist produced by a waterfall, while a predominantly positive charge was carried by the larger droplets. Droplets can be formed by a number of mechanisms including application of an electric field to a liquid surface (see §2.4), forcing liquid through an orifice or splashing it against a surface. Charge densities of 10^{-3} to 10^{-5} C m^{-3} are generated, depending on the mechanism of droplet formation. If a liquid droplet is charged, the charge resides on the surface and exerts an outward force which counteracts the surface tension. This sets an upper limit to the amount of charge on a droplet known as the Rayleigh limit. The condition is reached when the charge, q, is given by the equation

$$q = (64\pi^2\varepsilon_0\gamma a^3)^{1/2}.$$

This corresponds to a maximum charge-to-mass ratio

$$q/m_{max} = (36\varepsilon_0\gamma/a^3 D)^{1/2}$$

where D is the density of the liquid and γ is its surface tension. The validity of this relationship has been confirmed by Hendricks (1962). The Rayleigh limit for droplet charge is higher than the Gaussian or Pauthenier charge limits, as shown in figure 2.18. If charge is added to a liquid drop until the Rayleigh limit is reached, the particle disrupts to form smaller particles. 95 % of the liquid mass and 77 % of the charge remain in one droplet, and the rest goes to make several very much smaller satellite droplets (Schweizer and Hanson 1971).

Five mechanisms may be responsible for the production of charge on liquid drops:

(i) disruption of the double layer which occurs at the liquid–air interface;
(ii) disruption of the double layer at any solid–liquid surface (e.g. in an orifice);

(iii) charge transfer from contact potentials at the liquid and any solid it may contact during atomisation;

(iv) charge separation within the bulk liquid in an electric field;

(v) charging due to division of the random distribution of ions within the liquid.

Droplet formation by splashing has been studied by Iribane and Mason (1967), Jonas and Mason (1968) and Levin and Hobbs (1971). Levin and Hobbs demonstrated that the most important charging mechanism is disruption of the double layer at the liquid–air interface. Most of the charge separation in splashing results from the ejection of particles of about 10 μm in radius from the surface of the liquid. It was shown theoretically that the role of contact potentials would be small and this was confirmed by Vos (1971) who could find no significant difference in the charge produced on the aerosols created when a jet impinged on different metal surfaces.

Iribane and Mason showed that the charge, q, on a droplet is given by the equation

$$q = I\tau[1 - \exp(-t/\tau)]$$

where I is the charging current calculated from double-layer theory, τ is the charge relaxation time and t is the droplet formation time. For insulating liquids, where the relaxation time is much larger than the formation time, this reduces to

$$q = I\tau.$$

When droplets are formed and suspended in the air their charge cannot leak to earth. Therefore, relatively conducting liquids will still form a charged mist. In work on aqueous solutions it is observed that the charge increases with decreasing conductivity. This can be attributed both to the effect of the thickness of the double layer and to a decrease in the backflow of current which occurs as the droplet breaks off from the liquid stream. Vos (1971) proposed that the total charge generated by a jet of liquid of velocity u impacting on a metal sphere will obey the simple formula

$$I = c^*u^2$$

where I is the charging current and c^* is the charging tendency. c^* will depend on the properties of the double layer, the surface roughness of the sphere, the design of the nozzle producing the jet and other external parameters. He proposed a linear relationship between the thickness of the double layer and c^* which would result in a dependence of I on conductivity, of $\sigma^{-0.5}$. He in fact measured an exponent of 0.4 with considerable scatter in his results. Figure 2.32 shows the charge produced when $NaNO_3$ solutions of

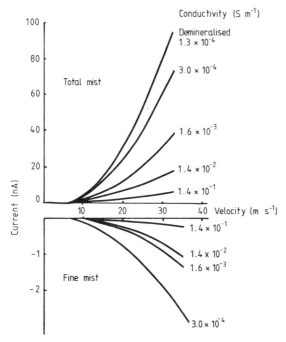

Figure 2.32 Current produced during atomisation of NaNO$_3$ solutions of different conductivities as a function of the velocity of the jet (from Vos 1971).

various concentrations were sprayed through a brass nozzle 0.55 mm in diameter (Vos 1971). The charge was approximately proportional to the velocity squared and was higher for the more resistive solutions. Vos also found that surface active agents could have a profound effect on the charging as shown in figure 2.33.

The charge produced on 2–20 μm droplets produced by ultrasonic atomisation of water-based liquids has been studied by Bassett (1975), who compared demineralised water (conductivity $< 4 \times 10^{-4}$ S m^{-1}) and a sodium nitrate solution (conductivity 1.7×10^{-3} S m^{-1}). In both cases the droplets were charged, but the aerosol contained droplets of both polarities and the majority of droplets had a very low charge. (The mean charge was 43 electrons per droplet.) Bassett concluded that statistical charging (mechanism (iv) above) dominated in his experiments. When an electric field was applied, the mean value of charge shifted to the polarity of the field. At low fields the charge was proportional to the electric field but at high fields (above approximately 3 kV m^{-1}) the charge levelled off.

Most experimental work has concentrated on the spraying of water-based liquids, however some results have been reported from experiments in which hydrocarbons were sprayed. For example, Vos found that some oils (with

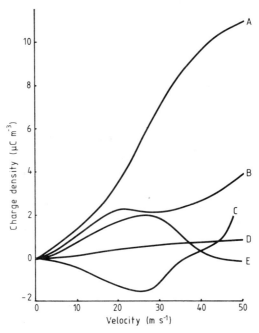

Figure 2.33 Charging of solutions of surface active agents during atomisation as a function of jet velocity (from Vos 1971): A, demineralised water; B, 50/50 ppm Fixanol C/Na aerosol OT; C, 1000 ppm Na aerosol OT; D, tap water; E, 100 ppm Fixanol C.

conductivities in the range $1-6 \times 10^{-8}$ S m^{-1}) produced similar charge levels to those he had measured in aqueous solutions. Lundquist *et al* (1971) measured currents up to 6.3 μA carried by solvents and paints with resistivities between 10^4 and 10^{11} Ω m when they were sprayed from a non-electrostatic airless spray gun. The size of the current was not directly related to the electrical conductivity of the paint and no detailed analysis was carried out to identify the source of charging, as the aim was simply to make safety recommendations.

Mixtures of oil and water have been shown to produce considerably more charge than either separately. Table 2.6 shows the effect of increasing water concentration in a crude oil and figure 2.34 shows the effect of 5 % water in kerosene sprayed through a 3 mm hole. In this case the charge level increased by a factor of 3000.

If the liquid surface is disrupted in an electric field the droplets will acquire an additional charge due to induction. The surface of the liquid gains an induced charge due to the electric field in the same way as described in §2.4. For liquids of suitable viscosity and electrical conductivity, the electrostatic

Table 2.6 Current produced by spraying crude oil–water mixes.

Mixture	Conductivity $(10^{-9} \, S \, m^{-1})$	Current at $40 \, m \, s^{-1}$ (nA)
Crude oil	57	-0.95
Crude oil + 0.5 % water	—	-0.55
Crude oil + 1.0 % water	71	-6.6
Crude oil + 2.0 % water	68	-6.0
Crude oil + 5 % water	64	-51
Crude oil + 10 % water	52	-57
Crude oil + 50 % water	—	-300 to -400

force on the charged surface causes it to rise up into a cone (the Taylor cone) and charged droplets are ejected from the apex. The liquid can thus be atomised by electrostatic forces alone. A high electric field will also cause a jet of liquid from a capillary to break up into charged droplets. Electrostatic atomisation is discussed in §5.1.

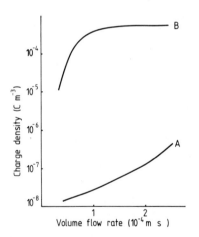

Figure 2.34 The charge generated by a jet of: A, kerosene; B, kerosene + 5 % water (from Gibson 1971).

REFERENCES

Abedian B and Sonin A A 1982 Theory for electric charging in turbulent pipe flow *J. Fluid Mech.* **120** 199–217

Adamson A W 1976 *Physical Chemistry of Surfaces* (New York: Interscience)

Akande A R and Lowell J 1985 Contact electrification of metals by polymers *J. Electrostatics* **16** 147–56

Anderson P W 1958 Absence of diffusion in certain random lattices *Phys. Rev.* **109** 1492–505

Arridge R G C 1967 Static electrification of nylon *Brit. J. Appl. Phys.* **18** 1311–16

Austin I G and Mott N F 1969 Polarons in non-crystalline materials *Adv. Phys.* **18** 41

Awakuni Y and Calderwood J H 1972 Water adsorption and surface conductivity of materials *J. Phys. D: Appl. Phys.* **5** 1038–45

Barnes C, Lederer P G, Lewis T J and Toomer R 1981 Electron and ion transfer processes at insulator surfaces *J. Electrostatics* **10** 107–14

Bassett J D 1975 Study of the charging mechanisms during the production of water aerosols *J. Electrostatics* **1** 47–60

Bauser H 1974 Static electrification of organic solids *Dechema Monograph* vol 72 (Frankfurt: Verlag Chemie) pp 11–29

Bauser H, Klopffer W and Rabenhorst H 1970 On the charging mechanism of insulating solids *Proc. 1st Conf. on Static Electricity* (*Vienna*) (Brussels: Auxilia) pp 2–9 (*Adv. Static Electricity* vol 1)

Chapman D L 1913 Theory of electrocapillarity *Phil. Mag.* **25** 475–85

Chowdry A and Westgate C R 1974a The role of bulk traps in metal insulator contact charging *J. Phys. D: Appl. Phys.* **7** 713–25

—— 1974b Comments on contact charging of polymers *J. Phys. D: Appl. Phys.* **7** L149

Clift R 1983 Fundamental processes in gas filtration *Mech. Eng. Trans. Institution of Engineers, Australia* ME8

Cooke B A 1954 *PhD Thesis* University of London

Coste J and Pechery P 1977 Contribution to the study of charges generated by friction between metals and polymers *Proc. 3rd Int. Conf on Static Electricity* (*Grenoble*) *1977* (Paris: Societé de Chimie Industrielle Paris) pp 4a–f

—— 1981 Influence of surface profile in polymer metal contact charging *J. Electrostatics* **10** 129–36

Cross J H, Haig I and Cetronio A 1977 Electrostatic hazards from pumping insulating liquids in glass pipes *Proc. 3rd Int. Conf. on Static Electricity* (*Grenoble*) *1977* (Paris: Societé de Chimie Industrielle Paris)

Cunningham R G 1970 Electrification of insulating belts passing over grounded rollers *J. Colloid and Interface Sci.* **32** 401–6

Cunningham R G and Hood H P 1970a The relation between contact charging and surface potential difference *J. Colloid and Interface Sci.* **32** 373–6

—— 1970b A new method of measuring contact electrification characteristics of materials *J. Colloid and Interface Sci.* **32** 444–8

Davies C N 1966 *Aerosol Science* (New York: Academic)

Davies D K 1967a Examination of the electrical properties of insulators by surface charge measurements *J. Sci. Instrum.* **44** 521–4

—— 1967b The generation and dissipation of static charge on dielectrics in vacuum *Static Electrification* (*London*) (Inst. Phys. Conf. Ser. 4) pp 29–36

—— 1969 Charge generation on dielectric surfaces *J. Phys. D: Appl. Phys.* **2** 1533–7

—— 1970 Charge generation on solids *Proc. 1st Conf. on Static Electricity* (*Vienna*) (Brussels: Auxilia) pp 10–21 (*Adv. Static Electricity* vol 1)

Davison S W and Gentry J L 1983 Fundamental hypotheses on charging of ultra-fine particles by diffusion of ions *Pacific Region Meeting of the Fine Particle Society (Honolulu) 1983* pp 1–5 (Tulsa, Oklahoma: Fine Particle Society)

—— 1985 Difference in the diffusion charging of dielectric and conducting ultra-fine aerosols *Aerosol Sci. and Tech.* **4** 157–63

Donald M B 1958 Electrostatic separation of minerals *Research* **11** 19–25

Duke C B and Fabish T J 1976 Charge induced relaxation in polymers *Phys. Rev. Lett.* **37** 1075–8

Duke C B, Salaneck W R, Fabish T J, Ritsko J J, Thomas H R and Paton A 1978 Electronic structure of pendant-group polymers: molecular ion states and dielectric properties of poly(2-vinylpyridine) *Phys. Rev.* B **18** 5717–39

Dukhin S S 1974 Electrokinetic phenomena *Surface and Colloid Science* vol 7, ed E Matjevic (New York: Wiley) ch 1

Edmonson H 1961 *PhD Thesis* University of Leeds

Eisberg R M 1961 *Fundamentals of Modern Physics* (New York: Wiley) ch 7

Fabish T J and Duke C B 1977 Molecular charge states and charge exchange in polymers *J. Appl. Phys.* **48** 4256–66

—— 1978 Molecular charge states in polymers *Polymer Surfaces* ed D T Clark and W J Feast (New York: Wiley) ch 6

Fabish T J, Saltsburg H M and Hair M L 1976 Charge transfer in metal-atactic polystyrene contacts *J. Appl. Phys.* **47** 930–9

Felici N J 1966 Forces et charges de petits objets en contact avec une electrode affectée d'un champ electrique *Rev. Générale de Éléctricité* **75** 1145–60

—— 1984 Conduction and electrification in dielectric liquids: two related phenomena of the same electrochemical nature *J. Electrostatics* **15** 291–7

Frisch H L and Lloyd S P 1960 Electron energy levels in a one dimensional disordered lattice *Phys. Rev.* **120** 1175–89

Furhmann J and Kurschner J 1981 Time dependent transient and intermittent contact electrification *J. Electrostatics* **10** 115–20

Gavis J and Koszman I 1961 Development of charge in low conductivity liquids flowing past surfaces—a theory of the phenomenon in tubes *J. Colloid Sci.* **16** 375–91

Gibbings J C and Hignett E T 1966 Dimensional analysis of electrostatic streaming current *Electrochim Acta* **11** 815

Gibson N 1971 Static in fluids *Static Electrification (London) 1971* (Inst. Phys. Conf. Ser. 11) pp 71–83

Gibson N and Lloyd F C 1970 Electrification of toluene flowing in large diameter metal pipes *J. Phys. D: Appl. Phys.* **3** 563–73

Gouy G 1910 Constitution of electrical charge at surface of an electrolyte *J. Physique* **9** 457

Haenen H T M 1976 Experimental investigation of the relationship between generation and decay of charges on dielectrics *J. Electrostatics* **2** 151–73

Harper W R 1967 *Contact and Frictional Electrification* (Oxford: Clarendon Press)

Haydon D A 1974 The electrical double layer and electrokinetic phenomena *Recent Progress in Surface Science* vol 1, ed J F Danielli, K G A Pankhurst and A C Riddiford (New York: Academic) pp 94–153

Hays D A 1974 Contact electrification between mercury and polyethylene—effect of surface oxidation *J. Chem. Phys.* **61** 1455–62

Helmholtz H 1879 Studiern uber electrische Grenzschichten *Weid. Ann. Phys.* **7** 337–82

Hendricks C D 1962 Charged droplet experiments *J. Colloid Sci.* **17** 249–59

Hennecke M, Hoffmann R and Furhmann H 1979 Simulation of contact electrification of polymers by an analogue model *J. Electrostatics* **6** 15–27

Hewitt G W 1957 The charging of small particles for electrostatic precipitation *AIEE Trans. Commun. Electron.* **76** 300

Hignett E T 1967 Particle charge magnitudes in electrostatic precipitation *Proc. IEE* **114** 1325–8

Homewood K P, Lowell J and Rose-Innes A C 1983 Charge accumulation in repeated contacts—the role of conduction *Electrostatics (Oxford)* 1983 (Inst. Phys. Conf. Ser. 66) pp 225–30

Hull H H 1949 A method for studying the distribution and sign of static charges on solid materials *J. Appl. Phys.* **20** 1157–9

Iribane J V and Mason B J 1967 Electrification accompanying the bursting of bubbles in water and dilute suspensions *Trans. Faraday Soc.* **63** 2234–45

Jeans J 1962 *An Introduction to the Kinetic Theory of Gases* (Cambridge: CUP)

Jewell-Thomas S R C 1957 *PhD Thesis* University of London

Jonas P R and Mason B J 1968 Systematic charging of water droplets produced by break up of liquid jet and filaments *Trans. Faraday Soc.* **64** 1971–82

Klinkenberg A 1964 Elektrische aufladung schlecht leitender flussigkeiten bei turbulenter stromung *Chim. Ing. Tech.* **36** 283–90

Klinkenberg A and van der Minne J L 1958 *Electrostatics in the Petroleum Industry* (Amsterdam: Elsevier)

Kornfeld M I 1969 The nature of frictional electrification *Sov. Phys.–Solid State* **11** 1306–10

Koszman I and Gavis J 1962a Development of charge in low conductivity liquids flowing past surfaces: engineering predictions from the theory developed for tube flow *Chem. Eng. Sci.* **17** 1013–22

—— 1962b Experimental verification and application of the theory developed for tube flow *Chem. Eng. Sci.* **17** 1023–40

Krämer H 1981 Electrostatic charging of poorly conducting liquid systems—suspensions, emulsions and solutions—by agitating *J. Electrostatics* **10** 89–97

Kraemer H F and Johnstone H F 1955 Collection of aerosol particles in the presence of electrostatic fields *Ind. Eng. Chem.* **47** 2426–34

Krupp H 1971 Physical models of the static electrification of solids *Static Electrification 1971* (Inst. Phys. Conf. Ser. 11) pp 1–17

Lebedev N N and Skal'skaya I P 1962 Force acting on a conducting sphere in the field of a parallel plate condenser *Z. Tekh. Fiz.* **32** 375–8

Leonard J T and Carhart H W 1969 *US Naval Research Lab. Report* 6952

Levin Z and Hobbs P V 1971 Splashing of water drops on solid and wetted surfaces: hydrodynamics and charge separation *Phil. Trans. R. Soc. London* A **269** 555–85

Lewis T J 1978 The movement of electrical charge along polymer surfaces *Polymer Surfaces* ed D T Clark and W J Feast (New York: Wiley–Interscience) ch 4

Lowell J 1976 The electrification of polymers by metals *J. Phys. D: Appl. Phys.* **9** 1571–85

—— 1979 Tunnelling between metals and insulators and its role in contact electrification *J. Phys. D: Appl. Phys.* **12** 1541–54

Liu B Y H and Yeh H C 1969 *Planetary Aerodynamics* (New York: Gordon and Breach) ch 11.6, pp 187–95

Lundquist S, Fredholm O and Lövstrand K G 1971 Dangerous electrostatic charging during airless paint spraying *Static Electrification (London) 1975* (Inst. Phys. Conf. Ser. 11) pp 260–70

Montgomery D J 1959 Static electrification of solids *Solid State Phys.* **9** 139–96 (New York: Academic)

Moore A D 1973 *Electrostatics and its Applications* (New York: Wiley–Interscience)

Mott N F 1968 Electrons in disordered structures *Adv. Phys.* **16** 49–144

Mott N F and Gurney R W 1948 *Electronic Processes in Ionic Crystals* (Oxford: OUP)

Murphy A T, Adler F T and Penney G W 1959 A theoretical analysis of the effects of an electric field on the charging of free particles *Trans. Am. Inst. Electronic Eng: Commun. and Electronics* **78** 318–26

Nielson K A and Hill J C 1976a Collection of inertialess particles on spheres with electrical forces *Ind. Eng. Chem. Fund.* **15** 149–56

—— 1976b Capture of particles on spheres by inertial and electrical forces *Ind. Eng. Chem. Fund.* **15** 157–64

O'Dwyer J J 1973 *The Theory of Electrical Conduction and Breakdown in Solid Dielectrics* (Oxford: Clarendon)

Ohara K 1979 Contribution of the molecular motion of polymers to frictional electrification *Electrostatics (Oxford) 1979* (Inst. Phys. Conf. Ser. 48) pp 257–64

Ottewill H 1975 Electrostatics in colloid science *Static Electrification (London) 1975* (Inst. Phys. Conf. Ser. 27) pp 56–73

Parsons R 1971 The electric double layer, electrode reactions and static *Static Electrification (London) 1971* (Inst. Phys. Conf. Ser. 11) pp 124–37

Pauthenier M M and Moreau-Hanot M 1932 La charge de particules spheriques dans un champ ionisé *J. Phys. Radium Ser. 7* **3** 590–613

Penney G W and Lynch R D 1957 Measurement of the charge imparted to fine particles by a corona discharge *AIEE Trans. Commum. Electron.* **76** 294–9

Peterson J W 1954a Contact charging between a borosilicate glass and nickel *J. Appl. Phys.* **25** 501–4

—— 1954b Contact charging between non-conductors and metals *J. Appl. Phys.* **25** 907–15

Postnikov S N 1978 *Electrophysical and Electrochemical Phenomena in Friction, Cutting and Lubrication* (New York: Van Nostrand)

Ruckdeschal F R 1973 *PhD Thesis* University of Rochester, USA

Sampuran-Singh 1981 Charging characteristics of some powders used in electrostatic powder coating *IEEE Trans. Ind. Appl.* **IA–17** 121

Schon G 1965 *Handbuch der Raumexplosionen* ed H H Frytag (Weinheim Bergstr.: Verlag Chemie)

Schweizer J W and Hanson D N 1971 Stability limit of charged drops *J. Coll. Interface Sci.* **35** 417–23

Seanor D A 1972 *Polymer Science* vol 2, ed A D Jenkins (Amsterdam: North-Holland) p 1187

Shaw P E and Jex C S 1928 Triboelectricity and friction–glass and solid elements *Proc. R. Soc. A* **118** 97–112

Shinbrot T 1985 A look at charging mechanics *J. Electrostatics* **17** 113–25

Smith W B and McDonald J R 1976 Development of a theory for the charging of particles by unipolar ions *J. Aerosol Sci.* **7** 151–66

Stern O 1924 Theory of the electrolytic double layer *Z. Electrochem.* **30** 508

Szirmai S 1980 The dispersion of powders by intense electrostatic fields *J. Appl. Phys.* **51** 5215–22, 5223–27

—— 1981 The dispersion of powders by intense electric fields *PhD Thesis* University of NSW, Australia

Toomer R and Lewis T J 1980 Charge trapping in corona charged polyethylene films *J. Phys. D: Appl. Phys.* **13** 1343–56

Touchard G 1978 Streaming currents generated by laminar and turbulent flow *J. Electrostatics* **5** 463–76

Touchard G and Dumarque P 1978 Transport of electric charges by convection of a dielectric liquid in a cylindrical metal tube *J. Electroanal. Chem. Interfacial Chem.* **88** 387–405

Vos B 1971 Electrostatic charge generation—mechanical studies *Static Electrification (London) 1971* (Inst. Phys. Conf. Ser. 11) pp 184–95

Vos B, Ramakers L and Van der Weerd J M 1974 Electrostatic charging of suspensions during agitation *Proc. 1st Int. Loss Prevention Symposium (Amsterdam)* (Amsterdam: Elsevier) pp 381–4

Wagner P E 1956 Charge separation at contacts *J. Appl. Phys.* **27** 1300–10

Walmsley H L 1982 The generation of electric currents by the turbulent flow of dielectric liquids. I: Long Pipes *J. Phys. D: Appl. Phys.* **15** 1907–34

—— 1983a The generation of electric currents by the turbulent flow of dielectric liquids. II: Pipes of finite length *J. Phys. D: Appl. Phys.* **16** 533–72

—— 1983b Charge generation in low dielectric constant liquids *Electrostatic Phenomena (Oxford) 1983* (Inst. Phys. Conf. Ser. 66) pp 45–52

Walmsley H L and Woodford G 1981a The generation of electric currents by the laminar flow of dielectric liquids *J. Phys. D: Appl. Phys.* **14** 1761–82

—— 1981b The polarity of current generated by the laminar flow of a dielectric liquid *J. Electrostatics* **10** 283–8

Webers V J 1963 Measurement of triboelectric position *J. Appl. Polymer Sci.* **7** 1317–23

Whipple F J W and Chalmers J A 1944 On Wilson's theory of the collection of charge by falling drops *Quart. J. R. Meteriol. Soc.* **70** 103

Whitby K T and Liu B Y H 1966 The electrical behaviour of aerosols *Aerosol Science* ed C N Davies (New York: Academic) ch 3

White H J 1963 *Industrial Electrostatic Precipitation* (Oxford: Pergamon)

Williams M W 1964 Effect of polymer structure on its triboelectric properties *IEEE 7th Conf. of Industrial Applications Society (Pittsburg) 1964*

—— 1976 The dependence of triboelectric charging of polymers on their chemical composition *J. Macromolecular Sci. Rev. Macromol. Chem.* **C14** 251–65

Wintle H J 1974 Contact charging of polymers *J. Phys. D: Appl. Phys.* L128–31

Zimmer E 1970 Die elektrostasche aufladung von hochpolymeren isolierstoffen *Kunstoffe* **60** 465–8

Zisman W A 1932 A new method of measuring contact potential differences in solids *Rev. Sci. Instrum.* **3** 367–70

Chapter 3　Measurements and Instrumentation

<hr>

3.1 INTRODUCTION

In a conventional electric circuit the voltage is held constant by a power supply or battery, and the rate of flow of charge (the electric current) is determined by the resistance of the circuit. There is no charge separation or accumulation because the circuit elements are conductors. In an electrostatic system there is no charge flow, i.e. the fixed parameter is the electrostatic charge. The definition of capacitance is

$$C = q/V. \tag{3.1}$$

Therefore, if q is constant, the voltage V will vary as the capacitance changes. It follows that measurement of a voltage gives no indication of the extent of static electrification unless the capacitance of the system is also known. The charge which has accumulated is the fixed quantity which must be defined but it is not always accessible to measurement and it may be necessary to measure the voltage or field created by the charge and calculate the charge itself.

The electric field E must also be measured in order to calculate the force acting on a charged object, which is given by the equation

$$F = qE. \tag{3.2}$$

The electric field is defined as the rate of change of the potential with distance d. For a simple planar geometry this is:

$$E = V/d. \tag{3.3}$$

The electric field, the charge and the potential are related to each other by very simple equations and it is often possible to use the same instrument to measure all three parameters.

91

3.2 POTENTIAL DIVIDERS AND RESISTANCE PROBES

In electrodynamic measurements an electric potential may be measured with a potential divider, i.e. the unknown voltage, V, is applied across two resistors, R_1 and R_2, in series. The voltage V' across the smaller resistor R_2 is then given by:

$$V' = VR_2/(R_1 + R_2).$$

If R_1 is $1000 \times R_2$, the voltage measured across R_2 is effectively 10^{-3} times the applied voltage and can be measured with a low-voltage meter.

The potential divider method may be used in electrostatics only if the stored charge is not significantly depleted by the current flow. Essentially this means that the method is only suitable for measuring the voltage of power supplies. Electrostatic power supplies are required to give a high voltage, but only a low current and, for safety reasons, they are often designed so that if a high current is drawn the voltage falls. Measurement of the voltage of this type of supply therefore requires a high-resistance potential divider to limit the current flow. For example, if it is required to draw only $1\ \mu A$ while measuring 100 kV, then the total resistance of the potential divider is calculated from Ohm's law to be:

$$R = R_1 + R_2 = V/I$$
$$= 10^{11}\ \Omega.$$

If R_1 is $10^{11}\ \Omega$ then R_2 must be $10^8\ \Omega$. Unfortunately, most voltage meters do not have an impedance which is significantly greater than $10^8\ \Omega$ and cannot be used to measure the voltage across R_2. An alternative way of using the resistor chain, which overcomes this problem, is to measure the current flowing through the known resistance to earth. The voltage is then found using Ohm's law. The resistance must still be of the order of $10^{11}\ \Omega$ to limit current flow. Most commercial high-voltage probes have a resistance of the order of 10^8 or $10^9\ \Omega$ and are not suitable for electrostatic power supplies. $10^{10}\ \Omega$ resistors which will withstand 15–20 kV are readily available and ten of these, mounted in series in a plastic tube, may be used to measure voltages up to 100 kV. For higher voltages the resistors must be immersed in oil to prevent electrical breakdown across the surface and between resistors.

It is not possible to draw a current from an isolated charged object without depleting its charge and either a non-contacting voltmeter or an electrostatic voltmeter must be used to measure its potential.

3.3 ELECTROMETERS AND ELECTROSTATIC VOLTMETERS

There is no fundamental difference between an electrometer (which measures charge) and an electrostatic voltmeter. Since $C = q/V$, measurement of voltage using an instrument with a known capacitance automatically gives the charge. Electrometers are designed to withstand lower voltages and are more sensitive instruments than electrostatic voltmeters.

3.3.1 The quadrant electrometer or electrostatic voltmeter

The quadrant electrostatic voltmeter makes use of the electrostatic force of repulsion to measure voltage. Typically the instrument has two interleaving sets of vanes, with one set fixed and the other mounted on a spring or fibre and attached to a pointer, as illustrated in figure 3.1. On application of a voltage the mobile vanes on the spring are repelled from the stationary vanes, by a force which is proportional to the square of the potential. The pointer moves across the dial and stops when the electrostatic force equals the restoring torque of the spring. The only current flowing to the meter is that required to charge the capacitance represented by the vanes. The input resistance of the instrument is theoretically infinite, but in practice it is limited by the resistance of the insulators on which the vanes are mounted. The deflection is usually measured by detecting the movement of a beam of light reflected from the moving parts. The scale is non-linear and rather cramped at low voltages, but this disadvantage is offset by the very high input impedance and the ability of the instrument to measure both DC voltages and the root mean square of an AC voltage.

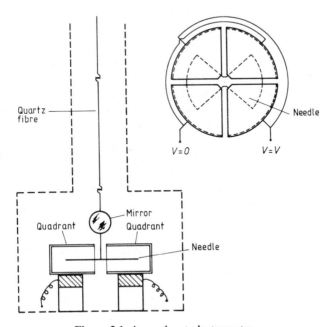

Figure 3.1 A quadrant electrometer.

Instruments designed to measure voltages up to about 60 kV normally have a capacitance between 2 and 20 pF. Unless the capacitance of the object whose voltage to be measured is very much larger than the meter capacitance, a correction must be made for the charge which flows to the meter. For example, if the capacitance of the meter is C_m, and the capacitance of the object whose potential is to be measured is C_1, then the combined capacitance C, of the two in parallel is given by

$$C = C_1 + C_m.$$

No additional charge is created by connecting the meter, therefore the original charge, q, on the article is shared between the two capacitances and the voltage must fall.

In the absence of the meter the true potential V_t of the article is related to its charge, q, and its capacitance, C_1, by the equation

$$C_1 = q/V_t.$$

After connection of the meter

$$C_1 + C_m = q/V_m$$

where V_m is the measured voltage. Therefore the relationship between the true voltage and the measured voltage is

$$V_t = V_m(C_1 + C_m)/C_1.$$

3.3.2 The Kelvin absolute electrometer

An absolute electrometer measures charge or voltage in terms of the basic units of mass, length and time, by comparing an electrostatic force with a gravitational force. The Kelvin electrometer, shown schematically in figure 3.2, consists of a parallel-plate capacitor in which the central portion of one plate is mounted on a spring which allows it a small independent movement. When a charge or voltage is applied to the bottom plate the top plate will be attracted towards it. This force is counteracted by decreasing the mass M on the movable section of the top plate until it is returned to its equilibrium position, indicted by an accurate pointer.

The electrostatic force of attraction between unit area of two plates in air, with a voltage V applied between them is

$$F = \varepsilon_0 V^2/2d^2 \tag{3.4}$$

when this is equated to the gravitational force, mg (due to a change in mass of m kg) it is found that

$$V = \left(\frac{2mg}{\varepsilon_0}\right)^{1/2} d. \tag{3.5}$$

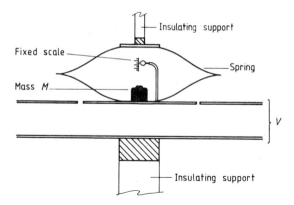

Figure 3.2 An absolute electrometer.

All the quantities on the right-hand side of the equation are known in terms of mass, length and time. The constant ε_0 determines the system of electrical units used. For V to be given in the conventional units of volts, ε_0 is $8.85 \times 10^{-12}\,\mathrm{F\,m^{-1}}$.

The sensitivity of this instrument increases with voltage. It is therefore most suitable for measuring very high voltages. However, it may be used for lower voltages, of the order of a few kilovolts, if an auxiliary constant potential is applied between the upper plate and the ground, and the pointer is set to zero under this condition. Small changes in potential can then be accurately registered.

A modern electrometer based on the attractive plate principle, which measures potentials between 3 kV and 200 kV, uses a variable current flowing through a coil between the poles of a magnet to provide the force which opposes the electrostatic attraction. The coil current is proportional to the force and hence to the square of the applied voltage (Davies 1974).

3.3.3 The electroscope

The gold leaf electroscope, illustrated in figure 3.3, was one of the earliest electrical instruments. A rigid central conductor carrying a fibre or foil, attached at one end only, is mounted on insulators in a conducting container. If a charge is applied to the rod, the foil is repelled from the rod towards the walls of the chamber. The deflection of the foil is a measure of the amount of charge applied to the rod. The instrument has a very small capacitance (of the order of 1 pF) therefore very little charge is drawn to it. It will measure very small quantities of charge of the order of $10^{-14}\,\mathrm{C}$.

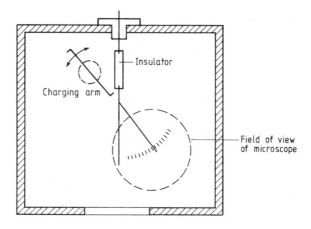

Figure 3.3 A gold leaf electroscope.

3.3.4 Modern electrometers

The essential characteristics of an electrometer are a very high input impedance, so that there can be no charge leakage to earth, and a known capacitance. This may be achieved using solid state circuitry. FET input amplifiers are able to achieve an input impedance of 10^{15} Ω which is nearly as good as achieved in practice with the insulators in electrostatic electrometers. Modern electrometers measure the voltage developed across one of a range of standard capacitors using an FET input amplifier. Charges down to approximately 10^{-13} C can be measured in this way.

3.4 FIELD METERS AND NON-CONTACTING VOLTMETERS

3.4.1 Introduction

Electrostatic field meters and non-contacting voltmeters have a sensing area which is effectively at earth potential. Therefore, if the meter is held a distance d in front of a plane surface which has a potential V there is a field at the meter which is equal to

$$E = V/d.$$

Measurement of the electric field at the meter therefore gives the surface potential and measurement of the surface potential allows the field to be calculated. The distinction between a non-contacting voltmeter and a field meter is thus slight, but it can be significant if the field is non-uniform or where a voltmeter cannot be used at the distance specified by the manufacturer. A voltmeter is calibrated in volts and a field meter in volts/metre but unfortunately not all manufacturers adhere strictly to this rule because under normal circumstances the instruments can be used equally for either measurement.

Field meters/voltmeters are probably the most versatile electrostatic instruments, but some calculation is normally required to transform from the measurement of the electric field in the presence of the meter to find the charge and potential which would be there in its absence. The main problem is that the meter is a fairly large, essentially grounded, object which, unless it is able to be placed in a position of zero potential (such as in the earthed walls of a container), distorts the field it is attempting to measure. In simple geometries the effect of the meter can easily be calculated, but in more complex situations the true field must be found from the measured field at various positions using a computer model (Chubb and Butterworth 1979, Diserens *et al* 1978). Field meters typically measure between 1 and $10^3 \, \text{kV m}^{-1}$.

3.4.2 The induction field meter

The simplest type of field meter/non-contacting voltmeter is the induction field meter, illustrated in figure 3.4. A metal sensor plate of area A, is charged by induction in the electric field to a surface charge density, Q_s (in C m^{-2}), which is proportional to the electric field (see equation (1.35)).

$$Q_s = \varepsilon_0 E. \tag{3.6}$$

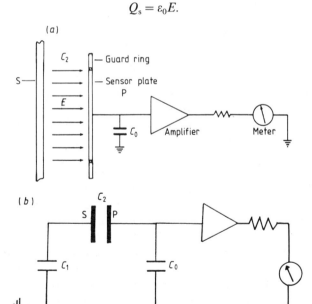

Figure 3.4 An induction field meter. (*a*) C_1 is the capacitance between the surface and earth in the absence of the field meter. (*b*) The equivalent circuit of the arrangement in (*a*).

A total charge $q = Q_s A$ flows from ground to the plate and charges the meter capacitance C_0 to a voltage V_0:

$$V_0 = q/C_0 = \varepsilon_0 EA/C_0. \tag{3.7}$$

V_0 is thus proportional to the charge induced on the plate which is proportional to the electric field E.

V_0 is small compared with the surface voltage which provides the field, i.e. the sensor plate is close to earth potential. An earthed ring can therefore be placed round the sensor plate to act as a guard. This ensures that the electric field across the sensor plate is uniform and there is no field intensification at its edges.

The induction field meter is very simple in concept and requires only a plane probe and an electrometer. However, in practice, it tends to suffer from zero drift problems as a result of signals generated by the bias current requirements of the amplifier. In addition the meter capacitance will be charged, not only by induction in the electric field, but also by collecting stray free charge. Hence the induction field meter is not suitable for measuring fields in the presence of charged, particles or ions. It is not sufficiently stable for continuous monitoring, but gives a useful indication of the electric field, provided the measurement can be made only a short time after setting the zero. It is possible to make induction probes with a very small sensor plate for high-resolution measurements of the surface charge and induction meters with a resolution approaching 50 μm have been reported (Scruton and Blott 1973, Toomer 1979).

3.4.3 The rotating-vane field mill

The most widely used instrument for measuring electric fields is the rotating-vane field meter. In principle, this is an induction field meter with a grounded butterfly rotor placed in front of the sensor plate as shown in figure 3.5. As the rotor turns, the sensor plate is alternately exposed to the field and shielded from it, so an alternating voltage is generated across the meter capacitance. The peak voltage is proportional to the electric field and independent of the rotor speed. A phase-sensitive detector, which uses the shutter rotation for the reference frequency, extracts the field information. The sensitivity of the instrument is changed by altering the value of the internal capacitance. The amount of free charge able to reach the collector plate in a single cycle (<0.01 s) is negligible and the amplifier is AC coupled, therefore this instrument does not suffer from the drift problems of the induction meter and may be used in an environment with free charge. The input impedance of the amplifier, used to measure the voltage built up across the capacitor, does not have to be as high as for the simple induction meter, as it is only necessary that the charge decay rate is slow compared with the periodic time of the alternating signal. In practice an input resistance of the order of 10 MΩ is sufficient.

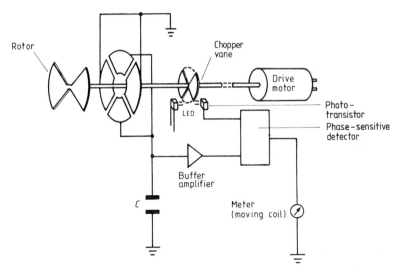

Figure 3.5 A rotating-vane field meter.

There are a wide variety of rotating-vane field meters commercially available. In the majority, a small electric motor is used to drive the vanes, however, for hazardous environments, clockwork or air turbine drives are available in instruments with intrinsically safe electronics. Air purging of the sensing area may also be introduced for dusty environments. A number of refinements to the basic instrument are reported in the literature (Chubb 1983, Collacott 1981).

3.4.4 The vibrating field meter

An oscillatory signal is also provided by vibrating field meters. These instruments are designed with an aperture in front of the sensor plate. The extent to which the field penetrates to the plate, and hence the charge induced on it, depends on the spacing between the aperture and the sensor plate. Either the aperture or the sensor plate vibrates. The signal detected at the plate is then proportional to the displacement between the sensor plate and the aperture, and to the electric field. An oscillatory signal is produced on the plate from which the electric field can be found. Vibrating field meters tend to be more compact than rotating-vane instruments and may have a sensing area as small as a millimetre across, whereas rotary field meters are normally several centimetres in diameter.

A modification of the vibrating field meter has been designed where the system has a feedback loop so that a voltage is applied to the sensing plate until the field measured is zero. This voltage is then equal to the voltage on the surface which created the electric field. This meter is therefore, strictly speaking, a voltmeter rather than a field meter.

A vibrating field meter has been designed which will operate at temperatures up to 1000 °C and 0.6 MPa (Lohman *et al* 1981).

3.4.5 The radial field mill

A schematic diagram of a radial field mill is shown in figure 3.6. It operates on the same principle as the flat-plate rotating field mill. The rotor consists of 16–24 segments with alternate segments connected together. One set of segments is earthed and the other set provides the output signal via a carbon brush. The outer cylinder, the stator, is perforated with slots. The rotor is driven at speeds of 10^4 rpm and the signal induced on it provides the data for the measurement of the electric field at the stator surface. The induced charge due to the electric field and free charge are easily distinguished in the displayed signal. This instrument is of interest primarily because it can form part of the active central electrode in a coaxial corona system and be used for study of the corona discharge (Waters 1972).

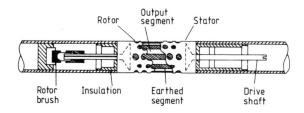

Figure 3.6 A radial field meter. Alternate segments of the rotor are connected to the rotor shaft which is earthed by the rotor brush. The remaining segments provide an output signal (after Waters 1972).

3.4.6 Measurement of surface potential and charge

A charged surface generates an electric field, with the relationship between charge and field given by the Gauss law. An infinite isolated conducting plane with a surface charge density of Q_s C m^{-2} is shown in figure 3.7. Field lines cannot exist in a metal and they will approach a metal surface at right angles. If we imagine a small cylinder, with cross sectional area ΔA, protruding through the surface, it encloses a charge $Q_s \Delta A$. Applying the Gauss law to the cylinder, there are no field lines parallel to the surface and the field perpendicular to the surface at the area ΔA is given by:

$$E \Delta A = \frac{Q_s \Delta A}{\varepsilon_0}.$$

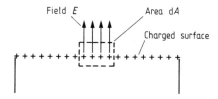

Figure 3.7 The electric field above a charged surface.

For a uniform charge, integrated over the whole surface, this may be written as

$$E = Q/\varepsilon_0. \tag{3.8}$$

Thus the surface charge can easily be found by measuring the electric field.

In practice the situation is complicated by two factors:

(i) Insertion of the field meter will change the electric field.

(ii) With an insulating material field lines may also exist in the material itself. The field above the surface will still be proportional to the charge on the surface but the constant of proportionality will not be ε_0.

The equivalent circuit for an induction-type field meter (which also applies to the rotating-vane and oscillating models) is shown in figure 3.4(b). The charged surface S has a capacitance C_1 to earth and there is a capacitance C_2 between the surface S and the sensor plate P of the field meter a distance d from the surface, which is given by

$$C_2 = \varepsilon_0 A/d.$$

The input capacitance of the field meter is C_0.

(a) *Measurement of surface voltage*
Let us assume that a potential V is applied to the surface S. This voltage must be shared between the two capacitances C_2 and C_0 which are in series giving a potential V_0 at the plate:

$$V_0 = C_2 V/(C_0 + C_2). \tag{3.9}$$

If the meter capacitance is much larger than C_2 this is approximately

$$V_0 = C_2 V/C_0 = (\varepsilon_0 A/C_0) \times (V/d)$$

V_0 is small and the meter may be considered to be effectively at earth potential. The electric field at the meter is

$$E = (V - V_0)/d \simeq V/d$$

and

$$V_0 = (\varepsilon_0 A E/C_0) = KE \tag{3.10}$$

where K is a calibration constant of the meter.

The meter reading V_0 is proportional to the electric field and the potential V on the surface can be found directly by multiplying the measured field by the spacing between the meter and the surface S. It can be seen, however, that if C_2 cannot be neglected in comparison with the meter capacitance then the relationship between the applied potential, V, and the meter reading, E, is not given by $E = V/d$ and the potential must be calculated using equation (3.9). In practice this situation only arises with the high-resolution field probe where the sensor plate must be within $30\ \mu m$ of the surface to achieve the maximum resolution. With conventional field meters, which are held a few centimetres from the charge surface, C_2 is less than 0.1 pF which is several orders of magnitude lower than the input capacitance of the meter.

(b) *Measurement of surface charge*

The field meter may be used to measure the electrostatic charge on an insulating surface. In this case the charge on the surface is constant and the surface potential may vary according to the total capacitance between the surface and earth. This capacitance depends on both C_1 and C_2, i.e. on the position of both the surface and the meter.

The charge q on the surface S is shared between the capacitance C_1, which takes a charge q_1, and the capacitance represented by C_2 and C_0 in series, which will each have a charge q_2:

$$q = q_1 + q_2$$

i.e.

$$q_1/C_1 = q_2/C_2 + q_2/C_0 = V \tag{3.11}$$

and

$$V_0 = q_2/C_0. \tag{3.12}$$

Writing these equations in terms of q and the three capacitances

$$V_0 = \frac{q}{C_0 C_1 (1/C_2 + 1/C_0 + 1/C_1)}. \tag{3.13}$$

As before C_0 is much larger than C_1 and C_2 and so the middle term in the brackets is negligible compared with the other two terms:

$$V_0 = \frac{q}{C_0 C_1 (1/C_2 + 1/C_1)}. \tag{3.14}$$

It can be seen that the field meter reading is proportional to the surface charge, and the constant of proportionality depends on all three capacitances. It therefore depends on the position of the surface and the meter. In many practical situations either C_1 or C_2 dominates equation (3.14).

For example, if the charge is to be measured on a thin film passing over a roller the capacitance between the surface and the roller will dominate and $C_1 \gg C_2$

$$V_0 = qC_2/C_1C_0.$$

Combining this expression with equation (3.10), which applies if $C_0 \gg C_1$

$$V = q/C_1 = Ed.$$

Since

$$C_1 = \varepsilon\varepsilon_r A/d'$$

(where ε_r is the relative dielectric constant of the film and d' its thickness) the charge per unit area on the surface is

$$q/A = \varepsilon_0\varepsilon_r E.$$

If the charged surface is well isolated, and the meter is held close to the surface, then $C_2 \gg C_1$. All the field lines go from the surface to the meter and C_0 takes the full charge q, i.e.

$$V_0 = q/C_0.$$

From equation (3.10)

$$V_0 = \varepsilon_0 A E/C_0$$

therefore

$$q/A = \varepsilon_0 E.$$

The meter reading is constant, independent of the meter spacing, provided it is close enough for the approximation that $C_2 \gg C_1$ to apply. In practice, a dependence on meter spacing is measured and the calculation above gives only an approximation to the surface charge.

3.4.7 Volume charge density using an electrostatic field meter

The volume charge density of a powder cloud or a mist can also be measured using an electrostatic field meter. The electric field at the surface of a volume containing a total charge, $\Sigma\, q$, is given by the Gauss law:

$$\int E\, dA = \sum q/\varepsilon_0.$$

A field meter in the earthed walls of the container can therefore be used to measure a uniform charge density inside. In some industrial situations it is unpractical to measure a volume charge density in this way. For example, it may be unacceptable to make a suitable entry point in the walls of the container, or the field may be screened by the presence of earthed girders, or the charged cloud may be unconfined so the total charge $\Sigma\, q$ and the surface A are not easily defined. In these circumstances a field meter can be placed in the walls of an earthed metal mesh box which is lowered into the container of charge. Ideally the charged dust passes through the mesh which acts as a screen between the meter and the external charge. The mesh provides the surface A in the Gauss equation. Provided the charge is uniformly dispersed in the container the field at its surface will be uniform and the total charge enclosed will be given by:

$$q = E\varepsilon_0 A.$$

If the charge density within the container is non-uniform the field is also non-uniform and this method cannot be conveniently used.

The field meter can also be used to measure the space potential in a charged cloud. Van der Weerd (1971) showed that if a field meter was lowered into a charged cloud and a potential applied until the reading of the meter was zero the potential gave a good measure of the space potential at that position.

3.4.8 The radioactive voltmeter

The radioactive non-contacting voltmeter works on a rather different principle. Figure 3.8 shows the instrument being used to measure the voltage on

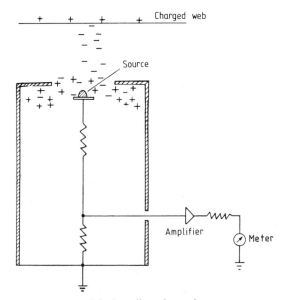

Figure 3.8 A radioactive voltmeter.

a charged web. An alpha source in the meter ionises the air so that the paths between the radioactive source and ground, and the source and the charged web, are weakly conducting. These two paths form a potential divider so the voltage at the source assumes a value which is a fraction of the voltage on the charged web according to the relative resistances of the two paths. The voltage of the source is measured using a potential divider with a much higher resistance than the ionised paths. The radioactive volt-meter must be used at a fixed distance from the charged surface so that the length of the two ionised paths is the same as when the instrument was calibrated. The sensitivity of the instrument may be adjusted by changing the spacing to a new value for which a calibration has been made, or by changing the size of the aperture through which the external electric field enters the ionisation chamber. The radioactive source is polonium 210, which is an α-particle emitter. α-particles are absorbed by only a few cen-timetres of air so the instrument presents no radiation hazard. It is however forbidden for some applications, because of the slight risk of polo-nium contamination. Polonium 210 has a half-life of 138.4 days therefore the source must be replaced regularly. The radioactive voltmeter has a response time of several seconds and therefore is not useful for rapidly varying fields.

3.4.9 Spark gaps for measurement of voltage

In 1889 Paschen showed that the sparking potential of the gap between two spheres depended on the sphere diameter, the sphere spacing and the density of the air. It is therefore possible to estimate potentials by measuring the minimum gap between a test sphere and a voltage source at which a spark occurs. Providing the voltage source has no sharp protru-sions, and, at the position of closest approach can reasonably be repre-sented as either a sphere or a plane, the approximate breakdown potential of the gap in air can be found from standard tables. More accurately, two spheres are set up in a sealed container and the voltage source is connected to one while the other is grounded. The spheres are mounted so that there is no insulation closer than one sphere diameter to the gap. The earthed sphere is moved towards the high-voltage sphere until a spark occurs. It is found that there is a random variation in this spacing which can be reduced by the presence of the UV light which helps to initiate the spark (UV light also reduces the breakdown potential of a gap by about 3.5 %). The breakdown voltage for different sphere diameters and spacings is given in table 3.1. Spark gaps are most often used to measure high voltages about 100 kV.

Table 3.1. Flashover voltages: one sphere grounded†

Sphere–gap spacing	Sphere diameter (cm)											
	2	5	6.25	10	12.5	15	25	50	75	100	150	200
0.05	2.8											
0.10	4.7											
0.15	6.4											
0.20	8.0	8.0										
0.25	9.6	9.6										
0.30	11.2	11.2										
0.40	14.4	14.3	14.2									
0.50	17.4	17.4	17.2	16.8	16.8	16.8						
0.60	20.4	20.4	20.2	19.9	19.9	19.9						
0.70	23.2	23.4	23.2	23.0	23.0	23.0						
0.80	25.8	26.3	26.2	26.0	26.0	26.0						
0.90	28.3	29.2	29.1	28.9	28.9	28.9						
1.0	30.7	32.0	31.9	31.7	31.7	31.7	31.7					
1.2	(35.1)	37.6	37.5	37.4	37.4	37.4	37.4					
1.4	(38.5)	42.9	42.9	42.9	42.9	42.9	42.9					
1.5	(40.0)	45.5	45.5	45.5	45.5	45.5	45.5					
1.6		48.1	48.1	48.1	48.1	48.1	48.1					
1.8		53.0	53.5	53.5	53.5	53.5	53.5					
2.0		57.5	58.5	59.0	59.0	59.0	59.0	59.0	59.0			
2.2		61.5	63.0	64.5	64.5	64.5	64.5	64.5	64.5			
2.4		65.5	67.5	69.5	70.0	70.0	70.0	70.0	70.0			
2.6		(69.0)	72.0	74.5	75.0	75.5	75.5	75.5	75.5			
2.8		(72.5)	76.0	79.5	79.5	80.0	81.0	81.0	81.0			

| | (75.5) | (79.5) | 84.0 | 85.0 | 85.5 | 86.0 | 86.0 | 86.0 | 86.0 | 86.0 | 86.0 |
	(82.5)	(87.5)	95.0	97.0	98.0	99.0	99.0	99.0	99.0	99.0	99.0
3.0	(75.5)										
3.5	(82.5)										
4.0	(88.5)	(95.0)	105	108	110	112	112	112	112		
4.5		(101)	115	119	122	125	125	125	125		
5.0		(107)	123	129	133	137	138	138	138	138	
5.5			(131)	138	143	149	151	151	151	151	
6.0			(138)	146	152	161	164	164	164	164	
6.5			(144)	(154)	161	173	177	177	177	177	
7.0			(150)	(161)	169	184	189	190	190	190	
7.5			(155)	(168)	177	195	202	203	203	203	
8.0				(174)	(185)	206	214	215	215	215	
9.0				(185)	(198)	226	239	240	241	241	
10.0				(195)	(209)	244	263	265	266	266	266
11.0					(219)	261	286	290	292	292	292
12.0					(229)	275	309	315	318	318	318
13.0						(289)	331	339	342	342	342
14.0						(302)	353	363	366	366	366
15.0						(314)	373	387	390	390	390
16.0						(326)	392	410	414	414	414
17.0						(337)	411	432	438	438	438
18.0						(347)	429	452	462	462	462
19.0						(357)	445	473	486	486	486
20.0						(366)	460	492	510	510	510
22.0							489	530	555	560	560
24.0							515	565	595	610	610
26.0							(540)	600	635	655	660
28.0							(565)	635	675	700	705

†Kilovolts peak at 20 °C, 1013 mbar.

3.5 CHARGE MEASUREMENT—THE FARADAY CUP

The Faraday cup (or can) is a double-walled vessel of any suitable shape. The outer wall is grounded and forms an electrical screen which prevents stray external charges from affecting the measurement. The inner wall is connected to an electrometer which measures charge by detecting the voltage built up across a known capacitance. The principle of the instrument is illustrated in figure 3.9. If a charged object, of any form or conductivity, is placed in the container, an equal and opposite charge is induced on the inner wall. This charge leaves behind an equal and opposite charge on the capacitor of the electrometer which can be measured to give the charge inside the container. It does not matter whether charge flows between the object and the inner wall of the Faraday cup so that the object is neutralised, or whether the charges remain separate but paired. The Faraday cup can therefore be used to measure charge on either conductors or insulators.

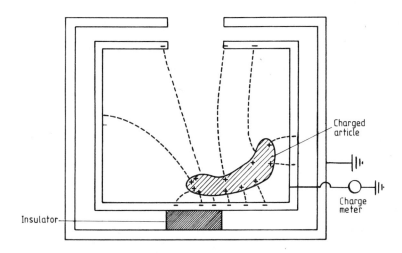

Figure 3.9 A Faraday cup.

If the electrometer is set to zero (i.e. its capacitor discharged) while the charge is still in the cup, subsequent removal of this charge frees the induced charge on the container wall which flows back to the electrometer. The capacitor will therefore recharge, but the meter will show the opposite polarity. If there has been some neutralisation between the article and the induced charge on the wall, the charge measured on removal of the article will be less than the original value.

The insulation between the inner and outer containers of the Faraday cup must be extremely high, i.e. there should be no decay of charge when a charged article is left in the cup.

The Faraday cup is obviously not able to be used when the charge is stored on a moving belt or a large article but it is useful for estimating the charge on liquid or powder samples. Care must be taken that the means by which the liquid or powder is introduced into the chamber does not produce additional charge. The sample must enter the cup directly and not through a tube or funnel which is not part of the inner container. When powder is collected from a gas stream the inner can is provided with holes to allow the air to escape and is lined with a filter to collect the powder. It is unimportant whether the filter is insulating or conducting. Figure 3.10 shows a modified Faraday cup, used to measure the charge on dust sampled isokinetically from a gas stream. In this case a sampling pipe is necessary but it is connected electrically to the inner vessel so if charge separation occurs at its walls both charges are measured and there is no net effect. The sampling pipe is covered with an earthed shield to prevent measurement of frictional charge from collision of dust particles with the outside of the sampling tube. With uniform sampling, the charge can be found by measuring the current for a fixed time (1 C = 1 A flowing for 1 s). A current meter has a low impedance which eliminates the need for an extremely high-insulation resistance

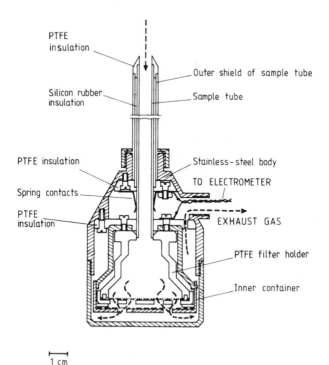

PTFE insulation

Silicon rubber insulation

Outer shield of sample tube

Sample tube

PTFE insulation

Stainless-steel body

TO ELECTROMETER

Spring contacts

PTFE insulation

EXHAUST GAS

PTFE filter holder

Inner container

1 cm

Figure 3.10 A Faraday cup for dust sampling.

between the inner and outer cans. In the design illustrated, the current to the sampling pipe and to the cup itself can be measured separately. More than 50 % of the total current may be measured at the sampling tube walls although very little dust usually remains in the tube. Charge-to-mass ratios between 10^{-10} and 10^{-1} C kg^{-1} may be measured by connecting this sampling cup to a suitable electrometer or current meter. By convention, the charge on a powdered sample is expressed in C kg^{-1} whereas on a liquid it is expressed in C m^{-3}. Since the charge on a powder particle depends on its surface area rather than its volume, a higher charge-to-mass ratio is achieved the smaller the particle size.

3.6 MEASUREMENT OF THE CHARGE AND MOBILITY OF INDIVIDUAL PARTICLES

3.6.1 The Millikan method of charge measurement

The charge on an individual particle can be measured by observing the way in which it moves under the influence of gravity and an electric field. The technique was developed by Millikan, who used an electric field opposing gravity for the first determination of the charge on an electron. More recently, the method has been used to measure the charge on small particles by McDonald *et al* (1980) and by Cross and Peterson (1984).

A charged particle is introduced into the space between two horizontal plane electrodes and its motion observed using a telescope or long focal length microscope. In Millikan's original experiments the time taken by an oil droplet to fall between two grid lines in the field of view of the telescope was measured using a stop watch. With modern techniques the particle can be displayed on a television screen and its movement timed automatically (Cross and Peterson 1984). Two measurements are taken. First, a voltage V_s is applied between the two electrodes to oppose the force of gravity and hold the particle stationary. The voltage is then switched off and the time taken for the particle to fall a fixed distance under gravity is noted to give the velocity, u_g.

When the particle is stationary the force due to gravity just balances the electrostatic force, i.e.

$$qE = mg$$

where q is the particle charge and g is the acceleration due to gravity. The mass m may be written:

$$m = \tfrac{4}{3}\pi a^3 D$$

and the field $E = V_s/d$ where D is the particle material density and d is the electrode spacing, i.e.

$$qV_s/d = \tfrac{4}{3}\pi a^3 Dg. \tag{3.15}$$

When the particle is falling under gravity and has reached its terminal velocity it experiences no acceleration. The force due to gravity is therefore balanced by the drag force. For particles greater than about 1 μm Stokes's law may be assumed:

$$mg = 6\pi\eta a u_g = \tfrac{4}{3}\pi a^3 Dg. \tag{3.16}$$

Provided the viscosity of air, η, and the particle density, D, are known the only unknowns in equations (3.15) and (3.16) are the particle radius and charge. The equations may therefore be solved for these unknowns.

For small particles, less than 1 μm in diameter, the Cunningham correction must be applied to the drag force and equation (3.16) becomes

$$mg = 6\pi\eta_{av}/C \tag{3.17}$$

where

$$C = 1 + A\lambda/a. \tag{3.18}$$

Here, λ is the molecular mean free path and $A = 1.25 + 0.4\exp(-1.1a/\lambda)$.

Theoretically the upper limit of the particle size for which this method may be used is fixed by the breakdown field of air, which limits the decelerating voltage applied to the particle as it falls under gravity. In practice particles greater than about 6 μm in diameter (depending on density) fall too fast to be able to use a manual voltage adjustment to hold them in the field of view.

The electric field can be applied perpendicular to gravity. With this geometry the vertical component of the velocity, u_v, gives the radius from the equation:

$$4\pi a^3 Dg/3 = 6\pi\eta a u_v/C$$

and the horizontal velocity u_h gives the charge from the equation:

$$6\pi\eta a u_h/C = qE.$$

The motion of the particle is observed by a telescope and cinecamera. A chopping system may be introduced so the light illuminating the droplets is synchronised with the film speed and a clear image of the droplet position is produced. Bassett (1975) used this method to look at water droplets up to 20 μm in diameter.

In both these methods it is important to be able to introduce a representative sample of the charged particles into the measurement cell without changing their charge. Cross and Peterson (1984) observed that introducing particles through a small hole in the upper electrode was not satisfactory as the most highly charged particles were deflected from the hole by the electrostatic lens effect illustrated in figure 3.11. Blowing or sucking particles into the cell tended to set up air currents, which gave the particles a sideways motion so they drifted out of the field of view of the microscope. With the crossed-field design of Bassett the introduction of the particles is not a

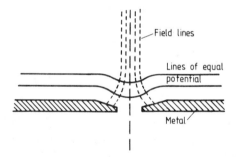

Figure 3.11 The electrostatic lens effect.

problem but the analysis is more complicated and normally requires development of a film and so cannot be carried out at the time of the measurement.

3.6.2 Particle mobility

It is not necessary to know the charge on a particle in order to assess its motion in an electric field. It is sufficient to know only its mobility. The mobility of a particle is a direct measure of its ability to move in an electric field and is defined by the equation:

$$b = u/E$$

where u is the particle velocity and E is the field in which it moves. The individual particle techniques described above may be used to measure mobility by measuring only the velocity in the direction of the electric field. Deflection methods have also been used to measure the mobility of particles in a gas stream.

A number of devices were reviewed by Whitby (1979). For example, Penney and Lynch (1957) passed an aerosol between parallel plates designed to minimise turbulence as shown in figure 3.12. A variable voltage was applied between the plates and a particle in the electric field experienced an electrostatic force proportional to the applied voltage. Ideally the particle, which is initially travelling in an air flow parallel to the plates, acquires a constant component of velocity perpendicular to the plates and the efficiency of collection of the plates is proportional to the applied voltage. In practice there is always some turbulence or other disturbing effect which reduces the efficiency when it rises above about 80 %.

Penney and Lynch found that a graph of collection efficiency against voltage was linear over much of its range. Extension of the linear portion to a collection efficiency of 100 % gave the voltage, V, required to move the particle across the distance, d, between the plates in the time, t, for which the

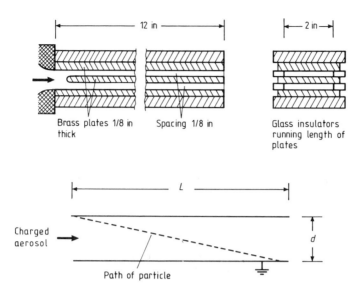

Figure 3.12 Parallel plates for measurement of particle mobility (from Penney and Lynch 1957).

particle remained between the plates:

$$t = L/u_a$$

where u_a is the air velocity and L is the length of the plates. The mobility of the particle is then given by:

$$b = d/Et = d^2/tV$$

so that

$$b = d^2 u_a/LV.$$

This measurement gives the mobility of the particle under the combined effect of the electrostatic force and the drag of the air. To compute the charge from the mobility, an independent measurement of particle radius must be made.

Coury and Clift (1984) suggested a modification of the Penney and Lynch method, suitable for larger particles with lower mobility, where long deflection plates would be required for total collection. Their design is illustrated in figure 3.13. Dust-laden air is introduced through a slit in the centre of a duct through which filtered air is flowing. The gases pass between parallel plates across which a voltage is applied and the distance migrated by the particle, across the air flow, is proportional to its mobility. The particles are collected by a battery of collector plates between which high-voltage wires are suspended. These act as small electrostatic precipitators and ensure that

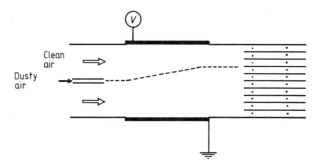

Figure 3.13 Measurement of particle charge (from Coury and Clift 1984).

all particles passing between the two plates are collected. The particles are classified according to the plate on which they are collected. This method allows a single deflecting voltage to be used instead of the range of different potentials used by Penney and Lynch.

With deflection techniques it is important to ensure that particles are not re-entrained from the deflector plates. A check can be made by making sure that the same result is obtained for a given potential difference, regardless of the absolute voltage of the system. Alternatively the charge on particles which fall out under gravity can be measured. The charge on particles which fall out should be low and should not be changed by reversing the polarity of the plates.

3.6.3 Particle charge or mobility by laser Doppler anemometry

The laser Doppler velocimeter measures the velocity of particles without disturbing the electric field or the particle motion. It can be used to measure the velocity of a particle in an electric field, to obtain the mobility. Laser Doppler systems were originally designed to measure fluid flows and to detect the distribution of the velocities in a cloud of particles. The instrument normally integrates the signal from a large number of particles, building up a velocity distribution over a timescale which is much longer than the timescale of fluctuations in the flow. However, it is also possible to measure the velocity of individual particles (Sato 1980, Ross 1981). The basic system is illustrated in figure 3.14. Light from a laser is split into two parallel beams which are focused by a lens to the measurement point. Light scattered from a moving dust particle suffers a Doppler frequency shift. It is gathered at the forward scattering position by a microscope system where it combines with the reference beam forming a beat pattern which is detected by the photomultiplier and displayed on an oscilloscope.

The velocity of the particle is given by

$$u = (\lambda/2T) \sin(\theta/2) \tag{3.19}$$

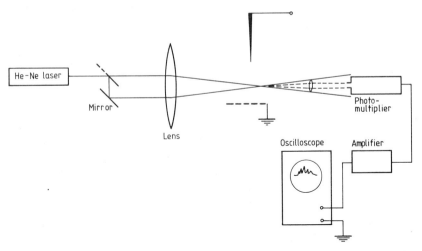

Figure 3.14 The experimental arrangement for measuring the particle velocity in a corona discharge by laser Doppler anemometry (from Sato 1980).

where λ is the wavelength of the laser beam, T is the period of the beat signal and θ is the angle between the two beams. Mobility is then found from the equation

$$b = u/E.$$

In order to find the charge on the particles, either the radius must be known, or two velocity measurements must be made with different values of the electric field as described above. It is possible to estimate the size of the particles from the intensity of the signal detected by the photomultiplier of the velocimeter. Theoretically, if light is scattered according to the Mie scattering theory, the amplitude of the signal is proportional to the cross sectional area of the particle. Real particles seldom obey this theory exactly and the constant of proportionality depends on the refractive index of the particles, but an estimate of particle diameter can be made by comparison with standard particles, or calibrated apertures, at the focus of the lens.

3.7 FIELD AND POTENTIAL PROBES

Any probe inserted into an electric field distorts the field. An isolated probe will become polarised and a probe which is connected to a source of current will be charged and take up a potential V_p. In general this potential is not the same as V_s, the space potential in the absence of the probe, and V_s must be found by calculating the field distortion produced by the probe. A potential probe is normally set up so that there are free ions available and can change its charge and potential freely to reach equilibrium.

3.7.1 The corona probe

The simplest type of probe is a very fine wire. A corona discharge occurs from the tip until the potential difference between the wire and the space is equal to the corona onset voltage, V_0. If the wire is made extremely fine the onset voltage is very low and the final potential of the probe is close to the space potential. The probe may be calibrated to find its onset potential and a correction applied to obtain the space potential more precisely. The voltage on the probe is either measured directly with an electrostatic voltmeter, or the space potential is found by a null technique, in which the voltage on the probe is increased until the corona discharge ceases. This voltage is then $V_s - V_0$. With this type of probe no adjustment is made for field distortion which must therefore be minimised. A conducting wire will always be an equipotential, therefore the probe is introduced along an equipotential line. A full analysis of the corona probe has been carried out by Wilson (1970). A corona probe may be used to measure voltages which lie between the corona inception and the voltage of conveniently available power supplies, typically 100 kV.

3.7.2 The potential probe in an ionised field

If the field is ionised a potential probe can be used which does not itself provide a source of ions. This type of probe is used for measuring the field and space potential in a corona discharge. The principle of the potential probe can be illustrated by considering the behaviour of a sphere inserted into an ionised field.

If an isolated conducting sphere is placed in an ionised electric field, the field is distorted and the sphere will collect ions until it reaches the limiting Pauthenier charge described in §2.2. If the spherical probe is connected to a power supply and its voltage varied, the current which flows to it is a function of the probe voltage, V_p, the space potential, V_s, the electric field which was present in the absence of the probe E_0, and the density and mobility of the positive and negative ions. When the sphere is at the space potential the field distortion is symmetrical as shown in figure 3.15(a). Positive ions flow down the field lines in the direction of the arrows and negative ions or electrons flow along the lines in the reverse direction. Positive and negative ions are therefore collected over separate hemispheres of the probe. In a bi-ionised gas, with positive and negative ions of the same mobility, the sphere will remain neutral and no current will flow. If more ions of one polarity are present, or one polarity of charge has a higher mobility (i.e. travels faster along the field lines), then one half of the hemisphere will collect more ions, and a current will flow to the probe.

Figure 3.15(b) shows the sphere with a positive applied potential. The area collecting positive ions has decreased and the area collecting negative ions has increased. A current will then flow even when the two polarities of charge

(a)

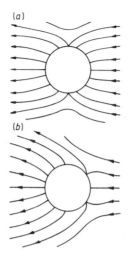

(b)

Figure 3.15 Field lines for a spherical probe in a uniform field: (a), $V_p = V_s$; (b), V_p positive.

have equal densities and mobilities. The current flowing to the probe can be found by calculating the field distortion for any probe voltage.

In general, for any shape of probe, the current of ions of one polarity which flows to a small section of a probe with an area ΔS at any time is

$$\Delta I = JE_n \Delta S/E_0 \tag{3.20}$$

where J is the current density of the ions of the appropriate polarity in the absence of the probe, E_n is the component of the distorted field which is perpendicular to the element of surface ΔS. J/E_0 may be regarded as the conductivity of the medium in the absence of the probe.

The total current, I, which will flow to a probe at any potential is found by calculating the field normal to the probe at all positions on the probe and integrating over the surface of the probe. The field is found by solving Laplace's equation as described in Chapter 7, i.e.

$$\nabla^2 V = 0 \quad \text{and } E = -\nabla V.$$

The solution is subject to the following boundary conditions:

(i) the potential at infinity is undistorted by the probe;
(ii) the potential at the surface of the probe is the applied probe potential.

A number of assumptions are made in this type of calculation:

(i) In using Laplace's equation, it is assumed that the density of ions is great enough to allow a current to flow to the probe, but not so great that Poisson's equation must be used rather than Laplace's equation. The validity of this assumption may be tested by calculating the order of magnitude of the electric field due to the presence of the ions, by applying Gauss's law to a sphere of the volume of the system. This must be much less than the externally applied field if Laplace's equation is to be valid.

(ii) It is assumed that the undistorted electric field in the region over which the probe collects ions is uniform.

(iii) It is often necessary to simplify the geometry of the system in order to find an analytical solution to Laplace's equation.

(a) *Measurement of the space potential in a mono-ionised electric field*
With a spherical probe the simplifying assumption is made that the probe support and the electrical connections by which the current is measured do not affect the field round the probe. The sphere is supposed to be far from any other electrode. The Laplace equation can then be solved as shown in Chapter 7.

When the sphere is at the space potential and the field lines are symmetrical, the field as a function of the angle θ round the sphere is given by

$$E_n = 3E_0 \cos \theta.$$

The field therefore ranges from a maximum value of $3E_0$ at $\theta = 0$ to zero at $\theta = \pi/2$. If ions of only a single polarity are present they are collected over the hemisphere $\theta = \pm \pi/2$ and the current flowing is:

$$I = \frac{J}{E_0} \int^{\text{hemisphere}} (3E_0 \cos \theta) \, dS \tag{3.21}$$

$$= \frac{2\pi a^2 J}{E_0} \int_0^{\pi/2} (3E_0 \cos \theta) \sin \theta \, d\theta$$

$$= 3\pi a^2 J. \tag{3.22}$$

Thus if the current density of ions in the absence of the probe (J) is known, the space potential can be found by finding the potential which must be applied to the probe in order to have a symmetrical field distribution, i.e. the potential for which the current flow is $3\pi a^2 J$.

(b) *The current–voltage characteristic of a spherical probe in a uniform field*
The full current–voltage characteristic for a sphere of potential V_p in a uniform mono-ionised field has been calculated by Collins *et al* (1979).

The distorted field at the probe surface is

$$E_n = (V_p - V_s)/a - 3E_0 \cos \theta.$$

The first term on the right-hand side is the field due to the potential difference between the probe and space, and the other term is the distortion of the uniform field by the sphere.

The field will be inwardly directed and the probe will collect positive ions when E_n is positive, and will be outwardly directed and collect negative ions when it is negative. The values of $\cos \theta$ where E_n is positive depend on the probe potential. A critical angle θ_c may be defined where $E_n = \theta$. This defines the boundaries of the areas collecting positive and negative ions:

$$\cos \theta_c = (V_p - V_s)/3E_0 a.$$

The probe characteristic can be considered in two regions depending on whether V_p is close to the space potential or far from it.

(i) $|V_p - V_s|$ *is large.*
For sufficiently large values of the difference between V_p and the space potential V_s, $\cos \theta = 1$ or -1 and the probe collects one polarity of ion over all of its surface. Increasing the probe potential difference still further cannot increase θ and the integration of the electric field is carried out for one polarity of ion over the entire surface of the sphere

$$I = (J/E_0) \int^{\text{sphere}} E_n \, dS$$

i.e.

$$I = (J/E_0) \int_{-\pi/2}^{\pi/2} [\,(V_p - V_s)/a - 3E_0 \cos \theta]2\pi a^2 \sin \theta \, d\theta$$

$$I = \frac{4\pi J a}{E_0}(V_s - V_p) \tag{3.23}$$

i.e. when the probe potential is far from the space potential the current of ions attracted to the probe is proportional to the probe potential. With only one polarity of ion present the current–voltage characteristic will have only one linear portion as shown in figure 3.16. If this linear portion is

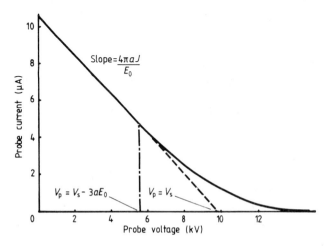

Figure 3.16 The current–voltage characteristic for a spherical probe in a mono-ionised uniform field.

extrapolated to intercept the voltage axis, the point of intersection is $V_p = V_s$. The slope of the line is $4\pi a J / E_0$. If there is only one polarity of ion present, J is known from the current in the external circuit, therefore E_0 and the space potential can be found.

With both polarities of ions present the characteristic has two linear portions. The external current gives only the sum of the positive- and negative-ion currents. The ratio of the slopes of the linear portions of the current–voltage characteristic, obtained when $V_p \gg V_s$ and $V_p \ll V_s$, gives the ratios J_+/E_0 and J_-/E_0.

(ii) When $V_s - 3aE_0 < V_p < V_s + 3aE_0$.

In this region the probe collects both polarities of ion and the integration must be carried out for each polarity over the areas bounded by $\pm \theta_c$. The current to the probe is the difference between the arithmetic value of the two currents. When this integration is carried out the result is a curve which smoothly joins the two linear portions of the probe characteristic. With only one polarity of ion present the probe characteristic curves down to zero as the potential increases to repel more and more ions as shown in figure 3.16.

Only the linear portion of the characteristic is required to find the electrostatic parameters of the system. However, in these regions the distortion of the electric field is greatest and the system, as a whole, is far removed from the conditions in the absence of the probe. The unknown parameters may also be found by performing a least-squares fit of the data over the whole characteristic.

(c) *The current–voltage characteristic of a cylindrical probe in front of a plane*
The spherical probe has two disadvantages:

(i) It is frequently required to use the probe near the plane in a corona discharge and Laplace's equation for a sphere in front of a plane cannot be solved simply.

(ii) In any real system a spherical probe must have a connection to mount it in the correct position and to serve as an electrical connection for current measurement. The geometry cannot therefore be totally spherical.

To overcome these problems a cylindrical probe can be designed, with an electrically guarded section. This is mounted along an equipotential line with the electrical connection and mounting system forming an extension of the cylinder. The Laplace equation for the case of a cylindrical probe in front of a plate in a uniform field can be solved using bipolar coordinates. The current is found by substituting this field in equation (3.20) and integrating as before (Cross and Barton 1984).

With the cylindrical geometry the current–voltage characteristic of the probe again consists of two linear regions, where ions of only one polarity are collected, smoothly joined by a curve whose form can be calculated. The linear portions have the equations

$$I_- = \frac{2\pi J_-(V_p - E_0 b)}{E_0 X} \qquad \text{where } V_p + E_0 b > 4E_0 bX \exp(-X) \qquad (3.24)$$

$$I_+ = \frac{2\pi J_+(V_p + E_0 b)}{E_0 X} \qquad \text{where } V_p + E_0 b < -4E_0 bX \exp(-X) \qquad (3.25)$$

where b and X are geometric parameters of the bipolar coordinate system such that b cosech X is the probe radius and b coth X is the probe-to-plate spacing. If the probe radius is much smaller than the probe-to-plane spacing, coth X is $\simeq 1$ and b is very close to the probe-to-plane spacing.

The ratio of the slopes of the two linear portions of the current–voltage characteristic gives the ratio of positive to negative ions. Where the sum of the positive and negative current densities is also known (by measurement of the current in the external circuit) the field and the number density of each polarity can be found.

When the probe potential is close to the space potential, integration must be carried out separately over the areas bounded by θ_c. The equation for this part of the characteristic may be found in the paper by Cross and Barton (1984).

If only one polarity of ions is present and the probe potential is equal to the space potential, the current to the probe is given by:

$$I = 8Jb \exp(-X).$$

The space potential in a mono-ionised field may therefore be measured by finding the probe potential at which the current is defined by this equation.

3.7.3 The bipolar current probe

The number of ions of each polarity present in an electric field, may also be measured using a bipolar current probe (Masuda and Nonogaki 1981). The probe, which may be cylindrical or spherical, is divided into three sections as shown in figure 3.17. The three electrodes are all connected to the same probe potential, V_p, but the current to each section is measured separately. When the probe is at the space potential, V_s, the field lines will be distributed symmetrically. One side of the probe will collect positive ions and the other negative ions. Masuda shows that at the true balance potential, when $V_p = V_s$, the currents I_- and I_+, measured by the sides of the probe collecting negative and positive ions respectively, will be

$$I_- = 3\pi a^2 J_- \cos^2(d/2a) \qquad (3.26)$$

$$I_+ = 3\pi a^2 J_+ \cos^2(d/2a) \qquad (3.27)$$

where a is the radius of the probe, d the width of the central electrode and J_+ and J_- the current densities of positive and negative ions respectively.

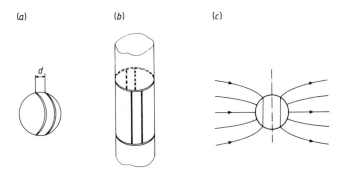

Figure 3.17 Bipolar current probe (after Masuda and Nonogaki 1981): (a), sphere radius = 2.3 mm, d = 1.2 mm; (b), cylinder radius = 3.0 mm, d = 1.0 mm; (c), field configuration at balance point.

In general, the mobility and current density of the two polarities are not equal and the current to the central section is not zero when $V_p = V_s$. The true balance potential (when $V_p = V_s$) may be calculated from the quasi-balance potential (defined as the probe potential when the current to the central section of the probe is zero) by dividing by a factor k which is given in figure 3.18. When the probe potential is set to the value found from this figure the currents to the two outer sections give the density of ions of each polarity according to equations (3.26) and (3.27).

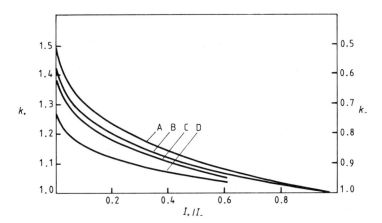

Figure 3.18 Correction factors k_+ and k_- plotted against I_+/I_- (after Masuda and Nonogaki 1981): A, $d/2a = 0.33$ spherical; B, $d/2a = 0.25$ spherical; C, $d/2a = 0.33$ cylindrical; D, $d/2a = 0.20$ cylindrical.

3.7.4 The ballistic probe

A spherical probe which has no electrical connections was proposed by Cooperman in 1956 and its performance has been analysed in detail by Corbett and Bassett (1971) and Corbett (1972). A small metal sphere is fired at high speed through a mono-ionised field, E, and collected in a charge measuring can. The charge on the sphere of radius a, after its passage through the field, is given by Pauthenier's theory (discussed in §2.2). For a mono-ionised field, where the transit time of the sphere is sufficiently long for the full charge to be attained the charge is:

$$q = 12\pi\varepsilon_0 a^2 E_0. \tag{3.28}$$

If the field is not uniform, it is assumed that the sphere acquires a charge related to the maximum field through which it passes. If the probe does not remain in the field long enough to reach equilibrium the charge on the particle is given by

$$q = 12\pi\varepsilon_0 a^2 E_0 t/(t + \tau) \tag{3.29}$$

where the time constant is

$$\tau = 4\varepsilon_0 E_0/J \tag{3.30}$$

t is the dwell time for which the probe remains in the ionised field and J the current density of the charging ions (assumed to be of single polarity). These equations can be combined to give

$$\frac{1}{q} = \frac{1}{(12\pi\varepsilon_0 a^2)E_0} + \frac{1}{(3a^2 J)t} \tag{3.31}$$

i.e. there should be a straight-line relationship between the reciprocal of the dwell time and the reciprocal of the charge. The intercept of this line will give J and the slope of the line will give the electric field, E_0.

This type of probe is highly sensitive to the presence of minority carriers which greatly reduce the charge on the probe.

3.7.5 The displacement electrostatic probe

The displacement probe was developed for measuring space potentials by Schwaiger (1925). A potential was applied to a fibre of silk or glass and varied until no deflection of the probe could be seen through a telescope. The probe was then at the space potential. This type of probe does not require the presence of ions to operate. Its sensitivity can be varied by changing the length of the fibre. The deflection, in mm kV^{-1}, is proportional to the fourth power of the probe length. The method has been studied more recently by Gosho (1967a,b) and his work has been discussed by Takuma (1969). It was shown that the probe should be as fine as possible and positioned along an equipotential to minimise field distortions. Gosho found that great care was needed to avoid mechanical vibration and the probe was sensitive to ripple in the applied field. The method may be used to measure potentials between a few tens of volts to the limit of conveniently available bias power supplies.

3.8 USE OF THE KERR AND POCKELS EFFECT FOR MEASUREMENT OF ELECTRIC FIELDS

In some materials the refractive index is a function of an applied electric field. The field induces a change in refractive index in the direction in which it is applied and this leads to a difference in speed for the components of light polarised parallel and perpendicular to the field. In materials where the change in refractive index is proportional to the square of the electric field the phenomenon is known as the Kerr effect. If it is linearly proportional to the field the effect is named after Pockels. For the Kerr effect

$$n_\parallel - n_\perp = \lambda B E^2 \tag{3.32}$$

and for the Pockels effect

$$n_\parallel - n_\perp = \lambda A E \tag{3.33}$$

where $n_\parallel$ and $n_\perp$ are parallel and perpendicular refractive indices, λ is the wavelength of the transmitted light, E is the electric field and A and B are the Pockels and Kerr coefficients of the material respectively.

B ranges from 10^{-21} m V^{-2} for helium gas to 10^{-7} for bentonite in water. For nitrobenzene, which is commonly used in Kerr cells because of its high dielectric strength, B is 10^{-12} m V^{-2}.

Kerr and Pockels cells may be used to measure electric field or voltage and are particularly useful for rapidly changing or pulsed signals.

Ettinger and Venezia (1963) described a pulsed-voltage measuring system using a Kerr cell and a much improved system was later described by Wunsch and Erteza (1964). They showed that the frequency response of the system was flat to 100 MHz.

Figure 3.19 shows a Kerr cell, installed between crossed polarisers. With this arrangement no light is transmitted through the cell until there

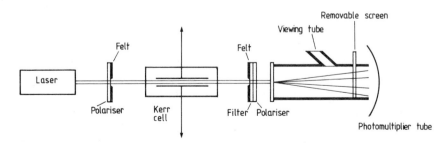

Figure 3.19 Kerr cell for measurement of high voltages.

is an electric field between the electrodes. This then changes the state of polarisation of the light beam and allows light to be transmitted. The light beam may be spread over the entire area of the cell and the light pattern produced, observed as a function of position, to obtain the spatially resolved electric field, or the beam may be collimated and the light transmitted at a fixed position observed as a function of time.

The intensity of the light passing through the cell at a position where the electric field is E is related to the strength of that field by the equation

$$I/I_m = \sin^2(\pi/2)(E/E_m)^2 \tag{3.34}$$

where I_m is the maximum intensity transmitted by the system and E_m is the field strength required to produce the first transmission maximum. The form of this equation is shown graphically in figure 3.20. For measurement of a pulsed voltage applied to the plates, the light intensity transmitted through the cell is measured as a function of time during the applied voltage pulse using a photomultiplier and an oscilloscope. V is determined from E/E_m from equation (3.30) and the relationship

$$V = (E/E_m)(E_m d). \tag{3.35}$$

The product of E_m, the field to produce maximum transmission, and d, the interelectrode distance, is the cell constant, which is found by calibration. Techniques for calibration are described by Cassidy *et al* (1968, 1970).

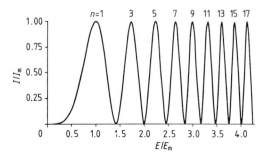

Figure 3.20 Relative transmitted light intensity, I/I_m, as a function of relative field strength E/E_m (from Cassidy *et al* 1968).

The system described above is normally operated with a voltage applied to the electrodes to bias the cell to its first transmission minimum. This serves several purposes.

(i) It reduces the danger of internal arcing by conditioning the cell for application of a high voltage.

(ii) It increases E/E_m so that more oscillations in intensity are produced for a given voltage and the sensitivity is increased.

(iii) It facilitates calibration of the system.

Field non-uniformities at the edge of the cell can give a component of the electric field which is parallel to the direction of polarisation of the light. These regions give rise to fringes called isoclinic fringes which may be useful when mapping the electric field throughout the interelectrode area but which complicate the measurement of applied voltage. They are eliminated by quarter-wave plates, placed before and after the cell.

Thompson *et al* (1976) have developed an interferometric technique which improves sensitivity. Linearly polarised light, with components parallel and perpendicular to the electric field, is passed through the Kerr cell where a relative phaseshift occurs. The emergent beam is divided by a beam splitter. Vertically polarised light is passed by a polariser on one path and horizontally polarised light is passed on the other path. Quarter-wave plates then change the polarisation of one beam and the two beams are brought together again to form an interference pattern. This is photographed, and compared with the fringes obtained with zero field, to obtain the spatially resolved measurements of the field within the cell. Temporally resolved measurements are obtained by observing the movement of the fringes as a function of time. Kerr cells have been used to measure voltages between a few kV and several hundred kV.

Figure 3.21 shows an example of a Pockels device used for measuring electric field (Hidaka and Kouno 1982). A laser beam is linearly polarised and passed through a Pockels cells at the position where the field is to be measured. The two components of light (polarised parallel and perpendicular to the field) travel at different speeds and there is a phaseshift between them. The light intensity, I, detected by the photodetector is in this case given by:

$$I = a \sin(bE) + c \qquad (3.36)$$

where

$$b = 2\pi n_0^3 A l / \lambda$$

a and c are constants, n_0 is the refractive index without the field, l is the crystal length along the light beam and A is the Pockels coefficient.

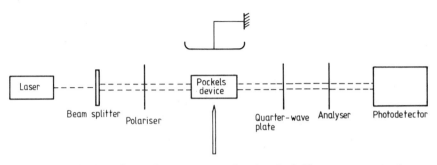

Figure 3.21 The experimental arrangement for electric field measurement using a Pockels device.

Figure 3.22 shows the response of a ZnS Pockels crystal to an impulse voltage applied to a plane-parallel gap. The oscillatory response is believed to be attributable to natural vibration of the crystal caused by the piezoelectric effect in the Pockels crystal. The crystal is able to respond to electric field changes at frequencies up to 10^9 Hz (Hertz 1985).

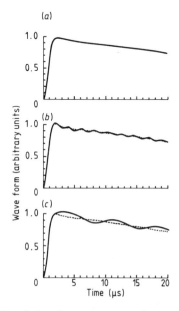

Figure 3.22 Use of Pockels cell to measure a voltage pulse (after Hidaka and Kouno 1982); (*a*), applied field; (*b*), output from ZnS crystal; (*c*), output from KH_2PO_4 crystal.

An ideal Pockels crystal should have the following properties:

(i) a large Pockels effect,
(ii) a dielectric constant which is close to that of the medium in which the field is being measured (so that field distortion is minimised),
(iii) a high volume and surface resistivity,
(iv) a small piezoelectric effect (because the piezoelectric effect produces an oscillatory signal on the output of the photodetector),
(v) no natural birefringence (i.e. the components of light travel at the same velocity in the absence of the electric field).

ZnS and KH_2PO_4 crystals were used by Hidaka and Kouno (1982) with ZnS giving the lower piezoelectric oscillations.

3.9 CAPACITANCE METERS

The electrical capacitance of an object defines the potential to which it will rise when it is given a charge, q. It is thus defined by the equation

$$C = q/V. \tag{3.37}$$

Capacitance can be measured accurately using an AC circuit balancing technique, such as the Schering bridge shown in figure 3.23. C_1 and R_1 are the unknown capacitance and its associated resistance. The variable capacitance and resistance R_2 and C_2 are changed until the current flowing through the meter A is zero. At this balance point the unknown capacitance and resistance are given by the equations

$$C_1 = C(R_2/R) \tag{3.38}$$

$$R_1 = R(C_2/C) \tag{3.39}$$

where C and R are the standard fixed capacitance and resistance of the bridge.

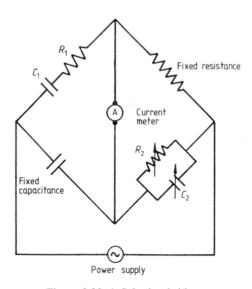

Figure 3.23 A Schering bridge.

Capacitance is a function of frequency, and for high-frequency measurements a more sophisticated bridge is required. However, in electrostatics, the capacitance is usually required to estimate the amount of charge or electrostatic energy that can be stored, and a low-frequency measurement is suitable. Bridge techniques are discussed by Scaife (1971).

Most bridges require that neither terminal is earthed, whereas in electrostatics problems it is frequently required to measure the capacitance to earth. In this case the measurement can be made using the principle that the frequency of an oscillating circuit is proportional to the capacitance in the tuning circuit. The capacitance meter consists of two oscillating circuits, tuned to the same frequency. The unknown capacitance is added to one circuit and the frequency difference between the two oscillations is detected.

Capacitance may also be measured by finding the time taken for a voltage on a charged capacitance to fall when it is connected to earth through a known resistance. The voltage will fall exponentially with a time constant of RC, i.e.

$$V = V_0 \exp(-t/RC) \qquad (3.40)$$

$$\ln V = \ln V_0 - t/RC \qquad (3.41)$$

therefore a graph of $\ln V$ against time has a slope of $-1/RC$.

3.10 MEASUREMENT OF RESISTANCE AND RESISTIVITY

3.10.1 The resistance of a path to earth

The resistance, R, of a path is defined as the ratio of the voltage applied across it to the current which flows:

$$V = IR. \qquad (3.42)$$

Resistance is measured by detecting the current flow when a known voltage is applied. For conductors the resistance is constant for any voltage (i.e. Ohm's law is obeyed), but for insulators or powdered samples, the resistance often depends on the applied voltage and it is necessary to measure the resistance at approximately the voltage applicable to the problem. For example, if it is required to estimate whether an electrostatic charge can build up to a hazardous level of several kilovolts, the measurement is best made with a megohm meter or other equipment which has a voltage source of the order of 1 kV. The recommended resistance of a path to earth is frequently in the range of 10^5 to 10^9 Ω because this is usually sufficiently conducting to prevent electrostatic charge accumulation, but protection is provided against shock from mains electricity. A high voltage is usually required to measure these resistances so that sufficient current flows to be easily detected.

The resistance between personnel and earth may be measured without applying a high voltage by means of the circuit shown in figure 3.24. The person stands on a conductive plate and grasps a handle. The bias of the transistor changes according to the resistance between the handle and the plate. The output of the transistor may be amplified and displayed or it can operate a relay which switches off a green light and switches on a red light

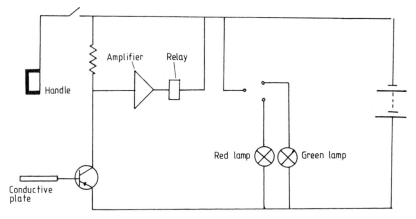

Figure 3.24 An arrangement for checking earthing of personnel.

to indicate a hazardous high-resistance path to earth. This type of instrument provides an easy way of checking the conductivity of antistatic footwear, particularly in environments where the soles may become contaminated with paint or some other insulating material.

3.10.2 Volume resistivity

The resistance of an object depends on its dimensions. Resistivity is defined as the resistance of unit length of a sample of unit area. It is thus a property of the material itself, regardless of the dimensions of the sample. The resistivity, ρ, of a block of material, is related to the resistance, R, measured when a voltage is applied across it, by the equation

$$\rho = RA/d \qquad (3.43)$$

where A is the sample area and d its length. The ratio of resistivity to resistance is known as the cell constant. By definition resistivity is a measurement of a block of solid or liquid and cannot be applied to a surface. The units are ohm metres.

Liquids are often measured in a cell consisting of concentric cylinders. The cell constant, K, depends on the ratio of the radii of the two cylinders and is given by

$$K = 2\pi \log r_1/r_0 \qquad (3.44)$$

where r_0 and r_1 are the radii of the inner and outer cylinders.

Solids and powders are usually measured in a parallel-plate cell. The surface of a solid is often more conducting than the bulk. The passage of current between the electrodes via the surface is prevented by guard rings at the same potential as the electrodes, as shown in figure 3.25. No current flows

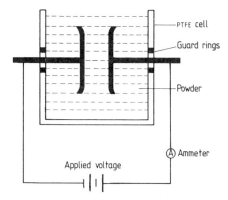

Figure 3.25 A parallel-plate cell for the measurement of powder resistivity.

between the central electrode and the guard because there is no potential difference. The guard rings also prevent field intensification at the edges of the electrodes which would increase current flow in these regions.

Insulating materials may have resistivities up to 10^{18} Ω m. It is therefore necessary to apply a high voltage to achieve even a small current flow. The resistance measured will depend on the effectiveness of the contact between the sample and the electrodes. With solid materials the electrodes can be painted onto the surface with conducting paint. The resistivity measured between metal electrodes pressed to a surface depends on the pressure applied and will be lower than that measured with painted electrodes. It is possible to avoid the effect of contact potential by using a four-terminal technique as shown in figure 3.26.

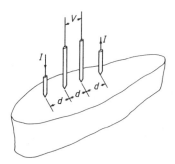

Figure 3.26 Volume resistivity measurement with four-point probe (from Blythe 1979).

A known current density, J, is established in the sample by applying a potential across the outer electrodes. The voltage drop, V, between two inner electrodes of spacing x is then measured. The resistivity ρ is given by

$$\rho = J/E$$
$$= \frac{I/A}{V/x}. \qquad (3.45)$$

(a) *Resistivity from point contacts*

The methods of resistivity measurement described above require the sample to be in the form of a block of material. In some situations, for example, the measurement of moulded items, or *in situ* tests on large samples, the sample is not available in block form and a measure of resistivity must be obtained from point contacts on to the sample. Moon and Spencer (1961) have shown that if a pair of hemispherical electrodes are in contact with a large sample, and their separation d is much greater than their radius r, as shown in figure 3.27, then the resistivity ρ is related to the measured resistance R by the equation

$$R = \rho/\pi r. \qquad (3.46)$$

According to this equation the resistance is independent of the spacing between the electrodes. This happens because nearly all the potential drop occurs close to the tips of the electrodes where the field is highest. It follows that the method is not very reliable, because the result depends so much on the small sample of material close to the tip, and the way in which the contact is made.

A more satisfactory measure of volume resistivity is obtained using the four-contact method illustrated in figure 3.28. A potential is applied across the outer two electrodes so that a current I flows. The potential is then measured across the inner two electrodes. If the electrodes are equally spaced by a distance d the voltage, V, between the central electrodes is related to the volume resistivity by the equation

$$V = I\rho/2\pi d. \qquad (3.47)$$

There is no dependence on electrode area, provided the electrode radius is much smaller than the spacing d.

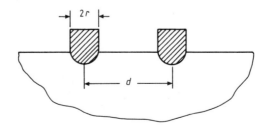

Figure 3.27 The two-terminal method for measuring resistivity.

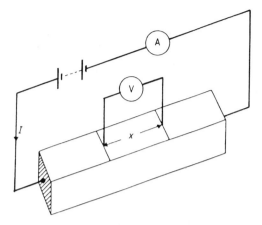

Figure 3.28 The four-terminal method of resistivity measurement.

If the sample has finite boundaries, a correction must be applied depending on the geometry of the sample (Uhlir 1955, van der Pauw 1961). Point contact methods are not suitable for highly resistive materials. One problem is that the input resistance of the voltmeter which measures the voltage between the central electrodes must be much greater than the resistance of the material between these two points. In practice the method is usually limited to resistivities below approximately 10^8 Ω m.

(b) *Resistivity by measurement of the displacement current*
When a voltage is first applied to a high-resistance material there will be an initial high current flow which gradually decays to a steady level. The high current is the displacement current, which flows because of the energy which is absorbed to polarise the atoms of the insulator. The final steady current is the leakage current through the resistance of the sample from which the resistivity of the sample is found. The displacement current will decrease approximately exponentially with the time constant of the decay, given by $\varepsilon_r \varepsilon_0 \rho$. ρ changes very much more between samples than ε_r, therefore the rate at which the current settles to a steady value gives a measure of the sample resistivity.

3.10.3 Surface resistivity

The resistance of the surface of a solid is measured by applying a voltage between parallel electrodes placed on the surface so that the spacing between electrodes is equal to their length. Provided the electrode spacing and length remain equal, the same resistance is measured, whatever the dimensions chosen. The resistivity of the surface is expressed in ohms. The distinction between the resistance of a surface of arbitrary size and the surface resistivity, which is the resistance of a square of material, is sometimes made by expressing the units as ohms/square. However, this is purely a way of indicating the way in which the measurement was made and it is incorrect to express surface resistivity as ohms/square metre, which has the units of $\Omega\,\mathrm{m}^{-2}$ rather than Ω.

Surface resistivity may also be measured using concentric cylindrical electrodes. The surface resistivity ρ_s is related to the measured resistance between the rings by

$$\rho_s = 2\pi R \ln(r_2/r_1). \tag{3.48}$$

This resistivity still has the units of ohms and will have the same value as the resistivity measured with square parallel electrodes.

3.10.4 Surface resistivity of antistatic films

It is sometimes desirable to measure the conductivity of a surface without making contact. (For example, films with antistatic coatings could be damaged by the forces necessary to achieve good electrode contact or by painted electrodes.) One approach is to use the electrical screening effect of a conductor as described in British Standard 2782 (1976). The film is clamped at the edges in an earthed metal ring and interposed between a high-voltage electrode and a detector electrode connected to an electrometer. If the film is a conductor it will shield the detector from the high voltage and the electrometer reading will be reduced to zero. The time taken for the shielding effect to develop is proportional to the resistivity of the film. For a film with a surface conductivity of $10^{-10}\,\mathrm{S\,m^{-1}}$, which is typical of a plastic film with an antistatic treatment, the time is about 0.3 s.

This time is too long for automatic monitoring of the conductivity of moving films and a method suitable for this application has recently been described by Blythe (1983). The detector is placed next to the high-voltage electrode, in the direction of travel of the film, as shown in figure 3.29. If the

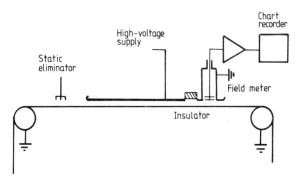

Figure 3.29 A scanning conductivity gauge for antistatic film (after Blythe 1983).

high voltage is positive it will induce a negative charge on the film which, when the film emerges from beneath the electrode, will decay with a time constant proportional to the film resistivity. The detector measures the residual charge.

The field, E, measured by the detector is given in terms of the surface conductivity, σ, by the equation

$$E = \frac{-V}{d} \frac{C_2}{C_1 + C_2} [1 - \exp(-L\sigma/ufC)] \exp(-L'\sigma/ufC) \qquad (3.49)$$

where V is the voltage on the electrode, d is electrode–film distance, C_1 is film-to-electrode capacitance, C_2 is the film-to-earth capacitance, $1/C = 1/C_1 + 1/C_2$, f is a geometric factor, L is the length of the electrode, L' is the electrode–detector distance and u is the film speed.

Blythe (1983) suggests several variations of this basic design to suit particular applications. For example, for low-conductivity films, the signal-to-noise ratio can be improved by switching the high-voltage periodically and detecting the charge using a phase-sensitive detector.

3.10.5 Charge decay rate

If Ohm's law is obeyed, the rate of flow of charge through a material to earth is proportional to the potential of the material (and therefore to the amount of charge on it). The current flow therefore decreases with time as the charge level falls. The charge density on the material falls exponentially with time, i.e.

$$Q = Q_0 \exp(-t/\tau) \qquad (3.50)$$

where Q_0 is the initial charge density and τ is the charge decay time constant:

$$\tau = \varepsilon_r \varepsilon_0 \rho$$
$$= RC. \qquad (3.51)$$

Equation (3.50) may also be written in the form

$$\ln Q = -t/\tau + \ln Q_0. \qquad (3.52)$$

Therefore the natural logarithm of Q, plotted against time, gives a straight line whose slope is the reciprocal of the time constant and whose intercept with the $t = 0$ axis is the initial level of charge. The charge on a surface may be monitored using an electrostatic field meter and the time constant found from this graph.

The dielectric constant, ε_r, of most non-metallic solids lies in the range one to ten, whereas the resistivity varies over several orders of magnitude. Similarly the resistance of a path to earth is likely to vary much more than the capacitance on which a charge is stored. Measurement of the charge decay rate can therefore give an estimate of electrical resistivity or the resistance of the path to earth, and a measurement of resistivity allows the charge decay time to be estimated. However, for most insulators, Ohm's law is not obeyed and plotting ln Q against time does not give a straight line. The effective resistivity increases as the amount of charge stored decreases. Charge decay times are therefore usually longer than predicted by measurement of the resistivity at high voltages, and a small residual charge may remain long after the expected decay time. Since the relationship between the charge decay and the resistance or resistivity is, in practice, not a simple exponential, it is often preferable to measure the form of the charge decay using a field meter rather than to quote a single resistivity to characterise charge decay.

3.11 ENERGY OF ELECTROSTATIC SPARKS

The electrical energy stored in a capacitor, C, charged to a voltage V is given by

$$U = \tfrac{1}{2}CV^2. \tag{3.53}$$

When the capacitor discharges by means of an arc, a flammable atmosphere can be ignited. The ability of an electrostatic spark to ignite a given atmosphere depends on the energy dissipated. For example, the minimum energy needed to ignite the vapour of many hydrocarbon solvents is of the order of 0.2 mJ.

3.11.1 Electrical measurement of spark energy

When a charged metal object, or capacitive electronic component, discharges by means of a spark, more than 95 % of the energy is released. Provided there is no series circuit resistance all this energy will be dissipated in the spark itself and the spark energy can be reasonably assumed to be approximately equal to the total stored energy given in equation (3.53). Other types of discharge (for example, a spark from a person) do not release such a high proportion of the energy stored and equation (3.53) overestimates the spark energy.

The power, or amount of energy per second dissipated in an electrostatic spark, is the product of the current flowing and the voltage across the spark gap, i.e.

$$dU/dt = IV$$

and

$$U = \int IV \, dt.$$

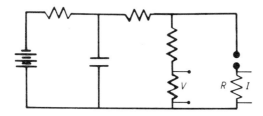

Figure 3.30 A circuit for measurement of spark energy.

The energy, U, may thus be measured by detecting the instantaneous values of the current and voltage in the spark gap and integrating the product of the two over time. Figure 3.30 shows a simple circuit which can be used to make this measurement. The voltage is measured at the high-voltage electrode using a potential divider and oscilloscope and the current flowing in the circuit is detected by measuring the voltage across resistor R. (This resistor can be the 50 Ω input resistor of the oscilloscope but for high-energy sparks it may be necessary to use a lower resistance.)

When the spark is initiated, the potential across the gap drops sharply and the current rises. For most of the duration of the current flow the voltage holds a steady value of the order of a few hundred volts and, provided the total duration of the spark is long compared with its risetime, a reasonable approximation to the energy is obtained by multiplying the area of the current trace by this steady voltage.

There are a number of problems in obtaining an accurate measurement of spark energy, particularly when the spark originates from an isolated capacitor and is very fast, with a duration of only a few nanoseconds.

(i) Since the spark risetime is fast, an extremely fast oscilloscope is required to detect the signals. The duration of the signal is less than the chopping time of most dual-beam oscilloscopes, therefore the instrument must have two independent time bases if it is to measure both the current and the voltage from the same signal.

(ii) Commercial potential dividers do not have the frequency response required to give an accurate measure of the voltage. It has been suggested that this problem may be overcome by using a Pockels cell for the measurement of voltage (Hertz 1985).

(iii) The current flowing in the external circuit is not instantaneously the same as the current flowing in the spark gap. For example, if there is a significant capacitance between the electrodes, current flows through the resistor, R, and charge is stored in this capacitance as the voltage builds up. When the spark occurs this charge neutralises by current flow across the gap but the associated current does not now have to flow through the detection resistor R. The importance of this effect has been investigated by Mills and

Haighton (1982). They carried out experiments in which a charged ball was allowed to fall towards a plate. The current flow measured at the plate is shown in figure 3.31. It can be seen that the total charge transferred was significantly larger than the charge passing through the resistor during the discharge itself. In their geometry the total charge on the sphere was 10 nC and the sphere was 19 mm in diameter. With larger total charge transferred or smaller interelectrode capacitance the effect would be less severe but measurements always tend to underestimate the charge transferred and hence the spark energy.

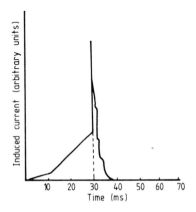

Figure 3.31 Current induced to a grounded electrode as a function of time prior to and during a spark (from Mills and Haighton 1982). Sphere released at time, $t = 0$.

This problem may be overcome by arranging for the spark to occur to a small isolated probe in the earthed electrode (Marode 1975, Chubb and Butterworth 1979). The charge induced on this small area is negligible compared with the total charge transferred and the total charge passing through the resistor is an accurate measure of the total charge crossing the gap. Marode (1975) also suggested that the charge can be measured capacitively at the high-voltage electrode and obtained information concerning the formation mechanism by comparing measurements at the two electrodes.

3.11.2 Spark energy by measurements of ignitability

The precise determination of the spark energy for safety purposes is seldom critical. A safety margin must always be allowed and the ignitability of a spark depends on factors other than the total energy dissipated (see §6.2.2). For example, long-duration sparks are more incendiary than short-duration sparks. The ignitability of a spark may be measured by defining the flammable mixture that the spark will just ignite. A spark which is difficult to measure electrically can then be compared with a more easily defined spark. Measurement of the equivalent spark energy in this way has been applied most frequently to sparks from insulator surfaces where the charge is drawn from a significant area of surface and the surface potential is hard to define.

3.11.3 Lichtenberg figures

Sparks from an insulating surface can be evaluated using Lichtenberg figures. These are the charge patterns made visible by dusting the surface with a powder. The technique was first discovered by Lichtenberg in 1777 and reported to the Royal Society of Göttingen as a new method of investigating the electric fluid. More recently the figures have been studied by Morris Thomas (1951) and Reynolds (1960).

The form of the patterns depends on the polarity and magnitude of the surface voltage and on the nature and pressure of the gas in which the discharge occurs. Discharges from a negative surface in air produce star-like patterns which develop branches with increasing voltage. Discharges from a positive surface are smaller at any given voltage, and are fan shaped or circular without discrete channels. (The same patterns can be observed by developing a photographic film to which a spark has occurred.)

The use of Lichtenberg figures as a measurement tool has been limited, but a considerable body of work has been carried out by Bertein (1973, 1975, 1977) showing that quantitative information may be obtained from the pictures. For example, for a discharge between a negative metal electrode and a positively charged sheet of insulator, of thickness d, placed on a second electrode, a circular Lichtenberg figure is produced and the energy, W, of the partial discharge is given by:

$$W = \frac{\varepsilon_r \varepsilon_0 r_0^2}{2d} (V_a - V_r)^2.$$

Here V_r is the voltage across the gap at which the discharge extinguishes, V_a is the voltage at which the surface breaks down and r_0 is the radius of the discharge pattern. V_a and V_r can also be estimated from the discharge pattern.

Lichtenberg figures have also been used to measure the time of occurrence, the polarity and the magnitude of voltage surges on transmission lines (Peters 1924). A historical review has recently been published by Takahashi (1979).

3.11.4 The spark calorimeter

The energy of a single spark may be measured using a calorimeter. One possible design has been described by Merritt (1978). The calorimeter consisted of two sealed volumes between which was mounted a sensitive differential pressure transducer. When a spark was produced between two electrodes in one of the volumes, the heat released resulted in an expansion of the gas, which was detected by the pressure transducer. The pressure change was compared with the pressure of a sealed reference volume, rather than against atmospheric pressure air, because the short-term pressure changes in atmospheric air are comparable with the small pressure change produced by a low-energy spark.

3.11.5 Light intensity measurements

There is evidence that the energy of an electrostatic spark is related to the light emitted. Measurements of sparks between two 6 mm diameter hemispheres and between a 1 mm point and an 18 mm sphere for sparks between 6 and 270 mJ suggest that the total output from a photomultiplier, integrated over the duration of the spark is proportional to the spark energy (Pude and Hughes 1982). However, more extensive tests are required with different geometries and spark generation circuits to evaluate the range of conditions over which this applies.

3.11.6 Radio emission measurements

The presence of an electrostatic discharge can be detected by the radio emission which may be picked up on any simple radio receiver. A system tuned to about 40 MHz is sensitive to sparks with energies well below the minimum ignition energy of hydrocarbon air mixtures and are relatively insensitive to corona discharges which are non-incendiary. It is possible to use the radio emission to find the position of the spark but studies have found no general relationship between the radio signal and the energy of the spark (Chubb *et al* 1973).

REFERENCES

Bassett J D 1975 Research on electrostatic hazards associated with tank washing in very large crude carriers (supertankers). (II) Study of charging mechanisms due to the production of water aerosols *J. Electrostatics* **1** 47–70
Bertein H 1973 Charges on insulators generated by breakdown of gas *J. Phys. D: Appl. Phys.* **6** 1910–16
—— 1975 Explosion of hydrocarbons by partial discharges *Electrostatics* (*London*) *1975* (Inst. Phys. Conf. Ser. 27) pp 290–300
—— 1977 The importance of electrostatic laws for understanding partial discharges *Proc. 3rd Int. Conf. for Static Electricity* (*Grenoble*) *European Federation of Chemical Engineers* pp 2a–f

Blythe A R 1979 *Electrical Properties of Polymers* (Cambridge: Cambridge University Press

—— 1983 A new conductivity gauge for antistatic films *Electrostatics (Oxford) 1983* (Inst. Phys. Conf. Ser. 66) pp 117–22

British Standard 2782 1976 Antistatic behaviour of films (part 2 method 250C)

Cassidy E C, Cones H N and Booker S R 1970 Development and evaluation of electrooptical high-voltage pulse measurement techniques *IEEE Trans. Instrum. Meas.* **IM-19** 395–402

Cassidy E C, Cones H N, Wunsch D C and Booker S R 1968 Calibration of a Kerr cell system for high-voltage pulse measurements *IEEE Trans. Instrum. Meas.* **IM-17** 313–20

Chubb J N 1983 Developments in electrostatic fieldmeter instrumentation *J. Electrostatics* **14** 349–59

Chubb J N and Butterworth G J 1979 Instrumentation and techniques for monitoring and assessing electrostatic ignition hazards *Electrostatics (Oxford) 1979* (Inst. Phys. Conf. Ser. 48) pp 85–96

Chubb J N, Erents S K and Pollard I E 1973 Radio detection of low energy electrostatic sparks *Nature* **245** 206–7

Collacott S J 1981 A novel method for deriving the reference signal in electrostatic field mills *J. Electrostatics* **9** 389–93

Collins L F, Linde Y and Self S A 1978 Spherical probes for corona discharges *J. Electrostatics* **4** 377–89

Cooperman P 1956 A new technique for the measurement of corona field strength and current density in electrostatic precipitation *Trans. Am. Inst. Elec. Eng. Pt. 1 (Commun. and Electron.* **75** 64–7)

Corbett R P 1972 *PhD Thesis* University of Southampton

Corbett R P and Bassett J D 1971 Electric field measurements in ionic and particulate clouds *Static Electrification (London) 1971* (Inst. Phys. Conf. Ser. 11) pp 307–19

Coury J and Clift R 1984 The distribution of electrical charge between airborne solid particles *Int. Symp. on Electrical and Magnetic Separation and Filtration Techniques (Antwerp)* pp 27–35

Cross J A and Barton N G 1984 Cylindrical probe measurements in a corona discharge *J. Electrostatics* **15** 15–29

Cross J A and Peterson L 1984 Evaluation of the Millikan method to measure the relationship between the electrostatic charge and aerodynamic radius of brown coal fly ash *Proc. 8th Int. Clean Air Conf. (Melbourne, Australia) 1984* (Melbourne: Holmes)

Davies D K 1974 Progress in measuring techniques for industrial and scientific investigations *Proc. 2nd Int. Conf. on Electrostatics (Frankfurt) 1974* (Dechema monograph vol 72 pp 45–53)

Diserens N J, Smith J R and Bright A W 1978 A preliminary study of electric field problems in plastic tanks and their theoretical modelling by means of a finite difference computer program *J. Electrostatics* **5** 169–82

Ettinger S Y and Venezia A C 1963 High voltage pulse measurement system based on the Kerr effect *Rev. Sci. Instrum.* **34** 221–4

Gosho Y 1967a Measurement of potential distribution in discharge gap by the electrostatic probe *Elect. Eng. Japan* **87** 55–65

_____ 1967b Characteristics of electrostatic probe *Inst. Phys. Chem. Res.* **61** 7–19

Haenen H T M 1976 Potential probe measurement analysis and charge distribution determination *J. Electrostatics* **2** 203–22

Helstrom R 1984 Private communication

Hertz H M 1985 Capacitively coupled KD*P Pockels cell for high voltage pulse measurement *J. Phys. E: Sci. Instrum.* **18** 522–5

Hidaka K and Kouno T 1982 A method for measuring electric field in space charge by means of a Pockels device *J. Electrostatics* **11** 195–211

Lohman R C, Venselaar H C J, Haighton E J and Van Laar W A 1981 A meter for the measurement of electrostatic fields at high temperatures *J. Sci. Instrum.* **14** 1296–8

McDonald J R, Anderson M H and Mosley R B 1980 Charge measurement on individual particles existing in laboratory precipitators with positive and negative corona at various temperatures *J. Appl. Phys.* **51** 3632–43

Marode E 1975 The mechanism of spark breakdown in air at atmospheric pressure between a positive point and a plane 1. Experimental nature of the streamer track *J. Appl. Phys.* **46** 2005–15

Masuda S and Nonogaki Y 1981 Sensing of back discharge and bipolar ion current *J. Electrostatics* **10** 73–80

Merritt L R 1978 A spark calorimeter *J. Phys. E: Sci. Instrum.* **11** 193–4

Mills J S and Haighton E J 1982 Electrostatic discharges: charge transfer measurement techniques *J. Electrostatics* **13** 91–7

Moon P and Spencer D E 1961 *Field Theory for Engineers* (London: Van Nostrand)

Morris Thomas A 1951 Heat developed and powdered Lichtenberg figures *Brit. J. Appl. Phys.* **2** 98–109

van der Pauw 1961 Determination of resistivity tensor and Hall tensor of anisotropic conductors *Phillips Research Rep.* **16** 187–95

Penney G W and Lynch R D 1957 Measurement of charge imparted to fine particles by a corona discharge *Trans. AIEE* **76** 294–9

Peters J F 1924 The klydonograph *Electronics World* **83** 769

Pude J R G and Hughes J F 1981 Spark energy measurement using an optical technique *IEEE Conf. Industrial Applications Society* 1201–6

Reynolds S I 1960 The measurement and influence of surface charges on the inception voltage between dielectric and metal dielectric surfaces *Trans. AIEE* **79** 310–14

Ross J N 1981 A laser Doppler anemometer using photon correlation to measure the velocity of individual particles *J. Phys. E: Sci. Instrum.* **14** 1019–23

Sato T 1980 Drift velocity measurements of charged particles under corona discharge in an air gap *J. Electrostatics* **8** 271–8

Scaife B K P 1971 *Complex Permittivity, Theory and Measurement* (London: London University Press)

Schwaiger 1925 *Elektrische Festigkeitslehre* 188

Scruton B and Blott B H 1973 A high resolution scanning probe *J. Phys. E: Sci. Instrum.* **6** 472–4

Takahashi Y 1979 Two hundred years of Lichtenberg figures *J. Electrostatics* **6** 1–13

Takuma T 1969 Comments on measurement of potential distribution in discharge gap by the electrostatic probe *Elect. Eng. Japan* **89** 78–9

Thompson J E, Kristiansen M and Hagler O M 1976 Optical measurement of high electric and magnetic fields *IEEE Trans. Instrum. Meas.* **IM-25** 1–7

Toomer R 1979 *PhD Thesis* University of Wales

Uhlir A 1955 The potentials of an infinite system of sources and numerical solutions of problems in semiconductor engineering *Bell Systems Tech. J.* 105–28

Van der Weerd J M 1971 Electrostatic charge generation—measurements and interpretation *Static Electrification 1971* (Inst. Phys. Conf. Ser. 11) pp 158–78

Waters R T 1972 Cylindrical electrostatic fluxmeter for corona studies *J. Phys. E: Sci. Instrum.* **5** 475–8

Whitby K T 1979 in *Fine Particles* ed B Y H Lui (New York: Academic)

Wilson A D 1970 *PhD Thesis* University of Reading

Wunsch D C and Erteza A 1964 Kerr cell measuring system for high voltage pulses *Rev. Sci. Instrum.* **35** 816–20

Chapter 4 Electrostatics in Gas Filtration

4.1 INTRODUCTION

The electrostatic force on a body with a charge q in a field E is

$$F_e = qE. \tag{4.1}$$

Both the charge and field are limited by the breakdown strength of air and electrostatic forces tend to be rather weak. However, the maximum charge which can be applied to a body is proportional to its surface area, therefore as the body becomes smaller its charge-to-mass ratio increases, and eventually the electrostatic force exceeds the force due to gravity. It is therefore possible to make use of electrostatic forces to control and direct the movement of small charged particles or liquid droplets. Small particles are also affected by aerodynamic forces. The range of particle size for which electrostatic forces dominate both aerodynamic and gravitational forces can easily be calculated.

The force on a sphere of radius a and density D due to gravity is

$$F_g = \tfrac{4}{3}\pi a^3 Dg. \tag{4.2}$$

The maximum electrostatic force is

$$F_e = q_{max} E_{max}.$$

The maximum charge per unit area can be calculated from Gauss's law and is 2.64×10^{-5} (see §1.5). Therefore, for a sphere of radius a:

$$F_e = 2.64 \times 10^{-5} \times 4\pi a^2 E_{max}. \tag{4.3}$$

The electrostatic force will exceed the force due to gravity when $F_e > F_g$, i.e.

$$a < 8 \times 10^{-6} E_{max}/D. \tag{4.4}$$

144

Thus, for a material whose density is 10^3 kg m^{-3}, in a field at the breakdown limit of air ($E_{max} = 3 \times 10^6$ V m^{-1}):

$$a < 24 \times 10^{-3} \text{ m}. \tag{4.5}$$

In practice, it is not possible to maintain a stable electric field very close to breakdown, and the practical upper limit of the field in air is about 5×10^5 V m^{-1}. The maximum radius for which electrostatic forces dominate in practice is therefore about an order of magnitude less than is calculated assuming that the charge and field can both hold their maximum values.

The limiting velocity, u, of a charged particle in an electric field in air can be calculated by equating the electrostatic force on the particle to the drag provided by the air.

Assuming the drag of the air obeys the Stokes law:

$$6\pi\eta au = 2.64 \times 10^{-5} \times 4\pi a^2 E \tag{4.6}$$

where η is the viscosity of air $\simeq 1.8 \times 10^{-5}$ N s m^{-2}

$$u = 1.76 \times 10^{-5} aE\eta^{-1}$$

$$u \simeq Ea. \tag{4.7}$$

Thus, for the maximum practical field of 5×10^5 V m^{-1}, the maximum velocity is 50 m s^{-1}, for a 100 μm radius particle, and 0.5 m s^{-1} for a particle with a radius of 1 μm.

It can be seen that submicron particles travel very slowly in an electric field and will be influenced more by air flow than by electrostatic forces. The range of particle radii where electrostatic forces may be greater than gravitational or aerodynamic forces, is therefore between about 1 μm and 2 mm. Within this range, particle motion can be controlled by charging the particles and directing them by means of electric fields.

In addition to the Coulomb force, which acts on a charged particle in a uniform electric field (described by equation (4.1)), there is a force on a neutral particle in a non-uniform electric field. This dipole or 'dielectrophoretic' force is operative in either DC or AC fields. It is smaller than the Coulomb force but can be significant and has a number of interesting applications, particularly in liquids.

Electrostatic systems are used commercially in a wide range of industries, the most important in commercial terms being filtration and separation for pollution control, metal finishing, and printing and copying processes. In this chapter electrostatic filtration and separation in a gaseous medium is discussed. Electrostatic precipitators are by far the most common electrostatic devices used in pollution control, but a number of other techniques have been proposed, some of which have been tested to at least pilot scale. None has yet received the intensive study which has been given to electrostatic precipitators in their hundred year history, and none has yet achieved general acceptance to the same extent. However several of the techniques have shown considerable promise in laboratory pilot scale tests and a number are commercially available. A review of electrostatic gas-cleaning devices with over eighty references is given by Henry *et al* (1982) and a manual covering electrostatic gas cleaning in general is published and updated monthly, under the title *The Electrostatic Precipitator Manual.*

4.2 ELECTROSTATIC PRECIPITATION

4.2.1 Introduction

The first major application of electrostatic forces in industry was the electrostatic precipitator. The collection of smoke using electrostatic forces was first demonstrated in 1824, by Hohlfeld in Germany, but the idea was not put to practical use until the 1880s when Oliver Lodge patented a precipitator for collecting smelter fumes. The early precipitators were not very successful, because power supplies were inadequate, and the first working precipitator was finally operational in 1907.

In the simplest type of precipitator a high voltage is applied to a wire on the axis of an earthed cylinder through which dusty gas passes. A corona discharge forms at the wire, and ions which have the same polarity as the wire are repelled towards the cylinder. The bi-ionised discharge zone is limited to a small region near the wire, and the majority of the interelectrode space is filled with ions of a single polarity. These ions are attracted to dust particles because of the distortion in the electric field which is caused by the difference in the relative permittivity of the particles compared with that of the gas. The theory of this process was discussed in §2.2.3. The dust particles collect ions until they reach a limiting charge q_{max}, when the repulsive field due to the charge on the particle balances the field distortion. The charged particles experience a force in the electric field which carries them to the earthed electrode. Insulating particles cannot lose their charge on contact with the electrode and they adhere to it until they are removed by rapping or washing. Conducting particles will lose their charge, and recharge to the opposite polarity by induction, as discussed in §2.4. Precipitation is therefore only applicable to relatively insulating powders or liquid droplets. Insulating particles agglomerate during deposition and when the collector electrode is rapped the agglomerated dust falls under gravity rather than being redispersed in the gas stream.

Large precipitators are usually designed with a negative high-voltage electrode because this allows a higher voltage to be applied without an arc. However, small precipitators, such as those designed for the removal of cigarette smoke in rooms, may have a positive high-voltage electrode, to minimise the production of ozone.

4.2.2 Theory of precipitation in laminar flow

Consider a stream of dust travelling vertically up a cylindrical electrostatic precipitator with a velocity u. The electrostatic force on a particle in a field E_0 is given by

$$F_e = qE_0. \qquad (4.8)$$

For particles of radius a ($a > 1$ μm) Pauthenier's charging theory may be assumed to apply. It was shown in §2.2.3 that this leads to a maximum charge given by

$$q_{max} = 4\pi\varepsilon_0 p E_c a^2 \qquad (4.9)$$

where E_c is the electric field in which the particle is charged, $\varepsilon_0 = 8.8 \times 10^{-12}$ F m^{-1} and $p = 3\varepsilon_r/(\varepsilon_r + 2)$. For a material of dielectric constant $\varepsilon_r = 2$, $p = 1.5$ whereas for a metal ($\varepsilon_r = \infty$), $p = 3$. Therefore the electrostatic force on a fully charged dielectric particle is

$$F_e = 6\pi\varepsilon_0 a^2 E_c E_0. \qquad (4.10)$$

The particle is given a transverse acceleration of F_e/m (where m is the mass of the particle), and rapidly reaches its terminal velocity, w, where the electrostatic force is balanced by the aerodynamic drag.

The aerodynamic drag force on the particle is given by the Stokes law:

$$F_d = 6\pi\eta a w \qquad (4.11)$$

where η is the viscosity of air, i.e.

$$F_d = 6\pi\eta a w = F_e = 6\pi\varepsilon_0 a^2 E_c E_0$$

and

$$w = \varepsilon_0 a E_c E_0/\eta. \qquad (4.12)$$

If the particles are smaller than about 1 μm then the drag force must be adjusted by the Cunningham correction factor and diffusion charging must be included in the calculation of the particle charge (see §2.2.7).

The collection time t, during which a particle with a charge q_{max} must remain in the electric field in order to travel the distance d to the collector, is given by

$$t = \frac{d}{w} = \frac{\eta d}{\varepsilon_0 a E_c E_0}. \qquad (4.13)$$

Typically, $E_c = E_0 \simeq 3 \times 10^5$ V m^{-1}, $\eta = 1.8 \times 10^{-5}$, $d = 150$ mm and $\varepsilon_0 = 8.8 \times 10^{-12}$, then the time taken for a particle 5 μm in radius to drift to the collector is

$$t = 0.68 \text{ s}.$$

It was shown in §2.2.3, that the time, t', for a particle to reach a charge q is given by

$$q/q_{max} = t'/(t' + \tau)$$

where

$$\tau = 4\varepsilon_0 E/J.$$

The particle has 50 % of its charge after a time τ and 90 % of its charge after 9τ. For $E = 3 \times 10^5$ V m^{-1} and $J = 10^{-4}$ A m^{-2} (typical of large precipitators), $\tau = 0.1$ s. (For small devices the current density can be an order of magnitude higher giving faster charging times.)

A residence time of several seconds is normally allowed to achieve a good collection efficiency with efficient charging and enough time for the particles to migrate to the collector.

In practice the majority of electrostatic precipitators are used in large-scale gas-cleaning operations, with by far the largest single use being the cleaning of fly ash from flue gas in coal-burning power stations. In these installations gas flow is not laminar and a duct-type precipitator is used with rows of wire electrodes between parallel plates.

4.2.3 Non-laminar flow—the Deutsch equation

A theory for precipitators with turbulent flow was developed by Deutsch in 1922 (Deutsch 1922). The precipitator is assumed to consist of two zones, a laminar boundary layer very close to the earthed electrodes and a turbulent core extending over the rest of the precipitator. Turbulent mixing is assumed to bring about a uniform distribution of particles, which then have a uniform concentration C_p throughout a given cross section. When the particle is within the laminar boundary layer it experiences an electrostatic force which gives it a velocity, w, towards the wall. This is called the migration velocity. In a time dt particles which are within a distance $w\,dt$ of an area of the wall dA will be collected. This reduces the particle concentration by dC_p.

Equating the rates of particle loss from the gas to the rate of particle arrival at the surface, we have

$$u_g\,dC_p = -wC_p\,dA$$

where u_g is the volume flow rate of the gas, i.e.

$$\frac{1}{C_p}dC_p = -\frac{w}{u_g}dA.$$

Integrating this expression gives the efficiency ξ:

$$\xi = \frac{1 - C_{out}}{C_{in}} = 1 - \exp(-Aw/u_g)$$

where C_{in} and C_{out} are the inlet and outlet concentrations and A is the total collecting area. A/u_g is called the specific collecting area α, i.e.

$$\xi = 1 - \exp(-\alpha w). \tag{4.14}$$

This is known as the Deutsch equation.

If we assume that the Pauthenier charging theory applies, then the migration velocity is given by the same expression as the drift velocity in equation (4.12). Deutsch's equation can then be written in the form:

$$\xi = 1 - \exp\left(\frac{-\varepsilon_0 a E_0 E_c \alpha}{\eta}\right). \tag{4.15}$$

Making the approximation that $E_c E_0 = V^2/d$ and taking logarithms of both sides this becomes

$$\ln(1 - \xi) = \frac{\varepsilon_0 a V^2 \alpha}{\eta d}. \tag{4.16}$$

White (1963) makes the empirical approximation that $E_c E_0$ is proportional to the corona power (i.e. the product of current and voltage). The corona current I is related to the applied voltage V by the equation,

$$I = KV(V - V_c)$$

where V_c is the corona inception voltage and K is a constant. It can be seen that these two criteria are not equivalent and White's approximation leads to a V^3-dependence of migration velocity at high voltages. With high-resistivity ashes the current is distorted by back-ionisation, which will be discussed later, and $E_c E_0 = V^2/d$ is probably the better approximation. In either case we have an equation for the efficiency in terms of known or measurable parameters.

4.2.4 Validity of the Deutsch equation

It has long been known that the Deutsch equation overestimates the efficiency of full-scale precipitators (White 1963). An equation of the general form of the Deutsch equation is normally obeyed, i.e.

$$\xi = 1 - \exp(\alpha w_e)$$

but the effective migration velocity, w_e, is lower than expected from equation (4.12), and is dependent on the linear gas velocity. The validity of the Deutsch equation, in the form of equation (4.16), can be tested by plotting $\ln \xi$ as a function of αV^2. This should produce a straight line with a slope which is proportional to the particle radius. This is known as the performance line. The efficiency of a large number of different Australian coals has been measured in a cylindrical pilot scale precipitator, and plotted in this way, by Potter and Paulson (1974). A reasonably straight line was obtained for most samples, but when the slope of the line was plotted as a function of the mass median particle diameter, measured with a Bahco sizer which measures aerodynamic radius, the line obtained was substantially removed from the position predicted from equation (4.16) (Cross and Paulson 1983), see figure 4.1.

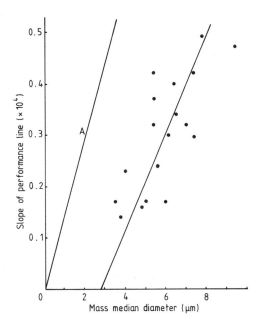

Figure 4.1 Slope of the performance line as a function of mass median diameter (after Cross and Paulson 1983). ●, Experimental points for fly ashes from different Australian coals. The line A shows result of theory from the Deutsch equation using $E_c E_p = V^2/R^2$, $p = 1.5$.

A large number of approximations are made in the derivation of equation (4.16), so it is, perhaps, not surprising that it provides only a general approximation for the behaviour of a real precipitator. The approximations of the theory are summarised below:

(i) The particle concentration across the precipitator cross section is assumed to be uniform. In practice there is a relatively dust-free zone near the discharge electrode which broadens as the dusty gas moves through the precipitator (Moore 1973).

(ii) The product of charging field and migration field is assumed to equal V^2/d.

(iii) The particles may be represented by a single-particle diameter (the mass median diameter).

(iv) All particles within the distance $w\,\mathrm{d}t$ of the wall are collected, i.e. the particles are not re-entrained after deposition and the capture efficiency is one.

In practice, photographic observations of a surface collecting high-resistivity dust have shown that significant re-entrainment does occur, starting after only a few seconds of deposition onto a clean electrode (Cross and Bassett 1974). Felder and Arce Medina (1980) have studied fly ash re-entrainment in a pilot scale precipitator, using irradiated fly ash as a tracer. They found that, under the conditions of their experiments, re-entrainment due to the friction of gas was negligible, but when the gas contained dust the re-entrainment was significant.

Numerous attempts have been made to improve upon the Deutsch equation as a means of predicting the size of precipitator required for a given efficiency. A common modification is to write the Deutsch equation as

$$1 - \xi = \exp[\,-(\omega_k \alpha)^k] \tag{4.17}$$

where k is a constant of the order of 0.5 and ω_k is the equivalent of a migration velocity. ω_k accounts for a multitude of non-ideal effects and varies widely with dust resistivity, particle size, etc. For example, for a high-resistivity dust it may be $12\text{--}15\ \mathrm{m\ s}^{-1}$, and for a lower resistivity material $60\text{--}70\ \mathrm{m\ s}^{-1}$. Although this modification to the Deutsch equation has no theoretical basis, it does account for some of the experimentally observed deviations from the Deutsch equation. It has proved useful in sizing precipitators from pilot scale tests because ω_k (unlike w_e) remains constant, independent of gas throughput (Watson 1979). The collecting area required is proportional to ω_k, and the value of ω_k, identified on the pilot scale applies to the full-scale precipitator.

4.2.5 The effect of dust properties on precipitation

At present, the only satisfactory way of predicting the size of precipitator required to collect a particular dust efficiently is to scale up results from pilot scale tests, using either the ω_k method or the performance line method described by Potter (1978, 1981). The Deutsch theory predicts that only the particle radius and dielectric constant will affect particle precipitability, but experience shows that other dust properties are of major importance. For example, high-resistivity dusts are found to require a substantially larger precipitator than more moderately resistive materials. With a resistive dust, both the collection efficiency at a given voltage and the maximum voltage attainable without an arc are reduced. Both effects are attributable to an electrical breakdown phenomenon within the deposited dust, known as back-ionisation (see below).

Measurements of particle size distribution and electrical resistivity can give an indication as to whether a dust is likely to be easy or difficult to collect, but do not give sufficient information to allow a precipitator to be sized accurately. It appears that some dusts are stickier than others, and suffer less re-entrainment, but, as yet, it has not proved possible to quantify this, or to predict precipitability from a knowledge of coal or ash chemistry.

A few parts per million of a flue gas additive can substantially improve precipitator performance (Potter and Paulson 1974, Dismukes 1976). The additives usually reduce the electrical resistivity of the ash, but there is evidence that they can also affect the agglomeration of the dust and its re-entrainment (Cross *et al* 1987). The effect of fly ash additives are discussed in a number of papers given at *The 3rd Symposium on the Transfer and Utilisation of Particulate Control Techniques* (1982) (EPA-600/9-82-005).

4.2.6 Back-ionisation

Back-ionisation is the name given to the electrical breakdown which occurs when a layer of charged dust is deposited on an earthed surface. It is extremely important both in the collection of high-resistivity dusts in a precipitator and in the electrostatic powder coating process, discussed in Chapter 5.

The electrical breakdown strength of a deposited layer of powder or dust is between 10^6 and 10^7 V m^{-1}. The field that builds up across the layer in the absence of free ions within the layer can be estimated from the resistivity ρ and the current density J flowing through it by Ohm's law, i.e.

$$E = \rho J \qquad (4.18)$$

where ρ is the electrical resistivity and J is the current density. Typically the current density at the collector plate of an electrostatic precipitator is 10^{-4} A m^{-2}. Therefore, the field across the layer reaches the breakdown strength when the resistivity exceeds 10^{10}–10^{11} Ω m.

When an electrical discharge occurs within the layer, positive ions and electrons will be created. Assuming the precipitator has a negative high-voltage electrode, the electrons will move through the layer towards the collector and the positive ions will be attracted across the interelectrode space towards the high-voltage electrode. These positive ions discharge the dust particles in the precipitator and therefore reduce its efficiency. When there is back-ionisation in the system the current in the external circuit increases substantially. (Positive ions travelling to the wire give the same polarity current as negative ions travelling in the opposite direction and the field due to the positive space charge increases the current in the negative corona.) Figure 4.2 compares the current–voltage characteristic of a point-to-plane corona discharge, with a clean metal plane and with a back-ionising layer on the plane. In the absence of back-ionisation the current I is propor-

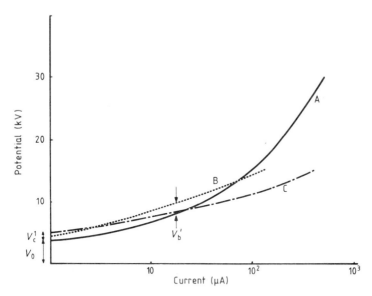

Figure 4.2 The current–voltage characteristic of a point-to-plane corona discharge with and without back-ionisation. A, no back-ionisation; B, moderate back-ionisation; C, high back-ionisation. V'_b and V'_c represent the voltage built up across layers b and c respectively at the point at which back-ionisation begins. V_0 is the corona inception voltage in the absence of a layer.

tional to $V(V - V_c)$ where V_c is the corona inception voltage. With back-ionisation this linearity is lost as shown in figure 4.3.

The source of the additional current flowing during back-ionisation has been studied by Cross (1985). When the normal negative corona discharge current is measured using a fast oscilloscope, it is found to consist of a series of regular, repetitive, pulses superimposed on a small steady current (see Chapter 7). For a given geometry, the steady current is a fixed proportion of the total integrated current (i.e. the current which is measured with a DC meter). The pulses can be identified with the motion of electrons near the high-voltage electrode. When the current increases due to back-ionisation, the frequency of the pulses increases. This increase accounts for nearly all of the additional current. Only at high levels of back-ionisation is there also a measurable increase of a few per cent in the steady component of the current. This means that most of the additional current flowing during back-ionisation is due to the movement of additional electrons near the high-voltage electrode. This increase is believed to be due to a reduction of the negative-ion space charge, by positive ions created in the back-ionising layer. The positive ions are not seen directly in the current measured in the external circuit, because this is dominated by the movement of high-mobility particles in the high-field region as discussed in Chapter 7. The oscilloscope also

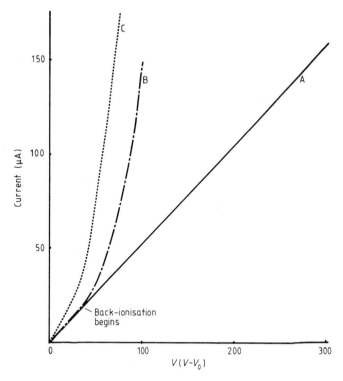

Figure 4.3 The current–voltage characteristic for a point-to-plane corona discharge with and without back-ionisation: A, no back-ionisation; B, moderate back-ionisation; C, high back-ionisation.

detects individual breakdown events in the back-ionising layer, but only with high-current densities flowing through a highly resistive fly ash layer is there a significant amount of current associated with these pulses. In this case streamers crossed from the layer to the high-voltage electrode and could be seen as a faint glow in the interelectrode space.

These results show that the current increase during back-ionisation cannot necessarily be assumed to give a direct measure of the number of positive ions released. An estimate has been made of the percentage of back-ions from tissue paper surfaces by Masuda and Nonogaki (1981) and Cross and Barton (1984), using electrostatic probes. Both found that approximately 20 % of the total current density near the plane can be attributed to positive ions. The maximum charge q'_{max} that a particle can achieve in a bi-ionised field with a current density J_f of forward ions and J_b of back-ions was shown in §2.2.7 to be

$$q'_{max} = q_{max}\frac{(1 - \xi)}{(1 + \xi)} \tag{4.19}$$

where q_{max} is the charge in a monoionised field and $\xi = (J_b/J_f)^{1/2}$ i.e., when

J_b is 20 % of the total current $J_b/J_f = 0.25$, and the maximum charge which can be achieved is reduced by a factor of three.

Back-ionisation discharges in the insulating layer can be seen with an image intensifier. They take the form of general glow over the surface and bright spots of light which may move around the surface. The light emission is associated with re-entrainment of dust from the layer, with the bright spots being associated with fountains of dust leaving the surface and the glow with individual particle movement (Cross and Bassett 1974). This movement in the layer makes it difficult to obtain repeatable results from real powder layers, and tissue paper or pinholes in solid insulators have frequently been used to model a powder layer in back-ionisation studies. The bright spots of light from a back-ionising layer have been shown to be the source of streamers which cross the interelectrode gap. These provide an ionised path which lowers the breakdown voltage (Cross 1986, Masuda and Mizuno 1977a, 1978).

The decrease in collection efficiency when back-ionisation begins has been measured by Sampuran-Singh *et al* (1979). Figure 4.4 shows the mass of powder deposited on a plane when a high-resistivity polymer powder was blown past a high-voltage point, towards the plane, in a point-to-plane corona discharge. The rate of deposition dropped substantially after the first few seconds of deposition, and this drop in efficiency could be correlated with the onset of back-ionisation.

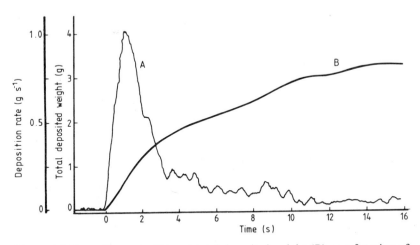

Figure 4.4 Deposition rate (A) and total deposited weight (B) as a function of time (from Sampuran-Singh *et al* 1979).

4.2.7 Electrical resistivity of the dust

Back-ionisation is more severe the higher the electrical resistivity of the dust. One might therefore expect a correlation between dust resistivity and precipitator performance. However attempts to measure this correlation have not been conclusive. Two basic methods are used to measure electrical resistivity. In one, dust is placed in a cell in a controlled environment with two plane-parallel electrodes a few mm apart. A voltage, V, of a few kV is applied between the electrodes and the current, I, flowing through the dust is measured to give the resistivity, ρ:

$$\rho = AV/Id$$

where A is the electrode area and d is the electrode spacing.

The second method allows the resistivity during a corona discharge to be measured *in situ*. The surface potential V_s of an electrostatically deposited dust layer of thickness d is measured while a known current density, J, from a corona discharge flows through it. The resistivity is given by

$$\rho = V_s/dJ.$$

The surface potential is found by probe techniques (e.g. Goard and Potter 1981, Cross and Barton 1984) or by observing the shift in the corona onset voltage (White 1963). In either case the measurement runs into problems when back-ionisation occurs. Back-ionisation produces additional ions, therefore a high current flows for the same applied voltage, i.e. after the onset of back-ionisation the effective resistivity of the layer is substantially reduced although the phenomenon itself is caused by a high dust resistivity. Back-ionisation can occur at low currents and for very thin dust layers (Cross 1986). This limits the usefulness of this method of measuring resistivity to relatively conducting dusts, where back-ionisation is low, such as ashes produced by high-sulphur coals.

The electrical resistivity of a precipitator dust is usually required in order to predict the tendency of a dust to back-ionise. However since the relationship between electrical resistivity and back-ionisation is not well understood it is more satisfactory to use the current–voltage characteristic of a corona discharge to detect the extent of back-ionisation directly. In the absence of back-ionisation the current in a corona discharge is proportional to $V(V - V_0)$ (where V_0 is the corona inception voltage). Thus a graph of I against $V(V - V_0)$ will produce a straight line. The voltage at which this graph deviates from a straight line and the extent of the deviation gives a measure of the extent of back-ionisation. More accurately, an allowance must be made for the voltage, V', built up on the surface of the insulating layer due to the current flowing through it. This can be taken to be the difference in potential between the current–voltage characteristic with back-ionisation and that without back-ionisation at the current where the characteristic plotted in the form of figure 4.3 first deviates from a straight line. I is then plotted against $V(V - V_0 - V')$.

Although it is accepted that back-ionisation plays a major role in the precipitability of different dusts, no direct correlation between precipitability and back-ionisation, measured in this way, has been reported in the literature.

4.2.8 Effect of aerodynamic forces

The aerodynamic requirements in the design of a large-scale electrostatic precipitator are:

(i) the total pressure drop through the precipitator must be minimised;

(ii) the gas must be decelerated from the duct velocity (usually $\geqslant 15 \text{ m s}^{-1}$) to the precipitator velocity ($1-2 \text{ m s}^{-1}$);

(iii) the decelerated dust must be evenly diffused into the collection chamber (in sizing a precipitator it is assumed that the gas is uniformly distributed across the cross section of the device);

(iv) gas flow at the bottom of the collection chamber, where the collected dust is stored, must be minimised;

(v) gas must be evenly accelerated out of the collection chamber.

It is important to achieve a uniform gas velocity because the effective migration velocity of the particles is a function of the gas flow rate (Groves and Smith 1980) (probably because re-entrainment is also a function of gas velocity). Substantial drops in overall efficiency have been reported owing to peaks in the velocity distribution at different positions in a precipitator (White 1963).

It has been shown, both theoretically and experimentally, that precipitator efficiency is higher the more laminar the flow. In fact, with moderately turbulent flow, precipitators should be more efficient than is predicted by the Deutsch equation (which assumes high turbulence) or than is ever observed in practice (Leonard *et al* 1982). The reason for the poor performance of aerodynamically well designed precipitators has not been identified but is usually assumed to be re-entrainment.

Flow modelling can achieve useful improvements in precipitator design (Griesco and Fortune). However, modelling cannot accurately reproduce the flow patterns within a real precipitator because of the ion wind. This is the bulk movement of the neutral gas molecules in the direction of the electric field owing to momentum transfer from the ions. This can result in a bulk velocity of the gas of $1-2 \text{ m s}^{-1}$ which is comparable with the mean velocity of the dirty gas through the precipitator. The flow pattern induced by the corona wind will depend on the geometry of the corona discharge and will change as dust is deposited on the electrodes. Experiments to measure the ion wind in model precipitators have been reported by Athwal *et al* (1983) and Masuda and Dri (1975).

4.2.9 The effect of applied voltage

In large-scale precipitators, operating at approximately 150 °C and atmospheric pressure, a negative high voltage is applied to the wire, because this allows a higher voltage to be applied without an arc. For small precipitators, where it is less important to minimise the size of the device, a positive high voltage may be applied because less ozone is created. Positive wire voltages are also preferred for some applications of gas cleaning at high temperatures and pressures because, under these circumstances, the arc-over voltage becomes higher for positive polarities (Brown and Walker 1971). Theoretically, the efficiency of collection depends on the square of the applied voltage, and optimum precipitator performance is obtained by using as high a voltage as possible. In practice it has been found that the undulating wave form from imperfectly filtered rectifiers gives a better performance than a smooth direct voltage. The relatively long delay between the peaks in the voltage allows time for sparks to extinguish, and a higher mean operating potential can be achieved than is possible with a smooth direct voltage. In order to maximise the mean operating voltage it is generally desirable to allow some sparking at the peak of the voltage wave form, but too much sparking reduces efficiency. The power supplies of large installations are frequently controlled to give a fixed spark rate of about a hundred sparks per minute. With very highly resistive dust it has been found that the reduction in efficiency at high voltages due to back-ionisation is greater than the improvement due to the increased voltage. In these cases a control method which holds the voltage at a level below severe back-ionisation is preferred (Truce 1981).

The occurrence of a spark in a precipitator depends on local variations in coating thickness, and is essentially a random process. The probability that a spark will occur from a corona wire therefore increases with the length of the wire. It can be shown that the optimum operating voltage for n sections of a precipitator, V_n, can be described in terms of the optimum voltage for a single section, V_1 by the equation

$$V_n = V_1 - \ln n/b \qquad (4.20)$$

where b is an empirical constant of the order of one.

There is therefore some advantage to be gained by dividing the precipitator into as many sections, each powered by different supplies, as is compatible with costs. This is also advantageous because the smaller the section powered by one supply, the smaller the electrostatic energy stored, and the less disruptive the arc when it does occur. The number of power supplies required is also dictated by their ability to deliver sufficient current to power the precipitator without losing voltage. All these requirements are discussed by White (1963).

In recent years it has been proposed that improved efficiency may be obtained by applying a voltage with a pulsed wave form. If a short duration pulse is superimposed onto the DC voltage it is possible to obtain a higher peak voltage without sparkover, and particle charging is improved. It is also possible to have high peak voltages without high mean currents. The current may therefore be held below the threshold for back-ionisation without reducing the particle migration velocity. Pulses with a number of different forms have been tested. Improvements corresponding to an increase in ω_k

(from equation (4.17)) by a factor of up to 2.5 have been reported. This can mean up to 85 % reduction in the particulate emissions from a stack. The improved efficiency is obtained only for medium- and high-resistivity dusts but it is these dusts which are most difficult to collect and are in greatest need of improvement. The main use of pulse energisation has been to upgrade existing precipitators to meet new emission regulations, or to allow a precipitator designed for one dust to be used for another which is more resistive and more difficult to collect.

In the system developed by F L Schmidt, (Petersen and Lausen 1979, Lausen *et al* 1979) a pulse lasting 50–200 μs, with a repetition frequency of 25–400 pulses per second was applied. The DC voltage was held just below the corona threshold and the peak voltage was of the order of 90 kV. Full-scale tests showed that ω_k was increased by a factor of 1.2 for a non-back-ionising dust, and by a factor of 2 for a severely back-ionising dust. Research Cottrell (1979) claim improvement factors of up to 2.5 with highly resistive dusts. They apply a fast risetime short pulse on top of the conventional partially rectified signal (figure 4.5(*b*)). The fast risetime leads to a more uniform discharge at the high-voltage electrode and eliminates local regions of high current density. Stomberg and Lundquist (1983) show that a much improved current distribution is also obtained when radio frequency oscillations are superimposed on the direct voltage. Masuda *et al* (1975) quote considerably improved efficiencies with a sharp square-wave pulse applied to

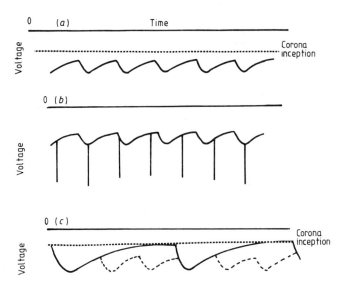

Figure 4.5 Pulse energisation wave forms (voltage as a function of time). (*a*), Conventional 50/60 Hz voltage wave form; (*b*), Research Cottrell pulsed wave form; (*c*), Semipulse concept (full curve) compared with conventional energisation (broken curve) (from Porle 1985).

a three-electrode precipitator. Their pulse had a risetime of 5 μs, a falltime less than 500 μs, a width of 10–10 000 μs, a height of 40 kV and a repetition frequency of 5–1000 pulses per second. Again the improvement was attributed to a more uniform current distribution and the ability to regulate the current without reducing the peak voltage.

Recently Porle (1985) compared two systems of energisation. The first, called the SPC, 'semipulse concept' is compared with conventional energisation in figure 4.5(c). The conventional wave form is achieved by rectification of a 50- or 60-cycle AC signal. In the SPC only one in three of these waves is allowed to pass and the mean current is decreased to one third of its previous value. This results in a substantial power saving and a slightly improved collection efficiency. The major advantage of this type of energisation is that it can be achieved with a conventional power supply, simply by modifying the controls. It leads to significantly better collection with very highly resistive ashes where back-ionisation is a major problem.

Greater improvements in efficiency were obtained with the 'multipulse concept' (MPC). This wave form is shown in figure 4.6 and consists of about eight short pulses, in bursts, with a gap of the order of milliseconds between each burst. The gap between individual pulses in a burst is not long enough for the precipitator to recover if a spark occurs, therefore each pulse is slightly smaller than the one before. The gap between the bursts of pulses is of the same order of magnitude as the time taken for an ion to cross the precipitator. The MPC increased ω_k for dusts whose resistivity exceeded about 10^{11} Ω m. The improvement increased, with dust resistivity reaching a factor of 2.5 for dusts with a resistivity of 10^{13} Ω m. This is approximately the same improvement as given by the Research Cottrell design.

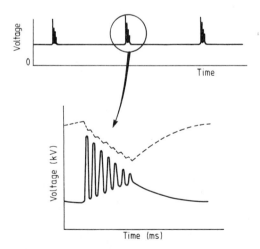

Figure 4.6 Pulse energisation for electrostatic precipitation. The multipulse concept (MPC) (from Porle 1985).

It is generally agreed that short pulses give the best improvement in efficiency and that there should be a long time between pulses, i.e. 50–100 ms is required for back-ionisation to disappear once it has begun.

4.2.10 The effect of precipitator geometry

In a cylindrical precipitator all gas and dust must pass through the treatment zone, whereas with a duct geometry, which has banks of plates with wires between them, there is always a small amount of sneakage round the top and bottom of the plates. However, large-scale precipitators are invariably designed with parallel plates and wires as in this way it is possible to have a much larger active volume in the same space and therefore to minimise costs. Numerous designs of electrode have been treated, including straight or twisted wires, and barbed or saw tooth geometries. No preference for one design rather than another has emerged from the tests, and the differences between the geometries are much reduced as the electrode becomes coated with dust during operation. It appears that wires with substantial barbs, or a saw tooth construction, remain cleaner and produce a discharge at regular intervals down the electrode, but a plain wire electrode, once it is coated with dust, produces a uniform glow down its entire length, and the advantages of the pointed electrode are reduced. In many cases the design of the electrode is defined by mechanical considerations rather than by electrical performance.

In 1956 Heinrich noticed that particle migration velocities were higher in precipitators designed with a duct width of 350 mm rather than the conventional 250 mm (Heinrich 1979). Tests were therefore carried out in which every other plate in a wire plate precipitator was removed and the discharge electrodes were rearranged. In this way the spacing was doubled and the applied voltage could be doubled for the same discharge current. The precipitator efficiency remained unchanged or even slightly increased although the Deutsch equation would predict a drop in efficiency due to the smaller collecting area. There appeared to be an increase in the effective migration velocity which was proportional to the electrode spacing. There have been several suggestions for the cause of this phenomenon, including the effect of different dust concentration gradients on turbulent diffusion, and the influence of the higher electric fields due to the large space charge cloud.

In order to take full advantage of the wider electrode spacing it is also necessary to double the discharge electrode spacing (Darby 1982). (The spacing between discharge wires in a wire plate precipitator should not be less than half the plate-to-plate spacing.) Economically, the savings made by reducing the collecting area and number of wires must be balanced against the increased costs and greater insulation difficulties associated with doubling the voltage.

4.2.11 Two-stage precipitators

Two-stage precipitators have been proposed as a means of overcoming the problem of back-ionisation for high-resistivity ashes. In the first, precharger stage, particles are charged, but not allowed to collect on the earthed electrode. In the second stage there is an applied field but no corona discharge, so the current flowing through the layer is minimised. Back-ionisation is therefore minimised in both sections. The design of prechargers is discussed in §4.6.4.

Two-stage precipitators have two problems:

(i) There is a limit to the amount of charge which can be applied to a dust cloud because the electric field due to the cloud cannot exceed the breakdown strength of the gas. In a two-stage system charge is lost as soon as the particles leave the precharger and for a large system this limitation can be severe.

(ii) Back-ionisation can still occur in the collector section, even without a corona current flowing through the layer, owing to the charge carried by the dust itself (Sampuran-Singh *et al* 1979). With large-scale systems two-stage precipitators have not given sufficient improvements to warrant the additional cost.

4.2.12 Small precipitators

Small-scale precipitators are used to remove cigarette smoke from hotels and as dust filters in air conditioning units. A fan draws air from the room into a charging zone and particles are removed by electrostatic forces as before. Small units do not usually have automatically cleaning collector electrodes, and are frequently designed as two-stage systems, with the collecting section sliding out as a replaceable module. Thus room precipitators frequently consist of a short charging section with a row of wires between parallel plates, and a rather longer collector section, consisting of parallel plates with alternate plates connected to earth and to a high voltage.

Room precipitators remove particulates but leave odours in the air stream, thus the fog from cigarette smoke is removed but not the smell. It is also necessary to ensure that they do not create ozone. The production of ozone can be reduced by using a positive corona discharge, however, even with this precaution the amount of ozone released can exceed the threshold limit value if the precipitator is to be used in an unventilated area. The ozone and odours can be removed by a carbon filter in the output duct.

It has recently been suggested that the collection efficiency of small two-stage precipitators can be significantly improved by placing an earthed grid between the two stages (Cucu and Lippold 1985) (figure 4.7). The improvement was attributed to three factors: (i) increased ionisation between the charging electrodes and the grid, (ii) an additional electric field between the

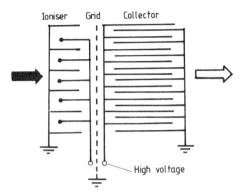

Figure 4.7 A two-stage electrostatic precipitator (from Cucu and Lippold 1985).

ionising section and the collecting section, (iii) the grid itself acting as an additional collector.

Recently a precipitator has been designed which will collect carbon soot from diesel engines. Carbon is particularly difficult to collect in a precipitator because of its very small particle size and high electrical conductivity (Masuda and Moon 1983). The soot precipitator has three stages, a precharger, which applies a high electrostatic charge to the particles, a precoagulator, in which the soot is agglomerated to reach a size of about 1 μm which can be collected by the precipitator, and a collector. The precoagulator consists of closely spaced parallel planes, on which the dust is first deposited then removed. The efficiency of the full system increased from 75 % without a precoagulator to 95 % with a precoagulator. Faulkner *et al* (1979) have also observed that a precipitator collecting diesel soot first coagulates it, and they also found that a second collector stage was required.

4.3 ELECTRON BEAM DESULPHURISATION AND DENITRISATION

Electrostatic precipitators do not collect gaseous pollutants. However it has been shown that direct irradiation of flue gases by a high-energy electron beam converts SO_x and NO_x pollutants into an aerosol which can easily be removed (Kawai and Aoki 1972, Machi and Kawai 1973). 80–90 % efficiency can be achieved with short irradiation times (0.1–1.0 s). The presence of the SO_2 is found to enhance the removal of NO_x and the addition of ammonia is also beneficial. The reaction products are $(NH_4)_2SO_4$ and NH_4NO_3, which are easy to remove and may be used as a fertiliser. The system was originally envisaged as a two-stage process with an irradiation chamber and an electrostatic precipitator but Masuda *et al* (1976) have shown that a field can be applied within the irradiation chamber. This not only allows the whole process to take place in a single vessel but also enhances the speed of desulphurisation and denitrisation. The main problem with the process is the high initial cost of the electron beam source, but in Japan the system is seen as economically promising, and two pilot scale plants have been constructed, one for heavy oil combustion gases at the central laboratory of the Ebara Company and the other for exhaust gases from a sintering furnace of the Nippon Steel Corporation.

4.4 ELECTROSTATICALLY ENHANCED CYCLONE SEPARATORS

Cyclone separators provide a reasonably effective means of removing dust particles exceeding 5 μm in diameter from a gas stream, but their efficiency falls off rapidly as the particle size of the dust decreases. Significant improvements in efficiency have been reported with an electrostatically enhanced cyclone. For example, Petroll and Langhammer (1962) demonstrated an

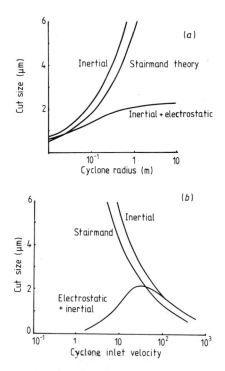

Figure 4.8 Predicted cut size of cyclone, with and without electrostatics, as a function of (*a*), cyclone radius; (*b*), cyclone inlet velocity (from Dietz 1982).

improvement in performance in a conventional reverse-flow cyclone when an electrostatic field was added, and achieved a reduction in penetration of 28 %. Reif (1977) and Thibodeaux *et al* (1976) showed a similar improvement with an axial-flow cyclone. Even in the absence of an applied field electrostatic charges on the particles enhance cyclone efficiency (Giles 1979).

A theoretical model of an electrostatically enhanced cyclone has been developed by Dietz (1982). The cyclone cut sizes (defined as the particle size for which 50 % of the particles are collected), with and without electrostatic enhancement, predicted by this model are shown in figure 4.8. It can be seen that, for high gas velocities, the cut point was not changed by the presence of the electrostatic force, but at low gas velocities a substantial improvement was predicted. The electrostatic forces do not give a better cut point than would be achieved by running the device at high velocities, but they do have

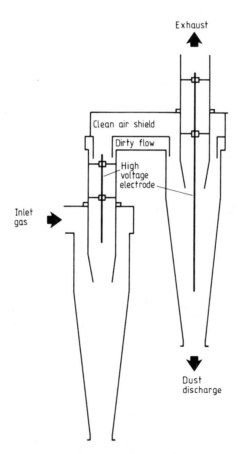

Figure 4.9 Schematic diagram of an electrocyclone (from Boericke *et al* 1982).

the advantage that the electrostatic force does not fall off as the size of the cyclone is increased therefore large electrocyclones can be as effective as small ones.

An electrocyclone with a double inlet, which provides a clean air sheath between the inlet for dusty gas and the outlet for clean gas, is shown in figure 4.9. The performance of this device was described by Boericke *et al* (1982). They suggest that the maximum size of an electrocyclone will be limited by space charge considerations to 1.5–1.8 m and that corona quenching will limit inlet dust loadings to 4.5 g m^{-3}.

Electrocyclones have the inherent difficulty that aerodynamic collection requires as high a gas velocity as possible and electrostatic collection requires low gas velocities. It is therefore not possible to optimise the device for both collection mechanisms simultaneously.

4.5 ELECTROSTATIC SCRUBBERS AND GRANULAR BED FILTERS

4.5.1 Introduction

Scrubbers, fixed- and moving-bed filters and fabric filters all collect small pollutant particles on larger spheres or cylinders and the fundamental theory of the collection of small particles on larger ones is relevant to all of these devices.

If both the pollutant particles and the collector particles are uncharged, the pollutant may be collected by four processes (Davies 1966). These are gravity, interception, inertial impaction and Brownian diffusion. In the particle size range relevant to pollution control (0.1–10 μm) the most important

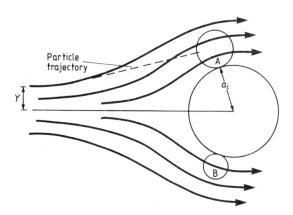

Figure 4.10 Collection by inertial impaction (particle A) and interception (particle B).

collection processes are inertial impaction and Brownian diffusion (Clift *et al* 1981, Alexander 1978). Inertial impaction is illustrated in figure 4.10. An inertialess particle is carried by the air stream round the collector and will only be collected if the streamline passes close enough to the collector for the particle to contact it. A particle with inertia will fail to be diverted and will collide with the collector. Collection by Brownian diffusion occurs when the thermal motion of fine particles brings them into contact with the collector. Collection as a result of this mechanism increases as the diffusivity increases, i.e., as the particle size decreases. In the absence of electrostatic forces Brownian diffusion dominates for very fine pollutants and inertial impaction for larger particles. Theories of the four processes are reviewed by Clift (1983).

When the particle and/or the collector is charged there are five different electrostatic forces of attraction (Ranz and Wong 1952). These are:

(i) the Coulomb attraction between a charged particle and an oppositely charged collector;

(ii) the dipole attraction between a charged particle and the dipole that this charge induces on the collector;

(iii) the dipole attraction between the charged collector and the dipole induced upon the particle;

(iv) the space charge repulsion of the cloud of charged particles;

(v) the attraction between the charged particle and the earthed collector, which carries an image charge, induced by the space charge of the surrounding aerosol.

Dimensionless groups governing these processes have been identified by Kraemer and Johnstone (1955).

If an electric field is applied so that the collector particles, although uncharged, are polarised, two more forces must be added. These are:

(vi) the force of attraction due to the distortion of the electric field by the presence of the particle (this is Pauthenier charging as described in §2.2);

(vii) the dipole attraction owing to the interaction between the dipole induced on the aerosol particle by the applied field and the non-uniform electric field in the vicinity of the collector. This is the dielectrophoretic effect discussed in Chapter 5.

The theory of filtration by particles or fibres involves evaluating the relative importance of the electrical and mechanical collection processes for a single collector, estimating how the processes combine (when a single dominating force cannot be identified), then finding a model for the efficiency of a large number of collector particles in terms of the single collector efficiency. At all stages of this process a large number of approximations must be made and accurate theoretical prediction of the efficiency of electrostatically enhanced particle collection techniques is not yet possible. The different collection techniques are therefore best evaluated experimentally, rather than theoretically, although for some devices surprisingly simple models have proved to be satisfactory.

An order of magnitude calculation can be carried out to identify which mechanisms, mechanical or electrical, are likely to have to be considered in any situation. For example, following Bertinat (1980), we can compare the inertial and electrostatic forces in the absence of an applied field. In the following analysis the subscript 'c' refers to a collector sphere and 'p' to a pollutant particle.

A sphere of radius a_c and charge q_c moving with a velocity u through a dust-laden gas imparts an acceleration to the gas in pushing it aside. This will be of the order of u^2/a_c. A particle of mass m_p, which is in the dust stream, therefore requires a force of the order of $m_p u^2/a_c$ to keep it in the gas stream as it is diverted round the particle. This can be seen as an inertial force pulling the dust particle towards the collecting sphere:

$$F_i \simeq m_p u^2/a_c = 4\pi a_p^3 D_p u^2/3a_c. \tag{4.21}$$

Thus the force due to inertial impaction is proportional to the cube of the particle radius and decreases rapidly as the particle size decreases. The Coulomb force F_e between two charged particles is given by

$$F_e = q_c q_p/4\pi\varepsilon_0 r^2 \tag{4.22}$$

where r is the distance between them. Assuming the collector particle is a liquid droplet charged to the Rayleigh limit (see §2.5.10) then

$$q_c = 8\pi(\gamma\varepsilon_0 a_c^3)^{1/2}. \tag{4.23}$$

For water this gives

$$q_c = 20 \times 10^{-6} a_c^{3/2}.$$

Assuming the pollutant particle is charged to the Gaussian limit:

$$q_p = 4\pi\varepsilon_0 a_p^2 E_b$$

where E_b is the breakdown field of air (3×10^6 V m^{-1}) and

$$F_e = \frac{60 a_c^{3/2} a_p^2}{r^2}. \tag{4.24}$$

If both particles are charged to the Gaussian limit

$$F_e = \frac{4\pi\varepsilon_0 a_p^2 a_c^2 E_b^2}{r^2}. \tag{4.25}$$

If the pollutant particle is uncharged there is still a force of attraction to the sphere, due to the dipole induced on the pollutant particle by the field of the charged collector. This dipole force is given by

$$F_d = p(dE_c/dr) \tag{4.26}$$

where p is the dipole moment of the dust particle induced by the field due to the collector E_c.

For a conducting particle in air

$$p = \pi a_p^3 \varepsilon_0 E_c \qquad \text{(see §7.5.4)} \qquad (4.27)$$

and

$$E_c = q_c/4\pi\varepsilon_0 r^2.$$

and therefore

$$F_d = \frac{-2q_c a_p^3 E_c}{r^3} = \frac{8a_c^3 a_p^3 \pi \gamma}{r^5}. \qquad (4.28)$$

If the gas velocity is assumed to be 1 m s^{-1} and the density of the pollutant particle is $3 \times 10^3 \text{ kg m}^{-3}$ the force for inertial impaction, given by equation (4.21), is

$$F_i \simeq \frac{1.2 \times 10^4 a_p^3}{a_c}.$$

The three forces F_i, F_e and F_d have a different dependence on the distance between the particles, therefore it is not possible to combine them by simple addition, and computer techniques must be used when a dominant force cannot be identified. For a particle at the surface of the collector $r = a_c$:

$$F_e/F_d = 15a_c^{3/2}/2a_p$$
$$F_e/F_i = 10^{-2}a_c^{1/2}/2a_p$$
$$F_d/F_i = 6 \times 10^{-4}/a_c.$$

For a dust particle of 1 μm in diameter and a collector of 200 μm these ratios are 15 : 100 : 6. For a 0.2 μm particle the ratios are 75 : 500 : 6.

Similar calculations can be carried out to identify the dominant force in other situations, e.g. in the presence of an electric field. Further calculations of single sphere efficiencies for different mechanisms and combinations of mechanisms are given in the Appendix to this chapter.

4.5.2 The charged droplet scrubber

In a conventional scrubber, water droplets are sprayed through a polluted gas stream and particles are collected by inertial impaction. The collection efficiency for fine pollutant particles is poor as these tend to follow the gas streamlines round the collector particles. The collection of micron and submicron particles is greatly improved by charging the pollutant and the droplets to opposite polarities and some improvement is still obtained if only the collector particles are charged. Direct visual observation has shown that wettable particles are collected inside the droplets and unwettable particles are held on the surface, in some cases dendrites build up on the droplet surface (Sumuyoshilani *et al* 1984).

The electrostatic spray scrubber was first patented by Penney in 1944. Water droplets were charged by induction or by ions from a corona discharge, and pollutant particles were charged to the opposite polarity by a corona discharge. With a water loading of 5 gallons per 1000 ft³ of gas, the addition of electrostatic forces increased efficiency from 13.8 to 44.8 %. Improved figures have been reported as time has progressed and many new patents have been granted. For example, Pilat *et al* (1974) tested a 140 ft³ h⁻¹, two-chamber scrubber with a 7 s residence time, illustrated in figure 4.11. The improvement in efficiency obtained by charging the droplets

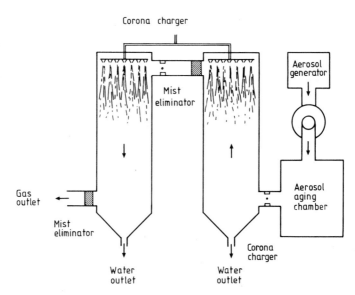

Figure 4.11 Schematic diagram of an electrostatic droplet spray scrubber (after Pilat *et al* 1974).

and the particles to opposite polarities is shown in figure 4.12. The overall particle collection efficiency for 1.05 μm dioctylphthalate particles, increased from 68.8 to 93.6 % when the particles were charged. The collection efficiency of 0.3 μm particles increased from 35 to 87 %. More recent work with scrubbers of similar design which are now commercially available quote even better results (Allen 1982).

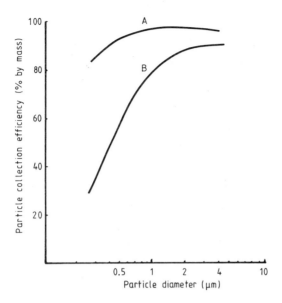

Figure 4.12 Particle collection efficiency of an electrostatic spray scrubber as a function of particle size (after Pilat *et al* 1974). A, droplets and particles charged oppositely; B, no charge.

In an alternative design, based on an ioniser patented by Schwab and Goodson (1978), the high-voltage electrode is situated in the throat of a venturi (figure 4.13). The high gas velocity in the throat allows intense electric fields to be applied which are up to three times the normal arc-over value. Droplets of the opposite charge to the particles are produced downstream by atomisation in the field between the electrode and the earthed casing. The collection efficiency for 0.5 μm TiO$_2$ particles typically improved from 80 %, without charging, to between 91 and 95 % with charging (Allen 1982). A number of other commercial designs are discussed by Allen, and an evaluation of four particle collection devices has been carried out by Calvert *et al* (1978).

Electrostatic collection is greatest for low relative velocities and for small drops and particles whereas inertial impaction requires the opposite conditions. It is therefore not possible to optimise collection by both mechanisms simultaneously. The electrostatic requirement for both small droplets and low velocities is also difficult to attain in practice. The improvement due to electrostatics, quoted above, must therefore take into account that the design of the scrubber was not the optimum for purely mechanical collection. The value of electrostatics lies in greatly improved efficiency of collection for the particles of the order 0.1 to 1 μm, where the collection efficiency due to inertial impaction is low, but Brownian diffusion does not yet dominate mechanical collection processes.

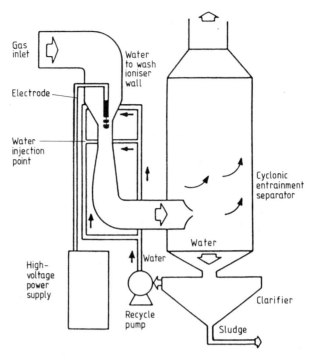

Figure 4.13 Electrostatic scrubber (after Schwab and Goodson 1978).

Two slightly different approaches to the theory of droplet scrubbers appear in the literature. Bertinat (1980) shows that if both the collector and the particle are charged the Coulomb force dominates the collection processes. He then assumes that in a time dt a single droplet, moving with velocity u relative to the gas stream, sweeps clean a volume dv given by

$$dv = \pi y^2 u \, dt. \tag{4.29}$$

If there are n_p particles per cubic metre, the number of particles collected is $n_p\pi y^2 u \, dt$ and the rate of collection of particles is

$$G = n_p\pi y^2 u \tag{4.30}$$

where y is the initial offset from the collector centre of a particle which has just been collected and is given in the Appendix to this chapter by equation (A5), namely

$$y^2 = \frac{4(q_c q_p)C}{(6\pi\eta a_p)(4\pi\varepsilon_0)u}. \tag{4.31}$$

Thus in a time dt, n_c m^{-3} droplets of gas, collect $n_c n_p\pi y^2 u \, dt$ m^{-3} particles of gas, i.e. the fractional change in concentration is

$$dc/c = -n_c \pi y^2 u \, dt.$$

Therefore

$$c_{out}/c_{in} = 1 - \xi = \exp(-\langle\!\langle n_c \pi y^2 u \rangle\!\rangle t) \tag{4.32}$$

where $\langle\!\langle\rangle\!\rangle$ denotes an average over all volume elements of the scrubber, ξ is the collection efficiency and t is the residence time in the scrubber.

Melcher *et al* (1977) assume that flow in a scrubber is so turbulent that it is not reasonable to consider particles as if they were stationary and swept up by moving droplets. They suggest that particles will be brought into the vicinity of the droplets by the turbulent motion of the gas and will be collected if, on arrival, they find an inwardly directed electric field. This will depend on the amount of charge already collected by the droplet compared with its saturation charge. According to this model a collector particle with charge q_c collects particles at a rate, G, which depends on the droplet's charge compared with its maximum saturation charge $q_{c\,max}$:

$$G = 3\pi a_c^2 E n_p b_p (1 - |q_c/q_{c\,max}|)^2. \tag{4.33}$$

If substitutions are made for $q_{c\,max} = 12\pi\varepsilon_0 E a_c^2$ and $b = q_p/6\pi\eta a_p$ (see equations (A1) and (A3)), it can be seen that equations (4.30) and (4.33) are similar in form but Bertinat's theory contains the relative velocity of the droplets in the gas stream, and Melcher has a term $(q_{c\,max} - q_c)^2/q_{c\,max}$ instead of q_c.

Practical design of electrostatic scrubbers is normally dictated not by a consideration of capture efficiencies of individual particles, but by two major theoretical limitations of the devices, self-precipitation and the Gaussian limit on the maximum charge which can be carried by a cloud of particles.

Self-precipitation is the collection of the droplets on the walls of the scrubber due to the force associated with the space charge field of the droplets themselves. The importance of self-precipitation can be evaluated by considering a characteristic time for precipitation of the droplets in comparison with a characteristic time for the collection of particles on the droplets (Melcher *et al* 1977).

The electric field at the wall of a cylindrical scrubber of radius R, filled with droplets of charge q_c, is given by Gauss's law:

$$E(2\pi R) = n_c \pi R^2 q_c / \varepsilon_0$$

$$E = nq_c R / 2\varepsilon_0.$$

The field can be written in terms of the collector velocity u_c and its mobility b_c:

$$E = u_c/b_c$$

i.e.

$$u_c = R/t = n_c q_c R b_c / 2\varepsilon_0.$$

Thus the characteristic time for a droplet to be precipitated out is given by

$$t = \varepsilon_0 / n q_c b_c. \tag{4.34}$$

The time, t', for a particle to be collected is found by assuming that the particle is a distance x from a droplet with charge q_c, i.e. the field due to the droplet charge is

$$E = q_c / 4\pi\varepsilon_0 x^2$$

$$u_p = E b_p = x/t'$$

therefore

$$t' = 4\pi\varepsilon_0 x^3 / q_c b_p. \tag{4.35}$$

If the initial spacing between the particle and the drop is taken as half the distance between the drops:

$$(2x)^3 = 1/n$$

$$t' = 2\pi\varepsilon_0 / n_c q_c b_p. \tag{4.36}$$

The mobility of a charged particle is found by equating the electrostatic force to the aerodynamic drag given by the Stokes law modified by the Cunningham correction factor C:

$$qE = 6\pi\eta a u / C$$

$$u/E = b = Cq/6\pi\eta a.$$

Assuming the particle is charged to the Gaussian limit, i.e. $q = 4\pi\varepsilon_0 a^2 E_b$:

$$b = 2C\varepsilon_0 a E / 3\eta.$$

The mobility is proportional to the particle radius, therefore the collector mobility is much greater than the particle mobility and the characteristic time for precipitation of the droplets is shorter than the time required for collection of the particles. This problem may be overcome in a number of ways. Bertinat (1980) suggests that the dust will spend a longer time in a less dense droplet cloud if the scrubber is designed with cross flow rather than counter flow, i.e. the gas flow is arranged to be parallel to the electric field and perpendicular to the droplet stream. Melcher *et al* (1977) propose a design in which the dusty gas makes several passes through the scrubbing region.

The second fundamental limitation in scrubber design is the Gaussian limit to the maximum charge that can be carried by a cloud of charged particles before the field at the outside of the cloud reaches the breakdown limit of air (see §2.1.15). To minimise this field, in a cylindrical geometry, a low droplet density over a long length of tube is required or the scrubber can be divided into sections so there are a number of small spray chambers. The problem of the Gaussian limit may also be overcome by operating with macroscopic charge neutrality, i.e. equal numbers of positive and negative drops (Melcher *et al* 1977). Although the droplets neutralise each other, the characteristic time for neutralisation is similar to the characteristic time for self-precipitation of unipolar drops, and the loss of droplets by the two mechanisms is similar. A scrubber can also operate in a precipitation mode, by giving the dust and droplets the same polarity of charge and using the field due to the charged droplets to repel the particles to the walls. Theoretically this has the same efficiency as a scrubber operated with one polarity of charge on the drops and the other on the particles. The theoretical and measured efficiency of an experimental system operated in the three modes is shown in figure 4.14 (after Melcher *et al* 1977).

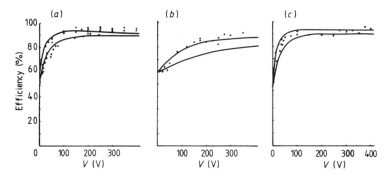

Figure 4.14 Efficiency of collection of particles by charged water droplets as a function of droplet charger voltage for different values of the parameter $Q_R = 6\pi\eta a_c \varepsilon_0 u / L N_0$ where u is the mean gas velocity and L the interaction length: (*a*), charged droplet scrubber, single-polarity droplets; (*b*), charged droplet scrubber, bipolar droplets; (*c*), charged droplet precipitator. Upper curves, $Q_R = 1.27 \times 10^{-14}$, lower curves, $Q_R = 2.03 \times 10^{-14}$ (after Melcher *et al* 1977).

Scrubbers require that pollutant particles should have a longer residence time than precipitators. Therefore, they seldom compete favourably in the removal of purely particulate pollutants. However, where scrubbers are required for other reasons (e.g. to remove gaseous pollutants) electrostatic forces can considerably improve their performance.

4.5.3 Electrostatic granular beds

In granular bed filters the pollutant particles are collected on solid granules. There are three basic types of filter, fixed bed, fluidised bed and moving bed.

In most designs the collector particles are not given a net charge, but an electric field is applied across a bed of granules so that they become polarised. Each then has a positive and a negative region and they can be considered to form miniature electrostatic precipitators. Charged pollutant particles are collected by Coulomb attraction and uncharged particles by dipole attraction.

A review on the state of the art of conventional granular bed dust filtration theory and experiment was given by Tardos, Abauf and Gutfinger in 1978 (Tardos *et al* 1978). Electrostatic effects due to natural charging of the dust particles were shown to be important even in conventional beds, where there is no intentional addition of electrostatic charge. Tardos *et al* reported a marked increase in the collection efficiency of a packed bed as soon as the gas velocity exceeded the minimum fluidisation velocity. The efficiency then remained more or less constant with increasing gas velocity and it was conjectured that this was due to electrostatic effects, with increased electrostatic forces at higher gas velocities counterbalancing the decrease in efficiency due to gas bypassing. Electrostatic effects in conventional fluidised-bed filters are discussed by Tardos *et al* (1979) and Katz and Sears (1969). A review is given by Coury (1983).

A number of tests of electrostatic granular collectors have been caried out. For example, a 100 mm × 100 mm × 200 mm electrostatic fixed bed of alumina spheres 6 mm in diameter has been used to collect fly ash at a loading of between 2.3 and 46 g m^{-3} from flue gas with a velocity in the range of 0.03 and 0.18 m s^{-1} (Self *et al* 1979). The filter efficiency for 1 μm particles was increased from 20 to 80 % by the application of an electric field of 4×10^5 V m^{-1} across the bed, provided that the inlet dust was charged.

Melcher and co-workers (Johnson and Melcher 1975, Zahedi and Melcher 1976, 1977, Melcher and Rhoads 1981) investigated the collection of dioctylphthalate particles 0.4 to 0.7 μm in diameter in packed and fluidised beds of sand with DC and AC fields applied parallel and perpendicular to the air flow. The sand was mixed with air at 50–90 % relative humidity, and had an electrical relaxation time of 10^{-1}–10^{-3} s. The gas velocity was of the order of 2 m s^{-1} and the applied field typically less than 5×10^5 V m^{-1}. They obtained efficiencies exceeding 90 % with a gas residence time less than 50 ms and a pressure drop of 1 kPa. They found reasonable agreement with the 'plug flow' theoretical model, discussed below. Figure 4.15 shows the collection efficiency as a function of bed parameters compared with Zahedi and Melcher's theoretical model. In co-flow fluidised beds (where the electric field is applied parallel to the gas flow) the electrical screens break up gas bubbles but in cross flow beds the bed does not expand uniformly as the fluidisation velocity increases and there is some bypassing due to bubbling. This causes a decrease in efficiency which, if large vertical channels form, may be as much as 30 % (Zahedi and Melcher 1977).

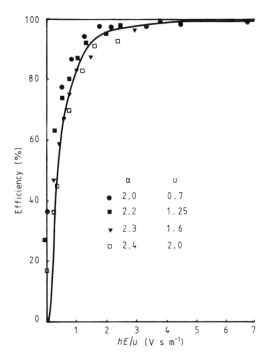

Figure 4.15 Collection efficiency of an electrostatic fluidised bed for different packing density and gas velocity (h is the bed height, E is the electric field, u is the free stream gas velocity). Bed height is 80 mm. α is a measure of the packing density of the bed such that αa is the mean distance between the centres of bed particles of radius a (after Zahedi and Melcher 1976).

The feasibility of operating an electrofluidised bed with 60 Hz AC energisation was demonstrated by Alexander and Melcher (1977). Provided the frequency of energisation was below a critical cut-off frequency, the collection was not reduced below its DC value. Theory and experiment showed that 60 Hz lay in this low-frequency region.

Fixed- and fluid-bed filters are batch systems which must be stopped when an excessive cake has built up, to remove the granules for cleaning. In moving-bed filters the granules are continuously removed and replenished, typical methods by which this may be achieved are illustrated in figure 4.16. A simple commercial, electrostatic moving-bed filter is shown in figure 4.17. The granules move downwards at a velocity of 2–3 m h^{-1} between concentric louvred cylindrical tubes. An electrostatic grid, in the form of a cage, is located within the granular medium and a field is applied between the grid and the tubes. The movement of the pea-sized granules against the louvres prevents the formation of a dust cake. The particle-laden granules are

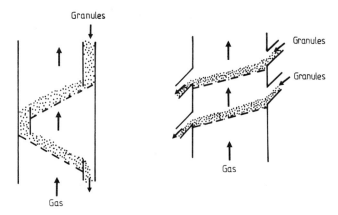

Figure 4.16 Dry-plate scrubbers with moving granules.

continuously removed from the bottom of the system and are transported pneumatically up a vertical pipe. This action separates the particles from the granules which are recycled to the top of the scrubber. A two-stage system is illustrated in figure 4.18. Here the coarse particles are collected in the bottom stage, which incorporates a fast face screen design. This is a perforated annular screen a small distance inside the louvres. Granules are fed

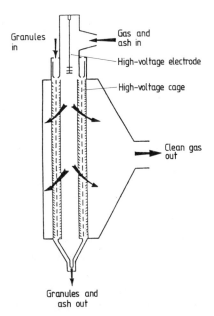

Figure 4.17 Electrostatic granular bed filter EFB Inc/GE (after Parquet 1982, General Electric Co 1981).

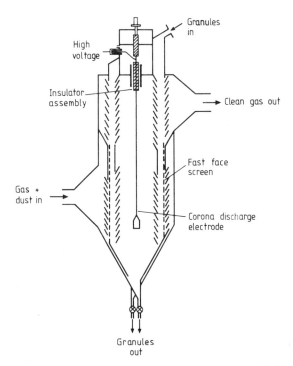

Figure 4.18 Electrostatic granular bed (after Presser and Alexander 1982, General Electric Co 1981).

down both sides of this screen with the media adjacent to the front face moving faster than that in the bulk of the bed. This helps to eliminate plugging at the front face. The partially clean gas flows up the centre of the unit, where the fine particles are charged. They enter the second stage which has a central grid providing an electrostatic field. The dust particles are collected on the granular filter medium which moves downwards and is removed for cleaning. Collection efficiencies in excess of 99 % have been reported with this design.

Electrostatic moving-bed filters have been in use in industry for five different applications since 1981. Figure 4.19 shows the particle capture efficiency at two different grid voltages in a pilot scale system collecting KCl fumes with 80 % of particles in the submicron range. The collection efficiency is lower for smaller particles, but electrostatic enhancement is substantial (Parquet 1982). Electrostatic granular beds have been considered for cleaning hot gases from pressurised fluidised-bed combustors. A detailed evaluation has been carried out considering both the hot and cold operation of moving-bed systems (General Electric Company 1981). At high temperatures it is not possible to incorporate a high-voltage electrode in the granular

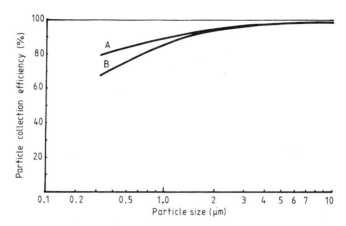

Figure 4.19 Experimental collection efficiency as a function of grid voltage (curve A, 60 kV; curve B, 40 kV) in a granular bed filter (from Parquet 1982).

medium because of conduction losses. However, electrostatic charging of the dusty gas is still effective.

Figure 4.20 illustrates the operation of an electrostatic dry-plate scrubber (Parker *et al* 1981). The dirty gas is charged in a corona discharge before it enters the scrubber. The electric field between the two grids either polarises the granules, or charges them by induction (depending on whether they are insulating or conducting). The device has been operated in all four possible modes, i.e. uncharged particles and neutral collectors, uncharged particles and polarised collectors, charged particles and neutral collectors and charged particles and polarised collectors. The best collection efficiency was

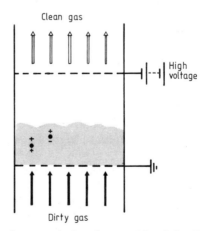

Figure 4.20 An electrostatic dry-plate scrubber (after Parker *et al* 1981).

obtained with polarised collectors and charged particles and the worst from unpolarised collectors and uncharged particles. In bench scale tests the collection efficiency for particles less than 5 μm in diameter ranged from 97.9 to 98.8 %. This design has the advantage that only one electrode is in contact with the granular bed, therefore it is possible to collect conducting pollutants without the high power loss which normally occurs when a conducting path forms between the electrodes.

In a granular bed the collector particles are close together and it is not reasonable to ignore the interaction between neighbouring granules as in the theoretical treatment of the droplet scrubber. A unit cell approach to the theoretical analysis of the collection process was first proposed by Happel (1958) and Kuwabara (1959). The bed of granules is modelled as an assemblage of unit cells each comprising a granule and the surrounding gas. The cell is assumed to be spherical and its radius R is related to the void fraction of the bed α and the granule radius a_c by the equation

$$R = a_c(1 - \alpha)^{-1/3}. \tag{4.37}$$

The single-cell efficiency is defined as the ratio of the number of particles collected by the granules, to the number of particles entering the unit cell. The relative importance of inertia, interception, gravity, diffusion and electrostatics for collection at low Reynolds numbers, of particles between 0.1 and 1.0 μm in diameter has been investigated by Snaddon (1982). He identified dimensionless numbers for all the processes and plotted the single-cell efficiency as a function of Stokes's number for each process. He concluded that, when conditions allowed the application of fields greater than 10^5 V m^{-1}, forces owing to the applied field dominated collection. The improvement in performance due to electrostatics was most significant for particles in the size range 0.1 to 1.0 μm, between the inertia- and diffusion-dominated regions.

When the dust is charged, but no external electric field is applied, the only electrostatic force of attraction is the image force. This still gives a significant improvement in the collection efficiency compared with the case with no charging, but the electrostatic forces do not dominate to the extent that other mechanical mechanisms can be ignored. In particular, diffusion plays an increasingly important role at smaller particle sizes.

Kallio and Dietz (1981) and Coury (1983) have analysed the particle trajectories using the unit cell approach and obtained figures for combined inertial impaction and electrostatic forces. Malcher *et al* (1984) propose a simple model in which mechanical and electrostatic collection are treated independently and the efficiency of the bed is given by

$$\xi = 1 - \exp[\alpha + \Delta\alpha + (k - 1)(\beta + \Delta\beta)]$$

where the filter consists of k close-packed layers and α is the filtration coefficient of the outer two layers and β of an internal layer. $\Delta\alpha$ and $\Delta\beta$ are the additions due to electrostatic enhancement. Their experimental results justify the validity of presenting data in this way and they evaluate the filtration coefficients of an experimental bed. In their work electrostatic enhancement was greatest for particles in an intermediate size range of 20–40 μm than for particles of 5–20 or greater than 60 μm, i.e. the particles collected were much larger than in most of the other studies.

An alternative approach to the theory of filtration by packed beds uses the constricted-tube model (Payatakes *et al* 1973). In this model, flow channels through the bed are assumed to be pores with entrance and exit diameters larger than the diameters at their centres. The model appears to be more realistic than the single-cell approach under conditions where diffusion dominates but calculations of inertial impaction are sensitive to the shape assumed for the tube wall. This model has not been extended to include electrostatic effects.

There are several different approaches to obtaining an estimate of the total bed efficiency from the single-particle or single-cell efficiency. In the plug flow model, the collection efficiency, ξ, of a fluidised bed is expressed in terms of the single-particle collection rate, G, the unfluidised-bed height, L_0, the superficial gas velocity, u, and the radius of the collector particle, a_c (Zahedi and Melcher 1976):

$$\xi = 1 - \exp\left(-\frac{GL_0}{8nua_c^3}\right). \tag{4.38}$$

The rate of collection of particles is given by

$$G = 3c\pi a_c^2 b_p n_p E \tag{4.39}$$

where b and n are the mobility and number density of the pollutant particles. This efficiency equation has been verified for co-flow, where the electrical screens ensure that conditions approximate to the theory, but is inadequate for beds where bubbles form.

Snaddon suggests an equation relating bed efficiency ξ_{bed} to cell efficiency ξ_{cell}:

$$\xi_{bed} = 1 - \exp[(3\xi_{cell}L_0)/4(1-\alpha)^{2/3}a_c]. \tag{4.40}$$

Thambimuthu *et al* (1978) give

$$\xi_{bed} = 1 - f' \exp[3\xi_{cell}(1-\alpha)L_0/2a_c] \tag{4.41}$$

where f' is a factor which accounts for anomalous filtration at the entry and exit of the bed. With the constricted-tube approach, where the bed is considered to be a series of units of length l and efficiency ξ_u:

$$\xi_{bed} = 1 - \exp\{L_0[\ln(1-\xi_u)]/l\}. \tag{4.42}$$

All these equations have an exponential dependence on the bed height but have different dependences on the other factors, such as the void fraction of the bed.

The above theories apply to the initial stages of filtration, when the collector particles are clean. As dust accumulates, the structure and operation of the bed changes. In some applications the pollutant collects as a cake on the upstream surface of the filter. The cake then essentially forms a fixed-bed filter in addition to the normal granules. The formation and structure of dust cakes has been studied by Coury (1983).

At present the theory of granular bed filtration is not sufficiently developed to be able to predict performance and evaluation of the technique must rest on experimental results.

4.6 ELECTROSTATICALLY ENHANCED FABRIC FILTERS

4.6.1 Introduction

When a dust-laden gas flows past a single fibre, particles are captured, first on the fibre, then on the dust itself, and dendrites build up. In the presence of an electrostatic field the rate at which particles accumulate is greatly increased and the dendrites form in straight chains rather than the irregular shapes formed in the absence of electrostatic fields. The efficiency of collection by a single fibre can increase by a factor of twenty when electrostatic forces are present (Wang *et al* 1980).

The theory of particle collection by clean single cylinders was considered by Nielson and Hill (1976a,b) and Nielson (1978a,b). More recently the same authors have developed a two-dimensional theory for dendritic deposition of inertialess particles on single fibres in the presence of electrostatic forces (Nielson and Hill 1980). This has been extended to a three-dimensional model by Auzerais *et al* (1983). The most frequently used model for combining the effects of the individual fibres to describe fabric performance is the Kuwabara model, which is also used to describe the performance of granular beds (Kuwabara 1959), but some aspects of this theory have been questioned by Henry and Airman (1981, 1982), and models are still being developed. In an operating filter, the dust cake which builds up in and on the fabric surface plays a major role in the filtration process and the efficiency of individual fibres is of only minor relevance to the overall efficiency.

The collection efficiency of a fabric filter is higher than for most other pollution control systems and improved efficiency is required only for a few particularly fine and toxic materials. However, the high efficiency of a fabric filter is achieved at the expense of a high-pressure drop across the filter medium; and in most applications it would be useful to be able to reduce this so that higher gas flows could be used and the devices could be made smaller. Electrostatic forces improve both the collection efficiency of fine particles and the way the dust cake builds up, and considerable reductions in the pressure drop have been reported in electrostatically assisted filters. The improved collection efficiency can also be used to allow a less dense fabric to be chosen, for a required collection efficiency. This also reduces the pressure drop.

Three different techniques of electrostatic enhancement of fabric filters can be identified:

(i) The fibre material can be chosen to provide electrostatic forces.

(ii) Charging electrodes can be embedded in filter bags.

(iii) The dust entering the filter can be given an electrostatic charge in a precharger.

4.6.2 Electrostatic fabrics

The earliest use of special fabrics, which produced electrostatic effects to enhance filtration, was in the Hanson filter used in respirators. The filter is made of wool, dusted with resin particles. Friction between the wool and the resin charges the two materials to opposite polarities and the efficiency of the filter is significantly increased.

Permanent electrostatic charges can be built into fibres by using an electret material. Electrets are the electrical counterparts of magnets, i.e. they are dielectrics which carry a strong inbuilt positive and negative charge. Electret films have been available for some years, but fibres are a relatively recent development. They are manufactured by producing a thin extruded film (usually a polyolefin such as PVDF) which is heated and stretched, before being charged positive and negative on opposite faces. When the film is cooled, this charge is frozen in. The film is fibrillated and chopped to form a staple, which is made into a non-woven felt, with the individual fibres polarised across their axes. An electret filter provides a relatively long-range force of attraction between the fibres and the pollutant particles, which allows the filter fibres to be further apart for the same collection efficiency. With a conventional fibre, the filter efficiency increases with time as the dust cake builds up and takes part in the filtering process. In an electret filter, the efficiency tends to decrease as the electrostatic forces are reduced by the coating of dust on the fibres. Electret filters are designed so that mechanical capture of particles dominates after a certain amount of dust has accumulated. They have a high collection efficiency, combined with a low pressure drop, and a 25 % higher dust-holding capacity than a conventional filter material of the same efficiency (Van Turnhout *et al* 1980).

Non-woven filter fabrics can be manufactured from electrostatically produced fibres as described in §5.9.4. If the polarity of the spray equipment is periodically reversed it is possible to form a fabric which has alternate layers of positive and negative fibres which give electrostatically enhanced filtration.

Since an electrostatic force holding the dust to the filter makes cleaning difficult, electrostatic fabrics are normally used in replaceable filters such as in face masks and air conditioning units. The use of electrostatic fabrics in dust respirators is discussed by Brown (1980).

4.6.3 Bag electrodes

A number of attempts have been made to improve fabric filtration performance using electrodes embedded in the filter material. The Textile Research Institute in the USA have applied a field parallel to the fabric surface, using a harness wrapped round the outside of a bag, with alternate wires raised to high positive and negative potentials (Greiner *et al* 1981). The aim of this design is to impart sufficient force perpendicular to the gas stream that the particles will be removed from it earlier and be collected further upstream in the fabric. This should reduce blinding due to the penetration of fine particles into the cloth and also reduce penetration. Laboratory and pilot scale tests confirmed that the pressure drop developed across Teflon bags, collecting fly ash, was approximately halved by the addition of the electrodes. With glass fibre bags, the effect was less pronounced. This was attributed to the surface structure of the bag and, in general, electrostatic enhancement was greatest when the filter fabric had a surface layer of loose fibres. In pilot scale studies, the electrostatic forces lead to a reduced pressure drop for a given face velocity, and a lower rate of pressure drop increase, compared with a conventional filter. The electrostatically enhanced filter could be operated at up to about twice the face velocities of the conventional baghouse (VanOsdell *et al* 1985).

Miller *et al* (1978) also chose to apply an electric field perpendicular to the flow, following calculations which showed that this would give the highest enhancement of collection efficiency for both charged and uncharged particles. However, an electric field applied parallel to the flow also improves the collection efficiency, and this design has been used in high-efficiency filter installations in applications such as nuclear plants where very high efficiencies for very fine particles are required (Fielding *et al* 1975, Nelson *et al* 1978). The porosity of the filter cake was enhanced, possibly because the dendrites on the filter surface were aligned preferentially, parallel, rather than perpendicular to the flow.

4.6.4 Particle precharging

The pressure drop across a filter is also reduced if the particles are given an electrostatic charge before they reach the filter. A number of processes may contribute to this. For example, the charge particle may be decelerated as it approaches the charge cake and hence form a more loosely packed layer. A precharged dust produces a more porous dust cake with a much rougher surface than an uncharged dust, but the roughness does not occur if the velocity of filtration is doubled (Iinoya and Mori 1982). Precharging may also cause the adhesion of the particles in the cake to be reduced so that more is removed during cleaning (Chudleigh 1982). Helstrom *et al* (1985) have recently shown from pilot scale tests that a substantial proportion of the reduced pressure drop, when an electrostatic precharger was in use, occurred because charged dust was precipitated out as it entered the baghouse and less dust was deposited on the bag. They showed that the electric field due to a typical charged dust cloud was easily large enough to produce this self-precipitation in the baghouse.

The same designs of electrostatic precharger are used both in two-stage precipitators and in electrostatically augmented fabric filters. They are usually designed so that dust does not collect significantly in the precharger. This is important for two reasons:

(i) the cost of having a dust removal system for the precharger is high;
(ii) if the dust is resistive, back-ionisation on the collector will reduce the charging efficiency.

In any two-stage device, the maximum charge that can be usefully applied to the dust is limited by the maximum charge that can be carried along the duct from the precharger. This is fixed by the Gaussian limit, i.e. the maximum electric field that can be tolerated without breakdown. The maximum charge per unit volume, in a cylindrical duct of radius R, was calculated in §2.1.15 and is given by

$$Q = 2E_b\varepsilon_0/R. \tag{4.43}$$

The charge density therefore decreases as the duct radius increases. This can provide a severe limitation in large-scale installations unless the duct is divided into a number of units of smaller radius.

(a) *Cooled-electrode precharger*
A precharger is usually designed to produce a high charge density within a short residence time. The maximum charge which can be applied to a single spherical particle of radius a by a corona discharge is

$$q_{max} = 4\pi\varepsilon_0 pEa^2$$

and the residence time required for charging (the time taken for a particle to reach half of its charge) is given by

$$\tau = 4\varepsilon_0 E/J \quad \text{(equation (2.16))}.$$

The current density, J, in a corona discharge is proportional to the square of the applied electric field, E^2, therefore high fields and current densities are required to give short charging times. However, a high current density will produce a high potential drop across any deposited dust layer which collects on the earthed electrode and back-ionisation becomes a problem. This may be reduced by making the dust more conducting, for example, by using cooled electrodes (Humphries *et al* 1984). Even when the dust is conducting, very high current densities lead to a reduced breakdown voltage and the advantages of small size and a short charging time must be balanced against the problems created by a high current density, particularly when any dust collects on the precharger electrodes.

A precharger consisting of parallel high-voltage wires between earthed plates is being used to reduce the pressure drop across a baghouse on a commercial lead smelter (Helstrom *et al* 1985). The device is similar in design to an electrostatic precipitator but the gas velocity is about 12 m s^{-1} to reduce dust deposition in the precharger.

(b) *High-intensity ioniser*
The high-intensity ioniser consists of a venturi tube with a sharp-edged disc in the throat (figure 4.21). The diameter of the venturi is 250–300 mm and the applied potential 80–100 kV. The gas velocity in the charging zone is 25 m s^{-1} but in spite of this high velocity, some dust is deposited, causing back-ionisation problems with highly resistive dusts. For dusts where this problem does not arise, very high charge levels are quoted which are 40 % higher than predicted from classical charging theory (Tassiker and Schwab 1977).

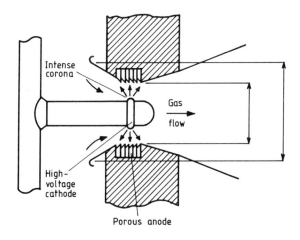

Figure 4.21 A high-intensity ioniser (after Tassiker 1975).

(c) *A trielectrode precharger*
A trielectrode precharger has been proposed by Pontius *et al* (1978). This is a wire/plate corona charging system, with grids carrying a small bias voltage of the same polarity as the corona wires, situated 20 mm from the surface of the plates. If back-ionisation occurs from the plates the ions are intercepted

by the grid, and do not reach the charging area. Some dust is likely to collect on the grid itself and this is still able to produce back-ions. However, analysis by McLean *et al* (1981) shows that the grid gap and bias voltage can be controlled to suppress back corona and good charging of the inlet particles is possible.

(d) *The boxer charger*

The principle of the boxer charger is illustrated in figure 4.22. A sinusoidal or square-wave potential, at a frequency of 50–500 Hz is applied between electrodes A and B, which are also ion sources. During the first half-cycle, the ion source at A is excited and ions with the same polarity as A travel towards electrode B. For the second half-cycle the ion source at B is excited, but the field is now reversed so the ions attracted towards A are the same polarity as before. Particles between the two electrodes are thus charged by ions of the same polarity approaching from both sides. Since the field regularly reverses, there is no net force towards either electrode. Figure 4.23 shows a design in which the ions are produced by a high-frequency voltage (1.5–20 kHz) applied to strip-discharge electrodes. This is capacitively coupled to the slower signal through a 0.2 mm insulating plate. A high-frequency corona is created at the edges of the discharge electrodes and a plasma appears over the whole surface of the electrode to provide the ion source. The boxer charger can operate with an order of magnitude higher current density than is possible in a conventional corona charging system,

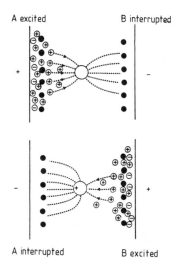

Figure 4.22 Principle of the boxer charger (after Masuda *et al* 1979). ⊕, positive ions; ⊖, negative ions; ●, discharge and ion collecting electrode.

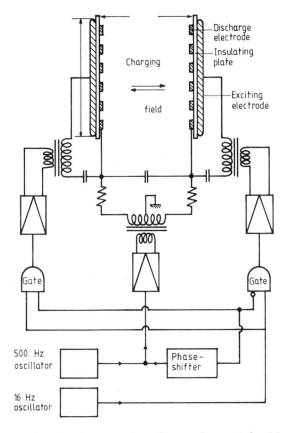

Figure 4.23 Circuit and construction of boxer charger (after Masuda *et al* 1979).

and high mean field strengths of 8×10^5 V m^{-1} exist in the charging region. This results in a high charging efficiency with a short charging time constant of about 5 ms. The boxer charger has been shown to operate well, even with the electrodes covered with high-resistivity dust, presumably because the surface charge is eliminated by the plasma formed on the electrodes.

APPENDIX

Collection efficiency of a single charged sphere

The collection efficiency, X, of a single sphere is defined as the ratio of the cross sectional area from which particles are collected to the cross sectional area of the sphere. The equation of motion for a small spherical particle is

$$\tfrac{4}{3}\pi a_p^3 D_p \frac{du_p}{dt} = \frac{-6\pi\eta a_p}{C}(u_p - u_0) + F_e$$

where u_0 is the velocity of the gas and u_p is the velocity of the particle. F_e is the force due to the combined electrical forces, listed in §4.5.1. The trajectory of the particle can be calculated analytically only for simple cases, for example, for inertialess particles (Nielson and Hill 1976a) or when there are no electrostatic forces (Cheng 1973).

In the general case, for a particle which has inertia and for which more than one electrostatic collection mechanism is significant the equation must be solved numerically, e.g. Nielson and Hill (1976b).

Inertialess charged particles—charged collector in an electric field

The collection of inertialess charged particles by a spherical collector with a charge q_c, in an electric field, E, is the Pauthenier charging problem discussed in §2.2.3. The effect of an air stream on the charging process has been calculated by Whipple and Chalmers (1944). They show that, for collector spheres charged to below the Pauthenier limit, q_c, and inertialess particles which have a net velocity towards the collector spheres, the efficiency of collection is not affected by the air flow. The Pauthenier charge q_c is given by

$$q_c = 12\pi\varepsilon_0 E a^2 \tag{A1}$$

and the collection efficiency in an air stream of velocity u, in the same direction as the ion flow is given by

$$X = b(3Ea^2 + q/4\pi\varepsilon_0)^2/3Ea_c^2(u + bE) \tag{A2}$$

where b is the particle mobility. The mobility of a charged particle is found by equating the electrostatic force to the Stokes drag:

$$b = Cq_p/6\pi\eta a_p. \tag{A3}$$

Slightly different equations apply when the particle and the collector move in opposite directions or the particle has more charge than the Pauthenier limit.

If both the collector particles and the pollutant particles are highly charged to opposite polarities, and the pollutant particles are small, this approximation can provide a reasonable estimate of the collection efficiency of a single sphere.

Inertialess charged or uncharged particles, charged collector, no electric field

Kraemer (1954) investigated theoretically and experimentally the collection of negatively charged dioctylphthalate particles ($0.8\,\mu$m diameter) onto charged metal spheres 6.4–11 mm in diameter. Following this work Kraemer and Johnstone (1955) calculated the single-sphere collecting efficiency by equating the forces of fluid resistance to the electrostatic forces. Inertial impaction and Brownian diffusion were neglected (as they were in Whipple's calculation) but the fluid flow equations were taken into account more precisely and the case where only one of the particles was charged was also considered. The equations of motion were solved numerically but approximate solutions were given for collection by the Coulumb force and the force between a charged collector and a neutral particle. Kraemer and Johnstone obtained an efficiency equation for the Coulomb force of

$$X = 4K_E$$

where

$$K_E = q_c b / 4\pi\varepsilon_0 a_c^2 u = Cq_c q_p / 4\pi\varepsilon_0 a_c^2 (6\pi\eta a_p) u_c \qquad (A4)$$

where u_c is the relative velocity between the air stream and the collector. (This is the same as the Whipple and Chalmers equation when the particle velocity in the applied field is less than the air velocity and the applied electric field is zero.) For a 0.2 μm diameter dust particle and an oppositely charged 0.2 mm diameter collector particle, both charged to their limits, $X = 12$. By definition $X = y^2/a_c^2$, i.e. the sphere will collect particles whose initial offset y from the centre line of the sphere is

$$y^2 = \frac{4(q_p q_c)(C)}{(4\pi\varepsilon_0)(6\pi\eta a_p)u}. \qquad (A5)$$

When only the collector is charged Kraemer obtained an efficiency of

$$X = (\tfrac{15}{8} K_i)^{0.4}$$

where

$$K_i = \frac{(\varepsilon - 1)8Ca_p^2 q_c^2}{(\varepsilon + 2)4\pi\varepsilon_0 a_c^2 6\eta a_c u}.$$

Extension to particles with inertia

Nielson and Hill (1976a,b) extended the work to particles with inertia and gave an empirical formula

$$X = [2(-K_E)^{1/2} - 0.8K]^2$$

where K is the Stokes number

$$K = 2CD_p u_0 a_p^2 / 9\eta a_c$$

K_E is the dimensionless force parameter for the Coulomb attraction which is

$$K_E = Cq_c q_p / 24\pi\varepsilon_0 \varepsilon_r a_p a_c^2 \eta u$$

u_0 is the free stream velocity. This equation was found to be accurate to within 3 % providing

$$0 < K < -0.3K_E \text{ and } 1.5 < -K_E < 10.$$

Nielson and Hill (1976a,b) also solved the equation of motion for the particles numerically and plotted the single-sphere collection efficiencies as a function of Stokes number for each of the electrostatic forces.

Snaddon (1982) computed equivalent curves for gravity, inertial impaction and diffusion in comparison with the external field force and the force due to a charge on the particles with a neutral collector.

Sparks (1971) calculated the efficiency of a single sphere by solving numerically an equation of motion proposed by Sparks and Pilat (1970) for a particle in a gas flowing round a sphere. This equation included Brownian diffusion and inertial impaction as well as electrostatics. However, he considered collection only on the upstream surface of the collector sphere and his results do not agree with the predictions made with the equations of Bertinat (1980) and Kraemer and Johnstone (1955).

REFERENCES

Alexander J C 1978 Electrofluidised beds in the control of fly ash *PhD Thesis* MIT Department of Electrical Engineering

Alexander J C and Melcher J R 1977 Alternating field electrofluidized beds in the collection of submicron aerosols *Ind. Eng. Chem. Fundam.* **16** 311–17

Allen R W K 1982 Electrostatically augmented wet dedusters *Filtration and Separation* **19** 334–40

Athwal C C, Coventry P F and Hughes J F 1983 Implications of ion wind and back-ionisation on precipitator performance *Electrostatics (Oxford) 1983* (Inst. Phys. Conf. Ser. 66) pp 167–72

Auzerais F, Payatakes A C and Okuyama K 1983 Dendritic deposition of uncharged aerosol particles on an uncharged fibre in the presence of an electric field *Chem. Eng. Sci.* **38** 447–67

Bertinat M P 1980 Charged droplet scrubbing for controlling submicron particle emissions *J. Electrostatics* **9** 137–58

Boericke R R, Kuo J T and Murphy K R 1982 Technical and economic evaluation of two novel particulate control devices *Proc. 3rd Symp. on the Transfer and Utilisation of Particulate Control Technology* US EPA Research Triangle Park (North Carolina) EPA 600/9-82-005 vol III 353–62

Brown R C 1980 The behaviour of fibrous filter media in dust respirators *Ann. Occ. Hygiene* **23** 367–80

Brown R F and Walker A B 1971 Feasibility demonstrated of precipitation at 1700 °F *J. Air Pollution Control Association* **21** 617–20

Calvert S, Young S C, Barbarika H and Patterson R G 1978 Evaluation of four novel fine particle collection devices *US Environmental Protection Agency Report* EPA/600/2-78-062

Cheng L 1973 Collection of airborne dust by water sprays *Ind. Eng. Chem. Proc. Res. Devel.* **12** 221–5

Chudleigh P W 1982 Fabric filter performance: effect of dust charge and cleaning efficiency *Filtration and Separation* **19** 388–92

Clift R 1983 Fundamental processes in gas filtration *Proc. 8th Australasian Fluid Mechanics Conf., University of Newcastle (Inst. Mech. Eng. Aust.* **ME-8** 181–91) (also EPA 600/2-76-154a 1976 Evaluation of APS electrostatic scrubber)

Clift R, Ghadiri M and Thambimuthu K V 1981 Filtration of gases in fluidised beds *Progress in Filtration and Separation* vol 2, pp 75–123, ed R J Wakeman (Amsterdam: Elsevier)

Coury J R 1983 Electrostatic effects in granular bed filtration of gases *PhD Thesis* University of Cambridge

Cross J A 1985 An analysis of the current in a point-to-plane corona discharge and the effect of a back-ionising layer on the plane *J. Phys. D: Appl. Phys.* **18** 2463–71
—— 1986 Back-ionisation in a negative point-to-plane corona discharge *J. Electrostatics* **18** 327–44

Cross J A and Barton N 1984 Cylindrical probe measurements in a corona discharge *J. Electrostatics* **15** 15–29

Cross J A and Bassett J D 1974 Observations of back ionisation in electrostatic powder coatings *Trans. Inst. Metal Finishing* **52** 112–4

Cross J A and Paulson C A J 1983 Investigation of the causes of the variation in efficiency in electrostatic precipitators collecting fly ash from different coals *Proc. Int. Clean Air Conf.* (Paris: IAUPPA) *1983* pp 409–16

Cross J A, Paulson C A J and Raper J 1987 The effect of additives on the agglomeration of flyash particles suspended in a gas stream *J. Air Pollution Control Association* submitted

Cucu D and Lippold J 1985 High efficiency oil mist filtration with electrostatic precipitation *J. Electrostatics* **17** 109–12

Darby K 1981 Use of pilot precipitators in the field and in the laboratory *Int. Conf. on Electrostatic Precipitation (Monterey) 1981* (Pittsburg: Air Pollution Control Association) pp 592–626

Davies C N 1966 *Aerosol Science* (New York: Academic)

Deutsch W 1922 Bewegung und Ladung der elektrizitatstrager im zylinderkondensator *Ann. Phys., Lpz* **68** 335

Dietz P W 1982 Electrostatically enhanced cyclone separators *Powder Technol.* **3** 221–6

Dismukes E B 1976 Techniques for conditioning fly ash *Symp. on Particulate Control in Energy Processes* US EPA Research Triangle Park (North Carolina) EPA 600/7-76-010

Faulkner M G, Dismukes E B, McDonald J R, Pontius D H and Dean A H 1979 Assessment of diesel particulate control: filters, scrubbers and precipitators US EPA Research Triangle Park (North Carolina) EPA-600/7-79-232a

Felder R M and Arce Medina E 1980 Radio tracer measurement of particle deposition and reentrainment in an electrostatic precipitator *Int. J. Appl. Radiation and Isotopes* **31** 761–7

Fielding G H, Thompson J K, Bogardus H F and Clark R C 1975 Dielectrophoretic filtration of solid and liquid aerosol particles *Proc. 68th Annual Meeting of Air Pollution Control Association (Boston)* Paper 75-35.2

General Electric Company 1981 Electrostatic granular bed filter development program Report DOE/ET/1549-18, DE82 004487

Griesco G and Fortune O Flow modelling—key to more effective precipitation *Research Cottrell Technical Bulletin TB* 202, *Utility Gas Cleaning Division Brook Bound (New Jersey)*

Giles W B 1979 *Proc. 1st Symp. on the Transfer and Utilisation of Particulate Control Technology* US EPA Research Triangle Park (North Carolina) EPA 600/9-82-005 vol III, 291

Goard P and Potter E C 1981 The resistive impediment from particles collected in the electrostatic precipitator *J. Electrostatics* **10** 237–42

Greiner G P, Furlong D A, VanOsdell D W and Hovis L S 1981 Electrostatic stimulation of fabric filtration *Control Technology News* **31** 1125–30

Groves J F and Smith C R 1980 Gas flow distribution effects in electrostatic precipitators *J. Electrostatics* **8** 342–53

Happel J 1958 Viscous flow in multiparticle systems: slow motion of fluids relative to beds of stationary particles *AIChE J.* **4** 197–201

Heinrich D O 1979 Electrostatic precipitator collector spacings above 300 mm *Atmos. Environ.* **13** 1707–11

Helstrom R, Blenman N and Humphries W 1985 *J. Electrostatics* Submitted

Henry F and Airman T 1981 The effect of neighbouring fibres on the electric field in a fibrous filter *J. Aerosol Sci.* **12** 137–49

Henry F and Airman T 1982 A staggered array model of a fibrous filter with electrical enhancement *Proc. 3rd Int. Symp. on the Transfer and Utilisation of Particulate Control Technology* US EPA Research Triangle Park (North Carolina) EPA 600/9-82-005 vol III, 301–10

Henry R F, Podolski W F and Saxena S C 1982 Electrostatically augmented devices for gas cleaning *Proc. IEEE Conf. Industrial Applications Society* 1050–60

Humphries W, Madden J J and Micelli M 1984 Effect of particle precharging on the performance of fabric filters collecting lead smelter dust *Aerosol Sci. Tech.* **3** 381–95

Iinoya K and Mori Y 1982 Fundamental study of a fabric filter with a corona precharger *Proc. 3rd Int. Symp. on Particulate Control Technology* US EPA Research Triangle Park (North Carolina) EPA 600/9-82-005 vol III, 181–92

Johnson T W and Melcher J R 1975 Electromechanics of electrofluidized beds *Ind. Eng. Chem. Fund.* **14** 146–53

Kallio G A and Dietz P W 1981 Image charge collection of fine particles in granular beds *Gas Borne Particles* (Inst. Mech. Eng. London) pp 101–10

Katz H and Sears J T 1969 Electric field phenomena in fluidised and fixed beds *Can. J. Chem. Eng.* **47** 50–3

Kawai K and Aoki S 1972 Research on the application of radiation beam to flue gas desulphurization *J. Atomic Energy Soc. Japan* **14** 597

Kraemer H F 1954 *PhD Thesis* University of Illinois

Kraemer H F and Johnstone H F 1955 Collection of aerosol particles in the presence of electrostatic fields *Ind. Eng. Chem.* **47** 2426–34

Kuwabara S 1959 The forces experienced by randomly distributed parallel circular cylinders or spheres in viscous fluid at small Reynolds number *J. Phys. Soc. Japan* **14** 527–32

Lausen P, Henriksen H and Petersen H H 1979 Energy conserving pulse energisation of precipitators *IEEE Ind. Appl. Soc. Conf.* (Cleveland, Ohio)

Leonard G L, Mitchner M and Self S A 1982 Experimental study on the effect of turbulent diffusion on precipitator efficiency *J. Aerosol Sci.* **13** 271–84

Machi S and Kawai K 1973 Control of gaseous pollutants in flue gas by the use of radiation beam *Atomic Energy Industries* **19** 25

McLean K J, Herceg Z and Boccola R I 1981 Electrical transparency of a corona triode *J. Electrostatics* **9** 221–32

Malcher J, Sycinska-Trojniak A, Szaynok A T and Zuczkowski R 1984 Influence of electric field on model spherical bed filter efficiency *J. Electrostatics* **16** 107–15

Masuda S and Dri I 1975 Recent progress in electrostatic precipitation *Static Electrification (London) 1975* (Inst. Phys. Conf. Ser. 27) pp 154–72

Masuda S, Aoyama M and Shibuya A 1975 Bias controlled pulse charging system for electrostatic precipitator *Staub Reinhalt Luft* **36** 19–26

Masuda S, Ishiga N and Akutsu K 1976 Experiments on electrostatic precipitation of aerosols by the use of electron beam irradiation: part I and part II *Proc. Ann. Conf. Inst. Elec. Eng. (Japan) 1976* Paper No 464, 465

Masuda S and Mizuno A 1977a Light measurement of back discharge *J. Electrostatics* **2** 375–96

—— 1977b Initiation condition and mode of back discharge *J. Electrostatics* **4** 35–52

—— 1978 Flashover measurements of back discharge *J. Electrostatics* **4** 215–33

Masuda S and Moon Jae-Duk 1983 Electrostatic precipitation of carbon soot from diesel engine exhaust *IEEE Trans. Ind. Appl.* **IA-19**

Masuda S, Nakatani H and Mizuno E P A 1979 Boxer charger, a novel charging device *1st Symp. on Transfer and Utilisation of Particulate Control Technology (Denver) 1979* (US EPA Research Triangle Park, North Carolina)

Masuda S and Nonogaki Y 1981 Sensing of back discharge and bipolar ionic current *J. Electrostatics* **10** 73–80

Melcher J R and Rhoads K G 1981 Macroscopic models for electrically induced particles collection in packed and fluidised beds *Symp. on Ind. Aerosol Technology Formation, Measurement and Control AIChE 91st Meeting (Detroit, Michigan)* p 127

Melcher J R and Sachar K S Method for inducing agglomeration of particulate in a fluid flow *US Patent Specification* 3755122

Melcher J R, Sachar K S and Warren E P 1977 Overview of devices for control of sub-micron particles *Proc. IEEE* **65** 1659–69

Miller B, Lamb G and Costanza P 1978 Studies of dust cake formation and structure in fabric filters *US Environmental Protection Agency Report* EPA 600/7-78-095

Moore A D 1973 *Electrostatics and its Applications* (New York: Wiley–Interscience)

Nelson G O, Bergman W, Miller H H, Taylor R D, Richards C P and Bierman A H 1978 *Am. Ind. Hygiene J.* **38** 472

Nielson K A 1978a Collection of inertialess particles on circular cylinders with electrical forces and gravitation *J. Colloid and Interface Sci.* **64** 131–42

—— 1978b Collection of inertialess particles on elliptical and irregular cylinders with electrical forces and gravitation *J. Colloid and Interface Sci.* **65** 345–51

Nielson K A and Hill J C 1976a Capture of inertialess particles on spheres with electrical forces *Ind. Eng. Chem. Fund.* **15** 149–56

—— 1976b Capture of particles on spheres by inertial and electrical forces *Ind. Eng. Chem. Fund.* **15** 157–63

_____ 1980 Particle chain formation in aerosol filtration with electrical forces *AIChE J.* **26** 678–86

Parker R, Jain R, Le T and Calvert S 1981 Dry plate scrubber for particulate control *Proc. High Temp., High Pressure Particulate and Alkali Control in Coal Combustion Process Streams: Conf.* 810249 (*Morgan Town, WV*) (Washington, DC: US Department of Energy)

Parquet D 1982 The electroscrubber filter—applications and particulate control performance *Proc. 3rd Symp. on the Transfer and Utilisation of Particulate Control Technology* US EPA Research Triangle Park (North Carolina) EPA 600/9-82-005 vol III, 363–72

Payatakes A C, Tien C and Turian R M 1973 A new model of granular porous media—Part 1 model formation *AIChE J.* **19** 58–67

Petersen H H and Lausen P 1979 Precipitator energisation utilising an energy conserving pulse generator *Proc. 2nd Symp. on the Transfer and Utilisation of Particulate Control Technology* US EPA Research Triangle Park (North Carolina) EPA 600/9-80-039c

Petroll J and Langhammer K 1962 *Freiberg Forschungsh.* **A220** 175–96

Pilat M J, Jaasund S A and Sparks L E 1974 Collection of aerosol particles by electrostatic droplet spray scrubbers *Env. Sci. Tech.* **8** 360–2

Pontius D H, Vann Bush P and Smith W B 1978 A new system for electrostatic precipitation of particulate materials having high electrical resistivity *APCA Meeting* (*Houston, Texas*) (Pittsburg: Air Pollution Control Association)

Porle K J 1985 Reduced emission and energy consumption with pulsed energisation of electrostatic precipitators *J. Electrostatics* **16** 299–314

Potter E C 1978 Electrostatic precipitator technology: a different viewpoint *J. Air Pollution Control Association* **28** 40–6

_____ 1981 Pilot-scale units for precipitator sizing—an Australian approach *Int. Conf. on Electrostatic Precipitation* (*Monterey, California*) (Pittsburg: Air Pollution Control Association) pp 577–91

Potter E C and Paulson C A J 1974 Improvement of electrostatic precipitator performance by carrier gas additives and its graphical assessment using the extended Deutsch equation *Chemistry in Industry* 532–3

Presser A M and Alexander J C 1982 Non-plugging retaining structure for granular bed filter for HTHP applications *Proc. 3rd Symp. on Transfer and Utilisation of Particulate Control Technology* (*Denver*) *1982* US EPA Research Triangle Park (North Carolina) vol IV

Ranz W E and Wong J B 1952 Impaction of dust and smoke on particles *Ind. Eng. Chem.* **44** 1371–81

Reif 1977 *US Patent Specification* 4010011

Research Cottrell 1979 *Technical Bulletin Air Pollution Control Div.* 300-3510-9019

Schwab J J and Goodson D B 1978 Apparatus for ionising gases and electrostatic charging of particles or ionising gases for removing contaminants from gas streams *US Patent Specification* 4903430

Self S A, Cross R H and Eustis R H 1979 Electrical augmentation of granular bed filters *Proc. 2nd Symp. on the Transfer and Utilisation of Particulate Control Technology* vol. 111 (EPA-600/9-80-039c pp 309–43)

Sampuran-Singh S, Hughes J F and Bright A W 1979 Discharges in electrostatically deposited films *Electrostatics* (*Oxford*) *1979* (Inst. Phys. Conf. Ser. 48) pp 17–25

Snaddon R W L 1982 Electrically enhanced collection of respirable aerosols in granular bed filters at low Reynolds number *Annual Meeting of the IEEE Industrial Applications Society* pp 1045–9

Sparks L E 1971 Effect of scrubber operating and design parameters on the collection of particulate air pollutants *PhD Thesis* University of Washington (Seattle)

Sparks L E and Pilat M J 1970 Effect of diffusiophoresis on particle collection in wet scrubbers *Atmospheric Environment* **4** 651–66

Stomberg H and Lundquist S 1983 Pulsed radio frequency resonance operation of electrostatic precipitators *Electrostatics (Oxford) 1983* (Inst. Phys. Conf. Ser. 66) pp 161–6

Sumuyoshilani S, Okada T, Hara M and Akasaki M 1984 Direct observations of collection process for dust particles from an air stream by charged water droplets *IEEE Trans. Ind. Appl.* **IA-20** 274–81

Tardos G I, Abauf N and Gutfinger C 1978 Dust deposition in granular bed filter theories and experiments *J. Air Pollution Control Association* **28** 354–63

Tardos G I, Gutfinger C and Pfeffer R 1979 Triboelectric effects in the filtration of small dust particles in a granular bed *Ind. Eng. Chem. Fund.* **18** 433–5

Tassiker O J 1975 Electrostatic precipitation research in Australia *J. Air Pollution Control Association* **25** 122–7

Tassiker O J and Schwab J 1977 High intensity ioniser for improved ESP performance *EPRI J.* **56** 55–61

Thambimuthu K V, Doganoglu Y, Farrokhalaee T and Clift R 1978 Aerosol filtration in fixed granular beds *Symp. on Deposition and Filtration of Particles from Gases and Liquids, Society of Chemical Industry (London)*

Thibodeaux D P, Baril A and Reif R B 1976 *IEEE Ann. Meeting of the Industrial Applications Society* pp 333–9

Truce R J 1981 Back corona and its effect on optimisation of precipitator control *Proc. 7th Int. Clean Air Conf. (Adelaide, Australia)* (Ann Arbor Science) pp 223–237

VanOsdell D W, Furlong D A and Hovis L S 1985 Pilot plant study of the effect of surface electric field on fabric filter operation *IEEE Trans. Ind. Appl.* **IA-21** 62–8

Van Turnhout J, Adamse J W C and Hoeneveld W J 1980 Electret filters for high efficiency cleaning *J. Electrostatics* **8** 369–79

Wang C S, Ho C P, Makino H and Iinoya K 1980 Effect of electrostatic fields on the accumulation of solid particles on single cylinders *AIChE J.* **26** 680–3

Wang P K, Grover S N and Pruppacher H R 1978 On the effect of electric charges on the scavenging of aerosol particles by small raindrops *J. Atmospheric Sci.* **35** 1735–43

Watson K S 1979 Collection of fly ash from low sulphur coals. An overview of Australian experience *Clean Air Conference (Pretoria) 1979* (Pretoria: CSIR) paper no 3

Whipple F J W and Chalmers J A 1944 On Wilson's theory of the collection of charge by falling drops *Quart. J. Meteorol. Soc.* **70** 103–9

White H J 1963 *Industrial Electrostatic Precipitation* (Oxford: Pergamon)

Zahedi K and Melcher J R 1976 Electrofluidised beds in the filtration of submicron particles *J. Air Pollution Control Association* **26** 345–52

—— 1977 Collection of submicron particles in bubbling electrostatic fluidized beds *Ind. Eng. Chem. Fund.* **16** 248–54

Chapter 5   Miscellaneous Applications

5.1 ELECTROSTATIC ATOMISATION

5.1.1 Droplet formation

Electrostatic forces can be used to disrupt a liquid surface to form a fine highly charged stream of droplets, or to produce a finer more uniform spray when a liquid is atomised mechanically. Electrostatic atomisation and electrostatically assisted atomisation are used in many diverse applications, including paint spraying, crop spraying and electrostatic printing. Electrostatic atomisation has been proposed as a mechanism for the propulsion of space vehicles.

When a liquid is subjected to an electric field, a charge is induced on the surface and mutual charge repulsion results in an outwardly directed force. Under suitable conditions, this electrostatic pressure at the surface forces the liquid up into a cone and surplus charge is ejected by the emission of charged droplets from the tip. The emission process depends on the viscosity, surface tension and conductivity of the liquid and the environment in which atomisation takes place (For example, in air the process may be affected by corona discharges from the tip of the cone.). The presence of a cone on the surface of a liquid in an electric field was first recorded by William Gilbert in 1600 but an explanation was not found until the 1960s when Taylor (1964) showed theoretically that a cone will form, and that it is stable only if its semivertical angle is 49.3°. His experimental work confirmed that the angle formed in practice was very close to this value. Taylor also showed that when an uncharged drop is placed in an electric field it will elongate until the droplet is 1.85 times as long as its equatorial diameter, then form conical ends from which small droplets can be ejected.

The effect of electrostatic forces on mechanical atomisation of a liquid was first studied in detail by Rayleigh (1882, 1892) who investigated the hydrodynamic stability of a jet of liquid, with and without an applied electric field. More recent studies are reviewed by Grant and Middleman (1966). Rayleigh considered the way in which a filament, or film of liquid, is disrupted by centrifugal, aerodynamic or hydraulic forces. He showed that when a jet of liquid is forced through an orifice (in the absence of electrical forces) its surface assumes a regular undulating wave form which is stationary in space. Some distance away from the orifice, surface tension forces cause this undulating jet to break up into droplets. The length of the waves depends on the way in which the jet is disturbed at the orifice, but even if every effort is made to remove the source of disturbance, the friction of the liquid is sufficient to produce undulations.

Rayleigh showed that the condition for the amplitude of the disturbance to grow so that droplets were formed was

$$\lambda > 2\pi r$$

where r is the orifice radius and λ is the wavelength of the jet disturbance.

If the wavelength is less than this limit the disturbance decays and the jet breaks up randomly. The maximum growth rate of the disturbance has been calculated to be

$$\psi = \left[\left(\frac{8Dr^3}{\gamma} \right)^{1/2} + \frac{6\eta r}{\gamma} \right]^{-1} \tag{5.1}$$

where D is the fluid density, η is the dynamic viscosity and γ is the surface tension.

If a smooth circular orifice is used, and external disturbances are suppressed then the jet travels a maximum distance before breaking up and the droplets are fairly regular. An irregular orifice produces irregular droplets, closer to the orifice, but the distribution is always polydisperse.

There have been a large number of experimental studies on electrostatic atomisation (e.g. Bose 1745, Zeleny 1914, Margavey and Outhouse 1962, Hendricks 1962, Bailey 1981). It is found that, under suitable conditions, the liquid from a surface or a capillary is drawn out into a Taylor cone of semivertical angle 49.3°. In many cases a filament then forms which breaks up into droplets. The length of the filament depends on the viscosity of the liquid (Zeleny 1917 and figure 5.1). With a conducting liquid, at a critical potential, the filament throws off a fine stream of fairly uniform droplets. Non-conducting liquids throw off occasional larger droplets (Taylor and Van Dyke 1969). The effect of the relative permittivity, viscosity and electrical resistivity of the liquid on the size distribution of droplets, produced electrostatically from a hypodermic syringe, has been studied by Bailey (1981). He found that increased viscosity or resistivity both lead to larger droplets, but that the resistivity had the greater effect on the particle size.

Low resistivities (of the order of 10^5 Ω m) produced a broader range of sizes than higher resistivities (of the order of 10^9 Ω m). Hendricks (1962) measured a log normal particle size distribution of oil droplets sprayed from a capillary. The radii of the particles lay in the range of 0.2 to 10 μm with the peak of the distribution at a droplet radius of 2 μm.

(a)   Alcohol   (b)   Glycerol

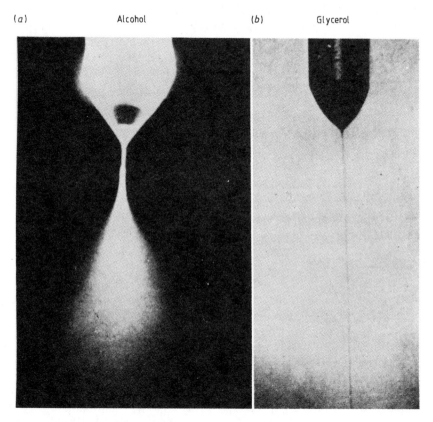

Figure 5.1 Electrostatic spraying of liquid from a capillary (from Zeleny 1917). The glycerol breaks up into drops after a distance of 15 mm. Alcohol sprays out after travelling a much shorter distance.

If the liquid flows slowly out of a capillary, rather than being forced out under pressure, then large uniformly sized droplets are produced, accompanied by very small satellite droplets produced from the fine liquid threads, which form between the drop and the capillary. The radius, r, of the uniform droplets is found by equating the gravitational force on the droplet to the capillary force:

$$\tfrac{4}{3}\pi a^3 Dg = 2\pi r_0 \gamma K \tag{5.2}$$

where K is a constant $\simeq 1$ and r_0 is the neck radius, which is approximately the internal radius of the capillary tip.

Substituting for the constants and the properties of water, it can be seen that the smallest drop which can be produced is of the order of 1 mm.

An electric field can be applied to the system, either by immersing an electrode in the liquid, or by directing the capillary towards a plate carrying a potential, or by applying a potential to a metal capillary. The electrostatic charge at the surface of the liquid creates a pressure which counteracts the surface tension. γ is reduced and the droplet size, calculated from equation (5.2), decreases. An electrostatic capillary can produce uniform-sized droplets between fifty and several hundred microns in diameter, accompanied by small satellite droplets.

At some critical applied voltage the form of atomisation changes and in addition to the stream of uniform droplets there is a wide cone of monodispersed mist. This phenomenon is known as electrodynamic spraying. If the voltage is applied by immersing an electrode in a liquid, the mist is formed only if the applied voltage is positive, and only for liquids with a resistivity in the range 10^{11}–10^4 Ω m. However, if a metal capillary is attached to a voltage source, and the liquid sprayed towards an earthed plane, the mist is produced for both polarities and for a wider range of liquid resistivities.

Uniform droplets can be produced from a capillary if the jet is modulated at a frequency which corresponds to that at which the maximum growth rate occurs (Lindbald and Schneider 1965). For a low-viscosity liquid this corresponds to a wavelength

$$\lambda = 9.016r$$

where r is the radius of the jet. The length of the jet before the droplets are detached is then

$$L = (u/\psi) \ln(r/\gamma) \tag{5.3}$$

where ψ is the maximum growth rate defined by equation (5.1) and u is the velocity of the jet. The droplet radius is given by $a = 1.89r$. This method of producing uniform droplets is limited to a narrow range of particle sizes because excitation is only possible close to the natural frequency of the jet, equivalent to the wavelength λ. However, uniform droplets of a controlled size can be produced electrostatically by applying a suitable alternating field (Sato 1984). Sato (1980c) first investigated the formation of gas bubbles at a capillary immersed in a liquid and showed that when a voltage was applied to the capillary, the size of the bubbles was reasonably uniform, with a mean which varied with the applied field. An alternating applied voltage produced even more uniform bubbles (Sato 1980b, Sato *et al* 1981). When an AC voltage was applied to a liquid issuing from an orifice, very uniform droplets were formed, synchronously with the applied voltage, with a droplet formed at the peak voltage of each cycle. As the voltage increased from 0 to 3000 V the droplet diameter decreased. It was then constant for the next 1300 V. For voltages above 4500, numerous finer droplets of irregular size were produced. For voltages within the synchronous region (up to 4500 V) the diameter was controllable within the range 28 μm to 2.4 mm.

5.1.2 The charge on electrostatically atomised droplets

A net electric charge on a liquid resides at the surface and exerts an outward force which opposes the surface tension. If sufficient charge is added to a drop of liquid it becomes unstable and disrupts. Rayleigh (1882) showed that the electrostatic force equalled the surface tension force and disruption occurred when the charge on a droplet of radius a was given by

$$q^2 = 64\pi^2 \varepsilon_0 \gamma a^3. \tag{5.4}$$

The maximum charge-to-mass ratio is

$$q/m = (36\varepsilon_0 \gamma / a^3 D^2)^{1/2}. \tag{5.5}$$

The validity of this relationship has been confirmed by Hendricks (1962). In his measurements of the charge-to-mass ratio of oil droplets sprayed from hollow-steel needles, he found a broad distribution of charge ranging from the Rayleigh limit to a factor of twenty below it. The Rayleigh limit lies above the Gaussian limit (see Chapter 2) and discharging to the Gaussian limit could account for the range of observed charge. Schweizer and Hanson (1971) observed a single charged droplet balanced against gravity in an electric field. They found that disruption occurred within 4 % of the theoretical Rayleigh limit. When a droplet disrupts it does so by ejecting several very small daughter droplets. The 20 μm diameter droplet studied by Schweizer and Hanson retained 95 % of the mass and 77 % of the charge after disruption. These figures were confirmed by Roth and Kelly (1983) who observed the disruption of liquid droplets as their radius was decreased by evaporation.

Not all observations follow these simple rules. For example, Williams and Bailey (1985) have recently measured the charge and radius of droplets formed as glycerol dripped from a metal capillary under the influence of an electric field. They found that, for a given droplet size, the charge on the droplet was a function of the capillary size with a larger capillary giving a higher charge. They also found two anomalies illustrated in figure 5.2.

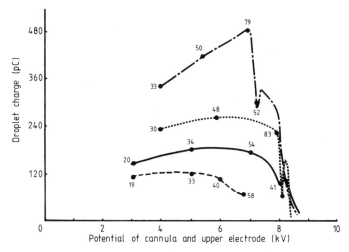

Figure 5.2 Droplet charge as a function of cannula and upper electrode potential. Numbers on curves are percentages which refer to the Rayleigh limit (from Williams and Bailey 1983).

(i) There was an abrupt decrease in droplet charge as the field at the capillary increased beyond a critical limit.

(ii) When the potential approached the value for electrodynamic spraying, some droplets of reverse polarity were measured.

Williams and Bailey (1985) proposed a number of possible mechanisms which could account for these results including changes in the charge and mass of the satellite droplets, corona discharges from the droplets or back-ionisation processes from the accelerating electrode.

5.1.3 Energy requirements for electrostatic atomisation

The atomisation process requires energy to be supplied which is expended in three ways (Bailey 1974).

(i) Energy is required to form a new surface (U_s).
If there are n droplets of radius a the surface energy of the ensemble is

$$U_s = n4\pi a^2\gamma.$$

The total mass of the droplets is

$$m = n4\pi a^3 D/3.$$

Therefore the surface energy per unit mass of the droplets is

$$U_s' = 3\gamma/Da.$$

If the droplets were formed from a liquid surface of radius R, then the initial surface energy was

$$U_0 = 3\gamma/DR.$$

$R \gg r$, therefore the original surface energy is very much smaller than the energy of the droplets and can be neglected. The energy to form the new surface may therefore be taken to be

$$U_s = 3\gamma/Da \qquad \text{per unit mass.} \qquad (5.6)$$

This is called the formation energy.

(ii) Energy is required to overcome the viscous forces of the liquid (U_v). This has been calculated by Monk (1952) who assumed that in the atomisation process, shown in figure 5.1, liquid could be considered to flow into the large end of a conical section and out of the small end, with increased velocity. He found the energy lost per second due to viscous forces was given by

$$U_v/t = 8\eta R^2 d_1^2/3\pi L d_2^4 \qquad (5.7)$$

where d_1 is the input diameter of the cone, d_2 is the output diameter of the cone, L is the length of the cone, η is the liquid viscosity and R is the volume flow rate. Viscous effects are usually smaller than the energy required to form the new surface.

(iii) There are also always energy losses. In the case of electrostatic atomisation, the most important losses are due to Joule heating of the liquid and to electrical breakdown processes, such as corona discharges. Joule heating leads to an energy loss of $U = I^2 R$.

Sufficient energy for these three energy needs must be supplied to the system before atomisation can occur. For low volumes of liquid, sufficient energy may be supplied by electrical energy alone, but for high-volume atomisation it is normally necessary to force liquid under pressure through an orifice to augment the electrical energy by mechanical means.

5.1.4 Electrostatic emulsification

A liquid can be electrostatically sprayed into another liquid in which it is immiscible to produce an emulsion (Nawab and Mason 1958). Watanabe *et al* (1978) carried out an experimental and theoretical analysis of the emulsion formed from an immersed capillary. They photographed the droplets as they emerged from the capillary, using the apparatus shown in figure 5.3. As the voltage on the capillary increased, the droplet size decreased, and at a critical voltage a shower of very fine droplets was produced, together with a few larger particles. The critical voltage depended on the relative conductivity of the liquids and was larger when the liquids had a similar conductivity. (It was necessary for the dispersed phase to have a higher conductivity than the continuous phase.) The maximum concentration which can be produced with an immersed electrode is about 1 % (Nawab and Mason 1958). To produce

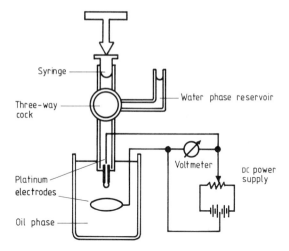

Figure 5.3 Schematic diagram of apparatus for capillary emulsification (after Watanabe *et al* 1978).

higher emulsion densities, the atomiser can be held above the liquid and the droplets stirred in.

An emulsion which is produced electrostatically has a narrower size distribution than one produced mechanically, and uses less energy than a mechanical system producing the same particle size. The electrostatic emulsion remains dispersed for a much longer time than an emulsion produced mechanically (Watanabe *et al* 1978).

The rate of production of the emulsion is limited by the rate at which energy can be supplied for the creation of the new surface, as described in §5.1.3 above. However, Hughes and Pavey (1981) have reported pilot scale experiments in which an emulsion, with droplet sizes close to 2 to 3 μm, was produced at a rate of 20 kg h^{-1}, giving an emulsion of a furniture wax suitable for aerosol can application.

5.1.5 The ink jet printer

It was shown in §4.1 that if the particle diameter lies between about 1 μm and 2 mm, electrostatic forces dominate over gravitational and aerodynamic forces. Electrostatic forces are therefore used in a number of industrial processes to direct liquid droplets. The precision with which this may be achieved is illustrated by the ink jet printer, which can produce good quality printing at very high speeds. The term 'ink jet printer' covers a range of non-impact printers in which a computer-controlled stream of charged droplets is sprayed on to a substrate in a dot matrix pattern. These are mostly based on work carried out by Sweet in the 1960s (e.g. Sweet 1965). Advantages of this form of printer are summarised in table 5.1.

Table 5.1 Advantages of ink jet printing (Keeling and Pullen 1981).

---

(1) Variable data
Input data can be continuously variable and can be alphanumeric or graphics.

(2) Non-contact
The process prints directly on to the substrate and requires no subsequent fusing.
There is no contact with the surface therefore delicate or uneven substrates such
as fabrics, tissues, corrugated card, foodstuffs etc can be printed.

(3) Versatile
The process operates with a wide range of specially developed inks on to virtually
any substrate.

(4) Multicolour
Multinozzle systems can be set up to print several colours simultaneously.

(5) High speed (typically $1–10 \text{ m s}^{-1}$).

(6) No moving parts (other than the substrate feed).

The very high accuracy of ink jet printers requires a stream of accurately
uniform, equally spaced droplets, with a closely controlled charge. In the
example illustrated in figure 5.4, this is achieved by forcing liquid through a
small nozzle (typically 35–80 μm) which is piezoelectrically stimulated at a
wavelength of 9.016 times the jet radius. If the jet is stimulated at this
optimum wavelength, the oscillation dominates the disruption process and a
uniform stream of droplets, one for each cycle, is produced (Lindbald and
Schneider 1965). The liquid jet passes through the centre of a charging
electrode to which a potential is applied. The jet and charging electrode form
a coaxial cylindrical capacitance, therefore a voltage on the charging electrode induces a charge on the jet. The system is arranged so the jet breaks up
into droplets within the charging electrodes, thus the droplets are charged as
they form. The voltage on the charge electrode is varied at the same rate as
the droplets are produced, so every droplet is individually charged and
every drop can be individually programmed. Typically the drops are produced at a frequency between 50 and 150 kHz and require 2 to 4 μs to reach
their full charge. It is important to be able to control the voltage so that the
drop has reached its full charge at the moment at which it breaks away from
the jet.

The charge per droplet can be calculated from the known capacitance of
the coaxial geometry and applied voltage and is given by

$$q = \frac{8\pi V \varepsilon_r}{3a^2 \ln(b/a)} \tag{5.8}$$

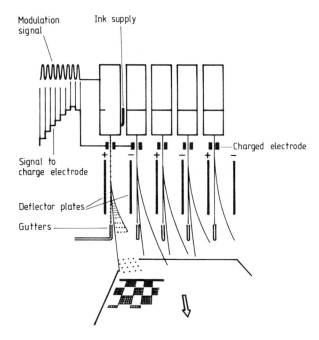

Figure 5.4 Operation of an ink jet printer (after Keeling and Pullen 1981).

where a is the particle radius and b is the radius of the ring electrode. The charged droplets pass through electrostatic deflector plates which deflect them by an amount proportional to their charge, then impinge on a substrate which is travelling at a high speed at right angles to the direction in which the drops are deflected.

A bank of nozzles may be used to produce pages of graphics or fabric prints. With multinozzle systems it is imperative that deflections of each jet should butt up against one another and therefore that the mass and charge on the drops from each nozzle should be the same (Fillimore and Van Lokeren 1982). An electronic system, which detects the deflection of the droplets before they reach the paper may be used to make corrections in liquid pressure or charging voltage to achieve optimum printing conditions (Keeling and Pullen 1981, Ream 1982).

A printer which does not need separate nozzles is described by Ichinose *et al* (1985). The ink issues from a slit, constructed from two flat panels with tapered ends. Recording electrodes (one for each dot) are located along the inside of the slit. A counter electrode in the form of a roller is placed behind the paper, 570 μm from the recording head. When a voltage pulse is applied between a recording electrode and the counter electrode, a jet is formed at that position, and a dot is recorded. More than one recording electrode can be driven at any one time and a dot pattern is formed in response to programmed signals. Ink jet printers are used as line printers and multicoloured systems are being developed for fabric printing.

5.1.6 The colloid thruster

The colloid thruster uses an intense electric field to atomise a dielectric liquid into small droplets which are accelerated to a high velocity, producing enough thrust to manoeuver a communications satellite. The first colloid thruster engine was built in 1963. The principle is illustrated in figure 5.5.

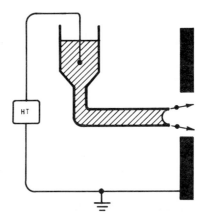

Figure 5.5 The electrostatic colloid thruster (after Bright 1974).

A voltage of about 10 kV is applied between a capillary containing dielectric liquid and an extractor electrode. The liquid forms Taylor cones and atomises into the vacuum. Since the droplets are sprayed into a vacuum they charge to the Rayleigh limit, given by equation (5.4), and the limiting charge-to-mass ratio is given by equation (5.5). There is no aerodynamic drag on the particles, and their terminal velocity, u, is found by equating the kinetic energy to the electrostatic energy

$$\tfrac{1}{2}mu^2 = qV$$

i.e.

$$u = [2(q/m)V]^{1/2}$$

$$u = \left(\frac{12V(\varepsilon_0 \gamma)^{1/2}}{Da^{3/2}}\right)^{1/2}.$$

Fields up to 10^8 V m^{-1} can be applied without breakdown, and droplet velocities have reached 30 km s^{-1} for an applied potential of 10 kV. (This is

significantly faster than achieved by conventional rockets (Bright 1974).)
Early experimental work used glycerol, doped with sodium iodide to provide
the correct electrical conductivity, as a propellant. Some successful experiments were also carried out with low-melting-point metals, such as gallium
and indium. These showed that even higher thrusts could be obtained by
spraying single ions from a needle (at a cost of increased power consumption). This device was known as the ion thruster. Calculations showed that
electrostatic thrusters were more suitable than gas jets or chemical rockets
for the purpose of maintaining a satellite in geostationary orbit, because of
their low fuel consumption. A few ion thrusters flew. For example, a mercury
ion thruster was successfully flown by NASA in 1970 and the Russian
Voskhod 1, launched in 1964, had a caesium ion thruster. The colloid
thruster was never flown because no satisfactory solution was found to the
problem of electrochemical errosion of the platinum electrodes during the
atomisation process.

5.2 ELECTROSTATIC SPRAY COATING

5.2.1 Introduction

There are a number of important applications of electrostatics where a
charged cloud of droplets or powder particles is sprayed towards an earthed
substrate and deposited on it. Particle charging techniques and the forces
which act on the particles are common to all these processes and are summarised here before the different processes are treated separately.

Droplets may be charged as a result of the natural charge separation
which occurs as they form, or this charge can be increased by induction or
a corona. Powder particles may be charged by friction or corona or, if they
are electrically conducting, by induction. These mechanisms were discussed
in detail in Chapter 2. The maximum charge levels which may be acquired by
particles of radius a are summarised in table 5.2, and the charge, and charge-
to-mass ratio, for particles in the range of $1-100\ \mu m$, which are most frequently used in electrostatic spraying, are plotted in figures 5.6 and 5.7
respectively. It can be seen that a $10\ \mu m$ radius particle, charged to the
Gaussian limit has a maximum charge of $8 \times 10^{-3}\ C\ kg^{-1}$ or $8\ \mu C\ g^{-1}$.
Thus $1\ g\ s^{-1}$ of powder flow requires only $8\ \mu A$ of charging current to reach
its limiting charge.

A particle with a charge q, which is sprayed in a cloud of similarly charged
particles towards an earthed substrate and is in a uniform field E, will
experience the following forces.

(i) A force F_e due to an externally applied field E:

$$F_e = qE. \tag{5.9}$$

Table 5.2 Maximum charge levels.

	Charge	Charge-to-mass ratio
Liquid droplet (Rayleigh limit)	$(64\pi^2\varepsilon_0\gamma a^3)^{1/2}$ $(7.5 \times 10^{-5})\gamma^{1/2}a^{3/2}$	$(36\varepsilon_0\gamma a^{-3}D^{-2})^{1/2}$ $(1.78 \times 10^{-5})\gamma^{1/2}a^{-3/2}D^{-1}$
Frictional charge (Gaussian limit)	$4\pi a^2\varepsilon_0 E_b$ $(3.3 \times 10^{-4})a^2$	$3E_b\varepsilon_0 D^{-1}a^{-1}$ $(7.92 \times 10^{-5})D^{-1}a^{-1}$
Corona charge (Pauthenier limit) (conductor) $E = 5 \times 10^5$ V m^{-1}	$12\pi\varepsilon_0 a^2 E_c$ $(1.66 \times 10^{-4})a^2$	$9\varepsilon_0 E_c D^{-1}a^{-1}$ $(3.96 \times 10^{-5})D^{-1}a^{-1}$
Corona charge (Pauthenier limit) (insulator) $E = 5 \times 10^5$ V m^{-1}	$6\pi\varepsilon_0 a^2 E_c$ $(8.3 \times 10^{-5})a^2$	$4.5\varepsilon_0 E_c D^{-1}a^{-1}$ $(1.98 \times 10^{-5})D^{-1}a^{-1}$

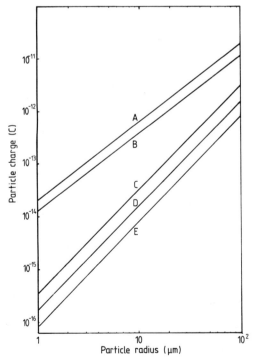

Figure 5.6 Charge as a function of particle radius for different charging mechanisms: A, Rayleigh limit for water; B, Rayleigh limit for solvent; C, Gaussian limit; D, Pauthenier limit for conductor, $E = 5 \times 10^5$ V m^{-1}, E, Pauthenier limit for insulator, $E = 5 \times 10^5$ V m^{-1}.

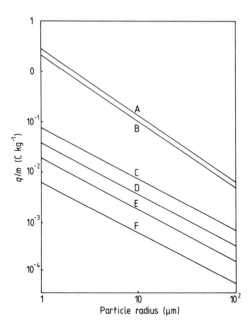

Figure 5.7 Charge-to-mass ratio as a function of particle radius for different charging mechanisms: A, Rayleigh limit for water; B, Rayleigh limit for hydrocarbon liquid; C, Gaussian limit; D, Pauthenier limit for conductor, $D = 1$, $E = 5 \times 10^5 \text{ V m}^{-1}$; E, Pauthenier limit for insulator, $D = 1$, $E = 5 \times 10^5 \text{ V m}^{-1}$; F, Pauthenier limit for insulator, $D = 3$, $E = 5 \times 10^5 \text{ V m}^{-1}$.

(ii) A force F_p due to the repulsion of the rest of the cloud of particles:

$$F_p = qE_p. \tag{5.10}$$

The field E_p due to a cloud of particles is given by the Gauss law and is:

$$E_p = QR/3\varepsilon_0 \tag{5.11}$$

where Q is the charge per unit volume in the cloud and R is the radius of the charged cloud. (If E_p exceeds $3 \times 10^6 \text{ V m}^{-1}$ the particles will discharge until the field is reduced to this limiting value.)

(iii) An image charge force F_i between the charged particle and its image in the earthed substrate:

$$F_i = q^2/16\pi\varepsilon_0 d^2 \tag{5.12}$$

where d is the particle-to-substrate spacing. This may be written

$$F_i = qE_i$$

with

$$E_i = q/16\pi\varepsilon_0 d^2. \tag{5.13}$$

These equations for the image force apply only if the particle is more than a few diameters from the substrate. At closer distances the position of the charge within the particle must be taken into account. The particle is polarised as it approaches its image, i.e. the charge and its image move closer together and the image force is increased. Calculations for the image charge force when the particle is very close to the substrate are given in §6.8.5.

In addition to these electrical forces a small particle will be affected by the air flows in the system. These are:

(i) the force due to external air flows or air flow from the spray gun,
(ii) the force due to the movement of air in the ion wind. The ion wind is the bulk movement of air in a corona discharge which occurs because the ions created in the discharge can impart their momentum to the neutral molecules. The ion wind normally flows at about 1 m s^{-1}.

The motion of particles is governed by a combination of these forces. Usually different forces govern the motion of the particles over different parts of their path. For example, if we assume the particle moves in an applied corona field of $3 \times 10^5 \text{ V m}^{-1}$, the image field, E_i, is greater than an applied field when

$$q/16\pi\varepsilon_0 d^2 > 3 \times 10^5.$$

If q is the Gaussian limiting charge this reduces to

$$d^2 < 2.5a^2$$

i.e. the image force is only important within a few particle diameters of the surface. At these close spacings it is increased by polarisation effects, as discussed above, and can be substantially higher than the force due to the applied field. The space charge field will exceed an applied field of 3×10^5 when

$$QR/3\varepsilon_0 > 3 \times 10^5$$

i.e.

$$Q > 8 \times 10^{-5} \text{ C m}^{-3}$$

e.g. a charge of $10^{-3} \text{ C kg}^{-1}$, on dust at a density of 80 g m^{-3} in a cloud of radius 0.1 m, will give a field which equals $3 \times 10^5 \text{ V m}^{-1}$.

The particles travelling under the influence of electrostatic forces rapidly reach their terminal velocity, u, where the electrostatic force is balanced by the aerodynamic drag: i.e.

$$qE = 6\pi\eta au \tag{5.14}$$

and

$$u = qE/6\pi\eta a.$$

The terminal velocity is plotted as a function of charging mechanism and particle radius in figure 5.8. It can be seen that velocities range from a few centimetres per second to a few metres per second therefore air velocities of a few metres per second will affect the particle motion, and in some circumstances dominate it.

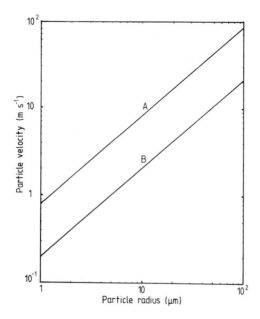

Figure 5.8 Particle velocity in a field of 5×10^5 V m^{-1} as a function of particle radius: A, particle charged to Gaussian limit; B, dielectric particle charged to Pauthenier limit.

Where there is no air motion, so electrostatic forces dominate, the particles follow the electric field lines to the substrate. This results in a high deposition efficiency and particles reach the back of the substrate which would normally be shielded (see figure 5.9(a)). However, it is difficult to coat inside recessed areas and there is a 'Faraday cage effect', illustrated in figure 5.9(b). There can also be a thicker coating on the edges of the substrate because of the additional particles pulled in by the electrostatic forces (figure 5.9(c)). In the paint industry this is known as window paning. Air motion can be used to force particles to regions which are electrostatically unfavourable and can reduce the Faraday cage effect. Effective coating is achieved by balancing the aerodynamic and electrostatic forces to achieve the required deposition.

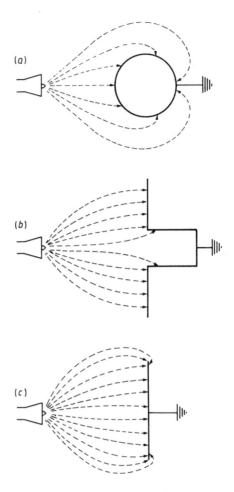

Figure 5.9 Electrostatic spraying: (*a*), wrap round; (*b*), the Faraday cage effect; (*c*), window paning.

5.2.2 Electrostatic paint spraying

When paint is applied by a conventional air spray gun the wastage can amount to as much as 70 % (Walberg 1977). The idea that efficiency could be improved, by applying an electrostatic charge to the droplets, so they were attracted to the work piece, was first patented by Pugh in 1932 and the first commercial electrostatic spray gun was produced in the 1940s. Electrostatic spraying of wet paints now holds a few per cent of the total spray coating market.

In an automatic electrostatic spray system the articles to be coated are hung on an earthed conveyer by metal hangers. Reciprocating spray guns are mounted about 30 cm away, and paint droplets are electrostatically charged by corona or induction from a high-voltage electrode at a potential of between 80 and 120 kV. The paint droplets move along the electric field lines and are attracted to the earthed work piece. The greatest savings are achieved with articles, such as furniture frames, where the electrostatic forces allow paint to be deposited on the surface facing away from the gun, but improvements from 40 % efficiency to 70 % have been reported with flat surfaces.

The work piece must be adequately earthed, both to prevent sparks, which could ignite a flammable solvent, and because a voltage, built up on the work piece reduces the electric field, and hence reduces the deposition efficiency. For the same reason the work piece must be a reasonable conductor. The maximum acceptable resistance between the work piece surface and earth can be calculated using Ohm's law ($V = IR$). For example, if the spray gun provides 100 μA of current, and a maximum potential of 100 V can be tolerated on the surface of the work piece, the resistive path to earth must be less than 10^6 Ω.

It has proved possible to coat some relatively insulating materials, either using a conducting primer or by heating (Moore 1973). For example, glass becomes conducting when heated to about 200 °C.

(a) *Spray gun types*
An electrostatic spray gun atomises and charges the paint. There are four common methods of atomisation and the droplets may be charged by corona or induction.

The paint can be atomised and charged simultaneously, using electrostatic forces alone. For example, in figure 5.10 paint is passed over a blade to which a high voltage is applied. The paint is atomised into a fine stream of droplets by the electric field between the blade and the work piece and is charged by induction as it leaves the blade. A stream of droplets is formed, which is uniformly distributed over the surface of the blade. Paints formulated for a purely electrostatic gun must have a resistivity in the range between 10^4–10^7 Ω m^{-1}. More conducting paints can be charged by induction, but form very uneven droplets. Paints with resistivity above about 10^7 Ω m will not charge well by induction. The viscosity also affects the atomisation process.

True electrostatic spray guns produce fine particles, with a close particle size distribution, and the particles are charged very efficiently. However, the energy required to atomise the paint is relatively high and these spray guns are limited to low-flow applications (typically of the order of a $10\,l\,h^{-1}\,m^{-1}$). The paint droplets from a purely electrostatic gun form a slow moving cloud, which moves under the influence of electrostatic forces alone. The droplets follow the electric field lines closely. They

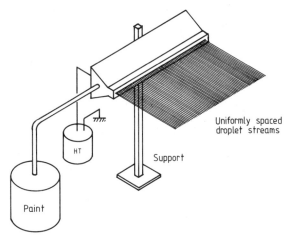

Uniformly spaced
droplet streams

HT

Support

Paint

Figure 5.10 Electrostatic blade paint spray gun.

therefore give good wrap round but have poor penetration into recessed areas.

When a higher paint flow rate is required, the droplets are normally formed by mechanical means. The original electrostatic paint guns used air atomisation to produce the droplets. These guns are not as efficient as purely electrostatic guns because the aerodynamic forces do not allow the electrostatic forces to have their full effect. However, the spray pattern can be varied in order to direct the paint into areas which are electrostatically dead, and it can prove to be more economic overall to use an air atomised gun rather than to touch up regions where an electrostatic gun gives a poor coating.

An airless spray gun atomises the paint by forcing it at high pressure through an orifice. This type of gun has a higher transfer efficiency than an air atomised gun and builds up a thicker coating in a single pass. It can also cope with high-viscosity paints, but requires high air pressures for successful operation. The pressure requirement may be reduced by using an air-assisted spray. For example, the paint can be forced through the nozzle which mechanically changes it to a thin hollow filament which is then converted to droplets by a tangential stream of air. This vortex air does not affect the axial speed of the droplets and hence the electrostatic forces are not significantly lower than in a pure electrostatic gun.

The droplets produced by air atomised and airless spray guns may be charged by corona from a needle at the tip of the gun or by induction at a high-voltage electrode as the paint leaves the gun.

A high transfer efficiency is also achieved by spinning-disc or spinning-bell spray guns. In the disc design, the paint is fed to the centre of a horizontal spinning disc, to which a high voltage is applied. It is driven to the periphery of the disc in a fine sheet by the centrifugal force and atomised by a combination of centrifugal and electrostatic forces. At low disc speeds (less than approximately 3000 rpm) the electrostatic forces play a substantial part in the atomisation process, but in the guns with high disc speed, which may operate at speeds up to about 50 000 rpm, the centrifugal forces dominate the atomisation process. The electrostatic forces produce a more uniform spray than purely centrifugal atomisation and also force the droplets to spread out so a wider band is painted. The spinning disc allows control of the droplet size as faster speeds produce finer droplets. The paint is charged by induction as it leaves the disc, therefore the system requires that the paint has some electrical conductivity, but there is not the close tolerance on conductivity that is required for pure electrostatic guns and conducting paints, such as waterborne coatings atomised effectively at high disc speeds. The theory of atomisation by a combination of electrostatic and centrifugal forces is analysed by Balachandran and Bailey (1982).

(b) *Power supplies*

Power supplies for electrostatic paint spray guns are usually separate, freestanding units, but a few commercial spray guns have the power supply within the gun itself. There are two types of generator used in this way. One is an electrogasdynamic (EGD) generator and the other a turbine generator. In an EGD generator (discussed in more detail in §5.12.3) a high voltage is built up as compressed air forces a charged aerosol against a voltage of a few kilovolts. Mechanical energy is thus converted to electrical energy creating a high-voltage low-current source. In the turbine generator, compressed air drives a small turbine in the gun head, which produces a low AC voltage. This is rectified and regulated before being multiplied by conventional voltage multipler circuits. The whole power supply is within the gun itself, which requires only compressed air for operation (Malcolm 1980, 1981). These designs avoid the necessity of heavy high-voltage cables between the gun and power supply.

(c) *Safety of electrostatic paint spray systems*

Although electrostatic spray guns operate at a high voltage, they will not give a dangerous electric shock if the current which may be drawn is limited. For example, if there is a resistor of 200 MΩ between a 100 kV power supply and the gun tip, then a current of 0.5 mA will cause a potential of 100 kV to be dropped across the resistor, i.e. if a person with a resistance of 10 MΩ touches the end of the gun tip, which is at 100 kV, virtually all the voltage is dropped across the internal resistance, and the current flowing through the person cannot exceed 500 μA. The limiting resistor is often situated in the gun head itself, as close as possible to the tip, but some designs use a distributed resistance down the length of the high-voltage cable.

If an electrostatic spray gun is used to spray paints based on hydrocarbon solvents, the energy of any spark from the gun must be limited to below

0.2 mJ to avoid ignition of the flammable vapours. The energy, U, of a spark is related to the gun voltage, V, and the capacitance, C, on which the voltage is stored by the equation

$$U = \tfrac{1}{2}CV^2. \tag{5.15}$$

The limiting resistor isolates the capacitance of the tip of the gun from the rest of the system, therefore only the capacitance of the part of the system after the resistor need be considered when calculating spark energy.

When a gun with a corona charging system and an internal resistance is brought up towards an earthed work piece the current rises, therefore the potential dropped across the internal resistance also rises and the potential at the gun tip falls. It is possible to design the gun so that, by the time it is close enough to an earthed surface for a spark to occur, the energy available at the gun tip is less than 0.2 mJ. Many commercial guns are certified safe and do not produce a hazardous spark capable of igniting flammable solvents. Precautions must also be taken to ensure that charge cannot build up on isolated conductors in the working area. For example, the work piece must remain earthed and the hangers by which it is connected to the conveyor must not become insulated by coatings of paint. Personnel must wear conducting footwear and operators of hand held guns should not wear rubber gloves which isolate them from the earthed gun.

Induction charging is very efficient but it requires a conducting paint to be in contact with the high-voltage electrode. This usually means that the paint pot will be at a high voltage, and must be isolated from earth and from the operator. The paint and its pot have a significant capacitance to earth which can store a large amount of energy which could discharge in a spark. If the paint droplets are charged by a corona discharge from a sharp point in the gun head, the electrostatic system and the paint flow system do not need to be in direct electrical contact. The paint pot can be grounded and the capacitance of the high-voltage electrode can be kept very low so the energy of any spark is below the ignition of a solvent vapour. Corona charging is not as efficient as induction charging, but it will allow a charge to be applied to insulating materials which cannot be charged by induction.

5.2.3 Electrostatic powder coating

Electrostatic powder coating is a method of metal finishing in which a paint layer is applied in dry powder form without the use of solvents (Hughes 1985, Harris 1981, Golovoy 1973a,b). A diagram of a conventional powder coating spray system is shown in figure 5.11. The powder is usually a resin, mixed with suitable pigments, free-flow agents, curing agents etc, which is ground to a mean size of about 40 μm diameter. This is pneumatically conveyed to the gun where it is sprayed past a high-voltage needle. The corona discharge between the needle and the earthed work piece creates a stream of unipolar ions, which charge the powder (as described in §2.2) so it is attracted to the work piece. The electric field which carried the particles to the work piece is provided both by the potential difference between the high-voltage-gun electrode and the earthed work piece and by the charged powder cloud. The powder is electrically insulating, therefore it retains its charge, and adheres to the work piece, which is moved to an oven where the coating is fused to form a continuous film.

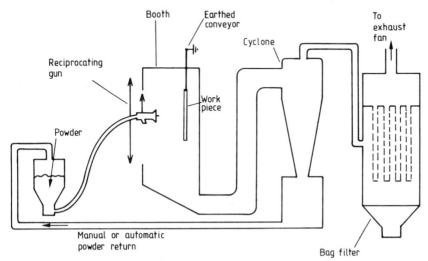

Figure 5.11 A schematic diagram of an electrostatic powder coating system.

While the work piece is in front of the gun the particles are held on to the surface by the electric field from the gun. When the field is removed, the charged particles are still held to the surface, attracted by image charges in the substrate. The charged particle and its image form a positive and negative pair which have no net effect some distance from the surface. The charge and its image can be considered to be opposite plates of a capacitor, i.e. all the field lines lie between the plates and none extend into space. There is, therefore, no repulsive field due to an infinite charge layer on a conducting surface. It is interesting to note that if a field meter is placed above the surface, a field will be measured because there is a capacitance between the meter and the charged surface. The charge which previously appeared across the capacitance between the surface and the earthed substrate is shared between the two capacitances and a field exists above the surface as a result of the presence of the meter.

A powder coating spray gun is conventionally given a negative voltage of about 80 kV, but nylon powders have a high tendency to charge positive by friction, and are usually sprayed using positive polarity. The current drawn

Table 5.3 Advantages and disadvantages of different types of powder coating.

Material	Advantages	Disadvantages
Acrylic	High durability, good hardness, excellent chemical resistance	Poor flow, moderate adhesion, brittle
Cellulose acetate	Excellent flow, good gloss and colour, excellent chemical resistance	Moderate adhesion soft film, discolours at high temperatures
Chlorinated polyethers	Excellent corrosion, mechanical and electrical resistance, self-extinguishing flame, good dimensional stability	Poor exterior durability, high cost, fair adhesion
Epoxies	Excellent adhesion, high alkali, abrasion and corrosion resistance	Chalking and yellowing in exterior applications, high cost
Fluorocarbons	High exterior durability and service temperature, low coefficient of friction, excellent chemical and electrical resistance	Poor adhesion, requires high curing temperature, high cost

Material	Advantages	Limitations
Nylon	Low coefficient of friction, high dielectric strength, chemical and abrasion resistance	Films below 100 μm difficult, poor adhesion, high cost, low service temperature
Polyester	Thermoplastic and thermoset available, intermediate cost	High curing temperature
Polyethylene	Good chemical resistance and electrical insulation, excellent flexibility, low water absorption, resists low temperatures, low cost	Poor adhesion and durability, poor exterior durability, and abrasion resistance, low service temperature
Polypropylene	Similar to polyethylene	Similar to polyethylene but higher service temperature
Polyurethane	High chemical resistance, excellent hardness, good gloss and flow	Poor adhesion, high water sensitivity, chalks and yellows in exterior use
Vinyls	High chemical resistance, high dielectric strength, long-term durability, good abrasion resistance, intermediate cost	Poor adhesion, only thick films 175 μm, maximum service temperature 105 °C

Table 5.4 Advantages and disadvantages of powder coating.

Advantages

(1) There are no solvents which are toxic and must evaporate from the coating.
(2) Powders are less flammable than solvents requiring an order of magnitude more energy to ignite them.
(3) Gives tougher more abrasion- and chip-resistant product.
(4) Thick coatings can be applied in a single operation.
(5) Smooth finishes can be produced over rough substrates.
(6) Resins which are not easily dissolved can be deposited.
(7) With a well designed system there is very little wastage.
(8) Special textured finishes can be easily applied.
(9) Allows faster conveyor speeds and closer spacing on conveyors.

Disadvantages

(1) Powder coating is usually only competitive where high volume and quality are required.
(2) Very thin coatings are difficult to produce.
(3) The temperature required for curing may degrade soft solder joints etc.
(4) It is difficult to achieve colour matching and uniformity.
(5) It is difficult to achieve good flow uniformity from the gun.
(6) Expensive to achieve fast, frequent colour change.
(7) Will not coat plastics or materials of high electrical resistance.
(8) Cannot be used where components contain rubber seals etc that cannot withstand the fusing temperature (usually 120 °C minimum).

is usually of the order of 50 μA therefore the power requirement of the spray system is only about 4 W, which is negligible compared with the requirement of the oven used to fuse the coating.

The oversprayed powder can be collected and reused and 98 % overall material usage is claimed in some installations. Usually the recovery system consists of a cyclone, followed by a fabric filter to remove the last traces of dust from the air. When powder is recycled, frequent colour changes obviously present a problem, as the booth and recovery system must be completely cleaned of all traces of the previous colour. Some systems have a separate recovery system for each colour, some change only the filter unit and others find it more economical to design the spray system for maximum powder usage and dispense with recovery. For example, the aerodynamics of the booth may be designed so the oversprayed powder remains suspended and can be recharged by auxiliary electrodes. A recent system has no cyclone and has a separate filter module, for each colour, which bolts onto the booth.

The powders in electrostatic coating systems are usually polymers, either thermosets or thermoplastics, and the process has proved particularly useful for epoxies and other materials which do not lend themselves well to solvent-based coatings. The epoxy and its hardener are mixed before the powder is ground and the final reaction occurs as the powder is fused at a temperature of about 120 °C. A particularly good bond is formed to the substrate and the paint layer tends to have good chip resistance. A summary of the more common types of polymer powder coating materials, with their advantages and disadvantages, is given in table 5.3. Recently, methods have been found of producing vitreous powders which have a sufficiently high resistivity to adhere to the substrate and the porcelain enamel industry is moving towards powder coating. The advantages and disadvantages of powder compared with wet paint are given in table 5.4.

(a) *Back-ionisation*

The phenomenon of back-ionisation was described in §4.2.4 as a problem which occurs during the electrostatic precipitation of dusts with high electrical resistivity. The electrical resistivity of the powders used for coating is several orders of magnitude higher than that of most dusts commonly collected by electrostatic precipitation and back-ionisation is an intrinsic part of the coating process. With polymer powders, back-ionisation begins as soon as there is a monolayer of powder on the surface (Sampuran-Singh *et al* 1979). As the layer builds up and electrical discharges in the layer create positive ions, the efficiency of powder deposition falls as shown in figure 4.4 and at high coating thicknesses very little powder is deposited. This has the obvious disadvantage that there is a high overspray after the first few seconds of coating, but it does mean that powder tends to be deposited on regions where the layer is thinnest, giving some degree of coating uniformity, i.e. the coating is to some extent self-limiting. The thickness at which the layer limits is greater, the greater the particle size and the lower the current density. It is also a function of the powder cloud density and when there is a high rate of arrival of powder a thicker coating is deposited (Bassett *et al* 1975).

Back-ionisation limits the field across the layer to 10^6–10^7 V m^{-1}. Thus, the potential drop across a layer which has an unfused thickness of 0.2 mm is of the order of 100 to 1000 V. This gives only a small reduction in the deposition field and the reduced efficiency in the presence of a deposited layer is due to back-ions from the discharges in the layer, not to repulsion by the charge accumulated on the surface, or to a decrease in the deposition field. Severe back-ionisation causes pinholes, moon craters and orange peel in the finished coating. These are different forms of surface blemish, which are formed as powder which has been deposited on the surface is thrown off as a result of the discharges in the layer. The details of which type of blemish is formed, and why, are not fully understood, but it is known that pinholes which penetrate through to the substrate are more likely with positive gun potentials and that surface blemishes are a bigger problem with more resistive powders and higher current densities. This has two practical consequences:

(i) It is difficult to coat protuberances on the work piece because field intensification directs higher currents to these regions (figure 5.12).

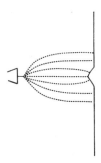

Figure 5.12 Field intensification at a protrusion from a work piece.

(ii) Particularly bad blemishes are created if the gun is moved closer to the work piece, after the coating has been deposited, so the current density is increased above the level for which the layer was stable. Figure 5.13 shows a surface before and after back-ionisation was increased by turning up the gun voltage, and a frame taken from a cinefilm of the disruption of the coating.

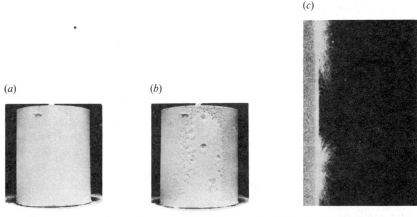

Figure 5.13 Formation of surface blemishes by back-ionisation. (*a*) Relatively smooth coating produced when back-ionisation is low. (*b*) Coated cylinder after voltage was increased showing moon craters and pin holes. (*c*) Fountains of powder leaving cylinder surface when back-ionisation is increased by increasing the gun voltage.

(b) *Measurements in powder coating systems*
For effective powder coating five things are required:

(i) a uniform powder flow from the gun;
(ii) a high voltage to create a corona current and a deposition field;
(iii) an effective earth so the work piece does not become charged and repel the powder;
(iv) an insulating powder which retains its charge at the work piece;
(v) a corona discharge from the sharp electrode which charges the powder;
(vi) a suitable balance between aerodynamic and electrostatic forces;
(vii) a well formulated powder.

(c) *Powder flow*
Although there is a degree of self-limiting, the thickness of a deposited powder layer depends on the powder flow rate. Therefore, when coating uniformity is critical it is important to have a uniform powder flow rate. Uniformity of flow is also an economic advantage as it is then possible to adjust the system for the minimum coating thickness required rather than having to allow for short-term fluctuations and a gradual decrease in flow with time as powder accumulates in the pipes to the gun. The powder flow is provided by a venturi feed from a fluidised- or fixed-bed powder hopper or occasionally by a screw feed. The powders are normally treated so they are free flowing, but fluidised systems tend to give the best flow characteristics for the widest range of powders. There is always a burst of powder when a gun is first switched on, because of powder settled in the pipe work but, once this has cleared, short-term variations within ± 10–15% can be achieved with a conventional system. Recently a powder feed system has been developed in which the powder and air flow rates are detected by means of pressure transducers and a feedback system maintains constant flow. Extremely uniform powder flow rates which remain constant to within 1.5–2.5 % are claimed for this system (Boyce 1985).

(d) *Voltage and current*
Most gun power supplies indicate both the voltage applied to the gun and the current drawn from the supply. Both are normally measured on the earth side of the circuit, therefore the current will include any leakage current as well as the corona current, and the voltage will not indicate any potential drop between the supply and the gun tip. If a fault is suspected the voltage must be measured at the gun tip using an electrostatic voltmeter or a potential divider which draws a current which is low enough not to cause the potential to fall, as described in Chapter 3. (A potential divider of resistance of $10^{11}\,\Omega$ draws 1 μA at 100 kV.)

The true corona current can be checked by measuring the current which

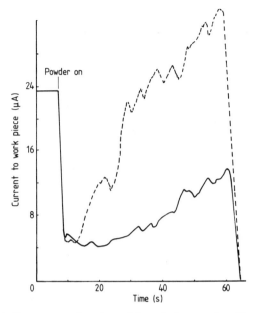

Figure 5.14 Current as a function of time during coating (from Cross *et al* 1980).

flows when the gun (without powder flow) is directed towards a flat sheet of metal which is connected to earth through a current meter.

A useful indication of a number of coating parameters can be obtained by monitoring the current which flows during coating, with the gun voltage held constant. Typical curves are illustrated in figure 5.14. The first portion of the curves show the steady corona current in the absence of any powder. When the powder is introduced the current falls because the powder particles are much more slow moving than the ions and form a space charge cloud which reduces the corona current from the gun. The size of this decrease depends on the total surface area of the powder in front of the corona needle and the uniformity of the current gives a measure of the uniformity of powder flow. After a few seconds of coating, the current rises as back-ionisation occurs. If the current remains low it does not necessarily mean there is no back-ionisation, it may indicate that the powder flow rate is too high, and the space charge cloud of powder has reduced the corona current so that charging is inefficient. The current may also be low if the high-voltage point becomes coated with powder so the corona is inhibited.

(e) *Earthing*

The work piece is normally earthed through the conveyor, and hangers may have to be completely stripped or replaced after a few passes through the system in order to maintain an effective earth. If it is assumed that a maximum potential of 1 kV can be tolerated, without introducing a potential hazard due to an electrostatic spark or decreasing the potential difference between gun and work piece significantly, then for a current of $50\,\mu A$ a resistance of $2 \times 10^7\,\Omega$ is acceptable. If the electrical path to earth registers on a megohm meter, the earth is adequate for coating purposes. Electrostatic powder coatings can be applied to materials such as glass and porcelain and the application of shatter-resistant coatings to glass bottles is a major potential application of powder coating.

(f) *Powder resistivity*

Charge decays from the deposited powder with a time constant τ:

$$\tau = \varepsilon_0 \varepsilon_r \rho \qquad (5.16)$$

$$\simeq 10^{-11} \rho.$$

Powders with a resistivity exceeding $10^{13}\,\Omega$ m retain their charge for several minutes. Conducting particles ($\rho < 10^{10}\,\Omega$ m) lose their charge rapidly and reverse polarity by the induction process, so they are repelled back to the gun. With a reasonably dry compressed-air system, polymer powders nearly always have sufficient resistivity to adhere to the work piece, but vitreous enamels require special treatment to reduce the water absorption on the surface and raise their resistivity.

Electrostatic deposition of conducting particles is only possible under one of the following conditions:

   (i) the surface is sticky;

   (ii) the particles are very small so that the molecular adhesion forces exceed the electrostatic removal forces;

   (iii) the conducting particles are a small percentage of the powder so that individual conducting particles are insulated from the substrate by the resin particles.

Electrostatic powder coating has been used to apply aluminium layers to steel which has been precoated with an adhesive layer. The electrostatic forces serve the purpose of ensuring a uniform dispersion of the aluminium powder (Taylor 1972).

(g) *Powder charge*

The powder used for electrostatic powder coating is usually in the size range of 5–50 μm diameter and is charged by corona. Referring to figure 5.7, it can be seen that for polymer particles of radius 20 μm, which pass through a monoionised field of the order of $5 \times 10^5\,V\,m^{-1}$, the charge-to-mass ratio will be

$$q/m = 1 \times 10^{-3}\,C\,kg^{-1} = 1\,\mu C\,g^{-1}.$$

This corresponds to a current of 1 μA for each g s^{-1} of powder flow. In practice, there must be many more ions than are necessary to charge the powder particles and, for a powder flow of a few g s^{-1}, currents of 20–50 μA are common. These additional ions must be removed before the charge on the powder can be measured. The charge-to-mass ratio on powder samples is normally measured using a Faraday cup as described in Chapter 3 and the free ions are removed by means of an earthed grid across the entrance of the outer cup, as shown in figure 5.15. The high-mobility ions are collected by the wide-mesh grid (3–10 mm spacing) whereas the powder passes undeflected to the measurement cup. After a few seconds of measurement, the grid becomes coated with powder and the positive ions created by back-ionisation at the grid considerably reduce the charge on the powder. The charge-to-mass ratio must therefore be measured within the first few seconds, before the grid has become coated. Back-ionisation from the grid can be eliminated by using a grid consisting of wires down which water is allowed to flow (Moyle and Hughes 1983).

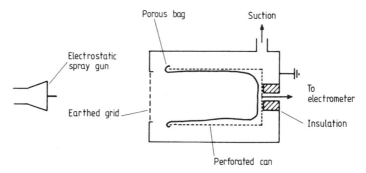

Figure 5.15 Measurement of the charge on powder from an electrostatic powder coating spray gun.

O'Neill (1977), using a dry grid to collect ions, showed that the charge on the powder from a commercial gun, operating at low powder flow rates (<1 g s^{-1}) was close to the Pauthenier limit for a field of 1×10^6 V m^{-1}, reaching 2.5×10^{-3} C kg^{-1}. (If the charge was less than 0.2×10^{-3} C kg^{-1} the powder would not adhere to a work piece.) Moyle and Hughes, using a water-washed grid but a different powder, measured a charge of 7×10^{-4} C kg^{-1}.

The presence of a water-washed grid between the gun and work piece in a coating system, both eliminates the free ions and shields the work piece from the gun voltage. The powder is deposited under the influence of self-repulsion and image forces alone. This improves the quality of the coating because back-ionisation from the work piece is substantially reduced. The coating is smoother and the powder is more uniformly deposited round a cylindrical work piece. Figure 5.16 shows wrap round with and without a water grid (Moyle and Hughes 1983). The coating thickness immediately in front of the gun decreased but the coating on the back of the work piece increased because the reduction in back-ionisation increased the powder charge so the electrostatic forces, tending to direct powder to the back of the work piece, were greater.

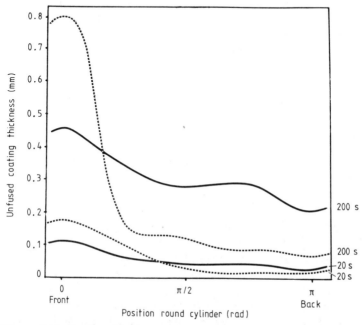

Figure 5.16 Coating thickness round a cylinder with and without a water-washed grid after 20 and 200 s (from Moyle and Hughes 1983) (dotted curves, without grid; full curves, with grid).

Lacchia (1974) separated the charge carried by free ions and powder by applying suction to a standard Faraday cup. The suction velocity was varied but held above the level where all the powder was collected. The number of free ions entering the cup with the powder was proportional to the suction velocity and the charge on the powder was proportional to the powder mass. The powder and ion currents could therefore be separated.

(h) *Aerodynamic forces*
The velocity of air from the gun and air flow within the booth reach speeds of several metres per second. Measurements, using laser Doppler anemometry, have shown that electrostatic forces only dominate the motion of powder particles within about 10 mm of the work piece (Sampuran-Singh and

Bright 1977). In the absence of air from the gun the ion wind dominates the motion of the particle near the gun (Sato 1980c). For optimum coating efficiency the air from the gun must be low enough to allow electrostatic forces to have their full effect at the work piece, but must be sufficient to ensure that the particles reach the work piece, rather than being swept away by the booth air. The minimum velocity of the booth air is fixed by two requirements, the legally permissible booth face velocity to keep powder effectively within the booth and the requirement that the mass of dust per unit volume of air in the recovery system must be below the explosive limit. (10–20 g m^{-3} for most polymers). Good control of the air flow pattern from the gun can also help to overcome the Faraday cage effect.

(i) *Powder formulation*

The size and shape of the powder particles affects both the final coating appearance and the powder handling characteristics. For example, good quality thin coatings require a narrow particle size range. Early coating systems suffered from excessive orange peel appearance and this has now largely been overcome by controlling the molecular structure of the polymer to give a low melt viscosity, and by varying the amounts of plasticiser, pigment and other chemicals which are added to the resin when it is formulated.

Very small amounts of contamination in powders can spoil the finish. Tiny hairs from dust contamination collect powder particles and form nibs in the finished coating, and contamination due to insufficient care during colour change can cause unsightly specks.

Practical experience shows that some powders coat more efficiently than others. In some cases this can be explained by measurements of the powder properties. For example, powders with a high concentration of TiO_2 tend to have a high dielectric constant and charge slightly more efficiently (Sampuran-Singh 1981). Powders with an extremely high electrical resistivity tend to charge poorly. (It is not clear whether this is due to an inability of the charge to spread over the surface of the powder or to a requirement for polar groups on the surface of the powder if it is to retain charge.) Resistivities much above 10^{15} Ω m cannot be measured using the simple powder resistivity cell which is described in Chapter 3, and therefore the correlation between resistivity and poor charging characteristics has not been fully investigated.

Poor transfer efficiency has also been found for powders which charge well. It has been shown that this can be due to a high tendency for the powder layer to back-ionise but, in an example quoted by Cross *et al* (1980), this could not be correlated with particle size, dielectric constant, charging efficiency or electrical resistivity. The effect of powder formulation on powder and coating properties is one of the most important current areas of research in powder coating.

(j) *Safety*

The principles for avoiding fires and explosions in electrostatic powder coating plant are similar to those which must be enforced in a paint spray plant, but the minimum spark energy which can ignite a typical coating powder is an order of magnitude higher than the ignition energy for a paint, so that safe operation is easier to achieve. The capacitance of the gun, following the limiting resistor, is kept low to limit the energy of a spark from the gun and, as before, the work piece must be sufficiently well earthed to prevent a potential building up to beyond a few hundred volts.

Powder clouds are only explosive above a density of about $10 \, \mathrm{g \, m^{-3}}$ therefore, where possible, powder clouds in the system are kept below this limit. For example, the recovery system should be designed so the air flow is sufficient to maintain the powder density below the explosive limit. There is usually a cloud of explosive density within the booth, near the gun, but this cloud is small and unconfined so in the event of a spark (for example, from a poorly earthed work piece) there is usually only a quick flash fire which is extinguished immediately. The greatest hazard arises if hot fragments from a booth fire are carried through to a bag filter or some other part of the recovery system where a high powder density might arise, and so these parts must be suitably vented or given explosion protection.

(k) *Alternative powder coating systems*

Although the most common powder coating technique is the corona spray system, described above, there are a number of other types of system available. For example, the powder may be charged by friction by passing it at high speed through a bank of plastic tubes in the gun head. The tubes are made of a highly insulating material, but there is sufficient charge leakage to allow the charging process to continue indefinitely. The limiting charge which can be applied by friction is the Gaussian limit, defined by the breakdown field of the air. The radius of the tubes in the gun head is small, so the field at the tube walls remains below the breakdown field, and the charge on particles can reach the single-particle Gaussian limit. Reference to figure 5.7 shows that this is higher than the charge typically applied to a polymer powder by corona. For a suitable powder, which charges well by friction, this is confirmed experimentally. A frictional charging gun does not produce large numbers of free ions therefore back-ionisation is reduced. It is not eliminated completely, but the discharges have a different form, and a greater thickness is deposited before efficiency falls (Sampuran-Singh *et al* 1979).

There is no applied voltage at the gun tip, and the force directing the particles towards the work piece is provided by the cloud of charged particles and the air flow from the gun. Guns which charge by friction tend to perform better with re-entrant samples than corona guns, both because there is no externally applied field and because the high charge per unit volume of the powder cloud gives a high space charge field and particles transported into a re-entrant region by aerodynamic forces experience a larger self-repulsion to the walls. Unfortunately, frictional charging is not effective with all powder formulations and can be upset by contamination or changes in humidity.

The powder may also be charged by a corona discharge inside the gun. In this system a voltage of 5 to 10 kV is applied to electrodes inside the gun and the powder is charged as it passes between them. The electrodes are designed so the high-speed air flow prevents powder deposition on the earthed electrode and back-ionisation in the charging zone is minimised. The number of free ions which emerge with the powder is lower than from a conventional gun, and there is no externally applied field between the gun and the work piece. The field directing the particles is due to the charged cloud itself. The Faraday cage effect and back-ionisation are therefore low. This type of gun is often combined with precipitating plates inside the booth, i.e. a voltage is applied to plates on the booth walls which repel powder back towards the work piece. This improves deposition efficiency and the system is normally sold without powder recycling equipment for applications requiring frequent colour change.

For small components, or wire coating, a fluidised bed may be more suitable than a spray system. The principal of an electrostatic fluidised bed is illustrated in figure 5.17. In the simplest design high-voltage corona electrodes are placed in the bottom of a fluidised bed of powder and an earthed work piece is held over the bed. The electric field between the electrodes and the work piece lifts the powder from the bed and the work piece is coated. Fluidised-bed coatings have a high charging and coating efficiency and give

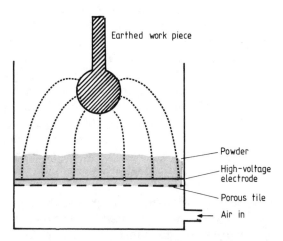

Figure 5.17 A schematic diagram of a simple electrostatic fluidised-bed coating system.

good penetration. There is also no reclaim problem and expensive powder recovery equipment is eliminated. However, there is some tendency for powders to stratify, with the finest powder fraction forming the coating. The simple design shown in the diagram is not suitable for use with explosive powders, as the cloud density in the bed is above the explosive limit, and a work piece hanging incorrectly could cause a spark. However, intrinsically safe fluidised beds are available. For example, the electrodes may be designed to limit the energy available in a spark, or may be placed below the porous tile so that the gas ions flow through the tile to charge the powder. A commercial unit operating with this system is shown in figure 5.18. Ionised air fluidises twin beds and the earthed work piece passes between them. The continuous process takes place in a covered tunnel and powder recovery needs are minimal.

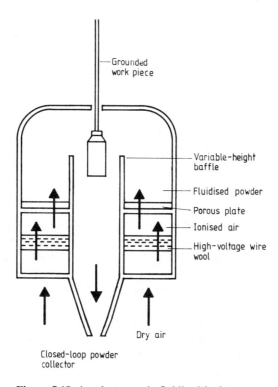

Figure 5.18 An electrostatic fluidised-bed coater.

5.2.4 Crop spraying

Electrostatics forces may be used to improve the deposition of pesticides (in liquid or powder form) on crops. The process has the same advantages and problems as electrostatic paint and powder spraying. Electrostatic forces can considerably improve the deposition efficiencies, particularly on the underside of leaves. Liquid pesticides are usually chemicals dispersed in water. They may therefore be charged by induction as the liquid contacts a high-voltage electrode but must be atomised mechanically to produce a uniform spray. The droplets produced in the presence of an electric field are more uniform than those formed by purely mechanical methods, and the repulsion between the droplets tends to distribute them evenly. For applications where the spray nozzle can be held within half a metre of the foliage, the electric field between the high voltage on the spray gun and the plant (which is effectively an earthed collector) provides a force which carries the droplets all round the foliage. The velocity imparted to the droplets by electrostatic forces is of the order of 1 m s^{-1}. This is less than the wind speeds in which the device must frequently operate and the droplets are usually carried to the vicinity of the foliage by air from the spray gun. The electrostatic forces are then able to reduce drift and improve the collection efficiency and uniformity of coating. In practice the spray unit is often not close to the foliage and the field between the gun and the leaves is low. The deposition force is then due to the field of the charged cloud of droplets, and to the image charge force between the charged droplet and the charge this induces in the earthed leaf. The order of magnitude of these forces was discussed in §5.2.1, where it was shown that the image charge is only significant when the particles are very close to the surface of the leaf. Electrostatic charging significantly increases the probability that a particle passing close to a leaf will be captured.

Typically, droplets of 20–50 μm radius are chosen for crop spraying to give a reasonable charge-to-mass ratio and electrostatic velocity (see figures 5.7 and 5.8 respectively). The charge-to-mass ratio on the droplets is approximately $10^{-3} \text{ C kg}^{-1}$, i.e. the current requirement is 1 mA per kg s^{-1} sprayed. Thus for a gun at 50 kV the power requirement is 50 W for each kg s^{-1} or 50 W for each 1 s^{-1} sprayed.

Electrostatic forces have also been applied to crop dusting, where the electrostatic effects not only aid the uniform dispersion of the powder, but also add to the adhesion forces holding it to the leaves.

Field tests show significant improvements with electrostatic charging of both droplets and powders. The Agricola Company carried out tests with a pesticide dust doped with 4 % copper to aid analysis. Their results (presented in table 5.5) showed that electrostatic spraying greatly increased dust deposits, with greater uniformity on both sides of the leaf. Liquid systems have been used both for ground level plants and for trees. Law and his co-workers at the Agricultural Engineering Department of Georgia University have carried out a considerable number of laboratory and field trials of electrostatic systems over the last fifteen years. Generally, an improvement by a factor of between two to four in the amount of pesticide deposited on

Table 5.5 Efficiency of electrostatic crop dusting. A copper doped crop dusting powder was sprayed on to *Solanum* plants in the open air at a distance of ten yards. The figures in the table relate to the weight of copper, in micrograms per square centimetre of leaf, with charged and uncharged powder.

	Leaf at front of bush (μg cm^{-2})			Leaf at back of bush (μg cm^{-2})		
	Upper surface	Lower surface	Total	Upper surface	Lower surface	Total
Uncharged	5.3	0.5	5.8	2.5	0.2	2.7
Charged	6.5	4.6	11.1	5.8	2.8	8.6

ground crops is reported. The deposition efficiency depends on the structure of the plant, with more pesticide deposited on smooth plants, such as cabbages, than on plants with more pointed leaves such as broccoli (Law and Lane 1981). In most cases, the deposition efficiency at first increases with increasing voltage applied to the gun, then levels off at higher voltages, but for cotton plants there appears to be an optimum voltage with a significant decrease in the effectiveness of electrostatic spraying at high gun voltages. This has been reported both for liquid sprays (Law and Lane 1981) and for electrostatically deposited powdered pesticides (Webb and Bowen 1970).

When there is a cross wind it may be advantageous to shield the spray area. An earthed metal shield will obviously collect charged droplets and reduce the amount of pesticide reaching the crops. However, if a voltage is applied to the shield to repel the particles, the shield will provide a deposition field. In still air, a charged shield does not give significantly more deposition than an unshielded system (Anantheswaran and Law 1981) but in a cross wind a shield is useful. Anantheswaran and Law (1981), investigating a system for spraying turf grass, have shown than an effective screen can be made using a highly insulating sheet such as mylar or polyethylene. The shield in the geometry tested, charged when spraying first began and provided a field equivalent to a metallic shield with an applied voltage of 30 kV. Figure 5.19 shows the deposition efficiency for a metal and a dielectric screen, compared with deposition in the absence of a shield where the deposition field is provided by the self-field of the droplet cloud.

Inculet and Castle (1981) have investigated a system designed to spray an orchard. Very fine liquid droplets were created and charged by induction at an air shear nozzle. The electrostatic field was produced by the charge cloud itself and its image in the collecting foliage. With this system, electrostatic forces made no difference to the amount of pesticide applied in the lower part of the trees but the foliage at the top of the tree contained 85 % more pesticide with electrostatic rather than with mechanical spraying.

Electrostatic forces produced a more uniform distribution of pesticide, with the upper parts of the tree having 97 % of the coverage of the lower parts with electrostatic forces, against 51 % without electrostatic assistance. Electrostatic crop sprayers have been designed both as backpacks and as tractor-operated systems (Coffee 1974).

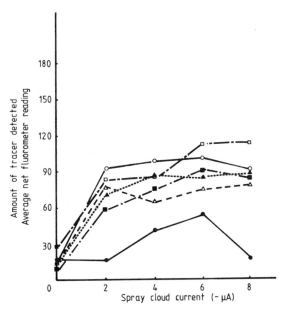

Figure 5.19 Spray deposition achieved with different methods of electrostatic coating on to planar targets (from Anantheswaran and Law 1981): ●, 0 kV; △, − 10 kV; ■, − 20 kV; ○, − 30 kV (on metal plate); □, dielectric plate; ▲, no external precipitator.

5.2.5 Electrostatic conditioning

Electrostatic forces may be used to apply surface treatments to powders or granules for a number of different purposes. The conditioning agent (in the form of a fine powder or a liquid spray) is spread more evenly under the influence of electrostatic forces and, under some circumstances, selective conditioning of granules in a mixture is possible. For example, conducting and non-conducting mineral particles have been oppositely charged by friction and dispersed in an aerosol of oleic acid dissolved in carbon tetrachloride to give a selective coating to aid froth flotation. The aerosol was given an electrostatic charge appropriate to the mineral it was required to coat. The process gave significant improvements in the flotation behaviour of the mineral mixture compared with the same amount of additive applied non-electrostatically (Balint and Flemming 1964).

5.2.6 Control of fugitive dust

Dust emissions from sources such as rock crushing, coal stock piles and open belt conveyors are commonly controlled by spraying the dust with a fine water spray. The spray is most effective when the water droplets are approximately the same size as the dust particles therefore, to remove the respirable fraction, a droplet particle size of less than 10 μm is required. Fine dust is usually electrostatically charged and attachment between the droplets and the dust can be improved by charging the water spray to the opposite polarity (Hoenig 1977). An independent evaluation of two commercial electrostatic foggers is reported by Brookman and Hartshorn (1982). They found that the effectiveness was improved by between 10 and 40 % by the addition of an electrostatic charge. In these tests the authors report that insufficient water was used for the scale of the dust source and this may have contributed to the discrepancy between these results and the manufacturer's field trials which achieved 78 % improvement (Mathai 1981). Castle *et al* (1983) have suggested that the charged water spray can also be used to impart a charge to neutral fumes and dust to enable it to be collected in an electric field between collector plates.

5.3 ELECTROSTATIC SEPARATION

5.3.1 Introduction

Electrostatic separation processes sort particles according to their size, shape, density, electrical conductivity or the polarity of the frictional charge acquired (Inculet *et al* 1982, Inculet 1984). The particles are charged by friction, induction or corona (or a combination of these processes) and are separated because their motion in an electric field depends on their charge-to-mass ratio.

For example, consider a particle of charge q and mass m falling under gravity between vertical-plate electrodes, with a field E between them (figure 5.20). The electrostatic force on the particle is

$$F_e = qE.$$

The gravitational force on the particle is

$$F_g = mg.$$

There is a transverse acceleration on the particle equal to F_e/m and the

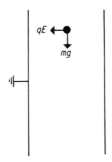

Figure 5.20 Forces on a particle falling in a transverse electric field.

particle rapidly reaches its terminal velocity where the electrostatic force is balanced by the aerodynamic drag. This horizontal velocity is given by

$$u_h = qE/6\pi\eta a.$$

The particle travels a distance d in a time $t = u_h/d$. In the vertical plane the terminal velocity is

$$u_v = mg/6\pi\eta a$$

and the height fallen in the time t is

$$h = u_v/t.$$

The ratio of the distance travelled horizontally under the influence of the electrostatic force and the distance travelled vertically is

$$d/h = qE/mg = F_e/F_g.$$

The limiting field which can be applied in practice without electrical breakdown is about 1×10^6 V m^{-1} and the limiting charge is the Gaussian limit which is a surface charge density $Q_s = 2.64 \times 10^{-5}$ C m^{-2}:

$$F_e = 4\pi a^2 Q_s E$$
$$F_g = \tfrac{4}{3}\pi a^3 Dg$$

i.e.

$$\frac{F_e}{F_g} = \frac{d}{h} \simeq \frac{8}{aD}.$$

Thus if the collection process requires that the particles of positive and negative charge be separated by 100 mm in a fall of 300 mm then each polarity must travel 50 mm and the maximum particle size will be given by the equation:

$$d/h = 8/Da = \tfrac{1}{6}.$$

The maximum particle size that will be separated for a density of $D = 3 \times 10^3 \ \mathrm{kg \ m^{-3}}$ is therefore 13.3 mm.

5.3.2 Triboelectric separation

Triboelectric separation is the separation of two insulating materials which charge to opposite polarities by friction. Frictional charge may be applied by a number of different systems.

(i) The fluidised bed
The two materials are dispersed in a fluidised bed and charge to equal and opposite polarities as a result of the interparticle contacts. In practice there is also charge exchange when two particles of the same material contact each other, so that this technique tends to give rather poor charge separation between the two materials. This problem can be overcome by reinforcing the action of the fluidised bed by an applied electric field. A system of this type, which has been used to separate iron ore from silica, is shown in figure 5.21 (Inculet and Bergougnou 1973). Iron ore tends to charge positively when in contact with silica and, since it is relatively conducting, it can also be charged by induction. The stainless-steel porous plate at the base of the fluidised bed is therefore given a positive potential. The Fe_2O_3 particles which contact it acquire an additional positive charge by induction, whereas the more insulating silica particles are unaffected. This reinforces the positive charging of the

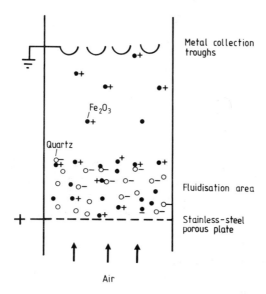

Figure 5.21 An electrostatic fluidised-bed separator (from Inculet and Bergougnou 1973).

iron ore which moves in the electric field to the top of the bed where it can be collected. Laboratory tests on synthetic mixtures of iron and glass powders, 15–55 μm in diameter, recovered more than 60 % of the iron (Kiewlet *et al* 1978).

(ii) Rotating drum

Two powders may be charged by mixing them in a rotating drum. This suffers from the same problems as the fluidised bed, because charging is primarily due to particle–particle contact. However, it has the advantage that the drum can also be a kiln when hot separation is required, and in this case the less efficient charging may be acceptable.

(iii) Vibrating chute

When powder falls down a vibrating chute charge is transferred by contact between the particles and the surface of the chute. The material of the chute can therefore be chosen so that the two materials to be separated charge to opposite polarities. The amount of charge transferred is a function of the work done during the contact (see Chapter 2) therefore the vibrating chute tends to give rather a low charge and higher charges are achieved by techniques giving higher frictional speeds.

(iv) Air cyclone

Cyclones produce high levels of charge and have been used in a number of different systems. Pearce and Pope (1976, 1977) tested the separation of a number of materials in the laboratory, using a cyclone diameter of 10 cm operating at 0.25 g s^{-1}. They give a triboelectric series for minerals (table 5.6) and quote results for the separation of quartz from dolomite, fluorite, barite, galena/fluorite and galena/barite. With a surface treatment to modify the triboelectric properties they also separated quartz and calcite, and quartz and apatite.

A cyclone triboelectric separator has also been reported by Masuda *et al* (1983). They found that for efficient separation of coal from mineral matter, it was necessary to select a cyclone wall material specific to the nature of the mineral inclusions and, in some cases, to make cascaded combinations of cyclones with different wall materials.

The electrocyclojet, illustrated in figure 5.22, and a tribocyclone, have been used on a laboratory and a pilot scale by Carta *et al* (1981) to separate various minerals and to reduce the ash content and sulphur content of coals. The essential feature of the electrocyclojet is the automatic recycling of the middlings, which has been found to improve separation efficiency significantly.

In a new type of tribocharger, recently patented by Ciccu (1984), particles are charged by impaction. The apparatus consists of a high-speed rotating wheel, surrounded by a cylindrical, or cone-shaped, surface. Mineral particles fed to the wheel are thrown off by centrifugal forces and impact against the surface.

Table 5.6 The triboelectric series of various minerals on different charging surfaces. A and B designate different samples of the same mineral species.

Charge	Copper	Tin	Zirconium	Brass	Nickel
Highest negative	Biotite	Biotite	Biotite	Biotite	Biotite
	Muscovite	Muscovite	Muscovite	Muscovite	Muscovite
	Quartz	Quartz	Quartz	Quartz	Quartz
	Albite	Ilmenite	Tourmaline	Albite	Petalite
	Orthoclase	Arsenopyrite }	Albite	Petalite	Albite
	Tourmaline	Petalite	Orthoclase}	Orthoclase	Orthoclase
	Petalite	Albite }	Petalite	Ilmenite	Tourmaline
	Arsenopyrite	Tourmaline	Arsenopyrite	Arsenopyrite	Ilmenite
	Ilmenite	Chalcocite	Ilmenite	Tourmaline	Arsenopyrite
	Galena	Galena	Galena	Cassiterite }	Red Hematite
	Cassiterite }	Orthoclase	Cassiterite	Galena	Galena
	Chalcocite }	Cassiterite	Chalcocite	Calcite	Cassiterite
	Red Hematite	Red Hematite	Red Hematite	Red Hematite	Apatite
	Apatite	Specularite	Specularite	Chalcocite	Calcite
	Specularite	Calcite	Calcite	Apatite	Chalcocite
	Celestite	Dolomite (A)	Apatite	Specularite	Specularite
	Dolomite (A)†	Apatite	Dolomite (A)	Dolomite (A)	Dolomite (A)
	Barite (A)	Celestite	Barite (A)	Celestite	Celestite
	Fluorite (B)	Fluorite (B)	Fluorite (B)	Barite (A)	Barite (A)
	Barite (B)	Barite (A)	Celestite	Fluorite (B)	Fluorite (B)
	Calcite	Barite (B)	Barite (B)	Barite (B)	Barite (B)
	Fluorite (A)	Fluorite (A)	Fluorite (A)	Fluorite (A)	Fluorite (A)
Highest positive	Dolomite (B)	Dolomite (B)	Dolomite (B)	Dolomite (B)	Dolomite (B)

†The charge obtained on dolomite was unstable when copper was used as a charging medium.

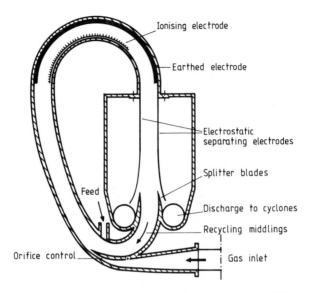

Figure 5.22 The electrocyclojet (from Carta *et al* 1981).

The range of materials which can be separated in a tribocharger can be extended by chemical pretreatment (Pearce *et al* 1977, Alfano *et al* 1985, Earnst and Singewald 1981). For example, sodium salts can be separated from potassium salts by giving the mixture a chemical pretreatment with dodecylamine or Pamak (a trade name for alkali-metal salts of oleic acid). These additives selectively change the surface conductivities of the two materials.

Temperature can also be important. For example, the triboelectric separation of phosphorous pentoxide from carbonate gangue is practically insignificant at room temperature, but becomes progressively more effective as the temperature is increased. Tests showed that at 150 °C the phosphorous pentoxide fraction reached 30 % with a 70 % recovery. This was attributed to differences in the surface electrical properties of the two materials as water was released (Alfano *et al* 1985).

5.3.3 Induction separators

A very simple induction separator can be demonstrated by placing a mixture of metal and insulating spheres between two parallel plates, the upper of which has a central hole. When a field of a few kV cm^{-1} is applied between the plates the conducting particles are charged by induction and bounce back and forth between the plates as discussed in §2.4. The insulating particles become polarised but gain no net charge therefore they do not leave the

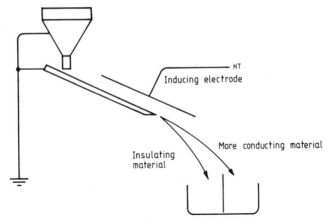

Figure 5.23 A chute separator.

lower electrode. The result is that only conducting particles pass through the hole in the upper plate. The particles will also separate if the plates are inclined with respect to each other. The particles which charge by induction travel along curved field lines between the two electrodes and experience a centrifugal force which moves them outwards to where the plates are furthest apart.

A continuous separator, that operates by induction alone, is shown in figure 5.23. The particles pass down the earthed chute and conducting particles are charged by induction in the field between the chute and the high-voltage electrode. This gives them a force of attraction towards the upper electrode, so they follow a different path as they fall off the chute. A similar principle operates in the screen electrostatic separator used to separate zircon from rutile shown in figure 5.24.

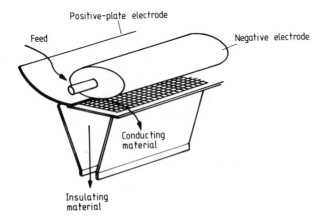

Figure 5.24 A screen electrostatic separator.

Particles with similar conductivity may sometimes be separated by shape. Two types of grass seed have been separated in the laboratory in an inclined-plate induction separator, because one type of seed had a fine fibre at one end. When an electric field was applied both types of seed were aligned in the field. The type without the hair charged by induction and left the electrode, but the seed with the hair would not take a high charge, because a corona discharge occurred from the tip of the hair. This type of seed therefore remained in the high-field region.

5.3.4 Corona separators

Figure 5.25 shows a rotating-drum separator which uses both corona and induction charging and separates materials according to their conductivity or size. The particles pass through a corona discharge and acquire a charge which depends on the particle radius and dielectric constant and the field of the corona discharge, as discussed in §2.2.4. Both insulating and conducting particles are charged, but the conducting particles are able to lose their charge to the earthed drum. As the drum rotates the conducting particles fall off under gravity, are thrown off by centrifugal forces or are pulled off as they charge by induction in the field of the second sphere. Insulating particles do not lose their charge, and are not charged to the opposite polarity by induction, therefore they are held to the drum until they are brushed off.

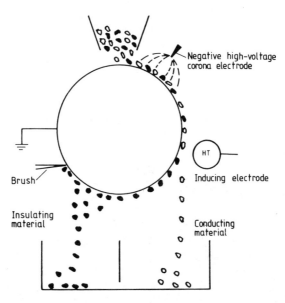

Figure 5.25 A rotating-drum electrostatic separator.

The electrostatic force which holds an insulating particle on to the drum is

$$F_e = qE + qE_i$$

where E is the applied electric field and E_i is the field due to the image charge. The speed of the drum for which the particles will just be held to the drum can therefore be calculated by equating the centrifugal force to the electrostatic force:

$$mu^2/r = q(E + E_i)$$

where m is the particle mass and r is the drum radius

$$u^2 = qr(E + E_i)/m. \tag{5.17}$$

It can be seen that the speed of the drum for which a particle will be thrown off is proportional to the square root of the charge-to-mass ratio of the particle. The charge is proportional to the square of the particle radius and the mass to the cube of radius, therefore the charge-to-mass ratio is inversely proportional to particle radius and larger particles will be thrown off at lower speeds. Non-spherical particles will also have a different adhesion force to spheres and it may be possible to choose a drum speed to separate on shape as well as on size or material.

A first approximation to the image charge field can be calculated by assuming that the charge resides at the centre of the particle. The field acting on a particle with a charge q, resting on a surface, due to the image of that particle is then

$$E_i = q/4\pi\varepsilon_0(2a)^2. \tag{5.18}$$

In practice the sphere will be polarised and the charge and its image will be closer than $2a$. A more accurate calculation of image charge adhesion is given in §6.8.5. There will also be forces of adhesion between the charged particles and the drum surface, due to charge exchange at the interface, molecular forces and forces due to absorbed water layers. These will usually be significant only for fine particles, less than 50 μm in diameter. For larger particles an adequate estimate of the required drum speed can usually be made using equation (5.17).

Fine particles are difficult to separate because of strong interparticle forces and because they tend to be affected by the windage of drum rotation. The drum method is normally considered to be applicable to a minimum size of 50–100 μm (depending on density) and a maximum of about 10 mm, but Lawyer and Dyrenforth (1973) claim to have achieved separations of particles down to 5 μm by using a pulsed corona discharge and high drum rotation speeds.

The separation of fine particles may also be achieved using a vibratory fluidised-bed tribocharger (described above), where aerodynamic forces separate the individual particles. However very fine particles (less than about 40 μm in diameter) tend to be entrained in the gas flow and for these particles Inculet *et al* (1977) have proposed a system in which the material is circulated in a loop, which is illustrated in figure 5.26. The particles are charged either by friction or by corona. The flow in the separation region is quasi-laminar and the particles move across the streamlines, according to their electric charge. A pilot scale system 8 m high has been tested, with a 100 mm diameter pipe on the upwards section. The ash content of the coal was reduced from 10 to 2 %. The system has also been used to remove carbon from fly ash.

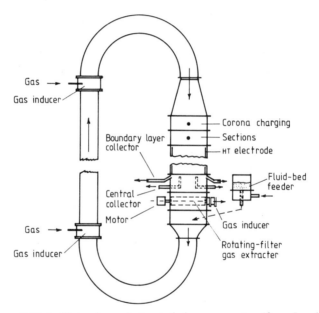

Figure 5.26 A dilute-phase electrostatic loop separator (from Inculet *et al* 1977).

Electrostatic systems are able to separate materials which vary only moderately in conductivity. Charge decay follows an exponential law and the charge q remaining after a time t is given by

$$q = q_0 \exp(-t/\tau). \tag{5.19}$$

τ is the time taken for the particle to reach about 37 % of its initial charge and depends on the resistivity and the dielectric constant of the particles:

$$\tau = \varepsilon_0 \varepsilon_r \rho \tag{5.20}$$

e.g. for quartz $\rho = 10^{17}$ and τ is therefore about 10^6 s whereas for pyrites τ is about 10^{-3} s.

5.3.5 Industrial applications

The first patents on electrostatic separators were taken out in the 1870s for the separation of lightweight constituents from cereals. Ground wheat was passed under a rubber roller which was electrified against a felt pad. The lightweight chaff was attracted to the roller and separated from the heavier grain. The technique was applied to the separation of minerals in 1886, when Carpenter patented the use of a triboelectrically charged belt for concentrating dry sands containing pyrites and galena, and Edison (1892) patented a separator for the concentration of gold. The first major commercial success was in 1912 when a system was set up to beneficiate lead and zinc ores. The interest in triboelectric separation decreased with the development of the froth flotation process early in the twentieth century, and in spite of the difficulties of dewatering, flotation became the most common separation technique in the minerals industry. However by the 1950s commercial electrostatic processes included separation of small diamonds from gangue, quartz from feldspar, phosphate rock from silica sand, seeds and nuts from their shells, rubber from fabric, gypsum from marl and zircon from rutile and ilmenite. This early work is reviewed in the book by Ralston (1961). In 1965 a large corona separation plant was installed in Canada to supplement gravity concentration of iron ore. The ore was crushed and concentrated when wet by gravity. The product was then further concentrated by electrostatics. This plant processed six million tons of ore a year and reduced silica from 8 to 2 % (Dyrenforth 1978).

Tests were carried out in Sweden, which showed that electrostatic techniques were the most successful way of removing phosphorous as well as silica from iron ore, and a dry electrostatic iron ore concentration plant has been built by the LKAB company at Malmberget. Triboelectric separation is used extensively in the potash mineral salt industry of Western Germany (Lebaron and Kropf 1958). In one system (Moore 1973), deflecting electrodes 10 m long are used to separate mixtures of salts at 200–300 t h^{-1}. 100 kV is applied between the electrodes and a current of 1 mA is drawn. A similar technique has been used to beneficiate 57 % pure coal with a feed size of 800 μm (Singewald 1976). The system operates at a feed rate of 5 t h^{-1} and, with the middlings recycled, recovers 88 % in the form of a concentrate containing 94.7 % pure coal, with a reject containing 14 % coal. Advanced Energy Dynamics are using a rotating-drum separator between a pulveriser and the boiler of a power station for coal benefication. Evidence from pilot scale tests suggests that ash-forming minerals and sulphur can be removed from coal more effectively by electrostatics, than by other conventional benefication techniques.

Electrostatic separation is also used extensively in the minerals industry (Lawyer 1969, Kelly and Spottiswood 1982). Pearce *et al* (1977) published a table of triboelectric mineral separations reported in the literature to

December 1976 and triboelectric separators used in the USSR are discussed by Olofinskii (1978). Although the minerals industry is the largest user of electrostatic separators, they are also in operation in the food industry and in the separation and beneficiation of municipal wastes (Takahashi *et al* 1980, Grubbs and Ivey 1972).

5.4 ELECTROKINETIC PHENOMENA IN LIQUIDS

5.4.1 Introduction

A liquid–solid, liquid–liquid or liquid–gas interface develops a charge double layer, as described in §2.5.2. Therefore, the surface of particles or bubbles in a suspension will be charged, and will be surrounded by a loosely bound diffuse layer of liquid ions of the opposite polarity. If an electric field is applied the particles will move in one direction and the liquid in the other. The movement of a particle in the field is called electrophoresis and the movement of the liquid electro-osmosis. The potential at the slippage plane is defined as the zeta potential.

A neutral particle will not experience a force of translation in a uniform field, but it will polarise and align with the field. There will only be a net force on the particle if the electric field is non-uniform. The movement of a neutral particle in a non-uniform field is called dielectrophoresis. There is also a force on a liquid, even in the absence of particles, due to the action of the electric field on ions or dipolar molecules, which is transmitted to the bulk of the liquid by intermolecular collisions. This electrohydrodynamic effect is called electroconvection.

No attempt will be made to give a detailed review of the theory of these processes and this section will concentrate on stating the basic equations governing the processes and discussing the applications in industry. More detail may be obtained from the review by Dukhin and Derjaguin (1974).

5.4.2 Electrophoresis and electro-osmosis

Electrophoresis and electro-osmosis were demonstrated by Reuss (1809), soon after the discovery of electrolysis. Liquid motion was observed when a field was applied to water in a vertical U tube, the bottom of which was blocked off by a porous quartz plug. No motion was observed in the absence of the plug and it was therefore assumed that the liquid was electrified by contact with the quartz. Electrophoresis was demonstrated in a second experiment in which quartz particles suspended in water were observed to move in an applied electric field. The first quantitative work was carried out nearly fifty years later when it was shown that the volume velocity of liquid flow in electro-osmosis was proportional to the electric current (Wiedemann 1852).

Soon afterwards Quincke (1859) demonstrated that a phenomenon opposite to electro-osmosis exists, and a potential difference is set up by the flow of a liquid through a porous plug. He found that the direction of the electric field depended on the direction of flow and was the same for plugs made of all the materials tested. Electro-osmosis causes liquid to rise up a capillary tube when a potential is applied and in the reverse process a potential is measured as a liquid flows through a capillary. This potential is known as the streaming potential.

There is also a reverse process to electrophoresis, and a sedimentation potential is set up when particles fall under gravity or move under the influence of a mechanical force. In this process the mobile part of the diffuse double layer tends to lag behind the particle as it moves, generating a potential across the sedimentation tube.

A theory for electro-osmotic flow in capillaries, when the double-layer thickness is small compared with the radius of the capillary, was developed by Smoluchowski (1921) (Dukhin 1974). According to Smoluchowski, the volume velocity of electro-osmotic flow is proportional to the current density I and also depends on the zeta potential ζ, the specific electrical conductivity σ, the viscosity η and the relative dielectric constant ε_r, i.e.

$$u = I\varepsilon_0\varepsilon_r\zeta/\eta\sigma. \tag{5.21}$$

The hydrostatic pressure generated by electro-osmosis in a capillary of radius a and length l is given by

$$P = 8\zeta\varepsilon_r\varepsilon_0 E/a^2 l. \tag{5.22}$$

This agrees with the data from Quincke's experiments in which the pressure was measured for different tube radii and electric fields.

Provided the double layer is thin, the electrophoretic velocity of a particle is given by a similar formula to the electro-osmotic liquid velocity, i.e.

$$u = E\zeta\varepsilon_r\varepsilon_0/\eta. \tag{5.23}$$

This applies provided the double-layer thickness is much smaller than the radius of curvature of the particle, so that the particle can be considered to be a flat surface for which the electro-osmotic slip is given by equation (5.21).

As the double-layer thickness increases, the electric and hydrodynamic phenomena cannot be considered separately inside and outside the double layer, and the electrophoretic motion becomes dependent on the shape and size of the particle.

Smoluchowski also developed the first theory for the sedimentation potential built up as particles settle through a liquid and obtained the equation

$$V_s = \frac{4\pi\varepsilon_0\varepsilon_r a^3(D - D')g}{3n\sigma} \tag{5.24}$$

where $D - D'$ is the density difference between the particles and the liquid.

Reviews of electrokinetic phenomena, including discussions of the derivations of these formulae, are given by Dukhin and Derjaguin (1974).

Electrophoresis and electro-osmosis depend, not only on the electrostatic forces which cause the migration of the particle and liquid towards the appropriate electrode, but also on the chemical and electrical exchange reactions which occur at the electrodes. For example, electrode reactions can destabilise a suspension and cause it to precipitate out at the electrode. Frequently there are a number of electrode reactions in competition and the overall kinetics of the process is complicated. The boundary layers near the electrodes are in general different from the bulk liquid and the passage of components through the layers may be diffusion limited.

Electrophoresis and electro-osmosis have widespread uses in the separation of the particulate and liquid phases of colloids, for example in dewatering coal sludge or the separation of clay from water (Grebenyuk *et al* 1975, Yukawa *et al* 1979, Lockheart 1983, 1984). The processes have also been discussed as a means of sewage treatment (Sunderland and Ellis 1981) and for stabilisation in civil engineering (Farmer and Bell 1975). Electrodialysis, which is the transport of ions through a membrane by an electrical driving force, has been used in the demineralisation of sugar and whey solutions in the food industry. Electrophoresis and electro-osmosis are also the basis of electropainting which is used to apply primer in most of the automotive industry.

5.4.3 Electropainting

Electropainting, or electrophoretic coating is a method of dip coating for water-based paints where electrical forces are used to transport the paint components, in solution or suspension, to the work piece. The work piece is lowered into a bath containing an electrode, and a potential of a few hundred volts is applied between the electrode and the work piece. The components of the paint migrate to the work piece where various electrochemical reactions take place and the paint precipitates out. Areas close to the electrode are coated first but as the resistive layer of paint builds up the current starts to flow to clean areas of the work piece. Coating is complete after about two minutes and the article is removed and rinsed. The paint film is fused and hardened by baking in an oven. The process provides a paint film with good corrosion resistance particularly in box sections. In 1977 it was claimed that 40–45 % of the new automobiles in the United States were electropainted and in Europe and Japan 90 % were electroprimed (Hopp 1977, Anon 1976b). A number of reviews of different aspects of electropainting are published in the *Advances in Chemistry* series, published by the American Chemical Society (No 119, Electrodeposition of Coatings) and a review and bibliography is given by Chandler (1978, 1981).

The paint is a mixture of the following components.

(i) Organic salts of polymers; these are made water soluble by the addition of a suitable acid or base (depending on the nature of the resin) and form ions in solution. The ions have large molecular weights and multiple charges, therefore they are surrounded by an atmosphere of counter ions.

(ii) Pigment particles; these are surrounded by resin particles and emulsifiers and also carry a charge.

(iii) Ions of emulsifying agents.

(iv) Ions of water.

(v) Contaminants.

When an electric field is applied, the positive ions and particles migrate to the cathode and the negative particles and ions to the anode. At the electrodes a number of reactions occur in competition and a chemical equilibrium is reached.

The early systems were all anodic, i.e. the resin was acidic in nature and charged negatively. For an acid resin [RCOOH] solubilised by a base [KOH] the electrode reactions are as follows.

(i) At the cathode

$$K^+ + e \rightleftharpoons K$$

$$2K + 2H_2O \rightleftharpoons 2KOH + H_2$$

$$2H^+ + 2e \rightleftharpoons H_2.$$

Hydrogen gas is evolved and the base regenerated.

(ii) At the anode (which is the article to be painted)

$$RCOO^- + H^+ \rightleftharpoons RCOOH \qquad \text{(the paint is deposited)}$$

$$4OH^- - 4e \rightleftharpoons 2H_2O + O_2 \qquad \text{(oxygen is evolved)}$$

$$M - e \rightleftharpoons M^+ \qquad \text{(the anode dissolves)}.$$

The pigment particles migrate to the electrode in the electric field and are embedded in the collecting layer. The water created at the anode moves out of the deposited layer by electro-osmosis which also makes the paint layer denser.

It can be seen that the base is regenerated but paint is constantly removed from the bath. Therefore it is necessary to continuously top up the bath with a base-deficient paint. Alternatively, the alkali is isolated in a box near the cathode where it is removed by flushing with water.

The build-up of paint obeys Faraday's laws of electrolysis, i.e. the weight of film deposited is proportional to the charge carried through the paint. Higher voltages therefore give a faster coating and better penetration into box sections. The voltage is limited by film disruption, which occurs when the current rises to a level where too much heat is created by the current passing through the resistive layer.

The electron exchange reactions can only occur at the metal interface with the film. Ions then carry the charge through the insulating film under the influence of the high field which builds up across it. The kinetics of the deposition of the paint film depend not only on the electrical forces carrying material to the electrodes, but on diffusion-limited processes in the layer and on the way that heat created in the layer is dissipated. It is therefore very difficult to predict theoretically how the process will behave and how the coating will build up with time.

The paint film which builds up is relatively insulating and the voltage drop across it is significant compared with the applied voltage. There is therefore a strong tendency for deposition to occur on the areas with the thinnest coating. As the areas closest to the cathode become coated with the insulating layer, the potential drop across them increases until the field drops below a threshold value. The coating process then ceases in that area and the current flow moves to areas further away. This will include areas inside box sections which cannot be reached by spraying. The ability of the coating to penetrate inside such sections is called the throwing power. The high throwing power is the most important advantage of electropainting systems.

Other advantages are high paint utilisation, because there is no overspray, and a very even film thickness.

With the anodic process described above, light-coloured paints cannot be deposited easily because the metal anode, or its phosphate pretreatment, are dissolved, and tend to stain the deposited paint. This problem is reduced by cathodic deposition where the paint is formulated so that it charges positively and moves to the cathode where there is no metal dissolution (Wessling *et al* 1972).

The reactions at the cathode are typically

$$2H^+ + 2e \rightleftharpoons H_2$$
$$OH^- + RNH^+ \rightleftharpoons RN + H_2O.$$

The nitrogen atoms in the resin give it a basic character so that it forms a water-soluble salt in the presence of an acid.

The gas evolved at the coated electrode is hydrogen, rather than oxygen, therefore the possibility of corrosion during coating is reduced. With cathodic deposition a good protective layer is built up with 15–20 μm of coating rather than 25–35 μm typical of anodic deposition therefore there is an overall energy saving. Anodic deposition uses typically 30 kW h per 100 m^2 of steel, where cathodic deposition uses 18–19 kW h. These advantages of cathodic deposition were foreseen for some years before the process was used commercially because some difficulty was experienced in finding suitable resins that could be charged appropriately and produce a coating of the correct resistivity. However, the first cathodic deposition plant was installed in the United States in 1977 and now cathodic electropriming is widespread in the automobile industry.

Although initial reports on cathodic deposition were highly favourable, as time progressed, it was found that it did not entirely live up to the early claims. In particular, the metal was not as inert as had been expected, and staining could still occur (Anderson *et al* 1978). The corrosion resistance of cathodic-deposited layers was still found to be greater than that of anodic-deposited layers, but this is probably due as much to the quality of the resin as the process by which it is applied (Schenck and Stoelting 1980). Problems have also been reported to arise as a result of the corrosive nature of the paint (Murphy 1978). Since the paint is acidic, corrosive-resistant pumps and pipework are required. In the anodic deposition system the whole tank often forms the cathode but with the acid paints of the cathodic system the tank is normally lined to prevent corrosion and stainless-steel anodes are inserted which are isolated from the tank. The anodes have an area which has a ratio of at least one to four of the cathode area to be coated.

A theory of film growth, applicable to both anodic and cathodic coating, has been presented by Pearce *et al* (1978), who found that there was a great similarity between the growth kinetics of a paint film and an inorganic oxide film.

Throwing power can be defined as the ability of an electrodeposited paint to be deposited in the interior of an object where auxiliary electrodes are not provided. For penetration into deep tubes, with a reasonable coating time, auxiliary electrodes must be used, or holes must be provided in the section to be coated. An understanding of the throwing power of the system is important to enable the position of these to be defined. Honig (1977) investigated throwing power using a series of plates in a long coating bath illustrated in figure 5.27. The cathode was set up at one end of a long tank and the current

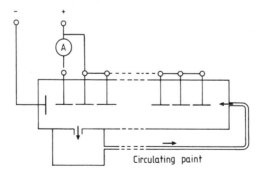

Circulating paint

Figure 5.27 Apparatus for measuring throwing power (after Honig 1977). The positive potential is applied to all plates and the current measured to each individually.

flowing to each anode plate in the row was recorded as a function of time. When electropainting started the current flow to the first segment increased rapidly to a peak where the paint started to deposit. The current decreased slowly as the resistive layer built up until, at a certain point, paint started to deposit on the next segment (figure 5.28). By plotting the time for the current maximum against the number of the segment, S, he found an equation of the form

$$t = AS^3/PV^{4/3} \qquad (5.25)$$

where A is a constant which is a function of the experimental geometry and V is the deposition voltage. This equation defines P, the throwing power. The most significant factors which control the throwing power of a paint are its specific conductivity, its coagulation properties and the rate of build-up of film resistance (Honig 1977).

Throwing power has also been studied by Furuno and Ohyabu (1977), and Haagan (1976) reviews ten different measurement techniques. Although the throwing power is primarily a property of the paint, factors such as the geometry of the measuring system and the methods used to remove heat from the deposited layer may affect the result and it is best to choose a system which resembles the product to be coated to evaluate the throwing power of different paints.

Since the resistivity of the system changes as the layer is deposited, either the current or the voltage must also change. Systems may be operated at either constant current or constant voltage. Electrodeposited coatings can also be applied using a current supply which is periodically interrupted. (The

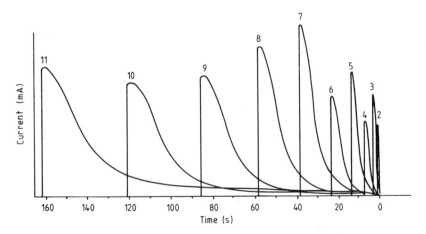

Figure 5.28 Current flow to the various anode segments (denoted by numbers on the curves) in figure 5.27 as a function of time (after Honig 1977). The differences in deflection reflect different sensitivity ranges of the current meter.

voltage is applied for a few seconds then interrupted for a few seconds (Brown 1974, 1975).) This has been found to allow higher voltages without film rupture because the pause allows the heat created in the layer to be dissipated. The voltage must normally be interrupted several times before sufficient paint has built up to reduce the current to a level where heating does not occur. The interrupted-current method gives thicker limiting coatings, which are smoother and more uniform, because the gas bubbles produced at the electrode are smaller. A small increase in the throwing power has been reported and in some cases an improvement in corrosion resistance is also found.

The rate of film growth can be accelerated using a cationic powder suspension with macroscopic rather than microscopic resin particles. In this way a film of 40–80 μm is built up in 15–60 s rather than a film of 15–35 μm in 1.5–4 min with conventional electropainting (Saatwerber 1979). Electropainting has also been used to produce composite films with powdered materials added to electroplating baths. For example, wear-resistant coatings have been produced by codepositing metal carbides and borides in a metal matrix (Addison and Kedward 1977).

5.4.4 Electrophoretic separation and electro-osmotic dewatering

Electrophoretic separation dates back to investigations by Pauli in 1924. The electrophoretic force can be used to increase the settling rate of suspended fine particles and electro-osmosis simultaneously thickens the sludge. The theory of electrically enhanced sedimentation is discussed by Yukawa *et al* (1979) and Lee (1978). Bier (1957) developed a force flow electrophoresis technique involving a membrane to concentrate biological substances and Moulik *et al* (1967) investigated forced-flow electrofiltration to separate clay and water. In the forced-flow processes, the field is applied parallel to the flow in a filter press with the direction of the field designed to move the particles in the opposite direction to the liquid flow. This system is used to treat industrial liquid wastes and also in the separation of emulsions, such as latexes produced by emulsion polymerisation processes (McCann *et al* 1973).

Giddings (1966) and Grushka *et al* (1973) investigated a system where the electric field was applied perpendicular to the direction of flow to fractionate particles according to their physical characteristics. Cross flow filtration was investigated by Harland *et al* (1978), but only very low filter rates were achieved. However, when forced-flow electrophoresis, in which a field is applied to force particles to migrate away from the filter surface, is added to the cross flow filtration process, which uses the fluid shear force tangential to the filter medium, to minimise particle accumulation on the filter interface, a comparatively high and steady filtration rate is achieved (Henry 1972, Henry and Jacques 1977). Henry's work was extended to non-aqueous systems by Lee (1978). The current drawn by the liquid in relatively resistive non-aqueous systems is much lower than flows through water, therefore high electric fields may be applied.

Figure 5.29 shows the principle of a cross flow electrofilter (Lee 1978). The filter is a porous metal plate or tube. A potential is applied between this porous electrode and a non-porous electrode (which is a second plate in a duct system, or a wire down the centre of the tube in a cylindrical system). The polarity is set so that the particles are attracted to the non-porous electrode and the fluid flows in the reverse direction. The particles are drawn away from the porous surface and do not block it or build up a cake to cause a pressure drop. Lee showed that above a critical applied potential a clear boundary layer formed at the filter surface. This depended on the Peclet number and electrophoretic mobility of the particles and on the rate of filtration. The system was shown to be feasible for the removal of micron-sized particulates from non-aqueous slurries such as are generated in coal liquefaction processes.

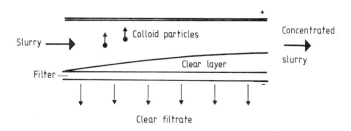

Figure 5.29 A cross flow filter (after Han 1975).

Electro-osmotic dewatering of cláys, by electrodes placed in stationary tanks of sludge, has recently been studied by Lockheart and Stickland (1984). They looked at different voltages and sample depths, and studied the effects of salt, acid, alkali and flocculant on the process. The rate of dewatering was a function of the current flow and it was more effective to dewater small depths repeatedly than to treat a deep tank. They found that additives could be beneficial and that the suspension was desalted as well as dewatered. Normally, the clay particles travelled to the anode and the water to the cathode. The large-scale dewatering of tailings ponds at coal mines has been shown to be feasible in two separate studies in the United States and Australia (Kelsh and Sprite 1982, Lockheart and Stickland 1984).

For example, in one trial, Lockheart and Stickland (1984) used three horizontal electrodes to dewater 570 tons of tailings to spadeable consistency (67 % solids) in two weeks. The applied voltage was 26–33 V and the system consumed 9 kW h t^{-1} on a wet basis and 20 kW h t^{-1} on a dry basis.

5.4.5 Electroflotation

Colloid particles can also be removed from liquids by electroflotation. In this process the bubbles of gas, created by electrolysis, scavenge particles and carry them to the surface. The process was first applied to sewage treatment in 1919, but the electrodes tended to collect a scale which stopped the current flow. The elimination of this problem and the theory of the process has recently been discussed by Fukui and Yiu (1985).

The collection process depends on the size of the particles and the bubbles, the electrostatic charges on both the bubbles and the particles, and the hydrophobicity of the particles. Collection is least efficient for small particles with a diameter of about 1 μm. Above this diameter hydrodynamic reactions give a dependence of the rate of flotation on radius of $r^{1.5}$, but below it, the collection efficiency again begins to increase as a result of increasing influence of Brownian diffusion (Reay and Ratcliffe 1973).

The effect of electrostatic charge has been investigated by Derjaguin and Shukakidse (1961). They found that the rate of flotation dropped sharply when the zeta potential was increased beyond a critical value and several experiments indicate that flotation is more effective the lower the zeta potential of the particles (Collins and Jameson 1977).

5.4.6 Electroconvection

When an electric field is applied to a liquid, free ions, which may be due to dissociation, or to injection from the electrodes, will move. They transfer momentum to neutral molecules and this results in bulk movement of the liquid, which is known as electroconvection (Gemant 1929). The first mathematical formulation of the phenomenon was put forward by Ostroumov (1915), who combined the conduction equation, with the Navier–Stokes hydrodynamic equation and arrived at the conclusion that electrical conduction would be non-Ohmic and that liquid motion would occur, which would be laminar at low fields, but become turbulent at high fields.

In addition to the Coulomb force on free charges in a DC field, there will be a dipole force on liquid molecules which have a natural dipole moment or are polarised in the applied field. This will lead to liquid motion in both AC and DC non-uniform fields.

The total force on a volume of liquid with a charge per unit volume, Q, may be written

$$F = QE + (P \cdot \nabla)E. \tag{5.26}$$

For a simple medium, with constant dielectric constant, the polarisation, P, is proportional to the electric field, E (see Chapter 7):

$$P = \varepsilon_0(\varepsilon_r - 1)E \tag{5.27}$$

and

$$F = QE + \tfrac{1}{2}\varepsilon_0(\varepsilon_r - 1) \ \mathrm{grad} \ E^2. \qquad (5.28)$$

Electroconvection can be used to enhance the heat transfer in liquid systems, to provide a pumping force or to increase the viscosity of a liquid, introducing the possibility of electrically controlled mechanical coupling. The IEEE Industrial Applications Society have held a number of conferences on electrohydrodynamic effects where the latest research in these areas is published (Cambridge (USA) 1969, Fort Collins 1978, Mexico 1983).

5.4.7 Injection pumping

Electrostatic pumping of liquids can be demonstrated in the apparatus shown in figure 5.30 (Pohl 1958). Liquid is attracted to the wire by dielectrophoretic forces, and charge is injected as a result of the high field at the wire surface. The liquid is then repelled and, if the wire protrudes through the liquid surface and a voltage exceeding a critical value is applied, an upward jet of liquid is formed. Jets up to 2 m high, with a narrow cone angle of 3–5° have been reported. Calculations showed that the electromechanical conversion in the laboratory demonstration was 50 % efficient.

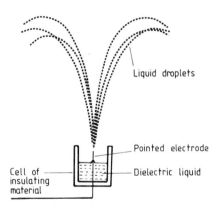

Figure 5.30 Pumping action of strong non-uniform field (after Pohl 1958).

The same process will also operate as a powder pump but the cone is normally more diffuse. A wide range of poorly conducting liquids and powders have been pumped in this way, including $CuSO_4 \cdot 5H_2O$, talc, alumina, silica and PVC (Pohl 1958).

This demonstration forms the basis of the cofield pump of Middendorf and Brown (1958) and the ion drag pump of Stuetzer (1959, 1960, 1961, 1962). Theoretical and experimental analyses show that the pressure built up by an ion injection pump is very approximately proportional to V^2 (Pickard 1965). However, the 'constant' of proportionality contains a factor which takes account of emission processes at the electrode surface, which are relatively unstable and difficult to predict and are a function of the applied voltage. It is found that the pumping action can take several hours to reach stable operating conditions, probably because of changes in the electrode emission characteristics with time. Although pumps using electroconvection and dielectrophoresis are reasonably efficient they have not found practical industrial application.

5.4.8 Electrically assisted heat transfer

The transfer of heat from a solid to a fluid by convection depends on the properties of the fluid and its velocity. Newton's law of cooling states that the rate of loss of heat per unit area is proportional to the temperature difference ΔT:

$$\frac{\mathrm{d}H}{\mathrm{d}t} = h\Delta T. \tag{5.29}$$

Here, h is defined as the heat transfer coefficient and has the dimensions of $\mathrm{J\,m^{-2}\,K^{-1}}$ and H is the heat per unit area. The heat transfer coefficient may itself be a function of temperature.

The earliest detailed study of the use of electrical forces to induce a movement of molecules, and hence introduce a form of forced convective heat transfer, was due to Senftleben (1932, 1934) and Senftleben and Braun (1936). They found that the convective heat transfer between a hot wire at the centre of a cylinder of gas increased by 50 % when a field was applied, provided the gas molecules had a permanent dipole moment. Molecules of gas in an electric field will have a dipole moment, which may be induced or permanent. The magnitude of the dipole moment per unit volume depends on the density of the gas, with a colder, denser, gas having more molecules per unit volume and hence a higher dipole moment. The dipoles experience a force in a non-uniform electric field which is proportional to the dipole moment so that a cold element will experience a higher force than a hot element (Kronig and Schwarz 1949). Although several patents appear in the literature, the phenomenon does not have much practical application in gases, as highly non-uniform electric fields are required, and the gas atoms must be polar for the effect to be large. Heat transfer in gases, when the field is high enough to create a corona discharge, is discussed further in §5.6.

Aschmann and Kronig (1950) repeated Senftleben's work, using an insulating liquid rather than a gas, and again measured an enhanced heat transfer when an electric field was applied. Mascarenhas published a series of papers in the nineteen fifties examining the apparent increase in the thermal conductivity of liquids in the presence of direct and alternating fields and produced theoretical equations in good agreement with experimental results. Mascarenhas (1957), Bonjour and Verdier (1960a,b), and Bonjour *et al* (1962) have extended the work to higher temperatures (up to the liquid boiling point) and also considered semiconducting liquids. Electrically assisted heat transfer has been reviewed by Newton (1973), Poulson and Richardson (1976) and Jones (1977), and a detailed theoretical analysis was carried out by Turnbull in a series of seven papers between 1968 and 1971 (Turnbull 1968, 1969a,b, 1970, 1971a,b, Turnbull and Melcher 1969). The effect of the electric field on boiling and condensation has also been studied by Velkoff and Miller (1965).

Research has now identified five mechanisms by which heat transfer in a liquid is enhanced in an electric field.

(i) Forced convection due to the electrostatic force on free charges in the liquid. These may be present because of dissociation or the presence of impurities or may be injected from a sharp high-voltage electrode.

(ii) Forced convection due to the dielectrophoretic force on induced or permanent dipoles.

(iii) Stirring by the motion of solid particles in the electric field.

(iv) Changes in the motion of bubbles of vapour in the liquid during boiling.

(v) Condensation effects.

The first two effects can be treated together and are termed 'electrically forced convection'.

(a) *The theory of electrically forced convection*
The electrical conductivity, σ, of a liquid is related to the current density, J, by the equation

$$J = \sigma E. \tag{5.30}$$

The conductivity is a function of temperature, therefore the current density and charge density are also functions of temperature. The action of an electric field on this non-uniform charge distribution results in motion away from the hotter surface.

The charge density and dielectric constant of a liquid are both functions of temperature. Therefore, when there is a temperature gradient, equation (5.28) must be modified to account for the inhomogeneity of ε and Q. The forces acting on the liquid can be summarised in the equation

$$F_{el} = QE + \varepsilon_0(\varepsilon_r - 1)\ \mathrm{grad}\ E^2 - \tfrac{1}{2}\ \mathrm{grad}[\varepsilon_0(\varepsilon_r - 1)E^2] - \tfrac{1}{2}\ \mathrm{grad}[DE^2 \delta\varepsilon/\delta D]$$

$$\tag{5.31}$$

(Landau and Liftshitz 1960).
The first term represents the electrophoretic force on dissociated ions, the

second is the dielectrophoretic term due to a non-uniform field, the third is due to a non-uniform dielectric constant and the fourth is an electrostrictive term due to changes of dielectric constant with temperature and density.

There will be a net rotational force if curl $F_{el} = 0$ (Porter and Poulter 1970), curl grad $= 0$ so that the curl of equation (5.31) becomes

$$\text{curl } F_{el} = \text{grad } Q \wedge E + \tfrac{1}{2} \text{grad } \varepsilon \wedge \text{grad } E^2. \qquad (5.32)$$

This shows that in order to have a net rotational force due to electrophoretic effects, an inhomogeneous charge distribution and a field which is not parallel to the gradient of the charge is required and for the dielectrophoretic force to give circulatory movement both an inhomogeneous permittivity (for example due to a temperature gradient) and a non-parallel grad ε and grad E^2 are required.

Analysis of electrically enhanced heat transfer must also take account of processes which tend to inhibit the effect. For example, all liquids allow some current flow so there will be some Joule heating which will give an increase in heat proportional to I^2R. This limits effective heat transfer to moderately insulating liquids where the current flow is low. Heat transfer may also be inhibited if electrolysis causes gas bubbles to build up on the metal surfaces, insulating them from the liquid.

(b) *Experimental measurements of electrically forced convection*
Experimental studies of electrically forced convection examine the change in the heat transfer coefficient, h, in an electric field. Early research workers believed that the most important process involved was the movement of dipoles in a non-uniform electric field, but the work of Bonjour and Verdier (1960a,b) and Bonjour *et al* (1962) showed that polar liquids gave only a slightly greater increase in heat transfer than non-polar liquids and the electrical conductivity of the liquid was more important than its dielectric constant, (i.e. semiconducting liquids gave a higher heat transfer enhancement than good insulators). The most important enhancement mechanism is therefore believed to be the motion of free charges, i.e. the electrophoretic term in equation (5.31) dominates. There appears to be very little dependence on the polarity of the applied field (Watson 1961).

Electroconvection in alternating fields has recently been reviewed by Tobazeon (1984). Sharborough and Walker (1983) who investigated the cooling of transformer oil have observed liquid motion when 60 Hz fields of a few tens of kilovolts were applied across a few millimetres.

Turnbull published a series of papers (Turnbull 1968, 1969a,b, 1970, 1971a,b, Turnbull and Melcher 1969) in which he used Schlieren techniques to investigate bulk liquid motion, when a steady electric field was applied between parallel plates, the upper of which was heated. He showed that a threshold field must be applied before the liquid begins to move. At low fields it moves in a non-linear but uniform way, but at high fields the flow becomes turbulent. This behaviour was also found by Atten and co-workers (e.g.,

Atten and Honda 1982, Atten and Moreau 1972, Atten and Lacroix 1979) during their study of electroviscosity.

The heat transfer coefficient increased, by up to a factor of ten, when an electric field was applied. The same enhancement factor has also been achieved by other groups but factors of two to five are more common.

Newton (1973) also used Schlieren techniques to display liquid motion and showed that liquid tended to travel in discrete paths which he called 'streamers'. These occurred in the absence of a temperature gradient, but were modified by it, giving a periodic fluctuation in the motion. For most liquids there is a hysteresis effect with 10–20 % greater heat transfer measured when the voltage is being increased than when it is being decreased. This may be explained by space charge effects.

At high field strengths and moderate temperature differentials (of the order of 20 °C) the heat transfer saturates, with no further increase in heat transfer as the temperature is increased. Newton attributes this to a removal of the temperature gradients when the liquid motion becomes turbulent.

A number of workers using cylindrical geometries have noticed that at low fields, and low heat fluxes, heat transfer can be inhibited. This has been attributed to a conflict between natural and electrical convection or to gas formation at the electrodes, which inhibits heat transfer until the electric field is high enough to induce movement of the bubbles.

(c) *Heat transfer due to the motion of particulate impurities*

Solid particles dispersed in a liquid will move in a uniform electric field as a result of electrophoresis. Conducting particles will change charge by induction at each electrode in turn, and will oscillate between them. Particles will also experience a dielectrophoretic force in a non-uniform field, as described in §5.5. These effects produce a particle-induced fluid mixing.

Dietz and Melcher (1975) studied heat transfer in transformer oil with a temperature difference of 30 °C. In the absence of particles, an applied field increased the heat transfer coefficient by a factor of 1.5, but the addition of 300 μm metallic particles increased this to a factor of about ten. The augmentation at first increased with the number of particles, but when there were approximately 4×10^6 particles m^{-3}, interparticle effects caused the increase to level off. The ratio of the power requirement to give particle movement to the augmented heat transfer was $10^{-4}:1$.

(d) *Heat transfer in flowing liquids*

Heat transfer is often required from flowing liquids. Schmidt and Leidenfrost (1953) applied a radial electric field to laminar flow of transformer oil in an annular pipe, the inner surface of which was heated. The heat transfer coefficient increased by a factor of four and an increase in the axial pressure drop was also noted, (i.e. there was an effective increase in liquid viscosity). Similar effects were also described by Porter and Poulter (1970). Poulson and

Richardson (1976) measured the heat transferred from a hot wire with a heat flux of 32 kW m^{-2} to a non-polar oil flowing in a tube round the wire. The heat transfer coefficient increased by a factor of ten in a 6.3 mm tube and by a factor of six in a 4.7 mm tube. The enhancement decreased with faster flow rates and more turbulent liquid flow. The greater heat transfer which was achieved with the larger tube was attributed to the higher voltages which could be applied without breakdown. Detailed investigations of the flow showed that the field introduced an orderly secondary flow rather than turbulence. The heat transfer improvement was lower with a more viscous hydrocarbon oil, but the axial pressure drop induced by the field was higher. A review of heat transfer in flowing liquids has been given by Poulson and Richardson (1976).

(e) *Heat transfer during boiling*
Boiling can be divided into three regions, depending on the temperature.

(i) Natural convective boiling—vapour rises from the surface of the liquid but there are no bubbles.
(ii) Nucleate boiling—bubbles of vapour form at asperities on the heated surface and grow until they rise to the liquid surface.
(iii) Film boiling—a homogeneous film of vapour coats the hot surface. This occurs when there is a high temperature difference between the hot surface and the liquid, and decreases heat transfer, because of the insulating properties of the vapour film.

All three forms of boiling are affected by an electric field. Convective heat transfer is increased by forced convection owing to the movement of free charges and dipoles, as discussed in the previous section. Heat transfer in nucleate boiling is increased because the dielectrophoretic force helps to pull vapour bubbles from the heated surface. In addition, field intensification at surface asperities tends to increase the number of nucleation sites so more bubbles are formed. The bubble usually has a net charge (Asch 1966), so it moves faster through the liquid under the influence of Coulomb forces. Film boiling does not occur in an electric field and is replaced by intense nucleate boiling. This improves heat transfer because no continuous thermally insulating vapour film forms on the surface. A detailed analysis of heat transfer during boiling is discussed by Jones and Schaeffer (1976), Huband (1977), Choi (1962) and Markels and Durfee (1964, 1965).

(f) *Heat transfer during condensation*
Heat transfer during condensation can be enhanced by an electric field in a number of ways.

(i) If a discharge is formed in a vapour, the ions form nucleation sites increasing the transition from vapour to liquid.

(ii) Liquid droplets are usually charged, therefore they move more quickly to the surface on which they condense when there is an electric field.

(iii) The film of liquid which forms on the cold surface is destabilised, so there is improved heat transfer through the liquid film to the surface.

Velkoff and Miller (1965) looked at the condensation of freon vapour in the presence of a corona discharge. They studied the effect of the ion wind and a uniform field on the liquid layer. Although the corona discharge did improve the heat transfer, the process was not energetically favourable. However, a uniform, non-ionised field, produced by a grid above the liquid surface, increased the heat transfer by a factor of 2.5 and drew less than $2 \mu A$ of current. When a potential was applied to the grid, it became covered with liquid (although it was at the same temperature as the vapour). Velkoff suggested that this liquid was pulled off from the surface of the film on the condenser plate, increasing the heat transfer at the plate. The effect occurred only for high fields exceeding 25 kV cm^{-1}.

(g) *Heat pipes*

A conventional heat pipe contains a liquid which evaporates at the hot end and is condensed at the cool end, and is transported between the two ends by capillary action. Cosgrove (1967) and Abu-Romia (1971) inserted electrodes in a conventional heat pipe to induce electro-osmotic flow and substantially improved the performance. Jones (1974) has suggested that capillarity can be completely replaced by electro-osmotic flow, and investigated theoretically the feasibility of electrically assisted heat pipes (EHD) (Jones 1971). A schematic diagram of the system proposed by Jones is shown in figure 5.31. It consists of a thin-walled tube of aluminium, or some other good thermal and electrical conductor, with end caps made of an electrical insulator. An array of thin ribbon electrodes are stretched between the end caps inside the tube, running parallel to its axis. When a field of sufficient strength is applied, the insulating dielectric liquid collects in the high-field regions, bridging the area between the ribbons and the grounded tube. When heat is applied at one end evaporation causes a recession of the dielectric liquid as shown in the figure. At the other end of the pipe, condensation causes the interface to bulge outwards. This results in a liquid flow from the condenser to the evaporator. The vapour flow in the central core balances the liquid flow, carrying thermal energy stored as latent heat.

(h) *Summary*

Laboratory investigations indicate that a factor of ten improvement in the heat transfer is possible, achieved by applying an electric field in several of the systems, as discussed above, but practical applications of the phenomena have not reached a very advanced stage of development.

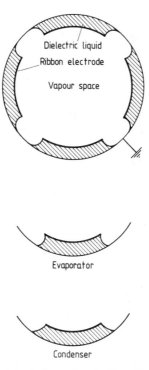

Dielectric liquid
Ribbon electrode
Vapour space

Evaporator

Condenser

Figure 5.31 A cross section of an electrically assisted heat pipe (EHD) (from Jones 1973).

5.4.9 The electroviscous effect

The electroviscous effect is the name given to a change in the apparent viscosity of a liquid in an electric field. The effect is small for most pure liquids but large increases in the apparent viscosity have been observed for solid/liquid suspensions, allowing the effect to be used for an electrically controlled clutch.

The first detailed observations of electroviscosity in pure liquids were made by Konig (1885). Later, Quincke (1897) studied the oscillations of a rotating sphere immersed in a liquid and observed the damping when an electric field was applied. His observations were confirmed by Pochettino (1903), who reported viscosity increases of up to 4 %, in liquids of low permittivity. The effect was studied by a number of authors in the 1930s (e.g. Bjornstahl 1935, Bjornstahl and Snellman 1937) and it was found that the effect was greatest with increasing electric field, liquid permittivity and conductivity. The presence of water in the liquid was found to be important. Polarity reversal gave rather irreproducible results but, with an alternating applied voltage, the greatest viscosity corresponded to a period which was close to the mean ion transit time of the system.

In the 1930s two different theories were discussed, one based on the build up of thick boundary layers by electrochemical effects at the electrodes, and the other on the effect of liquid motion induced by the electric field. Andrade and Dodd (1946, 1951) and Andrade and Hart (1954) found that electric fields could produce both increases and decreases in the viscosity and postulated a charge accumulation mechanism which caused a clustering of polar molecules which were then less free to move and increased the liquid viscosity. Hart and Merrilees (1963), and Atten and Honda (1982) rejected the boundary layer theory for electroviscosity. The latter proposed that the increase in viscosity was caused by electroconvection which arose as a result of the Coulomb force, acting on free charges in the liquid.

Free charges are created in liquids by dissociation and separation of ionic compounds and by injection from the electrodes. When a high voltage is applied to an electrode in a dielectric liquid, charge injection normally dominates. Atten *et al* (1982) showed that, for unipolar space-charge-limited injection from a single electrode in a system consisting of a liquid layer between two plane electrodes, the liquid layer cannot remain at rest when the dimensionless number T satisfies the following relation:

$$T = \varepsilon V/b\eta > 100 \qquad (5.33)$$

where V is the applied voltage, b is the ion mobility, η is the viscosity and ε is the liquid permittivity (Atten and Moreau 1972, Atten and Lacroix 1979).

Thus there is a critical voltage V_c, at which motion sets in, independent of the electrode spacing. V_c is about 11 V for nitrobenzene and about 130 V for a non-polar liquid.

The theory predicts that when the liquid is in motion, the transport of ions, i.e. the electrical conductivity of the liquid, is enhanced, and the current varies with voltage as $V^{5/2}$, until a transition voltage is reached, where the liquid motion becomes turbulent, and the current varies as V^2. Similar considerations apply to systems where space-charge-limited injection occurs from both electrodes, rather than from one electrode alone (Lacroix *et al* 1975). The predictions of the theory are confirmed experimentally, when charge injection dominates, but the picture is less clear under circumstances where dissociation dominates the charging processes. Theoretically, no motion would be expected in this case but, in practice, motion is observed.

Atten and Honda (1982) measured the change in pressure drop when a voltage was applied across liquids passing through a rectangular section with laminar flow. The electrodes were covered with a membrane, which allowed the permeation of only one type of ion, to encourage unipolar charge injection. A voltage of 5000 V, applied across a layer of nitrobenzene 1.06 mm thick, increased the pressure drop to twenty times its value in laminar flow in the absence of a field. This is higher than the increases observed by other workers who do not specifically enhance charge injection.

At low voltages, the pressure drop increased fairly slowly with voltage, but at higher voltages, it rose more rapidly. The transition between the two regimes corresponded approximately to the voltage for the transition between laminar and turbulent flow of electroconvection. The motion of the liquid was observed using Schlieren techniques and a strong relationship between electrically driven liquid motion, and pressure drop and apparent viscosity was confirmed.

Electroviscosity is also observed in insulating fluids which contain suspended particles. This was originally attributed to the dielectrophoretic force of attraction between the particles, which causes them to form chains aligned in the electric field (Winslow 1949). Klass and Martinek (1967) disputed this mechanism, because the electroviscous effect is virtually instantaneous. They believed it to be due to the induced polarisation of the electric double layer round the particles, which results in an interaction between particles, and an additional energy requirement for movement of liquid perpendicular to the electric field. They found that the strength of the electroviscous effect was higher for a silica dispersion than for a dispersion of calcium titanate, although the latter is ferroelectric and has a much higher particle polarisation, i.e. the interfacial and surface properties of the particles were more important than the bulk properties. This is confirmed by work showing that an electroviscous effect can be introduced to a system consisting of a suspension of dried particles in an insulating chlorine oil, by allowing water to adsorb onto the surface of the particles before they are suspended (Uejima 1972). The viscosity levelled off at a high water content and there was an optimum weight percentage of particles, with the relative viscosity (defined as the viscosity with and without an applied electric field) reaching a maximum when the liquid contained approximately 10 % of particles.

This differs from the observations of Klass and Martinek (1967) who found an increasing electroviscosity of a silica dispersion in naphthenic liquid up to a volume percentage of 46 %, and Sproston *et al* (1983) who obtained the greatest viscosities with 60 % particulates.

Electroviscous effects in particulate suspensions appear at the onset of current flow. The strength of the electroviscous effect increases with field strength and with temperature, but decreases with increasing frequency and shear rate. The viscosity is proportional to the square of the electric field and inversely proportional to the first power of the shear rate.

The use of electroviscous effects to make an electrically controlled clutch was first proposed by Winslow (1947). This clutch has been recently redesigned by Sproston *et al* (1983) and dynamic load tests carried out using a variety of fluids.

The clutch mechanism proposed by Sproston *et al* (1983) is shown in figure 5.32. It consisted of two brass plates, the upper one formed as a circular spigot and the lower one as a recess containing the liquid. Each plate was attached to a PTFE flange, bolted to an aluminium shaft. The lower shaft was fitted to a 13 mm diameter pulley, driven by a variable-speed AC motor. The upper shaft was loaded by means of a string, running over a bench-mounted pulley, then vertically to a weight holder. Electrical connection was made to each of the two plates by leaf springs. The torque was measured as a function of the voltage applied to the plates for a number of different fluids. It was found that with a mixture of silicone oil and starch with a paste-like consistency (a proportion of 1.5 : 1 starch to oil) the torque increased approximately linearly with applied voltage reaching approximately 0.24 N m with 5 kV applied across a 3 mm plate spacing. The shear force which the fluid could withstand became progressively higher with increasing voltage, until a point was reached at which the fluid would no longer flow. This limiting voltage was lower when the voltage was applied rapidly than when the limiting voltage was reached more gradually. The mechanism was able to operate as a brake or as a clutch, and it was possible to produce controlled slippage, with the output shaft moving at a slower speed than the drive shaft, by applying a voltage slightly lower than that needed for complete engagement of the plates. Recently Stevens *et al* (1985) have demonstrated the feasibility of using pulsed DC signals to activate the fluid. This enables the device to be linked to digital controls and has the added advantage that power consumption and the tendency for a spark to occur between the electrodes are both reduced.

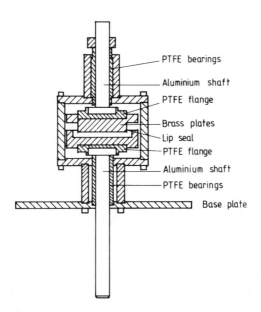

Figure 5.32 An electrostatic clutch (from Sproston *et al* 1983).

5.4.10 The electrical conductivity of dielectric liquids

The electrical conductivity in dielectric liquids is closely associated with electrokinetic effects, for example the irreproducibility with time and with polarity reversal can be observed in measurements of both electroviscosity and conductivity (Atten and Honda 1982). Dielectric liquids have a non-ohmic response to an electric field and the current flowing in a stationary liquid is proportional to the square of the applied voltage. When electroconvection sets in the liquid motion causes an increase in the electrical conductivity, which becomes proportional to $V^{5/2}$. Above the transition voltage, where electroconvection is turbulent, the current is again proportional to the square of the voltage, but the mobility of the ions is higher than when the liquid was stationary.

The presence of conducting particles which charge by induction and oscillate between the two electrodes obviously increases the liquid conductivity, but even insulating particles can increase the conductivity because they intensify the electric field locally. The conductivity of a dielectric liquid is proportional to the electric field to the power 2 or $\frac{5}{2}$ therefore the effect of the enhanced field does not average out over a rough electrode surface and the net conductivity is enhanced. An apparent increase in liquid conductivity is also measured when there is an insulating layer with pinholes on the electrodes because of field intensification at the pinholes.

5.5 DIELECTROPHORESIS

5.5.1 Introduction

Dielectrophoresis is the movement of an uncharged particle in a non-uniform field, by virtue of the dipole induced on the particle by the field. The first recorded observation of electrostatics in 600 BC was in fact an observation of dielectrophoresis, as small neutral particles were moved by the non-uniform field created by a frictionally charged amber rod.

The source of the dipole force and dielectrophoretic motion is illustrated in figure 5.33. The dipole is polarised in the field and develops a negative charge at one end, and an equal and opposite positive charge at the other end. In the example shown, the negative end of the dipole is in a higher field region than the positive end. The dipole therefore experiences a greater force in the direction defined by the negative charge, and moves towards the high-field region. The force on an isolated dipole is towards the higher field for both polarities of field, and both AC and DC fields produce dielectrophoretic motion.

The force on a particle in a field gradient dE/dx is given by

$$F = P \, dE/dx \tag{5.34}$$

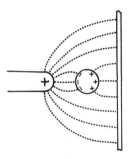

Figure 5.33 Force on a dipole in a non-uniform field. The negative end of the particle is in a higher field and therefore experiences a higher force than the positive end and there is a net translation towards the higher field.

where P is the particle dipole moment. The dipole moment of a sphere of radius a, in a field E and a field gradient dE/dx is derived in Chapter 7. The dielectrophoretic force on this particle is given by

$$F = 2\pi a^3 \varepsilon_1 \frac{(\varepsilon_2 - \varepsilon_1)}{(\varepsilon_2 + 2\varepsilon_1)} \nabla |E|^2. \tag{5.35}$$

It can be seen from this equation that if the particle has a lower dielectric constant than the surrounding medium, it will move to the lower field region. (A particle with a higher dielectric constant may also move to the low-field region if it has a permanent dipole moment and is spinning (Pohl 1978).) The dielectrophoretic force on a particle is proportional to the cube of the particle diameter and is larger, the greater the difference in dielectric constant between the particles and the medium in which they are suspended.

The source of the dipole in the applied field may be a permanent dipole moment, or a separation of charge within a conducting particle, but for a particle in a liquid the greatest component is frequently due to the mobile charge in the electric double layer.

Equation (5.35) was derived assuming the two components were perfect dielectrics. For lossy dielectrics, the effect of conductivity must be taken into account by replacing the dielectric constant in the equation with the complex permittivity (defined in Chapter 7). The non-ideal behaviour of real materials is discussed by Hawk (1967), Sher (1968), Feeley (1969) and Chen (1969).

The polarisation of a particle in an alternating electric field is a function of the frequency because the movement of charge to form a dipole takes a finite time, depending on the type of movement involved. For example, more time is required to rotate a polar molecule than to bias the electronic charge in a metal particle. This means that different dielectric constants apply at different frequencies and different forces are experienced. This may be used both to separate particles and to characterise them.

When two particles are present in a uniform electric field, each particle distorts the field locally as shown in figure 5.34. Each is therefore in a non-uniform field and there is a dipole force of attraction between them equal to

$$F = KE^2a^6/d^4 \qquad (5.36)$$

where K is a constant, E is the electric field, a is the radius of the two particles and d is the distance between them. The particles are therefore attracted to each other (Pohl 1978). If a non-uniform field is applied to a liquid containing particles, dielectrophoretic forces will cause the particles to agglomerate and drift towards the high-field region. The electrical double layer round the particles will provide an electrophoretic force in a DC field but it will also provide an electrostatic force of repulsion between the particles. The net force, when a field is applied to particles in a liquid, is a combination of all these effects. In a DC electric field the dielectrophoretic force is normally much lower than the electrophoretic force but there is no net electrophoretic motion in an AC field, which can therefore be used to make independent observations of dielectrophoretic effects.

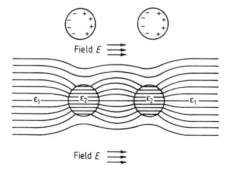

Figure 5.34 The force of attraction between two neutral particles in a uniform field when the dielectric constant of the particles exceeds that of the medium.

5.5.2 Non-uniform field geometries

Equation (5.42) shows that the dielectrophoretic force on a particle in a non-uniform field is proportional to $\nabla|E|^2$:

$$\nabla|E|^2 = 2E\nabla|E|.$$

Therefore for a high dielectrophoretic force one requires both a high field and a high field gradient. The most obvious electrode configurations which provide high field gradients are a concentric wire/cylinder geometry and a point at the centre of a hollowed electrode (which can be approximated to a spherical geometry). $\nabla|E|^2$ has been calculated by Pohl, for these two systems, and has been shown to be:

for the sphere

$$\nabla|E|^2 = \frac{-r_0 r_1^2 r_2^2 V_1^2}{r^5 (r_2 - r_1)^2} \tag{5.37}$$

and for the cylinder

$$\nabla|E|^2 = \frac{-2r_0 V_1^2}{r^3 (\ln r_1/r_2)^2} \tag{5.38}$$

where r_0 is a unit vector in the radical direction.

It can be seen that, for the case of the sphere, the dielectrophoretic force falls off with the fifth power of distance from the point, and for the cylinder, it falls off with the third power of distance from the wire. This rapid change of the dipole force with distance makes these geometries impractical for most applications. Electrodes can be designed to provide non-uniform fields which give a force which varies with distance as r^n where n lies between -3 and $+3$ (Pohl and Pollock 1978). A particularly useful geometry is the case for $n = 0$, which provides a force which is nearly constant over an extended region. This is referred to as an isomotive field and it is used in particle separation (Pohl 1960), particle levitation and in the determination of the dielectric constant of solids (Pohl and Pethig 1977). Pohl shows that such a field is provided by equipotentials having the equation

$$V = \frac{2}{3} \left(\frac{2F_1}{\alpha v} \right)^{1/2} r^{3/2} \sin(3\theta/2) \tag{5.39}$$

where F_1 is the force along the radius and v is the volume of a small test sphere. The equipotentials obeying this equation are shown in figure 5.35.

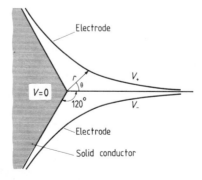

Figure 5.35 The electrode geometry for a field exerting a constant radial force (isomotive geometry) (from Pohl and Pollock 1978).

5.5.3 Applications of dielectrophoresis

Laboratory demonstrations of possible applications of the dielectrophoretic effect are described by Pohl (1958). For example, a simple apparatus, capable of separating carbon black from rubber or PVC, dissolved in di-isopropyl ketone, can be made from a wire on the axis of an earthed cylinder 0.1 m in diameter. Carbon particles collect on the central electrode within a few minutes of a voltage of 10 kV being applied. The same cell can be used to demonstrate dielectrophoretic agitation. If a voltage is applied to clumped, 1 : 1 carbon powder/alumina powder in carbon tetrachloride the particles are stirred into the liquid under the combined action of electrophoresis, dielectrophoresis and electroconvection.

Dielectrophoretic forces also take part in pumping of liquids and powders by electric fields (§5.4.7) and in the levitation of particles and droplets (§5.7.6). Although electrophoresis gives a much stronger force than dielectrophoresis, the latter can give useful separations of particles (§5.5.5). In the 1920s a system was devised for separating emulsions of water from petroleum (Dow 1926, Stevens 1925), and Pohl (1951) designed a system using dielectrophoresis for analysing plastic pigments.

5.5.4 Coalescence of emulsions

Electrostatic forces have been used to encourage coalescence in emulsions since the beginning of the twentieth century (Cottrell 1908). The surface of droplets in a liquid/liquid emulsion develop a double layer in the same way as solid particles in a suspension. This tends to produce an electrostatic force of repulsion between the droplets. However, when an electric field is applied, the droplets move electrophoretically and coalesce on a membrane placed in their path (Allan and Mason 1961). Typical migration velocities are 0.1 mm s^{-1} in a field of a few hundred volts per metre. An emulsion may also separate out at the electrodes as a result of the breakdown of emulsifiers in electrode reactions (Kuhn 1974).

Coalescence can occur in the liquid as particles moving at different speeds collide. This process is enhanced by dielectrophoresis, which provides a force of attraction between two polarised droplets as described above.

The majority of reported research in emulsion separation by coalescence concerns water-in-oil emulsions, which must be separated during the extraction of crude oil. In this application relatively high electric fields can be applied because of the low conductivity of the continuous phase.

The full expression for the force between two dipoles with a distance, d, between their centres has been given by Pohl (1978). For the case where the dielectric constant of the disperse phase, ε_d, is much greater than that of the continuous phase, ε_c (as in the case with a water-in-oil emulsion) this expression simplifies to

$$F = 24\pi\varepsilon_c(a/d)^4a^2E^2. \tag{5.40}$$

The dipole attraction is proportional to the square of the electric field, therefore one would expect that higher fields improve coalescence. In practice it is found that, if the field is too high, the droplets break up and re-emulsify (Williams and Bailey 1983). The transport phenomena do not obey the normal electrophoretic equation (Waterman 1965) and a critical field strength beyond which coalescence by collision is very rapid has been reported. It has been suggested that this critical field corresponds closely to the breakdown field of the oil and that the increase in coalescence could be caused by a discharge across the oil film between droplets (Brown and Hanson 1961).

An expression for the resolution time (i.e. the time required for the water to settle out of the oil) has been developed by Williams and Bailey (1983) and agrees reasonably well with experimental results for both AC and DC systems.

5.5.5 Dielectrophoretic separation

The use of dielectrophoresis in liquid/solid separation dates back to 1891 when Lowden patented an invention to remove metal particles from lubricating oil. More recently, Lockheart (1983) showed that clay particles could be separated from water using an alternating field. In addition to the movement of the particles he found that the water flowed to the high-field region with a flow rate that was proportional to the square of the voltage. He identified the dipole moment which caused the particle movement as due to surface polarisation of electrically bound cations in the double layer, whereas relatively free cations were responsible for electro-osmosis of the liquid.

For efficient separation of particles from a liquid, both a high electric field and a high field gradient are required. Electrode geometries which can provide these over large distances were discussed above. Alternatively, the combination of a high electric field and a high field gradient can be provided over small distances, using an assembly of highly comminuted electrodes or by a set of widely spaced electrodes, in which is placed a finely divided dielectric solid such as polyurethane foam or sintered ceramic. Matrices of dielectric fibres or spheres containing 50–95 % void space, concentrate the electric field lines, causing a field non-uniformity which extends a distance comparable with the particle radius. The field distortion is greatest for materials where there is a large difference in dielectric constant between the liquid and the collector particles. Barium titanate ceramics have been found to be particularly useful because they are ferroelectrics with a high dielectric constant and their electrical properties can be easily controlled by doping. The technique has been applied commercially in the petroleum industry and in the vegetable oil industry where contamination by small particles is a problem. A wide range of other applications, for example, in minerals separation, waste treatment and biochemical engineering are under investigation (Lin and Benguigui 1983).

A practical electrofilter which uses both sharp electrodes and a dielectric filler is shown in figure 5.36 (Hall and Brown 1966). This separator operates by a combination of electrophoretic and dielectrophoretic forces.

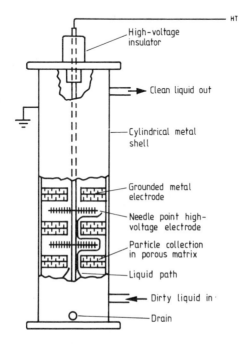

Figure 5.36 Electrostatic liquid cleaner (from Hall and Brown 1966).

5.5.6 Dielectrophoresis in biological systems

Dielectrophoresis has found a wide use in biological systems. Biological cells have complicated structures with different polarisabilities at different frequencies and the way in which cells move in an electric field is highly specific. For example, living and dead cells of the same organism can be separated (Pohl and Hawk 1966, Mason and Townsley 1971). Dielectrophoresis can be used to concentrate biological products, (Black and Hammond 1965) and to characterise single cells (Chen and Pohl 1974, Pohl 1978). Observation of the movement of biological particles as a function of frequency is widely used to study cell structure. For example, figure 5.37 shows the collection rate as a function of frequency from yeast and from spinach chloroplasts. The collection rate is a strong function of frequency and the collection rate spectrum is characteristic of the cell.

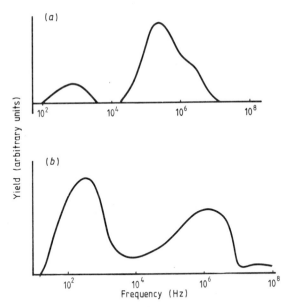

Figure 5.37 The dielectrophoretic collection rate as a function of frequency for: (*a*), yeast cells; (*b*), spinach chloroplasts (from Pohl 1978, also see Ting *et al* 1971).

Heller (1959) studied the response of a number of different unicellular organisms to high-frequency fields between 0.1 and 100 MHz. He observed the formation of chains by mutual dielectrophoresis, and cell orientation within preferential ranges of frequency. Some elongated cells exhibited a peculiar response and were aligned in the direction of the electric field at low frequencies, but at high frequencies became oriented perpendicular to the field lines. This was attributed to a strong internal dipole moment, owing to charge separation at cell boundaries, which was only operable at low frequencies. At high frequencies the cellular membrane formed a capacitor of high value. The energy of a capacitor is minimised when it is oriented perpendicular to the field (Fricke 1925, 1953, Cole *et al* 1935, 1936). Biological applications of dielectrophoresis are reviewed by Pohl (1978).

5.6 APPLICATIONS OF THE CORONA DISCHARGE

5.6.1 Introduction

When a high voltage is applied to a sharp electrode a corona discharge occurs as described in Chapters 2 and 7. Ionisation is limited to a region very close to the sharp electrode where the field is high, and over the rest of the interelectrode space only those charge carriers which are repelled from the high-voltage electrode will be found. For the case of a positive point these will be positive ions. For a negative point, electrons will emerge from the ionisation zone, but if the gas contains oxygen, or some other molecule with an affinity for negative charge, the electrons will rapidly attach to gas molecules to form negative ions.

The mobility of an ion in air is of the order of $2.2 \times 10^{-4} \, m^2 \, s^{-1} \, V^{-1}$ i.e. for a field of $3 \times 10^5 \, V \, m^{-1}$, typical of the drift region of a corona discharge, the ion velocity is of the order of $66 \, m \, s^{-1}$. For a typical ion current density of $10^{-3} \, A \, m^{-2}$ and a charge of one electron/ion ($1.6 \times 10^{-19} \, C/atom$) there will be 10^{15} ions m^{-3}. This compares with a density of neutral molecules of 2.6×10^{25} molecules m^{-3} at atmospheric pressure. The percentage of gas molecules which are ionised in a corona discharge is thus very small, but there are a large number of excited molecules and reactive molecular species, such as ozone and the nitrogen oxides, which take part in surface chemical reactions (Peyrous and Millot 1982). The number of excited neutral molecules is much higher than the number of ions, for example, Hartman (1976) estimated that at $70 \, \mu A$, 10 % of nitrogen molecules may be in an excited state.

The ions are similar in size to neutral molecules, therefore when the two collide momentum is transferred to the molecule and there is a bulk movement of the neutral gas in the direction of travel of the ions.

The most important use of DC corona discharge in electrostatics is to provide a source of unipolar ions for electrostatic charging of surfaces and particles as discussed in Chapter 2. Similarly an AC corona may be used to provide both polarities of ion to neutralise electrostatic charge as described in Chapter 6. The ions of a corona discharge are also used, as a source of current flow in a gas and to provide bulk movement of a neutral gas.

5.6.2 Corona conditioning

Although the energy of corona ions, arriving at the earthed electrode is low, a corona discharge can have a significant effect on the surface. Spectrometer studies have indicated that material is sputtered from the earthed electrode and there can also be considerable corrosion of metallic electrodes. Aluminium surfaces undergo severe pitting corrosion in a negative corona discharge in air if some moisture is present. The corrosion products have been identified as $Al-NO_3$ compounds and the excited neutral species have been shown to play an important role in the process (Sigmond *et al* 1980).

A corona discharge is used to treat polyethylene and other materials with a low surface free energy, to increase their wettability, so the surface can be printed or adhesives can be applied (Visking Corp 1952, Thi 1981). In a typical industrial process, plastic film travels at $30-40 \, m \, min^{-1}$ over an earthed roller which is sleeved in an insulating material. A high AC voltage (12–25 kV) is applied to an electrode held a few millimetres above the film and a region of intense corona discharge is created. The insulating sleeve on the roller prevents arc discharges through the film creating pinholes.

Studies of polymer films (mostly using materials without the normal commercial additives) show that the discharge creates some physical surface roughening (Kim and Goring 1971) and that the surface chemistry is altered, with unsaturated carbonyl and amino groups produced. The surface oxidises and x-ray photoelectron spectroscopy has identified the formation of a large number of peroxy cross links (Rossman 1956, Owens 1975, Rasmussen *et al* 1977, Blythe *et al* 1978, Briggs and Kendall 1982, Bird *et al* 1982).

Corona treatment has also been applied to wool, cotton and polyester fibres, and it is found to improve both the mechanical properties of the fibres and the way they accept a dye. The excited neutral species in the discharge play an important part in the changes, which are reduced by a factor of approximately four when the neutral species are removed.

5.6.3 The ion wind

The mean free path of an ion in air at atmospheric pressure (i.e. the distance it travels before a collision with a neutral molecule) is approximately 2×10^{-7} m. The mass of an ion is similar to the mass of a neutral molecule, therefore, when the two collide the momentum is transferred to the neutral gas molecule. After a collision the ion is accelerated by the field before colliding with another neutral molecule. Many such collisions occur before the ion reaches the earthed electrode, and the neutral molecules are given a component of velocity in the direction of the electric field. This is known as the ion wind. The wind is created by energy transfer from the ions and is not the movement of the ions themselves.

(a) *Calculation of the velocity of the ion wind*
Consider ions travelling from a point $x = 0$ to a plane at $x = L$. The energy of the electric field is transferred to the movement of a volume of gas. Conservation of energy therefore requires

$$\tfrac{1}{2}Du^2 = \int_0^L Q_V E \, \mathrm{d}x \qquad (5.41)$$

where D is the gas density, Q_V is the charge density and u is the velocity of the ion wind. From Poisson's law

$$\rho = \varepsilon_0 \operatorname{div} E$$

i.e.

$$u = \left(\frac{2\varepsilon_0}{D} \int_0^L (\operatorname{div} E) E_x \, \mathrm{d}x \right)^{1/2}. \qquad (5.42)$$

The velocity of the wind can therefore be found for any system if the electric field and the field gradient are known. If the system can be approximated to a one-dimensional system, where the field is V/L (where V is the applied voltage) then

$$\text{div } \boldsymbol{E} = V/L^2$$

and

$$u = (2\varepsilon_0 \boldsymbol{E}/D)^{1/2}. \tag{5.43}$$

In practice the electric field in a corona discharge is usually not known accurately, but measurements of the corona current and voltage are available. A slightly different form of equation (5.43) has therefore been derived by Robinson (1970) which relates the wind velocity to the current density J:

$$u^2 = \frac{2}{D} \int_0^L \frac{J}{b} \, \mathrm{d}x. \tag{5.44}$$

The current density is a function of x which depends on the geometry of the system. Robinson introduces a geometric factor g to account for this and a second constant K which allows for energy losses in a system where the air flow is bounded. The velocity of the wind is then related to the current I in the external circuit by the equation

$$u = g \left(\frac{I}{DbK} \right)^{1/2}$$

where b is the mobility of the ions.

An estimate of the maximum ion wind velocity can be made from equation (5.43), by substituting the maximum field, which is the breakdown field of air $(3 \times 10^6 \text{ V m}^{-1})$. This leads to a maximum wind velocity of 10.8 m s^{-1}. In practice corona fields are usually closer to 3×10^5 V m^{-1} and ion winds are of the order of 1–2 m s^{-1}.

The velocity of the ion wind increases with electric field and with current density, therefore higher ion winds can be achieved by changes in electrode geometry which increase current density. For example, increasing the number of points, in a system consisting of an array of points and a plane, will give an increase in current density, until the point spacing reaches about 1 cm. Closer spacings give no further increase in current density. The velocity of the wind increases as the mobility of the ions decreases, therefore a positive corona discharge gives a slightly higher wind velocity than a negative corona. In non-electron-attaching gases, such as nitrogen, only positive polarities give a significant wind, because the electrons have a very high mobility. The velocity of the ion wind depends on the product of gas density and ion mobility. Since ion mobility is inversely proportional to gas density, the wind speed is independent of gas density or pressure for a given gas.

The efficiency of energy conversion from the electric field to the ion wind is given by

$$\frac{\text{kinetic energy transferred to a mass } M \text{ of gas/unit time}}{\text{electrical power input}}.$$

This turns out to be about 1 % Robinson (1961).

(b) *Experimental measurements of the ion wind*
Robinson (1961) measured the wind velocity from a high-voltage point at the centre of a hemispherical grid, 38 mm in radius, and found winds up to 4 m s^{-1}, as shown in figure 5.38. When suitable constants for the geometric factor and the loss were introduced, these results agreed closely with the theory of equation (5.44).

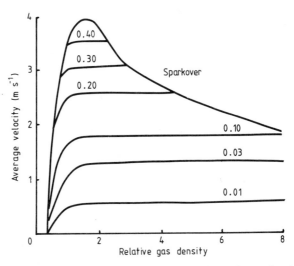

Figure 5.38 The ion wind velocity as a function of gas density and corona current (given on curves in mA) (from Robinson 1961).

Measurements of the ion wind above a plane target in a point-to-plane corona discharge with a potential spacing of 40 mm are shown in table 5.7. The earthed plane was divided into concentric segments, electrically isolated from each other, and the wind velocity and current density to each was measured. The velocity of the ion wind increased with point-to-plane spacing up to 60 mm although the current density to each segment decreased. At larger spacings there was considerable loss of current to the surroundings and the peak wind velocity decreased.

At 60 mm spacing, and voltages close to breakdown, a peak wind velocity of 5 m s^{-1} was measured but corona conditions were rather unstable and a

Table 5.7 Wind velocity and current of a corona discharge. Point-to-plane spacing 4 cm; mean field 5.5 kV cm^{-1}.

Segment number from	Negative						Positive	
	Array of fine points		Single fine point		Single coarse point		Single coarse point	
	Current (μA cm^{-2})	Wind (m s^{-1})	Current (μA cm^{-2})	Wind (m s^{-1})	Current (μA cm^{-2})	Wind (m s^{-1})	Current (μA cm^{-2})	Wind (m s^{-1})
1	0.5	1.8†	2.0	2.3†	1.8	1.8†	2.4	1.6†
2	1.1	1.6†	1.6	2.0†	1.7	1.7†	1.6	1.7†
3	1.4	1.8†	1.5	1.8†	1.5	1.9†	1.1	1.7†
4	1.3	2.1†	1.4	1.6†	1.3	1.7†	0.78	1.4†
5	1.2	1.9†	1.2	1.6	1.0	1.6	0.60	1.4
6	1.0	1.8†	0.85	1.4	0.75	1.3	0.45	1.3
7	0.89	1.8	0.60	1.3	0.59	1.2	0.39	1.2
8	0.68	1.8	0.45	1.1	0.43	1.2	0.32	1.1
9	0.53	1.8	0.32	0.9	0.31	1.1	0.26	1.0
10	0.45	1.5	0.23	0.9	0.23	0.9	0.14	0.9
11	0.30	1.3	0.15	0.8	0.17	0.8	0.10	0.7
Current outside 6 cm radius (μA)	21.5		10.5		11.5		3.5	
Total corona current to plate (μA)	88.9		75		68		39	

†Indicates values for which there was a strong fluctuation. The visual mean is quoted in the table.

steady velocity of about 2.5 m s^{-1} was the highest that could be practically maintained (Cross 1979). Higher velocities have been achieved by using a ring electrode, with a cross section of 10 mm and diameter of 20 mm, placed 50 mm from a high voltage point as shown in figure 5.39 (Hilpert and Kern 1974). A peak air flow of 7 m s^{-1} was measured on the axis of the ring. Blowers of this type may be cascaded to increase the velocity further (Hilpert and Kern 1975).

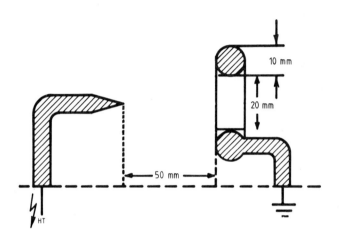

Figure 5.39 A ring electrode assembly for production of an ion wind (after Hilpert and Kern 1974).

(c) *Applications of the ion wind*

The power transfer efficiency of the ion wind is low, therefore although the wind may be used to drive a rotor for demonstration purposes, it is not a practical means of transferring electrical energy to mechanical energy. However, the ion wind may be useful where generation of air flow by other means is not possible, for example, in keeping solar mirrors dust free (Hoenig 1980, 1981).

The presence of the ion wind plays a significant part in corona deposition systems, and provides the major force acting on a particle in a corona discharge in the absence of external air flow.

The corona wind has also been used to assist heat transfer processes (Han 1975). Three techniques of corona-induced cooling are discussed in the literature.

(i) A decrease in temperature is observed when a high-voltage corona point is placed a few centimetres from a heated object. There is considerable evidence that the ion wind alone is responsible for this cooling. For example, it has been shown that cooling only occurs when a corona current flows and application of a field in the absence of a corona discharge does not enhance heat transfer (Franke 1969, O'Brien 1964). Kibler and Carter (1974) could detect no change in the heat transfer when the ions were removed from the corona wind. They also found that when air was blown from tubes with a velocity u the heat transfer was proportional to $u^{1/2}$. For the ion wind it was proportional to $I^{1/2}$. This is the relationship predicted by equation (5.44) if it is assumed that cooling is due to the ion wind alone. The velocity of the corona wind, measured with a hot-wire anemometer, is in close agreement with the velocity measured by a rotating-vane instrument. If the electric field produced any additional cooling the hot-wire anemometer would indicate an apparently higher air flow (Cross 1979). A comparison of the measured heat loss from a steel plate heated to 500 °C with that expected due to forced convection with an air flow at the velocity of the ion wind also showed that the measured heat loss corresponded to calculations of the effect of the ion wind alone (Cross 1979). However, observations of the thermal boundary layer round a heated cylinder, made using Schlieren techniques, showed distinct differences in the thermal boundary layer when cooling was due to a jet of air rather than to the ion wind. It can be seen from figure 5.40 that when a corona discharge was used to provide the wind a much thinner thermal boundary layer was formed. Although the efficiency of the ion wind is low, heat transfer can be doubled for a 5 % power increase.

(ii) The second approach to electrostatic cooling is to introduce wires close to an electrically insulated, heated substrate and connected alternately to a high voltage and to earth. Both wires create ions, and counter-rotating air currents are set up in the thermal boundary layer. The heat transfer theory for this system has been given by Persen (1965) and Mori and Uchida (1966). Velkoff and Ketcham (1968) have experimented with wires with an alternating voltage of 2 kV superimposed on 10 kV DC. The aim was to try to induce transition between laminar and turbulent conditions by varying the frequency of the AC signal, to couple it to the predominant oscillation of the thermal boundary layer. This was not found to be possible, giving further evidence that enhanced heat transfer in a corona discharge is due solely to ion wind.

(iii) The third technique makes the heated object the active electrode. Parsons (1929) observed that there was an abrupt decrease in temperature of a heated wire at corona onset and that the temperature decreased as the corona current increased. A detailed theoretical analysis of heat transfer from a heated object which is in corona has been carried out by Robinson (1970). The analysis is complicated by the difficulty of defining sensible values of mobility and velocity in the bi-ionised region of the corona discharge. The thickness of the corona glow region is of the same order as the thermal boundary layer and considerable disruption of this layer might be expected. Unlike the other two methods, enhanced cooling is obtained not only in stationary air, but also with forced flow. Heat transfer can be increased by 10 % with a forced flow of approximately 25 m s^{-1}.

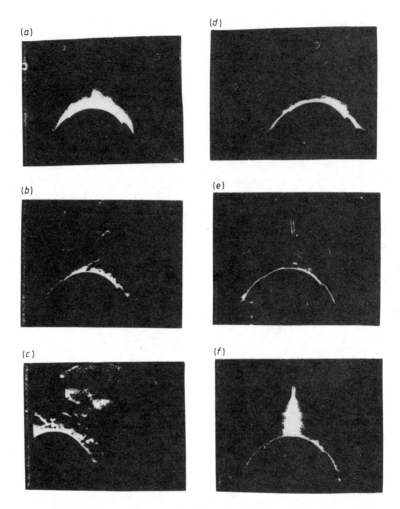

Figure 5.40 Schlieren pictures showing the relative air density round a heated cylinder during forced-convective cooling by an air jet and by the corona wind (from Cross 1979): (*a*), natural convection; (*b*), low-velocity air jet (0.5 m s^{-1}); (*c*), air jet of 2.0 m s^{-1}; (*d*), corona point at 10 kV, 3 cm spacing; (*e*), corona point 16.5 kV; (*f*), corona point 25 kV.

Morgan and Morrow (1980) measured the temperature of a wire at the axis of a cylinder as a function of voltage and found a pronounced drop in temperature at corona inception as shown in figure 5.41. The magnitude of the cooling was similar for positive, negative or AC energisation, although the corona process is different for the three cases. Morgan and Morrow's work was applied to studies of the heat transfer from overhead power lines.

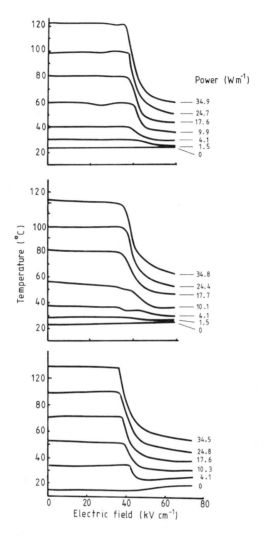

Figure 5.41 Electrostatic cooling of a high-voltage wire. Surface temperature as a function of heat input and electric field (from Morgan and Morrow 1980).

5.7 ELECTRODYNAMIC CONTAINMENT AND CONTROL OF PARTICLES

5.7.1 The control of electrons and ions

The paths of electrons and ions can be controlled very precisely by electrostatic fields. Beams of electrons or ions can be focused to very small diameter spots by electrostatic lenses, which are a series of grids, cylinders or plates with suitable applied potentials. Focused electron beams are used for the analysis of surfaces, for example in the electron microscopes and electron spectroscopes, and also in television tubes and cathode ray oscilloscopes. Ion beams are used for etching or implantation. In principle, any arrangement of electrodes which produces a regular curvature of equipotential surfaces will operate as an electrostatic lens. The simplest arrangement is two identical coaxial cylinders separated by a small gap, as shown in figure 5.42(a). The cylinders may be of different diameters, or may penetrate each other, producing differently shaped equipotentials and different focusing characteristics (figure 5.42(b)). Three-cylinder systems may be used to produce symmetrical lenses which are the optical equivalents of either, a combination of two concave with a convex lens, or vice versa, depending on whether the central element is at a lower or higher potential than the two outer elements. In either case the overall effect is convergent (figure 5.42(c)). The cylinders may be reduced to simple apertures as shown in figure 5.42(d).

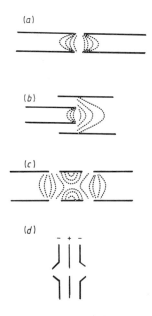

Figure 5.42 Electrostatic lenses: (a) and (b) are cylindrical lenses, (c) and (d) are symmetrical lenses (dotted lines are electric field lines).

Electrostatic lenses can be analysed in a similar way to optical lenses and their focal length and aberrations can be calculated and modified to obtain the desired beam properties. A comprehensive review of the design of electron and ion lenses as used in electron spectroscopy has been published by Harting and Read (1976). Twenty four lenses are treated, including double-

and triple-cylinder lenses, double- and triple-aperture lenses, double- and triple-rectangular-tube lenses and double- and triple-double-slit lenses. The focal and aberration properties are calculated for each system.

Electron and ion beams can also be controlled by magnetic fields. The force on a charged particle is proportional to the intensity of the magnetic field and the velocity of the particle and is in a direction perpendicular to both the velocity and the field.

5.7.2 Control of aerosol particles

The control of aerosol particles by magnetic fields is not practicable because the velocity of the particles is too low for the magnetic force to be significant. Particles must therefore be controlled by electrostatic fields alone. The mobility of a particle (defined as the velocity per unit applied electric field) is low, and the applied field is limited by the breakdown strength of air, therefore precise control of particles is difficult. It is not usually possible to apply high enough fields over suitable distances to focus particle beams using a conventional electrostatic lens design. Aerosol particles also usually vary in size, shape and electric charge, and therefore individual particles do not respond in an identical way to the applied field. If particle size, shape, charge and position are closely controlled, precise deflections of particle beams can be achieved. This is used in the ink jet printer discussed in §5.1.5. Less precise but still useful deflections are used in some electrostatic separators.

5.7.3 Particle suspension using quadrupole fields

The stable suspension of a charged particle by DC electric fields alone requires that there should be a three-dimensional potential minimum in space, so that any movement represents a gain in energy of the system. According to the Earnshaw theorem, this is fundametally impossible (see Chapter 7). However, particles may be held stationary by a combination of electrical and gravitational forces or may be held in dynamic equilibrium using a combination of AC and DC fields.

When a combination of AC and DC fields are used, the electrode configuration must provide a force which is proportional to the distance from a central origin and the applied voltage must vary sinusoidally with time. The simplest form of field with this property is the AC quadrupole field illustrated in figure 5.43. This configuration was studied by Paul and his co-workers in the development of a non-magnetic mass spectrometer for ions (Paul and Steinwedel 1953, Paul and Ralther 1955, Paul *et al* 1958) and by Straubel, who showed that a dust particle could be contactlessly held at the saddle point of AC quadrupole fields in air (Straubel 1955, 1967, 1968).

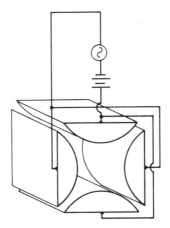

Figure 5.43 The electrode configuration for a two-dimensional quadrupole field.

Particle containment was studied theoretically and experimentally by Wuerker *et al* (1959). The circularly symmetric, potential distribution used in their work had the form

$$V = \left(\frac{V_{DC} - V_{AC}\cos\omega t}{z_0^2}\right)\left(z^2 - \frac{r^2}{2}\right). \tag{5.45}$$

V_{AC} is the peak of an alternating signal of angular frequency, ω, applied in series with the constant voltage, V_{DC}.

The equation of motion for a charged particle in the field provided by this potential distribution has a form which can be reduced to a standard differential equation (the Mathieu equation), which can be solved analytically and has stable solutions for fixed ranges of frequency and charge-to-mass ratio. Wuerker *et al* (1959) showed that experimental measurements of the motion agreed with theoretical predictions.

The system used to test this theory was evacuated to a pressure of twenty microns of mercury and the particles of approximately 20 μm in diameter were held within a stable region. The particles moved along a path which was a Lissajous' figure on which the driving frequency of 16.3 Hz was superimposed (figure 5.44). When a large number of particles were put into the system they could be made to take up stable arrays, each particle oscillating about its stable position under the influence of the alternating field. Reducing the frequency caused the stable array to disperse, reforming again when the frequency was increased.

Suspension in two-dimensional and three-dimensional quadrupole fields has also been studied by Masuda and Fujibayashi (1970).

Figure 5.44 A Lissajous' figure with oscillation frequency superimposed. The trajectory of a single aluminium particle suspended in an electrodynamic suspension system is shown (after Wuerker *et al* 1959).

5.7.4 Particle suspension by electrical and mechanical forces

A charged particle may be held stationary in space by applying a vertical electrostatic force to oppose gravity. If the field is applied between shaped electrodes, for example, a circular convex-top electrode and a matching concave-bottom electrode, the field between the electrodes has a horizontal component which tends to centre the particle. This method of centering the particle depends on the presence of a gravitational force, but gravity also limits the maximum size particle which can be suspended. A means of suspending charged drops and solid samples in the absence of gravitational fields has been developed by Rhim *et al* (1985), who were investigating techniques by which containerless, materials science experiments could be conducted in space. In the ring positioner, shown in figure 5.45, the outer rings of each electrode were maintained at a potential approximately 3.5 kV

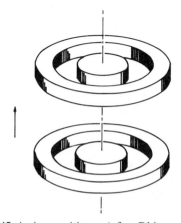

Figure 5.45 A ring positioner (after Rhim *et al* 1985).

higher than the central-disc electrodes and provided a force which tended to centre the particle. The vertical position was controlled by a servo control system that detected the position of the particle and provided an appropriate potential to centre it. A positioner with spheres at the corners of a tetrahedron allowed feedback control both horizontally and vertically. Rhim *et al* (1985) used charge coupled device cameras to detect the three-dimensional coordinates of the particle being levitated and this data was used to control an active feedback system which could hold the particle at any point in the levitation space. The ring and tetrahedral systems, operating at 20 kV, were able to lift particles of 0.15 g in a normal 1*g* environment. Rhim *et al* (1985) propose that samples exceeding 500 g could be held under the conditions which prevail in the space shuttle.

5.7.5 The electric curtain

The electric curtain is the name given to a particle suspension system developed by Masuda and co-workers at Tokyo University. A simple electric curtain is illustrated in figure 5.46. A set of parallel cylindrical electrodes, insulated from each other and connected to a single phase or a polyphase AC source forms a non-uniform, standing-or travelling-wave electric field, which acts as a contactless barrier or a contactless conveyor (Masuda *et al* 1972).

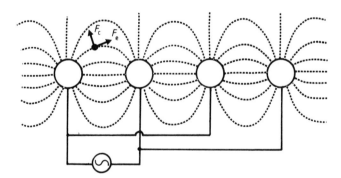

Figure 5.46 Principle of the electric curtain (after Masuda 1971). F_c is the centrifugal force acting on a particle and F_e the electrostatic force due to the lag between the oscillating field and the arrival of the particle.

For a stationary electric curtain, a single-phase AC signal is applied between pairs of rods. As the electric field oscillates, a charged powder particle will undergo a periodic motion, along the curved lines of force between two adjacent electrodes. It will be repelled from the electrode by two forces: (i) the centrifugal force due to the curved path of the particle and (ii) the force due to the change in the field intensity near the electrode coupled with the phase lag between the particle oscillation and the alternating field. The centrifugal force is perpendicular to the particle trajectories and the field force is tangential and the particle is held suspended above the electrode. If a polyphase signal is applied, the system provides not only suspension but transport, as the travelling-wave electric field moves particles from one electrode to the next. Particles can be transported in a tube by a series of ring electrodes along the wall.

The repulsive force on the particles, which holds them above the surface, and the transport velocity in a polyphase field, can be calculated by solving the equation of motion of the particle:

$$M \, d^2r/dt^2 + 6\pi\eta_a \, dr/dt = qE \cos \omega t + F \qquad (5.46)$$

where m is the particle mass, r is the particle position, η is the viscosity of air, q is the particle charge and F are the external forces, e.g. gravity.

The electric field changes in magnitude and space in a complicated manner therefore, unlike the case of the quadrupole field, the equation cannot be solved analytically. Masuda (1971) has obtained a solution to a linear approximation to the equation by making the assumption that the particle oscillation is small. He also obtained simulations of particle motion from a numerical solution of the equation. Measurements of particle trajectories in a ring type of electric curtain closely resembled the paths produced by the computer model.

For some applications, safety dictates that the cylindrical electrodes are not in direct contact with powder particles, and the electrodes are embedded in an insulating material. With this configuration it was observed that initially uncharged particles, in contact with the insulating material, could be violently ejected and transported. Since it appeared that contact with the sheet played an important role, this system was called the 'contact-type electric curtain'. A study of the behaviour of different powders showed that conducting particles charged by induction and were always ejected, but that some insulating particles charged by contact with neighbouring particles and were also active. A suitable mixture of two non-active powders could produce an active mixture (Masuda and Matsumoto 1974).

Masuda reports a number of applications of the electric curtain. For example, electrodes have been embedded in the walls of a powder coating spray booth, made of insulating material. When a three-phase AC signal was activated, oversprayed powder adhering to the booth walls was lifted and transported to a collecting hopper (Masuda *et al* 1975).

An electric curtain can be used to make a charged-particle filter which separates equally sized particles according to their charge (Masuda *et al* 1972), and has also been used in a dust collection device (Aoyama and Masuda 1971). Figure 5.47 shows a system based on contact and contactless electric curtains which was proposed by Masuda (1971) for producing a controlled beam of particles.

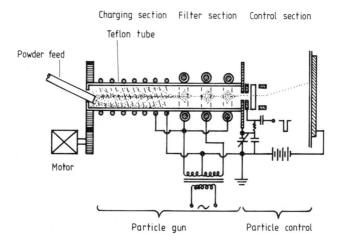

Charging section   Filter section   Control section

Figure 5.47 A particle beam system (from Masuda 1971). Particles are charged in a teflon tube which rotates inside a standing-wave electric curtain. The rotating action drives the particles into the filtering section. This acts as a band pass filter which passes particles of one charge-to-mass ratio. This beam can then be accurately deflected.

5.7.6 Dielectrophoretic levitation

A neutral particle may be suspended electrostatically, using the dielectrophoretic force. A particle will experience a force in a non-uniform electric field which moves it towards the high-field region if the dielectric constant of the particle is higher than that of the medium, and to the low-field region if the particle dielectric constant is lower than that of the medium. An extension of Earnshaw's theorem, due to Epstein (1965), states that an electric field maximum isolated from an electrode surface cannot exist, unless there is a space charge present. Therefore a particle which has a higher dielectric constant than the medium cannot be suspended by electrostatic forces alone. However, a three-dimensional field minimum can occur and a particle or bubble with a lower dielectric constant than the medium can be suspended by electrostatic forces alone (Jones and Bliss 1977).

The theory of dielectrophoretic levitation of low dielectric constant particles in a liquid, where both are assumed to have a finite conductivity, has been investigated by Jones and Kallio (1979). They showed that under certain circumstances, as detailed in table 5.8, there was a cut-off frequency above or below which levitation is no longer possible. Electrode configurations for dielectrophoretic levitation are discussed by Jones (1981) and Jones and McCarthy (1981).

Table 5.8 Tabulation of levitation conditions (Jones and Kallio 1979). σ_1 and σ_2, and ε_1 and ε_2 are the DC conductivity and the dielectric constants of materials 1 and 2 respectively.

	$\varepsilon_2 < \varepsilon_1$	$\varepsilon_2 > \varepsilon_1$
$\sigma_2 > \sigma_1$	Stable levitation at high frequencies only	No stable levitation
$\sigma_2 < \sigma_1$	Stable levitation at all frequencies	Stable levitation at low frequencies only

5.7.7 Movement of conducting particles between electrodes

When conducting particles are placed in an electric field between two electrodes, the particles oscillate between the electrodes, charging by induction at each in turn as discussed in §2.4.2. This technique has been used to disperse powders to allow uniform coatings to be applied to the particle surface (Szirmai 1984).

If the electrodes are in the form of inclined plates, the field lines between the two planes will be curved as sketched in figure 5.48. The field is non-uniform, but the field gradient is perpendicular to the direction of the electric field and hence perpendicular to the dipole moment of the particle. There is therefore no dipole force tending to move the particle to the higher field region. However, the particle experiences a centrifugal force as it moves along the curved field lines which moves it outwards to the lower field region. This can be used in electrostatic separators and has also been proposed as a means of moving powder across a surface to develop fingerprints.

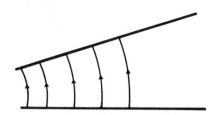

Figure 5.48 The field lines between inclined planes.

In the conventional method of developing a fingerprint the surface is brushed with aluminium powder which sticks to the fingerprint grease. However, the brush tends to smudge the prints. In the electrostatic technique, the conducting powder is placed on the surface on which fingerprints are to be developed, and an inclined electrode carrying 5–10 kV is held above the powder. Providing the surface has some electrical conductivity, the powder is dispersed, and moves around the surface as the electrode is moved. When the powder contacts an area of fingerprint grease it adheres and fingerprints are developed without use of a brush. The system works well with metal or glass surfaces, but painted surfaces are not sufficiently conducting to allow the particles to charge by induction and disperse.

Electrostatic and centrifugal forces are combined in the electrostatic conveyor, illustrated in figure 5.49 (Inculet and Castle 1985). A potential of approximately 20 kV is applied between edges A_1 and B_1 on phase 1, and between A_2 and B_2 on phase 2. B_1 and B_2 are also held 10 kV above earth. These potentials are maintained by a current flow along the plates which are made of a suitable resistive material. Curvilinear electric fields are generated, with a radius of curvature which depends on the length and spacing of the plates. When small charged particles are placed on the plane they oscillate in the AC field, along the curved paths. The centrifugal force pushes them along in the direction of the arrow. A time lag of $\pi/2$ between the two phases results in a travelling curvilinear field and the powder is conveyed along the tube. The conveying speed depends on the length of the plates and the frequency of the alternating field.

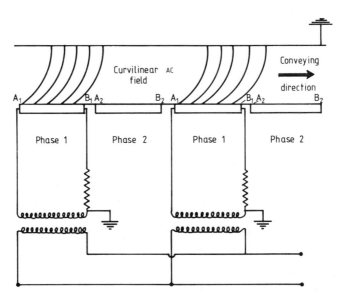

Figure 5.49 A schematic diagram of a two-phase travelling curvilinear AC electric field (after Inculet and Castle 1985).

5.8 APPLICATIONS OF ELECTROMECHANICAL FORCES

5.8.1 Electrostatics in fluidised beds

Spontaneous electrostatic charging occurs in fluidised beds of insulating particles and particle agglomeration has been widely observed. Frequently this is a nuisance, which is reduced by increasing the electrical conductivity of the particles, but electrostatic charging may also be turned to advantage. For example, fluidised beds can be used as charging devices in electrostatic separation. The mechanics of fluidised beds of semi-insulating particles are strongly affected by an applied electrostatic field. Electromechanical effects can be used in a number of different applications including electrostatic gas cleaning (Chapter 4), electrostatic separation (§5.3), commercial drying (Elsdon and Shearer 1977), heat transfer (Dietz 1978, Colver and Bosshart 1979) and fluidised-bed control (Johnson and Melcher 1975).

When the velocity of air passing through a packed bed of powder is increased, the pressure drop across the bed rises until a flow rate is reached at which the bed becomes fluidised, after which the pressure drop remains essentially constant. When an electric field is applied, the velocity required to fluidise the bed increases as illustrated in figure 5.50, but once the bed

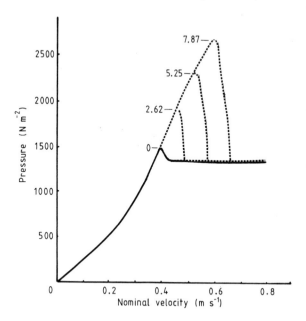

Figure 5.50 Pressure drop flow velocity characteristic for a fluidised bed with different applied fields (shown in kV cm^{-1}). The full curve corresponds to an applied field of 0 kV cm^{-1}.

fluidises, the pressure drop is essentially the same as in the absence of the field. The overshoot pressure required to achieve fluidisation is an approximately linear function of applied field and depends on particle resistivity. (The overshoot pressure is less for more insulating particles.) When the potential is increased across a bed which is already fluidised, a freezing potential can be reached, at which the bed loses its fluidised state. A bed which is fixed by application of field in this way is in a more expanded state than when there is no air flow and no field (Johnson and Melcher 1975).

Although the electric field has little effect on the pressure drop, once the bed is fluidised, it has a considerable effect on the appearance of the flow within the bed. When the electric field is applied perpendicular to the direction of the air flow, the formation of bubbles is inhibited, and the particles form two-dimensional laminae along the field lines which are distributed through the bubble as it propagates upwards. When the field is applied in the same direction as the flow, relatively conducting particles lift in the field and bounce between the electrodes. Particles form strings along the field lines which encourage channelling.

Electromechanical forces have been measured by studying the maximum angle of repose of a loosely packed bed of glass spheres across which an electric field is applied (Robinson and Jones 1984a,b). Electric fields of a few kilovolts per centimetre produced an electric stress of a few hundred N m^{-2}, in agreement with the values deduced from pressure drop measurements in fluidised beds.

When a DC field is applied to a fluidised bed, mixing is reduced and the heat transfer from a surface immersed in the bed falls (Dietz 1978). However, an alternating field applied perpendicular to the heated surface can increase heat transfer (Elsdon and Shearer 1977). This can be explained by assuming that the field causes the particles to oscillate so as to disturb the stagnant gas layer round the heated object. The movement of oppositely charged particles within the bed in opposite directions may also assist mixing.

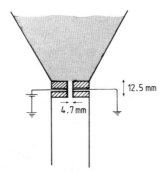

Figure 5.51 An electromechanical bed support (from Johnson and Melcher 1975). Reprinted with permission from Ind. and Eng. Chem. Fund. © American Chemical Society.

Electromechanical forces can be used to control the flow of powder through an orifice (Johnson and Melcher 1975). In the apparatus shown in figure 5.51, a field of $9 \, kV \, m^{-1}$ across the orifice prevented flow. When the potential was removed, powder flowed through the slit and the bed was lost within a few minutes. The bed can be supported with or without air flow. Electromechanical forces can be used to control an electrospouted bed, used for gas/solid reactions, as shown in figure 5.52. The bed has a draft tube and side exits to reduce gas bypassing. A high-voltage electrode ring, inserted below the draft tube, sets up electric fields between the ring and the draft tube and between the ring and the bed walls. These fields modify the flow of the particles, resulting in voltage-controlled particle entrainment and circulation (Talbert *et al* 1984).

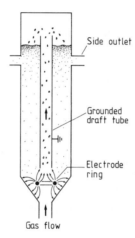

Figure 5.52 An electrospouted bed with an electrode ring near the inlet to control the particle circulation (from Talbert *et al* 1984).

5.8.2 Electrostatic holding

Electrostatic forces may be used to hold sheets of paper or fabric on to a platen and can be used to increase the friction between sliding surfaces. For example, electrostatic forces are commonly used to hold paper on to a pen recorder.

In one of the earliest devices a flat high-voltage electrode was fixed under an insulating sheet on which the paper was placed. A second earthed electrode was then rolled across the surface of the paper. The paper was polarised in the field as shown in figure 5.53. The positive charge, on the surface of the paper, was able to flow to earth through the roller, leaving the paper with a net negative charge, which attracted it towards the positive electrode.

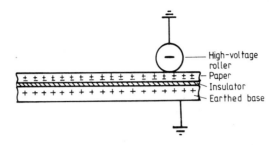

Figure 5.53 The principle of an electrostatic holding device.

In this system the force of attraction remained until the paper was discharged while there was zero voltage on the plane electrode. In later systems the force was removed when the power source was switched off. For example, in a system described by Stevko (1974), two interleaving sets of finger electrodes, with a potential of 4 kV between them, were placed beneath the surface of a semi-insulating material (resistivity $< 10^{13}\ \Omega\,m$). The fingers were approximately 20 mm wide with a spacing of about 10 mm. A small current, I, flowed between the two sets of electrodes through the semi-insulating sheet and across the paper surface. There was therefore a potential difference between the paper and the platen given by

$$V = IR$$

where R is the resistance of the contact.

This potential difference provided a force of attraction between the paper and the platen which was removed when the current flow ceased. There was also a dipole attraction, as a result of the strong field gradient at the edges of the finger electrodes.

A device which can be mounted on an existing, non-electrostatic platen is described by Sezako *et al* (1971). It consisted of an insulating sheet with a metallised layer on one side, and a semi-insulating layer which supported a conducting grid on the other side. A potential of between 500 and 1500 V was applied between the metallised layer and the grid. The paper, in contact with the grid, acquired the same polarity of charge, and was attracted through the spacing in the grid mesh towards the oppositely charged metallised layer.

Any of these holding systems can easily support a thick sheet of paper or fabric against gravity.

5.8.3 Electrostatic brakes

Electrostatic forces between two flat surfaces can be used to make an electrically operated brake. Johnsen and Rahbek (1923) discovered that there was an attractive force when an electric field was applied between a metal and a lithographic stone. The source of this effect is illustrated in figure 5.54. The true contact between the surfaces occurs at relatively small surface asperities, therefore, when a potential is applied, the current is constricted, creating regions of high field intensity. The semiconductor is polarised in the field and attracted to the regions of high field intensity at the asperities of the metal. This dielectrophoretic force is proportional to the square of the applied electric field and is independent of polarity. The effect has a time constant of about 10 μs therefore it can be seen for DC or slow AC fields. It is limited at high potentials by heating effects which begin to alter the interfacial structure and conductivity. Early attempts to make an electrically operated brake using this effect failed, because of the high wear between the metal and the semiconducting surface, but improved operation has been obtained using a polymer derived from cellulose as the semiconducting material (Duddings and Losty 1966). This is an electrically conducting polymer with good self-lubricating properties, whose electrical properties can be closely controlled by changing the temperature of the heat treatment.

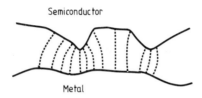

Figure 5.54 The Johnsen–Rahbek braking effect. Intense electric fields occur in the air gap at surface asperities with lower fields in the semiconductor.

5.9 ELECTROSTATIC COPYING

5.9.1 Electrophotography

In electrophotography a charge is applied to an insulating surface in the shape of the pattern to be copied. The latent image is developed by application of an ink or powdered toner (Schaffert 1975). In the most common system, illustrated in figure 5.55, the charged image is applied to a drum coated with a photoconducting material such as selenium. The drum is first charged to a uniform potential by a corona charging device such as a corotron. In its simplest form this is a high-voltage wire stretched between two supports but usually it has an earthed metal screen round three sides of the wire. The current flow to the drum depends on both the spacing between the wire and shield and the spacing between the wire and the drum. These are interdependent and there is quite a large variety in commercial designs.

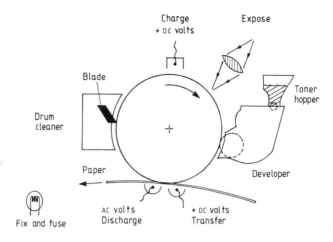

Figure 5.55 A schematic diagram of the automatic xerographic cycle.

With a positive corotron, hydrated protons, formed in the corona discharge, are neutralised at the surface of the drum resulting in positive holes trapped in surface states (Watson 1979). After charging, the drum is exposed to light from the optical image which is to be copied. The wavelength of the light chosen for illumination depends on the properties of the drum. Selenium is blue sensitive so an image of a blue line on white paper is poor, and green light, which is absorbed to some extent by most blue dyes, is chosen for illumination.

When the photoconductor is illuminated, charge carriers are generated, and move in the electric field so the surface potential is reduced approximately in proportion to the intensity of the illumination. The shadowed areas retain their charge producing the required electrostatic image. The latent image on the drum is developed by applying a toner by one of a number of different techniques (Thourson 1972). For example, the toner particles can be mixed with a carrier consisting of relatively coarse beads, which have a special surface, designed so that the toner acquires by friction a charge opposite in polarity to the drum. Usually the toner particles take a negative charge and the carriers the positive countercharge. The toner clings to the carrier beads, which are cascaded over the drum and the toner particles are transferred to the charged areas. The mechanisms by which the toner particles are transferred are not fully understood but both mechanical and electrostatic forces are believed to be involved (Donald and Watson 1972, Hays 1978). The developed image is then transferred to the paper which is heated to fix the image.

It is possible to develop an image, without using a carrier, by blowing the charged dust on to the surface. Powder is deposited in proportion to the amount of charge present. Other systems use a fur brush or a magnetic brush. The magnetic brush uses iron particles with a suitable polymer coating as a carrier. The toner is charged by friction against the polymer coating as before, but magnetic forces can be used to direct the carrier to the image. In some copiers the need for a carrier has been eliminated by making the toner itself magnetic by loading the resin with 50 % by weight of magnetite. The toner particles can then be transported using magnetic forces, for example, the particles may be held to a magnetic drum until charged by induction in the field between the magnetic drum and the charged surface. When the electrostatic force exceeds the magnetic retaining force the particle is attracted to the charged surface. Since this is insulating they do not discharge and remain adhering to it. For this method of development the toner particles must have some conductivity in order to charge by induction.

Early electrostatic copying machines were unable to reproduce large grey areas because of the low electric field above a uniformly charged surface on a conducting backing. (The field due to the surface charge acts mainly between the charge and its image in the substrate and there is very little field above the surface to attract the particles.) In the old machines the toner was therefore deposited preferentially in regions where the field gradient was high, i.e. on the boundaries of charged and uncharged areas. This problem was overcome by the use of a development electrode, in the form of an earthed plane electrode above the charged surface. This forces the charge to be shared between the substrate and the plane above the surface and intensifies the field above a large, uniformly charged area.

5.9.2 Electrographic printing

Electrostatic charged patterns can be produced on insulating surfaces in a number of non-photographic ways. For example an array of points can be held a few hundred micrometres above an insulating surface on a metal backing plate. When a voltage is applied to a pin there is a tiny electric spark which deposits a dot of charge on the dielectric. By pulsing combinations of pins in the array, numerals and alphabetical characters can be formed and developed using toners as before. The discharge lasts only a few microseconds and printing speeds of up to 5000 words/min are claimed.

For coarse patterns on insulating surfaces charge may be transferred by direct contact of electrodes on to the surface. This method has been used industrially to apply a dot pattern of heat-sensitive adhesive to interlining fabrics. After the charged dot pattern has been produced the interlining material is passed through a fluidised bed of the powdered adhesive to deposit a matrix of resin dots.

Powdered resins can be applied to a surface by a screen printing method. The powder is charged in a fluidised bed and suitable potentials are applied to screens held above the bed so the powder is pulled through to the surface to be printed. The screen may have closed areas as in conventional screen printing or may be treated with photoconducting film so the grid potential appears only in the required pattern.

5.10 ELECTROSTATICS IN THE TEXTILE INDUSTRY

5.10.1 Electrostatic spinning

An electrostatic field may be used in open-ended spinning to improve the fibre orientation (Kennedy 1949, Oglesby and Thomas 1955, Osaka Kiko Co. 1972, Unitika Co. 1973).

Figure 5.56 shows one type of electrostatic spinning machine. The fibres are conveyed by air, through a supply duct, into the gap between two electrodes which supply a non-uniform field. The fibres become polarised and align in the electric field and experience a dipole force which carries them towards the high-field region on the axis of the electrodes. The thread is inserted through the bottom electrode and protrudes into the high-field region. The fibres are attracted to the thread which is withdrawn through the lower electrode. The lower electrode is rotated to reduce the formation of bent fibres due to collisions between fibres rising from the anode and those falling from the cathode. The thread is twisted by a false-twist spindle. For efficient operation, the fibres must charge at the electrodes. They must therefore be slightly conducting. Optimisation of an electrostatic spinning

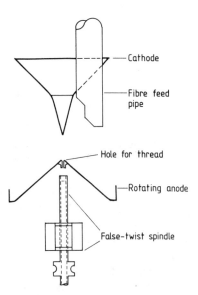

Figure 5.56 An electrostatic spinning machine (after Miura and Kaase 1980).

machine is discussed by Miura and Kaase (1980). The fundamental principles of electrostatic spinning are detailed in a series of four papers by Dogu (1975, 1976, 1977, 1984).

5.10.2 Electrostatic fibre formation

Figure 5.57 shows an electrostatic method for the manufacture of fibres for a non-woven cloth (Simm 1972). The bottom of a rotating disc is immersed in a solvent containing the resin from which the fibres are to be made and the disc picks up a liquid film as it rotates. A high voltage is applied to the disc which creates a strong electric field between the top of the disc and an earthed conveyor. A series of fine liquid threads are produced and pulled off the disc. The solvent evaporates leaving dry fibres which are carried by the electric field to the moving belts to form a non-woven cloth. This technique produces finer fibres than conventional technology (Brown 1980). The polarity of the disc can be periodically reversed to produce a fabric with inbuilt charge and enhanced filtration properties.

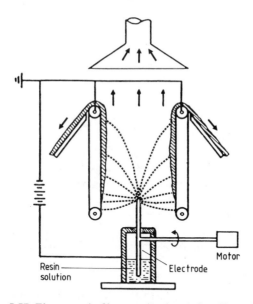

Figure 5.57 Electrostatic fibre production (after Simm 1972).

5.10.3 Electrostatic flocking

Electrostatic flocking is used to deposit fibres onto a surface to form a pile finish. A typical flock machine, used in carpet manufacture, is shown in figure 5.58. Polymer fibres are given a surface treatment to make them slightly conducting (i.e. the resistivity is reduced to approximately $10^9 \, \Omega \, m$)

and are brushed through a screen held at a high potential. The fibres charge by induction and fall towards an earthed substrate which is coated with an adhesive layer. Each fibre is polarised in the electric field and experiences a torque which aligns it with the field. It arrives at the earthed substrate in a vertical position and is held by the adhesive.

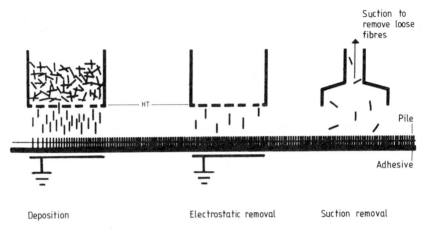

Figure 5.58 Electrostatic flocking.

In the absence of the adhesive, the particles would discharge at the earthed substrate, recharge by induction to the opposite polarity, and leave the substrate. The conductivity of the fibre is critical to obtaining a good dense-packed layer without treeing (strings of fibres building up on top of each other) and, for some fibres, the relative humidity must be maintained within a recommended range to obtain a satisfactory coating. The voltages used in electrostatic flocking machines range from 25 to 120 kV and the distance between the grid and substrate depends on the characteristics of the flock but is typically 120 mm for 80 kV. Flocking may be carried out with either AC or DC potentials. The AC fields tend to give a higher flock density for a given processing speed with less treeing and a more uniform flock distribution (Leimbacher 1966).

Electrostatic flocking is able to produce better orientation of the fibres than mechanical flocking and hence can achieve a better flocking density. However the conditioning of the surface of the fibre is more critical, and the mechanical design of the flocking machine, to incorporate the high-voltage electrodes, is more difficult.

Flock may also be applied by a spray gun where the fibres are either conveyed by air or thrown off a high-speed rotating electrode by centrifugal forces. The fibres are aligned in the field between the gun and the earthed substrate to produce the required pile finish.

The physical and mechanical performance of flocked materials is critically dependent on the flock density which is achieved. It can be shown that the maximum conceivable flock density is a close-packed hexagonal arrangement which would cover 90.7 % of the available surface. A hypothetical lower packing density, assuming every fibre is deposited so there is not quite enough room for another fibre next to it, is 30.2 %. With totally random packing about 50 % of the surface would be covered. In practice the maximum observed surface coverage is 12.1 % (Coldwell and Hersh 1978). Therefore it appears that it should be possible to achieve much greater packing densities than have been achieved in the past. Semenov *et al* (1983) have succeeded in improving coverage to 17.2 % by inserting a third electrode to increase the electric field as shown in figure 5.59. However the packing density is still well below the level expected from random packing. Although the coverage is much lower than is theoretically possible it is still sufficient to produce hard-wearing materials. The flocking density which can be achieved is a function of both the denier and the length of the flock and higher densities can be achieved with shorter flock lengths. It is important that fibres used for electrostatic flocking are of a uniform length. Longer flock particles will tend to sit above the surface and shield a local area from the field.

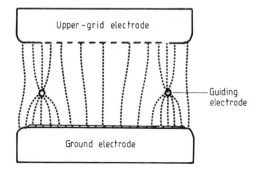

Figure 5.59 Flocking system with guiding electrodes and qualitative representation of electric field (after Semenov *et al* 1983).

There is very little published work on electrostatic flocking in the English language, and most research has taken place in Germany or Russia.

The first application of the flocking process was in the manufacture of sand paper, where electrostatic forces aligned the grit particles to produce the most abrasive surface possible. Now flocking is used in carpet manufacture, for producing a velour finish for car dashboards and novelty goods and to produce special effects on textiles. A recent patent suggests flock can be applied to electrical wiring to make it more suitable in interior design

(Batisse 1981). Electrostatic flocking has also been used to enhance the appearance of non-woven fabrics (Knoke *et al* 1982) and to prevent 'strike back' in fusible interlinings. In non-woven fabrics, fibres are held together in a felt by a binder. This impairs the fabric appearance and gives poor hot pressing characteristics. Electrostatic flocking is used to embed fibres vertically in the binder which is then crosslinked so the fibres are held permanently in position. The same process is used in fusible interlinings, which are adhesive-coated fabrics used as stiffenings which are hot pressed into collars etc in clothing manufacture. It is desirable to have the interlining as thin as possible but this tends to give strike back, i.e. the adhesive strikes through the interlining material on to the press. This is prevented by short vertical fibres without greatly adding to the weight of the fabric.

Early flocking machines could only coat automatically in one colour, but recently developments allowing three-colour automatic flocking have been reported (Anon 1983).

5.11 ELECTROSTATIC CRYSTALS

5.11.1 Introduction

Crystals which lack a centre of symmetry can have a net dipole moment per unit cell. Under normal circumstances, the charge imbalance across the crystal is neutralised by a surface charge, built up by internal conduction or by collection from the surrounding atmosphere. However the state of polarisation can be changed by reversing the electric field, by application of mechanical strain or by changing the temperature. Materials whose surface is changed by these three means are known as ferroelectrics, piezoelectrics and pyroelectrics respectively.

5.11.2 Ferroelectricity

Ferroelectrics are materials which have an electric polarisation in the absence of an applied electric field and also have the property that the direction of polarisation can be reversed by application of an electric field. When the electric field is removed, the ferroelectric material has a stable spontaneous polarisation in the new direction. They are the direct electrical equivalent of a ferromagnet. A graph of displacement ($D = \varepsilon_r \varepsilon_0 E$) against E exhibits hysteresis in a similar way to the graph of magnetic flux plotted against magnetic field. A good ferroelectric has a very square hysteresis loop, i.e. when an electric field is applied the direction of polarisation changes sharply and is stable in the new direction. Ceramics formed from lead zirconate and lead titanate can be polarised by relatively low voltages and are used as memory devices.

5.11.3 Piezoelectricity

A piezoelectric material lacks a centre of symmetry, so that when a mechanical strain is applied, the lattice distortion causes a net displacement between the positive and negative charges in the lattice and the crystal becomes polarised. The electric field produced is proportional to the applied force and the constant of proportionality is called the output coefficient.

Typical piezoelectric crystals are quartz, cadmium sulphide, zinc sulphide and zinc oxide. Other materials, such as polycrystalline, pressed ceramics, composed of barium titanate, and solid solutions of lead titanate and lead zirconate, can also exhibit strong piezoelectric effects if they are treated by subjecting them to 50–60 kV at elevated temperatures (Crawford 1961).

Some polymers, in particular polyvinylidene fluoride (PVDF) also exhibit piezoelectric and pyroelectric effects. PVDF is a semicrystalline polymer with three crystal forms. The piezoelectric and pyroelectric response depend strongly on the crystal form with the β-form producing the greatest effect (Klaase and van Turnhout 1979).

Piezoelectrics are used to couple electrical to mechanical signals, for example in cartridges for record players, where the variations in the record track are converted to electrical signals. The capacitance of a piezoelectric is low, therefore a fairly small mechanical force will produce sufficient charge to give a voltage of several kilovolts. Piezoelectric crystals have been connected to electrodes to produce sparks in gas igniters (Clevite Corporation 1968), or connected to a high-voltage point to produce a corona discharge. When a mechanical force is applied, the face of the crystal connected to the point acquires one polarity of charge and when the strain is released, ions of the other polarity are formed. A piezoelectric device is used as an electrostatic discharger gun for gramophone records. Piezoelectricity is discussed in detail by Cady (1964). This has been the standard text on the subject since the first edition was published in 1946. A more recent discussion is given by Nelson (1979).

5.11.4 Pyroelectricity

Pyroelectric materials are crystals with a net dipole moment per unit cell in which a change in temperature gives a proportional change in the polarisation.

Numerous devices have been designed using the pyroelectric effect including infrared and millimetre wave detectors, temperature sensors and thermal imagers. Among the more widely used pyroelectric materials are lithium tantalate single crystals and lead zirconate titanate ceramics.

5.11.5 Electrets

Electrets are materials in which a net polarisation is artificially built into the structure. The first electrets were made from a mixture of equal parts of carnuba wax and rosin (sometimes with some bees wax included). The mixture was melted and then allowed to solidify in the presence of a strong electric field. This is known as poling. When the field was moved the solid wax was polarised. When the electret was first removed from the mould its charge was of the heterocharge type, i.e. the surface which had been in contact with the positive electrode during solidification was negatively charged. However, this charge decayed to zero within a few hours and the surface began to exhibit homopolar charging, i.e. each surface had the polarity of the electrode with which it had been in contact. The surface finally reached a charge of the order of $2 \times 10^{-5} \, C \, m^{-2}$ (which is close to the maximum which can be achieved by friction) and maintained this charge for several years.

The heterocharges are believed to be due to volume polarisation of the dielectric and the homocharges due to trapped surface charges which are deposited during the poling process. The volume polarisation relaxes over a few hours but the trapped charge remains. The long-term electrification of electrets is thus due to the capture of electric charges in traps within the interior of the electret material (Perlman 1968).

Carnuba wax is a good electret but has rather poor mechanical properties. Thin-film electrets with desirable physical properties can be produced from various polymers including PTFE, PVDF and FEP (fluorinated ethylene propylene copolymer). Certain ceramics also make good electrets. Modern electrets may still be made by applying an electric field to a melt of the material but thin-film polymer electrets may also be formed by placing the film on an earthed electrode and establishing a corona discharge to the film.

The first application of an electret was in a condenser-type microphone in which a carnuba wax electret was used instead of the conventional high-voltage power supply. Modern electret microphones use a thin polymer diaphragm. As the sound waves impinge on the electret diaphragm it vibrates. The electric field to the counter electrode therefore varies and produces an electrical signal. Electrets have also been used as radiation detectors, memory storage units, vibration detectors, pressure gauges and in fabric filters (see §4.6.2).

5.12 ELECTROSTATIC GENERATORS

5.12.1 Introduction

Electrostatic generators convert mechanical energy to electrical energy by forcing charge to accumulate to build up a voltage. Normally they are low-current high-voltage supplies, which may be used for accelerators, x-ray sources or electrostatic applications such as paint spraying. The best known electrostatic generator is the Van de Graaff machine illustrated in figure 5.60. Charge is sprayed on to an insulating moving belt by corona points and removed from the belt by discharging points inside the high-voltage terminal. The charge accumulates on the high-voltage terminal until limited by flashover. The shape of this electrode is therefore designed to withstand a high voltage and is usually a sphere, surrounded by a second, concentric earthed sphere with a compressed gas between the two. Van de Graaff machines have been designed with current capabilities up to several milliamps (limited by the charge density which can be carried on the insulating belt) and voltages to about 5 MV. These machines have been used to power electron and ion accelerators used for high-energy physics research.

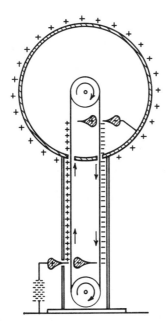

Figure 5.60 A Van de Graaff generator.

5.12.2 Cylindrical generators

The general form of a cylindrical generator is shown in figure 5.61. The rotating insulating cylinder is equivalent to the belt in the Van de Graaff machine. The cylinder is charged and discharged by corona, which is assisted by the inductors behind a glass cylinder. The cylinder rotates in hydrogen under pressure. (Hydrogen is chosen because of the high mobility of its ions.) These machines produce between up to 800 kV and tens of milliamps.

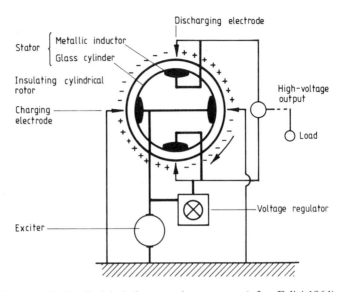

Figure 5.61 A cylindrical electrostatic generator (after Felici 1964).

5.12.3 Electrogasdynamic generators

An electrogasdynamic (EGD) generator is, in principal, similar to a Van de Graaff generator, but the charge is carried by an aerosol in a gas stream. The essential features are shown in figure 5.62. Aerosol particles are charged by corona from a needle and transported by compressed air to the collector. The air forces virtually all the charge to the collector, the attractor draws

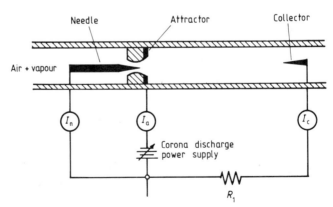

Figure 5.62 A simple single-needle EGD generator. The shaded area is metal and the hatched area dielectric.

very little current. Charge is collected from the particles by a corona discharge from the collector. The collector current, I_c, approximately equals the needle corona current, I_n, and a voltage builds up on the collector given by

$$V = I_c R_1.$$

The voltage is limited by the breakdown characteristics of the attractor–collector gap and by the dielectric strength of the gas vapour mixture but it considerably exceeds the potential applied to the corona needle.

The maximum power generated is limited by the maximum charge which can be applied to the particles. This is limited by the breakdown field of the gas which is related to the particle charge by Gauss's law. If the limiting field is E_b then from Gauss's law

$$E(2\pi r) = Q_v \pi r^2 / \varepsilon_0$$

where Q_v is the charge density in $C\,m^{-3}$. If the gas velocity is u then the current flow is

$$I = \pi r^2 u Q_v = 2\pi\varepsilon_0 Eur$$

and the power

$$VI = 2\pi\varepsilon_0 Eur V$$

where V is the voltage generated across the conversion section and r is the tube radius.

Although the power generated increases in proportion to the gas velocity, the frictional pressure drop across the conversion section increases in proportion to the square of the gas velocity and frictional losses in proportion to the cube of the velocity. Relatively low gas velocities therefore give the most efficient generation (Musgrove and Wilson 1970).

The main practical use of EGD generators is in paint spray guns where compressed air is already needed for transporting the paint and there are considerable advantages in minimising the power supply voltage.

5.12.4 Variable-capacitance generators

Variable-capacitance generators use the principle that the voltage on a component storing charge depends on the capacitance between that component and earth. A charged varying capacitor therefore produces a varying voltage. In the most effective design of these machines, electrodes in the form of blades on rotating discs are stacked in cylinders with alternate discs connected to the stator and the rotor. Rotation thus produces a bank of varying capacitors. A machine with one rotor and two stators of 50 cm diameter rotating at 10 000 rpm has produced 430 W at 24 kV (Moore 1973).

REFERENCES

Abu-Romia M M 1971 Possible applications of electro-osmotic flow pumping in heat pipes *Proc. 6th Thermophysics Conf. (Tullahoma, Tenn.) 1971* (New York: AIAA) AIAA paper No 71 p 423

Addison C A and Kedward E C 1977 The development of chromium based electro-deposited coatings *Trans. Inst. Metal Finishing* **55** 1–6

Alfano G, Carbini P, Carta M, Ciccu R, Del Fa C, Peretti R and Zucca A 1985 Applications of electrostatics in coal and ore beneficiation *J. Electrostatics* **16** 315–28

Allan R S and Mason S G 1961 Effect of electric field on coalesence in liquid–liquid systems *Trans. Faraday Soc.* **57** 2027–40

Anantheswaran R C and Law E S 1981 Electrostatic deposition of pesticide sprays onto planar targets *Trans. ASAE* **24** 273–6, 280

Anderson D G, Murphy E J and Tucci J 1978 Cathodic reactions and metal dissolution in cationic electrodeposition *J. Coatings Tech.* **50** 38–45

Andrade E N da C and Dodd C 1946 The effect of an electric field on the viscosity of liquids Part I *Proc. R. Soc.* A **187** 296–337

—— 1951 The effect of an electric field on the viscosity of liquids Part II *Proc. R. Soc.* A **204** 449–64

Andrade E N da C and Hart J 1954 The effect of an electric field on the viscosity of liquids Part III *Proc. R Soc.* A **225** 463–72

Anon 1976a Electrostatic separation system *Australian Mining*

Anon 1976b Powder, water, high solids electrocoat, radiation cure *Product Finishing, US* **40** 82–7, 164–73

Anon 1983 Automatic multicolor nonwovens flocking *Non Wovens Industry* **14** 29

Aoyoma M and Masuda S 1971 Characteristics of electric dust collector based on electric curtain *Proc. General Conf. Inst. Electr. Eng. Japan* No 821

Asch V 1966 Electrokinetic phenomena in boiling freon *J. Appl. Phys.* **37** 2654–8

Aschmann G and Kronig R 1950 The influence of electric fields on convective heat transfer in liquids *Appl. Sci. Res.* A **2** 235 (also corrigendum in 1951 *Appl. Sci. Res.* A **3** 83)

Atten P and Honda T 1982 The electroviscous effect and its explanation *J. Electrostatics* **11** 225–45

Atten P and Lacroix J C 1979 Non-linear hydrodynamic stability of liquids subject to unipolar injection *J. Mécanic* **18** 469–510

Atten P, Malraison B and Ali Kani S 1982 Electrohydrodynamic stability of dielectric liquids subjected to AC fields *J. Electrostatics* **12** 477–88

Atten P and Moreau R 1972 Electrohydrodynamic stability of insulating liquids subject to unipolar injection *J. Mécanic* **11** 471–520

Bailey A G 1974 Electrostatic atomisation of liquids *Sci. Prog.* **61** 555–81

Bailey A G and Balachandran W 1981 The disruption of electrically charged jets of viscous liquid *J. Electrostatics* **10** 99–107

Balachandran W and Bailey A G 1982 The dispersion of liquids using centrifugal and electrostatic forces *IEEE Ann. Meeting of the Industrial Applications Society* 971–5

Balint A and Flemming M G 1964 Selective conditioning of minerals in gaseous suspensions with the aid of electrostatic forces *Proc. 7th Int. Mineral Processing Cong. (New York)* ed N Arbiter (New York: Gordon and Breach)

Bassett J D, Corbett R P and Cross J A 1975 The self-limiting of electrostatic powder coatings *Static Electrification (London) 1975* (Inst. Phys. Conf. Ser. 27) pp 221–7

Batisse C 1981 Flocking electrically conducting wires *GB Patent 2080705*

Bier M 1957 New principle of preparative electrophoresis *Science* **125** 1084–5

Bird R, Blythe A R, Briggs D and Kendall C R 1982 Electrical discharge treatment of polymeric film surfaces *Proc. 7th Int. Conf. on Gas Discharges and Their Applications (London) 1975*

Bjornstahl K 1935 Viscosity of liquids in an electric field *Physica* **6** 257–64

Bjornstahl K and Snellman O 1937 Influence of electric field on the viscosity of pure liquids and colloid solutions *Kolloid Z.* **78** 258–72

Black B C and Hammond E G 1965 Separation by dielectric distribution *J. Am. Oil Chem. Soc.* **42** 931–6

Blythe A R 1978 *Electrical Properties of Polymers* (Cambridge: CUP)

Blythe A R, Briggs D, Kendall C R, Rance D G and Zichy V J I 1978 Surface modification of polyethylene by electrical discharge treatment and the mechanism of auto-adhesion *Polymers* **19** 1273–8

Bonjour E and Verdier J 1960a Interpretation of the effect of the action of electric fields on the transfer of heat in a liquid *C.R. Acad. Sci., Paris* **250** 76, 998–1000

—— 1960b Mécanism de l'ébullition sous champs éléctriques *C.R. Acad. Sci., Paris* **251** 924–6

Bonjour E, Verdier J and Weil L 1962 Electroconvective effects on heat transfer *Chem. Eng. Prog.* **58** 63–6

Bose G M 1745 *Récherches sur la Cause et sur la Véritable Theorie d'Éléctricite* (Wittenberg)

Boyce G M 1985 New automatic feed rate control; system for electrostatic powder coating *Powder Coating Conf. (Birmingham)* paper No 1

Briggs D and Kendall C R 1982 Derivatisation of discharge treated LDPE *Int. J Adhesives and Adhesion* **2** 13

Bright A W 1974 Modern electrostatics *Phys. Educ.* **9** 381–9

Brookman E T and Hartshorn W T 1982 Control of fugitive dust with electrostatically charged fog device—a status report *IEEE Conf. Industrial Applications Society* 982–6

Brown R C 1980 The behaviour of fibrous filter media in dust respirators *Ann. Occ. Hygiene* **23** 367–80

Brown W B 1974 Interrupted current electrodeposition of paints *US Patent Specification 3809634*

—— 1975 Current interruption methods of electrodepositing paints *J. Paint Technol.* **47** 43–7

Cady W G 1964 *Piezoelectricity* (New York: Dover)

Carta M, Alfano G, Carbini R, Ciccu R and DelFa C 1981 Triboelectric phenomena in mineral processing *J. Electrostatics* **10** 177–82

Castle G S P, Inculet I I and Littlewood R 1983 Ionic space charges generated by evaporating charged liquid sprays *Electrostatics (Oxford) 1983* (Inst. Phys. Conf. Ser. 66) pp 59–64

Chandler R H 1978 Advances in electrophoretic painting *Bibliographies in Paint Technology No 31* (Braintree, Essex: R H Chandler Ltd)

—— 1981 Advances in electropainting 1978–1980 *Bibliographies in Paint Technology No 36* (Braintree, Essex: R H Chandler Ltd)

Chen C S and Pohl H A 1974 Biological dielectrophoresis: the behaviour of lone cells in a nonuniform electric field *Ann. NY Acad. Sci.* **238** 176–85

Chen K W L L 1969 Dielectrophoresis of solids in aqueous solution *PhD Thesis* Oklahoma State University

Choi H Y 1962 Electrohydrodynamic boiling heat transfer *PhD Thesis* Massachusetts Institute of Technology (Dept. Mech. Eng.)

Cibrowksi J and Wlodarski A 1962 On electrostatic effects in fluidised beds *Chem. Eng. Sci.* **17** 23–32

Ciccu R 1984 *Patent* filed CCIA, Cagliari, Italy

Clevite Corporation 1968 A piezoelectric voltage source *GB Patent Specification* 1 124 166

Coffee R 1974 Depositional control of macroscopic particles by high-strength electric field propulsion *IEEE Trans. Ind. Appl.* **IA-10**

Coldwell R L and Hersh S P 1978 The influence of processing variables on the properties of flocked fabrics *IEEE Trans. Ind. Appl.* **IA-14** 177–91

Cole K S, Cole R H and Curtis H J 1935 *J. Gen. Physiol.* **18** 877

—— 1936 *J. Gen. Physiol.* **19** 609

—— 1938 Electrical impedance of single marine eggs *J. Gen. Physiol.* **21** 591–9

Collins G L and Jameson G J 1977 Double layer effects in flotation of fine particles *Chem. Eng. Sci.* **32** 239–46

Colver G M and Bosshart G S 1979 Heat and charge transfer in an AC fluidised bed *Proc. 2nd Multiphase Flow and Heat Transfer Symp. (University of Miami, Florida) 1979*

Cosgrove J H 1967 Operating characteristics of capillary limited heat pipes *J. Nucl. Energy* **21** 547–58

Cottrell F G 1908 Breaking and separating oil water emulsions *US Patent Specification* 895 729

Crawford A 1961a Lead zirconate–titanate ceramics *Brit. J. Appl. Phys.* **12** 529–34

—— 1961b Piezoelectric ceramic transformers and filters *Brit. J. Radio Eng. Inst.* **21** 353–60

Cross J A 1979 Electrostatically assisted heat transfer *Electrostatics (Oxford) 1979* (Inst. Phys. Conf. Ser. 48) pp 191–9

Cross J A, Sampuran-Singh and Abu Bakir 1980 Deposition efficiency of powder in the electrostatic powder coating process *J. Oil and Colour Chemists Assoc.* **63** 326–9

Derjaguin P N and Shukakidse N D 1961 *Trans. IMM* **70** 569

Dietz P W 1978 Heat transfer in bubbling fluidised beds *J. Electrostatics* **5** 297–308

Dietz P W and Melcher J R 1975 Field controlled change in heat transfer involving macroscopic charged particles in liquid *ASME J. Heat Transfer* **97** 429–34

Dogu I 1975 Fundamentals of electrostatic spinning: I. An analysis of the forces acting on a single fibre *Textile Res. J.* **45** 521–34

—— 1976 Fundamentals of electrostatic spinning: II. The mechanics of fibre transfer in the electrostatic zone of an electrostatic spinning machine *Textile Res. J.* **46** 676–91

—— 1977 Fundamentals of electrostatic spinning: III. The behaviour of fibres in the electrostatic zone of an electrostatic spinning machine *Textile Res J.* **47** 780–9

—— 1984 Fundamentals of electrostatic spinning: IV. Ionisation of atmospheric air under the action of an electrostatic field *Textile Res. J.* **54** 111–19

Donald D K and Watson P K 1972 Effects of electric fields on toner/carrier adhesion in xerographic development *IEEE Trans. Electron. Devices* **ED-19** 458–62

Dow D B 1926 *US Bureau of Mines Bull.* No 250

Duddings R W and Losty H H W 1966 Electrostatic clutches based on the Johnsen–Rahbek effect *GEC J.* **33** 2–9

Dukhin S S 1974 *Surface and Colloid Science* vol 7, ed E Matijevic (New York: Wiley) ch 1

Dukhin S S and Derjaguin B V 1974 Electrokinetic phenomena *Surface and Colloid Science* vol 7, ed E Matijevic (New York: Wiley) ch 2

Dyrenforth W P 1978 Electrostatic separation *Mineral Processing Plant Design, AIME* ed A L Muller and R B Bhappu 479–89

Earnst L and Singewald A 1981 Selective separation of minerals using surface conditioning *Z. Phys. Chem.* **124** 223

Edison T A 1881 *US Patent Specification* 245299

_____ 1892 *US Patent Specification* 476991

Elsdon R and Shearer C J 1977 Heat transfer in gas fluidised beds *Chem. Eng. Sci.* **32** 1147–53

Epstein L 1965 Electrostatic suspension *Am. J. Phys.* **33** 406–7

Farmer I W and Bell F G 1975 Methods of treatment of unstable ground (London: Butterworths)

Feeley C M 1969 Dielectrophoresis of solids in liquids of differing dielectric constant and conductivity *PhD Thesis* Oklahoma State University

Felici N J 1964 Cylindrical electrostatic generators *Radiation Sources* (New York: Pergamon)

Fillimore G L and Van Lokeren D C 1982 Multinozzle drop generator which produces uniform break up of continuous jets *IEEE Ann. Meeting of the Industrial Applications Society* pp 991–1001

Franke M E 1969 Effect of vortices induced by corona discharge on the convective heat transfer from a vertical plate *Trans. ASME Heat Transfer* **91** C 427–31

Fricke H 1925 A mathematical treatment of the electric conductivity and capacity of disperse systems *Phys. Rev.* **26** 678–87

_____ 1953 The electric permittivity of a dilute solution of membrane covered ellipsoids *J. Appl. Phys.* **24** 644–9

Fukui Y and Yiu S 1985 Removal of colloid particles by electroflotation *AIChE* **31** 201–8

Furuno N and Ohyabu Y 1977 Methods for measuring throwing power in electrodeposition coating *Prog. Organic Coatings* **5** 201–17

Gaudin A M 1971 Principles of electrical processing *Minerals Sci. Eng.* **3** 45–57

Gemant A 1929 Bewegungsercheinungenn an dielektriken unter hoten felden *Electrotech. Z.* **50** 1225–8

Giddings C J 1966 A new separation concept based on a coupling of concentration and flow nonuniformities *Separation Sci.* **1** 123–5

Gilbert 1600 de Magnete *Trans. P F Mottelay* (London: Peter Short) (On Readex microprint: Landmarks of Science 1967)

Golovoy 1973a Particle deposition in electrostatic spraying of powder coatings *J. Paint Technol.* **45** 68–71

_____ 1973b Growth of film thickness in electrostatic spraying of powder coatings *J. Paint Technol.* **45** 72–9

Grant R P and Middleman S 1966 Newtonian jet stability *AIChE J.* **12** 669–77

Grebenyuk V D, Kurilenklo O D, Dukhin S S and Sobolevskaya T T 1975 Electrofiltration of dispersions and electrokinetic phenomena *Coll. J. USSR* **37** 661–5

Grubbs M R and Ivey K H 1972 Recovery of plastics from urban refuse by electro-dynamic techniques *US Bureau of Mines Report* TPR 63

Grushka E, Caldwell K D, Myers M N and Giddings J C 1973 *Separation and Purification Methods* **2** 127–51

Haagan H 1976 Comparative investigations into methods of determining electropaint throwing power *Defazet* **30** 194–205

Hall H J and Brown R F 1966 New electrostatic liquid cleaner *Lubrication Eng.* **22** 488–95

Han C P 1975 Electrostatic cooling of metals and non metals *PhD Thesis* Department of Aerospace and Mechanical Engineering, Notre Dame, Indiana

Harland J R, McNaulty K J and Tomkins F C 1978 Research on cross flow filtration for solids removal from Coal Syncrudes *Final Report to US Department of Energy*

Harris S T 1981 *The Technology of Powder Coating* (New York: Portcullio)

Hart J and Merrilees P E 1963 The viscoelastic effect *Dielectrics* **1** 58

Harting E and Read F H 1976 *Electrostatic Lenses* (Amsterdam: Elsevier)

Hartmann G 1976 *Proc. 3rd Int. Conf. on Gas Discharges (London) 1974* (IEE Publication No 118 634–8)

Hawk I L 1967 Effect of non uniform fields on real dielectrics in water *PhD Thesis* Oklahoma State University

Hays D A 1978 Electric field detachment of toner *Proc. 3rd Conf. on Electrophotography (Phot. Sci. Eng.* **22** 232–5)

Heller J H 1959 *Digest of the 12th Ann. Conf. on Electronic Techniques in Medicine and Biology* (56 IRE, AIEE, ISA)

Hendricks C D 1962 Charged droplet experiments *J. Colloid Sci.* **17** 249–60

Henry J D 1972 Cross flow filtration in *Recent Developments in Separation Science* vol. II (Cleveland, Ohio: Chemical Rubber)

Henry J D and Jacques M T 1977 Charge characteristics of heavy particles in coal derived liquids *AIChE J.* **23** 607–9

Hilpert J and Kern J 1974 Electric wind in corona discharge *Arch. Elektr.* **56** 50–4

—— 1975 Studies of blowers in series to produce high velocity electric winds *Arch. Elektr.* **57** 55–8

Hoenig S A 1977 Use of electrostatically charged fog for control of fugitive dust *EPA* 600/7-77-131 (NTIS, Springfield, Virginia)

—— 1980 Electrostatic techniques for the protection of optical components in dusty environments *Appl. Opt.* **19** 694–7

—— 1981 New applications of electrostatic technology to the control of dust, smokes and aerosols *IEEE Trans. Ind. Appl. Soc.* **IA-17** 386–91

Honig H 1977 New methods of establishing the throwing power of electrodeposited paints *J. Oil and Colour Chemistry Association* **60** 173–80

—— 1978 New electrophysical measuring principle in the development and use of synthetic resins for electropainting *FATIPEC Congress Book* 279–83

Hopp M 1977 Application of paint films by cataphoresis *Surfaces* **108** 39–42, 45–6

Huband E J 1977 Boiling heat transfer with electric fields *Internal Report, Dept Mechanical Engineering, University of Bristol, UK*

Hughes J F 1985 *Electrostatic Powder Coating* (New York: Research Studies Press and Wiley)

Hughes J F and Pavey I D 1981 Electrostatic emulsification *J. Electrostatics* **10** 45–55

Ichinose S, Matsuki M and Higuchi K 1985 New ink jet recording for generating a plurality of ink jet streams *IEEE Trans. Ind. Appl.* **IA-21** 47–52

Inculet I I 1984 *Electrostatic Mineral Separation* (New York: Research Studies Press)

Inculet I I and Bergougnou M A 1973 Electrostatic beneficiation of mineral particles in a fluidised bed *Proc. 10th Int. Mineral Processing Congress (London) 1973* Paper 11 pp 1–14

Inculet I I, Bergougnou M A and Brown J D 1977 Electrostatic separation of particles below 40 μm in a dilute phase continuous loop *Trans. IEEE Ind. Appl.* **IA-13** 370–3

―― 1982 Electrostatic beneficiation of coal in *Physical Cleaning of Coal: Present and Developing Methods* ed Y A Lui (New York: Marcel Dekker)

Inculet I I and Castle G S P 1981 Deposition studies with a novel form of electrostatic crop sprayer *J. Electrostatics* **10** 65–72

―― 1985 Particle conveying with curvilinear electric fields generated by plane electrodes *J. Electrostatics* **17** 95–8

Johnsen A and Rahbek K 1923 A physical phenomenon and its application to telegraphy, telephony etc *J. IEE* **61** 713

Johnson T W and Melcher J R 1975 Electromechanics of fluidised beds *Ind. Eng. Chem. Fund.* **14** 146–53

Jones T B 1971 The feasibility of electrohydrodynamic heat pipes *Colorado State University, Fort Collins* NASA CR-114392

―― 1973 Electrohydrodynamic heat pipes *Int J. Heat and Mass Transfer* **16** 1045–8

―― 1974 An electrohydrodynamic heat pipe *Mechanical Engineering* **96** 27–32

―― 1977 *Electrical Engineering Department, Colorado State University, Fort Collins Research Report* NSF/ENG 74-24113/RR2/77

―― 1981 Cusped electric fields for dielectrophoretic levitation *J. Electrostatics* **11** 85–95

Jones T B and Bliss G W 1977 Bubble dielectrophoresis *J. Appl. Phys.* **48** 1412–7

Jones T B and Kallio G A 1979 Dielectrophoretic levitation of small spheres and shells *J. Electrostatics* **6** 207–24

Jones T B and McCarthy M J 1981 Electrode geometries for dielectrophoretic levitation *J. Electrostatics* **11** 71–83

Jones T B and Schaeffer R C 1976 Electrohydrodynamically coupled minimum film boiling in dielectric liquids *AIAA J.* **14** 1759–65

Kahn B and Gourdine M 1964 Electrodynamic power generation *J. AIAA* **2** 1423–7

Keeling M R and Pullen E A 1981 Ink jet printing *Inst. Phys. (UK) Seminar on Liquid Charging and Liquid Spraying* unpublished

Kelly E G and Spottiswood D J 1982 *Introduction to Mineral Processing* (New York: Wiley) ch 15

Kelsh D J and Sprite R H 1982 Electrokinetic densification of solids in a coal mine sediment pond—a feasibility study *US Bureau of Mines* RI 8666

Kennedy 1949 Electrostatic control of fibres *US Patent Specification* 2468827

Kibler K G and Carter H G 1974 Electrocooling in gases *J. Appl. Phys.* **45** 4436–40

Kiewlet C W, Bergougnou M A, Brown J D and Inculet I I 1978 Electrostatic separation of fine particles in vibrating fluidised beds *IEEE Trans. Ind. Appl.* **IA-14** 526–30

Kim C Y and Goring D A 1971 Corona induced bonding of synthetic polymers to wood *J. Appl. Polymer Sci.* **15** 1357–64

Klaase P T A and van Turnhout J 1979 Dielectric, piezoelectric and pyroelectric properties of materials *IEE Dielectric Materials Conf. Publ.* **177** 411–14

Klass D L and Martinek K W 1967 Electroviscous fluids: I. Rheological properties *J. Appl. Phys.* **38** 67–74, Electroviscous fluids: II. Electrical properties **38** 75–80

Knoke J, Bauchwald H and Fehlhaber J 1982 Fusible interlining with improved freedom from strike back and a process for its preparation *GB Patent Specification* 2111859

Konig W 1885 *Ann. Phys., Lpz* **25** 618

Kronig R and Schwarz N 1949 On the theory of heat transfer from a wire in an electric field *Appl. Sci. Res.* A **1** 35–45

Kuhn A T 1974 Electroflotation *Chem. Process* **20** 5–7

Lacchia P 1974 Contribution a l'étude de la charge d'un jet de particules microioniques dans le champ ionisé d'un systeme point plan *PhD Thesis* University Grenoble

Lacroix J C, Atten P and Hopfinger E J 1975 Electroconvection in a dielectric liquid subjected to unipolar charge injection *J. Fluid Mechanics* **69** 539–63

Landau L D and Lifshitz E M 1960 *Electrodynamics of Continuous Media* vol. 8 (Oxford: Pergamon) p 68

Law E S and Lane M D 1981 Electrostatic deposition of pesticide sprays onto foliar targets of varying morphology *Trans. ASAE* **24** 1441–5

Lawyer J K 1969 State of the art in electrostatic separation of minerals *J. Electrochem. Soc.* 57C–60C

Lawyer J E and Dyrenforth W P 1973 *Electrostatics and its Industrial Applications* ed A D Moore (New York: Wiley) ch 10

Lebaron I M and Kropf W D 1958 Application of electrostatics to potash beneficiation *Trans. AIME/SME* **211** 1081–3

Lee C H 1978 Electrophoretic separation of micron sized colloid particles suspended in non aqueous media *PhD Thesis* Illinois Institute of Technology

Leimbacher E M 1966 Electrostatic flock coating *American Dyestuffs Reporter* 334–5

Lin I J and Benguigui L 1983 High intensity, high gradient dielectrophoretic separation in *Progress in Filtration and Separation* ed. R J Wakeman (Amsterdam: Elsevier)

Lindbald N R and Schneider J M 1965 Production of uniformly sized liquid droplets *J. Sci. Inst.* **42** 635–38

Lockheart N C 1983 Electro-osmotic dewatering of clays *Colloids and Surfaces* **6** 229–69

—— 1984 Dry beneficiation of coal *Powder Technol.* **40** 1–3

Lockheart N C and Stickland R E 1984 Dewatering of coal washery tailings ponds by electro-osmosis *Powder Technol.* **40** 215–21

Lowden J J 1891 *US Patent Specification* 465822

McCann G D, Vanderhoff J W, Strichler A and Sacks T I 1973 Separation of latex particles according to size by continuous electrophoresis *Separation and Purification Methods* **2** 153–98

Malcolm D H 1980 Energy conversion unit for electrostatic spray coating apparatus and the like *US Patent Specification* 4219865

—— 1981 Spray gun having self-contained low voltage and high voltage power supplies *US Patent Specification* 42900921

Margavey R H and Outhouse L E 1962 Note on the break up of a charged liquid jet *J. Fluid Mechanics* **13** 151–7

Markels M and Durfee R L 1964 The effect of applied voltage on boiling heat transfer *AIChE J.* **10** 106–10

—— 1965 Studies of boiling heat transfer with electric fields *AIChE J.* **11** 716–23

Mascarenhas S 1957 Thermodynamic theory of thermal conduction of dielectrics under electric fields *Nuovo Cimento* **5** 1118–21

Mason B D and Townsley P M 1971 Dielectrophoretic separation of living cells *Can. J. Microbiol.* **17** 879–87

Masuda S 1971 Electric curtain for the confinement and transport of charged aerosol particles *Albany Conf. on Electrostatics (Albany, NY) 1971* (Electrostatic Society of America, American Meteorological Society and Institute of Electrical and Electronic Engineers)

Masuda S and Fujibayashi K 1970 Electrodynamic behaviour of charged dust particles in a quadrupole field *Proc. 1st Int. Conf. on Static Electricity (Vienna) 1970 (Advances in Static Electricity* vol 1 (Brussels: Auxilia) pp 384–97)

Masuda S, Fujibayashi K, Ishida K and Inaba H 1972 Confinement and transportation of charged aerosol clouds by electric curtain *Electron. Eng., Japan* **92** 43–52

Masuda S and Matsumoto Y 1974 Contact type electric curtain for electrodynamical control of charged dust particles *Proc. Int. Conf. on Electrostatic Charging (Frankfurt) 1973 (Dechema Monographien Band* 72 pp 1370–409 (Weinheim: Verlag-Chemie) pp 293–301)

Masuda S, Matsumoto Y and Ito M 1971 Theoretical characteristics of ring-type electric curtain with single-phase AC drive *Proc. Gen. Conf. Inst. Elect. Eng. Japan* Paper No 819

Masuda S, Mori S and Itoh T 1975 Applications of electric curtain in the field of electrostatic powder coating *Conf. of Electrostatic Society of America (University of Michigan) 1975* Unpublished

Masuda S, Toraguchi M, Takahashi T and Haga K 1983 Electrostatic beneficiation of coal using a cyclone tribocharger *IEEE Trans. Ind. Appl.* **IA-19** 789–93

Mathai C V 1982 A new charged fog generator for inhalable particle control *IEEE Conf. of Industrial Applications Society* p 976

Middendorf W H and Brown G H 1958 Liquid dielectrics in an electric field *Trans. AIEE* Part III **77** 795–9

Miura Y and Kaase S 1980 Study on electrostatic spinning *Textile Res. J.* 17–28

Monk G W 1952 Viscous energy dissipated during atomisation of a liquid *J. Appl. Phys. Lett.* **23** 288

Moore A D 1973 Electrostatics and its applications (New York: Wiley)

Morgan V T and Morrow R 1980 Cooling of heated cylinder in still air by electrical corona *Inst. Eng. Aust. Electr. Eng. Trans.* Paper E1027

Mori Y and Uchida Y 1966 Forced convective heat transfer between horizontal flat plates *Int. J. Heat and Mass Transfer* **9** 803

Moulik S P, Cooper F C and Bier M 1967 Forced flow electrophoretic filtration of clay suspensions *J. Colloid and Interface Sci.* **24** 427–32

Moyle B D and Hughes J F 1983 Corona charging of insulating particles *Electrostatics (Oxford) 1983* (Inst. Phys. Conf. Ser. 66) pp 155–60

Murphy E J 1978 Cationic electrocoating: myth vs reality *Plating and Surface Finishes* **65** 34–6

Musgrove P J and Wilson A D 1970 Charged aerosols for electrogasdynamic generators *Proc. 1st Int. Conf. on Static Electricity (Vienna) (Advances in Static Electricity* vol 1 (Brussels: Auxilia) pp 360–70)

320   *Miscellaneous Applications*

Nawab M A and Mason S G 1958 The preparation of uniform emulsions by electrical dispersion *J. Colloid Sci.* **13** 179–87

Nelson D F 1979 *Electric, Optic, and Acoustic Interactions in Dielectrics* (New York: Wiley)

Newton A C 1973 *PhD Thesis* Imperial College London

O'Brien R J 1964 Effect of electric field on the heat transfer from a vertical plate in various gases over a range of pressures *Wright Patterson Air Force Base, Ohio Air Force Inst. Tech.*

Oglesby S and Thomas A L 1955 Electrostatic method for collecting fibrous material and forming it into strands *US Patent Specification* 2711626

Olofinskii N F 1970 Electrical methods of ore dressing (Moscow: Nedra)

O'Neill B C 1977 Charging, deposition and self-limiting of electrostatic power coating *Proc. 3rd Int. Congress on Electrostatics (Eur. Fed. Chem. Eng.) (Grenoble) 1977* pp 25a–d

Osaka Kiku Co Ltd 1972 Apparatus for electrostatic spinning *Japan Patent Specification* 47-36217

Ostroumov G A 1915 *J. Tech. Phys. USSR* **24** 1954

Owens D N 1975 Mechanism of corona induced self-adhesion of polymer film *J. Appl. Polymer Sci.* **19** 265–71

Parsons S R 1929 The effect of corona current on the cooling of a hot wire *Phys. Rev.* **33** 75–80

Paul W and Ralther M 1955 The electrical mass filter *Z. Phys.* **140** 262–73

Paul W, Reinhard H P and von Zahn U 1958 The electrical mass filter as mass spectrometer and isotope separator *Z. Phys.* **152** 143–82

Paul W and Steinwedel 1953 Ein Neues masenspektrometer ohne magnetfeld *Z. Naturf.* **8a** 448

Pauli W 1924 Electrolyte free water soluble protein: I. Electrodialysis *Biochem Z.* **152** 355

Pearce M J and Pope M I 1976 The separation of quartz-dolomite powders using a triboelectric technique *Powder Technology* **14** 7–15

—— 1977 The triboelectric separation of quartz-calcite and quartz-apatite powders after chemical conditioning *Powder Technology* **17** 83–9

Pearce M J, Pope M I and Read A D 1977 Triboelectric separation—possibilities and limitations *Proc. XIIth Int. Mineral Processing Cong. (Sao Paulo) 1977*

Pearce P E, Kovac Z and Higginbotham C 1978 Kinetics and mechanisation of film growth during the electrodeposition process *FATIPEC Congress Book* pp 119–25

Perlman M M 1968 Review of phenomenological theories of electrets in *Electrets and Related Charge Storage Phenomena* (New York: Electrochemical Society of New York)

Persen L N 1965 A simplified approach to the influence of Gortler type vortices on heat transfer from a wall *Wright Patterson Air Force Base* Report ARL

Peyrous R and Millot R-M 1982 Gaseous products created by DC corona discharges in air or oxygen fed to a point to plane gap *Proc. 7th Int. Conf. on Gas Discharges and their Applications (London) 1982* (London: IEE) pp 173–6

Pickard W F 1965 Electrical force effects in dielectric liquids *Progress in Dielectrics* vol 6, ed J B Birks and J Hart (London: Temple Press) ch 1, pp 1–41

Pochettino A 1903 *Atti Accad. Nazl Lincei Rend. Classe Sci. Fis. Mat. Nat.* **12** 363

Pohl H A 1951 The motion and precipitation of suspensions in divergent electric fields *J. Appl. Phys.* **22** 869–71

—— 1958 Some effects of non-uniform fields on dielectrics *J. Appl. Phys.* **29** 1182–8

—— 1960 Non-uniform electric fields *Sci. Am.* **203** 106–12

—— 1978 *Dielectrophoresis* (Cambridge: CUP)

Pohl H A and Hawk I 1966 Separation of living and dead cells by dielectrophoresis *Science* **152** 647–9

Pohl H A and Pethig R 1977 Dielectric measurements using non-uniform field (dielectrophoretic) effect *J. Phys. E: Sci. Instrum.* **10** 190–3

Pohl H A and Pollock K 1978 Electrode geometries for various dielectrophoretic force laws *J. Electrostatics* **5** 337–42

Porter J E and Poulter R 1970 Electrically induced convection accompanying laminar flow heat transfer in an annulus *Chemca '70, Aust. Inst. Chem. Eng. and Aust. Acad. Sci. 1970* Session 3, pp 34–49

Poulson R and Richardson A T 1976 The electrohydrodynamic enhancement of heat transfer with single phase dielectric fluid in tubes *Department of Mechanical Engineering, Bristol University* Internal report

Quincke G 1897 *Ann. Phys. Chem.* **62** 1

Ralston O C 1961 *Electrostatic Separation of Mixed Granular Solids* (Amsterdam: Elsevier)

Rasmussen J R, Stedronsky E R and Whitesides G M 1977 Introduction, modification and characterisation of functional groups on the surface of low density polyethylene film *J. Am. Chem. Soc.* **99** 4736–45

Rayleigh J W S 1882 On the equilibrium of liquid conducting masses charged with electricity *Phil. Mag.* (Ser. 5) **14** 184–6

—— 1892 On the instability of a jet of a cylinder of viscous liquid under capillary force *Phil. Mag.* **34** 145–54

Ream G L 1982 Servo control of multinozzle ink jet operating point *IEEE Annual Meeting of the Industrial Applications Society* pp 993–8

Reay D and Ratcliffe G A 1973 Removal of fine particles from water by dispersed air flotation *Can. J. Chem. Eng.* **51** 178–85

Reuss F F 1809 *Memoires de la Societe Imperiale des Naturaklistes de Moscou* **2** 327

Rhim W K, Collender M T, Hyson M T, Simms W T and Elleman D D 1985 Development of an electrostatic positioner for space material processing *Rev. Sci. Instrum.* **56** 307–17

Richardson A T and Poulter R 1976 Electrophoretic instability in a diffusion-free dielectric liquid in an annular geometry *J. Phys. D: Appl. Phys.* **9** L45–8

Robinson K S and Jones T B 1984a Slope stability in electropacked beds *IEEE Trans. Ind. Appl.* **IA-20** 253–8

—— 1984b Particle wall adhesion in electropacked beds *IEEE Trans. Ind. Appl.* **IA-20** 1573–77

Robinson M 1961 Movement of air in the electric wind of the corona discharge *Trans. AIEE* **80** (*Communications and Electronics*) pp 143–50

—— 1970 Convective heat transfer at the surface of a corona electrode *Int. J. Heat and Mass Transfer* **13** 263–74

Rossman K J 1956 Bonding properties of polyethylene *Polymer Sci.* **19** 141–4

Roth D G and Kelly A J 1983 Analysis of disruption of electrostatically charged droplets *IEEE Trans. Ind. Appl.* **IA-19** 771–5

Saatwerber D 1979 Electropainting with cationic powder suspensions *Defazet* **33** 296–9

Sampuran-Singh S 1981 Charging characteristics of some powders in electrostatic powder coating *IEEE Trans. Ind. Appl.* **IA-17** 121–4

Sampuran-Singh S and Bright A W 1977 Laser anemometry studies of the powder deposition process *IEEE Meeting of the Industrial Applications Society* Paper 29G pp 729–32

Sampuran-Singh S, Bright A W and Hughes J F 1979 Discharges in electrostatically deposited films *Electrostatics (Oxford) 1979* (Inst. Phys. Conf. Ser. 48) pp 17–25

Sato M 1980a Cloudy bubble formation in a strong, non-uniform field *J. Electrostatics* **8** 285

—— 1980b The formation of gas bubbles synchronised with ac potential *J. Phys. D: Appl. Phys.* **13** L1

—— 1984 The production of essentially uniform droplets in gaseous or immiscible liquid media under applied ac potential *J. Electrostatics* **15** 237–49

Sato M, Miyaazaki S, Kuroda M and Sakai T 1981 The synchronised formation of uniform sized bubbles under applied ac potential *Kagaku Koguku Ronbunshu* **7** 115

Sato T 1980c Drift velocity measurement of charged particles under corona discharge in an air gap *J. Electrostatics* **8** 271–8

Schaffert R M 1975 *Electrophotography* (London: Focal) 2nd edn

Schenck H U, Spoar M and Marx M 1979 The chemistry of binders for electrodeposition *Prog. Organic Coatings* **7** 1–77

Schenck H U and Stoelting J 1980 Electrodeposition–anodic vs cathodic *J. Oil and Colour Chemists Association* **63** 482–91

Schmidt E and Leidenfrost W 1953 The effect of electric fields upon the heat transfer in liquid insulators *Frosch Hft Verdt Ing.* **19** 65–80

Schweizer J W and Hanson D N 1971 Stability limit of charged droplets *J. Coll. Int. Sci.* **35** 417–23

Semenov V A, Hersh S P and Gupta B S 1983 Increasing pile density in electrostatic flocking by introducing a guiding electrode *IEEE Trans. Ind. Appl.* **IA-19** 127–31

Senftleben H 1932 Influence of magnetic and electric field on heat transfer through gases *Z. Phys.* **74** 757–69

—— 1934 Influence of electric field on heat flow in gases *Phys. Z.* **35** 661–2

Senftleben H and Braun W 1936 Influence of electric field on heat transmission through gases *Z. Phys.* **102** 480–506

Sezako M, Nagayasu I and Sato H 1971 Electrostatic holding device for recording paper *GB Patent Specification* 1224155

Sharborough A H and Walker G W 1983 *Proc. IEEE Ann. Meeting on Industrial Applications (Mexico)* p 1160

Sher C D 1968 Dielectrophoresis in lossy dielectrics *Nature* **220** 695–6

Sigmond R S, Goldman A and Brenna D 1980 Corona corrosion of aluminium in air: electrochemical interaction between electrical coronas and metal surfaces *Proc. 6th Int. Conf. on Gas Discharges and their Applications (London) 1980* pp 82–5 (London: IEE)

Simm W 1972 *German Patent Specification* 2032072

Singewald A 1976 Process for the electrostatic separation of pyrite *US Patent Specification* 3941685

Smoluchowski M 1921 in *Handbuch der Elektrizitat und des Magnetismus* vol. 11, ed W Graetz (Leipzig: Johann Ambrosius Barth)

Sproston J L, Stevens N G and Page I M 1983 An investigation of torque transmission using electrically stressed dielectric liquids *Electrostatics (Oxford) 1983* (Inst. Phys. Conf. Ser. 66) pp 53–8

Stevens E W 1925 *US Patent Specification* 1533711

Stevens N G, Sproston J L and Stanway R 1985 The influence of pulsed DC input signals on electrorheological fluids *J. Electrostatics* **17** 181–93

Stevko P J 1974 Electrostatic holding device *GB Patent Specification* 1352715

Straubel H 1955 Millikan's oil drop experiment *Naturwissenschaften* **42** 506–7

—— 1967 Bestimmung der anzahl und grösse von aerosolteilchen *Chemie Ing. Tech.* **39** 977–81

—— 1968 Determination of the charge distribution of surfaces by stabilised electrically charged particles *Staub Reinhaltung der Luft* **12** 5–9

Stuetzer O M 1959 Ion drag pressure generation *J. Appl. Phys.* **30** 984–94

—— 1960 Ion drag pumps *J. Appl. Phys.* **31** 136–46

—— 1961 Ion transport high voltage generators *Rev. Sci. Instrum.* **32** 16–22

—— 1962 Magnetohydrodynamics and electrohydrodynamics *Phys. Fluids* **5** 534–44

Sunderland J G and Ellis D 1981 Electrokinetic thickening of slurry systems *Surf. Technol.* **12** 106

Sweet R G 1965 High frequency recording with electrostatically deflected ink jets *Rev. Sci. Instrum.* **36** 131–6

Szirmai S G 1984 Vapour coating of electrostatically dispersed powders *J. Appl. Phys.* **55** 4088–94

Takahashi T, Watabe Y, Tabei K and Haga K 1980 *IEEE Ann. Meeting of the Industrial Applications Society (Cincinnati) 1980* pp 1026–31

Talbert C M, Jones T B and Dietz P W 1984 The electrospouted bed *IEEE Trans. Ind. Suppl.* **IA-20** 1220–3

Taylor G I 1964 Disintegration of water drops in an electric field *Proc. R. Soc.* A **280** 383–97

—— 1966 The force exerted by an electric field on a long cylindrical conductor *Proc. R. Soc.* A **291** 145–58

Taylor G I and Van Dyke M D 1969 Electrically driven jets *Proc. R. Soc.* A **313** 453–75

Taylor J O 1958 Electrostatic applying and holding device *US Patent Specification* 2834132

Taylor R L S 1972 Aluminium coatings for steel—the evolution to and the development of the powder route *Industrial Finishing and Surface Coatings* pp 4–17

Thi M 1981 Etude de la modification de la mouillabilite d'un film de polyethylene soumis a l'action de la décharge couronne *PhD Thesis* Ecole Superieure d'Eléctricité, Paris

Thourson T L 1972 Xerographic development processes—A review *IEEE Trans. Electron Devices* **ED-19** 495–511

Ting I P, Jolley K, Beasley C A and Pohl H A 1971 *Biochem. Biophys. Acta* **234** 324

Tobazeon R 1984 Electrohydrodynamic instabilities and electroconvection in the transient and ac regimes of unipolar injection in insulating liquids—A review *J. Electrostatics* **15** 359–84

Turnbull R J 1968 Electroconvective instability with a stabilising temperature gradient *Phys. Fluids* **11** 2588–603

—— 1969a The effect of the dielectrophoretic forces on the Bernard instability *Phys. Fluids* **12** 1809–15

—— 1969b Free convection from a heated vertical plate in a direct current electric field *Phys. Fluids* **12** 2255–63

—— 1970 Thermal diffusion effects on the electrodynamic Rayleigh–Taylor bulk instability *Phys. Fluids* **13** 2615–6

—— 1971a Instability of a thermal boundary layer in a constant electric field *J. Fluid Mech.* **47** 231–9

—— 1971b Effect of a non-uniform alternating electric field on the thermal boundary layer near a heated vertical plate *J. Fluid Mech.* **49** 693–703

Turnbull R J and Melcher J R 1969 Electrohydrodynamic Rayleigh–Taylor bulk instability *Phys. Fluids* **12** 1160–6

Uejima H 1972 Dielectric mechanism and electrical properties of electro-fluids *Jap. J. Appl. Phys.* **11** 319–26

Unitiki Co 1973 Method and apparatus for using electrostatics *Japan Patent Specification* 48-13177

Velkoff H R and Miller J H 1965 Condensation of vapour on a vertical plane with a transverse electric field *Trans. ASME J. Heat Transfer* **87** 197–201

Velkoff H R and Ketcham J 1968 Effect of an electrostatic field on boundary layer transition *J. AIAA* **6** 1381–3

Visking Corporation 1952 *GB Patent Specification* 715914

Walberg A C 1977 Electrostatic application of waterborne and high solids coatings *American Electroplaters Society (Los Angeles) 1977*

Watanbe A, Higashitsuji K and Nishitzawa K 1978 Studies in electrostatic emulsification *J. Colloid Interface Sci.* **64** 279–89

Waterman L C 1965 Electrostatic coalescers *Chem. Eng. Prog.* **61** 51–7

Watson P K 1961 Influence of electric field on the heat transfer from a hot wire to an insulating liquid *Nature* **189** 563–4

Watson P K 1979 The scientific basis of electrophotography *Electrostatics (Oxford) 1979* (Inst. Phys. Conf. Ser. 48) pp 1–8

Webb B K and Bowen H D 1970 Electrical field breakdown phenomena in applying charged dust particles *Trans. ASAE* **13** 455–8

Wessling R A, Gibbs D S, Settinieri W J and Wagener E H 1972 Studies in cathodic electrodeposition *Adv. Chem.* **119** 118–26

Wiedemann G 1852 *Pogg. Ann.* **87** 321

Williams T and Bailey A J 1983 The resolution time of water in oil emulsions subjected to an external electric field *Electrostatics (Oxford) 1983* (Inst. Phys. Conf. Ser. 66) pp 39–44

—— 1985 Anomalous charging of droplets during electric fields accelerated dripping *Electrostatics* **16** 47–57

Winslow W M 1947 *US Patent Specification* 2417850

—— 1949 Induced fibration of suspensions *J. Appl. Phys.* **20** 1137–40

Wuerker R F, Shelton H and Langmuir R V 1959 Electrodynamic containment of charged particles *J. Appl. Phys.* **30** 342–9

Yukawa H, Kobayashi K, Yoshida H and Iwata M 1979 Studies of electrically enhanced sedimentation, filtration and dewatering processes *Progress in Filtration and Separation* vol 1, ed R J Wakeman (Amsterdam: Elsevier) pp 83–113

Zeleny J 1914 Discharge from liquid points and a method for measuring the electric field at their surfaces *Phys. Rev.* (Ser. 2) **3** 69–91

—— 1917 Instability of electrified liquid surfaces *Phys. Rev.* (Ser. 2) **10** 1–6

Chapter 6   Hazards and Problems

Unintentional charge accumulation can cause problems in industry ranging from a minor nuisance to a severe explosion risk. The small electrostatic spark experienced after walking across a nylon carpet in a dry environment contains more than enough energy to ignite a flammable vapour and electrostatic forces on powder particles or plastic films can interfere with industrial processes. In this chapter problems associated with electrostatic charging, and the means of eliminating them, are discussed.

6.1 FIRE AND EXPLOSION HAZARDS

6.1.1 Introduction

A flammable atmosphere may be ignited whenever sufficient energy is supplied to initiate a runaway oxidation reaction. A kernel of hot gas must be created, in which the heat generated exceeds the heat lost, for the flame to propagate. The energy may be supplied in a number of ways. By far the most common source of ignition in industrial fires and explosions is heat created during welding or cutting by means of a torch. This supplies a very high energy density which inevitably ignites any flammable material present. Hot surfaces (for example, from overheated machinery or self-heating dust deposits) provide another common source of ignition and a third source can be broadly described as 'sparks'.

There are four different types of phenomena which fall into this category.

(i) An electrostatic spark. This occurs when charge separates and accumulates so that a surface reaches a high potential creating an electric field which is sufficient to cause electrical breakdown in a gas. This is a high-voltage low-current phenomenon.

(ii) An electrical spark. This occurs when a low-voltage high-current circuit is broken (for example, in a switch or at the bushes of a motor commutator).

(iii) An impact spark. This is produced by the sharp impact of steel against steel or concrete.

(iv) An RF spark. This may be produced in plant which forms an adventitious aerial close to a high-power radio source.

Different materials have a different tendency to ignite, and tables are published of the ignitability of a material in terms of various parameters, according to the likely ignition source. For example, the flash point and the temperature for spontaneous combustion of gases and vapours is given. Sensitivity to electrical and electrostatic sparks is normally expressed in terms of the energy which must be dissipated in the spark which will just ignite the optimum flammable mixture. This is called the minimum ignition energy (MIE).

If the spark is caused by the release of charge stored on a capacitor, C, the stored energy is given by

$$W = \tfrac{1}{2}CV^2. \tag{6.1}$$

For energy stored in the magnetic field associated with the inductance, L, of an electrical circuit

$$W = \tfrac{1}{2}LI^2. \tag{6.2}$$

Most organic liquids and hydrocarbon gases in air have a minimum ignition energy of the order of 0.2 mJ, carbon disulphide, hydrogen and acetylene, in air can be ignited by approximately 0.02 mJ, while explosives can have minimum ignition energies as low as 0.001 mJ. A minimum ignition energy can also be quoted for oxidisable powders or liquid droplets, dispersed in air, but it is more difficult to measure and dependent on a number of factors such as the particle size distribution. Static-sensitive powders, such as sulphur and fine aluminium, can be ignited by sparks of a few millijoules, while other powders may require several joules of energy.

6.1.2 Minimum ignition energy of flammable vapours

Hazardous situations are classified according to the energy of the spark which could be released, and flammable mixtures are classified according to the minimum energy required to ignite them. The minimum ignition energy is therefore the basis of electrostatic hazard evaluation.

A mixture of air and a flammable vapour will only ignite if its composition lies within two limits, known as the lower and upper flammable limits. For

most hydrocarbon gases these are around 2 % to 10 % by volume but hydrogen, acetylene, ethylene and carbon disulphide are flammable over a much
wider range (BS 5345). Within this flammable range the energy in an electrostatic discharge which just ignites the mixture is a strong function of concentration as shown for example in figure 6.1. The energy corresponding to the
lowest point of the curve of ignition energy against concentration is the
minimum ignition energy. In general, the most ignitable mixture occurs
above a liquid which is being handled at a temperature which is just above
the liquid flash point.

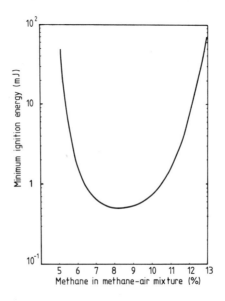

Figure 6.1 The effect of mixture composition on the ignition energy of a
methane–air mixture.

The concept of minimum ignition energy assumes that, if the thermal
energy is instantaneously delivered to a small volume, the minimum energy
to cause ignition is constant for a given gas mixture and geometry, regardless
of the way in which the energy is released. For gases this appears to be true
to a first approximation. For example, if a fine wire is broken to produce an
inductive spark from an electrical circuit, the minimum ignition energy required to ignite 8.5 % methane is 0.3 mJ (Berz 1961). This is very similar to
the value of 0.28 mJ obtained by Lewis and Von Elbe (1961) and by
Litchfield and Blanc (1959) using a capacitive discharge from the circuit
shown in figure 6.2. However, detailed measurements show that the ignitability of a spark depends not only on the total energy, but also, to some extent,
on the duration of the spark and the rate of discharge of the energy.

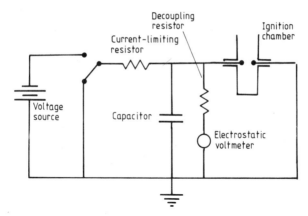

Figure 6.2 Equipment for production of sparks of known energy (BS 5958 Pt 1).

Rose and Priede (1958) found that when the duration of a spark in a hydrogen–air mixture was increased by means of a series resistance, there was an optimum resistance for ignition of about 10 kΩ. Riddlestone (1957) found the ignitability of methane–air mixtures was constant for $R < 100\ \Omega$, but the ignition was less likely to ignite if the resistance was increased to 1000 Ω. For higher resistances the incendivity began to rise slowly again. In these experiments, when the resistance was very low, the current was oscillatory as a result of the stray circuit inductance. As the resistance increased the oscillation was damped and the duration of the spark decreased, becoming a minimum at critical damping conditions. With a further increase in resistance the spark became aperiodic and increased in duration. The changes in incendivity were accompanied by visual changes in the way the flame kernel developed.

Kono *et al* (1976a) used a circuit in which a capacitive discharge was used to trigger a more extended DC discharge and showed that there is an optimum spark duration for hydrocarbons of about 50 μs (figure 6.3). The optimum spark duration increased with decreasing spark gap and mixture strength.

Sayers *et al* (1970) observed a strong dependence of the ignitability of sparks from a piezoelectric spark generator on the circuit series inductance (figure 6.4). (The spark from a piezocrystal is generally considered to be equivalent to a spark from a capacitor of about 50 pF.) Sayers suggests that this behaviour may be specific to piezoelectric igniters and due to a resonance phenomenon.

The increase in ignitability of a spark when a series inductance is included in the circuit, producing an oscillatory discharge, has also been studied by Kono *et al* (1976b). They simulated an oscillatory discharge by two

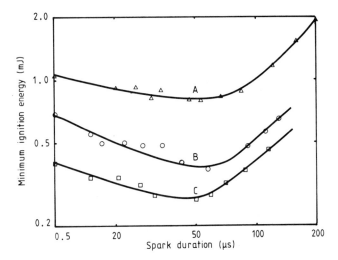

Figure 6.3 The effect of spark duration on minimum ignition energy for a gap width nearly equal to the quenching distance (from Kono *et al* 1976a). The percentages of propane in the propane–air mixtures were: A, 3.0; B, 3.2; C, 3.5.

short-duration pulses and showed that there was an optimum frequency of pulse for ignition which is equivalent to a spark interval of 10–50 μs.

The minimum ignition energy of a spark is a function of the value of the capacitance on which the charge is stored (Movilliat and Giltaire 1979, Guoxiang and Wang Changying 1982). With small capacitances, the minimum ignition energy does not depend greatly on the shape of the electrodes, but for larger capacitances the minimum ignition energy increases with in-

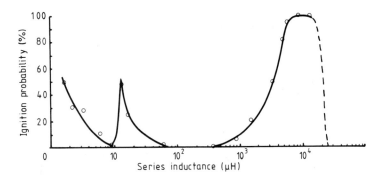

Figure 6.4 The effect of a series inductor on the ignition probability of a 12 % methane in air mixture with a piezoelectric igniter and a 3.5 mm spark gap (from Sayers *et al* 1970).

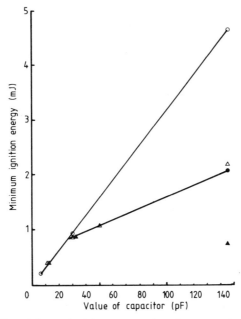

Figure 6.5 The minimum ignition energy of a mixture of air and CH_4 as a function of the capacitor on which the charge is stored (from Movilliat and Giltaire 1979). Electrodes: $\bigcirc$, spheres of 15 mm diameter; $\blacktriangle$, points; $\triangle$, spheres of 1.59 mm diameter; $\bullet$, spheres of 0.5 mm diameter.

creasing electrode diameter. With 15 mm diameter electrodes, the minimum ignition energy is proportional to capacitance as illustrated in figure 6.5.

The lowest minimum ignition energy for 8.5 % methane and 28 % hydrogen is obtained with very small capacitances of only a few picofarads. Movilliat and Giltaire (1979) obtained a minimum ignition energy of 0.21 mJ, for 8.5 % methane, which is below the accepted minimum of 0.28 mJ found by Lewis and Von Elbe (1961). For high capacitances of 146 pF, 0.75 mJ was required to ignite the same gas mixture. Evidence from experiments using items of unearthed equipment as the source of the spark gives a more confused picture (Tolson 1980).

The minimum ignition energy of a gas is a function of the electrode configuration. Small-diameter electrodes tend to give a corona discharge rather than a spark and measurements of minimum ignition energy may become erratic for electrodes below 2 mm in diameter. However, large-diameter electrodes absorb heat from the discharge, so more energy must be supplied to heat the gas to its ignition point. Different authors report different optimum electrode sizes for ignition, but generally the lowest energy is achieved from the smallest diameter electrode that can be used without a corona discharge forming. This is a function of a number of parameters, including the smoothness and sphericity of the electrode and the capacitance on which the charge is stored. (The capacitance governs the voltage across the spark gap for a given spark energy.)

Tests generally show little or no dependence of ignition energy on electrode material, unless very highly oxidising electrodes are used in which case reactions at the electrode surface may add to the heat put into the spark volume.

6.1.3 Quenching distance

The minimum ignition energy of a spark is a function of the electrode spacing. The optimum spacing is approximately equal to the quenching distance. (This is of the order of 2 mm for most hydrocarbons.)

The quenching distance has been defined in a number of ways (Potter 1960). It is essentially the minimum size which an inflamed volume at its normal flame temperature must attain in order to propagate. It is the size at which the heat created in the reaction zone just exceeds the heat loss from its boundaries. If the spacing between electrodes is less than the quenching distance, more energy must be supplied in a spark to cause an ignition, because energy is absorbed by the electrodes. Figure 6.6 shows the effect of electrode separation on the minimum ignition energy of an 11 % methane–air mixture using two sizes of electrodes (Sayers *et al* 1970). Above the quenching distance the two curves coincide. Below the quenching distance more energy must be supplied to the plane electrodes which absorb energy from the flame more effectively. There is a slight rise in the minimum ignition energy as the spark gap is increased beyond the quenching distance. Both the quenching distance and the minimum ignition energy increase with an increase in turbulence (Ballal and Lefebvre 1977). Increasing the temperature of a gas will decrease the energy required for ignition.

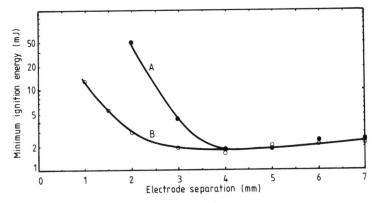

Figure 6.6 The effect of electrode separation on minimum ignition energy of 11 % by volume methane–air mixture obtained with two sizes of electrodes (from Sayers *et al* 1970). A, 10 mm diameter flat-faced electrodes; B, 4 mm diameter hemispherical electrodes.

It can be seen that a spark discharge circuit may be tailored to provide an optimum spark for ignition and industrial geometries may provide sparks of the same energy but quite wide ranging ignitability. However, electrostatic sparks are usually many times more energetic than the minimum ignition energy of a hydrocarbon vapour and the precise value of the ignition energy is seldom important for the evaluation of a hazard.

6.1.4 Maximum experimental safe gap

It has been found that a spark can ignite a gas only if the distance between the metal surfaces between which the spark occurs exceeds a minimum distance, known as the maximum experimental safe gap (MESG). When electrodes are closer than this critical spacing, most of the heat dissipated in the spark gap is absorbed by the metal surfaces and the flame does not propagate. The MESG for flammable hydrocarbons is of the order of 0.9–1 mm. It follows that there is a minimum potential below which a spark which causes ignition cannot occur. If it is assumed that a discharge requires a field of 3×10^6 V m^{-1}, then, in the absence of any field intensification, a spacing of 1 mm requires a voltage of 3 kV for breakdown. For hydrogen the MESG is smaller, and only a few hundred volts may be tolerable. British Standard code of practice (BS 5958) suggests that a potential of at least 300 V is necessary to initiate an incendiary discharge in normal industrial operations, but in explosives manufacture 100 V is considered to be hazardous. American NFPA Code 77 suggests sparks are unlikely to ignite a hydrocarbon vapour if the surface voltage is below 1500 V.

Measurements have shown that an incendiary spark of 0.2 mJ transfers at least 7.5×10^{-8} C of charge (Mason and Rees 1981).

In summary therefore a spark in a hydrocarbon vapour will be non-incendiary if it comes from a surface whose voltage is less than 300 V, if the available charge is less than 7.5×10^{-8} C or if the available energy is less than 0.2 mJ. In using the voltage criterion it must be remembered that the voltage on a surface may increase with no charge being added if its capacitance is decreased.

6.1.5 Minimum ignition energies of powders and dusts

The energy required to ignite a dust cloud is a function of the dust concentration, and there is a most ignitable concentration (usually in the range 200–500 g m^{-3}). In general, this is not the same as the concentration which gives the highest values for the maximum explosion pressure and the maximum rate of pressure rise, and it is significantly higher than the minimum explosive concentration, which is of the order of 10 g m^{-3}.

The minimum ignition energy of a powder cloud and the force of the resulting explosion are a strong function of the particle size distribution, the finer the dust the more easily it can be ignited. Theoretically the minimum ignition energy for spherical dusts of uniform particle diameter is proportional to the cube of the diameter of the particle, and experimental evidence, from the few tests which have been carried out with uniform particle size, supports this view (Kalkert and Schecker 1982). Test procedures normally specify that dust should pass through a 200 mesh sieve (particle size $< 75\,\mu$m) but variations in the fraction of fine particles, in the range 1–$10\,\mu$m, could give significantly different minimum ignition energies.

The minimum ignition energy of a dust cloud depends strongly on its temperature. Raising the temperature of a powder cloud which has a high minimum ignition energy (above 100 J), from 20 to 200 °C, can decrease the ignition energy by several orders of magnitude. If the ignition energy at 20 °C is in the range 10–100 mJ a decrease by one order of magnitude may occur (Glor 1985).

It is difficult to achieve and maintain an optimum dust concentration in the spark volume, and the dependence of the measured minimum ignition energy on the geometry of the spark gap and the circuitry producing the spark is more pronounced than for a gas. It is, therefore, more difficult to define a universal minimum ignition energy for a dust cloud than for a gas. Since the minimum ignition energy of many dusts is similar to the energy of many accidental electrostatic sparks, it is necessary to define reasonably clearly whether a dust is sensitive to static, in order to specify safe handling procedures.

(a) *Effect of electrode geometry on the minimum ignition energy of a dust cloud*

The minimum ignition energy of a dust cloud decreases with decreasing electrode size until a limit is reached where a corona discharge tends to form instead of an arc. The dependence of the ignition energy on electrode size is particularly pronounced for small gaps, presumably because heat is absorbed by the electrodes (Felstead *et al* 1983).

The quenching distance for dusts is much larger than for hydrocarbon vapours and is of the order of 7 mm. Figure 6.7 shows the effect of electrode spacing on the minimum ignition energy of four dusts, measured using a spark from a capacitive discharge. The optimum spacing for ignition was of the order of 11 mm, slightly greater than the quenching distance (Felstead *et al* 1983).

A small dependence of the minimum ignition energy on electrode material has also been observed for powders.

(b) *Effect of spark characteristics on the ignition of a dust cloud*

The minimum ignition energy of a dust cloud depends strongly on the duration of the spark. The formation of a flame kernel in a dust cloud relies on relatively slow chemical reactions and if the discharge time is short the shock wave of the discharge can disturb the mixture before the self-propagating

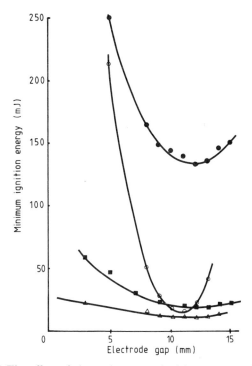

Figure 6.7 The effect of electrode gap on ignition energy using 3.5 mm diameter brass electrodes (from Felstead *et al* 1983): ●, sodium benzoate; ○, sulphamethazine; ■, adipic acid; △, octyl phenolic resin.

flame kernel can be established. The dependence of ignition energy on spark duration was investigated by Line *et al* (1959). They presented their results in terms of the spark energy above which every trial gave ignition and the energy below which no trial gave ignition. The frequency of ignition, based on ten trials, was plotted against the spark energy. Although this early work used sharp electrodes with a 6 mm gap, which is now known not be the optimum geometry, some interesting results emerged.

(i) There was a difference between the energy required to ignite a confined dust column one or two inches in diameter, and the energy required to ignite the column when it fell freely through an eight inch diameter chamber (the confined cloud required less energy).

(ii) With purely capacitive (short duration) sparks the curve of ignition frequency against energy was erratic (figure 6.8).

(iii) With sparks lengthened by an inductance or a resistance in series with the spark gap, the ignition frequency changed more regularly with spark energy, and the difference between the confined and wall free condition nearly disappeared (figure 6.8).

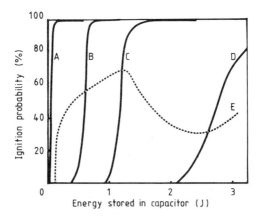

Figure 6.8 The effect of series resistor on ignition energy of lycopodium powder (from Line *et al* 1959). A, 10^5 Ω; B, 10^3 Ω; C, 10^6 Ω; D, 10^7 Ω; E, 0 Ω. © American Chemical Society.

(iv) The stored energy necessary for ignition decreased as the spark duration was increased by means of a series resistance, up to an optimum resistance of 10^5 Ω. (This is in spite of the fact that energy is lost in the resistance.) This was also found by Boyle and Llewellyn (1950) using different powders and a completely different experimental technique (figure 6.9).

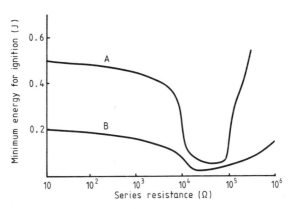

Figure 6.9 Ignition of dust clouds by capacitive sparks (of energy $\frac{1}{2}CV^2$) using an additional series resistance. Data after Boyle and Llewellyn (1950) from Eckhoff (1975). The powders used were: A, 90 % aluminium, 75 μm diameter; B, magnesium, 75 μm diameter.

The percentage of the energy from a capacitor which reaches the spark when there is a series resistor is shown in figure 6.10 (Eckhoff 1975). The energy dissipated in the spark whose duration was increased by a series resistance could be as low as 1 % of the total energy stored in the capacitor. The optimum spark duration for ignition was between 0.1 μs and a few microseconds, with a systematic increase in the optimum discharge duration with increasing spark energy.

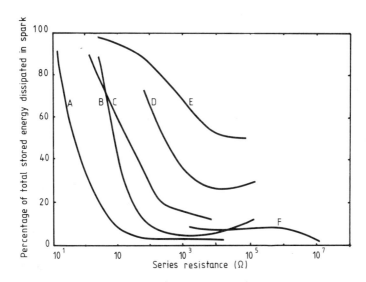

Figure 6.10 Percentage of total capacitor energy dissipated in the spark for a range of spark energies and series resistances (from Eckhoff 1975). The capacitor energies and capacitances were respectively: A, 12.75 mJ, 1000 pF; B, 255 mJ, 200 pF; C, 1.92 mJ, 100 pF; D, 0.115 mJ, 9 pF; E, 0.04 mJ, 4.2 pF; F, 18 mJ, 1000 pF.

As a result of this work, Eckhoff designed a circuit (shown in figure 6.11) to produce sparks with the optimum characteristics for ignition. The capacitance C is set to one of a range of values between 0.005 and 40 μF and the voltage can be varied up to 10 kV. The spark is initiated by the trigger circuit which induces a pulse of 15 kV in the secondary of the transformer. This causes the spark gap to break down and release the energy from the main capacitor. The diode causes the spark to follow a similar form to that from a circuit with a high series resistance.

The strong dependence of the minimum ignition energy of a dust cloud on the circuit producing the spark has lead to some difficulty in defining the

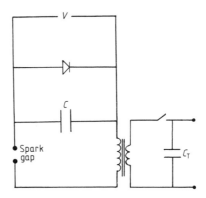

Figure 6.11 Eckhoff's ignition circuit (from Eckhoff 1975).

ignitability of dusts. There are two separate problems. In the first place a choice must be made between testing with a direct capacitor discharge or with a circuit which is optimised to give the lowest ignition energy. The former does not give the lowest possible ignition energy, but does represent the most common electrostatic spark which occurs in industry (the spark from an isolated conductor). The optimised circuit causes ignition at considerably lower energies, but it is questionable whether a spark of the optimum form would occur in practice. The second problem is that large numbers of powder mixtures have been tested by the US Bureau of Mines and the British Fire Research Station using the standard circuit shown in figure 6.12. The capacitance, C, is charged at a low voltage and discharged into the spark gap via the transformer. The energy dissipated in the spark is assumed to be $\frac{1}{2}CV^2$ and the energy lost in the transformer is ignored. The result is that the energy of the spark which actually ignites the dust is considerably lower than the quoted minimum ignition energy. The spark is not as short as from a capacitive discharge but neither is it optimised.

It is generally agreed that the US Bureau of Mines measurements may overestimate minimum ignition energies by a factor of between two and five, compared with the values found using a simple capacitive discharge from the

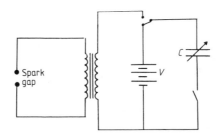

Figure 6.12 The ignition circuit used by the US Bureau of Mines.

Table 6.1 Minimum ignition energies of dusts measured with different circuits.

Material	Minimum ignition energy (mJ)		
	Ekhoff	Hartmann	Capacitance
Wheat	20	50–60	—
Lycopodium	7	40	25
Aluminium (5 μm)	1	15	7.5
Sulphur	0.3	10–15	3–5

circuit shown in figure 6.2. The minimum ignition energy of three dusts found by the circuit used by the US Bureau of Mines, by the direct capacitive discharge and by Eckhoff's optimum spark circuit are compared in table 6.1.

The most recent British Standard recommends that the minimum ignition energy of a dust should be measured by dispersing dust in a Hartmann apparatus, illustrated in figure 6.13, and that the spark should be applied by means of a direct capacitive discharge to electrodes which are as far apart as possible and certainly not less than 2 mm apart. The energy is taken to be

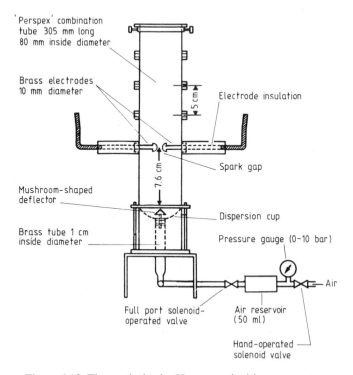

Figure 6.13 The vertical-tube Hartmann ignition apparatus.

$\frac{1}{2}CV^2$ and table 6.2 is provided to evaluate the results. This measurement applies to circumstances where the source of spark is likely to be an isolated conductor. If longer duration sparks are possible, sparks with considerably less energy could be hazardous. The method has the advantage that it measures the ignition energy in terms of industrially measurable quantities. Both the electrostatic voltage and the capacitance to earth of an isolated conductor can usually be measured.

Table 6.2 Guide to the evaluation of ignition sensitivity (BS 5958) (not applicable to high-resistivity powders in large insulating containers).

Minimum ignition energy (mJ)

500	Low sensitivity to ignition. All plant earthed when ignition sensitivity is below this level.
100	Personnel earthed when ignition energy is at or below this level.
25	The majority of ignition incidents occur when the ignition energy is below this level.
10	High sensitivity to ignition. Consider the restriction of the use of high-resistivity non-conductors when the ignition energy is below this level.
1	Extremely sensitive to ignition and precautions should be as for flammable liquids and gases when the ignition energy is below this level.

The dust-dispersal mechanism of the Hartmann apparatus has been criticised because the dust density changes considerably during a test and it is extremely critical at which point the spark is initiated. The effects of the walls of the tube are not well understood (Williams 1979).

Schmalz and Just (1968) have suggested that the minimum ignition energy may be evaluated indirectly, using a relationship between the minimum ignition energy of a dust and the induction time (defined as the time between the activation of the ignition source and the onset of an explosion). Ignition energies could then be found as part of the tests of dust explosibility (maximum pressure and rate of pressure rise etc). However, this is not yet sufficiently well tested to be recognised as a standard technique.

There is considerable controversy concerning the design of a standard piece of equipment to measure the minimum ignition energy of a dust cloud but the main aim of measurement is to define whether a particular dust is, or is not, liable to be sensitive to static sparks. Tables similar to table 6.2 can be drawn up for any of the measurement techniques, and the main requirement is to ensure that the table corresponds to the technique chosen for the measurement. The minimum ignition energies of clouds of organic powders are reported by Bartknecht (1979, 1981), Field (1982) and Berthold (1983).

(c) *Minimum ignition energy of layers of dust*

There is a minimum dust concentration below which a dust cloud will not explode, but there is no clearly defined upper limit of concentration. Layers of dust can be ignited by a static discharge and will burn with a bright flash, a glow or occasionally a flame. There is little correlation between the energy required to ignite a layer and a cloud (NFPA 77). In some cases more energy is required by the cloud and in other cases the layer is less ignitable.

6.1.6 Minimum ignition energies of hybrid mixtures of dusts and vapours

It has been shown that the minimum ignition energy of coal dust is considerably reduced by the presence of methane at concentrations below the minimum explosive limit of the gas (Bartknecht 1981, Pellmont 1979). This has been confirmed for other dusts and it has been found that the dust concentration which ignites most easily decreases as the concentration of flammable vapour increases. Figure 6.14 shows the effect of adding propane to five different dusts, including a PVC sample, which did not ignite in the absence of vapour. (The minimum ignition energies were measured using a capacitive discharge with a series inductance giving an oscillatory spark.) The minimum ignition energy of turbulent propane–air mixtures was considerably reduced by adding a readily ignitable dust (Bartknecht 1981).

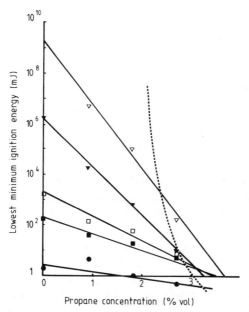

Figure 6.14 Influence of propane concentration on the minimum ignition energy of hybrid mixtures of different powders and propane (from Pellmont 1979). Sizes refer to diameter of powder: ●, hansa yellow, 20 μm; ■, cellulose, 27 μm; □, polyethylene, 125 μm; ▼, PVC, 20 μm; ▽, PVC, 125 μm; dotted curve, turbulent propane.

6.2 ELECTROSTATIC SPARKS

Charge may be generated by friction, induction, ion collection from a gas discharge process or double-layer separation. The theory of these processes was discussed in Chapter 2 so only a brief summary of the factors relevant to industrial hazards will be summarised here.

6.2.1 Charge generation by friction

(a) *Solids*
An electrostatic charge is transferred whenever two solids come in contact. If the charge transferred were to remain constant as the surfaces are separated again, the potential between the surfaces would increase. Therefore charge is driven back across the interface as the surfaces are pulled apart. If both the materials are conductors, this recombination is rapid and no significant charge remains on either material, but if *either* material is insulating, recombination cannot take place as quickly and some of the charge will remain on the separated surfaces. Rubbing tends to produce a higher charge than simple contact, because of the increased area of true contact between the surfaces and temperature effects. The maximum charge which can be acquired by an isolated surface in air is limited by electrical breakdown. The maximum charge density on a surface, when the electric field above the surface reaches the breakdown limit of air, can be calculated from Gauss's law and is $2.64 \times 10^{-5}\,\mathrm{C\,m^{-2}}$. In practice it is found that charge densities of a few times this value may be measured if there is no field intensification to initiate the breakdown process. Electrostatic effects are most significant for situations where the surface area of a solid is large compared with its mass, i.e. for powdered samples and films.

The total charge on a surface is proportional to its area, therefore the charge-to-mass ratio of a powdered sample increases as the particle size decreases. It is observed that the amount of charge generated during industrial processing of powders is more a function of the size distribution and the work done on the material than on the nature of the powder. Typical charge-to-mass ratios (or mass/charge densities) for an organic powder of medium resistivity are shown in table 6.3 (BS 5958 part 1).

Table 6.3 Charge generation on medium-resistivity powders $\rho \simeq 10^{12}\,\Omega\,\mathrm{m}$.

Operation	Charge-to-mass ratio $(\mu\mathrm{C\,kg^{-1}})$
Sieving	10^{-3} to 10^{-5}
Pouring	10^{-1} to 10^{-3}
Scroll feed transfer	1 to 10^{-2}
Grinding	1 to 10^{-1}
Micronising	10^{2} to 10^{-1}

Many experiments have been carried out to measure the charge acquired by powders in various processes. Work up to 1970 is reviewed by Lapple (1970). More recently, Jansen (1972), Boschung and Glor (1980) and Glor (1985) have compared the charge generated on a number of different powders. Boschung and Glor measured the charge on two hundred different powders, using an apparatus designed to simulate pneumatic transport. Charge densities ranged from 10^{-7} to 10^{-3} C kg^{-1} under the same experimental conditions. Some of this difference could be attributed to differences in the surface area of the powder, as shown in figure 6.15. Powders could be classified according to their tendency to charge, and the order of the classification was similar using two different frictional charging methods. However, it is difficult to relate these measurements to the level of charge which will be produced in an industrial installation. In an industrial process, Gauss's law limits not only the maximum charge on individual particles, but also the maximum charge density of a powder cloud, or powder flowing in a pipe. The charging capability of the powder then plays only a small part in defining the final charge.

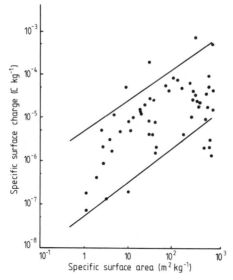

Figure 6.15 Influence of the specific surface area of powders on the charge determined by a laboratory scale pneumatic transport device (from Boschung and Glor 1980).

For some powders the polarity of charge acquired by friction is a function of the particle size (Cross and Farrer 1982). This has been observed, both in industrial installations where the polarity of the electric field is observed to reverse as the coarse particles settle out of a dust cloud, and in laboratory tests. Figure 6.16 shows the charge acquired by different size fractions of a powder passed through fans with polymer and metal blades respectively.

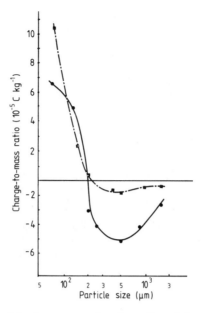

Figure 6.16 Particle charge as a function of particle size. Full curve, powder in contact with a plastic surface; broken curve, powder in contact with a metal surface.

(b) Gases

The movement of gases or gas mixtures creates little if any static electricity. However solid or liquid particles in a gas stream will charge. Thus the release of compressed air that contains small rust or dust particles, or water which condenses as the pressure is released, can build up a static charge. Aircraft charge as a result of contact with charged particles as they fly through the air (Odham 1970) and the release of liquefied carbon dioxide results in a carbon dioxide snow which can be very highly charged. Accidents have been reported in which a static discharge from a CO_2 portable fire extinguisher has re-ignited a fire which has just been put out. The design of extinguishers which avoid this problem has been discussed by Collocott *et al* (1980), Morgan *et al* (1981) and Butterworth and Dowling (1981).

(c) Liquids

Liquids build up a charge during relative movement at solid–liquid, liquid–liquid or liquid–gas interfaces. Single-phase resistive liquids, flowing in conducting pipes, carry a streaming current which has been shown empirically to have the form

$$I = K u^m d^n \tag{6.3}$$

where K is a constant, u is the velocity (m s^{-1}) and d is the pipe diameter (m)

(Schön 1965, Gibson and Lloyd 1970). *m* and *n* were assigned values of 2.4 and 1.6 by Gibson and Lloyd (1965), and were both found to lie between 1.8 and 2.0 by Schön (1965). Both forms of the equation predict similar magnitudes of streaming current, and may be considered to represent real fuel-loading facilities within a factor of about two (Rees 1981).

The charge density in an insulating liquid leaving a long pipe is nearly independent of liquid conductivity, and, if *m* and *n* in the equation above are taken to be two, the charge density is approximately proportional to the linear velocity of the liquid:

$$Q_v \simeq 5u \; \mu C \; m^{-3} \tag{6.4}$$

where *u* is measured in m s^{-1}. (A long pipe is considered to be one where $L > 3u\tau$ where τ is the time constant for charge decay $\tau = \varepsilon_r \varepsilon_0 \rho$.)

Very little data are available for liquid flow in insulating pipes. Information available in 1971 was reviewed by Gibson (1971). For low-conductivity liquids, 1–100 pS m^{-1}, flowing in plastic pipes, the streaming current is initially similar to that produced in a conducting pipe but it decreases as flow continues and the final equilibrium charge density is usually less than would be produced in a conducting pipe. The decrease in streaming current can be attributed to charge accumulating on the inner surface of the pipe wall, which can be sufficient for a spark to occur through the plastic tube, piercing it and allowing liquid to escape (Rees 1981). Both polarities of charge frequently appear in the same system and the streaming current is not necessarily nearly proportional to the velocity squared as it is in conducting pipes (Mason and Rees 1981).

When insulating liquids flow in glass pipes some leakage of charge is possible. In tests in a one inch Pyrex glass QVF system, the streaming current built up to a steady value over the first forty seconds of liquid flow, and the charge density in the liquid reached a level which was slightly lower than predicted by the 5*u* rule of equation (6.4). However, xylene which was sampled slowly through a narrow-bore tube only 200 mm long reached charge levels of 100 μC m^{-3}. With new glass pipes, potentials up to 18 kV built up on the metal flanges, and a spark capable of igniting xylene vapour could be drawn from them (Cross *et al* 1977).

Two-phase liquids or liquids containing a solid suspension or immiscible water tend to build up higher charges than single-phase liquids, particularly if there is a constriction in the flow. Water droplets introduced into large tanks during loading can generate enough charge as they settle through hydrocarbon liquids to generate a hazardous potential on the liquid surface. This potential is the 'settling potential' or 'sedimentation potential' discussed in §5.4 (Klinkenberg and van der Minne 1958, Holdsworth *et al* 1962). The presence of microfilters, i.e. fine filters of felt or paper, which have pore sizes of only a few micrometres, can increase charging by several orders of magnitude. Pumps, bends, gauze strainers and valves generally do not build up more charge on a single-phase liquid than flow in a long pipe. However, a simple gauze mesh strainer has caused problems when it was badly blocked by rust particles so it behaved like a microfilter (Strawson and Lyle 1975a).

Any relative motion produces charge separation and charge may be generated by settling, spraying, stirring or splashing. Splashing has not been found to produce very high charge densities but agitation of a powder in a low-conductivity liquid may be hazardous. For example, charge densities of $400-1500$ μC m^{-3} have been measured during the agitation of silica gel and polycarbonate granules in xylene (Krämer 1981). Charge levels exceeding $10-50$ μC m^{-3} were considered by Krämer to be potentially hazardous.

The atomisation of a liquid containing suspended powder particles can produce a much higher charge than the atomisation of the liquid alone. This can be a hazard during the filling of aerosol cans. Although the normal expulsion of the product through the spray nozzle does not usually create sufficient charge to be hazardous, accidental damage to pressure cans in which butane is used as the propellant, for example during filling at the factory, has resulted in a number of fires (Roberts and Hughes 1979).

6.2.2 Charge generation by corona and induction

Charging due to the collection of ions is seldom an industrial problem except during the operation of equipment which depends on a corona discharge, such as electrostatic spray guns. However, if high voltages are allowed to build up on objects with sharp edges the charge may be transferred to other isolated surfaces.

Induction charging is a result of charge separation within a conductor in an electric field. Direct contact with the charged surface which provides the electric field is not necessary. The mechanism by which a plant operator can charge by induction in an electric field, although the operator touches only earthed surfaces, was described in §2.4 and is illustrated in figure 2.21. Liquid droplets which are formed in an electric field will be charged by induction, and powder particles in contact with either the earthed or the high-voltage surface between which there is a field will also charge.

6.2.3 Industrial examples of electrostatic charge generation

There are a number of consequences of the above charging mechanisms which are often overlooked.

(i) Passage of a non-conducting powder or liquid through an earthed grid will in general tend to charge the material, not discharge it. The earthed grid is able to supply an indefinite quantity of charge to the insulating material, without itself charging up, but charge transferred during contact will not be able to flow rapidly enough from the insulating material to discharge it as it leaves the grid.

(ii) An isolated conductor in an electric field can be charged by induction without collecting charged particles and contacting nothing except an earth (see figure 2.21).

(iii) A relatively conducting liquid or powder, which would lose its charge within less than a second if it were stationary and in contact with earth, may acquire a high electrostatic charge during rapid motion because the charge transfer rate is faster than the charge decay rate. These materials will then retain their charge if they are not in contact with earth when they come to rest.

6.2.4 Charge accumulation

Electrostatic charge separation is hazardous only when charge accumulates so that sufficient energy is dissipated in one spark to cause ignition. The net charge on any sample is determined by a balance between the rate at which charge can be separated and the rate at which it is able to decay to earth or recombine. Charge decays exponentially, i.e. the charge, q, left on a sample a time t after charging has ceased obeys the equation

$$q = q_0 \exp(-t/\tau). \tag{6.5}$$

Here τ is known as the time constant and it is the time taken for the charge to reach $1/e$ (37 %) of its original value, q_0. The time constant depends on the resistance of the path to earth and may be described by one of two equations.

If the charge is accumulated on a single capacitor (or isolated conductor) which has a capacitance, C, and a resistance, R, to earth:

$$\tau = RC. \tag{6.6}$$

If the charge is dispersed in a medium of resistivity ρ and relative dielectric constant ε_r:

$$\tau = \varepsilon_r \varepsilon_0 \rho. \tag{6.7}$$

Since the capacitance of a charged object to earth usually remains reasonably constant, and the value of the relative dielectric constant does not differ greatly between materials, the rate of charge decay is dominated by the resistance to earth or the resistivity of the material.

(a) *The effect of relative humidity*
If water vapour is present in the air, it adsorbs onto surfaces and forms a slightly conducting surface layer. The extent to which the water adsorbs and

the increase in conductivity depends on the nature of the surface and the humidity of the atmosphere. For example, PTFE is hydrophobic and adsorbs only a few molecular layers even at very high humidities, whereas nylon surfaces may become relatively conducting in the presence of water vapour. There appear to be two critical levels of relative humidity. At humidities above about 40–50 % there is frequently a distinct drop in the level of charge which may be built up on an insulating surface (figure 6.17, Gibson and Harper 1981). Although there is not a definitive relative humidity where the conductivity of all materials changes, holding the relative humidity at about 65 % may significantly reduce electrostatic hazards without introducing an unpleasant environment.

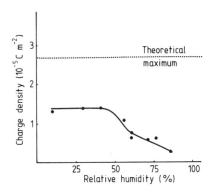

Figure 6.17 The effect of relative humidity on the charge density of a plastic surface ($5 \times 10^{11}\ \Omega$ at 25 °C) (from Gibson and Lloyd 1965).

In very cold climates, where the humidity can reach extremely low levels, the complete removal of water from surfaces can result in very high charge accumulation. For example, figure 6.18 shows the potential built up on the surfaces of two conveyor belts of different materials travelling at $5\ \mathrm{m\ s^{-1}}$ as a function of the moisture content of the air (Cross 1981). The more insulating belt showed a strong correlation between the potential and the absolute humidity (in grams of moisture/kg of dry air), but not between the potential and the relative humidity (i.e. the moisture content expressed as a percentage of the saturated vapour pressure at that temperature). In the worst case a very large potential of over 100 kV was built up. For this belt the resistance of the belt material measured at 25 °C and 50 % relative humidity was $1 \times 10^{12}\ \Omega$ measured across the surface and $5 \times 10^{11}\ \Omega$ measured through the belt. A belt whose resistance at 25 °C and 50 % relative humidity was $10^{9}\ \Omega$ did not charge significantly at any temperature.

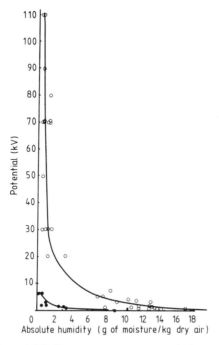

Figure 6.18 Potential built up on two conveyor belts as a function of absolute humidity: ●, antistatic belt ($10^9\,\Omega$ at 25 °C); ○, insulating belt ($5 \times 10^{11}\,\Omega$ at 25 °C). Each point represents measurements on a different day.

6.2.5 Sparks from isolated conductors

Charge stored on an isolated conducting body is mobile, and the entire charge can be drained in a single spark. The most hazardous situation in industry therefore occurs when the charge builds up on a conductor with a high resistance to earth. The circuit equivalent to this situation is a capacitor with a leakage resistance to earth as shown in figure 6.19(*a*).

Current decays exponentially from a capacitor C through the resistor R with a time constant RC. The voltage built up on the capacitor by a charging current I is thus given by

$$V = IR[1 - \exp(-t/RC)]. \tag{6.8}$$

If t is much greater than RC the exponential term becomes zero, i.e. the maximum potential built up on an article with a resistance R to earth, charged by a current I is

$$V = IR. \tag{6.9}$$

(a)

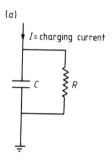

$I =$ charging current

C R

(b)

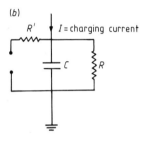

R' $I =$ charging current

C R

Figure 6.19 Equivalent circuits: (*a*), an isolated conductor with a leakage R to earth; (*b*), a person with a leakage R to earth and a skin resistance R'.

If the resistance is very high the final voltage built up when a charge q is stored on a capacitance C is given by

$$V = q/C. \tag{6.10}$$

A spark will occur across a gap of length d between the conductor and earth when the electric field reaches approximately 3×10^6 V m^{-1}, i.e. when

$$V/d = 3 \times 10^6 \text{ V m}^{-1}.$$

If it is assumed that all the energy stored in the capacitor is dissipated in the spark gap this energy is given by

$$W = \tfrac{1}{2}CV^2 = \tfrac{1}{2}qV = \tfrac{1}{2}q^2/C. \tag{6.11}$$

In terms of the charging current this may be written as

$$W = \tfrac{1}{2}CI^2R^2. \tag{6.12}$$

The capacitance can be measured using one of the methods described in Chapter 3, or can be estimated from the size of the object. For example an isolated sphere of radius r has a capacitance to earth

$$C = 4\pi\varepsilon\varepsilon_0 r$$

i.e. a 0.1 m radius sphere has a capacitance of

$$C = 11 \text{ pF}.$$

Approximate capacitances for industrial items, and the amount of charge and the voltage which is required to produce an energy of 0.2 and 5 mJ (typical of the energies required to ignite a hydrocarbon solvent and a static-sensitive dust cloud respectively) are given in table 6.4 (after BS 5958 Part 1).

Table 6.4 Hazardous charge and voltage accumulation.

Object	Capacitance (pF)	Charge (10^{-7} C) 5 mJ	0.2 mJ	Voltage (kV) 5 mJ	0.2 mJ
Small metal items: scoops, tools, etc	10	3.2	0.5	32	6.3
Small containers: buckets, etc	10–100	3–10	0.5–1.4	32–10	6–2
Medium-sized containers 250–500 l	50–300	7–17	1.0–2.4	14–5.5	2.8–1.7
Human body	100–300	10–17	1.4–2.4	10–5.5	2–1.7
Major plant items	100–1000	10–300	1.4–4.4	5.5–3	2–0.6

If the charged conductor has sharp edges, it may discharge by means of a corona rather than a spark. The energy density in a corona discharge is much less than in a spark and it will not ignite hydrocarbon vapours or powders. However, the ionisation of the air can enable sparks to form across much longer gaps than would normally be the case, for example, sparks have been observed to cross a gap of 200 mm between protrusions on an earthed surface and a corona point at 80 kV in an electrostatic spray gun. A corona discharge may also develop into a spark if the voltage is increased or the distance to earth decreased.

The energy, ΔW, dissipated in a spark in a small unit of time Δt, is the product of the current flowing between the electrodes and the potential difference across the electrodes during that time, i.e.

$$\Delta W = IV\Delta t.$$

Integrating over the duration of the spark

$$W = \int IV \, dt. \tag{6.13}$$

In principle, the true energy dissipated in the spark can be measured by recording the voltage across the spark gap and the current flowing through it during the spark. In practice, it is difficult to obtain an accurate measure of the voltage, which falls very rapidly from several kilovolts to a few hundred volts, and it is virtually impossible to get an accurate measurement for the short-duration spark from a capacitive discharge. Direct measurement is only realistically possible for long-duration sparks. For short-duration sparks from a simple capacitive discharge, it is assumed that the energy dissipated is the same as the energy stored. Experimental measurements have confirmed that, provided the energy is stored on an isolated metal conductor or in an electronic capacitor, less than 5 % of the energy remains after a single spark and, since there are no other circuit components where energy could be lost, the assumption that all the energy is dissipated in the gap is reasonable.

Earthing requirements

Hazardous sparks from conductors are eliminated by ensuring that any charge generated can flow to earth. According to British Standard Code of Practice (No 5958 Pt 1) a maximum potential of 100 V is acceptable for all explosive atmospheres. Charging currents range from 10^{-11} to 10^{-4} A. Therefore, the corresponding range of resistance, calculated from equation (6.9) is from 10^{13} to 10^{6} Ω. A resistance to earth of 10^{6} Ω will ensure safe dissipation of static charge in all circumstances, but charging currents are often less than 10^{-6} A, and a resistance to earth of 10^{8} Ω may be satisfactory.

Although the maximum resistance for electrostatic safety is specified to be 10^{6} Ω, other factors may also be taken into account in defining the earthing resistance for a given system. For example, some regulations specify a maximum resistance of 10 Ω or 100 Ω between metal plant and earth. Metals in direct contact should have a very low resistance between them, and should have no difficulty in remaining below a 10 Ω limit. A higher resistance is likely only if there is considerable corrosion which, with further deterioration, could rapidly lead to hazardous resistances. Where an earth path involves bearings, (e.g. a conveyor belt pulley), resistances of up to 10^{3} Ω are common. These cannot meet a 10 Ω limit but are not an electrostatic hazard.

The resistance specified for an earth path may take into account the following factors in addition to the electrostatic requirement of $R < 10^{6}$ Ω.

(i) A wish to detect the possibility of corrosion at an early stage.

(ii) Ease of measurement with a simple low-voltage resistance meter. (However resistances of 10^{6}–10^{8} Ω are measurable with a megohm meter which is a standard item of electricians' equipment.)

(iii) Compatibility with lightning regulations which specify a maximum resistance of 10 Ω.

(iv) In some processes it may be advantageous to have a resistance exceeding a few kΩ to prevent electrochemical corrosion.

The necessity of maintaining an adequate earth is well known, but frequently, modifications are made to equipment or to processes which inadvertently lead to an isolated conductor being formed. For example a flexible length of hose inserted into a system may isolate pipe work. Antivibration mountings or load cells can cause isolation and the build-up of paint on floors or earth clips can prevent adequate earth contact. (Processes which rely on manual placing of earth clips for electrostatic safety should be avoided wherever possible because failure to attach earth clips is so common.) Operators can acquire a static charge extremely easily and should wear antistatic footwear so that charge can leak to earth through the floor (which must of course also be of low resistivity).

Rubber-tyred vehicles can accumulate static if the tyres are dry. Passenger-carrying vehicles generally have tyres made of a rubber with a resistance of less than $10^9 \, \Omega$ but voltages of up to about 10 kV can build up under dry conditions. At one time drag chains were fitted to cars, to assist charge leakage, but these are not very effective unless the road is wet in which case the problem does not arise. Earth clips must always be fitted to road tankers when fuel is being transferred.

6.2.6 Sparks from personnel

A person, who is insulated from earth, can easily acquire sufficient charge to reach a potential of several thousand volts. The resultant spark is a nuisance but not physiologically harmful. However, it can be sufficiently energetic to ignite a flammable atmosphere.

A human being, with a capacitance C to earth, can be represented by the equivalent circuit shown in figure 6.19. R represents the leakage resistance through the shoes to earth and R' represents the contact resistance of the skin. C is of the order of 150–300 pF and potentials of 5 to 50 kV can be attained during the operation of industrial plant, therefore, according to equation (6.11), an energy of up to 375 mJ may be stored. This is considerably higher than the minimum ignition energy of flammable vapours and many dust clouds. The smallest energy of a spark which can be felt is about 1 mJ. Different people experience various degrees of discomfort as the energy of a static spark is increased above 10 mJ but accidents where people have been rendered unconscious have been estimated to be due to sparks involving several joules of energy.

Tests have shown that more energy must be stored on a person before a spark can ignite a flammable mixture than must be stored on a capacitor of the same value in a standard test apparatus (Tolson 1980, Movilliat and Giltaire 1979, Wilson 1977, 1979, 1983). There is some discussion in the literature, concerning both how much energy is required for ignition and why sparks from people are less likely to cause combustion than sparks from a standard optimum capacitor. Wilson (1977) passed a spark directly from a finger to an earthed sphere in an ignition chamber containing a methane–air mixture, and found that an energy of 18.6 mJ was required for ignition. However, if the capacitance of the person was reduced, by standing them on a thick plastic sheet, the energy for ignition was reduced to 1.7 mJ (Wilson 1979, 1983). This was still 4.3 times the minimum ignition energy of the gas mixture. Movilliat and Monomakhoff (1977) used an ignition chamber with two metal spheres, one of which was earthed and the other of which was grasped by the charged person. They obtained ignition of an optimum methane–air mixture with 5.8 mJ sparks. Tolson, using similar equipment, reduced the capacitance of the person to 86 pF and optimised the electrode size to obtain ignition at 1.1 mJ. In all cases, lower values of capacitance produced ignitions at lower values of stored energy. Charged isolated metal items gave a much less strong dependence of ignition energy on capacitance, and discharges from a person are slightly less likely to ignite a flammable atmosphere than sparks from a metal body of a similar size.

If the spark comes from a person, the energy necessary for ignition decreases as the capacitance between the person and earth decreases but the voltage required for ignition remains approximately constant (Wilson 1983, Tolson 1980). Under the conditions of Wilson's tests, where the sparks were produced between a finger and a 1 mm ball, the critical voltage was about 6 kV. With larger earthed spheres the critical voltage was higher. Tolson (1980) observed a sharp dependence of ignition energy on electrode size, with sharp electrodes igniting the gas with lower stored energy, and concluded that the low incendivity of sparks from personnel is due to a quenching effect. However, the work of Wilson (1983) indicates that the most important factors are energy lost in the body resistance and the fragmentation of the energy stored into a number of sparks, only the first of which contributes to the ignition hazard.

The accumulation of electrostatic charge on personnel can be avoided by providing a path to earth via footwear and floors. This ensures grounding at all times. The charge leakage path may be provided by either 'antistatic' or 'conducting' materials. The former will allow charge to disperse, but affords protection against 250 V, mains supply electrical shock. The resistance to earth of antistatic footwear on a non-insulating floor is in the range 5×10^4–5×10^7 Ω. Conducting footwear is suitable only where there is no danger of electrical shock. Specifications for footwear are given in BS 5451 and for flooring in BS 2050.

In general, any clothing is safe, provided the wearer is suitably earthed and the clothing is not removed. The exceptions to this are areas where there may be highly flammable gas mixtures (e.g. oxygen-enriched atmospheres or hydrogen-type gases), where explosives are handled or where static-sensitive electronic devices are handled. In these cases antistatic outer clothing is required. The removal of nylon or synthetic clothing frequently produces small discharges which produce an audible crackle. These are usually not able to ignite a propane atmosphere but the person is left with a high accumulated charge. Voltages up to 10 kV are common and with dry conditions and insulating flooring considerably higher voltages can be achieved. (A person with a capacitance of 200 pF to earth at 10 kV will produce a spark of 10 mJ.)

Recent tests have shown that sparks capable of igniting a 0.2 mJ atmosphere can be produced directly from 100 % polyester fabric, or 100 % cotton at a relative humidity of less than 33 %, if they are rubbed with nylon so the surfaces take up a negative charge. Sparks from a positively charged surface produced by friction with PTFE can ignite hydrogen mixtures but not propane mixtures. One can envisage that sitting on a nylon-covered seat could produce an incendiary discharge as the wearer of 100 % polyester clothing stood up, but with suitable antistatic flooring and footwear the charge would leak rapidly to earth. Brush discharges from insulating surfaces are discussed more fully in the next section.

6.2.7 Sparks from charge on insulating surfaces

The maximum charge density which can be applied to an insulating surface before the field above it reaches the breakdown limit of air can be calculated from Gauss's law and is 2.64×10^{-5} C m^{-2} (§2.2.2). When an earthed electrode approaches a charged surface it acquires an opposite charge by induction. The field increases as the two surfaces are brought closer together and eventually the air breaks down forming a multichannelled spark, known as a brush discharge. The charge is not mobile on the insulating surface and only a small area is discharged releasing a small amount of energy. The charge transferred and the energy released is a function of the size of the sphere up to spheres of 20 mm (Gibson and Lloyd 1965, Heidelberg 1967, Tabata and Masuda 1984). This size dependence occurs because the charge induced on the conducting sphere is proportional to the capacitance between the sphere and the charged surface, which in turn depends on the sphere diameter. Tabata and Masuda found that the charge transferred was related to the diameter, d, of a metal sphere by the empirical relationship

$$q \propto d^{1.7}$$

Sparks transferred from positively and negatively charged insulating surfaces are quite different in nature. This can be seen both in direct photographs of the spark and by Lichtenberg figures (the discharge patterns revealed by powdering the surface, see §3.11.3). A discharge to a positive surface causes essentially circular patches of negative charge to be deposited whereas, when the surface is initially positive, larger, filamentary, star-shaped negative deposits are created. This difference in appearance has been explained by Bertein (1973). In a discharge in which a negative site is deposited on initially positive surface, electrons are accelerated outwards along a decreasing field, leaving positive ions which reduce the field further. Streamers do not develop in the low field and the charge spreads out by a series of short steps, giving a uniform circular charge pattern. When a positive site is deposited on a negative surface, electrons accelerate inwards along an increasing field and the positive ions left behind also increase the field. The charge therefore spreads by discrete streamers creating a star-shaped pattern. Brush discharges from positively charged surfaces are much less incendiary than those from negative surfaces. For example, Tolson (1981) found that a charge density of 3.8 μC m^{-2} would ignite hydrogen and 7.4 μC m^{-2} would ignite propane if the surface was negative, whereas a charge density of 17 μC m^{-2} was required to ignite hydrogen if the surface was positive and no ignition of propane could be obtained with a positive surface. This result was also found in other tests (e.g. Lovstrand 1981).

Lovstrand also investigated the effect of the area of the charged surface on the ignitability of a spark. Discharges from small areas were found to be more intense than those from large areas but, with large charged areas, several discharge paths could form together, converging to a bright spot near the electrode. The probability of achieving an ignition decreases as the area of the insulating surface decreases, but a low probability of ignition is still found for areas as small as 12 cm^2 (Gibson 1983). German regulations suggest maximum safe areas of insulator which may be allowed in different environments (Schon 1982). No such recommendation is made in the British Code of Practice BS 5958, but BS 5501 Pt 1 (1977) suggests that there is a limiting safe surface resistance of 10^9 Ω at 23 °C and 50 % relative humidity. (Similar specifications for particular applications are given in BS 2050 (1978).)

Gibson (1983) suggests that, in zone 0, non-conducting plastics should be limited to areas of 4 cm^2 for 0.04 mJ atmospheres and 20 cm^2 for 0.2 mJ atmospheres. He suggests that greater areas are permissible in zone 1 provided:

(i) the normal operation of the plant does not lead to dangerously high levels of charge,

(ii) the frequency of occurrences which could lead to the accumulation of charge on the plastic (such as steam leaks) does not produce an ignition probability greater than that equivalent to zone 1 electrical equipment,

(iii) the insulator does not produce an isolated conductor.

(Definitions of the zones are given in the Appendix to this chapter.)

Brush discharges are a very variable phenomenon, with several spark channels forming between the sphere and the insulator. The first is generally the brightest, and presumably the most incendiary, but the occurrence of one channel which is apparently brighter is essentially a random phenomenon (Bertein 1977, Lovstrand 1981).

(a) *Estimation of the energy of brush discharges*
When the charge is stored on a metal surface it has a well defined potential and capacitance to earth. The energy released in the spark nearly equals the total energy stored in the capacitor, ($\frac{1}{2}CV^2$). The surface of an insulating material is not an equipotential and a capacitance cannot be defined, therefore the energy of a brush discharge cannot be defined in the same terms as the energy of a spark from an isolated conductor. A number of methods have been proposed for obtaining an estimate of the ignition energy of a brush discharge from measurable parameters of the charged surface. For example, Landers (1985) measured the charge transferred during a spark from an insulating surface to an earthed electrode by detecting the discharge current as a function of time, using an oscilloscope. The distribution of charge on the surface before and after the spark was measured using a capacitive probe. This allows a surface potential to be calculated from numerical field calculations (Landers 1979). The energy was then assumed to be $\frac{1}{2}qV$. Tabata and Masuda (1984) also suggest that the energy can be found from measurements of the surface potential before and after the spark and the current flowing during the spark using the formula

$$W = K(V_1 q - q^2/2C_d) \tag{6.14}$$

where K is a constant found by experiment, V_1 is the potential of the surface, q is the charge transferred and C_d is the differential capacitance, i.e. the ratio of the charge transferred and the fall in potential of the film.

Equation (6.14) agreed well with ignition tests for both hydrogen and propane mixtures for high film voltages (>30 kV) and $K = 0.08$. There was a minimum surface potential and sphere diameter which would lead to ignition. For hydrogen this was of the order of 4 kV and 2 mm.

Measurement of the total energy released in a spark from an insulating surface is of only limited value as an estimate of ignitability, because the duration and spatial distribution of the discharge differ considerably from sparks from an isolated conductor. It is more realistic to measure the ignitability of sparks from an insulator directly, by bringing an earthed sphere to a plastic sheet in a vessel containing a flammable atmosphere. A discharge from an insulator is said to have an equivalent energy, W, if it is just able to ignite a flammable mixture with the minimum ignition energy, W, determined by a capacitive spark discharge (Gibson and Lloyd 1965). The highest equivalent energy of a brush discharge has been reported by Glor (1981) who obtained a 40 % ignition probability of a propane–nitrogen mixture whose minimum ignition energy was 3.6 mJ. Previous results suggested that brush discharge channels carried less than 1 mJ of energy (Gibson and Lloyd 1965, Gibson 1983).

Tests have indicated that surface charge densities of at least 3 μC m^{-2} are required before a negative surface can give an incendiary spark and that a positive surface cannot ignite 0.2 mJ atmospheres but will ignite 0.04 mJ atmospheres (Lovstrand 1981, Tolson 1981). Charge densities can easily be reduced below this level by means of static eliminators.

Plastic pipes more than 10 mm in diameter may acquire similar charge densities to plastic surfaces and give sparks of similar incendivity. Hazardous discharges can occur from the surface of a plastic pipe when an insulating liquid is passed through it. Mason and Rees (1981) passed kerosine with a conductivity varying between 2 and 75 pS m^{-1} through a polyethylene pipe and measured the charge transferred from the outside of the pipe to a conducting sphere 28 mm in diameter. Tests were carried out both with an initially uncharged liquid and with a liquid which had passed through a microfilter and was therefore highly charged. Both positive and negative areas of charge built up on the pipe. The charge transferred to the sphere decreased as the liquid conductivity increased and was higher with negatively charged surfaces than positive. For low-conductivity highly charged liquids, a discharge occurred which punctured the pipe, allowing kerosine to escape. Mason and Rees concluded that an electrostatic hazard could exist for liquids whose conductivity was less than 100 pS m^{-1} and that the resistance through or along pipes carrying these products should not exceed $10^8 \, \Omega$.

(b) *Lichtenberg or propagating brush discharges*

If the charge density on an insulating surface can be increased above the normal Gaussian limit, then the surface can become more conducting and the charge can spread, so that a spark from an earthed electrode can discharge a large area of surface. This type of discharge is known as a Lichtenberg discharge or a propagating brush discharge. Lichtenberg discharges contain sufficient energy to ignite, not only flammable vapours, but also some flammable dusts.

The Gaussian limit to surface charge, which normally prevents the formation of Lichtenberg discharges, occurs because the field above the insulating surface is limited by the breakdown strength of the air. If a grounded metal plate is placed behind the insulating surface, the charges on the surface of the insulator are paired with image charges in the metal plate as shown in figure 6.20. The charged insulating surface and the metal backing plate effectively form a capacitance. A high field is built up across the insulator, which has a much higher breakdown field than air, and the field above the surface is reduced. In this way, very high charge densities can be built up without

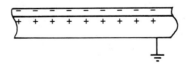

Figure 6.20 Charge pairing when a charged insulator is placed on an earthed backing.

breakdown. The maximum charge density on the surface is a function of the distance between the charged surface and the metal plate, i.e. of the thickness of the plastic sheet. Figure 6.21 shows the apparatus in which Heidelberg (1970) investigated the incendivity of Lichtenberg discharges. The plastic surface was charged by a corona discharge from needles at a potential of up to 75 kV. The charge density on the surface is plotted as a function of charging voltage and the thickness of plastic sheet in figure 6.22. Heidelberg (1970) found that the minimum charge density for a Lichtenberg discharge was $2.5 \times 10^{-4}\,\mathrm{C\,m^{-2}}$. The maximum distance between the plastic surface and the earthed metal backing which would allow this charge density was 8 mm. If the insulating layer is very thin, the electric field above the surface is low, and a conducting sphere must be brought very close to the surface before sufficient charge can be induced upon it to create a spark. If this distance is closer than the quenching distance, the probability of a spark causing ignition is reduced. Figure 6.23 shows the probability of ignition as a function of plastic thickness for a hydrocarbon vapour and for hydrogen as measured by Heidelberg (1970). This work indicated that layers less than 0.25 mm thick could not give a Lichtenberg discharge. However, Edwards and Underwood (1984) produced a charge density estimated to be $5 \times 10^{-3}\,\mathrm{C\,m^{-2}}$ on a $2.5 \times 10^{-2}\,\mathrm{m^2}$ area PVC sheet, only 0.15 mm thick, and the Lichtenberg discharge which occurred as a metal sphere was brought

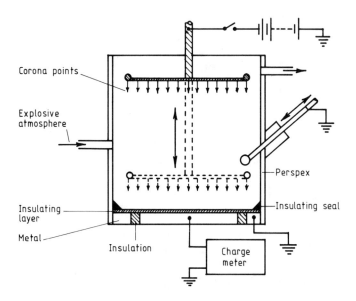

Figure 6.21 Apparatus for investigating brush discharges and Lichtenberg discharges from thin non-conducting layers on metal (from Heidelberg 1970).

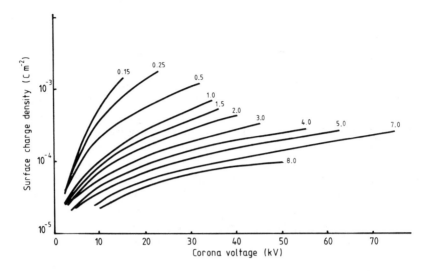

Figure 6.22 The charging of PVC on earthed metal (thickness of PVC layer is shown on each curve in mm) as a function of applied corona voltage. The maximum charge density produced by friction was 10^{-6}–3×10^{-5} C m^{-2}. Lichtenberg discharges began at 2.5×10^{-4} C m^{-2} (from Heidelberg 1970).

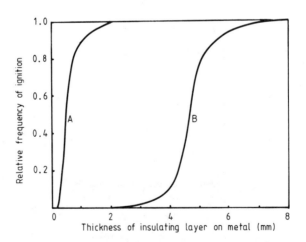

Figure 6.23 The ignition probability as a function of the thickness of the insulating layer (from Heidelberg 1970). A, hydrogen–air mixture; B, hexane–air mixture.

to within 20 mm of the surface-ignited anthraquinone powder (minimum ignition energy 2–10 mJ).

The probability of an incendiary discharge depends on the surface charge density and the thickness of the film and becomes less as the coating becomes thinner. The British Standard code of practice BS 5958 states that a completely safe thickness cannot be specified but that very thin layers such as paint films and thin epoxy coatings are unlikely to present a hazard. Separation of a highly resistive non-conducting coating from its substrate metal can cause an incendiary discharge between the two.

A high surface charge density, similar to that built up when there is an earthed metal backing plate, can also arise if a plastic sheet becomes polarised, with large opposing charges on its two surfaces. The net result of these charges is a near-zero field above the surface (a field meter will detect a low field of different polarities on the opposite sides of the sheet), but very high-energy sparks can be produced when sheets of plastic, charged in this way, are stacked.

Powders which are conveyed in plastic pipes can build up sufficient charge to produce a Lichtenberg discharge. In one incident, a PVC pipe (plastic drain pipe material) was used to convey chocolate crumbs. (This powder has a resistivity of the order of 10^{11} Ω m and a minimum ignition energy of the order of 100 mJ.) The plastic pipe was wrapped with an earthing wire and thus represented the classic case for the production of Lichtenberg discharges. The chocolate crumbs were ignited by sparks from the inner surface of the pipe to the earthing wire (Hughes *et al* 1975). Lichtenberg discharges approaching 1 m in length were observed from a section of 50 mm diameter polythene tube, conveying acrylic powder. In this case, the charge pairing which allowed the high-energy discharges to occur was believed to be due to a conducting layer of rain, water and snow on the outside of the pipe (Luttgens 1985).

Large energetic sparks can also form when a pile of charged insulating powder slides in a storage hopper (Maurer 1979a,b) or when charged powder stored in an insulating hopper is earthed (Blythe and Reddish 1979). This mechanism is discussed further in §6.2.10.

6.2.8 Sparks from charged liquids

Experimental work on the hazards of electrostatic charge accumulation in liquids has concentrated almost entirely on hydrocarbon liquids, particularly petroleum distillates, which have both low conductivities, so charge is retained for a long time, and flammable vapours.

The time constant for charge decay from a liquid is given by

$$\tau = \varepsilon_r \varepsilon_0 \rho_{eff}. \tag{6.15}$$

Liquid charging is conventionally considered in terms of the electrical conductivity σ, rather than its reciprocal, resistivity, and for hydrocarbons, where ε_r is of the order of two, the time constant is approximately

$$\tau \simeq 18/\sigma_{eff} \tag{6.16}$$

where σ_{eff} is the effective conductivity in pS m^{-1}.

The effective conductivity, which governs charge decay, can differ from the conductivity of the stationary liquid, measured in a laboratory cell, particularly for highly charged low-conductivity liquids, because the charging process significantly alters the number of free charge carriers present. Charge relaxation can therefore proceed much faster than predicted from the laboratory measurement of the conductivity of an uncharged liquid. Although theory would predict a hyperbolic charge relaxation law for liquids with a conductivity below 1 pS m^{-1} (Bustin *et al* 1964), in practice the effective conductivity can be assumed to be approximately half its rest value (Krämer and Schon 1975).

Single-phase liquids, with conductivities greater than 100 pS m^{-1}, are considered to be unlikely to accumulate charge, unless they are involved in a process including energetic stirring, mixing or microfiltration. In these cases 1000 pS m^{-1} is a recommended safe limit. With resistive liquids, static may be avoided by ensuring that the flow is slow. Different organisations suggest similar, but not identical, safe limits for the velocity; e.g. BS 5958 Pt 2 recommends

velocity (in m s^{-1}) × pipe diameter (in m) $\ngtr N$

where N is 0.38 for liquid conductivities < 5 pS m^{-1} and N is 0.5 for liquid conductivities > 5 pS m^{-1}. This is subject to the overall criteria that the flow velocity should not exceed 7 m s^{-1} for a single-phase liquid or 1 m s^{-1} for liquids below 50 pS m^{-1} when a second phase is present.

An alternative safety criterion is

$$Q/u\sigma < 12.6$$

where Q is the charge density in μC m^{-3}, u is the velocity of the liquid in m s^{-1} and σ is the conductivity of the liquid in pS m^{-1} (Rees 1981).

If the tank receiving a charged liquid is not earthed the charge in the liquid accumulates at the walls of the tank and at the surface of the liquid. After a filling time, t, the tank is raised to a potential, V, given by

$$V = IR[1 - \exp(-t/RC)] \tag{6.17}$$

where C is the tank capacitance, R is the tank resistance to earth and I is the streaming current.

The electric field strength in a tank made of insulating material may be three to four times higher than is measured when the same liquid is put into a metal tank (Bolton 1972) and the potential of the surface of the liquid will also be higher (Britton and Williams 1982).

An earthed filling pipe may be used to provide a path from the liquid to earth, providing that it extends to the bottom of the tank. (The rise of a charged liquid surface towards an earthed protrusion has a high probability of sparking.) The charge takes much longer to decay from a tank of an insulating material than from a metal tank even when the liquid is in contact with an earthed filling pipe.

Sparks from charged liquid surfaces are similar to sparks from insulating solid surfaces. The same polarity differences are noted, i.e. a negative surface gives a channelled spark and a positive surface, at the same potential, gives a more diffuse, less incendiary discharge. However, ignitions of 0.2 mJ atmospheres can be obtained from a positively charged liquid although they are not obtainable from a positive solid surface, other than by means of a Lichtenberg discharge.

An electric field of about 3×10^6 V m^{-1} is required to give spark breakdown in air, but earthed protrusions intensify the field to cause sparks when the uniform field is only just over a tenth of this value. An incendiary spark will be produced only when the earthed protrusion is above a critical diameter which has been variously reported to lie between 5 and 10 mm (e.g. Schön 1982, Asano *et al* 1977, Bright and Haig 1977, Britton and Williams 1982). For smaller diameters a corona discharge will form rather than a spark. A spark will not form if the protrusion is sufficiently close to the surface that a bridge of liquid is formed.

It has proved convenient in practice to relate the degree of hazard to the undisturbed surface potential of the liquid. The maximum safe voltage is a function of the liquid conductivity, as well as the electrode geometry. Table 6.5 summarises values of the minimum surface potential for which an incendiary spark has been obtained in different laboratories. There is a considerable variation between the measurements, some of which can be attributed to the different techniques used for measuring the surface potential and the liquid conductivity.

Table 6.5 Estimates of hazardous potential on a liquid surface.

Minimum spark voltage (kV)	Liquid conductivity (pS m^{-1})	Reference
20	7	Bright (1977)
25	18	Britton and Williams (1982)
27	1–10	Haig and Bright (1977)
45	4	Strawson and Lyle (1975b)
58	0.5	Krämer and Asano (1979)
60	1.0	Johnson (1977)

Once a safe potential has been defined, the inlet charge density which will produce this potential, for a particular geometry of tank and filling system, can be calculated using a computer model (Diserens *et al* 1975, Lees *et al* 1981, Butterworth and Brown 1982).

6.2.9 Sparks from charged-particle clouds

Dispersed charged particles will retain their charge by virtue of the insulation provided by the surrounding atmosphere. There is an electric field in and around a charged cloud which is a function of the charge density, the size and shape of the cloud and the size and shape of the vessel.

The electric field at the outside of a spherical charged cloud of powder with a charge density Q_V C m^{-3} is calculated from Gauss's law to be

$$E = Q_V r / 3\varepsilon_0$$

where r is the radius of the cloud.

If E exceeds the breakdown limit of air, it is plausible that ionisation could form conducting paths, through which the cloud could discharge in lightning-type sparks. However, there is no evidence that this does occur in any industrial situation and attempts to produce such a phenomenon, by introducing very highly charged dust clouds into a 3 m diameter storage vessel, have not succeeded (Boschung *et al* 1977). It seems likely that the air ionises and discharges individual dust particles in a non-catastrophic way and there is evidence that highly charged dust clouds rapidly lose their charge without causing ignition when the field rises above the Gaussian limit.

When an earthed probe is inserted into a charged cloud it will charge to the opposite polarity by induction. This will produce a more intense field near the probe which could initiate a hazardous discharge. The space potential at a spherical probe of radius a surrounded by a cloud of mist of radius r is given by

$$V = Q_V r^2 / 6\varepsilon_r\varepsilon_0. \tag{6.18}$$

For a cylindrical geometry the equation is

$$V = Q_V r^2 / 4\varepsilon_r\varepsilon_0 \tag{6.19}$$

(Klinkenberg and van der Minne 1958).

Experiments in which an earthed probe was inserted into a highly charged water mist, with space potentials up to 40 kV, failed to produce an incendiary spark (van der Meer 1971, van de Weerd 1971). Later theoretical work showed that the space potential must be at least 70 kV if a probe is to produce a spark that will ignite propane gas (van de Weerd 1972).

The hazard associated with an electrostatically charged mist was studied intensively in the early 1970s following a series of explosions in supertankers or very large crude carriers (VLCC). These explosions occurred when the empty tanks were being washed with very high pressure water jets, which created a highly charged water mist, in the flammable atmosphere from the residual oil. The possibility of arcs from the charged mist to earthed protrusions was investigated by van de Weerd (1972) and considered to be unlikely. A plausible explanation of the explosions is that a slug of water, falling through the charged mist, acquired an electrostatic charge and acted as a charged isolated conductor. Model experiments in a $2 \times 2 \times 1.5$ m^3 polythene tent, filled with propane, showed that the spark from a charged slug of water falling past an earthed sphere was capable of igniting a flammable mixture (Bright and Hughes 1975, Hughes *et al* 1973). A series of papers presenting the results of the studies on the supertanker explosions have been published in the proceedings of London Conference on Static Electrification (van der Meer 1971, van de Weerd 1971, Smit 1971, Vos 1971).

6.2.10 Sparks from bulk powders

As powders settle, the charge on individual particles is concentrated. This can result in very high charge densities in powders which have only a low level of charge on individual particles. A powder with a resistivity in the range 10^6–10^{12} Ω m, stored in an earthed metal container, will lose its charge with a time constant of less than 1 s, and incendiary sparks are unlikely. Powders with a resistivity above this range do not lose their charge effectively by conduction and a spark may occur from the bulking point (where particles first contact the heap) to the earthed walls of the vessel. Discharges have been observed to spread over the surface of the powder in radially directed discharge channels whose appearance changes considerably with slight changes in powder properties (Maurer 1979a,b, 1983). The probability of obtaining a discharge depends on the dimensions of the container and the mass flow rate, particle size and resistivity of the powder. A theoretical model suggests that discharges are only to be expected from rather coarse materials, whose size is in the range of 1–10 mm (Glor 1984). Since the energy of sparks produced by this mechanism is less than 10–30 mJ (Maurer 1983) the hazard of this type of discharge is greatest where coarse particles are handled with a fine dust of low minimum ignition energy.

Conducting powders (resistivity $< 10^8$ Ω m) can acquire a high charge density, which they retain as long as they are dispersed, but lose very rapidly as they are collected in an earthed metal container. Any powder stored in an insulating vessel is a potential hazard. The charge may be dissipated by means of earthing rods but these must be carefully designed to ensure that the field intensification due to the rod does not itself initiate a discharge (Blythe and Reddish (1979), BS 5958 Pt 2 (1982)). The normal methods by which liquids are made safer, i.e. reducing the transport velocity and increasing the electrical conductivity of the material are generally not available options in processes involving powders.

6.3 NON-ELECTROSTATIC SPARKS

6.3.1 Electrical sparks

When a circuit carrying an electrical current is broken, the current can continue to flow across the gap forming an arc. The incendivity of sparks produced in this way depends on the capacitance and inductance of the circuit, the voltage and current involved and the shape of the conductors between which the spark occurs. Generally the inductance of the circuit is the component which governs the energy released. When the circuit is complete and a current flows energy is stored in the magnetic field associated with the circuit inductance. When the circuit is broken the magnetic field collapses and this energy must be released. The energy stored in an inductor of value L is given by

$$W = \tfrac{1}{2}LI^2. \tag{6.20}$$

It has been found that there is a relationship between the inductance of the circuit and the minimum current for ignition:

$$LI^\alpha = \text{constant.} \tag{6.21}$$

Experiments assign a value of 1.79 to α and 0.00366 to the constant (Widgington 1968). For fine wires the minimum ignition energy is approximately the same for a break spark as for an electrostatic spark. Thicker wires require more stored energy before a given gas mixture is ignited.

6.3.2 Friction and impact sparks

When metal strikes against metal or against stone a spark may be produced. This spark has nothing to do with an electrical discharge and is a very hot fragment of material thrown off by the impact. Heat is created during the impact in two ways.

(i) There is a direct transfer of the kinetic energy of impact to heat at the impact point. The local temperature rise depends on the thermal conductivity of the material and its specific heat.

(ii) The heating of the impact area initiates an exothermic oxidation reaction which greatly increases the local temperature. The temperature is highest for easily oxidisable materials, such as magnesium, aluminium and iron and the temperature rise at the impact point is governed by the more easily oxidised material.

The temperature rise during friction has been calculated by Blok (1937), Jaeger (1942), Holm (1948, 1952), Archard (1959) and Chaudhri (1976). Measurements have been made by Bowden *et al* (1947), Bowden and Thomas (1954) and Bowden (1955) and more recently by Blickensderfer

(1975). The experimental work shows that sliding at speeds of $1-7$ m s^{-1} and loads of 0.1 to 10 kg can produce temperature rises of between 300 and 1400 °C, over an area of a few square millimetres from an actual contact area 10 μm in diameter. If oxidation occurs, the temperature can rise up to the melting point of the lower melting point material. The duration of the hot spot is a few milliseconds. In this time the slider used in the tests had moved away from the heated area, therefore the results are applicable to friction or impact (Bowden and Thomas 1954, Blickensderfer 1975).

A considerable amount of work has been carried out evaluating the ignitability of friction and impact sparks, mostly for the coal mining industry where cutting tools must be used and methane gas may be present. The ignition of gases and vapours by impact sparks has been reviewed by Powell (1969). The results can be summarised as follows.

(i) Hydrocarbon vapours can be ignited with difficulty by impact between steel and steel or steel and rock.

(ii) Hydrogen and other gases with a low minimum ignition energy can be ignited easily in these circumstances.

(iii) Hydrocarbon gases can be ignited easily if magnesium or aluminium is involved in the impact.

Less work has been carried out to evaluate the ignition probability of dusts subjected to sparks caused by the impact of steel against steel or concrete. The tests which have been made, have not managed to produce an ignition, either by dropping objects through a dust cloud on to a surface or by striking a deposited layer of powder (Morse 1958, Gibson *et al* 1968). In the experiments carried out by Morse, in which objects were dropped through clouds of grain dust, a bright kernel of flame was occasionally observed, but it did not propagate. The ignition of a powder cloud depends quite critically on the cloud density in the spark zone. This is very difficult to control in impact experiments and the fact that ignition has not been obtained with single impact sparks in the laboratory cannot be taken to mean that this ignition mechanism is impossible. The case histories of accidents (published, for example, by the National Fire Protection Association, Boston USA, or the Manufacturing Chemists Association) report the occasional dust explosion attributed to a single impact spark, but, in view of the difficulty in identifying the true source of an explosion from the debris, this cannot be taken to be conclusive. There is no doubt that multiple sparks and frictional heating, for example, when tramp metal enters a grinding or mixing machine, can cause a dust explosion (Billinge 1981).

(a) *The thermite reaction*

The thermite reaction occurs when a metal with a high affinity for oxygen comes into contact with the oxide of a metal with a lower affinity for oxygen. The most common combination is aluminium and rust. The chemical reaction is initiated by the heat generated in an impact and creates considerable additional heat. Only a smear of aluminium need be present on a surface to produce sufficient energy to ignite either hydrocarbon vapours or powders (Grice 1952, Gibson *et al* 1968). Some aluminium paints are able to give a thermite reaction when hit with rusty steel (Kingman *et al* 1952).

(b) *Non-sparking hand tools*
The temperature of hot spots produced by impact depends on the energy dissipated in the contact, the thermal conductivities of the impacting bodies and the tendency of the surfaces to oxidise. Non-sparking hand tools are made from materials which have a high thermal conductivity and a low tendency to oxidise. The chance of producing hazardous hot spots is therefore minimised. However, non-sparking hand tools can still produce impact sparks that will ignite a flammable vapour and the impact of a non-sparking hand tool on to a smear of aluminium on rusty iron can initiate a thermite reaction (Riddlestone and Bartels 1965).

6.3.3 RF sparks

When a plant structure forms an adventitious aerial in the vicinity of a powerful radio frequency transmission, incendiary sparks can be produced at any discontinuity of the structure. If these sparks coincide with a flammable atmosphere a fire could result. The first British standard on RF ignition hazards was published in 1974 and was based on established radio transmission theory rather than specific tests. Since publication of that standard considerably more experimental work on the risk of fires from RF sparks has been carried out (Hall and Burstow 1980, Excell *et al* 1978, Hall and Loveland 1980, Robertson and Loveland 1981). Much of this work was initiated as a result of concern about the proximity of the Royal Navy transmitting station at Crimond to the St Fergus North Sea gas processing plant in Scotland. Robertson and Loveland (1981) summarise the results of this work, which included both laboratory and site tests. The following factors were considered:

(i) the electrical behaviour of plant and its behaviour as an adventitious aerial,
(ii) the threshold power, energy or voltage required for an RF discharge at a discontinuity in a structure to be incendiary,
(iii) the effect of amplitude and pulse modulation of the RF source on the incendivity of a discharge,
(iv) the effect of multiple transmissions,
(v) the electromagnetic field strengths to which any structure might be subject and the effect of increases in field strength on the available power in the structure,
(vi) the effect of the frequency of the transmission.

Tests included both laboratory studies with equivalent circuits and models of aerial systems, and measurements at St Fergus on items of plant thought to be likely to form an efficient aerial. Structures which could behave either as loop aerials or long dipoles were considered. Both of these can be considered to be high-impedance sources but laboratory systems with an impedance of 50 Ω were also studied.

It was ascertained that the critical ignition parameter for an RF spark across a gap was the power and that the critical power varied with source impedance. With most electrode materials a minimum voltage of 300 V was required between the electrodes for ignition of methane–air mixtures, however, with well oxidised materials, ignition was possible at lower voltages.

The laboratory work indicated that strong radio frequency sources close to a flammable atmosphere could create an explosion hazard if a loop of the plant was adventitiously tuned to the wavelength of the transmissions or if part of the plant structure represented a long dipole. Site tests at St Fergus showed that real structures were usually rather inefficient aerials, presumably because of a rather low RF impedance to ground. The exception was an isolated loop structure, such as provided by a mobile crane. This gave the highest voltages of any structure on the site with voltages across a break reaching 36 V. No ignitions of a hydrogen–air test mixture were obtained.

A series of papers outlining the results of some of these tests have been published in *The Radio and Electronic Engineer* (Howson *et al* 1981, Burstow *et al* 1981, Rosenfeld *et al* 1981, Maddocks and Jackson 1981).

6.4 ELECTROSTATIC ELIMINATORS

6.4.1 Passive eliminators

Electrostatic eliminators reduce static charge by creating ions which increase the conductivity of the air and neutralise the problem charge. The simplest eliminator is an array of earthed points or an earthed wire. The electric field due to the problem charge is intensified at the points and a corona discharge forms, which creates ions of opposite polarity to the original charge. The discharge continues until the field at the points is reduced below the corona threshold. For points which are 10 mm from a surface this will be equivalent to a potential of about 5 kV on the surface. Thus a passive eliminator ceases to operate at moderate surface charge densities.

The threshold field that must be exceeded at a discharge point of radius r, before a corona is initiated, is given by

$$E_c = 18/r^{1/2}$$

where r is measured in cm and E_c is given in kV cm^{-1} (Cobine 1958). The threshold field at a wire of radius r, in a gas of relative density δ, is given by

Peek's semiempirical equation (Peek 1929)

$$E_c = \delta f [A + B/(r\delta)^{1/2}].\tag{6.22}$$

Here δ is the gas density relative to air at 1 atm and 25 °C, f is a roughness factor ($f < 1$) and A and B are constants, which for air have the values $A = 32.2 \times 10^5$ V m^{-1} and $B = 8.46 \times 10^4$ V m$^{-1/2}$.

Calculation of the potential difference required to produce the threshold field is complicated in all but the simplest of geometries. As a first approximation it can be assumed that the potential which must be applied between a single discharge point and a plane, to produce a field E_c at the surface, is independent of the spacing to earth and is given by

$$E_c = V_s/r.$$

Therefore $V_s = 18r^{1/2}$ with r in centimetres and V in kilovolts.

If the discharger is assumed to be a wire between two charged plates with a distance d between the wire and a plate, then the relationship between the corona threshold field and the potential on the surface is (Moore 1973)

$$E_c = V_s/r \ln(4d/r\pi)$$

i.e.

$$V_s = fr\delta[A + B/(r\delta)^{1/2}] \ln(4d/r\pi).\tag{6.23}$$

Passive eliminators are most efficient when the field above the surface for a given surface charge is high. Therefore they should be positioned where the charged surface is far from other earths. This is illustrated in figure 6.24. In position A, the charged belt is passing over the roller and the surface charge is paired with image charges in the roller so the field above the surface is low. At position B, the same surface charge produces a much higher electric field.

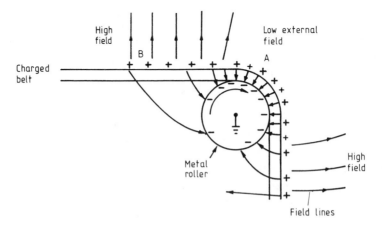

Figure 6.24 The electric field at the surface of a charged belt in the vicinity of an earthed roller.

At very high charge levels, a passive discharger will eliminate charge some distance before the earthed points. Some of the field lines travelling to the elimination zone, cross the surface, where it is already discharged, and ions, following the field lines recharge the surface. Therefore, at high initial surface charge levels, passive dischargers tend to overcompensate.

6.4.2 Active eliminators

An active eliminator neutralises a surface by producing ions of both polarities, either by means of a radioactive source, or by using an AC corona discharge. Radioactive eliminators most often use a polonium 210 source, deposited below the surface of silver foil. Alpha particles are emitted which have a range of 38.5 mm in air. The alpha particles do not themselves neutralise the charge, but they collide with air molecules and create a plasma of ionised air. A typical radioactive bar has an activity of 80 mCi, giving a discharge current of 8 μA m^{-1}. A radioactive eliminator tends to give more complete neutralisation than other active eliminators providing the charge level is low. However, and 80 mCi source cannot neutralise charge faster than 8×10^{-6} C s^{-1} for each metre width of charged belt. This is frequently insufficient for industrial applications, unless a passive neutraliser is first used to reduce charge. A major advantage of the radioactive neutraliser is that it has no power source and is therefore intrinsically safe. However, it is relatively expensive and cannot be used in environments where it would become dirty and require mechanical cleaning. The radioactivity of an eliminator is too low to be a radiation hazard but its use is forbidden in some applications because of the risk of polonium contamination. The half-life of a polonium 210 source is 138.4 d and radioactive eliminators must be changed as their activity falls.

An AC corona eliminator consists of an array of sharp points or a wire, to which an AC potential is applied. The points do not require to be particularly fine provided that the applied voltage divided by the radius of curvature of the points exceeds the corona threshold field. The AC corona discharge creates positive and negative ions on alternate halves of the cycle. At low frequencies each half-cycle behaves independently, as if there were two DC discharges. The current is not symmetrical and the polarity which produces the excess charge is a function of the point diameter and the applied voltage. For larger diameter wires and points, a given voltage produces more negative ions than positive ions. For small-diameter corona sources the reverse is true. AC eliminators are often designed with the high-voltage electrode within a grounded shield. Ions of both polarities are created in the discharge to the shield, and those required for neutralisation are pulled out of the shield by the electric field of the unwanted charge. Commercial devices vary considerably in dimensions, with shields between 5 and 50 mm from the corona source. A shield which is close to the corona source increases the total current but requires a higher electric field to deflect ions out of the shield.

A single corona point can produce up to a few hundred microamps of current. Each point in an array will act independently of its neighbour when the spacing between points is about twice the point-to-plane spacing. The total corona current produced by an array of points of fixed length increases as the number of points increases, until the spacing between points is reduced to about 10 mm. A corona wire can produce a current per unit length of up to about $10 \, \text{mA m}^{-1}$. Commercial eliminators usually operate at about $1 \, \text{mA m}^{-1}$, where the discharge is more stable. Only a small percentage of this current is normally required for neutralisation.

There is an optimum spacing between the eliminator and the charged surface to be neutralised. If the spacing is too small, the eliminator tends to deposit zones of positive and negative charge, if it is too large there is some recombination of the ions created in the two halves of the cycle, and the efficiency is reduced. The closer the eliminator to the problem charge, the more likely it is to overcompensate. When accurate neutralisation is required, a DC bias potential can be applied to the shield, controlled by feedback from measurements of surface charge downstream from the eliminator. Charge densities can be reduced to about 1 % of their initial level in this way (Lovstrand 1975). A combination of passive and active eliminators will also give good neutralisation with charge densities reduced to about $0.1 \times 10^{-6} \, \text{C m}^{-2}$. Low-frequency AC corona behaves very like two independent DC discharges, but at higher frequencies, where the time between polarity changes is less than the time taken for an ion to cross the gap, a positive space charge is formed and the arc-over voltage decreases. Commercial eliminators most commonly use 50 or 60 Hz sources, but frequencies up to a few kilohertz may be used without altering the form of the discharge, and higher frequencies will still give some neutralisation. For fast belt speeds (exceeding about $2 \, \text{m s}^{-1}$) 50 Hz eliminators leave equal and opposite bands of charge on a surface. (Some field meters would register this as zero charge.)

An alternative design for a corona eliminator is illustrated in figure 6.25. Positive- and negative-ion clouds are produced simultaneously from two separate arrays of corona points, one at a positive and the other at a negative potential. The points create a weak plasma in front of the charged surface from which the appropriate polarity for neutralisation is extracted. This type of device operates effectively at a larger and less critical spacing than the conventional AC eliminator, but it is more expensive, and takes up more room than the conventional device.

The jet ion generator, illustrated in figure 6.26, was originally designed to eliminate charge which was inaccessible to conventional AC eliminators. The AC corona discharge takes place in the throat of a nozzle and a high air flow ensures that the ions are carried out of the nozzle without being attracted to

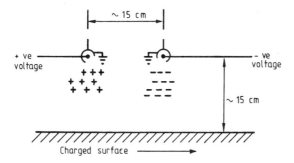

Figure 6.25 A bipolar static eliminator.

the walls. The ion current issuing from the device increases with velocity up to supersonic speeds. The efficiency of the jet ion generator is nearly an order of magnitude less than the conventional AC eliminator, possibly because the turbulence generated by the blast encourages recombination of the ions. Higher efficiency has been obtained using a supersonic nozzle, illustrated in figure 6.27 (Whewell *et al* 1970, Felici and Larigaldie 1980, Larigaldie and Giboni 1981). The sudden expansion of the air as it passes through the orifice causes very rapid cooling, so water particles are formed even when the air is fairly dry (down to 15 % relative humidity). Droplets tend to condense on ions, therefore a corona discharge point, placed at the point where the maximum cooling occurs, forms a cloud of very small charged droplets. These have a much lower mobility than the ions therefore recombination is greatly reduced. At 25 °C, the water droplets may be blown a distance of up to about 500 mm before they evaporate. The amount of water vapour introduced to the system with this device is negligible. The air jet issues from the nozzle very fast and the device is noisy. A jet eliminator is able to discharge a dispersed powder cloud which cannot be discharged by the conventional AC eliminator because of the large distances involved. Preliminary tests produced 4×10^{10} ions of each polarity per cubic metre in a room of volume

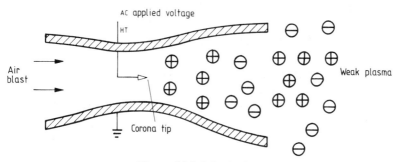

Figure 6.26 A jet ioniser.

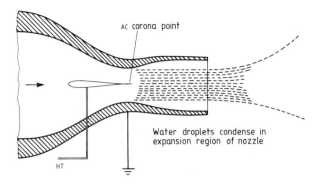

AC corona point

Water droplets condense in
expansion region of nozzle

HT

Figure 6.27 A supersonic jet eliminator (from Whewell *et al* 1970).

50 m^3. The charge density on a powder cloud was reduced by a factor of two
in 10 s and by a factor of ten in 2 min (Larigaldie and Giboni 1981).

Where a higher water content is acceptable, a charged water spray created
by conventional spraying techniques may be used to transport the ions
(Castle *et al* 1983). In large chambers, or at elevated temperatures, the
droplets evaporate leaving the ions available for neutralisation without damage to the charged surface.

Powder may be discharged as it emerges from a pipe, using a conventional
AC eliminator. However, the density of the powder flow tends to be high at
this point, and high discharging currents are necessary to produce a significant effect. AC eliminators have proved useful in removing the charge from
powders being put in tins in the food industry, and a considerable reduction
of charge in an industrial powder storage silo has also been reported. Passive
eliminators in the form of earthed rods or wires have been recommended to
reduce the level of the electric field in powder storage vessels. They are useful
when the charge density is of the order of 10 μC m^{-3} and the electric field
strength is close to the limit for the breakdown of air. The use of earthed rods
or wires at the bulking point of the powder can reduce discharge energies to
low values and will provide a charge leakage path if the powder is stored in
an insulating container (Blythe and Reddish 1979).

6.4.3 The safety of electrostatic eliminators

A passive eliminator may be used in flammable atmospheres where the
minimum ignition energy does not exceed approximately 0.2 mJ, but not in
more sensitive atmospheres such as oxygen-enriched atmospheres or hydrogen–air mixtures (BS 5958).

If an AC active eliminator is used in a flammable atmosphere it is necessary
to ensure that it cannot give a hazardous spark on the approach of an
earthed object. There are a number of ways this may be achieved.

(i) The earthed shield which surrounds the high-voltage wire in many AC eliminators can be designed to prevent any earthed object getting close enough to the active electrode to produce a spark.

(ii) The energy available in a spark can be minimised by installing a series resistor immediately before the corona electrodes. If the current from the corona electrode rises, the voltage drop across the resistor also rises, so the voltage at the corona point falls.

(iii) A decoupling capacitor may be used to isolate the eliminator from the transformer. This will protect personnel from electrical shock but the capacitance must be very small if it is to prevent sparks of 0.2 mJ which could ignite a flammable hydrocarbon vapour. The energy of a spark from the eliminator will be

$$W = \tfrac{1}{2}CV^2$$

where C is the capacitance of the device following any isolation resistor and V is the applied voltage. If the voltage applied to the corona electrode is 10 kV, and since the energy of the spark must be below 0.2 mJ, it can be seen that the capacitance of the points must be less than 4 pF.

(iv) An AC eliminator can be designed with the high-voltage electrodes completely encapsulated in insulating material as shown in figure 6.28. The high-voltage electrodes create an electric field so that a corona discharge is formed at the earthed sharp points, but no spark can be produced from the encapsulated electrodes whose potential is well below the breakdown potential of the insulating encapsulation.

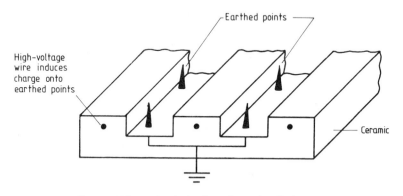

Figure 6.28 An intrinsically safe static eliminator.

(v) Jet eliminators have the point inside the nozzle where it cannot be touched, and the high air flow across its surface prevents a flammable atmosphere forming in the discharge area. These devices will not cause an ignition provided the air flow is always present before the discharge begins.

A survey of seven commercial AC eliminators has been carried out by Tolson (1980) of the Safety in Mines Research Establishment, UK. He studied both the efficiency of discharging and the safety of the devices for use in flammable environments. Some of the eliminators had exposed points and some were partially shielded, some were directly coupled and some AC coupled to the power source. He found that the discharging efficiency varied quite widely, but all seven removed most of the charge from a surface when operated at the distance recommended by the manufacturers. (This distance varied considerably from device to device.) None of the eliminators left a completely neutral surface, and the residual charge was opposite in polarity to the original charge. All the eliminators were less efficient at removing positive charge than negative, however, as discussed in §6.2.7, positive surfaces are less hazardous. At high levels of initial charge, where all AC eliminators left significant residual charge, a tinsel bar passive eliminator (made from a piece of Christmas decoration) compared quite well with the active, AC devices. At lower initial charge levels the AC devices were significantly more efficient than the passive eliminator. In the safety tests, four of the seven AC eliminators ignited propane gas; but one of these only did so because of a metal label which had been placed on the device after it had left the manufacturer. All but one device ignited hydrogen. In some cases, there was an incendiary spark between the charged surface and the earthed shield as the power was switched off. Some devices were nearly as efficient unpowered as powered, others were inefficient when unactivated but did not produce an incendiary spark. Unfortunately Tolson does not describe the design of the devices which had the desirable features but concludes that it is possible to design an AC powered eliminator which is safe to use in flammable atmospheres. Statistics show that the use of electrically powered eliminators reduces the incidence of fires.

6.5 ANTISTATIC AGENTS

6.5.1 Introduction

Antistatic agents are chemicals which can be added to liquids or solids to reduce the accumulation of electrostatic charge. The agents may function either by reducing the generation of charge, or by increasing the conductivity of the substance to which they are added, so as to increase charge leakage. Most additives operate by the second mechanism. The increased conductivity may be achieved by incorporating a conducting material such as metal, carbon or a more conducting polymer, or by causing a surface to absorb water from the atmosphere. There are 290 formulations of antistatic additives from the US patent literature 1966–1975 described by Johnson (1976) and a review of the mechanism of operation of different types of additive is given by Valko and Tesoro (1964).

6.5.2 Hydrophilic additives

A large number of commercial antistatic agents increase surface conductivity by increasing water adsorption at low relative humidities. An effective antistatic additive of this type must be present on the surface, rather than in the bulk of the material, and its efficiency depends on its durability, its ability to absorb moisture at low relative humidities (its hygroscopicity) and its ability to donate mobile ions to the adsorbed water to form a conducting surface layer. Most are surface-active agents which can be characterised by the general structure

$$R - S$$

where R is a hydrophobic group such as a hydrocarbon and S is a hydrophilic group. Antistatic agents may be classified as polymeric or non-polymeric and within each group as cationic, anionic, zwitterionic (having both charges) or non-ionic.

A non-polymeric cationic compound has the form:

$$[R—A^+]X^- \quad \text{or} \quad X^-[A^+—R—A^+]X^-.$$

Typical compounds of this type are quaternary ammonium salts (Johnson 1974).

Non-polymeric anionic compounds have the general form:

$$[R—B^-]M^+$$

where M^+ is a metal cation, R is a hydrocarbon and B^- is a carboxylate or sulphonate or similar, e.g.

Zwitterionic compounds have the general structure:

$$[R—A^+—B^-—R]$$

where A^+ and B^- are typical cationic and anionic groups. Typical compounds of this nature are (Hubu 1973):

An example of neutral antistatic additives are the aminophosphoric acid esters (Grabhofer 1969). Polymeric additives may also be divided into the same groups. The simplest compounds are polyether glycols (Pechmann 1970).

In all these examples, the antistatic additive is a surface-active agent oriented so its hydrophilic end protrudes into the air. These attract water molecules, which, under favourable conditions, form a continuous layer. It appears, however, that the water layer does not necessarily have to be continuous to give antistatic properties.

6.5.3 Antistatic additives in textile processing

When a synthetic yarn is first solidified and cooled from a molten polymer it is bone dry and very susceptible to electrostatic charging at the guides and pulleys of the rest of the process. An antistatic agent is normally applied during processing, often as a component of a lubricating oil.

Most antistatic additives not only adsorb water and donate ions to it but are soluble in water. They are therefore removed by washing. To avoid this problem hygroscopic antistatic agents can be chosen which form a crosslinked polymeric network which is insoluble in aqueous detergent solutions. The compound is deposited on the textile as a monomer and polymerised *in situ*. Commercial products are often ion exchange resins, formed by condensation polymerisation. Crosslinked additives usually increase fabric stiffness.

The conductivity of synthetic yarns may also be increased using a two-phase system in which an antistatic polymer, such as polyethylene glycol, is added as a disperse phase to a polymer which provides the fibre-forming properties. In nylon, addition of about 5 % of the antistatic material produces an increase in conductivity by a factor of about 10^3, and there is evidence that this is not entirely caused by an increase in moisture absorption (Grady and Hersch 1977). The conductive properties do not depend on the polyethylene glycol molecules being interconnected.

Antistatic properties of treated fabrics can be lost during storage, probably due to migration of the additive from the surface into the bulk of the polymer (Ward 1955).

Antistatic properties may be reapplied to textiles after laundering by using fabric softeners. The most effective fabric softeners are cationic softening agents, often based on quaternary ammonium salts. These are soluble in water and therefore wash out during laundering, however, they can be reapplied in the rinsing stage. After rinsing is complete the agents are firmly bound to the fibres. Softeners may also be sprayed on to fabrics during drying.

6.5.4 Antistatic additives for plastics

The durability of antistatic finishes is also a problem in the plastics industry, where a surface finish may be removed by rubbing. Durable antistatic additives for plastic materials are formed by incorporating the antistatic compound in the bulk plastic (at about a 0.1 % level) from where it gradually migrates to the surface (Aron 1964). In principle, the mechanism of this process is believed to be the same as the separation of two immiscible liquids. However, in the case of plastics, the separation is slowed down by the extreme viscosity of the medium and may take years to complete. Migration of the additive to the surface can thus extend over the useful life of the plastic. The compounds used are frequently amphipathic molecules, i.e. molecules with one polymer-compatible and one water-compatible end. They are often the same as the antistatic additives used for textiles, e.g. quaternary ammonium compounds, amine derivatives, phosphate esters and ethylene oxide condensates (Zichy 1974).

The potential uses of a conducting material with the mechanical properties of a plastic are great and there has been considerable work in recent years which attempt to develop such a material. Some polymers are naturally sufficiently conducting to dissipate static electricity. These have at least one ionisable group per monomer unit, an example is cellulose and its derivatives. Polyamides show pronounced ionic conduction at elevated temperatures (e.g. Nylon 6-6 has a conductivity exceeding $10^{-8} \, \Omega^{-1} m^{-1}$ at 100 °C). Plasticiser, for example in PVC, can reduce the conductivity sufficiently to prevent high storage of static charge. Molecular structures which provide higher conductivities are discussed by Blythe (1979). Although conducting polymers can be developed the mechanical properties of the materials are poor and the most useful formulations are still two-phase materials.

6.5.5 Metallised systems

Antistatic systems that use hydrophilic additives depend on the humidity of the atmosphere to provide water. A relative humidity of 25 % will usually be satisfactory, but in some applications this may not be available. A system based on metal conductivity is independent of atmospheric conditions. The conductivity of a composite is limited by the interparticle contact of the conducting phase, therefore it is normally necessary to use a metal which does not oxidise, to produce a reasonably conducting composite. Common metallic additives are silver and stainless steel.

Metallic additives have been used to reduce electrostatic problems from carpets. Three techniques have been used.

(i) The organic fibre is coated with a thin layer of metal and blended with the normal non-conducting fibres (Teijin 1968).

(ii) Very fine (4–12 μm) stainless-steel fibres are used at a percentage of the order of 0.1 to 1 %. The presence of this low percentage of steel in the carpet operates not by providing a continuous conducting path, but by limiting the electric field which can exist between shoes and the ground. The conducting fibre causes local field intensification and breakdown (Lowell and McIntyre 1978). This technique is effective, but the price of yarn with a steel fibre additive is high and there are problems associated with processing such yarns on standard equipment.

(iii) A metal fibre is woven in to the carpet backing.

Steel fibres, a few micrometres in diameter and 6 mm long have also been incorporated into plastics to provide a non-black antistatic plastic (originally required for the coal mining industry) and steel fibres are used in some needlefelt fabrics used for gas filtration.

Silver flakes are incorporated into some resins to make them electrically conducting, but by no means all silver-doped paints have this property. A highly doped silver paint can give a surface resistance of less than 1 Ω, whereas carbon-doped paints are normally quoted as less than 200 Ω.

Silver may also be incorporated into bulk plastics, but a high percentage is required to provide conducting properties so the material is expensive, and the desirable mechanical properties of the polymer are largely lost.

Silver-coated glass beads 1–1000 μm in diameter or silver-coated fibres may also be used as a filler in a plastic to provide conducting properties at a lower cost than the addition of pure silver.

6.5.6 Carbon black as an antistatic agent

Carbon black consists of very small carbon particles, less than 50 nm in diameter, which are formed (usually in small clusters or chains) in a furnace, or similar, by incomplete combustion of a hydrocarbon.

At low concentrations of carbon in a plastic, the conductivity of the composite is non-ohmic, and is dominated by electron tunnelling through gaps of the order of 5 nm between carbon particles.

An empirical equation relating the conductivity of the composite to the carbon concentration, for low concentrations is

$$\ln \sigma = (A/f)^{-p} \tag{6.24}$$

where f is the weight fraction of carbon, and A and p are constants. A and p vary for different blacks (Bulgin 1945). For example, high surface area carbon blacks produce a better conductivity for the same loading than low surface area blacks.

There is usually a sharp increase in conductivity as the loading is increased to about 15 % by weight. For example, the resistivity of high-density polyethylene decreases from 10^7 to 10^2 Ω m as the percentage of carbon black is increased from 7.5 to 11.3 %, and can be as high as 1 Ω m at 15 % loading. Higher loadings continue to produce a more conducting product but the increase is rather slower (see figure 6.29, Blythe 1979). At high concentrations of carbon the conductivity of the composite is ohmic.

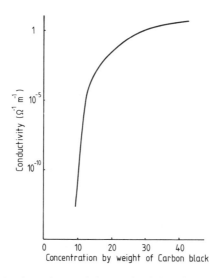

Figure 6.29 The dependence of the conductivity of a PVC composite on carbon black content (from Blythe 1979).

To achieve a high conductivity for the lowest carbon loadings the carbon particles must be uniformly dispersed, with gaps of only a few nanometres between neighbouring chains. The conductivity will obviously be highest if the carbon particles can be dispersed in a matrix through the polymer. This can be achieved by coating the particles of the moulding powder, by mixing them with carbon black, in a ball mill. If the subsequent process does not shear the mixture too much, the carbon black remains in a honeycomb structure and the conductivity is greatly enhanced over a uniform dispersion of the same amount of black. Overmixing of the additive always tends to reduce conductivity because it tends to increase the interparticle distance.

The presence of carbon black changes the physical properties of the polymer making it harder and stronger. It also pigments it black. Attempts have been made to use carbon black in fibres, but usually so much carbon is required to produce the required conductivity that the fibre-forming properties of the polymer are impaired (Boyd and Bulgin 1957). The presence of carbon black takes plastics into the resistivity range of semiconducting materials, but, unlike true semiconductors, the resistivity increases with increasing temperature.

6.5.7 Epitropic fibres

An epitropic fibre is a fibre whose surface contains partially, or wholly, embedded particles, which modify one or more of the fibre properties. They are made using bicomponent fibres in the form of a core and sheath, where the sheath has a lower softening point than the core. The sheath is softened by accurately controlled heat treatment, and conducting particles are embedded into it, without affecting the fibre core. Very good results are obtained if the particles are less than 5 μm in diameter. Carbon black has been embedded in the surface of both polyester and nylon. Approximately 2 % by weight of carbon is required to reduce the resistance of a polyester fibre by six orders of magnitude. A few per cent of an epitropic fibre, incorporated into a garment made of 100 % polyester, results in a similar decrease in the resistance of the fabric.

6.5.8 Charge control agents

An additive which operates by reducing the amount of static charge which is formed is known as a charge control agent. The charge generated by friction may be reduced to a very low level by incorporating a substance which generates a frictional charge of the same magnitude but opposite polarity to the original material (Bailey *et al* 1974). It is possible to choose an additive with a high charging tendency, so that the amount which must be incorporated to produce a significant reduction in charge generation is low. Charge control agents contain groups such as COOH or NR_3, which are neutral but which can easily be charged, forming COO^- or NR_3^+. These are similar to the groups in antistatic additives which attract water but are present in smaller quantities and perform a different function.

6.5.9 Antistatic additives in liquids

A high static charge is built up when a liquid has sufficient ions present for separation to occur, but an insufficient number to impart electrical conductivity to the liquid. The most hazardous conductivities lie in the range 0.1–10 pS m^{-1}. The conductivity needs to be raised only to 100 pS m^{-1} to reduce the chance of electrostatic charge accumulation greatly (provided the liquid is single phase). This may be achieved by adding as little as 1 PPM of a suitable antistatic agent. Since antistatic additives increase the number of ions present, they can also increase the amount of charge separation, and hence increase the charge on the liquid, if it is stored in an insulating container. However, proprietary additives exist which give low charge generation and bring the conductivity of hazardous hydrocarbon liquids to above the recommended safe limit of 100 pS m^{-1}.

6.6 ELECTROSTATIC PROBLEMS IN THE ELECTRONICS INDUSTRY

6.6.1 Modes of failure

Electronic devices can be easily damaged by electrostatic discharges. The fault is not always immediately detectable, but the device can be left in a state where it is much more susceptible to failure in future use.

Table 6.6 shows a list of static-sensitive devices and the voltages that may cause damage (Davies 1985). There are two modes of failure:

(i) discharges occur within the device, due to voltage build-up across thin insulating layers,

(ii) thermal damage occurs due to the flow of a current.

Table 6.6 Static-sensitive electronic devices (Davies 1985).

Device type	Voltage range for electrostatic charging (V)
VMOS	30–1800
EPROM	100 max
MOSFET	100–200
GaAs FET	200–300
JFET	140–17 000
SAW	150–500
OP AMPS	190–2500
CMOS	250–2000
Schottky diodes	300–2500
Film resistors	300–2500
Bipolar transistors	380–7000
ECL (Hybrid, PB level)	500–1000
SCR	680–1000
Schottky TTL	1000–2500

The first mode may be illustrated by considering a MOS device such as illustrated in figure 6.30. The device is operated by a small voltage of the order of 1 V applied to the metal gate which is insulated from the base silicon by a dielectric layer of the order of 0.1 μm thick. The dielectric layer is frequently SiO_2 which has a breakdown strength of the order of 10^9 V m^{-1}, i.e. a potential exceeding 100 V arriving at the gate, can cause failure. In practice there may be defects in the oxide layer so that breakdown can occur at slightly lower voltages. The discharge can puncture the oxide layer and introduce a conducting path through it. The capacitance of the gate of an MOS device is of the order of 0.02 pF:

$$V = q/C.$$

Therefore a potential of 100 V is built up if a charge of 2×10^{-12} C can be acquired by the gate, and extremely small discharges may damage a static-sensitive electronic component.

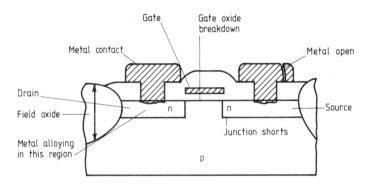

Figure 6.30 Structure and damage to a CMOS device; n and p refer to n- and p-type doped silicon respectively.

Breakdown damage can occur whenever there is a thin insulating layer separating conducting films, for example, when two metallic traces cross over or when they run close to each other. (This mode of failure occurs in SAW devices.) In VMOS devices, the layers are deposited in a V-shaped groove and the breakdown potential is even lower than in CMOS devices. Voltages of the order of 30 V are the maximum acceptable (Edwards *et al* 1979).

A current, I, flowing through a resistance, R, will dissipate heat energy, W, ($W = I^2R$). This can cause thermal damage in a number of ways. For example, the temperature increase in a thin film of silicon can cause thermal vaporisation. Thermal runaway can also occur in silicon which has a negative coefficient of resistance once the temperature rises above a critical level, which depends on doping.

Silicon dissolves in aluminium at a relatively low temperature, forming a solid solution, therefore heat dissipated in aluminium–silicon junctions can result in alloying or in the formation of a metal spike across the relatively insulating layer. Thin metal layers on insulating materials are unable to lose any heat dissipated in them and metallic tracks may partially melt.

Electrostatic problems increase as the dimensions of the structures in integrated circuits become smaller. For example, oxide layers can now be as thin as 0.02 μm, with a breakdown voltage of 26 V.

6.6.2 Sources of static

Unearthed personnel easily acquire voltages exceeding 10 kV and can store an energy of several hundred millijoules. A spark from a person with a capacitance of 150 pF charged to a potential of 10 kV will release 1.5×10^{-6} C of charge. These voltage and charge levels are several orders of magnitude higher than the threshold for damage to static–sensitive devices. Electrostatic charge on a person may be transmitted to the circuit directly, for example by contact with a pin of the device, or with a switch or keyboard to which the device is connected. It may also be coupled indirectly from a spark in the vicinity of the static-sensitive device because the rapid rate of rise of current in a spark induces a secondary current in nearby circuits by inductive coupling. For example, a spark to the outside of a well earthed cabinet can induce a current flow inside it, which can damage components. Discharges to metal parts on the outside of an insulating container may also be capacitively coupled to devices inside the container.

The second most common source of damage to electronic components is a discharge from a plastic surface. Although this stores much less charge than the human body it may reach a potential of about 10 kV. A discharge from the surface of a plastic bag may easily release 10^{-9} C of charge which would be sufficient to damage a static-sensitive device.

A charge may build up on the devices themselves by induction or by friction. For example it has been shown that sliding dual in-line devices along earthed metal strips can generate sufficient charge to cause a spark as the device leaves the strip (Davies 1985).

6.6.3 Protection

Integrated circuits are commonly designed with input circuits which protect the more sensitive components of the device from the effects of electrostatic discharges. These may include a combination of resistors, current-limiting transistors, diodes etc (Turner and Morris 1980, Bhatti *et al* 1978, Minear and Dodson 1977, Hickernell and Crawford 1977, Clark 1979, Phillip and Levinson 1979). Protection circuits are themselves vulnerable, and in some cases failure of a chip is due to a failure in the protection circuit.

Electrostatic problems may be eliminated from the electronics environment by minimising the presence of polymer materials and ensuring efficient earthing. Small electrostatic charges on personnel are the greatest hazard and the most efficient solution to this problem is to earth personnel by a wrist strap which has an impedance of 1 MΩ to earth, to prevent danger from electric shock. A work station for assembly of static-sensitive devices has a conductive bench and a floor mat. Stools do not have rubber feet or plastic seat covers and all trays and containers on which devices might be placed are conducting. Electrically conducting foams are available for device storage

(Jowett 1976). Static-sensitive devices are normally stored in containers which have an antistatic treatment but tests have shown that some of these are not effective (Davies 1985). Antistatic materials which prevent charge accumulation have a resistivity in the range 10^6 to 10^8 Ω m but materials required to provide electromagnetic screening must be continuous and metallic. Electrostatic eliminators are recommended by some experts but overcompensation can occur and there is a shortage of data on their effectiveness in the electronics environment.

Recommendations for the safe handling of static-sensitive devices are discussed in the *Electrostatic Discharge Control Handbook*, *Electrostatic Discharge Standard* and BSI 78/22265 DC draft standard code of practice for the handling of static-sensitive devices.

6.7 ADHESION

6.7.1 Introduction

The influence of electrostatic forces in the adhesion of particles and films has received a great deal of study but is still not well understood. For example, it is often difficult to define why one powder should be more cohesive than another, and both failure to flow and failure to pack with sufficient density have been attributed to electrostatic forces between particles. Adhesive forces between materials are important in the friction and wear properties of materials, the formation of compacts in powder metallurgy or the pharmaceutical industry, the production of powdered films in the coatings industry and the manufacture of ceramics. Cohesion and adhesion have also been studied with reference to filtration and separation. The literature on the subject is therefore vast and widespread.

Adhesive forces range from the light contact adhesion of particles which fall off a surface when it is given a slight tap, to forces comparable with the cohesion of a solid material. Strictly speaking, all the forces of cohesion and adhesion may be considered to be electrostatic in origin, as they result from the interaction of charges on either a macroscopic or atomic level. However, the term 'electrostatic force of adhesion' is generally taken to refer to the force of adhesion due to a macroscopic charge on surfaces, either due to an externally applied charge or to charge exhange at the contacting surfaces.

In the following sections different forces of adhesion will be discussed to put into perspective the influence of electrostatic forces. A summary of the order of magnitude of each force, together with its governing equations is given in table 6.7.

Table 6.7 Summary of the adhesion forces. In this table z is the separation and z_0 is the van der Waals separation ($= 0.4$ nm).

Force	Equation Sphere of radius a on plane	Magnitude (N) $a = 10 \ \mu m$
Gravity	$F = \frac{4}{3}\pi D a^3 g$	10^{-10}
van der Waals force		
Bradley theory (smooth rigid surfaces)	$F = aA/12z_0^2$	10^{-5}–10^{-6}
Derjaguin theory	$F = 4\pi \gamma a$	3×10^{-6}–10^{-4}
JKR theory (smooth elastic sphere)	$F = 3\pi \gamma a$	
Rough surfaces	Force is reduced by about two orders of magnitude	
Electrostatic forces		
Layer of particles	$F = qE$	10^{-7}
Charged to Gaussian limit	$F = 4\pi \varepsilon_0 a^2 E_b$	10^{-7}
Single particle charged to Gaussian limit	$F = \dfrac{\pi \varepsilon_0 E_b^2 a^3}{z[\psi + \frac{1}{2}\ln 2a/z]^2}$	10^{-5}–10^{-6}
Charge exchange	$F = \pi \varepsilon_0 a \varphi^2 / z_0$	1.7×10^{-7}
Surface tension	$F = 4\pi \gamma a \cos \theta$	7×10^{-6}

6.7.2 The van der Waals force (dispersion forces)

(a) *Rigid bodies*

The van der Waals force occurs between any two atoms and arises from the rapid fluctuations in electron density within an atom. At any instant, an atom has a net dipole moment, which induces a distortion in the charge distribution of a neighbouring atom so there is a mutual attraction. The force is strong at close range, but falls off very rapidly with distance. The force between two atoms is proportional to $1/d^7$ at distances less than 20 nm and $1/d^8$ at larger distances (Israelachvilli 1974).

For solid bodies, the combined effect of all the atoms must be considered and the following equations have been derived for the force, F, and energy of the interaction, U, between two smooth bodies (Bradley 1932). For two spheres of radius a:

$$U = -Aa/12z_0 \tag{6.25}$$

$$F = Aa/12z_0^2 \tag{6.26}$$

where A is the Hamaker constant and z_0 is the separation: for a sphere of radius a and a plane

$$u = -Aa/6z_0 \qquad (6.27)$$

$$F = Aa/6z_0^2 \qquad (6.28)$$

for two planes

$$U = -A/12\pi z_0^3 \qquad (6.29)$$

$$F = A/6\pi z_0^2. \qquad (6.30)$$

In order to calculate the force of adhesion between perfectly smooth bodies it is necessary to evaluate A and z_0.

The Hamaker constant, A, can be calculated for a given pair of materials if the refractive index, dipole moment and density of the materials is known (Lifshitz 1956, Krupp 1967). It usually lies between 10^{-19} and 10^{-18} J. The separation constant z_0 cannot be calculated, and is normally estimated by measurements of perfectly smooth surfaces or by modelling (Zimon 1969). It is generally taken to be of the order of 0.4 nm. Experimental verification of the Lifshitz theory, which allows the Hamaker constant to be calculated from bulk dielectric properties is not easy. The most direct measurements of the force between solid surfaces are those of Tabor and Winterton (1969) and Israelachvilli and Tabor (1972), who used cylindrical sheets of mica to obtain perfectly smooth surfaces. The disagreement between theory and experiment is significant at low separations (see figure 6.31), but it is not clear whether this is because of approximations inherent in the theory or because of the influence of other forces of adhesion (Tabor 1977).

The energy of adhesion may also be considered in terms of the energy required to create a new surface. If two parallel surfaces of materials 1 and 2 are in a medium of material 3, the surface free energy when the surfaces are in contact is γ_{12}. The surface free energy of the surfaces when separated is $\gamma_{13} + \gamma_{23}$; i.e. the change in energy on separation of the surfaces is

$$\gamma_{13} + \gamma_{23} - \gamma_{12}.$$

This can be equated to the adhesion energy of the two spheres given by equation (6.26):

$$\gamma_{13} + \gamma_{23} - \gamma_{12} = A_{12}/12\pi z_0^2. \qquad (6.31)$$

This gives a value for the Hamaker constant in terms of the surface free energy which is a measurable quantity. If

$$\gamma_{13} = \gamma_{23} = \gamma \qquad \text{and} \qquad \gamma_{12} \ll \gamma_{13}$$

then the force between a sphere of radius a and a plane is

$$F = 4\pi a\gamma. \qquad (6.32)$$

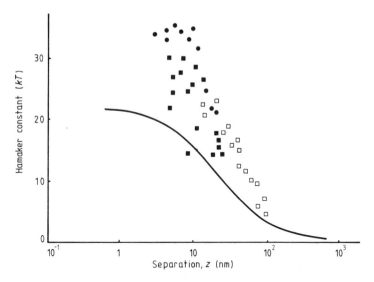

Figure 6.31 Hamaker constant in units of kT as a function of the separation for a sphere on a plane or crossed cylinders (from Tabor 1977). The full curve is prediction of the theory of Chan and Richmond and experimental points are due to Tabor *et al* in three different sets of experiments, see Tabor (1977).

The equivalence of the surface free energy approach and the equations derived by summing the effect of individual atoms, was first demonstrated by Bradley (1932), who showed that equations of the same form were obtained in calculating both the van der Waals adhesion and the surface free energy.

(b) *Elastic bodies*

In the derivations of the equations above it is assumed that the spheres are rigid. If they are able to deform elastically or plastically, the area in true molecular contact may be increased, leading to higher adhesive forces. At the same time an elastic stress built into the contact will aid the disruption force.

In 1896 Hertz derived an expression for the radius a of the contact area of two perfectly smooth spheres of radius r_1 and r_2 pressed together with a load P:

$$r^3 = \tfrac{3}{4}\pi(k_1 + k_2)aP \tag{6.33}$$

where $a = a_1 a_2/(a_1 + a_2)$, $k = (1 - v^2)/\pi Y$, Y is Young's modulus and v is Poisson's ratio. For a sphere pressing on to a flat surface the radius of the circle of contact is given by

$$r^3 = \tfrac{3}{8}\pi Pa(k_1 + k_2) \tag{6.34}$$

or where the two materials are the same by

$$r^3 = \tfrac{3}{4}\pi Pa(1 - v^2)Y^{-1}. \tag{6.35}$$

Derjaguin suggested that if the external force were reversed, the surfaces would separate when they reach their undeformed shape. In this case the pull-off force at the moment of separation is equal to its value for non-deformable solids:

$$F = 4\pi\gamma a. \tag{6.36}$$

If there were no adhesion, the contact area with zero applied load would be zero. With adhesion, the radius of the contact circle between a sphere and a plane of the same material, with no externally applied load is

$$r_0^3 = 3\pi a^2 \gamma (1 - v^2)/2Y \tag{6.37}$$

(Derjaguin *et al* 1975).

Roberts (1969) found that the contact area for low loads was larger than would be expected from the classical Hertz theory. However, this theory ignores the forces which are close to, but outside, the contact circle and also produces a deformed shape which is not compatible with the overall distribution of the surface forces, according to the principles of contact mechanics. When these factors are included, Johnson *et al* (1971) calculated that the radius of the contact area is given by

$$r^3 = \tfrac{3}{4}\pi a(k_1 + k_2)\{P + 6\gamma\pi aP + [12\gamma\pi aP + (6\gamma\pi a)^2]^{1/2}\}. \tag{6.38}$$

When the surface free energy $\gamma = 0$ this reverts to the classical Hertz formula. At zero applied load the contact area is finite and equal to

$$r_0^3 = 9\pi^2(k_1 + k_2)\gamma r^2. \tag{6.39}$$

The shape of the deformation at the contact region is shown in figure 6.32(*a*). According to the theory of Johnson, Kendall and Roberts, when the surfaces are pulled apart there is a sudden instability when the rate of release of mechanical energy in the contact zone exceeds the surface energy requirements and the surface parts when the force is given by

$$F = 3\pi\gamma r. \tag{6.40}$$

Israelachvilli *et al* (1980) simultaneously measured the adhesion and the area of contact between molecularly smooth surfaces of mica which were coated with adsorbed layers to change their surface free energy. They found that the theory of Johnson, Kendall and Roberts provided the correct value for the shape of the contact zone, but underestimated the force required to separate the surfaces. The separation force was better represented by Derjaguin's equation (equation (6.32)).

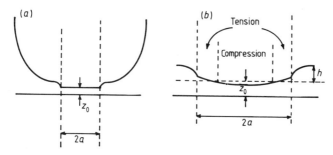

Figure 6.32 The interaction between an elastic sphere and a hard flat surface according to the Johnson–Kendall–Roberts theory. (*b*) is an enlargement of the contact area of (*a*) (from Tabor 1977).

The analysis of Johnson, Kendall and Roberts assumes linear elasticity applies and also that the force outside the contact zone is zero, i.e. in figure 6.32(*b*), $h \gg z_0$. Tabor (1977) showed that this assumption is valid down to radii of about $10^{-7}\ \mu$m for a hard material and $10^{-8}\ \mu$m for a thermoplastic material.

(c) *Rough surfaces*

The van der Waals force is essentially short range, therefore it is strongly dependent on the true area of contact between the surfaces, and sub-micrometre-sized surface asperities have a profound effect on the overall adhesive force.

As a first approximation, the van der Waals force for rough surfaces is estimated by taking the radius in the formulae above to be the radius of the surface asperities (Zimon 1969). The elastic constants of small asperities are not necessarily the same as the bulk material, for example, submicrometre asperities may remain under conditions where bulk deformation of the material occurs (Chives *et al* 1974). Fuller and Tabor (1975) measured the adhesion between optically flat rubber surfaces and roughened Perspex and showed that the adhesion was hardly altered for very small surface asperities but then fell suddenly (figure 6.33). Surface asperities which were much smaller than the bulk deformation of the rubber were able to reduce the force of adhesion significantly. If the surface roughness was assumed to be uniform and the force of adhesion is governed by the radius of the asperities, as suggested by Zimon, a linear relationship between the adhesion and the mean radius of the surface roughness would be predicted. Fuller and Tabor's result may be explained if it is assumed that the adhesion is dominated by a few high asperities which exert a high elastic force. It was shown that the adhesion depended on the ratio of the mean deviation of the asperity heights to the extension which an asperity junction can sustain before adhesion fails (Tabor 1977, Fuller and Tabor 1975).

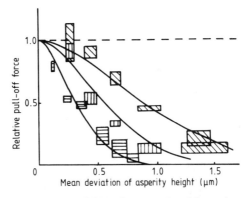

Figure 6.33 Relative pull-off force for smooth rubber spheres in contact with a flat perspex surface as a function of the surface roughness of the perspex. Full curves, theory; blocks, experimental measurements (Tabor 1977).

With hard solids, such as sapphire and diamond, the adhesion was very low, even when the surface roughness scarcely exceeded atomic dimensions, and the surfaces were extremely clean in a vacuum of 10^{-10} Torr.

Tabor defined a factor θ:

$$\theta = \frac{Yz^{3/2}a^{1/2}}{r\gamma} \tag{6.41}$$

and proposed that adhesion falls to a very low value when θ exceeds about ten. The denominator is a measure of the adhesive force experienced by a sphere of radius a, and the numerator (apart from a small numerical factor) turns out to be the elastic force required to push a sphere of radius a to a depth z in to an elastic solid of modulus Y.

As the load on a spherical asperity is increased a point is reached where the elastic limit of one of the materials is exceeded. This occurs at the region where the shear stresses are maximum, which turns out to be a point $0.6a$ below the centre of the circle of contact of radius r, as shown in figure 6.34. As the load is increased further, the region of plasticity grows rapidly, and full plasticity is reached at a load which is about sixteen times the load for the onset of plasticity.

The yield pressure, in $kg\,m^{-2}$, averaged over the contact area πr^2, was found to be $2 \times 10^7\,kg\,m^{-2}$ for copper and $2 \times 10^8\,kg\,m^{-2}$ for tool steel. For a copper particle of radius $10\,\mu m$ (or a spherical asperity of the same size), the area of contact at zero applied load calculated from equation (6.39) is about $2 \times 10^{-13}\,m^2$. Therefore a force of 4×10^{-4} N/particle is required to produce a plastic deformation. If we have a particle of radius $10\,\mu m$ with asperities of radius $1\,\mu m$ and the same elastic constants, a force of 1.8×10^{-5} N/particle would produce plastic deformation. These forces are rather larger than the van der Waals adhesion force itself and plastic deformation of a metal contact is only likely if an external force is applied.

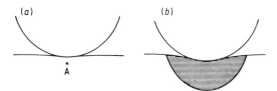

Figure 6.34 The plastic deformation of a flat surface by a harder spherical surface: (*a*), the onset of plasticity occurs at a point A; (*b*), the whole area round the contact flows plastically.

Summary

(i) The adhesion force for a perfectly smooth sphere of radius 10 μm with no deformation according to equation (6.28) is

$$F = Aa/6z_0^2.$$

For A between 1 and 10×10^{-19} J and $z_0 = 0.4$ nm:

$$F = 10^{-5} \text{–} 10^{-6} \text{ N.}$$

(ii) The adhesion force for a deformable sphere according to the Derjaguin theory is

$$F = 4\pi a\gamma$$

where γ ranges from approximately 25 mJ m^{-2} for a rubber to 1000 mJ m^{-2} for a hard solid, i.e. for a particle of radius 10 μm:

$$F = 3.1 \times 10^{-6} \text{–} 1.2 \times 10^{-4} \text{ N.}$$

(iii) The adhesion force of a deformable sphere according to the theory of Johnson, Kendall and Roberts is

$$F = 3\pi a\gamma$$

$$F = 2.3 \times 10^{-6} \text{–} 0.9 \times 10^{-4} \text{ N.}$$

For a perfectly smooth sphere of radius 10 μm, resting on a plane, forces up to 10^{-4} N could be explained by van der Waals' attraction. For realistic, rough particles maximum forces of up to 10^{-7} N are more likely.

6.7.3 Adhesion due to the presence of a liquid

The presence of water adsorbed onto surfaces affects the adhesion in several ways.

(i) The hardness of the suface is effectively reduced.

(ii) The true contact area is increased by condensation in surface pores.

(iii) For thick enough liquid films, the surface tension of a liquid film between two surfaces exerts a force binding them together.

(iv) With thick water films there is also a kinetic effect due to large frictional forces within the liquid, which must be overcome during separation of the adherents (Bikerman 1961).

The adhesion force between a smooth sphere and a solid surface in a saturated atmosphere (illustrated in figure 6.35) has been calculated by Bradley (1932), Derjaguin (1934) and Larsen (1958). The most important components of the force are:

(i) The force arising from the Laplace pressure in the liquid film. From Laplace's formula the pressure in the liquid film is

$$p = \gamma_{LV}(1/r_1 + 1/r_2). \tag{6.42}$$

The associated force is

$$F_L = p \times \pi r_1^2$$
$$= \pi \gamma a/(1 + \tan \varphi/2). \tag{6.43}$$

For small φ this reduces to

$$F_L = 4\pi a \gamma_{LV} \tag{6.44}$$

and for unwetted surfaces it becomes

$$F_L = 4\pi a \gamma_{LV} \cos \theta \qquad \text{where } \theta \text{ is the contact angle.} \tag{6.45}$$

(ii) The solid–solid force at contact (which is present in the absence of condensed liquid):

$$F_A = 4\pi \gamma_{SL} a. \tag{6.46}$$

(iii) The surface tension force at the liquid–vapour boundary is

$$F_T = 2\pi a \gamma_{LV} \sin \varphi \, \sin(\theta + \varphi). \tag{6.47}$$

If r_2 and $r_1 \ll a$, then θ and φ are very small and this force is negligible compared with the Laplace pressure force.

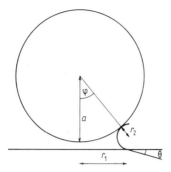

Figure 6.35 A sphere on a flat surface with liquid condensation.

Capillary condensation of water begins at a relative humidity of about 65 %, and a distinct rise in the force of adhesion between particles is observed at this level of humidity (Zimon 1969). Cross and Picknett (1963) found that the adhesion of a 200 μm particle was increased by a factor of thirty when the relative humidity was increased from 49 % to saturation, but a smaller increase was found with smaller particles (Corn 1961).

In practice the adhesion at 65 % relative humidity is only about 50 % of the value predicted for the force arising from the Laplace pressure. It then increases more or less linearly with relative humidity, but it remains below the level calculated from the Laplace pressure for relative humidities up to 97 %. Fisher and Israelachvilli (1981) investigated the increase in adhesion due to condensation for a range of liquids and found that the Laplace force dominated adhesion, provided the liquid–vapour surface tension exceeded the solid–vapour interfacial energy, and r_2 exceeded 10 nm. However, for water, the bulk laws of thermodynamics, which are used to calculate the Laplace pressure, applied only when $r_2 > 5$ nm, and this corresponded to partial pressures greater than 95 %. For cyclohexane, the classical calculations were applicable for r_2 at least as small as 1 nm, and equation (6.43) is applicable to much lower values of partial pressure.

For liquids with low surface tension, the adhesion is dominated by the surface–surface contribution, in spite of the presence of condensed liquid. Liquid forces can substantially alter the deformation of the surface but this has little effect on the measured adhesion (Fisher and Israelachvilli 1981).

Bhattacharya and Mittal (1978) investigated the effect of water vapour on the adhesion of particles, using an air jet to remove glass particles up to 10 μm in diameter from a surface. Although it is difficult to interpret their results in terms of an adhesion force, it was clear that the presence of water vapour considerably increased adhesion. Baking to 180 °C did not decrease the adhesion, perhaps because water was still held in small pores in the surface or perhaps because a bond was formed with salts present in the surface water film, present at high humidities.

Summary
The surface tension of water is about $73 \times 10^{-3} \, \text{N m}^{-1}$. Therefore for a 10 μm radius sphere contacting a plane (where both are hydrophilic so that $\theta = 0$):

$$F = 9.2 \times 10^{-6} \, \text{N}.$$

For glass, with a contact angle of 30°, this reduces to $7.8 \times 10^{-6} \, \text{N}$. At relative humidities of 65 % an adhesion of half this value might be expected, increasing approximately linearly with relative humidity. Capillary forces due to the condensation of water or other liquids do not depend on surface roughness and usually dominate all except chemical forces of adhesion when the relative humidity of the atmosphere exceeds 65 %.

6.7.4 Chemical forces

Materials (except those freshly cleaved in a high vacuum) are covered in surface layers such as oxides and physisorbed or chemisorbed gases. These satisfy the chemical bonds at the surface so no direct chemical bonding occurs at an interface. At high temperatures or pressures, the surface layers may be disrupted and chemical bonding can occur between atoms. As the temperature and pressure are increased plastic deformation of asperities occurs, eventually the contact grows by viscous flow and diffusion and the materials are sintered. In the early stages of sintering elastic stress is stored in the contact region but when this is relieved, the adhesion force is comparable with the bulk strength of the material. Sintering can begin at about 50 % of the melting point of a material. A review of sintering of metals and ceramics is given by Kuczynski (1972). The minimum sintering temperature of materials has been measured by Compo *et al* (1984).

Chemical forces can also be formed if one material diffuses into another, or if a chemical reaction occurs at an interface, for example oxidation between two touching metal surfaces may lead to the formation of a common oxide layer. Whenever chemical bonds are formed adhesion forces are considerably larger than van der Waals' or electrostatic forces.

6.7.5 Electrostatic forces of adhesion

Three types of electrostatic force may be distinguished;

(i) the force arising from a net charge carried by the surfaces,
(ii) the force arising from charge exchange at the interface between two contacting solids,
(iii) the force arising from an externally applied electric field.

(a) *Coulomb force due to a net charge on a surface*
It is shown in Chapter 7 that the force between any two charged bodies is given by

$$F = \tfrac{1}{2} \int \varepsilon_0 \varepsilon_r E^2 \, dA \qquad (6.48)$$

i.e. the force can be found by calculating the electric field between the bodies and integrating the square of the electric field over one of the surfaces.

For plane surfaces in a dielectric medium, ε_r, the force is simply

$$F = \tfrac{1}{2} \varepsilon_r \varepsilon_0 E^2 A.$$

In general the electric field must be found by solving Laplace's equation, as discussed in Chapter 7. A precise solution is available only for simple geometries and approximations must be made to estimate the size of the electrostatic force in most practical situations.

The adhesion force between two spheres, or between a sphere and a plane has been estimated in a number of different ways. In the simplest approximation the charge is assumed to be situated at a point at the centre of the sphere and the force of attraction between a sphere and a plane is then the force between the point charge and its electrical image in the plane.

The Coulomb force of attraction between a point charge q, and its image charge $-q$, is

$$F = -q^2/4\pi\varepsilon_0 d^2. \qquad (6.49)$$

If the sphere is in contact with the plane, the effective interaction distance between the charges is twice the particle radius and the Coulomb attraction is

$$F = -q^2/4\pi\varepsilon_0 4a^2 \qquad (6.50)$$

when the sphere is a distance z from the plane

$$F = -q^2/16\pi\varepsilon_0(a + z)^2.$$

For a particle charged to the Gaussian limit

$$q = 4\pi a^2 \varepsilon_0 E_b \qquad (6.51)$$

where E_b is the breakdown field of air. The Coulomb force between a particle of radius 10 μm in contact with a plane, calculated from equation (6.50) is

$$F = 2.5 \times 10^{-8} \text{ N}.$$

In practice, the charge will be attracted towards its image and the particle will be polarised. The effective distance between point charges is therefore less than $2(a + z)$ and equation (6.51) underestimates the force.

The equipotential surfaces for a point charge and its image, a distance x from a plane are not spheres, but take the form shown in figure 7.15. It can be seen that, if $x - a \ll a$, then a charged sphere near an earthed plane cannot be represented by a single point charge. However, in a two-dimensional approximation the equipotential surfaces for a point charge in front of a line are circles and the charge on the surface of the circle can be considered to be at a point P, where P is defined such that $b(d - b) = a^2$ (figure 6.36).

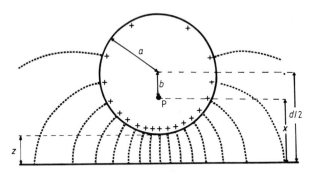

Figure 6.36 Polarisation of a charged circle near an earthed line. The charge acts as if it is situated at a point P where $b(d - b) = a^2$. This is directly applicable to a rod-shaped particle in front of an earthed plane and is an approximation to a sphere in front of a plane.

The force between two circles separated by a distance d, or between a single circle and a line at a distance $\tfrac{1}{2}d$ is

$$F = -q^2/16\pi\varepsilon_0 x^2.$$

Referring to figure 6.36, it can be seen that

$$x = \tfrac{1}{2}d - b.$$

where $b(d - b) = a^2$.

Combining these equations so the position of the point charge is expressed in terms of the sphere radius and the distance of its centre from the plane

$$x^2 = \tfrac{1}{4}d^2 - a^2.$$

but $\tfrac{1}{2}d = z + a$, i.e.

$$x^2 = z(z + 2a).$$

and

$$F = q^2/16\pi\varepsilon_0 z(z + 2a). \tag{6.52}$$

If $z \ll a$ then

$$F = q^2/8\pi\varepsilon_0 az. \tag{6.53}$$

This equation is an exact solution for the force per unit length of a cylinder, with a charge q per unit length, but it is only a rough approximation for a sphere near a plane.

A more precise calculation of the force between a sphere and a plane was carried out by Russel (1909). He considered the force between two charged spheres or a sphere and a plane in terms of the rate of change of stored energy as the surfaces were separated:

$$F = dU/dz$$

where the energy, U, between the bodies is given by

$$U = \tfrac{1}{2}CV^2.$$

He calculated the capacitance, C, between the sphere and the plane in air, to be

$$C = 4\pi\varepsilon_0 a(\psi + \tfrac{1}{2}\ln 2a/z) \tag{6.54}$$

where ψ is Euler's constant ($= 0.577$). Therefore

$$F = \frac{d}{dz}(\tfrac{1}{2}CV^2) = \pi\varepsilon_0 aV^2/z. \tag{6.55}$$

Since $C = q/V$, this may also be written as

$$F = q^2/[16\pi\varepsilon_0 az(\psi + \tfrac{1}{2}\ln 2a/z)^2]. \tag{6.56}$$

For a sphere of radius 10 μm with a separation distance of $z_0 = 0.4$ nm charged to the Gaussian limit the force calculated from equation (6.56) is

$$F = 1.7 \times 10^{-5}\,\text{N}.$$

If the separation is due to a 10 nm thick oxide layer the force is given by

$$F = 1.3 \times 10^{-6}.$$

At first glance all three approximations would seem to be reasonable, however, as z/a decreases they start to diverge markedly, as illustrated in table 6.8. When z is small, the assumption that the charge acts at the centre of the sphere underestimates the force, while the two-dimensional approximation gives an overestimate.

Davis (1969) calculated the force of adhesion for both conducting and dielectric spheres by solving Laplace's equation in bispherical coordinates to obtain the electric field round the sphere. He evaluated equation (6.48) numerically for the cases of a charged sphere and an uncharged sphere of

Table 6.8 Comparison of calculations for electrostatic adhesion forces between a sphere and a plane.

Equation	$z = 2a$	$z = a/100$	$z = a/1000$
(6.51)	$q^2/144\pi\varepsilon_0 a^2$	$0.06q^2/\pi\varepsilon_0 a^2$	$0.06q^2/\pi\varepsilon_0 a^2$
(6.52)	$q^2/128\pi\varepsilon_0 a^2$	$3.12q^2/\pi\varepsilon_0 a^2$	$31.2q^2/\pi\varepsilon_0 a^2$
(6.56)	$q^2/128\pi\varepsilon_0 a^2$	$0.60q^2/\pi\varepsilon_0 a^2$	$3.26q^2/\pi\varepsilon_0 a^2$

radius a in an electric field. He found that for $z < 0.01a$, the force of adhesion of an insulating sphere with a relative dielectric constant of two was an order of magnitude lower than the force for a conducting sphere. If $z < 0.001a$ the difference approached two orders of magnitude (z is the distance of closest approach of the sphere).

Davis assumed that insulating particles acted in the same way as conducting particles, except in so far as the dielectric constant affected the polarisation. However, the charge on the surface of an insulating material could remain trapped at the surface. Krupp carried out a calculation assuming that the charge on the sphere and the plane resided in layers with the space charge density decreasing exponentially from the surface, i.e. the charge a distance x from each surface is given by

$$q = q_0 \exp(-x/\delta)$$

where q_0 is the charge on the surface layer. Krupp estimated that, within an error of less than 25 %, equation (6.56) becomes

$$F = \frac{q^2}{16\pi\varepsilon_0 r\delta} \frac{\ln(1 + \delta/z)}{(\psi + \frac{1}{2}\ln 2r/z)[\psi + \frac{1}{2}\ln(2r/z + \delta)]}. \tag{6.58}$$

If δ is taken to be $1\ \mu m$ and $a = 10\ \mu m$ then the adhesion force is

$$F = 1.56 \times 10^{-7}\ \mathrm{N}.$$

If the characteristic depth of charge, δ, is 10 nm then

$$F = 3.0 \times 10^{-6}\ \mathrm{N}.$$

This calculation assumes undeformed surfaces of dielectric constant 1.

(b) *Multilayers of charged particles*
If a layer of charged particles is deposited on a surface there is an additional force due to the space charge of the other particles. The force on a particle of charge q is

$$F = qE$$

where E is the field due to the other particles. It can easily be shown that if every particle is charged to the Gaussian limit the field E would exceed the breakdown strength of air. Therefore the maximum practical force of adhesion is

$$F = qE_b.$$

For a particle of radius $10\ \mu m$, charged to the Gaussian limit, this is equivalent to a force of

$$F = 10^{-7}\ \mathrm{N}.$$

(c) *Charge exchange*
When two surfaces are in contact charge will flow from one to the other as described in Chapter 2. If both particles are electrical conductors charge will

flow until the potential built up is equal to the difference in the work functions of the two materials. This contact potential difference which is typically less than 0.5 V may be substituted for V in equation (6.55). The force of attraction due to charge exchange between a spherical conductor of radius 10 μm and a plane is then

$$F = 1.7 \times 10^{-7}\,\text{N}.$$

In this approximation it has been assumed that the particle is an undeformed conductor. Let us now assume that it is a deformable insulator and that the charge is transferred only where the materials are in contact. If the charge is supposed to be stored in a parallel-plate capacitor with an area equal to the contact area A then the force required to separate the plates is

$$F = dU/dz$$

where U is the energy stored in the capacitor, but

$$U = \tfrac{1}{2}Q^2/C.$$

If the diameter of the contact area is much greater than z

$$C = \varepsilon_0 A/z$$

i.e.

$$F = Q_s^2 A/2\varepsilon_0$$

where Q_s is the surface charge density. No assumption is needed about the trapping depth of the charge, but the approximation applies only to small z.

For a thermoplastic material $\gamma = 100\,\text{mJ m}^{-2}$, $Y = 10^9\,\text{N m}^{-2}$ and $v = 0.3$. The radius of the area of contact for a smooth sphere, 10 μm in radius, is given by equation (6.39) and is of the order of $10^{-7}\,\mu$m. If the surface density of charge, transferred while the surfaces are in contact, is taken to be $1 \times 10^3\,\text{C m}^{-2}$ (which is approximately the highest level measured when surfaces are separated under circumstances where breakdown is prevented) then

$$F = 2.3 \times 10^{-8}\,\text{N}.$$

This approximation will underestimate the true force for two reasons:

(i) there will always be some transverse charge migration beyond the true contact area,

(ii) the surface density of charge while the surfaces are in contact could be higher than the measured value after separation if back-tunnelling occurs.

(d) *The influence of charged double layers*
Electrostatic forces of adhesion may be affected by any charged double layers on the surface. In general these will weaken the force of adhesion

because the double layers on like surfaces will be oriented in the same direction. Roberts (1972) has measured surface double-layer repulsions of up to 10^6 N m^{-2}.

(e) *Dipole forces*
If a molecule or particle has a dipole moment it experiences a force in a non-uniform electric field. There is also a force of attraction between two dipoles (see §5.5.1). The adhesion due to the dipole force is considerably smaller than the van der Waals force and only begins to approach the same order of magnitude for strongly polar molecules (Czyzak 1952).

(f) *Adhesion in an applied electric field*
When a sphere is in contact with a plane in an applied electric field, current flow is constricted to the narrow contact area between the two and there is considerable field intensification around the contact zone which increases the force of adhesion between the particles. The force of adhesion in the presence of an external field is calculated from equation (6.48) by integrating the electric field over the particle surface.

The field round the surface of a sphere in contact with a plane, in the presence of an externally applied field, has been calculated using three different models.

(i) McLean (1977) calculated the field across the interface by assuming that there was a conduction current around the particle surface controlled by a surface resistivity ρ_s.

The resistance of an area of the sphere surface defined by the angle $\theta - \theta_0$ in figure 6.37 is given by

$$R_\theta = \frac{\rho_s}{2\pi} \int_{\theta_0}^{\theta} \frac{d\theta}{\sin \theta}.$$

The total potential drop across a hemisphere in a field E_0 is rE_0 and the potential drop across a portion of the sphere defined by an angle θ is

$$V = \frac{R_\theta a E_a}{R_{\pi/2}}.$$

The electric field, $E_z(\theta)$ at an angle θ is thus

$$E_z = V/z(\theta)$$

and the force of adhesion between two adjacent particles is given by

$$F = \tfrac{1}{2} \int \varepsilon_0 E_z^2 \, dA$$

where the integral is taken over the surface of the particle. McLean allowed the surface to deform according to Hertz's law and also allowed for the fact

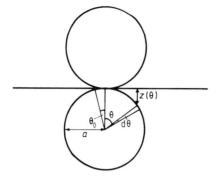

Figure 6.37 Two spherical particles in an electrical field.

that the field between the two particles cannot exceed a certain limit, E_{max}, without electrical breakdown occurring. The relevant equations were then solved numerically giving the result shown in figure 6.38.

(ii) Dietz (1978) followed the same procedure as McLean to find the electric field. He then solved the integral analytically but made no allowance for particle deformation. He found that the electrostatic force between two spherical particles was

$$F \simeq (0.415)4\pi\varepsilon_0 a^2 E_{max}^{0.8} E_0^{1.2}. \tag{6.59}$$

(iii) A general analysis, including both volume and surface conduction, has been carried out by Moslehi and Self (1984). They calculated the contact area, the maximum field and the adhesive pressure across the contact area for different ratios of the surface and volume resistivity. They found that for the case where volume conductivity dominates:

$$\theta_0 = D_v^{1/5} E_0^{2/5}$$

$$E_{max} = D_v^{-2/5} E_0^{1/5}$$

$$P = (\pi A_v \varepsilon_0 D_v^{-2/5} E_0^{6/5})/4$$

and where surface conductivity dominates:

$$\theta = D_s^{1/5}(E_0/K_s)^{2/5}$$

$$E_{max} = D_s^{-2/5}(E_0/K_s)^{1/5}$$

$$P = \tfrac{1}{4}\pi A_s \varepsilon_0 D_s^{-2/5}(E_0/K_s)^{6/5}$$

where θ_0 is the angle which defines the contact area, P is the average compressive stress across a layer of particles, $D_v = 3A_v\pi\varepsilon_0(1 - v^2)/4Y$, $A_v = 1.28$, $D_s = 3\pi\varepsilon_0 A_s(1 - v^2)/4Y$ and $A_s = 2.14$. K_s is a constant which decreases from 7.6 to 5.6 as the mean field E_0 increases from 10^4 to 10^6 V m^{-1}.

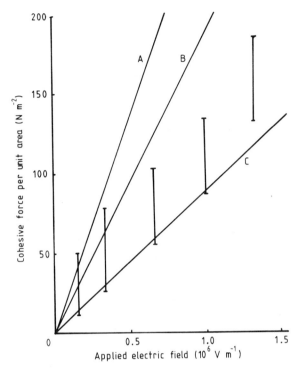

Figure 6.38 Variation of cohesive force with applied electric field. The full curves are calculated values (values of E_{max} (V m^{-1}) are: A, 3×10^7; B, 2×10^7; C, 10^7) and the bars are experimental values (after McClean 1977).

For the 10 μm polymer particle with $v = 0.3$ and $Y = 10^9$, discussed in the earlier example, in a field of 3×10^5 V m^{-1} the adhesive pressure is

$$P_v = 2.3 \times 10^3 \text{ N m}^{-2} \qquad \text{assuming volume conduction}$$

and

$$P_s = 3.6 \times 10^2 \text{ N m}^{-2} \qquad \text{assuming surface conduction.}$$

P is the average compressive stress therefore it must be multiplied by the cross sectional area of the particle to give the force per particle, i.e.

$$F_v = 7.2 \times 10^{-7} \text{ N}$$

$$F_s = 1.1 \times 10^{-7} \text{ N.}$$

These forces are higher for harder materials because the smaller contact area leads to greater field distortion, i.e. for a glass, Moslehi and Self calculate pressures of 1.3×10^4 and 2.0×10^3 N m^{-2} due to volume and surface conductivities respectively.

6.7.6 Experimental measurements of adhesion forces

The most precise measurements of adhesion, where the contact area is also known, have been carried out by Tabor and his co-workers at Cambridge, UK, and more recently, by Israelachvilli at Canberra, Australia. The adhesion between smooth surfaces, where external charging has been minimised can be explained to within 30 % by van der Waals' forces alone. The discrepancy could either be due to the influence of other forces, for example, due to charge exchange between the surfaces, or due to approximations inherent in the theory of van der Waals' forces. The van der Waals' force is short range and will be considerably reduced if the surfaces are rough. Electrostatic forces are longer range, and mutual charge repulsion to some extent reduces the effect of surface roughness, therefore electrostatic forces might be expected to play a more important role as the surfaces become rougher. Fuller and Tabor (1975) were able to explain their experimental measurements of adhesion between roughened Perspex and rubber on the basis of van der Waals' forces alone; however, a number of experiments have been carried out which indicate that, under some circumstances, electrostatic forces are important.

Derjaguin and Smilga (1967) summarised the experimental evidence for the importance of the role of a double layer of charge in the adhesion of films to surfaces as follows.

(i) Fast electron emission has been observed to accompany the peeling of a polymer film from a surface (Karassev *et al* 1953). The potential difference between the surfaces evaluated from measurements of this phenomena are able to account for the observed detachment force.

(ii) Siloxane compounds have been used to modify the adhesion between two surfaces and it has been found that there is a deep minimum in the adhesion in the region where the double-layer reverses polarity (Krotova and Morozova 1959).

(iii) The charges measured on peeled polymer surfaces, under circumstances where no gas discharge could occur, agreed with the results derived from the mechanical work required to peel the layer from the substrate (Derjaguin and Smilga 1958).

(iv) The dependence of the work of detachment of polymer films on the peeling rate and on the pressure and nature of the gas medium can be readily interpreted on the basis of electrostatic forces.

A number of attempts have been made to correlate the force of adhesion with the electrostatic charge on the surfaces after separation. The adhesion of particles to surfaces has been measured using centrifugal forces or by using vibration or an air jet. Measurements of the adhesion of large particles have also been made using the deflection of a cantilevered beam (Corn 1961, Uber *et al* 1984).

Donald (1972) measured the force required to remove fine particles from glass beads and the charge on the particles which had been removed. He found a strong relationship between the charge after separation and the adhesive force. Zimon *et al* (1964) showed that the charge measured on glass spheres was proportional to the force required to detach them from a painted surface. Derjaguin *et al* (1968) removed particles from a surface, using the impact from a pneumatically driven bullet, and measured the charge on the particles by measuring their deflection as they fell through an electric field. In this experiment the adhesive force and the charge on the particle both increased in proportion to approximately the square of the particle radius. Derjaguin explained his results assuming that there was an electrostatic force

$$F = 2\pi Q_s^2 A$$

where A is the contact area. In a similar experiment, Uber *et al* (1984) found no relationship between charge and adhesion. Although several authors have suggested that a relationship between the charge after separation and the adhesive force implies an electrostatic component of adhesion it should be noted that both the van der Waals force of adhesion and the amount of charge exchanged would be expected to increase with true contact area and the charge need not be the direct cause of the increased adhesion.

The influence of charge exchange forces can be investigated more directly by changing the double-layer properties of an interface and measuring the change in adhesion. For example, Schnabel (1970) illuminated the contact area of a CdS–Zr interface, to change the charge exchange properties of the CdS surface. The adhesion force changed by a maximum factor of about 2.6. This agreed well with the change in adhesion expected when the change in the work function of CdS, due to illumination, was substituted into equation (6.55).

A number of experiments have been carried out which indicate that the adhesion of particles is significantly increased if the particles are given a net electrostatic charge. Kottler *et al* (1968) measured the adhesion of polymer particles, with radii of the order of 20 μm, to selenium. The adhesion force rose with the amount of free charge applied to the particles and the authors were able to interpret their results by supposing that the electrostatic force compressed the surface asperities so that the van der Waals adhesion was increased. Charges of about 3×10^{-14} C/particle increased the adhesion by a factor of about twenty over an uncharged particle. The median adhesion force for 20 μm particles with a charge of 6×10^{-14} C, adhering directly to the selenium, was 2×10^{-6} N. The median particle-to-particle adhesion force in a multilayer was 8×10^{-7} N.

Cross (1975, 1979) measured the adhesion of layers of particles to metal and glass surfaces, using a centrifuge. The acceleration required to remove 50 % of the particles was multiplied by the mean particle mass to obtain a measure of the median adhesion force. The relative humidity was held below 25 %. Particles of a range of different materials with the particle radii in the range 5–50 μm were tested. The following results were obtained.

(i) The force required to remove 50 % of the layer (which was up to ten layers thick) lay in the range 1×10^{-8}–7×10^{-6} N. With some powders, some particles remained on the surface at the highest accelerations which were applied, i.e. the adhesion exceeded 10^{-5} N.

(ii) The adhesion was greater if particles were charged before deposition on the surface (even when the particles were sufficiently conducting that the charge had decayed to the earthed substrate before the adhesion measurement was made).

(iii) Smooth spherical particles adhered more strongly than ground powders of the same material.

(iv) A soft, spherical powder (Perspex) adhered more strongly than a hard, spherical powder, (glass with a hydrophobic surface), but the glass spheres were more adhesive than any of the ground polymers.

(v) Powders which were deposited in a corona discharge adhered more strongly than those charged by friction. This was shown to be due to the current of ions which had flowed through the deposited powder, rather than to the electric field. The adhesion of a frictionally charged layer could be increased by passing a corona current through it for a period of a few minutes.

(vi) The electrical resistivity of a charged powder had a strong effect on its adhesion and could be divided into four regimes.

(a) $\rho > 10^{14}\,\Omega$ m. Some of the powder charge was lost by discharge processes as the layer formed and back-ionisation occurred. Residual charge was retained while the measurements were made.

(b) $10^{10}\,\Omega$ m $< \rho < 10^{13}\,\Omega$ m. Discharges still occurred as the powder was deposited, but the residual charge decayed within about a minute of deposition, (i.e. before the adhesion measurement was made).

(c) $10^{7}\,\Omega$ m $< \rho < 10^{10}\,\Omega$ m. The charge on the powder in this range was lost rapidly and without back-ionisation.

(d) $\rho < 10^{6}\,\Omega$ m. These powders were metals without a significant insulating oxide layer.

Powders in groups (a) and (b) had a similar adhesion which was affected more by the particle shape than by its resistivity or hardness. PTFE and polyethylene, which have low surface free energies, had the smallest adhesion, however tests also showed that they charged less effectively than the other powders in a corona discharge. The adhesion of all the powders in group (c), which included oxidisable metals, such as aluminium, as well as calcium tungstate and a glass sample, was an order of magnitude lower than powders in groups (a) and (b). Powders deposited in a corona discharge gave a higher adhesion than those charged by induction, even though the charge decayed immediately on contact with the substrate. The powders in group (d) were removed by accelerations of only a few *g* and the rotor could not be moved from the deposition area to the centrifuge without dislodging the layer.

Clearly an external electrostatic charge can change the adhesion force by more than an order of magnitude. This could be due either to a direct electrostatic component of adhesion, or to an increase in the van der Waals force as a result of an increase in true contact area, produced by electrostatic forces. The observation that the passage of a current through a powder layer gives a permanent increase in adhesion and that increased adhesion remains after a charge has decayed supports the idea that an electrostatically enhanced van der Waals adhesion is involved. However, it is also possible to postulate current-enhanced charge exchange at the interface and the influence of electrostatic forces in adhesion cannot yet be quantitatively explained.

6.7.7 Cohesion of powders

The influence of electrostatic forces between particles on the flow properties of a powder is hard to define because charge differences within an agglomerated mass cannot usually be measured. However there is some evidence that, at least in some cases, electrostatic forces play a part. One investigation involved two PVC powders, both with a particle diameter of about 200 μm but manufactured by different methods. Each powder was free flowing but a mixture of the two had extremely poor flow properties. The electrostatic charge on the particles was evaluated by spreading the powder very thinly on a substrate and measuring the electric field with a high-resolution probe with a diameter of 75 μm. The electric field seen by the probe, as it was scanned across the powder, is shown in figure 6.39. It can be seen that the electrostatic activity was much greater for the powder mixture than for either powder alone and the difference was greater than is likely from slight height variations which arise from agglomeration. The use of a free-flow agent, which was an extremely fine alumina powder, reduced the electrostatic activity to a very low level, although the alumina was itself electrically insulating. This would seem to indicate that the use of free-flow agents, which are generally believed to act mainly by reducing the real contract area between particles, also affects the electrostatic charge exchange.

There is circumstantial evidence that electrostatic charging has a significant effect on flow during pneumatic conveying. Observations of increased pressure losses have been explained in electrostatic terms by Weaver *et al* (1982) and the discharge of accumulated charge is believed to explain violent upsets in the flow pattern (Larouere *et al* 1984). Joseph and Klinzing (1983) studied flow at the choking point (i.e. the transition between dilute-phase conveying and dense-phase flow where solids are carried by air slugs). The pressure drop and pressure fluctuations in the choking region were much more violent at low humidities where electrostatic effects were expected to be greatest.

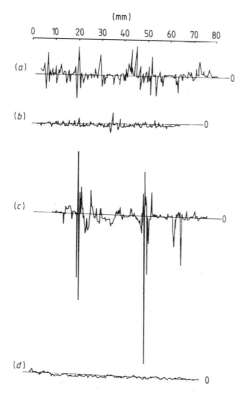

Figure 6.39 The electrostatic charge along a line across a single layer of PVC powder: (*a*), suspension PVC; (*b*), mass PVC; (*c*), mixture; (*d*), mixture + free-flow agent. The same arbitary scale is used for all samples.

Cohesion of powders in an electric field

A number of experiments have been carried out which show that the cohesion of a bed of particles is increased by the application of an electric field and this effect has been used to control the flow of powdered materials as described in §5.8.1. The following experiments have been carried out to quantify this effect.

(i) Johnson and Melcher (1975) measured the pressure drop across a packed bed of powder at incipient fluidisation as a function of electric field and obtained the results shown in figure 5.50.

(ii) Dietz (1976), and Dietz and Melcher (1978) measured the friction coefficient of a fluidised bed of powder using a modification of a Couette viscometer. The test cell consisted of two concentric cylindrical electrodes with the powder fluidised between them. The outer cylinder was rotated at a constant speed and the torque on the inner cylinder was measured as a function of applied electric field.

(iii) Robinson and Jones (1984a) measured the yield stress of a brass sled in packed beds of powder (glass beads and sand) when an electric field was applied perpendicular to the direction in which stress was applied.

(iv) The same authors (Robinson and Jones 1984b) measured the angle of repose of a packed bed of the same materials as a function of electric field.

All the experiments found that the normal stress was a linear function of the electric field but there was a considerable variation in the amount of stress applied by a given electric field. However, the experiments covered a wide range of different conditions and materials. For example, both particle–particle and particle–wall contacts contributed to the angle of repose experiments, while the brass sled yield locus experiments were dominated by particle–wall contacts.

A field of 5×10^5 V m^{-1} produced an electric stress of between 50 and 600 N m^{-2}. For example, Robinson and Jones found an effective electric stress of 200 N m^{-2} between glass spheres 600 μm in diameter. This is approximately 2×10^{-4} N/particle assuming close packing.

APPENDIX

Ten rules for the elimination of electrostatic hazards

(i) Design plant to minimise the extent and volume of any flammable atmospheres.

(ii) Reduce static by reducing velocities of separation.

(iii) Earth all metal plant and accessories (drums, funnels etc).

(iv) Provide all people who may come into contact with a flammable atmosphere with antistatic footwear.

(v) Floors in areas where flammable atmospheres exist should not be highly insulating and should be kept free from insulating materials such as paint residues.

(vi) Only the essential use of plastics should be permitted in hazardous areas.

(vii) Electrostatic eliminators, which are not themselves capable of producing incendiary sparks should be used on films or sheets of insulating material which must enter a flammable atmosphere.

(viii) Antistatic additives should be used where possible to increase the electrical conductivity of insulating liquids such as xylene and toluene preferably to a level of at least 100 pS m^{-1}.

(ix) Vessels which contain powder clouds of low minimum ignition energy should be provided with venting or explosion suppression facilities or some way of rendering the cloud inert.

(x) Earthed protrusions (dip sticks etc) must not approach the surface of a flammable liquid until it has had time to discharge.

Standards and codes of practice

British Standards

BS 358	1960	Method for the measurement of voltage with sphere gaps
BS 1259	1958	Intrinsically safe electrical apparatus and circuits for use in explosive at-
Amendment 3605	1981	mospheres
BS 1870 Pt 1	1979	Safety footwear
BS 2044	1984	Methods of determining resistivity of conducting and antistatic plastics and rubbers
BS 2050	1978	Electrical resistance of conductive and antistatic products made from flexible polymeric material
BS 4683	1971	Electrical apparatus for explosive at-
Amendment 4275	1983	mospheres
BS 5345 Pt 1	1976	Basic requirements of the code of practice for the selection, installation and maintenance of electrical apparatus for use in potentially explosive atmospheres
BS 5451	1977	Specification of electrically conducting and antistatic footwear
BS 5458	1977	Safety requirements for indicating and recording electrical measuring instruments and their accessories
BS 5501 Pt 1	1977	General requirements for electrical apparatus for potentially explosive atmospheres
BS 5501	1977	Electrical apparatus for potentially explosive atmospheres
BS 5783	1984	Electrostatic sensitive devices han-
Amendment 4705	1984	dling code
BS 5908	1980	Fire precautions in chemical plant

BS 5958 Pt 1	1980	Control of undesirable static electricity General considerations
BS 5958 Pt 2	1983	Recommendations for particular industrial situations
BS 6233	1982	Recommended method of test for volume and surface resistivities of insulating materials
Code of Practice 326	1975	The protection of structures against lightning
Code of Practice 1003	1960	Electrical apparatus and associated equipment for use in explosive atmospheres of gas or varpour other than mining applications
Code of Practice 3013		Fire precautions in chemical plant

International Electrical Commission

IEC 31		Electrical equipment for explosive atmospheres
IEC 79-1–79-11	1978	Electrical apparatus for explosive gas atmospheres
79-12		Classification of mixtures of gases or vapours with air according to their maximum experimental safe gaps and minimum ignition currents
IEC 79-1A	1975	Construction and test of flame-proof enclosure of electrical apparatus
IEC 93		Recommended method of test for volume and surface resistivities of insulating materials

National Fire Protection Association (USA)

1 Fire prevention code.
49 Hazardous chemical data.
68 Guide to explosion venting.
69 Explosion prevention systems.
63 Industrial plant–dust explosions.
77 Static electricity recommended practice.
325 The properties of flammable liquids, gases and solids.
493 Intrinsically safe apparatus.
704 The fire hazards of materials.

General
Highly Flammable Liquid and Liquefied Petroleum Gas Regulations 1972 (London: HMSO)
Dust explosions in factories *Health and Safety at Work Booklet No 22* (London: HMSO)

HSE Electrical Equipment Certification Guide 1982 (Issued by British Health and Safety Executive Electrical Equipment Certification Services)

Classification of hazardous areas

The classification of hazards is based on reducing the probability of an explosion to an acceptably low level. The degree of hazard depends on a combination of probabilities:

    (a) the probability that an explosive atmosphere will be present,

    (b) the probability that that atmosphere will ignite and

    (c) the expected extent of direct or indirect damage as a result of an explosion.

According to IEC 79-1 to 79-11 areas may be zoned as follows:

zone 2   explosive atmosphere not likely and of short duration,

zone 1   explosive atmosphere likely but not for long periods and

zone 0   explosive atmosphere present continuously (or frequently) for long periods.

Gas groups are classified by the IEC according to the maximum experimental safe gap (MESG) and the minimum ignition current (MIC) relative to the MIC of methane in a particular piece of apparatus described in IERC publication 79-1A. The groups are:

group I   methane endangered areas in coal mines,

group II   explosion endangered areas other than coal mines.

Group	MESG (mm)	MIC
IIA	> 0.9	> 0.8
IIB	0.5–0.9	0.45–0.8
IIC	> 0.5	< 0.45

(Some gases are close to the borderline of IIA and IIB which, in view of the statistical scatter of results, makes classification difficult. These may be referred to as IIA/B gases.) The British code of safe practice for the control of undesirable static electricity makes no distinction between gas types as gases from all three classes are capable of being ignited by electrostatic sparks of the energies frequently available.

Recommended safe levels

These are recommended limits at the time of publication of the data concerned. They are intended only as a guide to orders of magnitude. Tests are constantly reducing the limits which determine safe situations and the data below may have been superseded in more recent work unknown to the author. There is not necessarily agreement from country to country and, except where otherwise stated, the values are taken from research papers not the certifying or governmental bodies.

Insulating liquids must have a minimum conductivity of 100 pS m^{-1} (Loveland 1981), 50 pS m^{-1} (Gibson 1983) or 1000 pS m^{-1} if there is vigorous stirring or mixing (Loveland 1983, Gibson 1983). The charge build-up during agitation or dispersion in a liquid becomes potentially hazardous at charge levels of 10–50 μC m^{-3} (Krämer 1981). The maximum safe charge density on plastic surfaces in a 0.2 mJ atmosphere is -3 μC m^{-2} or $+5$ μC m^{-2} (Tolson 1981). The maximum safe voltage on personnel is less than 5 kV (Tolson 1980, Wilson 1983). The total surface area of plastics should not exceed the sizes given in the table below (Schön 1982, IEC 79).

Gas group	Zone 0	Zone 1	Zone 2
IIA	50	100	
IIB	25	50	No limit
IIC	4	20	

NB Smaller areas may cause an ignition. For example, an area of polyethylene of area 12 cm^2 had a probability of 0.001 of igniting a 0.2 mJ mixture (Gibson 1983).

Alternative criteria for zone 0 are 4 cm^2 for gases with a minimum ignition energy of less than 0.04 mJ, and 20 cm^2 for a gas of minimum ignition energy 0.2 mJ.

Surface resistance of a plastic should not exceed 10^9 Ω at 23 °C and 50 % relative humidity or 10^{11} Ω in specified extreme temperature and humidity conditions. (This does not apply to zone 0 or type-IIC gases.)

Liquid flow velocities must be less than 7 m s^{-1} for single-phase systems and less than 1 m s^{-1} for multiphase systems (Gibson 1983, BS 5958):

velocity (m s^{-1}) × pipe diameter (m) < 0.38   liquid conductivity
$\qquad\qquad\qquad\qquad\qquad\qquad\qquad\qquad\qquad$ < 5 pS m^{-1}

velocity (m s^{-1}) × pipe diameter (m) < 0.5   liquid conductivity
$\qquad\qquad\qquad\qquad\qquad\qquad\qquad\qquad\qquad$ 5–100 pS m^{-1} (BS 5958).

Earthing

A resistance to earth of 10^6 Ω is applicable to all plant (although a lower value may be chosen for convenience). Alternatively $R < 100/I$ (where I is the charging current and R the resistance to earth) is acceptable. (This is seldom able to be used in practice because of the difficulty of measuring I.) (BS 5958) Antistatic and non-metallic materials have a maximum permitted resistance of 10^6–10^8 (BS 5958, Gibson 1983).

REFERENCES

Archard J F 1959 The temperature of rubbing surfaces *Wear* **2** 438–55

Aron R B 1964 Antistatic agents *Modern Plastics Encyclopedia* (New York: McGraw-Hill) p 443

Asano K, Krämer H and Schön G 1977 Electrostatic fields around a sphere in a cylindrical tank partly filled with charged liquid *Proc. Inst. Electrostatics, Japan* 114

Bailey W J, Houle J F and Van Norman G R 1974 Multilayer radiation sensitive element having controlled triboelectric charging properties *US Patent Specification* 3850642 (See also US Patent Specification 388678 (1975))

Ballal D R and Lefebvre A H 1977 Ignition and flame quenching in flowing gaseous mixtures *Proc. R. Soc.* A **357** 163–81

Bartknecht W 1979 *Chemie Technik* **10** 493

—— 1981 *Explosions* (New York: Springer)

Bertein H 1973 Charges on insulators generated by breakdown of gas *J. Phys. D: Appl. Phys.* **6** 1910–16

—— 1977 The importance of electrostatic laws for understanding partial discharges *Proc. 3rd Int. Conf. for Static Electricity* (*Grenoble*) European Federation of Chemical Engineers Paper 2 (Paris: Societe de Chemie Industrielle) pp 2a–f

Berthold W 1983 *Proc. Int. Conf. on Safe Handling of Hazardous Dusts* (Nuremberg: VDI Berichte) No 494, p 105

Berz I 1961 On inductive sparks of high incendive power *Combustion and Flame* **3** 131–2

Bhattacharya S and Mittal K L 1978 Mechanics of removing glass particles from a solid surface *Surf. Technol.* **7** 423–5

Bhatti I S, Fuller E and Jenne F B 1978 VMOS electrostatic protection *Proc. 16th Ann. IEEE Reliability Physics Symp.* pp 140–5

Bikerman J J 1961 *The Science of Adhesive Joints* (New York: Academic)

Billinge K 1981 Frictional ignition hazards in industry—a survey of reported incidents 1958–1978 *Fire Prevention Science and Technology* **24** 13–19

Blickensderfer R 1975 Methane ignition by frictional impact heating *Combustion and Flame* **25** 143–52

Blok H 1937 *General Discussions on Lubrication* vol 2 (London: Institution of Mechanical Engineers)

Blythe A R 1979 *Electrical Properties of Polymers* (Cambridge: Cambridge University Press)

Blythe A R and Reddish W 1979 Charges on powder and bulking effects *Electrostatics* (*Oxford*) *1979* (Inst. Phys. Conf. Ser. 48) pp 107–14

Bolton P 1972 *Admiralty Oil Laboratories UK Report* 69

Boschung P and Glor M 1980 Methods for investigating the electrostatic behaviour of charged powders *J. Electrostatics* **8** 205–19

Boschung P, Higner W, Lutgens G, Maurer B and Widner A 1977 An experimental contribution to the question of lightning-like discharges in dust clouds *J. Electrostatics* **3** 303–13

Bowden F P 1955 Recent studies in metallic friction *Chartered Mechanical Engineer* **2** 86–101

Bowden F P, Stone M A and Tudor G K 1947 Detonation of explosives by friction *Proc. R. Soc.* A **188** 329–49

Bowden F P and Tabor D 1950 *Friction and Lubrication of Solids* (Oxford: Clarendon)

Bowden F P and Thomas P H 1954 The surface temperature of sliding solids *Proc. R. Soc* A **223** 29–40

Boyd J and Bulgin D 1957 The reduction of static electrification by incorporating viscous rayon containing carbon *J. Textile Inst.* **48** 66–99

Boyle A R and Llewellyn F J 1950 The ignitability of dust clouds and powders *J. Soc. Chem. Ind. London* **69** 170–81

Bradley R S 1932 Cohesion between surfaces and the surface energy of solids *Phil. Mag.* **13** 853–62

Bright A W 1977 Electrostatic hazards in liquids and powders *J. Electrostatics* **4** 131–49

Bright A W and Haig I G 1977 Safety criteria applicable to the loading of large plastic tanks *IEEE Conf. of Industrial Applications Society (Los Angeles) 1977*

Bright A W and Hughes J F 1975 Research on electrostatic hazards associated with tank washing in very large crude carriers —introduction and experimental modelling *J. Electrostatics* **1** 37–47

Britton L G and Williams T J 1982 Some characteristics of liquid–metal discharges involving a charged low risk oil *J. Electrostatics* **13** 185–207

Bulgin D 1945 Electrically conductive rubber *Trans. Rubber Industry* **21** 188

Burstow D J, Loveland R J, Tomlinson R and Widgington D W 1981 Radio frequency ignition hazards *Radio and Electron. Eng.* **51** 151–69

Bustin W M, Koszman I and Tobye I T 1964 New theory for static relaxation in high resistivity field *Hydrocarb. Proc.* **43** 209

Butterworth G J and Brown K P 1982 Assessment of electrostatic ignition hazards during tank filling with the aid of computer modelling *J. Electrostatics* **13** 9–27

Butterworth G J and Dowling P D 1981 Electrostatic effects with portable CO_2 fire extinguishers *J. Electrostatics* **11** 43–55

Castle G S P, Inculet I I and Littlewood R 1983 Ionic space charges generated by evaporating charged liquid sprays *Static Electrification (Oxford) 1983* (Inst. Phys. Conf. Ser. 66) pp 59–64

Chaudhri M M 1976 Stab initiation of explosions *Nature* **263** 121–22

Chives J, Mitchell L and Rowe G 1974 The variation of real contact area between surfaces with contact pressure and material hardness *Wear* **28** 171–85

Clark O M 1979 *Electrical overstress/Electrostatic discharge Symp. Proc. EOS.1 Reliability Analysis Centre* pp 193–7

Cobine J D 1958 *Gaseous Conductors* (New York: Dover)

Collocott S J, Morgan V T and Morrow R 1980 The electrification of operating powder fire extinguishers *J. Electrostatics* **9** 191–6

Compo P, Tardos G I, Mozzone D and Pfeffer R 1984 Minimum sintering temperatures of fluidisable particles *Part. Charact.* **1** 171–7

Corn M 1961 Adhesion of solid particles to solid surfaces *J. Air Pollution Control Association* **11** 523, 566, 584

Cross J A 1975 Adhesion of electrostatic powder coatings *Static Electrification (London) 1975* (Inst. Phys. Conf. Ser. 27) pp 202–14

—— 1979 Electrostatic effects in adhesion in *Surface Contamination* ed K Mittal (New York: Plenum)

—— 1981 Hazards in powder processing *Particulate Technology D1/E* (I. Chem. E. Symp. Ser. 63) pp 1–12

Cross J A, Cetronio A and Haig I G 1977 Electrostatic hazards from pumping insulating liquids in glass *Proc. 3rd Int. Cong. on Static Electricity (Grenoble) 1977* Paper 28

Cross J A and Farrer D 1982 *Dust Explosions* (New York: Plenum)

Cross N and Picknett R G 1963 The liquid layer between a sphere and a plane surface *Trans. Faraday Soc.* **59** 846–55

Czyzak C J 1952 On the theory of dipole interactions with metals *Am. J. Phys.* **20** 440–6

Davies D K 1985 Harmful effects and damage to electronics by electrostatic discharges *J. Electrostatics* **16** 329–42

Davis M H 1969 Electrostatic field and force on a dielectric sphere near a conducting plane *Am. J. Phys.* **37** 26–9

Derjaguin B V, Aleinikova I N and Toporov Yu P 1968 The adhesion of polymer particles to solid surfaces *Powder Technol.* **2** 154–8

Derjaguin B V and Krotova 1957 *Proc. 2nd Int. Conf. on Surface Activity (London) 1957*

Derjaguin B V, Muller V M and Toporov Yu P 1975 The effect of contact deformation on the adhesion of particles *J. Colloid and Interface Sci.* **53** 314–26

—— 1978 On the role of molecular forces in contact deformation *J. Colloid and Interface Sci.* **67** 378–9

—— 1980 On different approaches to contact mechanics *J. Colloid and Interface Sci.* **73** 293

Derjaguin B V and Smilga V P 1958 Electronic adhesion: the theory of metals joined by a semiconducting interlayer *Dokl. Akad. Nauk.* **121** 877

—— 1967 Electronic theory of adhesion *J. Appl. Phys.* **38** 4609–16

Derjaguin D K 1934 Unlersichungen uker die reibung und adhasion *Koll. Z.* **69** 155

Dietz P W 1976 Electrofluidised bed mechanics *PhD Thesis* MIT

—— 1978 Heat transfer in bubbling electrofluidised beds *J. Electrostatics* **5** 297–308

Dietz P W and Melcher J R 1978 Interparticle electrical forces in packed and fluidised beds *Ind. Eng. Chem. Fund.* **1** 28–32

Diserens N J, Smith J R and Bright A W 1975 A preliminary study of electric field problems in plastic tanks and their theoretical modelling by means of a finite difference computer program *J. Electrostatics* **5** 169–82

Donald D K 1972 Contribution of charge to powder particle adhesion *J. Adhesion* **4** 233–45

Eckhoff R K 1975 Towards a minimum ignition energy for dust clouds *Combustion and Flame* **24** 53–64

Edwards H R and Underwood M C 1984 The ignition of powder air mixtures by discharge of static electricity *J. Electrostatics* **15** 123–5

Edwards J R *et al* 1979 VMOS reliability *IEEE Trans. Electron. Devices* **ED-26** 43–7

Electrostatic Discharge Control Handbook (Washington, DC: Naval Sea Systems Command)

Excell P S, Butcher and Howson D P 1978 Performance of long dipoles as unintended antennas *Proc. Conf. on Electromagnetic Compatibility (Guildford)* (London: Institute of Electronic and Radio Engineers) pp 251–8

Felici N J and Larigaldie S 1980 Experimental study of a static discharger for aircraft with special reference to helicopters *J. Electrostatics* **9** 59–70

Felstead D K, Rogers R L and Young D G 1983 The effect of electrode characteristics on the measurement of the minimum ignition energy of dust clouds *Static Electrification (London) 1983* (Inst. Phys. Conf. Ser. 66) pp 105–10

Field P 1982 Dust explosions *Handbook of Powder Technology* vol 4, ed J C Williams and T Allen (Amsterdam: Elsevier)

Fisher L R and Israelachvilli J N 1981 Direct measurement of meniscus forces on adhesion *Colloids and Surfaces* **3** 303–19

Fuller K N G and Tabor D 1975 The effect of surface roughness on the adhesion of elastic solids *Proc. R. Soc.* A **345** 327–44

Gibson N 1971 Static electricity in fluids *Static Electrification (London) 1971* (Inst. Phys. Conf. Ser. 11) pp 71–84

—— 1983 Electrostatic hazards; a review of modern trends *Electrostatics (London) 1983* (Inst. Phys. Conf. Ser. 66) pp 1–11

Gibson N and Harper D J 1981 Evaluation of electrostatic hazards associated with non conducting materials *J. Electrostatics* **11** 27–41

Gibson N and Lloyd F C 1965 The incendivity of discharges from electrostatically charged plastics *Br. J. Appl. Phys.* **16** 1619–31

—— 1970 Electrification of toluene flowing in large diameter metal pipes *J. Phys. D: Appl. Phys.* **3** 563–73

Gibson N, Lloyd F C and Perry G R 1968 Fire hazards in chemical plant from friction sparks involving the thermite reaction *Proc. 3rd Symp. on Chemical Process Hazards* (Inst. Chem. Eng. (UK) Ser. 25)

Glaner T 1983 *PhD Thesis* ETH Zurich

Glor M 1981 Ignition of gas/air mixtures by discharges between electrostatically charged plastic surfaces *J. Electrostatics* **10** 327–33

—— 1984 Condition for the appearance of discharges from the gravitational compaction of powders *J. Electrostatics* **15** 223–35

—— 1985 Hazards due to the electrostatic charging of powders *J. Electrostatics* **16** 175–91

Grabhofer H 1969 *US Patent Specification* 3428456

Grady P L and Hersch S P 1977 The effect of internal additives on the electrical conductivity and activation energy of nylon fibres *IEEE Trans. Ind. Appl.* **IA-13** 379–85

Greason W D and Castle G S P 1984 The effects of electrostatic discharge on microelectronic devices—a review *IEEE Trans. Ind. Appl.* **IA-20** 247–52

Grice G S W 1952 *Safety in Mines Research Board, USA* 50/1952

Guoxiang Li and Wang Changying 1981 Comprehensive study of electric spark sensitivity of ignitable gases and explosive powders *J. Electrostatics* **11** 319–39

Haig I G and Bright A W 1977 Experimental techniques for the study of surface discharges from hydrocarbon surfaces *Proc. 3rd. Int. Cong. on Static Electricity SCI (Grenoble)* (Paris: Societe de Chemie Industrielle) pp 28a–f

Hall A and Burstow D J 1980 Risk of ignition of flammable gases and vapours by radio transmission *Electrotechnology* **8** 12–15

Hall A and Loveland R J 1980 Radio frequency ignition hazards *Conf. on Radio Transmitters and Modulation Techniques (IEE Digest* **40** 58–62)

Heidelberg E 1960 *Die Berufsgenossenschaft Betriebssicherheit* p 265

—— 1967 Generation of igniting brush discharges by charged layers on earthed conductors *Static Electrification (London) 1967* (Inst. Phys. Conf. Ser. 4) pp 147–54

—— 1970 Zundungen explosibler gemische durch statische elektrizitat *Advances in Static Electricity* (*Ostereichischer Verband ur Electrotechnik*) 351–9

Hickernell F S and Crawford J J 1977 Voltage breakdown characteristics of close spaced aluminium arc gap structures on oxidised silicon *Proc. 15th Ann. Reliability Physics Symp. (Las Vegas)* (New York: IEEE) pp 128–31

Holdsworth M P *et al* 1962 Electrical charging during white oil loading of tankers *Trans. Inst. Marine Eng.* **74**

Holm R 1948 Calculations of the temperature development in a contact, heated in the contact surface and application to the temperature rise in sliding contact *J. Appl. Phys.* **19** 361–6

—— 1952 Temperature development in a heated contact with application to sliding contacts *J. Appl. Mech.* **19** 369–75

Howson D P, Excell P S and Butcher G H 1981 Ignition of flammable gas/air mixtures by sparks from 2 MHz and 9 MHz sources *Radio and Electron. Eng.* **51** 170–4

Hubu T 1973 *US Patent Specification* 3743608

Hughes J F, Bright A W, Makin B and Parker I F 1973 A study of electrical discharges in a charged water aerosol *J. Phys. D: Appl. Phys.* **6** 966–75

Hughes J F, Corbett R P, Bright A W and Bailey A G 1975 Explosion hazards and diagnostic techniques associated with powder handling in large silos *Static Electrification (London) 1975* (Inst. Phys. Conf. Ser. 27) pp 264–75

Israelachvilli J N 1974 Van der Waals forces *Contemp. Phys.* **15** 159–79

Israelachvilli J N, Perez E and Tandon R K 1980 On the adhesion forces between deformable solids *J. Colloid Interface Sci.* **78** 260–1

Israelachvilli J N and Tabor D 1972 The measurement of Van der Waals dispersion forces in the range 1.5–130 nm *Proc. R. Soc.* A **331** 19–38

Jaeger J C 1942 Moving sources of heat *Proc. R. Soc. NSW* **76** 203–24

Jansen G 1972 *Dissertation* Universität Fredericiana, Karlsruhe

Johnson D D 1974 *US Patent Specification* 3811848

Johnson J K 1977 The ignition of vapour droplets by liquid to metal sparks *J. Electrostatics* **4** 53–65

Johnson K 1976 Antistatic additives for textiles and plastics *Noyes Data Corp. New Jersey*

Johnson N L, Kendall K and Roberts A D 1971 Surface energy and the contact of elastic solids *Proc. R. Soc.* A **324** 301–33

Johnson T W and Melcher J R 1975 Electromechanics of electofluidised beds *Ind. Eng. Chem. Fund.* **14** 146–53

Joseph S and Klinzing G E 1983 Vertical gas solid flow with electrostatics *Powder Technol.* **36** 79–87

Jowett C E 1976 *Electrostatics in the Electronics Environment* (London: Macmillan)

Kalkert N and Schecker H G 1982 Influence of particle size distribution on the minimum ignition energy of explodable dusts *Chem. Ing. Tech.* **52** (in German)

Karassev V V, Krotova N A and Derjaguin B V 1953 Investigation of the gas discharge during the separation of a film of a high polymer from a hard support *Sov. Phys.–Dokl.* **89** 109–12

Kingman F E T, Coleman E H and Rogowski Z W 1952 The ignition of flammable gases from sparks from aluminium, paint and rusty steel *J. Appl. Chem.* **2** 449–55

Klinkenberg A and van der Minne J L 1958 *Electrostatics in the Petroleum Industry* (Amsterdam: Elsevier)

Kottler W, Krupp H and Rabenhorst H 1968 Adhesion of electrically charged particles *Z. Angew. Phys.* **4** 219–23

Kono M, Kamagai S and Sakai T 1976a Ignition of gases by two successive sparks with reference to the frequency effect of capacitive sparks *Combustion and Flame* **27** 85–98

—— 1976b Optimum conditions for the ignition of gases by composite sparks *Proc. 16th Int. Combustion Symp. (Cambridge, Mass.) 1976* (Pittsburg: Combustion Institute) pp 757–66

Kragelski I V and Demkin N B 1960 Contact area of rough surfaces *Wear* **3** 170–87

Krämer H 1981 Electrostatic charging of poorly conducting liquid systems—suspensions, emulsions and solutions—by agitating *J. Electrostatics* **10** 89–99

Krämer H and Asano K 1979 Incendivity of sparks from electrostatically charged liquids *J. Electrostatics* **6** 361–79

Krämer H, Asano K and Schön G 1977 Criteria for the safe filling of tank vehicles—theoretical and experimental study to assess electrostatic hazards *Proc. 3rd Int. Cong. on Static Electricity (Grenoble) 1977* (Paris: Societe de Chemie Industrielle) paper 31

Krämer H and Schön G 1975 *Proc. of the 9th World Petroleum Cong. (Tokyo) 1975* vol 6, Special paper 6, pp 147–58

Krotova N A and Morozova L P 1959 *Dokl. Akad. Nauk.* **129** 149

Krupp H 1967 Particle adhesion—theory and experiment *Adv. Colloid and Interface Sci.* **1** 111–239

Kuczynski G C 1972 The physics and chemistry of sintering *Adv. Colloid and Interface Sci.* **3** 275–330

Landers E U 1979 Computation of asymmetric three dimensional electric fields with any input conditions *Int. Symp. on High Voltage Engineering (Milan)*

——1985 Distribution of charge and field strength due to discharge from insulating surfaces *J. Electrostatics* **17** 59–68

Lapple C E 1970 Electrostatic phenomena with particulates *Adv. Chem. Eng.* **8** 1–96

Larigaldie S and Giboni N 1981 A new device for the neutralisation of static electricity on pulverant materials *J. Electrostatics* **10** 57–64

Larouere P L, Joseph S and Klinzing G E 1984 Some stability concepts in relation to electrostatics and pneumatic transport *Powder Technol.* **38** 1–6

Larsen R I 1958 The adhesion and removal of particles attached to air filter surfaces *Am. Ind. Hygiene Assoc. J.* **19** 265–70

Lees P, McAllister D, Smith J R, Britton L G and Hughes J F 1981 Experimental and computational investigation of electrostatic fields in plastic tanks during filling with low conductivity oils *J. Electrostatics* **10** 267–73

Leonard J T 1981 Static electricity in hydrocarbon liquids and fuels *J. Electrostatics* **10** 17–30

Lewis B and Von Elbe G 1961 *Combustion, Flames and Explosion of Gases* (New York: Academic)

Lifshitz E M 1956 The theory of attractive forces between solids *Sov. Phys.–JETP* **2** 73–83

Line L E, Rhodes H A and Gilmer T E 1959 The spark ignition of dust clouds *J. Phys. Chem.* **63** 290–5

Litchfield E L and Blanc M V 1959 Recent developments in spark ignition *US Bureau of Mines Report No* 5461

Loveland R J 1981 Electrostatic ignition hazards in industry *J. Electrostatics* **11** 3–11

Lovstrand K G 1975 On the discharge of static electricity with induction eliminators *Static Electrification (London) 1975* (Inst. Phys. Conf. Ser. 27) pp 246–55

——1981 The ignition power of brush discharges. Experimental work on the critical energy density *J. Electrostatics* **10** 161–9

Lowell J and McIntyre J E 1978 Antistatic fibres in fabrics and carpets *J. Electrostatics* **4** 267–82

Luttgens G 1985 Collection of accidents caused by static electricity *J. Electrostatics* **16** 247–57

McLean K J 1977 Cohesion of precipitated dust in electrostatic precipitators *J. Air Pollution Control Association* **27** 1100–3

Maddocks A J and Jackson G A 1981 Measurement of radio frequency voltage and power induced in structures on St Fergus gas terminals *Radio and Electron. Eng.* **51** 187–94

Mason P I and Rees W D 1981 Hazards from plastic pipes carrying insulating liquids *J. Electrostatics* **10** 137–45

Maurer B 1979a Discharges due to electrostatic charges of particles in large storage silos *Ger. Chem. Eng.* **4** 189–95

—— 1979b *Chim. Ing. Tech.* **51** 98

—— 1983 *Proc. Int. Conf. on Safe Handling of Flammable Dusts* (Nuremberg: VDI Berichte) pp 119, 494

Minear R L and Dodson G A 1977 Effect of electrostatic discharge on linear bipolar integrated circuits *Proc. 15th Ann. IEEE Reliability Phys. Symp.* (New York: IEEE) pp 138–41

Moore A D 1973 *Electrostatics and its Industrial Applications* (New York: Wiley)

Morgan V T, Collocott S J and Morrow R 1981 The electrification of operating portable CO_2 fire extinguishers *J. Electrostatics* **9** 201–10

Morse A R 1958 Investigation of the ignition of grain dust clouds by mechanical sparks *National Research Council of Canada Report* NRC 4968 ERB 494

Moslehi G B and Self S A 1984 Electromechanics of precipitated particulate layers *IEEE Trans. Ind. Appl.* **IA-20** 1598–606

Movilliat P and Giltaire M 1979 Measure de l'énergie d'inflammation de mélanges gazeux par décharge capacitive. Inflammation par décharge d'une personne chargée d'electricité statique *J. Electrostatics* **6** 307–31

Movilliat P and Monomakhoff H 1977 *Int. Conf. of Safety in Mines Research (Varna, Bulgaria) 1977* paper C3

Odham G A M 1970 Electrostatic charging of aircraft in flight *Proc. 1st Int. Conf. on Static Electricity (Vienna) (Advances in Static Electricity* vol 1 (Brussels: Auxilia) pp 248–60)

Pechmann K 1970 *US Patent Specification* 3549375

Peek F W 1929 *Dielectric Phenomena in High Voltage Engineering* (New York: McGraw-Hill)

Pellmont G 1979 Explosions und zundverhalten von hybriden gemischen aus brennbaren stauben und brengasen *Dissertation* ETH Zurich No 6498 1979

Phillip H R and Levinson L M 1979 Transient protection with ZnO varistors. Technical considerations *Electrical Overstress/Electrostatic Discharge Symp. Proc. EOS 1 Reliability Analysis Centre* pp 193–97

Potter A E 1960 *Prog. in Combustion Sci. and Technol.* vol 1 (Oxford: Oxford University Press) pp 145–81

Powell F 1969 Ignition of gases and vapours by friction and impact *Ind. and Eng. Chem.* **61** 29–37

Reddish W 1970 *GB Patent Specification* 1201166

Rees W D 1981 Static hazards during the top loading of road trailers with highly insulating liquids—flow rate limitation proposals to minimise risk *J. Electrostatics* **11** 13–25

Riddlestone H G 1957 The effect of circuit resistance on the discharge energy required for the ignition of methane/air mixtures *ERA Report No* D/T 105

Riddlestone H G and Bartels A 1965 The relative hazards in the use of ferrous and non sparking hand tools *J. Inst. Petroleum* **51** 106–10

Roberts A D 1969 *Phd Thesis* University of Cambridge

—— 1972 Direct measure of electrical double layer forces between solid surfaces *J. Coll. Int. Sci.* **41** 23–4

Roberts J M C and Hughes J F 1979 Elimination of electrostatic charging in punctured aerosol cans *IEEE Trans. Ind. Appl.* **IA-15** 104–8

Robertson S S J and Loveland R J 1981 Radio frequency ignition hazards: a review *IEE Proc.* **128** 607–14

Robinson K S and Jones T B 1984a Particle–wall adhesion in electropacked beds *IEEE Trans. Ind. Appl.* **IA-20** 1573–7

—— 1984b Slope stability of electro-packed beds *IEEE Trans. Ind. Appl.* **IA-20** 253–8

Rose H E and Priede T 1958 Ignition phenomena in hydrogen air mixtures *Proc. 7th Symp. on Combustion* (London: Butterworth) pp 436–45

Rosenfeld J L J, Strachan D C, Tromans P S and Searson P A 1981 Experiments on the incendivity of radio frequency breakflash discharges *The Radio and Electronic Engineer* **51** 175–86

Russel A 1909 Coefficients of capacity and the mutual attraction and repulsion of two electrified spherical conductors when close together *Proc. R. Soc.* A **82** 524–31

Sayers J F, Tewari G P, Wilson J R and Jessen P F 1970 Spark ignition of natural gas, theory and practice *The Gas Council UK Research Communication* GC 171

Schmalz F and Just T H 1968 Measurements of ignition delays of hydrogen air mixtures under simulated conditions of supersonic combustion chambers *AGARD Adv. Components for Turbojet Eng.* Pt 2

Schnabel W 1970 Electrostatic double layer adhesion *Proc. 1st Int. Conf. on Static Electricity (Vienna)* (*Advances in Static Electricity* vol 1 (Brussels: Auxilia) pp 33–41)

Schön G 1965 *Handbuch der Raumexposionen* (Munich: Freytag Verlag Chemie)

—— 1982 Safety in industry: ignition hazards due to electrostatics *J. Electrostatics* **11** 309–17

Smit W 1971 Electrostatic charge generation—mathematical methods *Static Electrification (London) 1971* (Inst. Phys. Conf. Ser. 11) pp 178–84

Strawson H and Lyle A R 1975a The avoidance of hazards during the filling of road and rail tanker wagons *Proc. 2nd Int. Conf. on Electrical Safety in Hazardous Environments (IEE London) 1975*

—— 1975b Safe charge densities for road and rail tanker filling *Electrostatics (London) 1975* (Inst. Phys. Conf. Ser. 27) pp 276–89

Tabata Y and Masuda S 1984 Minimum potential of charged insulator to cause incendiary discharges *IEEE Trans. Ind. Appl.* **IA-20** 1206–11

Tabor D and Winterton R H S 1969 Direct measurement of Van der Waals forces *Proc. R. Soc.* A **312** 435–50

Tabor D 1977 Surface forces and surface interactions *J. Colloid and Interface Sci.* **58** 2–13

Teijin 1968 *South African Patent* 68/7302

Tolson P 1980 The stored energy needed to ignite methane by discharges from a charged person *J. Electrostatics* **8** 289–93

—— 1981 Assessing the safety of electrically powered static eliminators for use in flammable atmospheres *J. Electrostatics* **11** 57–69

Turner T E and Morris S 1980 Electrostatic sensitivity of various input protection networks *Electrical overstress/electrostatic discharge Symp. Proc. EOS2 Reliability Analysis Centre* pp 95–103

Uber A E, Hoburg J F and Penney G W 1984 Experimental investigation of electrostatic effects in the adhesion of dusts *IEEE Trans. Ind. Appl.* **IA-20** 148–54

Valko E I and Tesoro G S 1964 Antistatic additives *Encylopedia of Polymer Science and Technology* vol 2 pp 204–29

van der Meer J M 1971 Electrostatic charge generation during washing of tanks with water sprays: I. General introduction *Static Electrification (London) 1971* (Inst. Phys. Conf. Ser. 11) pp 153–58

van de Weerd J M 1971 Electrostatic charge generation during washing of tanks with water sprays: II. Measurements and interpretation *Static Electrification (London) 1971* (Inst. Phys. Conf. Ser. 11) pp 158–78

—— 1972 Can probe to cloud discharges be an ignition source in tanker explosions? *Shell Research NV External Report* AMSR 001672

Vos B 1971 Electrostatic charge generation—mechanical studies *Static Electrification (London) 1971* (Inst. Phys. Conf. Ser. 11) pp 184–94

Ward G R 1955 Antistatic action vs molecular structure *Am. Dyestuff Reporter* **44** 220–6

Weaver M L, Smeltzer E E and Klinzing G E 1982 *IEC Process Design Development* **21** 390

Whewell B R, Bright A W and Makin B 1970 The application of charged aerosols to the discharge of static from aircraft *Advances in Static Electricity (Proc. 1st Int. Conf. on Static Electricity (Vienna) (European Federation of Chemical Engineers))* (Brussels: Auxilia) pp 261–75)

Widgington D W 1968 Some aspects of the design of intrinsically safe circuits *Safety in Mines Research Establishment (Sheffield) Report No 256*

Williams R E 1979 Dynamics of the Lucite Hartmann bomb *Int. Grain Silo Symp.* (Sponsored by US Department of Agriculture)

Wilson N 1977 The risk of fire and explosions due to static charging on textiles and clothing *J. Electrostatics* **4** 67–84

_____ 1979 The nature and incendiary behaviour of spark discharges from the body *Electrostatics (Oxford) 1979* (Inst. Phys. Conf. Ser. 48) pp 73–83

_____ 1983 The ignition of natural gas by spark discharges from the body *Electrostatics (Oxford) 1983* (Inst. Phys. Conf. Ser. 66) pp 21–7

Zichy E L 1974 Antistatics for plastics *Dechema Monograph No* 1370–1409 vol 72 (*Elektrostatische Aufladung* pp 147–63)

Zimon A D, Dovnar N I, Belkina G A and Nozdrina G V 1964 in *Research in Surface Forces* (*Izd Nauka* 330)

_____ 1969 *Adhesion of Dust and Powder* (London: Plenum)

Chapter 7   Theory

7.1 FUNDAMENTAL LAWS OF ELECTROSTATICS

7.1.1 Coulomb's law

The theory of electrostatic fields and forces was mostly developed in the
second half of the nineteenth century, before the nature of matter or the
existence of electrons and ions had been discovered. The theory was based on
one experimentally derived law, Coulomb's inverse square law. This states
that the force between two charged bodies is proportional to the product of
their charges and inversely proportional to the square of the distance between them, i.e.

$$F = \frac{Kqq'}{r^2}. \tag{7.1}$$

The force on the charge q due to q' some distance away is said to be due to
the electric field of q' i.e. by definition the force on the charge q is given by

$$F = qE. \tag{7.2}$$

Thus the field due to q' may be written in the form

$$E = \frac{Kq'}{r^2}. \tag{7.3}$$

The electric field, like the force, is a vector quantity. It acts in the direction
of the force on a positive charge.

    Coulomb originally proposed that an inverse square law was applicable,
by analogy with magnetism, and he supported the proposition with direct
measurements of force and distance. Experimental measurements of this
type were necessarily subject to considerable experimental error. Cavendish
showed that if a conductor, which is placed inside a second, closed, hollow
conductor and in contact with it, is deprived of all electric charge, then the

inverse square law must be precisely true. Similarly, Laplace proved that it was the only law compatible with the observation that there is no electric field inside a charged hollow conductor. Our conviction of the accuracy of Coulomb's law is now based on experiments of this type, which may be made with very high accuracy, rather than on the direct measurement of force and distance.

For example, we can calculate the electric field at a point O within a spherical shell which has a surface charge density of Q_s C m^{-2}. Referring to figure 7.1, it can be seen that two cones of solid angle dω can be drawn from O to the surface. These intersect the shell in the elemental areas dS_1 and dS_2. It is assumed that the field falls with distance according to r^{-n}, i.e. Coulomb's law can be written as:

$$F = \frac{Kqq'}{r^n}.$$

Then the field at O due to the areas of charge dS_1 and dS_2 will be

$$dE = KQ_s\left(\frac{dS_1}{r_1^n} - \frac{dS_2}{r_2^n}\right).$$

However, the solid angle dω is given by

$$d\omega = \frac{dS_1\cos\theta}{r_1^2} = \frac{dS_2\cos\theta}{r_2^2}.$$

Therefore

$$dE = \frac{KQ_s\,d\omega}{\cos\theta}\left(\frac{1}{r_1^{n-2}} - \frac{1}{r_2^{n-2}}\right).$$

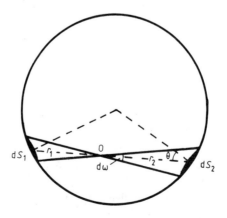

Figure 7.1 Proof of the inverse square law.

The whole surface of the sphere can be divided into elemental areas in this way. The vector resultant of these fields at O can only be zero if all the individual dE are zero, otherwise there would be a net component of electric field in some direction. Since $r_1 \neq r_2$ this can only be true if $n = 2$.

The constant of proportionality for Coulomb's law in air was originally taken to be one. With the force measured in dynes, the unit of electric charge was then defined by Coulomb's law and was called an electrostatic unit (ESU). If the charge is measured in the SI unit of coulombs, and the force is in newtons, then the constant in Coulomb's law is no longer one, but becomes $1/4\pi\varepsilon_0$. ε_0 has the units of farads per metre, and is a constant known as the permittivity of free space. ε_0 has the value $1/(36\pi \times 10^9)$ F m$^{-1} \simeq$ 8.81×10^{-12} F m^{-1}. Thus in SI units

$$F = qq'/4\pi\varepsilon_0 r^2 \tag{7.4}$$

and

$$E = q'/4\pi\varepsilon_0 r^2. \tag{7.5}$$

7.1.2 Electric potential

The electric potential at a point is defined as the work done on unit charge to move the charge from a position of zero potential (assumed to be at infinity) to the point in question.

In vector notation, the work done in moving a charge q a distance $d\mathbf{r}$ against a field E is

$$V = \mathbf{F} \cdot d\mathbf{r} = -q\mathbf{E} \cdot d\mathbf{r}. \tag{7.6}$$

(The negative sign arises because work must be done on the charge to move it against the field.)

The work done in moving unit charge from A to B is thus

$$V_{AB} = -\int_A^B \mathbf{E} \cdot d\mathbf{r}$$

V is called the potential difference between A and B. The work done in bringing unit charge from infinity (taken to be zero potential) to a point A is the potential of that point:

$$V_A = -\int_\infty^A \mathbf{E} \cdot d\mathbf{r}. \tag{7.7}$$

This may also be written

$$E = -dV/dr = -\text{grad } V. \tag{7.8}$$

The potential is measured in volts and is a scalar quantity.

It follows from equations (7.5) and (7.8) that V is given by

$$V = q'/4\pi\varepsilon_0 r. \tag{7.9}$$

7.1.3 Electric displacement

There can be no electric field in a conductor because, if charge is free to move, it will flow until the potential across the conductor is zero. However an electric field can exist in a dielectric (insulating) material. Charge cannot flow in a perfect insulator, but the atoms polarise and the positive and negative ions are displaced by the electric field. Overall neutrality is preserved, but one boundary becomes negative and the other positive, as shown in figure 7.2. This charge is called the induced charge and the induced charge per unit area is defined as the displacement D. D is proportional to the applied field and is a vector in the direction perpendicular to the surface charge, i.e. in the direction of the electric field, i.e.

$$\boldsymbol{D} = \varepsilon \boldsymbol{E} \tag{7.10}$$

where ε is known as the dielectric constant. D has the units of C m^{-2} and E is in V m^{-1}, therefore ε has the units of F m^{-1}. It can easily be shown that in air ε is ε_0 which is the constant in the Coulomb equation.

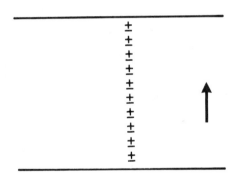

Figure 7.2 Polarisation of charge in an electric field results in one face becoming positive and the other negative.

Consider a charge q at the centre of an earthed sphere of radius R. Earth can be considered to be an infinite sink, or source, of charge, therefore an equal but opposite charge, $-q$, is able to flow from earth to the sphere, attracted by the charge, q, at its centre, i.e. there will be an induced charge $-q$ on the inside of the sphere. The induced charge per unit area is

$$D = q/4\pi R^2.$$

From equation (7.10)

$$D = \varepsilon E$$

but

$$E = q/4\pi\varepsilon_0 R^2 \qquad \text{(equation 7.5)}$$

so that

$$\varepsilon = \varepsilon_0.$$

When a dielectric medium is present, the field due to the charge q is reduced by the polarisation of the medium and ε is greater than ε_0. By convention ε is written as a multiple of the permittivity of free space,

$$\varepsilon = \varepsilon_r \varepsilon_0$$

where ε_r is the relative dielectric constant, or relative permittivity.

D is also known as the electrostatic flux density. It is possible to consider the direction of the lines of D as flux lines representing the flow of electrostatic flux through a surface. These do not have any physically real significance, but D can be treated mathematically as if the flux had a physical meaning similar to current density (current density has the units of $C\,m^{-2}\,s^{-1}$ or $A\,m^{-2}$ where displacement has the units of $C\,m^{-2}$).

7.1.4 Coulomb's law in a dielectric medium

When there is a dielectric medium between two charges, the force between them is modified as a result of polarisation of the medium. The atoms polarise so as to neutralise the field partially, so that the force is reduced below its value in vacuum, by a factor ε_r.

In a dielectric medium equations (7.4) and (7.5) therefore become

$$F = \frac{qq'}{4\pi\varepsilon_0\varepsilon_r r^2} \qquad (7.11)$$

$$E = \frac{q'}{4\pi\varepsilon_0\varepsilon_r r^2}. \qquad (7.12)$$

7.1.5 Gauss's law

Gauss's law states that if a closed surface S, of any shape, is constructed in a region in which an electric field is present, then the surface integral of the normal component of the displacement over the surface is equal to the net free charge enclosed by the surface: i.e.

$$\int D \cdot dS = \sum q. \qquad (7.13)$$

Since $D = \varepsilon_0\varepsilon_r E$ and in air the relative permittivity is one, this may be written

$$\int E \cdot dS = \sum q/\varepsilon_0. \qquad (7.14)$$

Thus Gauss's law can be used to estimate the electric field due to an assemblage of charge, or to calculate the total charge from a measured electric field.

Gauss's law may be derived from Coulomb's law and the definitions of D and E by considering a point charge $+q$ within an arbitrary surface as illustrated in figure 7.3.

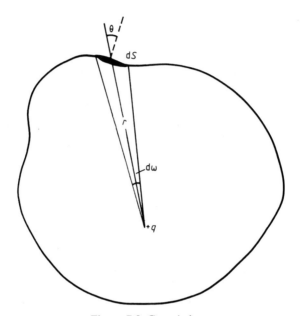

Figure 7.3 Gauss's law.

As before the displacement at a surface, a distance r from a point charge q, is

$$D = \frac{q\mathbf{r}}{4\pi r^3}.$$

Therefore, the normal component of D at the infinitesimal area of surface dS a distance r from a charge q is

$$D \cos \theta = q \cos \theta / 4\pi r^2.$$

Integrating over the surface,

$$\int D \cos \theta \, dS = \int \frac{q \cos \theta \, dS}{4\pi r^2}$$

but the solid angle subtended by dS is $d\omega$ where $d\omega = \cos \theta \, dS/r^2$, so that

$$\int D \cos \theta \, dS = \int \frac{q \, d\omega}{4\pi}.$$

The integral of a solid angle over a closed surface is 4π, therefore

$$\int D \cos \theta \, dS = q$$

or, in vector notation

$$\int \boldsymbol{D} \cdot d\boldsymbol{S} = q.$$

If the charge is expressed as a volume distribution of charge $Q_v \, \mathrm{C\,m^{-3}}$, Gauss's law is written

$$\int \boldsymbol{D} \cdot d\boldsymbol{S} = \int Q_v \, dv.$$

The expression $\int \boldsymbol{D} \cdot d\boldsymbol{S}/dv$ is the electrostatic flux through the surface per unit volume. The flux per unit volume is called the divergence of that quantity and Gauss's law may also be written in the form

$$\mathrm{div}\, D = \boldsymbol{V} \cdot \boldsymbol{D} = Q_v.$$

The divergence of a vector is a scalar quantity which expresses the growth of flux per unit volume.

Consequence of Gauss's law

(i) There can be no free charge within a solid conductor and any charge must reside at the surface. Consider the solid conductor shown in figure 7.4(a). By definition, a conductor is a material where electrons are free to move under the influence of an electric field. In equilibrium there is no current flow, therefore there can be no field within the conductor. Consider a Gaussian surface within the conductor, shown by the broken curve in figure 7.4(a). Since the field at every point on the surface is zero, the charge enclosed by the surface is also zero. The hypothetical Gaussian surface can be expanded until it lies just beneath the surface of the conductor, therefore there can be no free charge within the conductor.

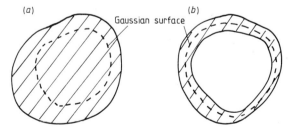

Figure 7.4 Illustration of the consequences of Gauss's law for: (a) an arbitrary solid conductor and (b) an arbitrary hollow conductor.

(ii) No configuration of charge outside a conducting cavity can give rise to a field inside, and a closed metal cavity acts as an electrostatic screen. Consider the hollow conductor of figure 7.4(*b*) with a free charge inside. The field at any Gaussian surface within the conductor must be zero, therefore there must be an equal and opposite charge on the inner surface of the conductor, so that the net charge enclosed by a Gaussian surface is zero. If there is no charge within the cavity, then the Gaussian surface can be distorted in any way and $\int E \cdot dS$ continues to be zero. This can only be true if the field is zero at all points within the cavity and the conductor. This is true whatever the charge outside the conductor. The reverse does not apply, i.e. with a charge q inside the cavity, there will be an equal and opposite charge on the inner wall of the conductor as discussed above. If the conductor is neutral this must be matched by a charge on the outer wall of the conductor which will give rise to an external field. If the conductor is earthed, the charge on the outer wall will flow to earth and there will be a net charge on the conductor but no external field or potential.

Gauss's law may be used to relate the field at the surface of a conductor to the surface charge density. Consider a hypothetical Gaussian surface in the form of a small pill box as shown in figure 7.5. There can be no field inside a conductor, therefore the portion of the surface inside the conductor

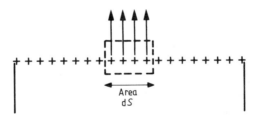

Figure 7.5 Gauss's law applied to a pill box at a metal surface.

makes no contribution to the integral of the field over the surface. At the surface of a conductor the field must be perpendicular to the conductor. (If there was a component of field parallel to the conductor charge would flow and there would be a current.) Therefore the sides of the pill box also make no contribution. The only contribution to the electric field comes from the area dS. From Gauss's law

$$\int E \cdot dS = \sum q / \varepsilon_0 \varepsilon_r$$

(where Σq is the total charge enclosed by the surface and ε_r is the relative dielectric constant of the medium outside the surface). If the surface density of charge is Q_s C m^{-2} this may be written in the form

$$E = Q_s/\varepsilon_0\varepsilon_r. \tag{7.15}$$

In air, the electric field is limited to 3×10^6 V m^{-1}. At higher fields, electrical breakdown of the air occurs, creating ions which discharge the surface. Therefore, substituting 8.8×10^{-12} for the permittivity of free space, it is found that the limiting charge is

$$q_{max} = 2.64 \times 10^{-5} \text{ C m}^{-2}.$$

7.1.6 Poisson's equation

Combining Gauss's law with the definition of electric potential (equation (7.6)) we have

$$\text{div } \boldsymbol{E} = Q_v/\varepsilon_0\varepsilon_r$$

and

$$\boldsymbol{E} = -\text{grad } V$$

i.e.

$$\text{div (grad } V) = \nabla^2 V = -Q_v/\varepsilon_0\varepsilon_r. \tag{7.16}$$

This is known as Poisson's equation.

If there is no free charge then Q_v is 0 and

$$\nabla^2 V = 0. \tag{7.17}$$

This is Laplace's equation.

In cartesian coordinates Poisson's equation is written

$$\frac{\partial^2 V}{\partial x^2} + \frac{\partial^2 V}{\partial y^2} + \frac{\partial^2 V}{\partial z^2} = -\frac{Q_v}{\varepsilon_0\varepsilon_r}. \tag{7.18}$$

In spherical polar coordinates it is

$$\frac{1}{r^2}\frac{\partial}{\partial r}\left(r^2\frac{\partial V}{\partial r}\right) + \frac{1}{r^2 \sin\theta}\frac{\partial}{\partial\theta}\left(\sin\theta\frac{dV}{d\theta}\right) + \frac{1}{r^2 \sin^2\theta}\frac{\partial^2 V}{\partial\varphi^2} = -\frac{Q_v}{\varepsilon_0\varepsilon_r} \tag{7.19}$$

and in cylindrical coordinates it is

$$\frac{1}{r}\frac{\partial}{\partial r}\left(r\frac{\partial V}{\partial r}\right) + \frac{1}{r^2}\frac{\partial^2 V}{\partial\theta^2} + \frac{\partial^2 V}{\partial z^2} = -\frac{Q_v}{\varepsilon_0\varepsilon_r}. \tag{7.20}$$

Coulomb's law, Gauss's law and Poisson's law are all different formulations of the same physical law. From these equations the electric field and potentials in any geometry can be found, provided the position of charges in the system (both free and those induced in conductors) are known. Solutions of these equations for different geometries are discussed in §7.4.

7.2 CAPACITANCE AND CAPACITORS

7.2.1 Definitions

If a charge q is given to an isolated conductor, its potential rises to a voltage V. The ratio of the charge to the voltage depends on the size and shape of the conductor and is called its capacitance, C:

$$C = q/V. \tag{7.21}$$

If a second conductor is brought close to the first one and earthed, an equal charge of the opposite sign will be induced on it, and the potential of the first sphere will fall. Since the first sphere is isolated, its charge remains constant, therefore the capacitance has increased. The two conductors together form a capacitor. The capacitance of a capacitor is defined as the ratio of the charge on either conductor to the potential difference between them.

If there is a dielectric medium between the conductors, the medium will be polarised and the polarisation charge will be opposite in sign to the induced charge as shown in figure 7.2. The effect of the applied charge q is reduced by a factor ε_r and the potential between the conductors is reduced by the same factor.

The relative permittivity of a medium, ε_r, may be defined as the ratio of the capacitance between two conductors in the presence of a dielectric medium to the capacitance between them in the vacuum.

7.2.2 Calculations of capacitance

The capacitance of a conductor, or a system of conductors, can only be calculated precisely if a relatively simple geometry is involved. The calculation involves defining the electric field, as a function of the position on the conductor, then calculating the work done to bring unit charge from infinity to the conductor. The capacitance is then the ratio of the charge to the potential. The principle of the calculations is illustrated in the following examples.

(a) *Isolated sphere*
Consider an isolated sphere of radius, a, and a charge, q, in an infinite dielectric medium, which has a relative permittivity ε_r. We apply Gauss's theorem over a spherical surface of radius r, concentric with the isolated sphere:

$$\int D \cdot dS = q.$$

D is constant over the spherical surface and therefore integrating we obtain

$$4\pi r^2 D = q = 4\pi \varepsilon_0 \varepsilon_r r^2 E$$

$$E = q/4\pi \varepsilon_0 \varepsilon_r r^2. \tag{7.22}$$

The potential of the sphere $(r = a)$ is

$$V = - \int_\infty^a E \, dr = q/4\pi\varepsilon_0\varepsilon_r a$$

$$C = q/V = 4\pi\varepsilon_0\varepsilon_r a. \tag{7.23}$$

(b) Two concentric spheres
With two concentric spheres of radius a and b respectively and charge q and $-q$ respectively the field at a Gaussian sphere of radius r (where $a < r < b$ as shown in figure 7.6) is given by equation (7.22). When r is outside the larger sphere the field at r is zero since the total charge enclosed by any surface larger than the outer sphere is zero.

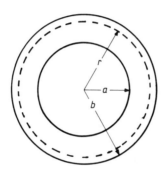

Figure 7.6 Concentric spheres.

The potential between the two spheres is therefore

$$V = - \int_a^b E \, dr = \frac{q}{4\pi\varepsilon_0\varepsilon_r} \left(\frac{1}{a} - \frac{1}{b} \right)$$

and

$$C = 4\pi\varepsilon_0\varepsilon_r \frac{ab}{b - a}. \tag{7.24}$$

(c) Parallel plates
The electric field between parallel plates, with a total charge q, separated by a distance d, which is small compared with their area A, is given by

$$E = V/d.$$

From equation (7.15)

$$q/A = \varepsilon_0\varepsilon_r E$$

so that

$$C = q/V = \varepsilon_0 \varepsilon_r A/d. \tag{7.25}$$

7.2.3 The energy stored in a capacitor

A system of charges contains potential energy because work must be done to bring the charges together. If we assume that the ith charge is increased from zero to q_i in infinitesimal steps so that at any time it has a charge αq_i (where α is a fraction less than 1), then the instantaneous potential at the position of the ith charge is αV_i (where V_i is the potential when the charges have reached their final level).

The work done in increasing the value of the ith charge by $q\, d\alpha$ is therefore

$$dU_i = \alpha V_i q_i \, d\alpha.$$

The total work done on all the charges is

$$U = \sum q_i V_i \int_0^1 \alpha \, d\alpha$$

$$= \tfrac{1}{2} \sum q_i V_i. \tag{7.26}$$

Applying equation (7.26) to a capacitor, which has a charge q and $-q$ on the plates, and a potential difference $V = V_1 - V_2$ between the plates

$$U = \tfrac{1}{2}(qV_1 - qV_2)$$

$$= \tfrac{1}{2}qV.$$

By definition, $C = q/V$ so that

$$U = \tfrac{1}{2}qV = \tfrac{1}{2}CV^2 = \tfrac{1}{2}q^2/C. \tag{7.27}$$

If we consider a parallel-plate capacitor, q may be written as the product of the surface density of charge Q_s and the area of the capacitor, A. C is given by equation (7.25); therefore

$$U = q^2/2C = Q_s^2 Ad/2\varepsilon_0 \varepsilon_r \tag{7.28}$$

but

$$Q_s = D = \varepsilon_0 \varepsilon_r E$$

i.e.

$$U = \tfrac{1}{2}DE(Ad) \tag{7.29}$$

and the energy per unit volume of dielectric in the capacitor is

$$U/v = \tfrac{1}{2}DE.$$

A more general proof is given by Bleaney and Bleaney (1965), who show that the energy is distributed in any dielectric medium with an energy density described by the equation

$$U/v = \tfrac{1}{2}\boldsymbol{D} \cdot \boldsymbol{E} \tag{7.30}$$

and

$$U = \tfrac{1}{2}\int \boldsymbol{D} \cdot \boldsymbol{E} \, \mathrm{d}v. \tag{7.31}$$

This equation applies to anisotropic dielectrics where D is not necessarily parallel to E, but assumes that D is always proportional to E.

The force between the plates of a capacitor
A force is required to separate the plates of a capacitor, which is equal to the rate of change of stored energy as the separation is increased:

$$F = \mathrm{d}U/\mathrm{d}x.$$

From equation (7.28)

$$\begin{aligned} U &= Q_{\mathrm{s}}^{2}Ax/2\varepsilon_0\varepsilon_{\mathrm{r}} \\ F &= \mathrm{d}U/\mathrm{d}x = Q_{\mathrm{s}}^{2}A/2\varepsilon_0\varepsilon_{\mathrm{r}}. \end{aligned} \tag{7.32}$$

From equation (7.31)

$$U = \tfrac{1}{2}\int\int \boldsymbol{D} \cdot \boldsymbol{E} \, \mathrm{d}A \, \mathrm{d}x$$

i.e.

$$F = \mathrm{d}U/\mathrm{d}x = \tfrac{1}{2}\int \boldsymbol{D} \cdot \boldsymbol{E} \, \mathrm{d}A. \tag{7.33}$$

For an isotropic dielectric this may be written in the form

$$F = \tfrac{1}{2}\varepsilon_0\varepsilon_{\mathrm{r}}\int E^2 \, \mathrm{d}A.$$

The force between any two charged bodies may thus be found by calculating the field at the surface of one body which arises from the charge of the other and integrating over the surface of the body.

7.3 POLARISATION

7.3.1 The electric dipole

An electric dipole consists of two charges of the same magnitude but opposite polarity, separated by a small distance. If the charge is q and the separation is a, then the dipole moment is defined as qa.

The potential a distance r from a dipole, in air, is the sum of the individual potentials from the two charges. With the notation of figure 7.7:

$$V = \frac{q}{4\pi\varepsilon_0}\left(\frac{1}{r_2} - \frac{1}{r_1}\right).$$

If $a \ll r$ so that terms of the order $(a/r)^2$ can be neglected then

$$V = \frac{q}{4\pi\varepsilon_0}\left(\frac{1}{r - \frac{1}{2}a\cos\theta} - \frac{1}{r + \frac{1}{2}a\cos\theta}\right)$$

$$\simeq \frac{qa\cos\theta}{4\pi\varepsilon_0 r^2}$$

$$= \frac{p\cos\theta}{4\pi\varepsilon_0 r^2} = \frac{\boldsymbol{p}\cdot\boldsymbol{r}}{4\pi\varepsilon_0 r^3}. \qquad (7.34)$$

The radial and azimuthal components of the field are

$$E_r = -\frac{\partial V}{\partial r} = \frac{1}{4\pi\varepsilon_0}\frac{2p\cos\theta}{r^3} \qquad (7.35)$$

$$E_\theta = -\frac{1}{r}\left(\frac{\partial V}{\partial\theta}\right) = \frac{1}{4\pi\varepsilon_0}\left(\frac{p\sin\theta}{r^3}\right). \qquad (7.36)$$

It can be seen that the electric field due to a dipole falls off with distance as r^3 and the potential as r^2, whereas the corresponding laws for a single charge are $1/r^2$ and $1/r$.

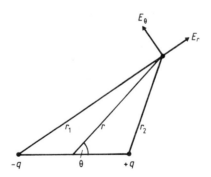

Figure 7.7 The electric field due to a dipole.

When a dipole is placed in a uniform electric field there is no net translational force on it, because the two charges experience equal and opposite forces, but there is a rotational force and the dipole will align in the direction of the electric field. If a dipole is placed in a non-uniform field it experiences a translational force as well as a couple. This force will now be calculated.

If E_x is the x-component of the electric field at the charge at position A then the field E'_x at position B will be

$$E'_x = E_x + \left(\frac{\partial E_x}{\partial x}\right)a_x + \left(\frac{\partial E_x}{\partial y}\right)a_y + \left(\frac{\partial E_x}{\partial z}\right)a_z$$

where a_x, a_y, a_z are the components of $\boldsymbol{a}$ in the direction of the three coordinate axes x, y and z.

The total force on the dipole is therefore

$$F_x = -qE_x + qE'_x$$
$$= qa_x\left(\frac{\partial E_x}{\partial x}\right) + qa_y\left(\frac{\partial E_x}{\partial y}\right) + qa_z\left(\frac{\partial E_x}{\partial z}\right).$$

Now

$$\frac{\partial E_x}{\partial y} = \frac{\partial}{\partial y}\left(-\frac{\partial V}{\partial x}\right) = \frac{\partial}{\partial x}\left(-\frac{\partial V}{\partial y}\right) = \frac{\partial E_y}{\partial x}$$

and similarly

$$\frac{\partial E_x}{\partial z} = \frac{\partial E_z}{\partial x}$$

so that

$$F_x = p_x\left(\frac{\partial E_x}{\partial x}\right) + p_y\left(\frac{\partial E_y}{\partial x}\right) + p_z\left(\frac{\partial E_z}{\partial x}\right). \tag{7.37}$$

Therefore there is a force on a dipole which is proportional to the rate of change of the electric field with distance. This can be written more generally as

$$F = (\boldsymbol{p} \cdot \nabla)E. \tag{7.38}$$

A neutral object will be polarised in an electric field so it becomes a dipole. If the field is non-uniform there is a translational force as described above. The movement of a neutral particle in a non-uniform field is called dielectrophoresis.

7.3.2 Polarisation of matter

Charge cannot flow in a perfect insulator but the electrons and ions will be displaced in an electric field and the atoms will polarise. The degree to which the material polarises is called its polarisability, α. The polarisability of an atom α_i is defined by the equation

$$p_i = \alpha_i E_{\text{loc}} \tag{7.39}$$

where p_i is the dipole moment of the atom and E_{loc} is the local electric field at the molecule. If the molecule is in a dielectric E_{loc} is not the same as E_0, the electric field applied to the dielectric.

The polarisation P, of a slab of dielectric is the induced dipole moment per unit volume of the material. i.e.

$$P = np_i$$

where n is the number of molecules per unit volume.

P can also be defined as the additional surface charge density produced when an electric field is applied to a slab of dielectric. The charge per unit area induced on the surface of a dielectric in an electric field was defined in §7.1.3 to be the displacement D, i.e.

$$P = D_r - D_0$$

where D_r is the displacement within a dielectric of relative permittivity ε_r and D_0 is the displacement in the absence of a dielectric. For an externally applied electric field E_0 this may be written as

$$P = \varepsilon_r \varepsilon_0 E_0 - \varepsilon_0 E_0$$
$$= \varepsilon_0 E_0 (\varepsilon_r - 1) \tag{7.40}$$

where $\varepsilon_r - 1$ is called the susceptibility, χ, of the medium.

The relationship between the polarisability, or the dipole moment, of an individual molecule and the dielectric constant may be found if the field inside the dielectric E_{loc}, can be related to the applied field E_0. This depends on the way in which the molecules are arranged in the dielectric. For a cubic array of molecules, or for a gas or liquid where molecules move at random and independently, the relationship is found to be

$$\frac{\varepsilon_r - 1}{\varepsilon_r + 2} = \frac{n_i \alpha_i}{3\varepsilon_0}. \tag{7.41}$$

This equation was first derived by Clausius and Mosotti and is named after them.

The dipole moment of a molecule in an electric field may arise from a number of sources.

(i) The electronic polarisability, which arises from the displacement of electrons in an atom relative to the positive nucleus.

(ii) The ionic polarisation due to the relative displacement of ions of opposite polarity within a solid.

(iii) The orientational polarisation, due to the rotation of molecules which have a permanent dipole moment. (This is highest in liquids where the molecules are able to rotate freely but is also significant in some solids.)

(iv) The interfacial polarisation, which arises from the accumulation of charge at a structural interface, e.g. grain boundaries in a solid, or the surfaces in powdered samples. Colloids have a charged double layer at the solid–liquid boundary and distortion of this can give rise to very high inter-facial polarisation.

(v) The nomadic polarisation, which arises from the response of thermally excited charges situated on long polymeric molecules. These electrons move over distances corresponding to one or more molecular lengths, much further than the movement of electrons in non-polymeric molecules (Pohl 1978).

A finite time, (different for each mechanism) is required after application of the field, before each of these dipoles is formed. The polarisability and the dielectric constant of the medium are therefore functions of frequency. The static dielectric constant is measured when sufficient time is allowed for all mechanisms to come into play and it is this quantity that defines the charge storage ability of a capacitor.

7.3.3 Complex permittivity

When an oscillating field is applied to a dielectric the displacement may lag the applied field by a phase δ, which depends on the mechanism of polarisation, i.e. for an applied field E,

$$E = E_0 \exp(i\omega t)$$
$$D = D_0 \exp[i(\omega t - \delta)].$$

It follows that

$$D/E = \varepsilon = (D_0/E_0 \exp i\delta)$$

i.e. the permittivity of the medium is complex and can be written

$$\varepsilon = \varepsilon' + i\varepsilon''$$

where ε' and ε'' are real numbers.

It is customary to express the ratio of the real and imaginary parts of the permittivity in terms of the angle by which they are out of phase;

$$\varepsilon''/\varepsilon' = \tan \delta. \tag{7.42}$$

7.3.4 The dielectrophoretic force

The net force on a body with dipole moment P per unit volume in a field E_0 is

$$F = (Pv \cdot \nabla)E.$$

For a body which is isotropically and linearly polarised

$$P = \alpha E_0$$
$$F = \alpha v(E_0 \cdot \nabla)E_0 = \tfrac{1}{2}\alpha v \nabla |E_0|^2 \tag{7.43}$$

where α is the polarisability of the medium.

It can be seen that the force is proportional to the volume of the sample, its polarisability and the gradient of the square of the electric field. Since the force depends on the square of the electric field it is independent of the field direction and there will be a force on a dipole in a non-uniform AC field.

The force on a small dielectric sphere in a non-uniform field
Consider a small sphere of radius a and dielectric constant ε_2, placed in a medium of dielectric constant ε_1 to which a non-uniform field is applied. It is assumed that the sphere is small compared with the dimensions of the field non-uniformity, i.e. the polarisation of the sphere can be calculated by assuming the field, E, is uniform over the dimensions of the sphere.

It will be shown in §7.5.4 that the dipole moment induced in the sphere in this situation is

$$p = 4\pi\varepsilon_1\varepsilon_0 a^3 E(\varepsilon_2 - \varepsilon_1)/(\varepsilon_2 + 2\varepsilon_1). \tag{7.44}$$

The force on a particle in a non-uniform field is

$$F = (p \cdot \nabla)E.$$

Therefore

$$F = 2\pi\varepsilon_1\varepsilon_0 \frac{a^3(\varepsilon_2 - \varepsilon_1)}{\varepsilon_2 + 2\varepsilon_1} \nabla|E^2|. \tag{7.45}$$

It can be seen that, if $\varepsilon_2 > \varepsilon_1$, the force is in the direction of the higher field, but if $\varepsilon_2 < \varepsilon_1$ the force changes sign. Bubbles of gas in a liquid, or liquid emulsions where the dispersed phase is of lower dielectric constant, will move to the low-field region. The force does not increase indefinitely as the dielectric constant of the sphere increases, but reaches a limit which is set by the dielectric constant of the surrounding medium.

When two spheres are close together in a dielectric medium in a uniform field, each will distort the field so the local field is non-uniform. There is therefore a force between two neutral spheres in a uniform electric field. The interaction energy and hence the force between the two spheres has been calculated by Pohl (1978).

7.4 IDENTIFICATION OF FIELD LINES AND EQUIPOTENTIALS

7.4.1 Introduction

The solution of a number of different types of electrostatic problems requires a knowledge of the electric field at all points in a system. For example, the field is required in order to define the paths of charged particles, to calculate the force between charged bodies or to define positions of electrical breakdown.

It is useful at this stage, to re-introduce the concept of the electric field line, which was discussed in Chapter 1, as this provides a means of visualising electrostatic interactions. An electric field line is an imaginary line along which the force between charged bodies is transmitted. It is the path followed by a free positive charge. A field line may be considered to start and end on free or induced charges and the density of field lines at a surface gives the surface charge density. The density of field lines in space is proportional to the magnitude of the electric field. Field lines are always perpendicular to equipotential surfaces.

If the electric charge distribution is known, in any system of conductors and insulators, the field and potential are uniquely defined, and can be found by a number of different techniques. These include construction methods, measurement in electrostatic models, or calculation using Gauss's law, Coulomb's equation or Poisson's equation.

7.4.2 Finding field lines and equipotentials by construction

If a system of charges can be divided into components for which the individual equipotentials are known, then the equipotentials for the combination of charges can be found by construction. For example, consider two small charged bodies with charges q_1 and q_2, in air.

The potential a distance r from the charge q_1 is

$$V = q_1/4\pi\varepsilon_0 r.$$

Therefore if V is set to 1, 2, 3, 4, etc a series of spheres can be drawn for which

$$r = q_1/4\pi\varepsilon_0 V.$$

These are a series of equipotentials for the charge q_1.

The same process can be carried out for the second charge, q_2, giving a second set of spheres which intersect the first set. At each point of intersection the potential due to each individual charge is known. Potential is a scalar quantity, therefore the resultant potential is the algebraic sum of the two components. The surface passing through the intersections for which the resultant potential is the same, is an equipotential of the combined system. On the right-hand side of figure 7.8 the dotted curves are the equipotentials due to two equal and opposite charges and the full curves show the equipotentials of the combined system. The inner equipotentials of the combined system are approximately spherical; however, they are not exactly spherical, and the equipotentials arising from two charged spheres are not the same as those arising from point charges located at the centres of the spheres.

Electric field   Equipotentials

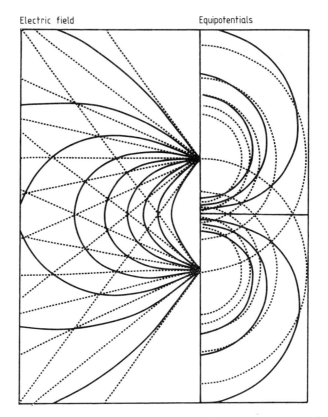

Figure 7.8 The electric field and equipotentials due to two equal and opposite point charges by construction. The dotted curves are the field and equipotentials due to the two charges individually and the full curves are the field and equipotentials of the combined system.

The electric field lines from a single centre of charge are straight lines radiating from the centre. The number of field lines is proportional to the charge. The number of field lines passing through an element of surface dS is equal to $\int E \cdot dS$. Field lines may be plotted by joining the points of intersection where the fields of the two individual charge systems are the same.

Figure 7.9 shows the field and equipotentials when the two charges have the same polarity but are in the ratio of four to one. Each point is surrounded by equipotentials which are nearly spheres. Any equipotential surface can be replaced by a conducting body of the same potential, without changing the form of the field or equipotentials. This diagram therefore shows the field due to two charged conductors which are nearly spherical and have charges in the ratio of four to one. The figure also shows the field lines due to an ovoid conductor (represented by one of the equipotentials which surrounds both charges). Since field lines originate at surface charges, the diagram illustrates the surface density of charge on an ovoidal charged body. It can be seen that this is greatest at the small end and less at the large end, with the lowest charge density in a circle rather nearer the small end than the large end.

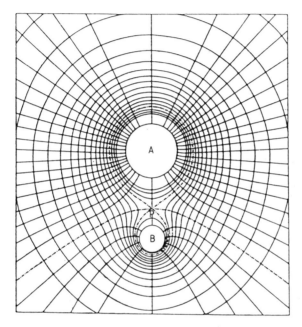

Figure 7.9 Field lines and equipotentials for two charges of the same polarity of value q and $4q$ (from Maxwell 1904).

Figure 7.10 shows the field lines and equipotentials due to a point charge in a field which, before the introduction of the charge, was uniform. This was found by combining the equipotentials and field lines of a point charge with those of a uniform field. This solution also applies to the field between two planes, one of which has a protuberance near its middle point, as shown by the bold curve in the figure. The extent of the protuberance is changed by choosing a different equipotential to represent the surface.

This method of combining the equipotentials of two systems can only be used if the charges in the combined system are in the same position as in the separate systems. For example, if two charged spheres are brought together they will polarise and the charges will not be in the same position as when the spheres were far apart.

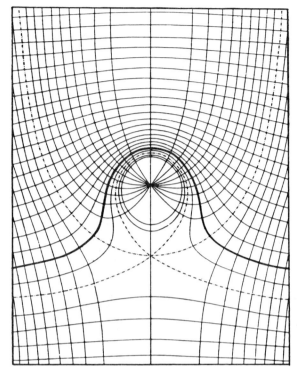

Figure 7.10 The electric field and equipotentials for a point charge in a uniform field (from Maxwell 1904). This represents the field at a protuberance on a plane in a uniform field.

7.4.3 Field lines and equipotentials by measurement

Field lines are the lines travelled by charged particles, therefore they may be found by setting up a model system where charge can flow and its path can be detected. The two most common methods use an electrolytic tank or resistive paper. In an electrolytic tank, electrodes in the form of the system to be modelled are placed in a conducting fluid and connected to an alternating current source. The current flow between the electrodes through the electrolyte follows the electric field lines and can be detected using a probe. Alternatively, the electrodes can be painted on to resistive paper, using a conducting silver paint. When a potential is applied to the electrodes, a current flows along the field lines. The potential drop along the resistive path can be measured using a simple meter and probe, and so the equipotentials can be plotted.

7.4.4 Fluid mapping techniques

It can be shown that, when a viscous liquid flows between closely spaced parallel plates, the average velocity is the gradient of a velocity potential which satisfies Laplace's equation in two dimensions. The paths of the fluid coincide with the streamlines of the velocity vector and can be made visible by colouring the fluid. A simple system for constructing a field map is shown in figure 7.11. Water leaves an elevated tank and enters the restricted flow

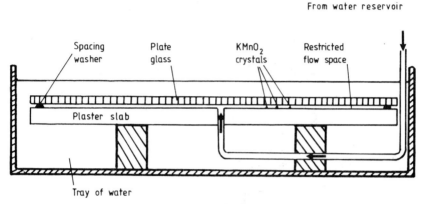

Figure 7.11 Apparatus for fluid flow mapping of an electric field (from A D Moore in Rogers (1954)).

space between a smooth plaster slab and a sheet of plate glass by means of holes in the plaster slab. A hole, where water enters the system, represents a positive charge (i.e. a source of field lines). A hole through which water leaves represents a negative charge. Fairly complicated systems can be visualised using this technique, for example figure 7.12 shows the field due to a central charged line surrounded by six symmetrically spaced lines representing a grid and a circular outer boundary representing a cylindrical conductor. With this technique, only the direction of the field is represented. The spacing between the lines is a function of the position of the potassium permanganate crystals used to dye the fluid and does not represent the number density of field lines in the system (Moore 1954).

7.4.5 Finding the electric field and potential using Coulomb's equation

(i) *A uniform line charge*
The potential due to a uniform line charge of λ C m^{-1} is shown in figure

Figure 7.12 The fluid flow map of the electric field due to a central wire and six-grid electrodes (from Rogers 1954).

7.13. From equation (7.9) the potential at a point P due to an elemental section of line dL in air is

$$dV = \frac{\lambda\,dL}{4\pi\varepsilon_0[(z-L)^2 + y^2]^{1/2}}.$$

Therefore the total potential is

$$V = \frac{1}{4\pi\varepsilon_0}\int_{-a}^{a}\frac{\lambda\,dL}{[(z-L)^2 + y^2]^{1/2}}$$

$$= \frac{-\lambda}{4\pi\varepsilon_0}[\ln\{(z-L) + [(z-L)^2 + y^2]^{1/2}\}]_{-a}^{a}$$

$$= \frac{\lambda}{4\pi\varepsilon_0}\ln\left(\frac{z+a+[(z+a)^2 + y^2]^{1/2}}{z-a+[(z-a)^2 + y^2]^{1/2}}\right). \tag{7.46}$$

Equipotentials may be plotted by substituting constant values for V and for each V plotting the values of z for each y.

Rearranging equation (7.46), it may be seen that

$$\frac{z+a+[(z+a)^2 + y^2]^{1/2}}{z-a+[(z-a)^2 + y^2]^{1/2}} = \exp\left(\frac{4\pi\varepsilon_0 V}{q}\right).$$

Denoting the right-hand side of this equation as k, this can be written as (Rogers 1954)

$$\frac{(k-1)^2}{(k+1)^2}\left(\frac{z}{a}\right)^2 + \frac{(k-1)^2}{4k}\left(\frac{y}{a}\right)^2 = 1.$$

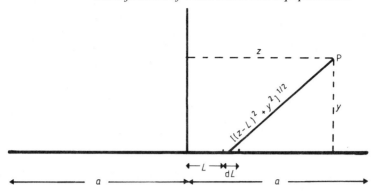

Figure 7.13 The electric field and potential arising from a uniform line charge.

Different values of V give different k and the equation represents a family of ellipses with a semi-major axis of

$$\frac{(k+1)a}{k-1}$$

a semi-minor axis of

$$\frac{2k^{1/2}a}{k-1}$$

an eccentricity of

$$\frac{k-1}{k+1}$$

and foci at $z = \pm a$. The field lines are then hyperbolas perpendicular to these ellipses.

(ii) *Two equal and opposite point charges*
The potential at any point P due to charges $+q$ and $-q$ a distance $2d$ apart is the sum of the potentials due to each charge individually, i.e. with the notation of figure 7.14;

$$V = \frac{q}{4\pi\varepsilon_0\varepsilon_r}\left(\frac{1}{[y^2 + (x-d)^2]^{1/2}} - \frac{1}{[y^2 + (x+d)^2]^{1/2}}\right). \qquad (7.47)$$

By setting $V =$ a constant and plotting y for each value of x, equipotentials are mapped out. The result is shown in figure 7.15. The inner curves are approximately circles and the $x = 0$ axis coincides with the equipotential $V = 0$. This is the same solution as found by construction in §7.4.2. The x-component of the electric field can be found by differentiating this expression with respect to x and similarly the y-component by differentiating with respect to y.

The equipotentials shown in figure 7.15 are nearly spheres. Any equipotential can be replaced by a conducting surface at that potential without altering the field or equipotentials of the system. If we consider two of these near spheres of radii a and b respectively, such that $a \ll d$ and $b \ll d$ then the

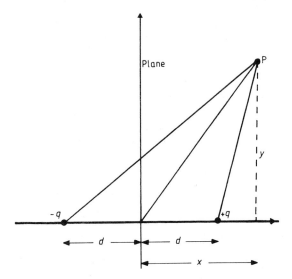

Figure 7.14 The image of a point charge in a plane.

charge is approximately at the centre of each sphere and the potential at the surfaces of a and b are approximately

$$V_a = \frac{q}{4\pi\varepsilon_0\varepsilon_r}\left(\frac{1}{a} - \frac{1}{2d}\right)$$

$$V_b = \frac{q}{4\pi\varepsilon_0\varepsilon_r}\left(\frac{-1}{b} + \frac{1}{2d}\right)$$

where higher powers of a/d or b/d are neglected.

The capacitance between the two near spheres with charges q and $-q$ respectively is thus

$$C = q/(V_a - V_b)$$

$$= 4\pi\varepsilon_0\varepsilon_r\left[\frac{1}{a} + \frac{1}{b}\left(1 + \frac{ab}{d(a+b)}\right)\right].$$

This approximation applies only when the spacing is large compared with the radii of the spheres.

It is also possible to replace the $V = 0$ equipotential by an infinite earthed plane, with no change to the equipotentials or field lines. The field on one side of the $x = 0$ axis, produced by the two charges, is identical to the field produced by a single charge, a distance d from an infinite conducting plane at earth potential. A charge in front of an earthed plane may be considered to have a mirror image charge of opposite polarity in the plane. This forms the basis of the image method of solving electric field problems, which is discussed in the next section. A method of calculating the capacitance between two spherical conductors, which can be applied to all radii and spacing, is given by Russel (1922).

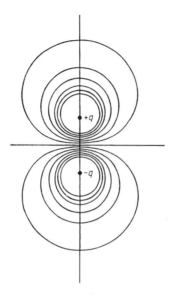

Figure 7.15 The equipotentials for two equal and opposite point charges or for a point charge in front of a plane.

7.4.6 The method of images

An electrical image is defined as 'an electrified point or system of points on one side of a surface which would produce on the other side of the surface the same electrical action which the actual electrification of that surface really does produce'. That is, the image charge replaces the total charge induced on the surface of a conductor without altering the field and potential distribution.

(i) *The image of a point charge in an infinite conducting plane*
When a point charge $+q$ is placed a distance d in front of an infinite plane, the surface charge induced on the plane terminates the field lines and the induced charge is equal in magnitude and opposite in polarity to the point charge. The infinite conducting plane and the point charge produce a field which is identical to that which would be produced by locating a charge $-q$ a distance d behind the plane.

The method of images can be used to calculate the surface density of charge on the plane as a function of position. The potential due to a point charge and a plane is the same as due to two point charges as discussed above and is given by equation (7.47). The x- and y-components of the electric field are found by taking the partial derivatives of this expression:

$$E_x = -\frac{\partial V}{\partial x} = \frac{q}{4\pi\varepsilon_0\varepsilon_r}\{(x-d)[y^2 + (x-d)^2]^{-3/2}$$
$$- (x+d)[y^2 + (x+d)^2]^{-3/2}\} \qquad (7.48)$$

$$E_y = -\frac{\partial V}{\partial y} = \frac{qy}{4\pi\varepsilon_0\varepsilon_r}\{[y^2 + (x-d)^2]^{-3/2} - [y^2 + (x+d)^2]^{-3/2}\}. \qquad (7.49)$$

At the plane $x = 0$, E_y vanishes and E_x becomes

$$E_x = -\frac{q}{2\pi\varepsilon_0\varepsilon_r} d(y^2 + d^2)^{-3/2}.$$

The induced charge per unit area, Q_s is the displacement D, i.e.

$$Q_s = E_x\varepsilon_0\varepsilon_r \qquad (7.50)$$

$$Q_s = -\frac{q}{2\pi} d(y^2 + d^2)^{-3/2}.$$

If this is integrated over the plane the total charge is q as required.

(ii) *The image of a point charge and a conducting sphere*
The image charge is not necessarily equal and opposite to the true charge. For example, consider the case of a point charge at a point P outside a conducting sphere of radius r, as shown in figure 7.16.

By symmetry, the image charge must lie on the line joining the centre of the sphere and the point charge. Let the value of the image charge be q' and its position be defined by the point P'. The potential at point Q on the surface

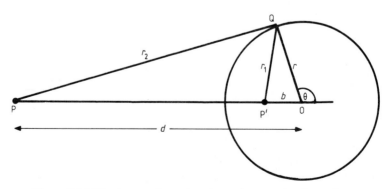

Figure 7.16 The image of a point charge in a conducting sphere.

of the sphere is then

$$V = \frac{1}{4\pi\varepsilon_0\varepsilon_r}\left(\frac{q}{r_1} + \frac{q'}{r_2}\right)$$

$$= \frac{1}{4\pi\varepsilon_0\varepsilon_r}\left(\frac{q}{(r^2 + d^2 + 2rd\,\cos\theta)^{1/2}} + \frac{q'}{(r^2 + b^2 + 2rb\,\cos\theta)^{1/2}}\right). \quad (7.51)$$

It is only possible to make $V = 0$ over the whole surface of the sphere if the functions in the denominators are similar functions of θ. Therefore b must be chosen so that

$$b/r = r/d. \quad (7.52)$$

When P and P' are related by these distances, they are called the inverse points of the sphere. It can be seen that the triangles POQ and P'OQ have a common angle. From equation (7.52), the adjacent sides of these triangles are proportional therefore the triangles are similar and it follows that

$$b/r = r/d = r_1/r_2. \quad (7.53)$$

The potential at Q due to point charges at P and P' is

$$V = \frac{q + (d/r)q'}{4\pi\varepsilon_0\varepsilon_r(r^2 + d^2 + 2dr\,\cos\theta)^{1/2}}.$$

This will be zero if we make $q' = -qr/d$. Therefore the image of a charge q in an earthed conducting sphere is a charge $-qr/d$ at the inverse point in the sphere.

If the sphere is an isolated conducting sphere and initially uncharged, its total charge must remain zero. In this case there must be a second charge $-q'$, at a position such that the surface remains an equipotential, i.e. $-q'$ must be at the centre of the sphere.

(iii) *Image of a point charge in two conducting planes*
If two conducting planes intersect at an angle π/n, and there is a point charge P between them, the system can be represented by a finite system of images. In figure 7.17, AO and BO are sections of the two planes with the angle $AOB = \pi/n$. A circle with radius OP and centre O is constructed. Q_1 is the image of P in OB, Q_2 is the image of P in OA, P_2 is the image of Q_1 in AO etc. The electrified point and the alternate images P_2 and P_3 are ranged round the circle at intervals of 2AOB with the images Q_1, Q_2, Q_3 at intervals of the same magnitude. If 2AOB is $2\pi/n$ where n is a whole number there will be a finite number of images and none will fall in the angle AOB. If the angle $AOB \neq 2\pi/n$ it will be impossible to represent the system by a finite number of points.

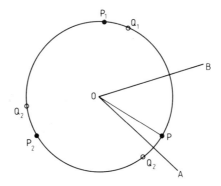

Figure 7.17 The image of a charge P in two planes.

7.4.7 Field and potential calculations using Gauss's law

(i) *Concentric cylinders*

The use of Gauss's theorem to find the field and potential between two concentric spheres was discussed in §7.2.2. The same exercise can also be carried out for coaxial cylinders, with radii a and b and a charge Q per unit length. From Gauss's law the field arising from length L of the inner cylinder is given by

$$\int E_A \, dS = QL/\varepsilon_0\varepsilon_r$$

i.e. at a Gaussian surface in the form of a cylinder of radius r, $(a < r < b)$ the field due to the inner cylinder of radius a is

$$E_A = Q/2\pi\varepsilon_0\varepsilon_r r. \qquad (7.54)$$

The field due to the outer cylinder is zero (since there is no field inside a charged conductor due to a charge on its surface).

Therefore the total field at r, E_r, is

$$E_r = E_A$$

$$V_x = -\int_{-\infty}^{x} E_r \, dr$$

$$V_b - V_a = V = \int_{a}^{b} E_r \, dr$$

$$V = \frac{Q}{2\pi\varepsilon_0\varepsilon_r} \ln b/a$$

and the capacitance between two coaxial cylinders

$$C = q/V = QL/V = 2\pi\varepsilon_0\varepsilon_r L[1/\ln(b/a)]. \qquad (7.55)$$

(ii) *Two parallel line charges*
From Gauss's law the field at a cylindrical surface a distance r_1 from a uniform line charge is

$$E = Q/2\pi\varepsilon_0\varepsilon_r r_1$$

and the potential a distance r_1 from a uniform line charge is

$$V = - \int E \, dr = \frac{-Q}{2\pi\varepsilon_0\varepsilon_r} \ln r_1 + \text{constant}$$

(we cannot assume the potential at infinity is zero because the line charge extends to infinity).

The potential due to two parallel line charges of strength Q and $-Q$ per unit length (shown in figure 7.18) is the sum of the potentials from the two

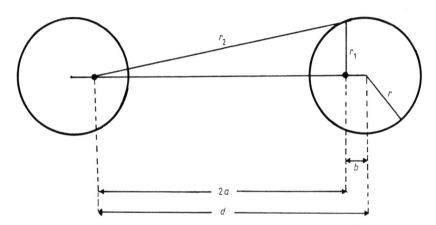

Figure 7.18 The field and potential due to two parallel line charges.

lines individually

$$V = \frac{Q}{2\pi\varepsilon_0\varepsilon_r} \ln \left(\frac{r_2}{r_1}\right) + \text{constant}. \tag{7.56}$$

To find the equipotential surfaces, V is set to be constant, therefore r_2/r_1 must be constant. This condition is fulfilled if Q and $-Q$ are positioned at inverse points of cylinders in which case $r_2/r_1 = d/r$ (where d and r are defined in figure 7.18). The equipotential surfaces given by equation (7.56), thus have the form of cylinders of radius r with the line charges at the inverse points, as shown in figure 7.19.

The position of the centres of the cylinders, a distance b from the inverse points can be found from the theorem of inverse points (equation (7.52))

$$bd = r^2.$$

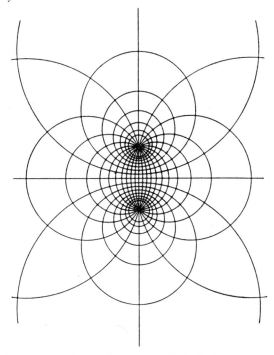

Figure 7.19 The equipotential lines and field lines for two equal and opposite line charges or for a line charge in front of an earthed plane.

The surface whose potential is zero is the median plane for which $r_1 = r_2$.

From figure 7.19 it can be seen that the field due to two cylinders or a cylinder and a plane can be found exactly by replacing the cylinders with line charges at the inverse points of the cylinders. (It will be remembered that the equipotentials due to point charges were not true spheres and field problems involving spheres cannot be accurately solved by replacing a sphere by a point charge.) It can also be seen that the problem of a line charge (or a cylinder) above a plane can be treated by the method of images.

(iii) *The capacitance between two parallel cylinders*

The capacitance between two parallel cylinders each of radius r with a distance $2a$ between their centres, is found by choosing points P and P' inside the cylinders so that these are the inverse points of a family of circles two of which correspond to the cylinders in question. The cylinders may then be replaced by line charges with a strength of Q and $-Q$ per unit length at P and P'.

With the notation of figure 7.20 the potentials at the surfaces of the two

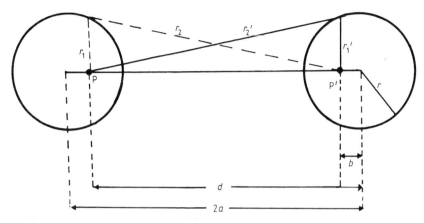

Figure 7.20 The capacitance between two parallel cylinders.

cylinders are then

$$V_Q = \frac{-Q}{2\pi\varepsilon_0\varepsilon_r} \ln\left(\frac{r_2}{r_1}\right) \qquad \text{where } r_2/r_1 = d/r$$

$$V_{Q'} = \frac{Q}{2\pi\varepsilon_0\varepsilon_r} \ln\left(\frac{r_2'}{r_1'}\right) \qquad \text{where } r_2'/r_1' = d/r.$$

Therefore

$$V = V_Q - V_{Q'} = \frac{Q \ln (d/r)}{\pi\varepsilon_0\varepsilon_r}$$

and

$$C = q/V = \pi\varepsilon_0\varepsilon_r/\ln(d/r). \tag{7.57}$$

where C is the capacitance per unit length. From figure 7.20 it can be seen that

$$d + b = 2a$$

but

$$db = r^2$$

i.e.

$$d^2 - 2ad + r^2 = 0.$$

Solving we have

$$d = a \pm (a^2 - r^2)^{1/2}$$

and since the value of d required is greater than a, the negative root can be neglected, and the potential difference between the two cylinders is given by

$$V_Q - V_{Q'} = V = \frac{a}{\pi\varepsilon_0\varepsilon_r}\left[\ln\left(\frac{a + (a^2 - r^2)^{1/2}}{r}\right)\right].$$

The capacitance per unit length is

$$C = \frac{Q}{V} = \frac{\pi\varepsilon_0\varepsilon_r}{\ln\{[a + (a^2 - r^2)^{1/2}]/r\}}.$$

When $a \gg r$ this approaches a limiting value of

$$C = \frac{\pi\varepsilon_0\varepsilon_r}{\ln 2a/r}. \tag{7.58}$$

(iv) *The field due to a volume distribution of charge*
Consider a uniform distribution of charge of density Q_v confined to a cylinder of radius a as shown in figure 7.21. At any Gaussian surface defined by the cylinder of unit length and radius b (where $b > a$)

$$\int D \, dS = \pi a^2 Q_v$$

$$D = \frac{a^2 Q_v}{2b} \qquad b > a$$

$$E = \frac{a^2 Q_v}{2b\varepsilon_0\varepsilon_r}.$$

At the Gaussian surface defined by a cylinder of radius c ($c < a$) the charge enclosed is $\pi c^2 Q_v$

$$D = cQ_v/2$$

$$E = cQ_v/2\varepsilon_0\varepsilon_r.$$

The solutions for D and E match at $c = b = a$.
The potential inside the cylinder is given by

$$V = -\int E \, dc.$$

Therefore for points inside the volume of charge

$$V = -\frac{c^2 Q_v}{4\varepsilon_0\varepsilon_r} + K$$

where K is the constant of integration. If we define $V = 0$ at $c = a$, then

$$K = \frac{a^2 Q_v}{4\varepsilon_0\varepsilon_r}$$

$$V = \frac{Q_v}{4\varepsilon_0\varepsilon_r}(-c^2 + a^2)$$

(a)

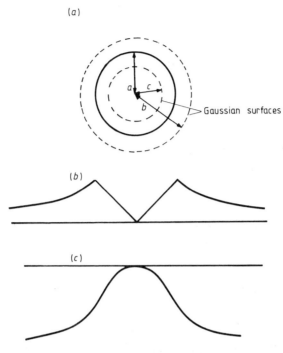

Gaussian surfaces

(b)

(c)

Figure 7.21 The field and potential due to a cylindrical volume distribution of charge: (a), notation; (b), displacement (D); (c), potential.

and at the centre of the cylinder where $c = 0$

$$V = \frac{a^2 Q_v}{4\varepsilon_0 \varepsilon_r}.$$

For points outside the cylinder

$$V = \frac{-a^2 Q_v}{2\varepsilon_0 \varepsilon_r} \ln\left(\frac{b}{a}\right).$$

Figure 7.21 shows the field and potential as a function of position. There is no discontinuity in the field at the boundary of the charge distribution. The region of maximum field is the outside of the cylinder of charge, where the field is

$$E = a Q_v / 2\varepsilon_0.$$

If E is limited by the breakdown of the air to

$$E = 3 \times 10^6 \text{ V m}^{-1}$$

then the maximum charge density is limited to

$$Q_v = \frac{5.29 \times 10^{-5}}{a} \, C \, m^{-3}.$$

This sets the maximum charge density that can be transported in a pipe without discharging. It can be seen that the maximum charge density increases for smaller pipes, i.e. the maximum charge density can be increased by subdividing a pipe.

7.5 ELECTRIC FIELD AND POTENTIAL BY SOLUTION OF LAPLACE'S EQUATION

7.5.1 Introduction

In principle the potential distribution due to any system of charges and conductors can be found using Poisson's equation:

$$\nabla^2 V = Q_v/\varepsilon_0\varepsilon_r. \tag{7.59}$$

When the charge density is zero this reduces to Laplace's equation:

$$\nabla^2 V = 0. \tag{7.60}$$

In practice, it is difficult to solve Poisson's equation analytically and even Laplace's equation can only be solved for particular geometries. The equations of Poisson and Laplace have a large number of possible solutions but, for a given system, there is only one solution that satisfies both the required equation and the boundary conditions (i.e. the fixed potentials applied to the conductors of the system). This statement is known as the uniqueness theorem. A proof is given by Rogers (1954).

In order to define the electric field and potentials of a system using Laplace's equation one must be able to express the physical position and the shape of the boundaries of the problem in a reasonably simple way. The surfaces of conductors are equipotentials, and electric field lines and equipotentials are orthogonal sets of curves, therefore one may be able to choose coordinate surfaces which are themselves field lines or equipotentials and transform Laplace's equation mathematically to this coordinate system.

Many electrostatic problems were actually first solved in reverse, i.e. solutions to Laplace's equation were found which gave a function for the potential. This function was then plotted to identify the electrode system represented.

The general procedure for finding the field and potential in any given system, by transformation of coordinates is as follows.

(i) Transform Laplace's equation into a coordinate system that fits the geometry of the problem.

(ii) Separate this equation into three ordinary differential equations.

(iii) Solve these equations.

(iv) Apply the known boundary conditions to find the unique solution to the problem.

The most difficult part of this procedure lies in the first three steps. However, general solutions to Laplace's equation, for a large number of different coordinate systems, have already been found. For example, Moon and Spencer (1961) give solutions to Laplace's equation in forty, three-dimensional coordinate systems, which cover most practical geometries for which a separable solution of Laplace's equation may be found. It only remains to substitute the known boundary conditions and transform back to conventional coordinate systems.

Before solving a problem using one of the less conventional coordinate systems the more conventional cartesian and cylindrical coordinates will be discussed, to illustrate the solution of Laplace's equation by the separation of variables and the application of boundary conditions.

7.5.2 Laplace's equation in cartesian coordinates

In cartesian coordinates Laplace's equation is given by

$$\frac{\partial^2 V}{\partial x^2} + \frac{\partial^2 V}{\partial y^2} + \frac{\partial^2 V}{\partial z^2} = 0. \tag{7.61}$$

The variables are said to be separable when the solution of the equation can be written as the product of three functions each of which is a function of only one of the variables, i.e.

$$V = X(x)Y(y)Z(z).$$

Equation (7.61) can then be written in the form

$$YZ\frac{d^2 X}{dx^2} + XZ\frac{d^2 Y}{dy^2} + XY\frac{d^2 Z}{dz^2} = 0 \tag{7.62}$$

and dividing by XYZ we obtain

$$\frac{1}{X}\frac{d^2 X}{dx^2} + \frac{1}{Y}\frac{d^2 Y}{dy^2} + \frac{1}{Z}\frac{d^2 Z}{dz^2} = 0. \tag{7.63}$$

The three terms are completely independent. We can therefore put

$$\frac{1}{X}\frac{d^2 X}{dx^2} = a^2 \tag{7.64}$$

$$\frac{1}{Y}\frac{d^2 Y}{dy^2} = b^2 \tag{7.65}$$

and

$$\frac{1}{Z}\frac{d^2Z}{dz^2} = c^2 \qquad (7.66)$$

where $a^2 + b^2 + c^2 = 0$.

These are ordinary differential equations and have only one variable. The solutions can be found in any mathematical text on differential equations e.g. Stephenson (1966). Two solutions are:

$$X_1 = A_1 e^{+ax}$$

and

$$X_2 = A_2 e^{-ax}.$$

The sums and differences of these functions are also solutions (see Appendix) therefore there are also pairs of solutions sinh ax and cosh ax, if a is real, and sin ax and cos ax, if a is imaginary.

A general solution of Laplace's equation in cartesian coordinates and three dimensions is given by

$$V = \sum A_i e^{\pm ax} e^{\pm by} e^{\pm cz} \qquad (7.67)$$

with

$$a^2 + b^2 + c^2 = 0.$$

There are eight different combinations of the polarity of the exponent and an infinite number of values of a, b and c. For each solution there is a different value of A_i. The correct combination of terms is found by substituting boundary conditions.

Many problems have a centre of symmetry so that the potential is independent of one of the coordinates. We then have

$$\frac{d^2X}{dx^2} = a^2X \qquad (7.68)$$

$$\frac{d^2Y}{dy^2} = -a^2Y. \qquad (7.69)$$

This has the solutions

$$X = A e^{ax} + B e^{-ax} \qquad (7.70)$$

$$\text{where } a \text{ is real}$$

$$Y = A \sin ay + B \cos ay \qquad (7.71)$$

$$X = A \sin ax + B \cos ax \qquad (7.72)$$

$$\text{where } a \text{ is imaginary}$$

$$Y = A e^{ay} + B e^{-ay} \qquad (7.73)$$

and

$$X = A + Bx \qquad \text{(7.74)}$$
$$\text{where } a^2 = 0.$$
$$Y = A + By \qquad \text{(7.75)}$$

The correct combination of terms is found by substituting the boundary conditions. Cartesian coordinate surfaces represent infinite planes which are seldom of physical significance in real electrostatic problems, therefore, this exercise will be carried out in the second example, in which cylindrical coordinates are used.

7.5.3 Cylindrical coordinates

Laplace's equation in cylindrical coordinates is written as

$$\frac{\partial^2 V}{\partial r^2} + \frac{1}{r}\frac{\partial V}{\partial r} + \frac{1}{r^2}\frac{\partial^2 V}{\partial \theta^2} + \frac{\partial^2 V}{\partial z^2} = 0. \qquad \text{(7.76)}$$

The coordinate surfaces are

$$r = \text{const} \qquad \text{concentric cylinders}$$
$$\theta = \text{const} \qquad \text{half-planes}$$
$$z = \text{const} \qquad \text{planes.}$$

When V is independent of z Laplace's equation becomes

$$\frac{\partial^2 V}{\partial r^2} + \frac{1}{r}\frac{\partial V}{\partial r} + \frac{1}{r^2}\frac{\partial^2 V}{\partial \theta^2} = 0. \qquad \text{(7.77)}$$

This equation is separable, i.e.

$$V = F_1(r)F_2(\theta).$$

Following the same procedure as for cartesian coordinates (or referring to Moon and Spencer 1961) the two ordinary differential equations which must be solved are

$$r^2 \frac{d^2 F_1}{dr^2} + r\frac{dF_1}{dr} = a^2 \qquad \text{(7.78)}$$

$$\frac{d^2 F_2}{d\theta^2} = b^2 \qquad \text{(7.79)}$$

where

$$a^2 + b^2 = 0.$$

When $a = 0$ the solutions to these two equations are

$$F_1 = A_0 r + B_0 \qquad (7.80)$$

$$F_2 = C_0 \theta + D_0 \qquad (7.81)$$

and if $a \neq 0$

$$F_1 = A r^a + B r^{-a} \qquad (7.82)$$

$$F_2 = C \cos a\theta + D \sin a\theta. \qquad (7.83)$$

The solution to Laplace's equation is therefore

$$V = (A_0 \ln r + B_0)(C_0 \theta + D_0) + (A_a r^a + B_a r^{-a})(C_a \cos a\theta + D_a \sin a\theta). \qquad (7.84)$$

In most physical problems the potential is a single-valued function of position, i.e. the potential at r and θ is the same as at r and $\theta + 2\pi$. In this case a has integer values only and $C_0 = 0$, so that

$$V = (A_0 \ln r + B_0) + (A_a r^a + B_a r^{-a})(C_a \cos a\theta + D_a \sin a\theta). \quad (7.85)$$

Let us now take the case of an earthed conducting cylinder of radius R, inserted into a uniform field E_0. If the potential at the origin (taken as the centre of the cylinder) is zero, then the potential as a function of θ and r in the absence of the cylinder is

$$V = -E_0 r \cos \theta.$$

We know the following boundary conditions.

(i) At large distances, where $r \gg R$ the cylinder has no effect and equation (7.85) must reduce to

$$V = -E_0 r \cos \theta. \qquad (7.86)$$

This establishes that $A_0 = 0$, $B_0 = 0$ and $a = 1$.

(ii) The potential is symmetrical about the z-axis, therefore the potential at r and θ is the same as at r and $-\theta$. Therefore $D = 0$ and $A \times C = -E_0$.

(iii) The potential is zero when $r = R$ therefore,

$$AR + BR^{-1} = 0.$$

When all these conditions are included the potential reduces to

$$V = -E_0(r - R^2/r) \cos \theta.$$

7.5.4 Spherical coordinates

The potential for a sphere in a uniform field is more difficult to solve because the solutions of the separated Laplace's equation in spherical coordinates are more complicated in form. A full analysis is beyond the scope of this book, however, the results are used in a number of practical situations, therefore a brief description of the method used to solve the problem and the simple formulae which eventually result, when common boundary conditions are substituted, are presented here.

Laplace's equation in spherical coordinates is given by

$$\frac{1}{r^2}\frac{\partial}{\partial r}\left(r^2\frac{\partial V}{\partial r}\right)+\frac{1}{r^2\sin\theta}\frac{\partial}{\partial\theta}\left(\sin\theta\frac{\partial V}{\partial\theta}\right)+\frac{1}{r^2\sin^2\theta}\frac{\partial^2 V}{\partial\varphi^2}=0. \quad (7.87)$$

A sphere in a uniform field has symmetry about the polar axis, therefore the potential is independent of φ

$$\frac{1}{r^2}\frac{\partial}{\partial r}\left(r^2\frac{\partial V}{\partial r}\right)+\frac{1}{r^2\sin\theta}\frac{\partial}{\partial\theta}\left(\sin\theta\frac{\partial V}{\partial\theta}\right)=0. \quad (7.88)$$

The variables are separable, i.e. V can be written as

$$V(r,\theta)=Z(r)P(\theta).$$

Substituting this expression for V, equation (7.88) becomes

$$\frac{1}{r^2}P(\theta)\frac{d}{dr}\left(r^2\frac{dZ}{dr}\right)+\frac{Z(r)}{r^2\sin\theta}\frac{d}{d\theta}\left(\sin\theta\frac{dP}{d\theta}\right)=0.$$

Dividing by $P(\theta)Z(r)$ we have

$$\frac{1}{Z}\frac{d}{dr}\left(r^2\frac{dZ}{dr}\right)=\frac{-1}{P(\sin\theta)}\frac{d}{d\theta}\left(\sin\theta\frac{dP}{d\theta}\right).$$

This may be assigned the value k and we have two differential equations, each with only one variable.

Consider first the equation in θ

$$\frac{1}{\sin\theta}\frac{d}{d\theta}\left(\sin\theta\frac{dP}{d\theta}\right)+kP=0. \quad (7.89)$$

This is known as Legendre's equation. The only acceptable solutions correspond to values of k for which $k=n(n+1)$, where n is a positive integer (Reitz and Milford 1960).

These solutions are designated by $P_n(\theta)$, and are Legendre polynomials in $\cos\theta$. The Legendre polynomials for the first four values of n are given in table 7.1.

Table 7.1 The Legendre polynomials

n	$P_n(\theta)$
0	1
1	$\cos\theta$
2	$\frac{1}{2}(3\cos^2\theta-1)$
3	$\frac{1}{2}(5\cos^3\theta-3\cos\theta)$

The radial equation obtained by separation of variables is

$$\frac{d}{dr}\left(r^2 \frac{dZ}{dr}\right) = n(n+1) Z. \tag{7.90}$$

This has two independent solutions

$$Z_n = r^n \quad \text{and } Z_n = r^{-(n+1)}.$$

Solutions to Laplace's equation are products of $Z_n(r)$ and $P_n(\theta)$, where Z and P must correspond to the same values of n, i.e.

$$V = r^n P_n(\theta) \quad \text{or } V = r^{-n(n+1)} P_n(\theta).$$

If the sphere is in a uniform field E_0, at large r, where the sphere has no influence, the potential must reduce to $V = -E_0 r \cos \theta$. Terms with a higher order of $\cos \theta$ are therefore not likely to contribute and $n = 0$ or 1. The solution to Laplace's equation may be written as

$$V = A + Br^{-1} + Cr \cos \theta + Dr^{-2} \cos \theta.$$

The first term represents the constant potential at the position of the sphere. The second term is a potential which falls off inversely with radius and is due to a net charge on the sphere. The third term is the potential of the uniform applied field and the fourth term represents the potential due to the charge induced on the sphere by the uniform field. If we take the centre of the sphere as our point of zero potential, $A = 0$. At large distances from the sphere, terms depending on $1/r$ and $1/r^2$ are negligible and $V = -E_0 r \cos \theta$, i.e.

$$-E_0 r \cos \theta = Cr \cos \theta$$

$$C = -E_0.$$

It is assumed that initially the sphere of radius a is conducting and held at zero potential. At $r = a$, $V = 0$ therefore and

$$0 = B/a - E_0 a \cos \theta + Da^{-2} \cos \theta$$

i.e.

$$B = 0 \text{ and } D = E_0 a^3$$

and so

$$V = -E_0 r \cos \theta (1 - a^3/r^3).$$

The radial component of the electric field E_r is

$$E_r = -\frac{\partial V}{\partial r} = E_0 \cos \theta + 2E_0 \frac{a^3}{r^3} \cos \theta \tag{7.91}$$

so that at $r = a$, $E_r = 3E_0 \cos \theta$.

If a potential V' is applied to the sphere then we must add a potential which equals V' when $r = a$, decreases radially from the sphere and is independent of θ, i.e. $B = V'a$, and the general solution for a conducting sphere of radius a held at a potential V' is

$$V = V'a/r - E_0 r \cos \theta (1 - a^3/r^3). \tag{7.92}$$

(i) The dielectric sphere in a uniform field

When the sphere is conducting, there is no electric field inside the sphere and we can assume that $V = 0$ at all positions in the sphere. When the sphere is insulating the potential will be finite inside the sphere and we must consider the regions $r < a$ and $r > a$ separately. The region outside the sphere is designated medium 1 and the sphere is medium 2.

On the basis of the solution of the problem for a conducting sphere, we first assume that the potential outside an uncharged dielectric sphere is

$$V_1 = -E_0 r \cos \theta + D_1 r^{-2} \cos \theta \tag{7.93}$$

and that inside the sphere it is

$$V_2 = C_2 r \cos \theta + D_2 r^{-2} \cos \theta. \tag{7.94}$$

The potential cannot tend to infinity at the centre of the sphere therefore D_2 must be zero.

At the surface of the sphere $(r = a)$ $V_1 = V_2$ and therefore

$$C_2 = D_1 a^{-3} - E_0. \tag{7.95}$$

The normal component of the displacement, D, at the surface of the sphere must also be continuous, i.e.

$$\varepsilon_1 (\partial V_1/\partial r)_{r=a} = \varepsilon_2 (\partial V_2/\partial r)_{r=a}$$
$$-C_2 = (\varepsilon_1/\varepsilon_2)(E_0 + 2D_1 a^{-3}). \tag{7.96}$$

The solutions of equations (7.95) and (7.96) are

$$C_2 = -\frac{3\varepsilon_1}{\varepsilon_2 + 2\varepsilon_1} E_0$$

$$D_1 = \frac{\varepsilon_2 - \varepsilon_1}{\varepsilon_2 + 2\varepsilon_1} E_0 a^3.$$

Thus the potential inside the sphere is

$$V_2 = -\frac{3\varepsilon_1}{\varepsilon_2 + 2\varepsilon_1} E_0 r \cos \theta \tag{7.97}$$

and the potential outside the sphere is

$$V_1 = -\left[1 - \frac{a^3}{r^3} \left(\frac{\varepsilon_2 - \varepsilon_1}{\varepsilon_2 + 2\varepsilon_1} \right) \right] E_0 r \cos \theta. \tag{7.98}$$

Therefore the field inside the sphere is parallel to the applied field E_0 and is of magnitude

$$E_2 = \frac{3\varepsilon_1 E_0}{\varepsilon_2 + \varepsilon_1}.$$

The potential outside the sphere is that of the uniform field with an additional potential V' superimposed:

$$V' = \frac{a^3}{r^3}\left(\frac{\varepsilon_2 - \varepsilon_1}{\varepsilon_2 + 2\varepsilon_1}\right) E_0 r \cos\theta. \tag{7.99}$$

If equation (7.99) is compared with equation (7.34) it can be seen that the additional component is equivalent to the potential due to a dipole at the centre of the sphere which has a magnitude

$$p = 4\pi\varepsilon_0 a^3 E_0 \left(\frac{\varepsilon_2 - \varepsilon_1}{\varepsilon_2 + 2\varepsilon_1}\right). \tag{7.100}$$

(ii) *The charge acquired by a sphere in a bi-ionised uniform field*

The use of Laplace's equation to solve electrostatic problems can be illustrated by the calculation of the residual charge on a conducting sphere of radius a in an AC corona discharge (assumed to be a uniform field in which both polarities of ion are present). The current density of positive ions is taken to be J_+ and the current density of negative ions to be J_-.

It was shown above that the solution of Laplace's equation gives the potential outside a conducting sphere in a uniform field E_0 to be equation (7.92):

$$V = V'a/r - E_0 r \cos\theta + E_0 a^3 r^{-2} \cos\theta.$$

The sphere acquires charge and reaches an equilibrium potential, V', which will be related to the final charge on the sphere, q', by the equation

$$q' = CV'$$

where C is the capacitance of the sphere.

$$E_r = -\frac{\partial V}{\partial r} = E_0 \cos\theta + V'\frac{a}{r^2} + 2E_0\frac{a^3}{r^3}\cos\theta$$

and at $r = a$

$$E_a = 3E_0 \cos\theta + V'/a.$$

There will be a position of zero field on the surface of the sphere at θ_c given by

$$\cos\theta_c = -V'/3E_0 a. \tag{7.101}$$

$\cos\theta_c$ is positive when θ_c lies between 0 and $\pi/2$ and negative when θ lies between $\pi/2$ and π.

In figure 7.22(b), V' is negative, therefore $\cos\theta_c$ is positive and positive ions will be collected over a larger fraction of the surface of the sphere than negative ions. (If the equilibrium potential of the sphere is positive, $\cos\theta_c$ is negative and θ_c lies between $\frac{1}{2}\pi$ and π. The sphere will then collect negative ions over a larger portion of its surface.)

The negative current flowing to the sphere is given by

$$I_- = \frac{J_-}{E_0} \int_0^{\theta_c} E_a 2\pi a^2 \sin \theta \, d\theta$$

$$= \frac{2\pi a^2 J_-}{E_0} \left(\int_0^{\theta_c} 3E_0 \cos \theta \sin \theta \, d\theta + \int_0^{\theta_c} \frac{V'}{a} \sin \theta \, d\theta \right)$$

$$= \frac{2\pi a^2 J_-}{E_0} \left[\tfrac{3}{2}E_0 \sin^2 \theta - V'a^{-1} \cos \theta \right]_0^{\theta_c}$$

and substituting from equation (7.101) for $\cos \theta_c$,

$$I_- = \frac{\pi a^2 J_-}{3E_0^2} \left(9E_0^2 + \frac{V'^2}{a^2} + \frac{6V'E_0}{a} \right)$$

$$= \frac{\pi a^2 J_-}{3E_0^2} \left(3E_0 + \frac{V'}{a} \right)^2. \qquad (7.102)$$

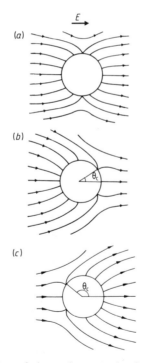

Figure 7.22 Collection of charge by a conducting sphere in a uniform electric field. (a) The sphere is neutral, and positive and negative charges are collected equally. (b) The sphere has a net negative charge. (c) The sphere has a net positive charge. Arrows designate the direction of positive field, i.e. the direction of movement of positive charge.

Similarly the positive current is given by

$$I_+ = \frac{J_+}{E_0} \int_{\theta_c}^{\pi} E_r 2\pi a^2 \sin\theta \, d\theta$$

$$= \frac{2\pi a^2 J_+}{E_0} [\tfrac{3}{2}E_0 \sin^2\theta - V_p a^{-1}\cos\theta]_{\theta_c}^{\pi}$$

$$= -\frac{\pi a^2 J_+}{3E_0^2}\left(3E_0 - \frac{V}{a}\right)^2. \tag{7.103}$$

The equilibrium potential is reached when the negative and positive currents are equal:

$$J_-\left(3E_0 + \frac{V}{a}\right)^2 = J_+\left(3E_0 - \frac{V}{a}\right)^2$$

$$(J_+^{1/2} - J_-^{1/2})3E_0 = (J_+^{1/2} + J_-^{1/2})\frac{V}{a}$$

$$V = \left(\frac{J_+^{1/2} - J_-^{1/2}}{J_+^{1/2} + J_-^{1/2}}\right)3E_0 a.$$

The capacitance of a sphere of radius a is given by

$$C = q/V = 4\pi\varepsilon_0 a$$

and therefore the equilibrium charge is given by

$$q = 12\pi\varepsilon_0 E_0 a^2\left(\frac{J_+^{1/2} - J_-^{1/2}}{J_-^{1/2} + J_+^{1/2}}\right). \tag{7.104}$$

7.5.5 Identifying coordinate systems by the method of conformal transformations

Conformal transformations have been widely used in two-dimensional field analysis to solve problems for which the boundary conditions cannot be simply expressed in cartesian or cylindrical coordinates. It is shown in the Appendix that any function of a complex variable

$$w = F(z) = F(x + iy)$$

is a solution of Laplace's equation in two dimensions.

If w is separated into its real and imaginary components

$$w = u + iv$$

then u and v are also solutions of Laplace's equation. It is also shown that lines of $u = $ constant and $v = $ constant are orthogonal, and can represent field lines and equipotentials. Maxwell (1904) solved a number of two-dimensional electrostatic problems by choosing a function $F(z)$, calculating equations for u and v in terms of conventional coordinates x and y, and plotting the lines of constant u and v to define field lines and equipotentials. He identified a number of functions which provide equipotentials which represent common practical geometries. Moon and Spencer (1961) show that this method can be used to solve three-dimensional field problems, by rotating a two-dimensional function about an axis of symmetry to form a rotational coordinate system, or by translating it to form a cylindrical coordinate system. An infinite number of coordinate systems may be generated in this way, but Laplace's equation is not necessarily separable in the new three-dimensional system. Moon and Spencer defined a number of coordinate systems for which Laplace's equation was separable, at least in situations with some symmetry. These may be used in problems where the boundaries may be simply defined in the new coordinates. The field and equipotential surfaces are often, but not always, the same as the coordinate planes.

The first step is to identify the functions, $F(z)$, which provide useful transformations. Twenty one are listed by Moon and Spencer, who also give maps of the lines of constant u and v. These may be used either to generate three-dimensional coordinate systems, as described above or, may be considered directly as field and potential lines which are particular solutions to Laplace's equation in a two-dimensional representation of the problem.

7.5.6 Examples of functions which provide useful coordinate systems

(i) *Parallel planes*
The simplest function which we know to be a solution to Laplace's equation is the function

$$z = x + iy.$$

In this case the lines $x = u = $ constant and $y = v = $ constant are straight lines parallel to the coordinate axes and these are the field lines and equipotentials between the plates of an infinite parallel-plate capacitor.

(ii) *Concentric circles*
The function $z = x + iy$ may equally be written in the form

$$z = x + iy = r(\cos\theta + i\sin\theta) = r\, e^{i\theta}$$

where

$$r = (x^2 + y^2)^{\frac{1}{2}}$$

and

$$\theta = \tan^{-1} y/x$$

as defined in figure 7.23.

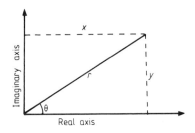

Figure 7.23 Definition of coordinates.

The function

$$F(z) = \ln z = \ln(x + iy) \tag{7.105}$$

is also a solution of Laplace's equation and may be written in the form

$$F(z) = \ln r\ e^{i\theta}.$$

and separating this into real and imaginary parts gives

$$\ln z = \ln r + i\theta. \tag{7.106}$$

$\ln(r) = $ constant defines a set of concentric circles which represent equipotentials and $\theta = $ constant defines a set of radial lines, which represent field lines. When this system is translated perpendicular to the x–y plane a three-dimensional coordinate system is produced, which can be used for the problems involving concentric conducting cylinders.

(iii) *Ellipses and hyperbolas*
If z is chosen so that

$$z = x + iy = a\ \cosh(u + iv) \tag{7.107}$$

then

$$x = a\ \cosh u\ \cos v \qquad \text{and} \qquad y = a\ \sinh u\ \sin v.$$

The lines of constant u are ellipses and the lines of constant v are hyperbolas as shown in figure 7.24.

This solution is particularly interesting because it may be used to treat two types of problems. If the ellipses represent equipotentials then figure 7.24 gives the field lines and equipotentials for an elliptical conductor (or in the limit a line charge). However, if the hyperbolas are the equipotentials then the solution can be used as a two-dimensional representation of a hyperbolic point and a plane, as shown by the bold curve in the figure 7.24.

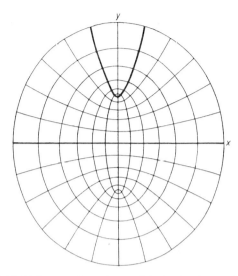

Figure 7.24 Field lines and equipotentials in the form of ellipses and hyperbolas. If the figure is rotated about the *y*-axis the bold curve represents a point in front of a plane, i.e. in this configuration the hyperbolas are the equipotentials and the ellipses are the electric field lines.

Three-dimensional coordinates where the point and plane are coordinate surfaces are obtained by rotating figure 7.24 about the *x*-axis. This produces prolate spheroidal coordinates described by

$$x = a \sinh \eta \sin \theta \cos \psi \qquad (7.108)$$

$$y = a \sinh \eta \sin \theta \sin \psi \qquad (7.109)$$

$$z = a \cosh \eta \cos \theta. \qquad (7.110)$$

The lines of $\theta = $ constant are hyperboloids with $\theta = \pi/2$ representing the plane at $z = 0$ (Moon and Spencer 1961). Surfaces of constant θ are equipotential surfaces and the potential is independent of η and ψ. For this situation Moon and Spencer give the solution of the Laplace equation:

$$V = A + B \ln \cot(\theta/2) \qquad (7.111)$$

$$V = A + C \ln \tan(\theta/2). \qquad (7.112)$$

(iv) *The fringing field of a capacitor*
Consider the functions

$$z = x + iy = a/\pi(w + 1 + e^w) \qquad \text{where } w = u + iv. \qquad (7.113)$$

This function is made up from sums or differences of other functions which are solutions of Laplace's equation, therefore it is itself a solution. It can be seen that

$$x = a/\pi(u + 1 + e^u \cos v) \tag{7.114}$$

$$y = a/\pi(v + e^u \sin v). \tag{7.115}$$

If we set $v = \text{const} = \pi$, then

$$y = a$$

$$x = a/\pi(u + 1 - e^u).$$

As u varies from $-\infty$ to 0, x varies from 0 to ∞. When u is positive, e^u is always greater than $u + 1$ and so x remains negative. Therefore the equipotential for which $v = \pi$ is a line a distance a from the origin, extending from $x = -\infty$ to 0. The equipotential for which $v = 0$ is an infinite line at the origin, parallel to the x-axis. Substituting for $v = 0.2\pi$, 0.4π, 0.6π etc, and computing for each v the values of x and y as u takes successive values allows a set of equipotentials and field lines to be drawn as shown in figure 7.25. If the lines for which $v = \text{constant}$ are taken to be the equipotentials of the system, the two half-planes at $v = \pi$ and $v = -\pi$ can be replaced by conductors and the diagram shows the fringing field of a parallel-plate capacitor in two dimensions.

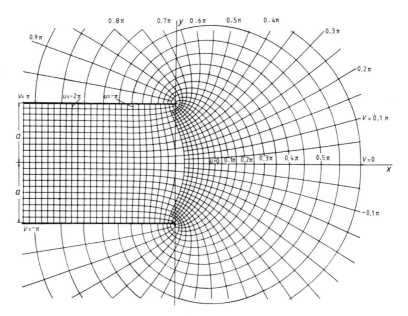

Figure 7.25 Field lines and equipotentials for the ends of two parallel plates (i.e. the fringing field of a parallel-plate capacitor).

This can be transformed to three dimensions by translating the figure parallel to the z-axis. Laplace's equation is then written in the form

$$\nabla^2 V = \frac{\pi^2}{a}(1 + 2\,\mathrm{e}^u \cos v + \mathrm{e}^{2u})^{-1}\left(\frac{\partial^2 V}{\partial u^2} + \frac{\partial^2 V}{\partial v^2}\right) + \frac{\partial^2 V}{\partial z^2} = 0.$$

If V is independent of z this reduces to

$$\nabla^2 V = 0 = \frac{\partial^2 V}{\partial u^2} + \frac{\partial^2 V}{\partial v^2}$$

which is the same as the equation obtained in rectangular coordinates and has the general solution given by equations (7.70)–(7.75).

(v) Rogowski profiles
It can be seen from figure 7.25, that the region of highest field (where the field lines are closest together) is at the ends of the parallel plates. In some cases (for example, when electrical resistivity is to be measured by applying a potential between parallel planes) it is important to ensure that the maximum field in a parallel-plate system is the uniform field between the plates. The field is unchanged if an equipotential is replaced by a conducting surface at that potential. Therefore, an equipotential is chosen so that the field will decrease for all values of x as one moves away from the $x = 0$ axis. Rogowski calculated that the first equipotential for which the maximum field occurs within the uniform-field central region was $v = \pi/2$. This equipotential is called the Rogowski profile.

7.5.7 Solution of Laplace's equation by numerical methods

Laplace's equation for complicated geometries which are not amenable to theoretical analysis may be solved using numerical methods. The finite-element method consists of four basic steps.

(i) A grid of numbered nodal points is established over the region of interest including the boundary. At the boundary either the potential V or its normal derivative, the field E, is known.
(ii) The nodes are interconnected to form a number of subregions within the volume of interest.
(iii) The potential is approximated by a continuous function over each subregion with continuity conditions imposed at the boundaries of the subregions.
(iv) The unknown potentials at the nodes are calculated by minimising the electrostatic energy.

To illustrate the method we consider the solution of Lees *et al* (1979) to the electric field in a silo as shown in figure 7.26. This problem is

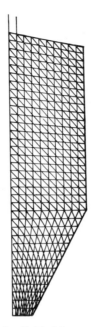

Figure 7.26 Diagram of silo divided into small volumes for numerical analysis (from Lees *et al* 1979).

axisymmetric and Poisson's equation which we wish to solve is given by

$$\frac{1}{r}\frac{\partial}{\partial r}\left(r\frac{\partial V}{\partial r}\right)+\frac{\partial^2 V}{\partial z^2}=\frac{Q_v}{\varepsilon_0\varepsilon_r}. \tag{7.116}$$

The boundary conditions are

$$V = 0 \qquad \text{at the silo walls}$$
$$E = 0 \qquad \text{on the central axis } (r = 0).$$

Lees *et al* (1979) divided the silo up into triangular subregions with nodes labelled i, j, k.

The potential over each triangle was approximated to

$$V = \alpha_1 + \alpha_2 r + \alpha_3 z$$

i.e. at node i

$$V_i = \alpha_1 + \alpha_2 r_i + \alpha_3 z_i.$$

The variables α_1, α_2 and α_3 can therefore be found in terms of V_i, V_j and V_k, and the coordinates of the nodes i, j and k. It then follows that

$$V = N_i V_i + N_j V_j + N_k V_k$$

where N_i, N_j and N_k are functions of r_i, r_j, r_k, z_i, z_j, z_k, r and z.

The nodal values of V are found by requiring

$$F = \int_A \left[r \left(\frac{\partial V}{\partial r} \right)^2 + r \left(\frac{\partial V}{\partial z} \right)^2 - \frac{2rQ_v V}{\varepsilon_0 \varepsilon_r} \right] dA$$

to be a minimum. This is equivalent to the requirement that V satisfies equation (7.116). Substitution of local expressions for V, $\partial V/\partial r$ and $\partial V/\partial z$ leads to a set of simultaneous equations in the nodal potentials for each triangle. These give a global set of equations which can be solved by standard techniques.

7.6 EARNSHAW'S THEOREM

Earnshaw's theorem states that a charged body placed in an electric field cannot rest in stable equilibrium under the influence of electric forces alone (Maxwell 1904).

This is equivalent to the statement that there cannot be a three-dimensional minimum in the potential. This follows as a direct consequence of Laplace's equation. For example, in cartesian coordinates the components of the electric field are dV/dx, dV/dy and dV/dz. The potential will be a maximum or minimum in the x-direction when $dV/dx = 0$.

This will be a maximum when d^2V/dx^2 is negative and a minimum when d^2V/dx^2 is positive. However, Laplace's equation states that

$$d^2V/dx^2 + d^2V/dy^2 + d^2V/dz^2 = 0.$$

Therefore the potential cannot have a three-dimensional maximum or minimum in the absence of a free charge.

7.7 CORONA DISCHARGE THEORY

7.7.1 Introduction

In many applications of electrostatics a charge is applied to a surface by means of a DC corona discharge. This gives a more controlled level charge than friction, and the phenomenon is less affected by environmental changes, such as variations in the relative humidity. A major treatise on corona discharge has been published by Loeb (1965) and reviews of recent work have been given by Goldman and Goldman (1978) and by Sigmond (1978).

A corona discharge occurs when a high voltage is applied between electrodes in a non-uniform field geometry. For example, a potential is applied to the wire at the centre of a cylinder or to a point facing a plane. With these geometries there is a high-field region close to the sharp electrode where ionisation of the gas occurs, but over most of the space between the electrodes the field is too low for ionisation and the region contains only ions which are repelled from the sharp electrode. In the ionisation region, electrons and positive ions are formed. If the sharp electrode is positive the electrons flow to it and positive ions are repelled. If the sharp electrode is negative electrons are repelled. When these no longer receive enough energy from the field to cause further ionisation, they will attach to any electronegative atoms present (such as oxygen or fluorine) and negative ions, rather than electrons, fill most of the interelectrode space. In pure nitrogen, or other gases to which electrons do not attach, the current in a negative corona will be carried by electrons and will be very much higher than is normally observed in air. In practical applications of electrostatics, there is invariably some electronegative gas present, and only the behaviour of the corona under these circumstances will be considered here.

The corona current density on a plane arising from a single-point electrode is typically 10^{-4}–10^{-3} A m^{-2}. The ion mobility in air is approximately 2×10^{-4} m^2 V^{-1} s^{-1}. At a corona field in the drift region of about 3×10^5 V m^{-1} the ions are therefore travelling at a velocity of about 66 m s^{-1} and the charge density in the gas is typically 1.5×10^{-6} C m^{-3}. This is equivalent to 10^{13} ions per cubic metre compared with 10^{23} neutral molecules per cubic metre. A corona discharge thus ionises only a very small percentage of the neutral gas molecules. The ions make many collisions with the gas molecules and impart momentum to them, creating the ion wind described in Chapter 5. There are also many metastable neutral molecules present, whose influence on the discharge process and on surface reactions in a corona discharge is not yet fully understood. Hartmann (1976) estimates that with a corona current of 70 μA about 10 % of the nitrogen molecules in a corona discharge were in an excited state.

7.7.2 The Townsend criterion

This criterion was formulated by Townsend (1915). If N_{e0} electrons with mobility b_e are released in a gas in an electric field E, they will drift with a velocity, $u = b_e E$, down a field line and collide with gas atoms. Each electron will produce α new electron–ion pairs and suffer η attachments per unit path length (where α and η are the primary ionisation and attachment coefficients). The change in the number of electrons in a path length dl is thus

$$dN_e = N_e(\alpha - \eta)\,dl$$

which is integrated to give:

$$N_e = N_{e0}\exp[(\alpha - \eta)\,dl].$$

Since there were initially N_{e0} electrons released, the number of new electron–

ion pairs is

$$N = N_{e0}[\exp(\alpha - \eta) \, dl - 1].$$

If the discharge is to be self-sustaining there must be a secondary process which replaces the initial electrons. The secondary processes are combined in the secondary ionisation coefficient, γ, defined as the number of replacement electrons produced per ionising collision in the ionisation region.

The number of secondary electrons is thus given by:

$$N_{es} = \gamma N_{e0}[\exp(\alpha - \eta) \, dl - 1].$$

The condition for the discharge to be self-sustaining is that there should be one secondary electron for every initial electron released, i.e.

$$\gamma[\exp(\alpha - \eta) \, dl - 1] = 1. \tag{7.117}$$

The coefficients α, η and γ are reasonably well known for many gases, and are defined functions of the local field. However the local field is non-uniform and a function of the space charge density. Determinations of the conditions for which a discharge is self-sustaining must therefore be made by computer modelling (e.g. Morrow 1985a,b).

7.7.3 Conditions for corona onset

The field strength necessary to initiate a corona discharge at the sharp electrode depends on the field required to accelerate the electrons sufficiently to produce ionising collisions in the gas present. Peek (1929) showed semi-empirically that the onset of corona from a perfectly smooth wire on the axis of a cylinder was given by:

$$E' = \delta' \left(A_g + \frac{B_g}{(r_0 \delta')^{1/2}} \right) \tag{7.118}$$

where r_0 is the wire radius in metres, δ' is the relative air density:

$$\delta' = \frac{T_0 P \delta_0}{T P_0}.$$

Here δ_0, T_0 and P_0 are the density, absolute temperature and pressure of the air at 1 atm and 25 °C, T and P are the actual temperature and pressure, and A and B are constants which are a function of the gas, g. For air, $A_g = 32.2 \times 10^5$ V m^{-1} and $B_g = 8.46 \times 10^4$ V m$^{-1/2}$.

In practice, wires are not perfectly smooth and it is customary to multiply the right-hand side of the equation by a roughness factor f, where f is less than one and usually between 0.5 and 0.9. (A roughness factor of 1 is a perfectly smooth wire.) With a suitable choice of constants, equation (7.118) has been shown to apply to numerous gases and gas mixtures and a variety of electrode geometries. However, it does not apply to negative corona in a

pure non-attaching gas and may considerably overestimate the corona inception field at high pressures.

At the corona inception field there is no space charge, therefore the corona
starting voltage may be found from the field using the relationship

$$V = -\int E \, dr.$$

For example, it is shown below that for a concentric wire/cylinder geometry
the voltage at any distance r from the axis is related to the field at that point
by the equation

$$E = \frac{V}{r \ln(r_0/r_1)} \tag{7.119}$$

where r_0 is the radius of the wire and r_1 is the radius of the cylinder.

The corona onset potential increases with increasing wire diameter and
ultimately a wire diameter is reached where the starting voltage equals the
sparkover voltage and corona is not possible. The voltage range between
corona initiation and a spark widens as the wire size is decreased.

7.7.4 The electric field in a corona discharge

The simplest corona geometry for analysis is a high-voltage wire on the axis
of a cylinder. In this case the field is radial and independent of z and θ:

$$E = -\frac{dV}{dr}. \tag{7.120}$$

Poisson's equation in cylindrical coordinates is given by

$$\frac{d^2V}{dr^2} + \frac{1}{r}\frac{dV}{dr} = \frac{Q_v}{\varepsilon_0}. \tag{7.121}$$

Prior to the onset of corona Q_v is zero and the solution is

$$V = A + B \ln r.$$

Assuming that the potential of the cylinder at radius r_1 is zero and the
potential of the wire of radius r_0 is V_0:

$$B = V_0 \ln (r_1/r_0)$$

$$E_0 = \frac{V_0}{r \ln(r_1/r_0)}. \tag{7.122}$$

The field decreases across the tube as shown in curve A of figure 7.27.

After corona onset Q_v is no longer zero. If we assume that the wire
produces a current J per unit length then

$$J = 2\pi Q_v b E \tag{7.123}$$

where b is the ion mobility. Combining equations (7.123), (7.121) and

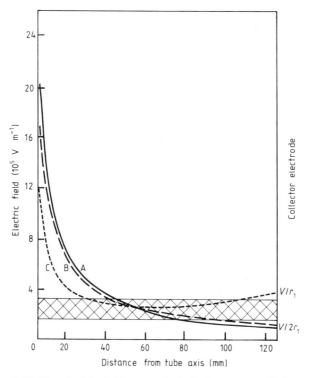

Figure 7.27 The electric field in a wire/cylinder corona discharge: A, prior to corona onset (equation (7.122)); B, with low space charge of corona ions (equation (7.124)); C, with high space charge, e.g. in the presence of charged particles. For reasonably high space charge densities the electric field lies approximately between V/r_1 and $V/2r_1$ for much of the discharge area. This figure was calculated assuming a wire current of $82\ \mu\text{A m}^{-1}$ and a wire potential of 40 kV. For curve C there was a density of $18\ \text{g m}^{-3}\ 6.6\ \mu\text{m}$ particles charged to the Gaussian limit (from Lowe and Lucas 1953).

(7.122) and integrating

$$E = \left[\frac{J}{2\pi\varepsilon_0 b} + \left(\frac{r_0}{r}\right)^2 \left(E_0^2 - \frac{J}{2\pi\varepsilon_0 b}\right) \right]^{1/2} \qquad (7.124)$$

where E_0 is the corona onset field.

The effect of the corona ions is to increase the field near the plane and decrease it near the point as shown in curve B of figure 7.27. For sufficiently large r and J equation (7.124) simplifies to

$$E = \left(\frac{J}{2\pi\varepsilon_0 b}\right)^{1/2} \qquad (7.125)$$

i.e. E is independent of radius and nearly uniform near the cylinder.

If the space charge density is very high, for example because there is a charged dust present, the field is raised still further close to the earthed electrode and depressed near the wire. This is shown in curve C of figure 7.27 (Lowe and Lucas 1953).

7.7.5 The current–voltage characteristic of the corona discharge

It has been found experimentally that the current, I, flowing in a corona discharge is related to the applied voltage, V, by an equation of the form

$$I = KV(V - V')$$
(7.126)

where V' is the corona starting voltage and K is a constant. This form for the current–voltage characteristic was first identified for a point-to-plane geometry by Warburg (1899), and was confirmed for cylindrical geometry by Almay in 1902. The cylindrical corona can be analysed mathematically because Laplace's equation, which relates charge, voltage and electric field, is two dimensional and easily solved. This calculation was carried out by Townsend (1915). He derived a relationship between the applied voltage V and the current per unit length of wire, J, by integrating equation (7.124):

$$\left(\frac{V - V'}{V'}\right) \ln\left(\frac{r_0}{r_1}\right) = (1 + Y)^{1/2} - 1 - \ln \tfrac{1}{2}[1 + (1 + Y)^{1/2}]$$
(7.127)

$$Y = \left(\frac{r_1}{E_c r_0}\right)^2 \frac{J}{2\pi\varepsilon_0 b}$$
(7.128)

where V' is the corona inception voltage and E' is the corona inception field. For low currents, near the corona threshold this may be simplified to

$$J = \frac{8\pi\varepsilon_0 b V(V - V')}{r_1^2 \ln(r_1/r_0)}.$$
(7.129)

For a point-to-plane geometry the mathematics is intractable. Lamo and Gallo (1974) carried out an experimental study of this geometry and proposed a formula

$$J = KV(V - V')/s^2$$
(7.130)

where s was the point-to-plane spacing. K was taken to be a constant although it had a weak dependence on the point radius.

The current in a point-to-plane corona discharge is concentrated in an angle of about $60°$ round the axis. Warburg (1899) showed that the current at the plane has the form

$$I = I_0 \cos \theta^5.$$
(7.131)

7.7.6 Pulsed phenomena in a corona discharge

If the current flowing in a corona discharge of either polarity is observed with a fast oscilloscope it may be seen to consist of pulses superimposed on a small steady current. For most of the voltage range of a negative corona discharge from a single point in an electronegative gas, the pulses are extremely regular and have a very fast risetime of the order of 1 ns. These pulses were first studied in detail by Trichel, and are known by his name. The size and shape of Trichel pulses are more or less independent of current but depend on the corona geometry. For a given geometry the pulse frequency increases linearly with current at low currents and slightly more rapidly at high currents (figure 7.28). The pulse shape depends on the gas. Figure 7.29 shows examples of oscilloscope traces of negative corona pulses in air and oxygen at different pressures and with different point radii. It can be seen that the pulses formed in air are superimposed on a steady current. Although this is only a very small percentage of the peak Trichel pulse current, it represents a significant proportion of the total current drawn from the power supply. Under the conditions shown in the figure the steady component was 46 % of the total current, the remaining 54 % being in the pulsed component. In oxygen the decay of the pulse is more gradual and it is not possible to define a steady component. The shape of the pulses is a function of point diameter, gas composition and pressure, and corona current and voltage (Cross *et al* 1986). For example, under some circumstances the Trichel pulse is found to have steps on its leading or trailing edges (Zentner 1970a,b, Cross *et al* 1986). Computer models of the phenomenon are now able to explain these features (Morrow 1985a,b).

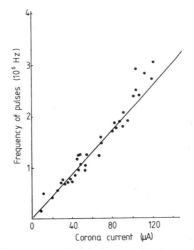

Figure 7.28 The frequency of Trichel pulses in air as a function of current. Negative point-to-plane corona. Point radius 0.08 mm, spacing 15 mm.

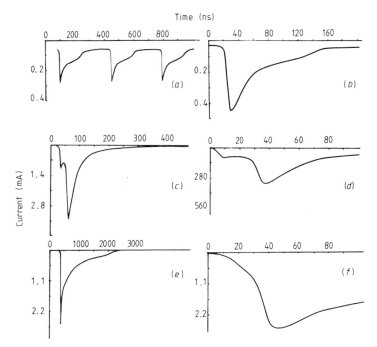

Figure 7.29 The shape of Trichel pulses in air and oxygen (*a*), air at atmospheric pressure, 100 μA, electrode radius 0.08 mm; (*b*), air at atmospheric pressure, 50 μA, electrode radius 0.08 mm; (*c*) and (*d*) oxygen at 50 Torr pressure 2 mm point, 50 μA; (*e*) and (*f*) air at 50 Torr pressure 2 mm point, 50 μA. The vertical axis is current in milliamps flowing instantaneously in the discharge.

At high pulse frequencies, when the pulse period approaches the pulse length, the discharge switches to a continuous glow mode. The conditions for the pulsed and glow modes are discussed further by Miyoshi (1964).

The time constants of the system used to measure the Trichel pulses is less than the time taken for electrons or ions to cross the gap. Changes in the electric field at the plane, due to the movement of electric charge in the system are transmitted at the speed of light; the charge itself moves more slowly. The effects of moving charges are therefore detected at the earthed electrode before the charges themselves arrive, and the current measured does not necessarily equal the number of charges arriving at the electrode at that instant. Integrating over time, charge is conserved, and the total current is equal to the average rate of arrival of charge.

The Trichel pulses detected in the current in the external circuit may be considered to be an induced current due to all the moving charges in the system. This gives rise to an induced charge on the electrode, which is neutralised as the ions arrive. The field driving the induced current is produced by moving charges and is not capacitive, therefore the electrode geometry is not important.

The problem has been analysed by Sato (1980) who showed that the instantaneous current arriving at the electrode was given by:

$$I = (e/V_0) \int (n_p u_p - n_i u_i - n_e u_e) E \, dv \tag{7.132}$$

where n is the density of charge carriers and u the component of their velocity in the direction of E. The subscripts p, i and e represent positive ions, negative ions and electrons; dv represents integration over the volume of the discharge and e is the electronic charge. V_0 is the applied voltage and E the Laplacian electric field (i.e. the field in the absence of a space charge).

The measured current is dominated by the movement of electrons, even though these are confined to a small volume near the point, because the electrons have a very much higher mobility than the ions and move in the high-field region of the discharge. It is the movement of electrons which gives rise to the sharp risetime of the Trichel pulse. As the electrons move from the point and form negative ions a negative space charge builds up which reduces the field near the point, so that the ionisation process ceases until sufficient time has elapsed for the negative ions to drift away in the field. The long tail of the corona pulse and the steady current between the pulses are due to the drift of the positive ions formed in the ionisation region towards the point and the negative ions to the plane. It has been suggested that there may be a steady discharge in addition to the normal pulsed discharge (Sigmond 1978). However, theories are not yet sufficiently far advanced to be able to define whether the movement of ions formed by attachment of Trichel pulse electrons can account for all of the experimentally observed steady current or whether there is an additional steady discharge.

Pulses in a positive corona discharge are larger and more irregular than negative corona pulses. Their dependence of current is opposite to that of the Trichel pulse as their amplitude is proportional to current and their frequency varies irregularly with voltage and current. Figure 7.30 shows the frequency of pulses as a function of voltage for a positive corona discharge and it can be seen that there are two voltage ranges for which pulses are observed with a region of steady glow between.

The pulses in a corona discharge are much more rapid than the time required for a surface to achieve its limiting charge at typical corona current densities. The pulsed nature of the discharge therefore has little practical significance to charging or discharging by means of a corona. However, in studies of back-ionisation (i.e. discharges in porous layers deposited on the plane electrode), it is important to realise that oscilloscope measurements of the corona current will not be able to identify separately the movement of positive and negative ions near the plane. Back-ionisation causes a significant increase in the current measured in the external circuit which, in a negative corona discharge, can be identified almost entirely with an increase in the frequency of Trichel pulses. Positive ions created at the plane have a significant effect on the surface charging efficiency but cannot be separately identified in the external current.

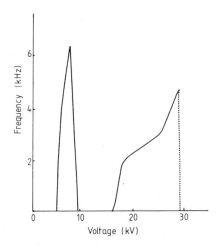

Figure 7.30 The frequency of pulses in a positive point-to-plane corona discharge as a function of applied voltage: spacing, 31 mm; needle radius, 0.17 mm (from Goldman and Goldman 1978).

7.7.7 The nature of corona ions

The mobility of a charge carrier in a corona discharge is defined as the velocity per unit field and is characteristic of the gas. Identification of the chemical nature of the ions by measurement of their mobility is impeded by the presence of the ion wind. However, it is possible to compensate for this and the presence of ions of a number of different mobilities have been detected (Goldman and Goldman 1978, Goldman *et al* 1976). In air the highest mobility ion is at 2.21×10^{-4} m^2 V^{-1} s^{-1}. This has been detected both by Goldman *et al* and by Cabine (1969) who used a different experimental technique. This mobility was tentatively identified with O_3^- ions. Goldman also identified mobilities of 1.03, 0.66 and 0.75×10^{-4} m^2 V^{-1} s^{-1} and Cabine found mobilities of 2.05, 1.55 and 1.35×10^{-4} m^2 V s^{-1}. These discrepancies could result from different environmental conditions or from the fact that the ages of the ions could differ in the two experiments. The nature of these slower ions were not specifically identified. The presence of moisture can significantly affect ion mobilities as the ions become hydrated by up to ten water molecules to form larger less mobile ions.

Experimental measurements of the chemical nature of the ions present in a negative corona in air have been made by Gardiner and Craggs (1977) and Shahin (1969). Both sampled ions from the chamber in which the discharge took place and measured their mass using a mass spectrometer.

Gardiner and Craggs limited their measurements to between 10 and 30 τ and found that the most common species at the anode in a negative discharge was CO_3^- but O_3^- (at lower pressures) and O^- (at higher pressures) were also significant. Shahin found that the predominant ion in a positive discharge in air with a water content of 0.65 mol % was $(H_2O)_n H^+$ with n up to 8. The number of water molecules decreased as the water content of the air decreased and for water contents less than 0.1 mol % $NO^+(H_2O)_n$ and $NO_2^+(H_2O)_n$ were found.

Computer modelling of a negative corona in air suggests that the main negative ion near the anode is CO_4^- but in the higher field regions near the point it is CO_3^- or O_3^- (Sigmond and Goldman 1978). In a positive corona the main ion was calculated to be O_2^+. The N_2^+ ion which is also created rapidly converts to NO^+ and O_2^+.

Bastien *et al* (1975) have published the results of computations in which 26 possible ionic and neutral species created in a corona discharge in air are followed to equilibrium under a variety of conditions. They looked at the effect of relative humidity and pressure, and investigated impurities created by the discharge (ozone and oxides of nitrogen). The same group have also shown experimentally that there are highly oxidising neutral species present other than ozone (Rippe *et al* 1974). The number of neutral metastable molecules considerably exceeds the number of ions produced by a corona discharge. They are believed to play an important part in the formation of ions in the discharge and in chemical reactions at the anode: however the details are not well understood (Lecuiller *et al* 1972).

APPENDIX: PROPERTIES OF SOLUTIONS TO LAPLACE'S EQUATION

Any function $F(z)$ of $(x + iy)$ is a solution of Laplace's equation. This may be seen by differentiating $F(z)$, i.e.

$$\frac{\partial F}{\partial x} = \frac{\partial F}{\partial z}\frac{dz}{dx} = \frac{\partial F}{\partial z} \qquad \frac{\partial^2 F}{\partial x^2} = \frac{\partial^2 F}{\partial z^2}$$

$$\frac{\partial F}{\partial y} = \frac{\partial F}{\partial z}\frac{dz}{dy} = \frac{i\,\partial F}{\partial z} \qquad \frac{\partial^2 F}{\partial y^2} = -\frac{\partial^2 F}{\partial z^2}. \tag{A7.1}$$

Therefore

$$\frac{\partial^2 F}{\partial x^2} + \frac{\partial^2 F}{\partial y^2} = 0$$

and F is a solution of Laplace's equation.

Separating $F(x + iy)$ into its real and imaginary parts:

$$F(x + iy) = U(xy) + iV(xy).$$

Both U and V must be solutions of Laplace's equation, but

$$\frac{\partial F}{\partial y} = \frac{i \, \partial F}{\partial x}$$

therefore

$$\frac{\partial U}{\partial y} + \frac{i \, \partial V}{\partial y} = i \left(\frac{\partial U}{\partial x} + \frac{i \, \partial V}{\partial x} \right)$$

and equating real and imaginary parts

$$\frac{\partial U}{\partial x} = \frac{\partial V}{\partial y} \qquad -\frac{\partial V}{\partial x} = \frac{\partial U}{\partial y}.$$

These equations express the fact that the surfaces $U(xy) = $ constant and $V(xy) = $ constant meet everywhere orthogonally. Therefore if $V(xy)$ satisfies Laplace's equation, then $V(xy) = $ constant represents a set of equipotentials and $U(xy) = $ constant gives the field lines.

Conjugate functions

If a function $(U + iV)$ is a function of $(x + iy)$, then U and V are said to be conjugate functions of x and y. If x and y are solutions of Laplace's equation so are its conjugate functions. A number of theorems have been proved giving rules for identifying conjugate functions. These allow new solutions of Laplace's equation to be found once one solution is identified. The proofs of the theorems of conjugate functions stated below are given by Maxwell (1904).

Theorem 1

If U_1 and V_1 and U_2 and V_2 are each conjugate with respect to x and y, then the functions $U_1 + U_2$ and $V_1 + V_2$ are also conjugate functions of x and y.

Theorem 2

If U_1 and V_1 and U_2 and V_2 are conjugate functions of x and y, then $X = U_1 U_2 - V_1 V_2$ and $Y = U_1 U_2 + V_1 V_2$ are also conjugate functions of x and y.

Theorem 3

If V is any function of x' and y' and if x' and y' are conjugate functions of x and y then

$$\int\int\left(\frac{\partial^2 V}{\partial x^2}+\frac{\partial^2 V}{\partial y^2}\right)dx\,dy = \int\int\left(\frac{\partial^2 V}{\partial x'^2}+\frac{\partial^2 V}{\partial y'^2}\right)dx'\,dy'.$$

The integrations are between the same limits.

Theorem 4

If x_1 and y_1, and x_2 and y_2 are conjugate functions of x and y then if $X = x_1 x_2 - y_1 y_2$ and $Y = x_1 y_2 + x_2 y_1$ then X and Y are conjugate functions of x and y.

Theorem 5

If V is a solution of the equation

$$\frac{d^2 V}{dx^2}+\frac{d^2 V}{dy^2}=0$$

and if

$$2R = \log\left[\left(\frac{dV}{dx}\right)^2+\left(\frac{dV}{dy}\right)^2\right]$$

and

$$P = -\tan^{-1}\frac{dV}{dx}\bigg/\frac{dV}{dy}$$

then R and P are conjugate functions of x and y.

From these theorems it can be seen that sums and products of solutions to Laplace's equation are also solutions. The general solution to the equation is therefore a series of a large number of possible terms with arbitrary coefficients which are defined by the boundary conditions of the problem.

REFERENCES

Bastien F, Haug R and Lecuiller M 1975 Simulation sur ordinateur de l'évolution temporelle des ions négatifs de l'air–application au cas de la décharge couronne négatif *J. Chimie Physique* **72** 105–12

Bleaney B I and Bleaney B 1965 *Electricity and Magnetism* (Oxford: Oxford University Press)

Cabine 1969 *Thèse Doctorat de 3ᵉ Cycle* Paris

Cross J A, Morrow R and Haddad G 1986 An analysis of the current in a point to plane corona discharge and the effect of a porous insulating layer on the plane *J. Phys. D: Appl. Phys.* **19** 1007–17

Gardiner P S and Craggs J D 1977 Negative ions in Trichel corona in air *J. Phys. D: Appl. Phys.* **10** 1003–9

Goldman M and Goldman A 1978 Corona discharges *Gaseous Electronics* eds M Hirsch and H J Oskham (New York: Academic) ch 4

Goldman A, Haug R and Latham R V 1976 A repulsive field technique for obtaining the mobility spectra of ion species created in a corona discharge *J. Appl. Phys.* **47** 2418–23

Hartman 1976 *Proc. 3rd Int. Gas Discharges Conf. (London) 1976* (IEE Publication No 118) pp 634–8

Lamo W L and Gallo C F 1974 Systematic study of the electrical characteristics of the Trichel pulses from the negative needle in a point to plane corona discharge *J. Appl. Phys.* **45** 103–13

Lecuiller M, Julien R and Pucheault J 1972 Etude par voie chimiques des ions produits par decharges couronnes *J. Chimie Physique* **69** 1353–9

Lees P, Bright A W, Smith J R, McAllister D and Diserens J 1979 Applications of numerical methods of field problems in silos *IEEE Conf. Ind. Appl. Soc. (Cleveland, Ohio)* pp 209–13

Loeb L 1965 *Electrical Coronas* (Berkeley, CA: University of California Press)

Lowe H J and Lucas D H 1953 The physics of the electrostatic precipitator *Br. J. Appl. Phys.* **4** Supp. 2 540–7

Maxwell J C 1904 *A Treatise on Electricity and Magnetism* 3rd edn (Oxford: Oxford University Press)

Miyoshi Y, Hosokawa T and Sakai O 1964 *Nagoya Inst. Tech. Bulletin 1964* (results summarised by Sigmond 1978)

Moon P and Spencer D E 1961 *Field Theory Handbook* (Berlin: Springer)

Moore A D in Rogers W E 1954 *Introduction to Electric Fields* (New York: McGraw-Hill) Appendix

Morrow 1985a A theory of the stepped corona pulse in a negative corona discharge *Phys. Rev.* A **32** 1799–809

—— 1985b Theory of negative corona in oxygen *Phys. Rev.* A **32**

Peek F W 1929 *Dielectric Phenomena in High Voltage Engineering* (New York: McGraw-Hill)

Pohl H A 1978 *Dielectrophoresis* (Cambridge: Cambridge University Press)

Reitz J R and Milford F J 1960 *Foundations of Electromagnetic Theory* (Reading, Mass: Addison-Wesley)

Rippe B, Lecuiller M and Koulkes-Pujo A-M 1974 Réactions d'oxydoreduction des solutions aqueuse par les éspece chimiques crées lors d'une décharge couronne *J. Chimie Physique* **71** 1185–90

Rogers W E 1954 *Introduction to Electric Fields* (New York: McGraw-Hill)

Russel A 1922 The problem of two electrified spheres *Proc. Phys. Soc.* **35** 10–22

Sato N J 1980 Discharge current induced by the motion of charged particles *Phys. Rev.* D **13** L3–L6

Shahin M M 1969 Ionic reactions in corona discharges in atmospheric gases *Chemical Reactions in Electrical Discharges* ed B D Blaustein (Advances in Chemistry Series 80) (Washington: American Chemical Society) ch 4

Sigmond R S 1978 Corona discharges *Electrical Breakdown in Gases* ed J M Meek and J D Craggs (New York: Wiley) ch 4

Sigmond R S and Goldman M 1978 Corona discharge physics and applications *Nato Advanced Study Institute Series B* vol 89, part B, pp 1–64

Stephenson G 1966 *Mathematical Methods for Science Students* (London: Longman)

Townsend J S 1915 *Electricity in Gases* (Oxford: Clarendon)

Warburg E 1899 *Weid Ann.* **67** 69

Zentner R 1970a Stufennimpulse der negativen koronaentladung *ETZ-A* **91** 303–5

—— 1970b Uber die anstiegszeiten der negativen koronaentladungsimpulse *Z. Angew. Phys.* **29** 294–301

Index

ABS, 43
AC corona, 371–2
AC eliminator, 371–6
AC field, 201, 265, 287, 291, 293–4
Accumulation of charge, 347
Acetate rayon, 30
Acetylene, 327–8
Active eliminators, 371–6
Additives, 152
  antistatic, 376–82
Adhesion, 245, 386–410
  in electric field, 402–5, 409
  measurement of, 405–8
Adhesives, 277
Adsorbed layers, 20, 390, 394
Aerodynamic force, 144–5, 147, 157, 212–13, 229, 232, 238
Aerosol, 82, 287
  cans, 346
Agglomeration, 152, 270, 295
Airless spray gun, 216
Alcohol, 200
Alpha particles, 371
Aluminium, 227, 367
  paint, 368
  powder, 336, 339
Amber, 10
Amorphous insulators, 22, 24
Anodic deposition, 252–3
Anthraquinone, 361
Antistatic
  additives, 44, 79–80, 376–82, 410

films, 134–5
footwear, 130, 354, 411
materials, 354, 376–82, 411
Antivibration mountings, 353
Aqueous solutions, 66
Atomisation, 62, 66, 81–5, 198–209, 215–7, 346

Back-ionisation, 152–6, 158, 162, 186, 188, 223–6, 228, 232
Ballistic probe, 123
Band theory of solids, 18–21, 34
Barium titanate ceramics, 274, 307
Beneficiation, 247
Bi-ionised field, 50, 54, 469–70
Biological systems, 275
Bipolar
  current probe, 121–2
  eliminator, 373
Bispherical coordinates, 399, 465–70
Boiling, 260, 263
Booth, 291
Boundary conditions, 461–70
Boxer charger, 188–9
Brakes, 268, 298–9
Brownian diffusion, 166–7, 171, 192, 257
Brush discharges, 355–6

Cadmium sulphide, 307
Calcium titanate, 267
Capacitance, 5, 8–9, 15, 91, 94, 276, 330, 349–53, 434–7, 473–5

measurement of, 128–9
of concentric spheres, 435
of isolated sphere, 14, 434
of parallel plates, 14, 435
of sphere and plane, 399
of two parallel cylinders, 456–7
Capacitive discharge, 327, 337, 349
Capillary condensation, 395
Carbon, 163, 273
Carbon black composites, 10, 380–1
Carbon dioxide, 344
Carbon disulphide, 327–8
Carpet, 380
Cartesian coordinates, 462–3
Cathodic deposition, 252–3
Cell constant, 130
Cellophane, 43
Centrifuge, 406
Charge control agents, 382
Charge decay rate, 135, 347, 361–2
Charge density, 13, 16, 103
Charge exchange, 400
Charge generation, 17–85, 342–7
by atomisation, 83, 85
by splashing, 82
Charge injection, 66, 266
Charge-to-mass ratio, 110, 202, 228, 342
Charge, measurement, 9, 93, 95, 102–3, 108–15, 228–9
Charged droplet scrubber, 169–75
Charging
of emulsions, 81, 84
of suspensions, 80
Chemical force, 396
Chute separator, 243
Clausius–Mosotti equation, 440
Clay, 274
Clothing, 354
Clutch, 267–8
CMOS device, 384
Cofield pump, 258
Coal, 246
mines, 367, 413
Coalescence, 273
Cohesion, 408–9
Collection efficiency
of fibre, 183
of granular bed, 176–7, 180–3

of precipitator, 148–51
of scrubber, 172–5
of sphere, 189–92
Colloid thruster, 208–9
Complex permittivity, 441
Composite materials, 10, 376, 380–1
Compressed air, 344
Concentric circles, 471
Concrete, 10
Condensation, 260, 263, 395
Conducting
foam, 385
materials, 354, 411
particles, 61–4, 227, 293
Conductivity, 10–11, 15–16, 20–1, 26, 44, 270, 414
of liquids, 25, 66, 130, 266, 269, 362
of powders, 131, 151–6, 159, 365, 407
Conformal transformations, 470
Conjugate functions, 488–9
Contact
area, 389, 390–1, 394, 405–6, 408
charging, 17–45
potential difference, 28, 35, 401
containment and control, 285
Conveyor belts, 348, 370
Cooling, 259–65, 282–5
Coordinate systems, 461–75
Copying machines, 301
Corona
charging, 46–60, 147, 180, 209–15, 218, 226, 232, 237, 277, 346, 460
conditioning, 277
deposition, 218–36, 282
discharge, 46–9, 146, 152–5, 158, 264, 276–85, 331, 351, 359, 363
onset, 153, 370, 479
probe, 116
separators, 244–7
wind, 264, 277–84, 486
Corotron, 300
Corrosion, 277, 352
Cotton, 10, 30, 31, 43, 278
Coulomb force, 60, 145, 168–9, 172, 191, 266, 397–402
Coulomb's law, 6, 10, 13–14, 65, 425–30, 430, 433, 443, 447–51
Crop spraying, 233–7

Crude oil, 85
Cunningham correction factor, 111, 147
Current–voltage characteristic, 118–21, 153–5, 482
Cyclone, 164–6, 222, 240
Cylindrical
    coordinates, 463–4
    generators, 309
    probe, 120–1

Dacron, 30
Debye length, 71
Deutsch equation, 148–51, 157
Dewatering, 255
Diamond, 32
Dielectric
    constant, 9, 428–9
    sphere in uniform field, 466–7
Dielectrophoresis, 248, 257–61, 269, 273, 276, 439–42
Dielectrophoretic
    force, 145, 258–61, 267, 271–5, 292
    levitation, 272, 292–3
    separation, 274–6
Diffuse charge layer, 65, 67, 70
Diffusion, 396
    charging, 55–7
Dioctylphthalate, 57, 170, 176
Dip sticks, 411
Dipole, 273, 436, 439
    force, 60, 167, 169, 257, 269, 270, 274, 402
Dischargers, 358, 369–76, 410
Dispersion, 64, 293–4
    force, 387
Displacement, 428–31
    current, 133
    probe, 123
Double layer, 27–8, 39, 40, 64–72, 81, 248–9, 270–1, 401–2, 405–6
    repulsion, 402
Droplets, 146, 174, 198–207, 364
Drum separator, 244
Dry scrubber, 178–80
Dual in-line device, 385
Duration of spark, 328, 334, 336–7, 355, 357

Dust
    cloud, 364
    respirators, 185
    sampling, 109
    suppression, 237

Earnshaw's theorem, 287, 477
Earthing, 129, 226, 352, 385, 410, 414
Ebonite, 31
Effective
    conductivity, 362
    migration velocity, 149, 157
Efficiency of collection, 148–9, 173, 181–191
EGD, 310–11
Elastic bodies, 389
Electret, 184, 308
    filter, 184
Electric
    curtain, 290–1
    field, 4–7, 14, 16, 91, 425–34
        measurement of, 96, 124–5
Electrical spark, 327, 366
Electrically enhanced
    sedimentation, 255
    fabric filters, 183–9, 303
    heat transfer, 259–65, 282–5
Electrically forced convection, 260–1
Electroconvection, 248, 257–9, 261, 266, 269, 273
Electrocyclojet, 240, 242
Electrocyclone, 165–6
Electrode
    configuration, 331, 334
    reactions, 70
Electrodialysis, 250
Electrodynamic
    spraying, 201, 203
    suspension, 289
Electrofilter, 255–6, 275
Electroflotation, 257
Electrofluidised bed, 175–7, 295–7
Electrogasdynamic generators, 217, 310–11
Electrographic machine, 301
Electrokinetic phenomena, 248
Electrolysis, 251–9
Electrolytic conduction, 24–5

Electromechanical forces, 295–6
Electrometer, 92–6, 108
Electromotive force, 6
Electron energies
  in insulators, 18–22, 29, 34–6
  in metals, 18–21
Electronic
  components, 383–6
  polarisation, 440
Electronics, 383–6, 411
Electro-osmosis, 248–50, 255–6, 264, 274
Electropainting, 250
Electrophoresis, 248, 249–50, 270, 273
Electrophoretic
  coating, 250–5
  force, 261, 271, 275
  mobility, 70
Electrophotography, 299
Electroscope, 1, 2, 95
Electrospouted bed, 297
Electrostatic
  adhesion, 396–408
  conditioning, 236
  conveyor, 290, 293–4
  copying, 299, 300
  crystals, 306
  fabrics, 184
  fluidised-bed coating, 232
  generator, 1, 308–11
  holding, 297–8
  lens, 112, 286
  painting, 209, 214–8
  powder coating, 209–33
  precharger, 162, 184–9
  precipitator, 146–64, 186
  probe, 115–21, 154–6
  screen, 432
  separation, 237–48, 255–7
  spark, 327, 342–66
  spinning, 302
  spraying, 198–237
  voltmeter, 92, 96
Electroviscosity, 265–9
Eliminators, 54, 64, 358, 369–76, 410
Ellipses and hyperbolas, 472
Emulsification, 204–5
Emulsions, 66, 81, 84, 255, 273, 345

Energy
  of adhesion, 388
  of atomisation, 203–4
  of brush discharge, 357
  of spark, 136–40, 327–31, 334
  stored in capacitance, 136–9, 276, 350–3, 435
  stored in inductance, 366
Epitropic fibres, 382
Epoxy resin, 80, 220
Equipotentials, 7–8, 397–8, 442–71
Equivalent energy, 357
ESU, 3, 6, 427
Ethyl cellulose, 30
Ethylene, 328
Exothermic reaction, 366
Explosion, 326
Exponential decay, 11–12, 135

Fabric
  filter, 166, 183–6, 222, 303, 308
  softeners, 378
Faraday
  cage effect, 213–14, 230, 232
  cup, 108–10, 288
Faraday's laws, 25, 251
FEP, 308
Fermi energy, 19–21, 35, 39
Ferroelectricity, 267, 306
Fibres, 303–4, 379, 381–2
Field, 6–8, 213–14, 224, 425, 427, 442–71
  due to charged cloud, 458–9
  in corona discharge, 480–1
  intensification, 365
Field
  lines, 4, 7, 50, 213–14, 442–7
  meter, 96–100, 103–4
Filters, 168, 303, 308, 345
Filtration, 144–90, 255–6
Finger print development, 293
Fire extinguishers, 344
Fixed-bed filter, 175, 177, 183
Flame-proof enclosures, 412
Flocking, 303–6
Flooring, 355, 410
Flue gas additive, 152
Fluid bed filter, 175–7, 182

Fluid flow mapping, 447
Fluidisation, 239, 295–7, 409
Fluidised-bed coating, 232
Fly ash, 150, 185, 246
Focusing, 285
Food industry, 248
Footwear, 130, 353–4, 411
Force
    aerodynamic, 144–5, 147, 157, 212–13, 229, 232, 238
    dielectrophoretic, 145, 258–61, 267, 271–5, 292
    due to gravity, 145, 387
    electrostatic, 6–14, 63–4, 94, 144–7, 168–9, 212–13, 238
Forced convection, 258–63
Four-probe technique, 131
Freon, 264
Friction spark, 366–9
Frictional charging, 17–46, 231, 237, 239–44, 342–3
Fringing field of capacitor, 473–4
Fugitive dust, 237

Gas filtration, 144–92
Gases, 344
Gauss's law, 16, 45, 100, 103, 144, 429–32, 443, 454
Gaussian limit, 45, 49, 168, 173–4, 202, 210–11, 213, 387
Gelatin, 30
Generators, 1, 217, 308–11
Glass, 10, 19, 26, 40, 44
Glass pipes, 345
Glycerol, 200
Gouy–Chapman model, 67–8
Grain dust, 367
Granular bed filter, 175–83
Grinding, 342, 367
Guard ring, 98
Gypsum, 4

Hamaker constant, 388
Hanson filter, 184
Hartmann apparatus, 339–40
Hazardous
    area classification, 413
    environments, 99

Hazards, 99, 217, 231, 326–69
Heat
    pipe, 264–5
    transfer, 259–65, 282–5
Helmholtz layer, 65–71
Heptane, 74–5, 77
Hexane, 360
High frequencies, 127
High-intensity ioniser, 187
High-resistivity powder, 152–7, 223, 230
High-resolution probe, 98
High-temperature filtration, 158, 179
Hybrid mixtures, 341
Hydrocarbon liquids, 70, 217, 345, 361
Hydrocarbon vapours, 327–33, 367
Hydrogen, 327–8, 331, 360, 367
Hydrophilic additives, 377

Ignitability, 138, 328–30
Image charge, 49, 58, 397, 450–4
    force, 60, 63, 211–12, 234, 245, 397
    of point charge in plane, 451
    of point charge in sphere, 452
    of point charge in two planes, 453
Impact spark, 327, 366
Induced charge, 4, 108, 355, 364, 428
Inductance, 328, 366
Induction
    charging, 61–4, 84, 180, 215–8, 237, 244, 269, 293, 346
    field meter, 97–8
    separators, 242–4
Inertial impaction, 166–71, 181, 192
Ink jet printer, 205–8
Insulating
    liquids, 414
    pipes, 77, 345, 358
    surfaces, 355–64
    tank, 362–3
Insulators, 18–21, 26
Integrated circuits, 384
Interception, 166
Interfacial polarisation, 440
Intrinsically safe apparatus, 375, 412
Ion
    drag pump, 258
    exchange resin, 378
    generator, 372

mobility, 277–9, 486–7
transfer, 39–40
wind, 48, 264, 277–84, 486
Ionic conduction
in liquids, 24
in solids, 26
Ionic polarisation, 440
Ioniser, 171
Ions in a corona discharge, 486–7
Iron ore, 239, 247
Isolated conductor, 349
Isomotive geometry, 272
Ivory, 10

Jet
eliminator, 375
ion generator, 372–3
JP-4 aircraft fuel, 76

Kelvin electrometer, 94–5
Kerosene, 85, 358
Kerr effect, 124–6

Laminar flow, 73
Laplace force, 394–6
Laplace's equation, 117, 399, 433, 460, 482, 487
Laser Doppler anemometry, 114–15
Layers of dust, 341
Lead titanate, 307
Lead zirconate, 307
Legendre equation, 466
Lenses, 112, 286
Levitation of particles, 272, 288–90, 293
Leydon jar, 2, 4
Lichtenberg
discharge, 358, 363
figures, 139, 355
Lightning, 2, 352, 412
Limiting charge, 50–3, 186, 202, 209–14
Liquid
charging, 64–77, 344–6
conductivity, 73, 75, 130, 260, 269
flowing in pipes, 70–9
Liquids, 24–5, 62, 64, 382, 394
Load cells, 353
Localised states, 21–3, 35
Lycopodium, 17, 336, 339

Magnesium, 367
powder, 336
Magnetic brush, 301
Maximum experimental safe gap 333, 413
Metal finishing, 209–33, 250–5
Metallised composites, 379–80
Metals, 18–21
Metastable molecules, 478, 487
Methane, 331, 332, 413
Method of images, 451–4
Mica, 10, 31, 389
Microfilters, 345
Micronising, 342
Migration velocity, 148–9, 151, 157, 161
Millikan method, 110
Minerals, 236, 241, 243, 247, 275
Minimum ignition energy, 231, 327–42, 357
Mist, 364
Mixing, 414
Mobility
of ions, 277–9, 486–7
of particles, 57, 110–15, 174, 287
Molecular crystals, 22
Monodisperse droplets, 201, 206
Moon craters, 223
MOS devices, 383
Moving-bed filter, 166, 175, 178–9
Municipal waste, 248

Nearly-free-electron model, 20
Neutralisation, 54, 369–76
Nitrobenzene, 266
NO_x, 163
Nomadic polarisation, 441
Non-contacting voltmeter, 96–7
Non-sparking hand tools, 368
Non-uniform field, 257, 259, 261, 270–2, 292
Non-woven fabric, 303, 306
Numerical methods, 475–6
Nylon, 10, 28–33, 43, 58, 219, 378

Odours, 162
Ohm's law, 15, 50, 92
Oil–water emulsion, 84, 85
Orange peel, 223
Orientational polarisation, 440

Orlon, 30
Oscillatory discharge, 328
Ovoid conductor, 445
Oxidation, 366
Oxygen, corona discharge in, 483
Ozone, 146, 486–7

Packed bed, 410
  filter, 176, 182
Paint, 209, 214–20, 251–2, 311, 361
Parallel cylinders, 455
Parallel line charges, 455
Parallel planes, 471
Parallel-plate capacitor, 435, 47–54
Particle
  charge, 110–14, 209–14
  containment, 285–8
  levitation, 287–94
  size distribution, 333, 365
Passive eliminators, 369–71, 374
Pauthenier
  charging, 147–9, 167, 460
  limit, 51, 53, 116, 210–211, 213
Pearl chain formation, 267
Peek's equation, 370, 479
Performance line, 150
Permittivity, 6, 9, 441
  of free space, 427
Personnel, 350–1, 354, 385
  resistance meter, 129–30
Perspex, 10, 29–31, 43
Pesticide, 233–6
PET, 29, 32–3, 36, 40–2
Phenol formaldehyde, 30
Phosphorus pentoxide, 242
Photoconductor, 300
Piezoelectric, 127, 307, 328, 330
Plastic
  deformation, 392
  film, 134, 370
  surface, 385
Plastics, 356, 379, 410, 414
Pneumatic conveying, 316, 343, 408
Pockels' effect, 124, 126–7
Poisson's equation, 433, 443, 460
Polar
  liquid, 9
  molecules, 402

Polarisability, 9, 440
Polarisation, 5, 212, 304, 397–400, 428–9, 436
Polarity, 355–6
Pollution control, 145
Polonium 210, 371
Polyacrylamide, 30
Polyacrylester, 34
Polyacrylic acid, 30, 43
Polyacrylonitrile, 31, 43
Polycarbonate, 29, 40
Polychlorinated ether, 29
Polyepichlorohydrin, 29
Polyester, 30, 43, 278, 382
Polyethylene, 10, 28–32, 40, 79, 277, 358, 381
Polyethylene glycol, 378
Polyethylene oxide, 29
Polyethylene teraphthalate, 29, 32–3, 36, 40–2
Polyimide, 29, 31
Polymer, 19, 23, 26–8, 32–44, 58, 135, 155, 221, 223, 303, 381
Polymethyl methacrylate, 29–31, 43
Polyphenyloxide, 43
Polystyrene, 29, 31
Polysulphone, 29
Polytetrafluoroethylene, 28–33, 36, 40, 185, 308, 348
Polyurethane, 30
Polyvinyl
  acetate, 29
  alcohol, 30–1, 43
  cabazole, 34
Polyvinyladene fluoride, 184, 308
Polyvinyl butyral, 29
Polyvinyl butyrate, 31
Polyvinyl chloride, 29, 31, 43, 341, 360, 381, 408
Potassium salts, 242
Potential 6–7, 427, 434
  divider, 92, 137
  probe, 115–122
  measurement of, 37–8, 92–4, 98–102, 105–7, 118–20, 123–8, 225, 411
Pouring, 342
Powder
  coating, 209, 218–33

Powder (*contd*)
  layers, 400
  resistivity, 131, 227
Power supplies, 92, 217
Precharging, 162, 184–9
Pressurised fluidised-bed combustor, 179
Printing, 205
Probes, 115–21, 154–6
Propagating brush discharge, 358–61
Propane, 330, 341
PTFE, 10, 28–33, 36, 40, 185, 308, 348
Pulse energisation, 158–60
Pumps, 258, 345
PVC, 29, 31, 43, 341, 360–1, 381, 408
PVDF, 184, 308
Pyrex glass, 77
Pyrites, 246
Pyroelectricity, 307

Quadrant electrometer, 93
Quadrupole field, 287
Quaternary ammonium compounds, 379
Quartz, 10, 246, 248, 307
Quenching distance, 332–4

RF sparks, 327, 368
Radial field meter, 100
Radio emission, 140
Radioactive
  eliminators, 371
  voltmeter, 104–5
Rayleigh limit, 56, 81, 202, 210
Re-entrainment, 152
Relative
  humidity, 347–8, 379, 395–6, 477, 487
  permittivity, 428–9
Resins, 222, 252
Resistance, 129
  probe, 92
  to earth, 352, 414
  series and parallel, 15
Resistivity, 10–11, 15–16, 20–1, 26, 44,
    270, 414
  effect on liquid charging, 73–8, 83
  measurement of, 129–35, 412
  of powder, 131, 151–6, 159, 365, 407
Road tankers, 353
Rogowski profile, 475
Rotating-drum separator, 240, 247

Rotating-vane field meter, 98–9
Rubber tyres, 353
Rutile, 243

SO_x, 163
Safety, 217, 231, 326–76
Sand paper, 305
Schering bridge, 128
Schlieren effect, 262, 267, 283–4
Schrödinger equation, 22
Screen printing, 301
Scrubber, 166–75
Sedimentation, 255
  potential, 249, 345
Selenium, 406
Self-precipitation, 173
Semiconductors, 21
Separation, 237–48, 250, 255–7, 273–5,
    293, 295
Sewage treatment, 250
Shoes, 353–4, 411
Sieving, 342
Silica, 239, 247, 267
Silicone oil, 268
Silk, 30–1
Siloxane, 405
Silver, 380
Sintering, 396
Sodium salts, 242
Solid–liquid interface, 65–7
Soot, 163
Space charge repulsion, 167
Spark, 158, 326, 342–69
  calorimeter, 139–40
  energy, 136–40, 327–31, 334
  from bulk powder, 365
  from capacitor, 337
  from dust cloud, 364
  from insulator, 139, 355–61
  from isolated conductor, 349
  from liquid surface, 361
  from personnel, 353
  gaps, 105–7, 411
Specific collecting area, 149
Specific surface area, 343
Spherical
  coordinates, 465–70
  probe, 118–20, 364

Spinning, 302
  disc, 216
Splashing, 82, 342
Spraying, 198–218, 346
Starch, 268
Static eliminators, 358, 369–76
Static-sensitive devices, 383–6, 411
Stern model, 68
Stirring, 79, 273, 345–6, 414
Stokes's law, 111
Strainers, 345–6
Streaming
  current, 72–7, 345
  potential, 249
Stress in capacitance, 436
Submicron particles, 56, 145, 170, 176,
    179, 181
Sulphur, 10, 17, 31, 339
Supertanker explosions, 365
Surface-active agents, 83
Surface
  charge, 17
    measurement of, 102–3
  free energy, 388–90
  potential, measurement of, 100–2
  resistivity, 133–4
  states, 23, 26–7, 36–9, 43
  tension, 387, 396
Suspensions, 80, 255, 267, 345

Taylor cone, 85, 198–9, 208
Temperature, 41, 259–65, 282–5, 332,
    334
Textiles, 302–6, 378
Thermal boundary layer, 283
Thermal conductivity, 259
Thermal damage, 383
Thermite reaction, 367
Three-electrode precipitator, 160
Throwing power, 252–5
Tight-binding approximation, 19
Time constant for charge decay, 11–12,
    16, 135, 347
Toluene, 74
Townsend criterion, 478
Tramp metal, 367
Transformer oil, 262
Tribocharging, 17–50, 231, 239–41

Triboelectric
  separation, 239–41
  series, 17, 28–31, 241
Trichel pulses, 153, 483–6
Trielectrode precharger, 187
Turbine generator, 217
Turbulence, 73–4, 332
Two-stage precipitator, 162–3, 186

Ultrasonic atomisation, 83, 206
Uniqueness theorem, 461

Valence band, 19
Valves, 345
Van de Graaff generator, 309
Variable-capacitance generator, 311
Venting, 411
Vibrating chute separator, 240
Vibrating field meter, 99
Viscose, 30–1
Viscosity, 265
Viscous flow, 396
VMOS device, 384
Voltage, 6–7, 427, 434
  measurement of, 92–7, 100, 104–7,
    124–6, 225, 411
Van der Waals' force, 387–94, 405

Water, 65, 83, 170, 201, 255, 376, 394,
    396
Wheat, 399
Wide-electrode precipitator, 161
Window paning, 214
Wood, 10
Wool, 30–1, 43, 184, 278
Work function, 20–1, 28, 32–7
  of insulators, 28, 30
Wrap round, 214

Xerographic process, 300
Xylene, 77–8, 80

Zeta potential, 66, 70, 72, 248, 257
Zinc oxide, 307
Zinc sulphide, 127, 307
Zircon, 243
Zones, 356, 413